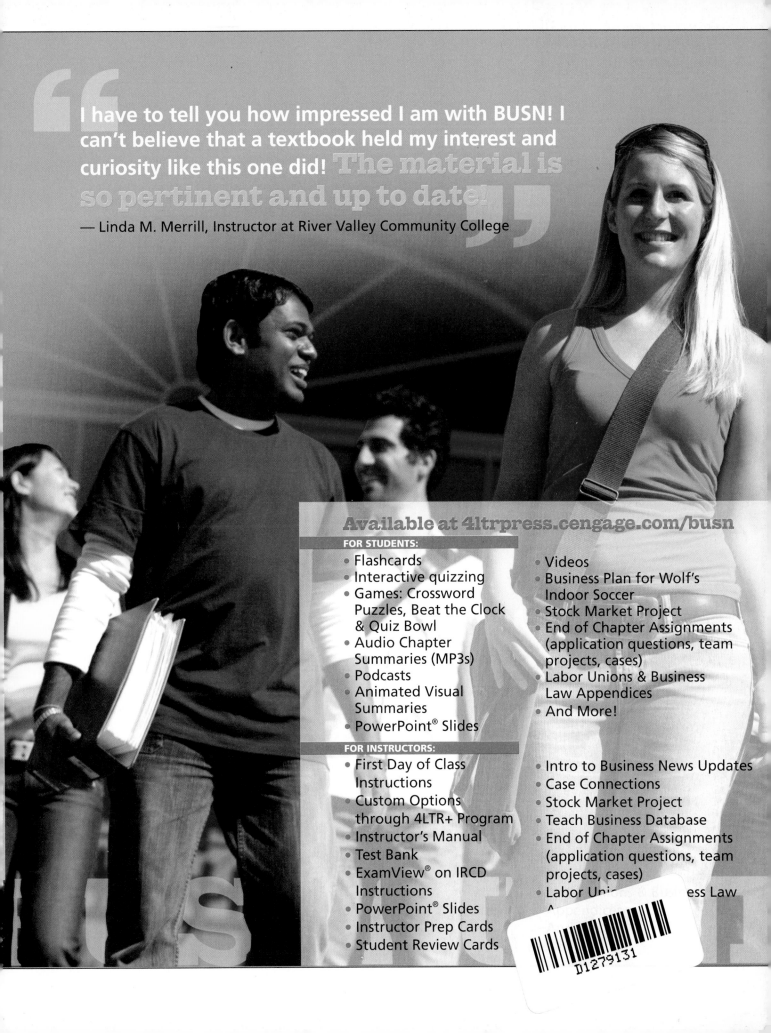

"I have to tell you how impressed I am with BUSN! I can't believe that a textbook held my interest and curiosity like this one did! The material is so pertinent and up to date!"

— Linda M. Merrill, Instructor at River Valley Community College

D1279131

**SOUTH-WESTERN**
CENGAGE Learning™

**BUSN 2008-2009**
**Marce Kelly, Jim McGowen**

Executive Vice President and Publisher, Business & Computers: Jonathan Hulbert

Vice President of Editorial, Business: Jack W. Calhoun

Editor-in-Chief: Melissa S. Acuña

Director, 4LTR Press: Neil Marquardt

Sr. Acquisitions Editor: Erin Joyner

Developmental Editor: Julie Klooster

Research Associate: Clara Goosman

Executive Marketing Manager: Kimberly Kanakes

Sr. Marketing Coordinator: Sarah Rose

Marketing Communications Manager: Sarah Greber

Sr. Content Project Manager: Martha Conway

Technology Project Manager: Kristen Meere

Sr. Frontlist Buyer: Beverly Breslin

Production House: Bill Smith Studio

Sr. Art Director: Stacy Jenkins Shirley

Internal Designer: Ann Small, A Small Design Studio

Cover Designer: KeDesign, Mason, OH

Cover Image: Corbis and Getty Images

Title Page Images: Getty Images

Photography Manager: Deanna Ettinger

Photo Researcher: Charlotte Goldman

Text Permissions Researcher: James Reidel

For product information and technology assistance, contact us at
**Cengage Learning Customer & Sales Support, 1-800-354-9706**

For permission to use material from this text or product,
submit all requests online at **www.cengage.com/permissions**
Further permissions questions can be emailed to
**permissionrequest@cengage.com**

The names of all products mentioned herein are used for identification purposes only and may be trademarks or registered trademarks of their respective owners. South-Western disclaims any affiliation, association, connection with, sponsorship, or endorsement by such owners.

Library of Congress Control Number: 2008938639
Student Edition ISBN 13: 978-0-324-58187-4
Student Edition ISBN 10: 0-324-58187-4

Student Edition with PAC ISBN 13: 978-0-324-58188-1
Student Edition with PAC ISBN 10: 0-324-58188-2

Instructor's Edition ISBN 13: 978-0-324-58968-9
Instructor's Edition ISBN 10: 0-324-58968-9

Instructor's Edition package ISBN 13: 978-0-324-58969-6
Instructor's Edition package ISBN 10: 0-324-58969-7

**South-Western Cengage Learning**
5191 Natorp Boulevard
Mason, OH 45040
USA

Cengage Learning products are represented in Canada by Nelson Education, Ltd.

For your course and learning solutions, visit **academic.cengage.com**
Purchase any of our products at your local college store or at our preferred online store **www.ichapters.com**

Printed in the United States of America
1 2 3 4 5 6 7 12 11 10 09

# Brief Contents

**CHAPTER 1**

Business Now: Change Is the
Only Constant 2

**CHAPTER 2**

Economics: The Framework
for Business 14

**CHAPTER 3**

The World Marketplace: Business
without Borders 28

**CHAPTER 4**

Business Ethics and Social
Responsibility: Doing Well
by Doing Good 42

**CHAPTER 5**

Business Communication: Creating and
Delivering Messages that Matter 56

**CHAPTER 6**

Business Formation: Choosing the
Form that Fits 68

**CHAPTER 7**

Small Businesses and Entrepreneurship:
Economic Rocket Fuel 82

**CHAPTER 8**

Accounting: Decision
Making by the Numbers 94

**CHAPTER 9**

Finance: Acquiring and Using Funds to
Maximize Value 108

**CHAPTER 10**

Securities Markets: Trading Financial
Resources 122

**CHAPTER 11**

Marketing: Building Profitable
Customer Connections 136

**CHAPTER 12**

Product Strategy: Delivering
More Value 152

**CHAPTER 13**

Distribution and Pricing: Right
Product, Right Person, Right Place,
Right Price 168

**CHAPTER 14**

Marketing Promotion: Delivering
High-Impact Messages 182

**CHAPTER 15**

Management, Motivation, and
Leadership: Bringing Business
to Life 196

**CHAPTER 16**

Human Resource Management: Building
a Top-Quality Workforce 210

**CHAPTER 17**

Managing Information and Technology:
Finding New Ways to Learn
and Link 224

**CHAPTER 18**

Operations Management: Putting
It All Together 238

**ENDNOTES** 253

**SUBJECT INDEX** 269

**TEAR-OUT CARDS**

Visit 4LTRPress.cengage.
com/busn to see the
online appendices.

Online Appendix 1:
Labor Union and
Collective Bargaining

Online Appendix 2:
Business Law

Online Chapter 11 –
updated AMA
definition of
marketing

© STOCKDISC PREMIUM/GETTY IMAGES

# ContentsContentsCont

## CHAPTER 1

### Business Now: Change Is the Only Constant 2

Business Now: Moving at Breakneck Speed 3  Business Basics: Some Key Definitions 3

The Evolution of Business: Putting It All in Context 4

Nonprofits and the Economy: The Business of Doing Good 5

Factors of Production: The Basic Building Blocks 5

The Business Environment: The Context for Success 7  The Economic Environment 7  The Competitive Environment 8  The Technological Environment 9  The Social Environment 10  The Global Environment 12

Business and You: Making It Personal 13

## CHAPTER 2

### Economics: The Framework for Business 14

Why Economics Matters 15  Macroeconomics Versus Microeconomics: Same Scene, Different Takes 15  Economic Systems: Different Ways to Allocate Resources 16

Capitalism: The Free Market System 16  The Fundamental Rights of Capitalism 17  Four Degrees of Competition 18  Supply and Demand: Fundamental Principles of a Free Market System 20

Planned Economies: Socialism and Communism 20  Socialism 21  Communism 21

Mixed Economies: The Story of the Future 22

Evaluating Economic Performance: What's Working? 22  Gross Domestic Product 22  Employment Level 23  The Business Cycle 23  Price Levels 24  Productivity 24

Managing the Economy Through Fiscal and Monetary Policy 25  Fiscal Policy 25  Monetary Policy 25

© JOHN MUTRUX/MCT/LANDOV, © GAVIN HELLIER/ROBERT HARDING WORLD IMAGERY/GETTY IMAGES

## CHAPTER 3

### The World Marketplace: Business without Borders 28

An Unprecedented Opportunity… 29

Key Reasons for International Trade 30  Competitive Advantage 31

Global Trade: Taking Measure 31  Balance of Trade 31  Balance of Payments 31  Exchange Rates 32  Countertrade 32

Seizing the Opportunity: Strategies for Reaching Global Markets 32  Foreign Outsourcing and Importing 33  Exporting 34  Foreign Licensing and Foreign Franchising 34  Foreign Direct Investment 34

Barriers to International Trade 35 Sociocultural Differences 35 Economic Differences 35 Political and Legal Differences 36

Free Trade: The Movement Gains Momentum 37 GATT and the World Trade Organization (WTO) 38 The World Bank 38 The International Monetary Fund 38 Trading Blocs and Common Markets 40

## CHAPTER 4

### Business Ethics and Social Responsibility: Doing Well by Doing Good 42

Ethics and Social Responsibility: A Close Relationship 43 Defining Ethics: Murkier Than You'd Think… 43 Universal Ethical Standards: A Reasonable Goal or Wishful Thinking? 44

Business Ethics: Not an Oxymoron 45

Ethics: Multiple Touchpoints 45 Ethics and the Individual: The Power of One 45 Ethics and the Organization:

It Takes a Village 46 Creating and Maintaining an Ethical Organization 46

Defining Social Responsibility: Making the World a Better Place 47 The Stakeholder Approach: Responsibility to Whom?  48

Ethics and Social Responsibility in the Global Arena: A House of Mirrors? 53

Monitoring Ethics and Social Responsibility: Who Is Minding the Store? 54

## CHAPTER 5

### Business Communication: Creating and Delivering Messages that Matter 56

Excellent Communication Skills: Your Invisible Advantage 57 Communication Barriers: "That's Not What I Meant!" 57

Nonverbal Communication: Beyond the Words 58 Active Listening: The Great Divider 59

Choose the Right Channel: A Rich Array of Options 59 Consider the Audience: It's Not about You! 60

Pick the Right Words: Is That Car Pre-Loved or Just Plain Used?! 60 Analyze Your Audience 60 Be Concise 61 Avoid Slang 61 Avoid Bias 62 Use Active Voice Whenever Possible 62

Write High-Impact Messages: Breaking through the Clutter 63 Strike the Right Tone 63 Don't Make Grammar Goofs 63 Use Block Paragraphs 64 Use Headings and Bulleted Lists Wherever Appropriate 64

Create and Deliver Successful Verbal Presentations: Hook 'Em and Reel 'Em In! 65 Opening 65 Body 65 Close 66 Questions 66 Visual Aids 66 Handling Nerves 66 Delivery 67

© BOB THOMASON/STONE/GETTY IMAGES

# CHAPTER 6

## Business Formation: Choosing the Form that Fits 68

Sole Proprietorships: Business at Its Most Basic 69
Advantages and Disadvantages of Sole
Proprietorships 70

Partnerships: Two Heads (and Bankrolls) Can Be Better
Than One 71 General Partnerships 71 Advantages
and Disadvantages of General Partnerships 71 Limited
Partnerships 72 Limited Liability Partnerships 72

Corporations: An Artificial Reality 73 Forming a General
Corporation 73 Ownership of General Corporations 74
The Role of the Board of Directors 74 Advantages
of General Corporations 74 Disadvantages of
Corporations 75

Other Types of Corporations: Same but Different 75

Corporate Restructuring 76 Mergers and Acquisitions 76

The Limited Liability Company: The New Kid on
the Block 77 Forming and Managing an LLC 77
Advantages of LLCs 77 Limitations and Disadvantages
of LLCs 78

Franchising: Proven Methods for a Price 78 Franchising
in Today's Economy 78 Advantages of
Franchising 79 Disadvantages of Franchising 80
Entering into a Franchise Agreement 81

# CHAPTER 7

## Small Businesses and Entrepreneurship: Economic Rocket Fuel 82

Launching a New Venture: What's in It for
Me? 83 Greater Financial Success 83 Independence 83
Flexibility 84 Challenge 84 Survival 84

The Entrepreneur: A Distinctive
Profile 85 The Entrepreneurial Mindset: A Matter of
Attitude 85 Entrepreneurial Characteristics 85

Opportunities and Threats for Small Business: A Two-
Sided Coin 87 Small Business Opportunities 87
Small Business Threats 87

Launch Options: Reviewing the Pros and Cons 89
Making It Happen: Tools for Business Success 89

Finding the Money: Funding Options for Small
Business 91 Personal Resources 91 Loans 91
Angel Investors 91 Venture Capital 91

Small Business and the Economy: An Outsized
Impact 92 Entrepreneurship around the World 93

# CHAPTER 8

## Accounting: Decision Making by the Numbers 94

Accounting: Who Needs It? 95

The Accounting Profession: More Than Just Recording Transactions 96 What Accountants Do 96 Qualifications for Accounting Positions 96

GAAP: Playing by the Rules of Financial Accounting 97 Role of the Financial Standards Accounting Board 97 Ethics in Accounting 98

Financial Statements: the Main Output of Financial Accounting 99 The Balance Sheet: What We Own and How We Got It 99 The Income Statement: How Did We Do? 100 Statement of Cash Flows: Show Me the Money 101 Other Statements 102

Interpreting Financial Statements: Digging Beneath the Surface 102 The Independent Auditor's Report: A Necessary Stamp of Approval 102 Notes to Financial Statements: Reading the Fine Print 103 Beyond the Statements: Horizontal, Vertical, and Ratio Analysis 104

Managerial Accounting: Inside Intelligence 104 Product Costing 105 Incremental Analysis 105 Budgeting 106

© JASON REED/PHOTODISC/GETTY IMAGES

# CHAPTER 9

## Finance: Acquiring and Using Funds to Maximize Value 108

What Motivates Financial Decisions? 109

Evaluating Performance: Where Do We Stand? 110

Financial Planning: Providing a Road Map for the Future 110 Basic Planning Tools: Pro Forma Statements and the Cash Budget 112

Managing Working Capital: Current Events 112 Managing Current Assets 112 Short-Term Financing 114

Capital Budgeting: In It for the Long Haul 116

Comparing Cash Flows That Occur at Different Times 116 Using Net Present Value to Evaluate Capital Budgeting Proposals 118

Choosing the Sources of Long-term Capital: Loaners vs. Owners 118 Sources of Debt Financing 118 Sources of Equity Financing 119 Financial Leverage: Using Debt to Magnify Gains (And Losses) 119

© AP IMAGES

## CHAPTER 11

### Marketing: Building Profitable Customer Connections 136

Marketing: Getting Value by Giving Value 137
   The Scope of Marketing: It's Everywhere! 138
   The Evolution of Marketing: From the Product to the Customer 139

The Customer: Front and Center 140  Value 140
   Customer Satisfaction 141  Customer Loyalty 141

Marketing Strategy: Where Are You Going and How Will You Get There? 141  Target Market 142
   Consumer Markets versus Business Markets 142
   Consumer Market Segmentation 142  Business Market Segmentation 143  The Marketing Mix 143  The Global Marketing Mix 144  The Marketing Environment 145
   The Global Marketing Environment 146

Customer Behavior: Decisions, Decisions, Decisions! 146  Consumer Behavior 146
   Business Buyer Behavior 147

Marketing Research: So What Do They REALLY Think? 147  Types of Data 147  Primary Research Tools 148  An International Perspective 148

Social Responsibility and Technology: A Major Marketing Shift 148  Marketing and Society: It's Not Just About You! 148  Technology and Marketing: Power to the People! 149


## CHAPTER 10

### Securities Markets: Trading Financial Resources 122

Basic Types of Financial Securities 123  Common Stock 123  Preferred Stock 124  Bonds 124

Trading Securities: The Primary and Secondary Markets 126  The Primary Securities Market 126
Secondary Securities Markets 127

Regulation of Securities Markets: Establishing Confidence in the Market 129  State Regulations 129
Federal Legislation 129  The Role of Self-Regulatory Organizations 130

Personal Investing 130  Choosing a Broker 131  Buying Securities 131  Strategies for Investing in Securities 131

Other Types of Securities-related Investments 133
Mutual Funds 133  Exchange Traded Funds 134

Keeping Tabs on the Market 134  Stock Indices 134
Tracking the Performance of Specific Securities 135

# CHAPTER 12

## Product Strategy: Delivering More Value 152

Product Definition: It's Probably More Than You Thought 153   Services: A Product by Any Other Name… 153   Goods versus Services: A Mixed Bag 154   Product Layers: Peeling the Onion 154

Product Classification: It's a Bird, It's a Plane… 155   Consumer Product Categories 155   Business Product Categories 156

Product Differentiation and Planning: A Meaningful Difference 156   Product Quality 156   Features and Benefits 157   Product Lines and the Product Mix 157   Branding 159   Packaging 161

New Product Development: Nuts, Bolts, and a Spark of Brilliance 162   Types of Innovation 162   The New Product Development Process 163   New Product Adoption and Diffusion 164

The Product Life Cycle: Maximizing Results over Time 165

# CHAPTER 13

## Distribution and Pricing: Right Product, Right Person, Right Place, Right Price 168

Distribution: Getting Your Product to Your Customer 169   The Role of Distributors: Adding Value 169   The Members of the Channel: Retailers versus Wholesalers 170

Wholesalers: Sorting out the Options 171   Merchant Wholesalers 171   Agents and Brokers 171

Retailers: The Consumer Connection 171   Store Retailers 172   Nonstore Retailers 174

Physical Distribution: Planes, Trains, and Much, Much More… 175   Transportation Decisions 176   Proactive Supply Chain Management 176

Pricing Objectives and Strategies: A High Stakes Game 177   Building Profitability 177   Boosting Volume 177   Matching the Competition 178   Creating Prestige 179

Pricing in Practice: A Real World Approach 179   Breakeven Analysis 179   Fixed Margin Pricing 180   Consumer Pricing Perceptions: The Strategic Wild Card 180

# CHAPTER 14

## Marketing Promotion: Delivering High-Impact Messages 182

Promotion: Influencing Consumer Decisions 183   Promotion in Chaos: Danger or Opportunity? 183

Integrated Marketing Communication: Consistency and Focus 184   Coordinating the Communication 184

A Meaningful Message: Finding the Big Idea 184   An International Perspective 185

The Promotional Mix: Communicating the BIG IDEA 186   Emerging Promotional Tools: The Leading Edge 186   Traditional Promotional Tools: A Marketing Mainstay 189

Choosing the Right Promotional Mix: Not Just a Science 195

Motivation: Lighting the Fire 199  Theories of
    Motivation 199  Motivation Today 201

Planning: Figuring Out Where to Go and How to Get
    There 202  Strategic Planning: Setting the Agenda 203

Organizing: Fitting Together the Puzzle Pieces 205
    Key Organizing Considerations 206  Organization
    Models 207

Leadership: Directing and Inspiring 208  Leadership
    Style 208

Controlling: Making Sure It All Works 209

## CHAPTER 16

### Human Resource Management: Building a Top-Quality Workforce 210

Human Resource Management: Bringing Business
    to Life 211

Human Resource Management Challenges: Major
    Hurdles 211  Older Workers 212  Younger Workers 212
    Women Workers 212  Need for Flexibility 212
    Wage Gap 212  Outsourcing 212  Lawsuits 212

Human Resources Managers: Corporate Black
    Sheep? 212  The Problem 212  The Solution 213

Human Resource Planning: Drawing the Map 213
    Recruitment: Finding the Right People 214
    Selection: Making the Right Choice 215
    Training and Development: Honing the Competitive
    Edge 217  Evaluation: Assessing Employee
    Performance 218  Compensation: Show Me the
    Money 219  Benefits: From Birthday Cakes to Death
    Benefits 220  Separation: Breaking Up Is Hard
    to Do 222

Legal Issues: HR and the Long Arm of the Law
    222  Affirmative Action: The Active Pursuit of Equal
    Opportunity 223  Sexual Harassment: Eliminating
    Hostility 223

## CHAPTER 15

### Management, Motivation, and Leadership: Bringing Business to Life 196

Bringing Resources to Life 197  Management Hierarchy:
    Levels of Responsibility 197  Management Skills: Having
    What It Takes to Get the Job Done 198

## CHAPTER 17

### Managing Information and Technology: Finding New Ways to Learn and Link 224

Information Technology: Explosive Change 225
Hardware and Software 225 Networks 226

Information Technology and Decision Making: A Crucial
Aid 226 Data and Information 226 Expert Systems 228

Information Technology and the World of
e-Commerce 228 Using Information Technology
in the B2C Market 229 Using Information Technology
in the B2B Market 231

Challenges and Concerns Arising from New
Technologies 231 Cookies, Adware, Spyware, and
Viruses 231 Spam and Phishing 232 Hackers 233
Ethical and Legal Issues 233

New Developments—What's around the Corner? 235
Radio Frequency Identification 235 New Hardware
Technologies 236 Internet2 236

## CHAPTER 18

### Operations Management: Putting It All Together 238

Operations Management: It Isn't Glamorous, But It
Definitely Matters… 239 Goods vs. Services 239
Effectiveness vs. Efficiency 240

What Do Operations Managers Do? 240 Facility
Location 240 Process Selection and Facility
Layout 241 Inventory Control: Don't Just Sit There 242
Project Scheduling 243

The Technology of Operations 244 Automation: Let the
Machines Do It 245 Software Technologies 245

Integrated Operating Systems: Coordinating
Efforts 245 How Operations Managers View
Supply Chains 245 Enterprise Resource Planning:
Creating One Big System 247

Focus on Quality 248 Waking Up to the Need for
Quality 248 How American Firms Responded to
the Quality Challenge 249 Quality Standards and
Quality Initiatives 250

Lean Production: Cutting Waste to Improve
Performance 251 Identifying Sources of Waste: Value
Stream Mapping 251 Reducing Investment in Inventory:
Just-in-Time to the Rescue 251 Lean Thinking in the
Service Sector 251

**ENDNOTES 253**

**SUBJECT INDEX 269**

**TEAR-OUT CARDS**

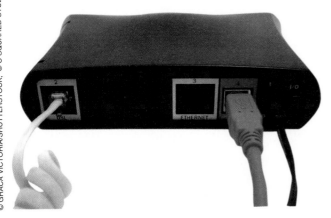

**Visit 4LTRPress.cengage.com/busn**
**to see the online appendices.**

**Online Appendix 1: Labor Union and**
**Collective Bargaining**

**Online Appendix 2: Business Law**

**Online Chapter 11 – updated AMA**
**definition of marketing**

© GRACA VICTORIA/SHUTTERSTOCK, © C SQUARED STUDIOS/PHOTODISC/GETTY IMAGES

To my family—
Scot, Justin, Lauren,
Allison, Cathy, and Shel.
You are my greatest blessing.

—Marce Kelly


To my parents,
Jim and Joy. Thank
you so much for your love,
encouragement, and support.

—Jim McGowen

# Letter to Students

The idea for this book—a whole new way of learning—began with students like you across the country. We paid attention to students who wanted to learn about business without slogging through endless pages of dry text. We listened to students who wanted to sit through class without craving a triple espresso. We responded to students who wanted to use their favorite gadgets to prepare for tests.

So we are confident that BUSN will meet your needs. The short, lively text covers all the key concepts without the fluff. The examples are relevant and engaging, and the visual style makes the book fun to read. But the text is only part of the package. You can access a rich variety of study tools via computer or iPod—the choice is yours.

We did one other thing we hope you'll like. We paid a lot of attention to students' concerns about the high price of college textbooks. We made it our mission to ensure that our package not only meets your needs but does so without busting your budget!

This innovative, student-focused package was developed by the authors—Marce Kelly and Jim McGowen—and the experienced Cengage Learning publishers. The Cengage team contributed a deep understanding of students and professors across the nation, and the authors brought years of teaching and business experience.

Marce Kelly, who earned her MBA from UCLA's Anderson School of Management, spent the first 14 years of her career in marketing, building brands for Neutrogena and The Walt Disney Corporation. But her true love is teaching, so in 2000 she accepted a full-time teaching position at Santa Monica College. Professor Kelly has received seven Outstanding Instructor awards from the International Education Center and has been named four times to *Who's Who Among American Teachers*.

Jim McGowen has served as chairperson of the Business Transfer Department at Southwestern Illinois College for the last 12 years. He earned his MS in Economics from Auburn University and has completed additional graduate work in economics, finance, accounting, and operations management. Professor McGowen has taught the Introduction to Business course at Southwestern Illinois for over 20 years. The Illinois Community College Trustees Association awarded him an Excellence in Teaching Award in 2007, the year he was also named Faculty Member of the Year at Southwestern Illinois College.

We would appreciate any comments or suggestions you want to offer about this package. You can reach Jim McGowen at jmcgowen4@gmail.com and Marce Kelly at marcekelly@ca.rr.com. We wish you a fun, positive, productive term, and look forward to your feedback!

**Marce Kelly**

**Jim McGowen**

## CHAPTER 1

# Business Now: Change Is the Only Constant

## LEARNING OBJECTIVES

After studying this chapter, you will be able to...

**LO1** Define business and discuss the role of business in the economy

**LO2** Explain the evolution of modern business

**LO3** Discuss the role of nonprofit organizations in the economy

**LO4** Outline the core factors of production and how they impact the economy

**LO5** Describe today's business environment and discuss each key dimension

**LO6** Explain how current business trends might impact your career choices

4ltrpress.cengage.com/busn

Playing it safe is the most dangerous thing
we can do. We have to get bolder.

—Steve Jobs, CEO of Apple

## LO1 Business Now: Moving at Breakneck Speed

Day by day, the business world simply spins faster. Producers pump out better goods more quickly and cheaply than ever before. Industries transform with the click of a mouse. Technologies forge instant connections across the globe. And powerful new trends surface and submerge, sometimes within a matter of months. In this fast-paced, fluid environment, change is the only constant.

Successful firms lean forward and embrace the change. They seek the opportunities and avoid the pitfalls. They take reasonable risks. They completely understand their market. Their core goal is to generate long-term profits by delivering unsurpassed **value** to their customers.

### Business Basics: Some Key Definitions

While you can certainly recognize a business when you see one, more formal definitions may help as you read through this book. A **business** is any activity that provides goods and services in an effort to earn a profit. **Profit** is the financial reward that comes from starting and running a business. More specifically, a profit is the money that a business earns in sales (or revenue), minus expenses such as the cost of goods, and the cost of salaries. But clearly, not every business earns a profit all of the time. When a business brings in less money than it needs to cover expenses, it incurs a **loss**. If you launch a music label, for instance, you'll need to pay your artists, buy or lease a studio, and purchase equipment, among other expenses. If your label generates hits, you'll earn more than enough to cover all your expenses and make yourself rich. But a series of duds could leave you holding the bag.

Just the possibility of earning a profit provides a powerful incentive for people of all backgrounds to launch their own enterprise. A recent survey reported that 47% of American adults have already taken steps to start their own business or supplement their income, and 21% have crafted a specific business plan. The numbers among your peers are probably even higher, since two-thirds of college students plan to launch their own business at some point in their career. People who risk their time, money, and other resources to start and manage a business are called **entrepreneurs**.[1]

The Forbes list of the richest Americans highlights the astounding ability of the entrepreneurial spirit to build wealth. The top ten—featured in exhibit 1.1—includes five entrepreneurs who made their fortunes in technology, a hotbed of opportunity over the past few decades.

**business** Any activity that provides goods and services in an effort to earn a profit.

**profit** The money that a business earns in sales (or revenue), minus expenses, such as the cost of goods, and the cost of salaries. Revenue – Expenses = Profit (or Loss)

**loss** When a business incurs expenses that are greater than revenue.

**entrepreneurs** People who risk their time, money, and other resources to start and manage businesses.

**Exhibit 1.1** The Richest Americans, *Forbes* Magazine[2]

| Name | Net Worth | Source of Wealth |
| --- | --- | --- |
| Bill Gates | $59 Billion | Microsoft |
| Warren Buffett | $52 Billion | Berkshire Hathaway |
| Sheldon Adelson | $28 Billion | Casinos, Hotels |
| Lawrence Ellison | $26 Billion | Oracle |
| Sergey Brin | $18.5 Billion | Google |
| Larry Page | $18.5 Billion | Google |
| Kirk Kerkorian | $18 Billion | Investments, Casinos |
| Michael Dell | $17.2 Billion | Dell |
| Charles Koch | $17 Billion | Oil, Commodities |
| David Koch | $17 Billion | Oil, Commodities |

**standard of living** The quality and quantity of goods and services available to a population.

**quality of life** The overall sense of well being experienced by either an individual or a group.

Interestingly, as entrepreneurs create wealth for themselves, they produce a ripple effect that enriches everyone around them. For instance, if your new music label becomes the next Interscope Records, who will benefit? Clearly, *you* will. And you'll probably spend at least some of that money enriching your local clubs, clothing stores, and car dealerships. But others will benefit, too, from the artists on your label, to the staff members who support them, to the contractors who build your facilities, to the government that collects your taxes. The impact of one successful entrepreneur can extend to the far reaches of the economy. Multiply the impact times thousands of entrepreneurs—each working in his or her own self-interest—and you can see how the profit motive benefits virtually everyone.

From a bigger picture perspective, business drives up the **standard of living** for people worldwide, contributing to a higher **quality of life**. Not only do businesses provide the products and services that people enjoy, but they also provide the jobs that people need. Beyond the obvious, business contributes to society through innovation—think cars, TVs, and personal computers. Business also helps raise the standard of living through taxes, which the government spends on projects that range from streetlights to environmental clean-up. And socially responsible firms contribute even more, actively advocating for the well being of the society that feeds their success.

## LO2 The Evolution of Business: Putting It All in Context

You may be surprised to learn that—unlike today—business hasn't always been focused on

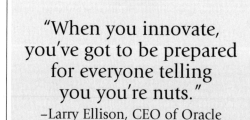

"When you innovate, you've got to be prepared for everyone telling you you're nuts."
–Larry Ellison, CEO of Oracle

what the customer wants. In fact, business in the United States has changed rather dramatically over the past 200 to 300 years. Business historians typically divide the history of American business into five distinct eras, which overlap during the periods of transition.

- **The Industrial Revolution:** Technological advances fueled a period of rapid industrialization in America from the mid-1700s to the mid-1800s. As mass production took hold, huge factories replaced skilled artisan workshops. The factories hired large numbers of semiskilled workers, who specialized in a limited number of tasks. The result was unprecedented production efficiency, but also a loss of individual ownership and personal pride in the production process.

- **The Entrepreneurship Era:** Building on the foundation of the industrial revolution, large-scale entrepreneurs emerged in the second half of the 1800s, building business empires. These industrial titans created enormous wealth, raising the overall standard of living across the country. But many also dominated their markets, forcing out competitors, manipulating prices, exploiting workers, and decimating the environment. Toward the end of the 1800s, the government stepped into the business realm, passing laws to regulate business and protect consumers and workers, creating more balance in the economy.

- **The Production Era:** In the early part of the 1900s, major businesses focused on further refining the production process and creating greater efficiencies. Jobs became even more specialized, increasing productivity and lowering costs and prices. In 1913 Henry Ford introduced the assembly line, which quickly became standard across major manufacturing industries. With managers focused on efficiency, the customer was an afterthought. But when customers tightened their belts during the Great Depression and World War II, businesses took notice. The hard sell emerged: aggressive persuasion meant to separate consumers from their cash.

- **The Marketing Era:** After World War II, the balance of power shifted away from producers and toward consumers, flooding the market with enticing choices. To differentiate themselves from their competitors, businesses began to develop brands, or distinctive identities to help consumers understand the differences among various products. The *marketing concept* emerged: a consumer orientation began to permeate successful companies in every department, at every level. This approach continues to influence business decisions today as global competition heats up to unprecedented levels.

- **The Relationship Era:** Building on the marketing concept, leading-edge firms now look beyond each immediate transaction with a customer and aim to build long-term relationships. Satisfied customers can become advocates for a business, spreading the word with more speed and credibility than even the best promotional campaign. And cultivating current customers is more profitable than constantly seeking new ones. A key tool is technology. Using the Web and other digital resources, businesses gather detailed information about their customers, and use this data to serve them better.

## LO3 Nonprofits and the Economy: The Business of Doing Good

Nonprofit organizations also play a critical role in the economy, often working hand in hand with business to improve the quality of life in our society. Focusing in areas such as health, human services, education, art, religion, and culture, **nonprofits** are business-*like* establishments, but their primary goals do not include profits. Chuck Bean, executive director of the Nonprofit Roundtable, explains: "By definition, nonprofits are not in the business of financial gain. We're in the business of doing good. However, nonprofits are still businesses in every other sense—they employ people, they take in revenue, they produce goods and services and contribute in significant ways to our region's economic stability and growth." Nationwide, nonprofits employ over ten percent of America's workforce, accounting for about 50% more paid workers than the entire construction industry, and more than three times as many as agriculture. And nonprofit museums, schools, theaters, and orchestras have become economic magnets for many communities, drawing additional investment.[3]

## LO4 Factors of Production: The Basic Building Blocks

Both businesses and nonprofits rely on **factors of production**—four fundamental resources—to achieve their objectives. Some combination of these factors is crucial for an economic system to work and create wealth. As you read through the factors, keep in mind that they don't come free of charge. Human resources, for instance, require wages, while entrepreneurs need a profit incentive.

- Natural resources: This factor includes all inputs that offer value in their natural state, such as land, fresh

**nonprofits**
Business-like establishments that employ people and produce goods and services with the fundamental goal of contributing to the community rather than generating financial gain.

**factors of production**
Four fundamental elements—natural resources, capital, human resources, and entrepreneurship—that businesses need to achieve their objectives. Some combination of these factors is crucial for an economic system to create wealth.

# Oops! What were they THINKING?!

### There's no such thing as a bad idea?

No question about it: creativity underpins virtually every business success. From high-profile innovation such as brand-new products to behind-the-scenes innovation such as better inventory management, creativity counts more than ever before. But since new ideas by their very definition have no track record, it's often hard to distinguish the good stuff from the garbage. A quick review of some bad new ideas can be both amusing and instructive:

- The helicopter ejection seat: Press the button and try to avoid the whirling steel blades! Someone just wasn't thinking...

- The high security briefcase: If the wrong person grabs this briefcase, it emits a piercing scream and delivers a high voltage electric shock. Too bad it doesn't come with lawsuit protection, too...

- An inflatable dartboard. Enough said...

Some say that about 50 ideas are rejected for every successful new product. So if you're mulling over new ideas, don't get discouraged. Cultivate your creativity knowing that even your bad ideas might someday provide entertainment for students just like you![4]

© PHOTODISC/GETTY IMAGES

## Partners with a Purpose

A growing number of firms have developed nonprofit partnerships with a profit-minded approach: using the same investment dollars to improve society and to support their own strategic mission. The key is finding the right fit. Here are three examples of business–nonprofit partnerships that represent a double win:

- *Kraft Foods:* The Kraft vision, spelled out on their Website, is "Helping people around the world eat and live better." In support of that mission, Kraft has partnered with America's Second Harvest, a nonprofit organization that aims to create a hunger-free America. In 2005 Kraft donated $400,000 to America's Second Harvest, mitigating the impact of a devastating social issue while raising their public profile...all in complete alignment with their fundamental vision.
- *Polo Ralph Lauren:* Ralph Lauren is known for its all-American image and its American flag logo, so investing in the flag itself made sense on a number of levels. The company recently donated $10 million to restore and promote the flag that inspired Frances Scott Key to write the national anthem. Promotion of the project supports the Ralph Lauren brand as it preserves an American treasure for the benefit of everyone.
- *Los Angeles Times:* No paper will survive without readers, yet California literacy rates are shockingly low. In a smart strategic move, the *L.A. Times* stepped in to meet the need with a focus on their future. They launched the Reading by 9 program, designed to ensure that all Southern California students are reading at grade level by the age of 9. By nurturing stronger readers, the *L.A. Times* is working to improve literacy, while building its own potential customer base.[5]

water, wind, and mineral deposits. Most natural resources must be extracted, purified, or harnessed; people cannot actually create them. (Note that agricultural products, which people do create through planting and tending, are not a natural resource.) The value of all natural resources tends to rise with high demand, low supply, or both.

- **Capital:** This factor includes machines, tools, buildings, information, and technology—the synthetic resources that a business needs to produce goods or services. Computers and telecommunications capability have become pivotal elements of capital across a surprising range of industries, from financial services to professional sports. You may be surprised to learn that in this context, capital does not include money, but clearly, businesses use money to acquire, maintain, and upgrade their capital.

- **Human Resources:** This factor encompasses the physical, intellectual, and creative contributions of everyone who works within an economy. As technology replaces a growing number of manual labor jobs, education and motivation have become increasingly important to human resource development. Given the importance of knowledge to workforce effectiveness, some business experts, such as management guru Peter Drucker, break out knowledge as its own category, separate from human resources.

- **Entrepreneurship:** Entrepreneurs are people who take the risk of launching and operating their own businesses, largely in response to the profit incentive. They tend to see opportunities where others don't, and they use their own resources to capitalize on that potential. Entrepreneurial enterprises can kick-start an economy, creating a tidal wave of opportunity by harnessing the other factors of production.

But entrepreneurs don't thrive in an environment that doesn't support them. The key ingredient is economic freedom: freedom of choice (who to hire, for instance, or what to produce), freedom from excess regulation, and freedom from too much taxation. Protection from corruption and unfair competition is another entrepreneurial "must."

Clearly, all of these factors must be in place for an economy to thrive. But which factor is *most* important? One way to answer that question is to examine current economies around the world. Russia and China are both rich in natural resources and human resources. And both countries have a solid level of capital (growing in China and deteriorating in Russia). Yet neither country is wealthy; both rank relatively low in terms of gross national income per person. The missing ingredient seems to be entrepreneurship, limited in Russia largely through corruption

In a recent survey more than 724,000 Americans reported that eBay entrepreneurship provides their primary or secondary source of income.

and in China through government interference and taxes. Contrast those examples to, say, Hong Kong. The population is small and the natural resources are severely limited, yet Hong Kong has consistently ranked among the richest regions in Asia. One key reason is that Hong Kong operated for many years under the British legal and economic system, which actively encouraged entrepreneurship, fueling, in turn, the creation of wealth. Recognizing the potential of entrepreneurship, China has recently done more to relax regulations and support free enterprise. The result has been tremendous growth, which may yet bring China into the ranks of the wealthier nations.[6]

## LO5 The Business Environment: The Context for Success

No business operates in a vacuum. Outside factors play a vital role in determining whether each individual business succeeds or fails. Likewise, the broader **business environment** can make the critical difference in whether an overall economy thrives or disintegrates. The five key dimensions of the business environment are the economic environment, the competitive environment, the technological environment, the social environment, and the global environment, as shown in exhibit 1.2.

### The Economic Environment

The U.S. economy is a global powerhouse, largely because the government takes active steps to reduce the risks of starting and running a business. As a result, free enterprise and fair competition flourish. One of the government policies that supports business is the relatively low federal tax rate, both for individuals and businesses. A number of states—from Alabama to Nevada—

**Exhibit 1.2**

Each dimension of the business environment impacts both individual businesses and the economy overall.

make their local economies even more attractive by providing special tax deals to attract new firms. The federal government also runs entire agencies that support business, such as the Small Business Administration. Other branches of the government, such as the Federal Trade Commission, actively promote fair competitive practices, which help give every enterprise a chance to succeed.

**business environment** The setting in which business operates. The five key components are economic environment, competitive environment, technological environment, social environment, and global environment.

Another key element of the U.S. economic environment is legislation that supports enforceable contracts. For instance, if you contract a company to supply your silk screening business with 1,000 blank tee shirts at $4.00 a piece, that firm must comply or face legal consequences. The firm can't wait until a day before delivery and jack up the price to $8.00 per piece because you would almost certainly respond with a successful lawsuit. Many U.S. residents take enforceable contracts for granted, but in a number of developing countries—which offer some of today's largest business opportunities—contracts are often not enforceable (at least not in day-to-day practice).

Corruption also plays a role in the economic environment. A low level of corruption and bribery dramatically reduces the risk of running a business. Fortunately, U.S. laws keep domestic corruption mostly—but not completely—at bay. Other ethical lapses can also increase the cost of doing business for everyone involved. But in the wake of ethical meltdowns at major corporations such as Enron and WorldCom, the federal government has passed tough-minded new regulations to increase corporate accountability. If the new legislation effectively curbs illegal and unethical practices, every business will have a fair chance at success.

Despite its overall strength, underlying issues threaten the U.S. economy. Personal income has grown, but economist Robert Gordon points out that "a lot of the goodies that we think of as raising living standards have gone to the people at the top at the expense of the broad mass of Americans in the middle." The national savings rate, another key indicator of economic health, fell below zero in 2005. In early 2008, *Newsweek* magazine reported that the average household owes 20% more than it makes each week, which helps to explain skyrocketing consumer debt. Meanwhile the federal debt continues to balloon, with the Treasury Department projecting a shortfall of about $400 billion in 2008 alone. Falling real estate prices and the subprime mortgage crisis have only exacerbated the issues. A record number of Americans are losing their houses to foreclosure, and key financial firms have foundered. These noteworthy weak spots in the U.S. economy may lead to a full-fledged recession that could severely impact business over the next decade. Upcoming chapters on economics and ethics will address these issues and their significance in more depth.[7]

## The Competitive Environment

value **The relationship between the price of a good or a service and the benefits that it offers its customers.**

As global competition intensifies yet further, leading-edge companies have focused on customer satisfaction as never before. The goal is to develop long-term, mutually beneficial relationships with customers. Getting current customers to buy more of your product is a lot less expensive than convincing potential customers to try your product for the first time. And if you transform your current customers into loyal advocates—vocal promoters of your product or service—they'll get those new customers for you more effectively than any advertising or discount program. Companies such as Southwest Airlines, Toyota, and Google lead their industries in customer satisfaction, which translates into higher profits even when the competition is tough.[8]

Customer satisfaction comes in large part from delivering unsurpassed **value**. The best measure of value is the size of the gap between product benefits and price. A product has value when its benefits to the customer are equal to or greater than the price that the customer pays. Keep in mind that the cheapest product doesn't necessarily represent the best value. If a 99-cent toy from Big Lots breaks in a day, customers may be willing to pay several dollars more for a similar toy from somewhere else. But if that 99-cent toy lasts all year, customers will be delighted by the value and will likely encourage their friends and family to shop at Big Lots. The key to value is quality, and virtually all successful firms offer top-quality products relative to their direct competitors.

Jack Trout, author, consultant, and 40-year veteran of marketing wars, sums up the current competitive environment by pointing out that markets he used to think were intensely competitive look like a tea party by today's standards. He recommends that companies cope by following four basic principles:

1. Avoid your competitors' strengths and exploit their weaknesses. Don't even try to beat them at their own game—instead, start a new one.
2. Always be a little bit paranoid about competition. This means never, ever underestimate your competitors.
3. Remember that competitors will usually get better if pushed. So don't assume that they won't fix their problems.
4. Don't forget that competitors are sometimes irrational when threatened. They may sacrifice their own profits to drive you out of business.[9]

A 2008 ranking study by *BusinessWeek* magazine and Interbrand consulting firm highlights brands that use imagination, innovation, and determination to deliver value to their customers. Exhibit 1.3 shows the winners and the up-and-comers in the race to capture the hearts, minds, and dollars of consumers around the world.

| **Exhibit 1.3** | Global brand champions and the ones to watch, *BusinessWeek* and Interbrand[10] |
| --- | --- |

| Most Valuable Brands | Biggest Gainers / Percentage Gain | |
| --- | --- | --- |
| 1. Coca-Cola | 1. Google | +43% |
| 2. IBM | 2. Apple | +24% |
| 3. Microsoft | 3. Amazon | +19% |
| 4. GE | 4. Zara | +15% |
| 5. Nokia | 5. Nintendo | +13% |
| 6. Toyota | | |
| 7. Intel | | |
| 8. McDonald's | | |
| 9. Disney | | |
| 10. Google | | |

© FRAZER HARRISON/GETTY IMAGES

## Creativity Counts!

For the past decade, economists have touted the Knowledge Economy—a new world order where nothing matters more than information and analysis, math and science, bits and bytes. But knowledge has become a commodity faster than anyone predicted. White-collar jobs have followed blue-collar jobs out of the country to far corners of the globe, landing with highly trained experts in places such as India, China, Russia, Argentina, and Hungary. In response, *BusinessWeek* magazine reports that the U.S. economy has shifted focus, concentrating on innovation and imagination to generate growth. American firms such as Procter & Gamble have demonstrated an uncanny ability to tap into consumer culture, generating breakthrough new products—such as the blockbuster Swiffer or the Tide-to-Go bleach stick—by figuring out what consumers want even before they do. The U.S. lead in consumer-focused creativity isn't surprising, given the enormous domestic market for consumer goods and the American tendency to think outside the box. But as other economies flex their creative muscles—and leverage firsthand knowledge of their local cultures—competition will clearly be fierce.[11]

**Leading Edge versus Bleeding Edge** **Speed-to-market**—the rate at which a firm transforms concepts into actual products—can be another key source of competitive advantage. And the pace of change just keeps getting faster. In this tumultuous setting, companies that stay ahead of the pack often enjoy a distinct advantage. But keep in mind that there's a difference between the leading edge and the bleeding edge. Bleeding edge firms launch products that fail because they're too far ahead of the market. During the late 1990s, for instance, in the heart of the dot-com boom, WebVan, a grocery delivery service launched to huge fanfare. But the firm went bankrupt in 2001, partly because customers weren't yet ready to dump traditional grocery stores in favor of cyber-shopping. Leading edge firms, on the other hand, offer products just as the market becomes ready to embrace them.[12]

Apple computer provides an excellent example of a leading edge company. You may be surprised to learn that Apple—which owns about 75% of the digital music player market—did not offer the first MP3 player. Instead, they surveyed the existing market to help develop a new product, the iPod, which was far superior in terms of design and ease-of-use. But Apple didn't stop with one successful MP3 player. Racing to stay ahead, they soon introduced the colorful, more affordable iPod mini. And before sales reached their peak, they launched the iPod Nano, which essentially pulled the rug from under the blockbuster iPod mini just a few short months before the holiday selling season. Why? If they didn't do it, someone else may well have done it instead. And Apple is almost maniacally focused on maintaining its competitive lead.[13]

**The Workforce Advantage** Employees can contribute another key dimension to a firm's competitive edge. A recent study found that investing in worker satisfaction can bring bottom line results. The researchers evaluated the stock price of 28 companies employing 920,000 people. In 2004, the stock price for companies with high morale rose an average of 16%, while the increase for their competitors with average morale was just 6%, and the jump for those with low morale was only 3%. A sense of fairness, a chance for achievement, and a team-oriented atmosphere seemed to be the three pivotal sources of employee satisfaction.[14]

Finding and holding the best talent will likely become a crucial competitive issue in the next decade, as the baby boom generation begins to retire. The 500 largest U.S. companies anticipate losing about half of their senior managers over the next 5 to 6 years. Replacing them will be tough: baby boomers include about 77 million people, while the generation that follows includes only 46 million. Firms that cultivate human resources now will find themselves better able to compete as the market for top talent tightens.[15]

## The Technological Environment

The broad definition of **business technology** includes any tools that businesses can use to become more efficient and effective. But more specifically, in today's world, business technology usually refers to computers, telecommunications, and other digital tools. Over the past few decades, the impact of digital technology on business has been utterly transformative. New industries have emerged, while others have disappeared. And some fields—such as travel, banking, and music—have changed dramatically. Even in categories with relatively unchanged products, companies have leveraged technology to streamline production and create new efficiencies. Examples include new processes such as computerized billing, digital animation, and robotic manufacturing. For fast-moving firms, the technological environment represents a rich source of competitive advantage, but it can clearly be a major threat for companies that are slow to adapt or to integrate new approaches.

The creation of the **World Wide Web** has transformed not only business, but also people's lives. Anyone, anywhere, anytime can use the Web to send and receive images and data. One result is the rise of e-commerce or online sales. Growing nearly five times

faster than total retail sales, retail **e-commerce** taps into a worldwide community of potential customers. Business-to-business selling is even more robust, comprising the vast majority of total e-commerce sales (and an even larger share of the profits). A growing number of businesses have also connected their digital networks with suppliers and distributors to create a more seamless flow of goods and services.[16]

Alternative selling strategies thrive on the Internet, giving rise to a more individualized buying experience. If you've browsed seller reviews on eBay or received shopping recommendations from Amazon, you'll have a sense of how personal Web marketing can feel. Online technology also allows leading edge firms to offer customized products at prices comparable to standardized products. On the Scion Website, for instance, customers can build their own car and "see it inside and out, with full rotation and zooming" while sitting at home in their pajamas.

As technology continues to evolve at breakneck speed, the scope of change—both in everyday life and business operations—is almost unimaginable. In this environment, companies that welcome change and manage it well will clearly be the winners.

## The Social Environment

The social environment embodies the values, attitudes, customs, and beliefs shared by groups of people. It also covers **demographics**, or the measurable characteristics of a population. Demographic factors include population size and density, and specific traits such as age, gender, race, education, and income. Clearly, given all these influences, the social environment changes dramatically from country to country. And a nation as diverse as the United States features a number of different social environments. Rather than cover the full spectrum, this section will focus instead on the broad social trends that most strongly impact American business. Understanding the various dimensions of the social environment is crucial, since successful businesses must offer goods and services that respond to it.

**Diversity** The American population has always included an array of different cultures, but the United States has become more ethnically diverse in recent years. Caucasians continue to represent the largest chunk of the population at nearly 70%, but the Hispanic and Asian populations are growing faster than any other ethnic groups. Looking ahead, the U.S. Census Bureau projects that those two groups will nearly double their size by 2050, while the Caucasian population will drop to only half of the U.S. population. The overall population breakdown would be as follows:

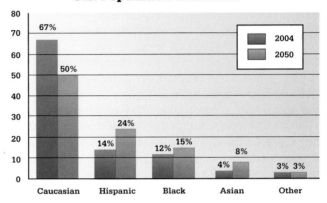

**U.S. Population Estimates[17]**

| | Caucasian | Hispanic | Black | Asian | Other |
|---|---|---|---|---|---|
| 2004 | 67% | 14% | 12% | 4% | 3% |
| 2050 | 50% | 24% | 15% | 8% | 3% |

But the national statistics are somewhat misleading, since ethnic groups tend to cluster together. African Americans, for example, currently comprise about 36% of the Mississippi population, Asians comprise about 58% of the Hawaiian population, and Hispanics comprise about 43% of the New Mexico population.[18]

So what does this mean for business? Growing ethnic populations offer robust profit potential for firms that pursue them. For instance, a number of major corporations such as AutoZone, Kellogg, Anheuser-Busch, PepsiCo, and Procter & Gamble have invested heavily in the Hispanic market over the past 5 years. A recent study shows that these heavy-hitters have realized an impressive $4 return on each $1 that they invested in Hispanic marketing. Targeting an ethnic market can also yield remarkable results for products that cross over into mainstream culture. Music mogul and entrepreneur Russell Simmons, for example, initially targeted his music and clothing to the black market, but

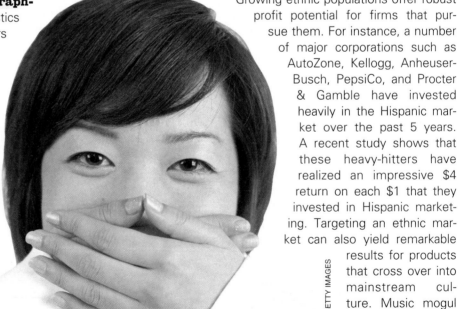

© RICHARD ROSS/RISER/GETTY IMAGES

his success quickly spilled over to mainstream culture, helping him build a hip-hop empire.[19]

Growing diversity also impacts the workforce. A diverse staff—one that reflects an increasingly diverse marketplace—can yield a powerful competitive advantage in terms of both innovation and ability to reach a broad customer base. From global behemoths such as General Electric to local corner stores, companies have taken proactive steps to hire and nurture people from a broad range of backgrounds. And that doesn't just reflect racial or ethnic roots. True diversity also includes differences in gender, age, religion, and nationality among others. Leading-edge firms have also taken proactive steps to train their entire workforce to manage diversity for top performance.[20]

Effectively managing diversity should only become easier as time goes by. Multiple studies demonstrate that young American adults are the most tolerant age group, and they are moving in a more tolerant direction than earlier generations regarding racial differences, immigrants, and homosexuality. As this generation gathers influence and experience in the workforce, they are likely to leverage diversity in their organizations to hone their edge in a fiercely competitive marketplace.[21]

**Aging Population** As life spans increase and birthrates decrease, the American population is rapidly aging. Its current median age is 35.9 years, and it's increasing month by month. Over the next 20 years, the size of our working population will shrink, while the number of retirees will explode. And the United States isn't alone in this trend. The population is aging across the developed world, from Western Europe to Japan. China faces the same issue, magnified by its huge population. Demographers estimate that by the middle of the 22nd century, China will be home to more than 400 million people age 65 or older.[22]

The rapidly aging population brings opportunities and threats for business. Companies in fields that cater to the elderly—such as healthcare, pharmaceuticals, travel, recreation, and financial management—will clearly boom. But creative companies in other fields will capitalize on the trend as well by re-imagining their current products to serve older clients. Possibilities include books, movies—maybe even videogames—with mature characters, low-impact fitness programs such as water aerobics, and cell phones and PDAs with more readable screens. Again, the potential payoff of age diversity is clear: companies with older employees are more likely to find innovative ways to reach the aging consumer market.

But surging retirement rates also pose significant threats to overall business success. With a smaller labor pool, companies will need to compete even harder for top talent, driving up recruitment and payroll costs. As state and federal governments stretch to serve the aging population, taxes may increase, putting an additional burden on business. And as mid-career workers spend more on elder care, they may find themselves with less to spend

## Innovation: For Better or for Worse

Creativity matters, not just for individual businesses, but also for the economy overall. And with global competition, the stakes are high. Encyclopedia Britannica recently explored creativity over time and across countries, compiling a list of the 100 greatest inventions of all time. The editors chose the winners—which they did not rank—based on how profoundly the innovations have impacted human life…for better or for worse. Before you read further, consider which inventions you would place on the list. Why have they impacted human life? How? What inventions would you expect to find in the future?

Many of the citations are not surprising. A few examples: the computer, eyeglasses, gunpowder, candles, vaccinations, and the atomic bomb. But other items are rather startling, including disposable diapers (which *have* improved the quality of life for millions of parents worldwide!), cat litter, bikinis, and the Monopoly board game. A few citations, such as Muzak (generic "elevator music"), Kool-Aid (powdered drink mix for kids), Astroturf (artificial grass), and Post-It notes are somewhat puzzling, although they have clearly permeated contemporary culture.

While most of the inventions are fairly recent, some are older than you might think. Flush toilets, for instance, have been around since the 1500s (thank you, Sir Harrington of England!), although toilet tissue wasn't invented until 1857. Vending machines were invented in Egypt sometime between 100 and 200 BC. And the construction nail was invented by the Sumerians in about 3,300 BC.

Interestingly, over the last century, corporations rather than individuals have been responsible for a growing number of key innovations. Examples include the camcorder (Sony), the laptop computer (Radio Shack), and Viagra (Pfizer). This trend is only likely to build momentum as global competition intensifies.

Among nations, the United States, despite our relatively short history, dominates the list of greatest inventions, with 162 of 325 citations, or just under 50%. One reason may be that our nation celebrates individuality, creativity, and, of course, the profit incentive. If we continue to flex our creative muscles, we could find ourselves with a competitive edge far into the 21st century.[23]

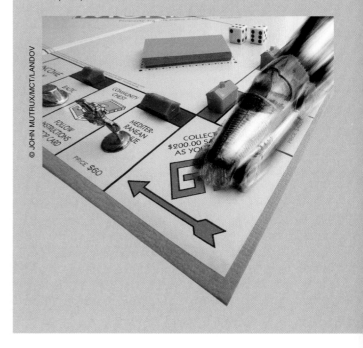

© JOHN MUTRUX/MCT/LANDOV

on other goods and services, shrinking the size of the consumer market.

**Rising Worker Expectations**   Workers of all ages continue to seek flexibility from their employers. Moreover, following massive corporate layoffs of the early 2000s, employees are much less apt to be loyal to their firms. A recent survey shows that only 59% of employees say they are loyal to their companies, and only 26% believe that their companies are loyal to them. As young people today enter the workforce, they bring higher expectations for their employers in terms of salary, job responsibility, and flexibility—and less willingness to pay dues by working extra long hours or doing a high volume of "grunt work." Smart firms are responding to the change in worker expectations by forging a new partnership with their employees. The goal is a greater level of mutual respect through open communication, information sharing, and training. And the not-so-hidden agenda, of course, is stronger long-term performance.[24]

**Ethics and Social Responsibility**   With high-profile ethical meltdowns dominating the headlines in the past few years, workers, consumers, and government alike have begun to hold businesses—and the people who run them—to a higher standard. Recent federal legislation, passed in the wake of the Enron fiasco, demands transparent financial management and more accountability from senior executives. And recognizing their key role in business success, a growing number of consumers and workers have begun to insist that companies play a proactive role in making their communities—and often the world community—better places. Nearly 80% of consumers, for example, consider corporate citizenship when making investment and purchasing decisions. And employee loyalty hits nearly 90% at companies that support social causes.[25]

> ❝
> We believe humor is essential to success. We applaud irreverence and don't take ourselves too seriously. We yodel.
> –Yahoo Core Value
> ❞

## The Global Environment

The U.S. economy operates within the context of the global environment, interacting continually with other economies. In fact, over the last two decades, technology and free trade have blurred the lines between individual economies around the world. Technology has forged unprecedented links among countries, making it cost effective—even efficient—to establish computer help centers in Bombay to service customers in Boston, or

## Are You Part of Generation C?

The C stands for *content,* but it could just as easily stand for *creative* or *control.* Generation C, identified by the widely respected *Trendwatching* Website, embodies a flood of consumers creating content for the Web, and customizing—even coproducing—the products they consume. According to the Pew Internet and American Life Survey, 44% of U.S. adult Internet users have created cyber content by building or contributing to Websites, creating blogs, and sharing files. This number will only increase as today's digitally literate kids hit age 18.

Savvy companies actively encourage Generation C to unleash the artist within by developing and promoting tools that make it easy. Canon ensures snap-happy amateurs that "professional digital photography is no longer just for the professionals." HP tells consumers that YOU should take pictures about YOU, and you should share them, and forward them, and print them, and (of course) post them on the Web. Xingtone lets consumers compose their own ring tones. Trekshare.com encourages travelers to post tips and travelogues. San Francisco's KYOU Radio receives about 15 listener-created podcasts each day. And Apple's blockbuster GarageBand program turns computer-based wannabes into virtual rock stars.

Business opportunities abound in this highly charged setting. Successful companies will delight Generation C with new tools, the training to use them, and the forum to showcase their efforts. And who knows? With so many resources, you might find yourself with more than just 15 minutes of fame.[26]

© BIG CHEESE PHOTO/JUPITERIMAGES

© DAVID SACKS/THE IMAGE BANK/GETTY IMAGES

**Global trade has forged unprecedented links among nations.**

**A Multipronged Threat** In the past decade alone, war, terrorism, disease, and natural disasters have taken a horrific toll in human lives across the globe. The economic toll has been devastating as well, impacting businesses around the world. The 9/11 terrorist attacks in New York and Washington, D.C., decimated the travel industry, and led to multibillion dollar government outlays for Homeland Security. More recently, Hurricane Katrina destroyed homes and businesses alike and brought the Gulf Coast oil industry to a virtual standstill. In 2002 a terrorist bombing at an Indonesian nightclub killed nearly 200 people, destroying tourism on the holiday island of Bali. The 2003 deadly epidemic of the SARS flu dealt a powerful blow to the economies of Hong Kong, Beijing, and Toronto. Less than 2 years later the Indian Ocean tsunami wiped out the fishing industry on long swaths of the Indian and Sri Lankan coastline and crippled the booming Thai tourism industry. And the war in Iraq—while a boon to the defense industry—has dampened the economic potential of the Middle East. With nationalism on the rise, and growing religious and ethnic tensions around the world, the global economy may continue to suffer collateral damage.[28]

to hire programmers in Buenos Aires to make Websites for companies in Stockholm. Not surprisingly, jobs have migrated to the lowest bidder with the highest quality—regardless of where that bidder is based.

Often, the lowest bidder is based in China or India. Both economies are growing at breakneck speed, largely because they attract enormous foreign investment. China has been a magnet for manufacturing jobs because of its large population and low wages—an average of 64 cents per hour versus $21.11 per hour in the United States. And India has been especially adept at attracting high-tech jobs, in part because of their world-class, English-speaking university graduates who are willing to work for less than their counterparts around the globe.[27]

The migration of jobs relates closely to the global movement towards **free trade**. In 1995, a renegotiation of the **General Agreement on Tariffs and Trade (GATT)**—signed by 125 countries—took bold steps to lower tariffs (taxes on imports) and to reduce trade restrictions worldwide. The revised agreement also established the **World Trade Organization (WTO)** to enforce its provisions and to further promote free trade. As a result, goods move more freely than ever across international boundaries. Individual groups of countries have gone even further, creating blocs of nations with virtually unrestricted trade. Mexico, Canada, and the United States have laid the groundwork for a free trade mega-market through the North American Free Trade Agreement (NAFTA), and 27 European countries have created a powerful free trading bloc through the European Union. The free trade movement has lowered prices and increased quality across virtually every product category, as competition becomes truly global. We'll discuss these issues and their implications in more depth in Chapter 3.

> In Asia, the average person's living standards are currently set to rise by 10,000% in one lifetime!
>
> —*NewsWeek*

## LO6 Business and You: Making It Personal

Whatever your career choice—from videogame developer, to real estate agent, to Web designer—business will impact your life. Both the broader economy and your own business skills will influence the level of your personal financial success. In light of these factors, making the right career choice can be a bit scary. But the good news is that experts advise graduating students to "Do what you love." And this is a hard-headed strategy, not soft-hearted puffery. Following your passion makes dollars and sense in today's environment, which values less routine abilities such as creativity, communication, and caring. Exercising these abilities tends to be more rewarding for most people than using routine, programmable skills that computers can easily emulate. Following your passion doesn't guarantee a fat paycheck. But it does boost your chances of both financial and personal success.[29]

# Economics:
## The
# Framework
### for Business

# 2

## LEARNING OBJECTIVES

After studying this chapter, you will be able to...

**LO1** Define economics and discuss the impact of economics on business

**LO2** Explain and evaluate the free market system and supply and demand

**LO3** Explain and evaluate planned market systems

**LO4** Describe the trend toward mixed market systems

**LO5** Discuss key terms and tools to evaluate economic performance

**LO6** Analyze the impact of fiscal and monetary policy on the economy

4ltrpress.cengage.com/busn

> In economics it is a far, far wiser thing to be right than to be consistent.
> —John Kenneth Galbraith, economist

## LO1 Why Economics Matters

Knowing economics won't make you money. But economics *will* give you a deeper understanding of the broad forces that impact both your business and your personal life. Knowing even basic economic principles can help you make better business decisions, and better decisions can certainly help you make more money.

The **economy** is essentially a financial and social system. It represents the flow of resources—natural resources, capital, human resources, and entrepreneurship—through society, from production, to distribution, to consumption. **Economics** is the study of the choices that people, companies, and governments make in allocating those resources.

From a business standpoint, a key goal of economics is to guide future decisions by applying a deep understanding of past choices. But economics is not a crystal ball. Economic predictions are often imperfect simply because the economy is so complex. Thousands of variables—general and specific—feed into the system, and most of those variables undergo constant flux. Examples include the price of oil, the attitude of consumers, the decisions of individual firms, the value of the dollar...even the weather! Yet despite the complexity and constant change, broad economic trends—such as inflation, employment, and growth—are clearly discernable, providing a context that impacts every business.

### Macroeconomics Versus Microeconomics: Same Scene, Different Takes

The field of economics falls into two core categories: macroeconomics and microeconomics. **Macroeconomics** is the study of a country's overall economic issues, such as the employment rate, the gross domestic product, and taxation policies. While macroeconomic issues may seem abstract, they directly impact your day-to-day life, influencing key variables such as what jobs will be available for you, how much cash you'll actually take home after taxes, or how much you can buy with that cash in any given month.

**Microeconomics** focuses on smaller economic units such as individual consumers, families, and individual businesses. Every day, you and your peers make microeconomic

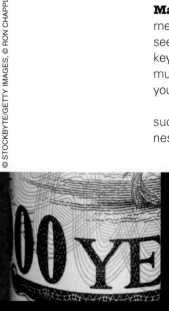

**economy** A financial and social system of how resources flow through society, from production, to distribution, to consumption.

**economics** The study of the choices that people, companies, and governments make in allocating society's resources.

**macroeconomics** The study of a country's overall economic issues, such as the employment rate, the gross domestic product, and taxation policies.

**microeconomics** The study of smaller economic units such as individual consumers, families, and individual businesses.

**economic system** A structure for allocating limited resources.

**capitalism** An economic system—also known as the private enterprise or free market system—based on private ownership, economic freedom, and fair competition.

choices. Imagine, for instance, that the price of coffee on your college campus suddenly increases by $2.00 per cup. What might happen? To predict the response, you'd need to consider a number of factors, including:

- How much of their excess cash do students spend on coffee? How would that change with the price increase?

- Is it easy to find other choices such as tea, water, soda and energy drinks? Are any of these options good substitutes for coffee? How do their prices compare to the new price of coffee?

- What about the timing? Is it finals week? The beginning of the semester? Or is it during summer break? How badly will people need their caffeine?

The answers to these questions would clearly influence how you and your friends respond to the price increase. And your responses matter—they could either make or break the campus coffee business. Through simple microeconomics analysis, the campus coffee vendor could figure out in advance how a price increase might affect profits. On a broader scale, the constant, changing interplay between micro- and macroeconomic factors—individual behavior

and broad trends—determines the shape of the entire economy.

## Economic Systems: Different Ways to Allocate Resources

It's a simple fact: everyone can't get everything they want all of the time. We live in a world of finite resources, which means that societies must determine how to distribute resources among their members. An **economic system** is a structure for allocating limited resources. Over time and around the globe, nations have instituted different economic systems. But a careful analysis suggests that no system is perfect, which may explain why there isn't one standard approach. The next several sections examine each basic type of economic system and explore the trend toward mixed economies.

## LO2 Capitalism: The Free Market System

**Capitalism** is also known as a private enterprise system or a free market system. Founded by Adam Smith in the 1700s, capitalism is based on private ownership, economic freedom, and fair competition. A core capitalist principle is the paramount importance of individuals, innovation, and hard work. In a capitalist economy—such as the United States—individuals, businesses, or nonprofit organizations privately own the vast

## TechNotes

## Tollbooths on the Information Superhighway?

On today's Internet, consumers sit in the driver seat: you, your friends, and everyone else who uses the Web determine which sites succeed—and which sites fail—depending on where you choose to go most often. Your Internet service provider (ISP) simply provides a connection between you and the Web sites of your choice. When you click on a site, information races from the site to you as fast as the network can send it, without regard to content. According to Vinton Cerf, Google's "Internet Evangelist," the success of the Internet stems largely from the lack of gatekeepers over new content or services. This concept is called network neutrality, and it has contributed to the amazing abundance of choice that we all enjoy on the Web.

But as cable companies and phone companies consolidate their control over high-speed Internet access, they may start deciding which information should move most quickly. And guess who will have the edge? The companies that can afford to pay for it. Sites that stop by the ISP tollbooth will swerve straight into the fast lane, while tiny start-up sites—such as Facebook and eBay were a few short years ago—will meander down the slow lane, doing their best to maneuver around the potholes. The New York Times believes that cable and phone companies might also limit access to new innovations, such as Vonage's cheap, popular Internet phone service, if they perceive a threat to their revenue.

The United States Senate recently began hearings on network neutrality. Advocates argue that neutrality is key for fostering a free, open network. Opponents, on the other hand, argue that the government shouldn't legislate neutrality, and that ISPs should be free to charge whatever they want for access to their networks. The basic question is whether users or ISPs—a handful of huge companies—should guide the evolution of the Internet. The answer to that question could shape the future of the world economy.[1]

# Oops! What were they THINKING?!

## Cracks in the Crystal Ball…

For thousands of years, forecasting the future has been the province of colorful fortunetellers, reading the stars and gazing into their crystal balls. But forecasters today are more likely to wear conservative suits and tote complex computer models as they predict the future of our complex, changing economy.

Despite their modern tools, economic forecasters are still far from perfect. Here are a few examples of predictions gone wrong:

- On March 6, 1999, the respected journal *Economist* predicted that the price of oil might soon fall as low as $5 per barrel, since the world was already "awash" in oil. Two weeks later, the price of oil had risen by 30%, and less than a year later it hit $25 per barrel. And by 2008, the price of oil was well over $100 per barrel. Oops.

- At the end of 2004, the majority of the American people in a Gallup poll predicted that 2005 "would be a year of economic difficulty." Even though it was a tough year for many, the unemployment rate hit a 30-year low, the economy continued to grow, and household wealth hit an all-time high. That's not bad for a "difficult" year!

- On January 1, 2005, Charles H. Ferguson, author of *Technology Review*, predicted, "Google will need brilliant strategy and flawless execution simply to survive." Google closed 2005 with a 267% increase in net income. If that were barely surviving, success would be something to see!

Although forecasting blunders can be downright embarrassing, making the effort is well worthwhile, since—at the very least—predictions spark discussion, which leads to greater understanding and better decisions. And when the crystal ball cracks, economic forecasters can always fall back on the defense of John Maynard Keynes: "When the facts change, I change my mind. What do you do, sir?"[2]

---

majority of enterprises (only a small fraction are owned by the government). These private sector businesses are free to make their own choices regarding everything from what they will produce, to how much they will charge, to whom they will hire and fire. Correspondingly, individuals are free to choose what they will buy, how much they are willing to pay, and where they will work.

To thrive in a free enterprise system, companies must offer value to their customers—otherwise, their customers will choose to go elsewhere. Businesses must also offer value to their employees and suppliers in order to attract top-quality talent and supplies. As companies compete to attract the best resources and offer the best values, quality goes up, prices remain reasonable, and choices proliferate, raising the standard of living in the economy as a whole.

## The Fundamental Rights of Capitalism

For capitalism to succeed, the system must ensure some fundamental rights—or freedoms—to all of the people who live within the economy.

- *The right to own a business and keep after-tax profits.* Remember that capitalism doesn't guarantee that anyone will actually *earn* profits. Nor does it promise that there won't be taxes. But if you do earn profits, you get to keep your after-tax income and spend it however you see fit (within the limits of the law, of course). This right acts as a powerful motivator for business owners in a capitalist economy; the lower the tax rate, the higher the motivation. The U.S. government strives to maintain low tax rates to preserve the after-tax profit incentive that plays such a pivotal role in the free enterprise system.

- *The right to private property:* This means that individuals and private businesses can buy, sell, and use property—which includes land, machines, and buildings—in any way that makes sense to them. This right also includes the right to will property to family members. The only exceptions to private property rights are minimal government restrictions designed to protect the greater good. You can't, for instance, use your home or business to produce cocaine, abuse children, or spew toxic smoke into the air.

**Women make about 80% of buying decisions in U.S. households. And they're likely to do more research and be less influenced by advertising than men.**

**pure competition** A market structure with many competitors selling virtually identical products. Barriers to entry are quite low.

**monopolistic competition** A market structure with many competitors selling differentiated products. Barriers to entry are low.

- *The right to free choice:* Capitalism relies on economic freedom. People and businesses must be free to buy (or not buy) according to their wishes. They must be free to choose where to work (or not work) and where to live (or not live). Freedom of choice directly feeds competition, creating a compelling incentive for business owners to offer the best goods and services at the lowest prices. U.S. government trade policies boost freedom of choice by encouraging a wide array of both domestic and foreign producers to compete freely for our dollars.

- *The right to fair competition:* A capitalist system depends on fair competition among businesses to drive higher quality, lower prices, and more choices. Capitalism can't achieve its potential if unfair practices—such as deceptive advertising, predatory pricing, and broken contracts—mar the free competitive environment. The government's role is to create a level playing field by establishing regulations and monitoring the competition to ensure compliance.

© GAVIN HELLIER/ROBERT HARDING WORLD IMAGERY/GETTY IMAGES

## Four Degrees of Competition

While competition is essential for the free market system to function, not all competition works the same. Different industries experience different degrees of competition, ranging from pure competition to monopolies.

- **Pure competition** is a market structure with many competitors selling virtually identical products. Since customers can't (or won't) distinguish one product from another, no single producer has any control over the price. And new producers can easily enter and leave purely competitive markets. In today's U.S. economy, examples of pure competition have virtually disappeared. Agriculture probably comes closest—corn is basically corn, for example—but with the dramatic growth of huge corporate farms and the success of major cooperatives such as Sunkist, the number of competitors in agriculture has dwindled and new farmers have trouble entering the market. Not only that, segments of the agriculture market—such as organic farms and hormone-free dairies—have emerged with hit products that command much higher prices than the competition.

> "You cannot help the poor by destroying the rich. You cannot lift the wage earner by pulling down the wage payer.
> –Abraham Lincoln

- **Monopolistic competition** is a market structure with many competitors selling differentiated products. Producers have some control over the price of their wares depending on the value that they offer their customers. And new producers can fairly easily enter categories marked by monopolistic competition. In fact, if a monopolistic category takes off, it typically attracts a number of new suppliers quite quickly. Examples of monopolistic competition include the clothing industry and the restaurant business. Think about the clothing business, for a moment, in local terms. How many firms do you know that sell tee shirts? You could probably think of at least 50 without too much trouble. And the quality and price are all over the board: designer tee shirts can sell for well over $100, but plenty of options go for less than $10. How hard would it be to start your own tee shirt business? Probably not hard at all. In fact, chances are strong that you know at least one person who sells tee shirts on the side. In terms of product and price variation, number of firms, and ease of entry, the tee shirt business clearly demonstrates the characteristics of monopolistic competition.

- **Oligopoly** is a market structure with only a handful of competitors selling products that are either similar or different. The retail gasoline business and the car manufacturing industry, for instance, are both oligopolies, even though gas stations offer very similar products, and car companies offer quite different models and features. Other examples of oligopoly include the soft drink industry, the computer business, and network television. Breaking into a market characterized by oligopoly can be tough because it typically requires a huge upfront investment. You could start making tee shirts in your kitchen, for instance, but you'd need a pretty expensive facility to start manufacturing cars. Oligopolies typically avoid intense price competition, since they have nothing to gain—every competitor simply makes less money. When price wars do flair up, the results can be devastating for entire industries.

- **Monopoly** is a market structure with just a single producer completely dominating the industry, leaving no room for any significant competitors. Monopolies usually aren't good for anyone but the company that has control, since without competition there isn't any incentive to hold down prices or increase quality and choices. Because monopolies can harm the economy, most are illegal according to federal legislation, such as the Sherman Antitrust Act of 1890 and the Clayton Antitrust Act of 1914. Microsoft is the latest example of an industry giant that ran afoul of antimonopoly laws due to its position and policies in the software business. Even though Microsoft is not an actual monopoly, it was convicted of "monopolistic practices" that undermined fair competition.

However, in a few instances, the government not only allows monopolies, but actually encourages them. This usually occurs when it would be too inefficient for each competitor to build its own infrastructure to serve the public. A **natural monopoly** arises. Cable television offers a clear example. Would it really make sense for even a handful of competitors to wire neighborhoods separately for cable? Clearly, that's not practical. . . just imagine the chaos! Instead, the government has granted cable franchises—or monopolies—to individual companies, and then regulated them (with mixed results) to ensure that they don't abuse the privilege. In addition to natural monopolies, the government grants patents and copyrights, which create artificial monopoly situations (at least temporarily), in order to encourage innovation.

**oligopoly** A market structure with only a handful of competitors selling products that are either similar or different. Barriers to entry are typically high.

**monopoly** A market structure with one producer completely dominating the industry, leaving no room for any significant competitors. Barriers to entry tend to be virtually insurmountable.

**natural monopoly** A market structure with one company as the supplier of a product because the nature of that product makes a single supplier more efficient than multiple, competing ones. Most natural monopolies are government sanctioned and regulated.

## A Cheesy Approach?

"Happy cows" in California—created by the California Milk Board to offer comical musings on the good life in the Golden State—have helped propel California cheese production from 281 million pounds in 1983 to more than 2 billion pounds in 2007. Although some might argue that a good cheddar is a good cheddar regardless of where it's from, the happy cow marketing campaign has created a clear perception of superiority for California cheese. In 1999 the California Cheese Board began sending those happy cows to other states, taking market share from (apparently) less happy cows in Wisconsin and elsewhere. In Washington State, the *Puget Sound Business Journal* notes that the motto of their homegrown Dairgold milk farm sounds downright grim in comparison: "Local cows, working hard." Chances are good that those California dairy farmers are the only ones more happy than their cows as they milk a campaign that creates a competitive edge.[3]

## Supply and Demand: Fundamental Principles of a Free Market System

**supply** The quantity of products that producers are willing to offer for sale at different market prices.

**supply curve** The graphed relationship between price and quantity from a supplier standpoint.

**demand** The quantity of products that consumers are willing to buy at different market prices.

**demand curve** The graphed relationship between price and quantity from a customer demand standpoint.

**equilibrium price** The price associated with the point at which the quantity demanded of a product equals the quantity supplied.

In a free market system, the continual interplay between buyers and sellers determines the selection of products and prices available in the economy. If a business makes something that few people actually want, sales will be low and the firm will typically yank the product from the market. Similarly, if the price of a product is too high, low sales will dictate a price cut. But if a new good or service becomes a hit, you can bet that similar offerings from other firms will pop up almost immediately (unless barriers—such as government-granted patents—prevent new entrants). The concepts of demand and supply explain how the dynamic interaction between buyers and sellers directly impacts the range of products and prices in the free market.

**Supply** **Supply** refers to the quantity of products that producers are willing to offer for sale at different market prices. Since businesses seek to make as much profit as possible, they are likely to produce more of a product that commands a higher market price, and less of a product that commands a lower price. Think about it in terms of pizza. Assume it costs a local restaurant about $5 to make a pizza. If the market price for pizza hits, say, $20, you can bet that restaurant will start cranking out pizza. But if the price drops to $6, the restaurant has much less incentive to focus on pizza and will probably invest its limited resources in cooking other dishes.

The relationship between price and quantity from a supplier standpoint can be shown on a graph called the **supply curve**. The supply curve maps quantity on the x-axis (or horizontal axis) and price on the y-axis (or vertical axis). In most categories, as the price rises, the quantity produced rises correspondingly, yielding a graph that curves up as it moves to the right. Exhibit 2.1 shows a possible supply curve for pizza.

**Demand** **Demand** refers to the quantity of products that consumers are willing to buy at different market prices. Since consumers generally seek to get the products they need (or want) at the lowest possible prices, they tend to buy more of products with lower prices and less of products with higher prices. Pizza and tacos, for instance, are both popular meals. But if pizza costs a lot less than tacos, most people will get pizza more often than tacos. Likewise, if the price of pizza were out of hand, people would probably order tacos (or some other option) more often, reserving their pizza-eating for special occasions.

The relationship between price and quantity from a demand standpoint can be shown on a graph called the **demand curve**. Like the supply curve, the demand curve maps quantity on the x-axis and price on the y-axis. But different from the supply curve, the demand curves for most goods and services slopes down as it moves to the right, since quantity demanded tends to drop as prices rise. Exhibit 2.2 shows how a demand curve for pizza could look.

**Equilibrium Price** It's important to remember that supply and demand don't operate in a vacuum. The constant interaction between the two forces helps determine the market price in any given category. In theory, the actual market price occurs at the point where the supply curve and the demand curve intersect (see exhibit 2.3). The price associated with this point of intersection—the point where the quantity demanded equals the quantity supplied—is called the **equilibrium price**.

| **Exhibit 2.1** | Supply Curve |

Supply Curve

*Y-axis: Price per Pizza ($), from 0 to 22*
*X-axis: Quantity of Pizza Supplied per Day (in Thousands), from 0 to 120*

## LO3 Planned Economies: Socialism and Communism

In capitalist economies, private ownership is paramount. Individuals own businesses and their personal fortunes

## Exhibit 2.2  Demand Curve

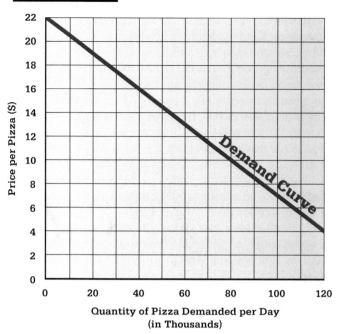

Demand Curve

Price per Pizza ($) vs. Quantity of Pizza Demanded per Day (in Thousands)

## Exhibit 2.3  Equilibrium

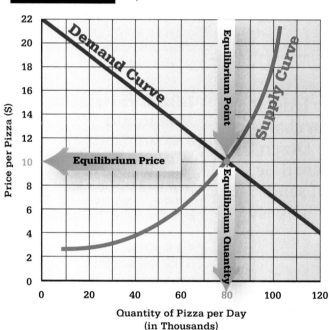

Demand Curve / Supply Curve / Equilibrium Point / Equilibrium Price / Equilibrium Quantity

Price per Pizza ($) vs. Quantity of Pizza per Day (in Thousands)

depend on their success in the free market. But in planned economies, the government plays a more heavy-handed role in controlling the economy. The two key categories of planned economies are socialism and communism.

### Socialism

**Socialism** is an economic system based on the principle that the government should own and operate key enterprises that directly affect public welfare, such as utilities, telecommunications, and healthcare. Although the official government goal is to run these enterprises in the best interest of the overall public, inefficiencies and corruption often interfere with effectiveness. Socialist economies also tend to have higher taxes, which are designed to distribute wealth more evenly through society. Tax revenues typically fund services that citizens in free enterprise systems would have to pay for themselves in countries with lower tax rates. Examples range from free childcare to free university education.

Most Western European countries—from Sweden, to Germany, to the United Kingdom—developed powerful socialist economies in the second half of the 20th century. But more recently, growth in these countries has languished. Although many factors have contributed to the slowdown, the impact of high taxes on the profit incentive and lavish social programs on the work incentive has clearly played a role. Potential entrepreneurs may migrate to countries that let them keep more of their profits, and workers with abundant benefits may find themselves losing motivation.

### Communism

**Communism** is an economic and political system that calls for public ownership of virtually all enterprises, under the direction of a strong central government. The communist concept was the brainchild

### The Cost of an Ice-Cold Coke

Most of us are used to the idea that a matinee costs a whole lot less than an evening at the movies. And even if we don't like it, we've accepted that the same airplane seat costs more if you buy it right before you fly. But in 1999, Coca-Cola took the laws of supply and demand just a little too far. The beverage behemoth announced its intention to install thermometers in its vending machines so it could charge more for a cold Coke on a hot day. But consumers were outraged at the very idea, forcing Coca-Cola to backpedal almost immediately. Tim Manners of *Reveries* marketing magazine suggests that Coke should have considered *lowering* their prices on hot days. Even if they didn't sell enough extra sodas to boost their profits, the bump in goodwill would have probably more than made up for the few lost cents per bottle.[4]

**mixed economies** Economies that embody elements of both planned and market-based economic systems.

**privatization** The process of converting government-owned businesses to private ownership.

**gross domestic product (GDP)** The total value of all final goods and services produced within a nation's physical boundaries over a given period of time.

of political philosopher Karl Marx, who outlined its core principles in his 1848 *Communist Manifesto*. The communism that Marx envisioned was supposed to dramatically improve the lot of the worker at the expense of the super rich.

But countries that adopted communism in the 1900s—most notably the former Soviet Union, China, Cuba, North Korea, and Vietnam—did not thrive. Most imposed authoritarian governments that suspended individual rights and choices. People were unable to make even basic choices such as where to work or what to buy. Without the free market to establish what to produce, crippling shortages and surpluses developed. Corruption infected every level of government. Under enormous pressure from their own people and the rest of the world, communism began to collapse across the Soviet Union and its satellite nations at the end of the 1980s, replaced with democracy and the free market. Over the past two decades, China has also introduced significant free market reforms across much of the country, fueling its torrid growth rate. And in the 1990s, Vietnam launched free market reforms, stimulating rapid, sustained growth. The remaining communist economic systems— North Korea and Cuba—continue to falter, their people facing drastic shortages and even starvation.

## LO4 Mixed Economies: The Story of the Future

In today's world, pure economies—either market or planned—are practically nonexistent, since each would fall far short of meeting the needs of its citizens. A pure market economy would make insufficient provision for the old, the young, the sick, and the environment. A pure planned economy would not create enough value to support its people over the long term. Instead, most of today's nations have **mixed economies**, falling somewhere along a spectrum that ranges from pure planned at one extreme to pure market at the other.

Even the United States—one of the most market-oriented economies in the world—does not have a *pure* market economy. The various branches of the government own a number of major enterprises, including the postal service, schools, parks, libraries, entire systems of universities, and the military. In fact, the federal government is the nation's largest employer, providing jobs for more than 4 million Americans. The government also intervenes extensively in the free market by creating regulations that stimulate competition and protect both consumers and workers.[5]

Over the past 30 years, most economies of the world have begun moving toward the market end of the spectrum. Government-owned businesses have converted to private ownership via a process called **privatization**. Socialist governments have reduced red tape, cracked down on corruption, and created new laws to protect economic rights. Extravagant human services—from free healthcare to education subsidies—have shrunk. And far-reaching tax reform has created new incentives for both domestic and foreign investment in once-stagnant planned economies.[6]

Unfortunately the price of economic restructuring has been a fair amount of social turmoil in many nations undergoing market reforms. Countries from France to China have experienced sometimes-violent demonstrations in response to social and employment program cutbacks. Change is challenging, especially when it redefines economic winners and losers. But countries that have taken strides toward the market end of the spectrum—from small players like the Czech Republic, to large players like China—have seen the payoff in rejuvenated growth rates that have raised the standard of living for millions of people.

> " If you put the federal government in charge of the Sahara Desert, in 5 years there'd be a shortage of sand.
> —Milton Friedman, economist "

## LO5 Evaluating Economic Performance: What's Working?

Clearly, economic systems are complex...very complex. So you probably won't be surprised to learn that no single measure captures all the dimensions of economic performance. To get the full picture, you need to understand a range of terms and measures, including gross domestic product, employment level, the business cycle, inflation rate, and productivity.

### Gross Domestic Product

Nominal **gross domestic product**, or GDP, measures the total value of all final goods and services produced within a nation's physical boundaries over a given period of time, not adjusting for inflation. All domestic production is included in the GDP, even when the producer is foreign-owned. The U.S. GDP, for instance, includes the value of Toyota pickup trucks built in Texas, even though Toyota is a Japanese firm. Likewise, the Mexican GDP includes the value of Whirlpool appliances built in Mexican factories, even though Whirlpool is an American firm.

GDP is a vital measure of economic health. Business-people, economists, and political leaders use GDP to measure the economic performance of individual nations and to compare the growth among nations. Interestingly, GDP levels tend to be somewhat understated, since they don't include any illegal activities—such as paying undocumented nannies and gardeners, or selling illegal drugs—which can represent a significant portion of some countries' production. The GDP also ignores legal goods that are not reported to avoid taxation, plus output produced within households. In 2007 the GDP of the United States was more than $13 trillion, with a 2.2% growth rate. Check out chapter 3 for a survey of the world's key economies according to total GDP and GDP growth rate.[6a]

## Employment Level

The overall level of employment is another key element of economic health. When people have jobs they have money, which allows them to spend and invest, fueling economic growth. Most nations track employment levels largely through the **unemployment rate**, which includes everyone age 16 and older who doesn't have a job and is actively seeking one. The U.S. unemployment rate from 2000 to 2007 has ranged between 4% and 6%, which is relatively low compared to both historical U.S. levels and the unemployment rates in other countries.[7]

Interestingly, some unemployment is actually good—it reflects your freedom to change jobs. If you have an awful boss, for instance, you may just quit. Are you unemployed? Of course, you are. Are you glad? You probably are, and the chances are good that you'll find another position that's a better fit for you. This type of job loss is called *frictional unemployment*, and it tends to be ultimately positive. *Structural unemployment*, on the other hand, is usually longer term. This category encompasses people who don't have jobs because the economy no longer needs their skills. In the United States growing numbers of workers in the past decade have found themselves victims of structural unemployment as manufacturing jobs have moved overseas. Often their only option is expensive retraining. Two other categories of unemployment are *cyclical,* which involves layoffs during recessions, and *seasonal,* which involves job loss related to the time of year. In some areas of the country, construction and agricultural workers are seasonally unemployed, but the best example may be the department store Santa who only has a job during the holiday season!

## The Business Cycle

The **business cycle** is the periodic contraction and expansion that occurs over time in virtually every economy. But the word "cycle" may be a little misleading, since it implies that the economy contracts and expands in a predictable pattern. In reality, the phases of the cycle are different each time they happen, and—despite the efforts of countless experts—no one can accurately predict when changes will occur or how long they will last. Those who make the best guesses stand to make fortunes, but bad bets can be financially devastating. The two key phases of the business cycle are contraction and expansion, shown in exhibit 2.4.

- **Contraction** is a period of economic downturn, marked by rising unemployment. Businesses cut back on production, and consumers shift their buying patterns to more basic products and fewer luxuries. The economic "feel-good factor" simply disappears. Economists declare an official **recession** when GDP decreases for two consecutive quarters. A **depression** is an especially deep and long-lasting recession. Fortunately, economies seldom spiral into full-blown depressions, thanks in large part to proactive intervention from the government. The last depression in the United States was the Great Depression of the 1930s. Whether a downturn is mild or severe, the very bottom of the contraction is called the trough, as shown in exhibit 2.4.

- **Recovery** is a period of rising economic growth and increasing employment, following a contraction. Businesses begin to expand. Consumers start to regain confidence, and spending begins to rise. The recovery is essentially the transition period between contraction and expansion.

- **Expansion** is a period of robust economic growth and high employment. Businesses expand to capitalize on emerging opportunities. Consumers are optimistic and confident, which fuels purchasing, which fuels produc-

**unemployment rate** The percentage of people in the labor force over age 16 who do not have jobs and are actively seeking employment.

**business cycle** The periodic contraction and expansion that occurs over time in virtually every economy.

**contraction** A period of economic downturn, marked by rising unemployment and falling business production.

**recession** An economic downturn marked by a decrease in the GDP for two consecutive quarters.

**depression** An especially deep and long-lasting recession.

**recovery** A period of rising economic growth and employment.

**expansion** A period of robust economic growth and high employment.

**Employment in the auto industry has decreased in the midwest and increased in the south.**

**inflation** A period of rising average prices across the economy.

**hyperinflation** An average monthly inflation rate of more than 50%.

**disinflation** A period of slowing average price increases across the economy.

**deflation** A period of falling average prices across the economy.

**consumer price index (CPI)** A measure of inflation that evaluates the change in the weighted-average price of goods and services that the average consumer buys each month.

**producer price index (PPI)** A measure of inflation that evaluates the change over time in the weighted-average wholesale prices.

**productivity** The basic relationship between the production of goods and services (output) and the resources needed to produce them (input), calculated via the following equation: output/input = productivity.

tion, which fuels further hiring. As exhibit 2.4 demonstrates, the height of economic growth is called the peak of the expansion. The U.S. economy had the longest growth spurt on record during the 10-year period from 1991 to 2001. After a relatively mild slowdown in 2001–2002, the U.S. economy has continued to experience slow but steady growth, even in the face of rising oil prices, war, and extreme weather.[8]

## Price Levels

The rate of price changes across the economy is another basic measure of economic well-being. **Inflation** means that prices on average are rising. Similar to unemployment, a low level of inflation is not so bad. It reflects a healthy economy—people have money, and they are willing to spend it. But when the Federal Reserve—the nation's central bank—manages the economy poorly, inflation can spiral out of control, which can lead to **hyperinflation**, when average prices increase more than 50% per month. In Hungary, for example, inflation in its unstable, post–World War II economy climbed so quickly that prices doubled every 15 hours in 1945–1946. More recently, prices in the war-torn former Yugoslavia doubled every 16 hours between October 1993 and January 1994.

When the rate of price increases slows down, the economy is experiencing **disinflation**, the situation in the United States in the mid-1990s. But when prices actually decrease, the economy is experiencing **deflation**, typically a sign of economic trouble that goes hand in hand with very high unemployment. People don't have money and simply won't spend unless prices drop. During the Great Depression in the 1930s, the U.S. economy experienced deflation, with prices dropping 9% in 1931, and nearly 10% in 1932. Despite some economic turmoil, inflation in the United States was relatively low from 2000–2007, hovering at around 3%. But inflation picked up in the first half of 2008, sparking concern among businesses and consumers alike.

The government uses two major price indexes to evaluate inflation: the **consumer price index (CPI)**, and the **producer price index (PPI)**. The CPI measures the change in weighted-average price over time in a consumer "market basket" of goods and services that the average person buys each month. The U.S. Bureau of Labor Statistics creates the basket—which includes hundreds of items such as housing, transportation, haircuts, wine, and pet care—using data from more than 30,000 consumers. While the market basket is meant to represent the average consumer, keep in mind that the "average" includes a lot of variation, so the CPI may not reflect your personal experience. If you don't have a pet, for example, changes in veterinary costs wouldn't affect you, although they would (slightly) impact the CPI.

The PPI measures the change over time in weighted-average wholesale prices, or the prices that businesses pay each other for goods and services. Changes in the PPI can sometimes predict changes in the CPI because producers tend to pass on price increases (and sometimes also price decreases) to consumers within a month or two of the changes.

## Productivity

**Productivity** refers to the relationship between the goods and services that an economy produces and the resources needed to produce them. The amount of output—goods and services—divided by the amount of inputs (e.g., hours worked) equals productivity. The goal, of course, is to produce more goods and services, using fewer hours and other inputs. A high level of productivity typically correlates with healthy GDP growth, while low productivity tends to correlate with a more stagnant economy.

Over the past couple of decades, the United States has experienced strong, sustained productivity growth,

**Exhibit 2.4** Business Cycle

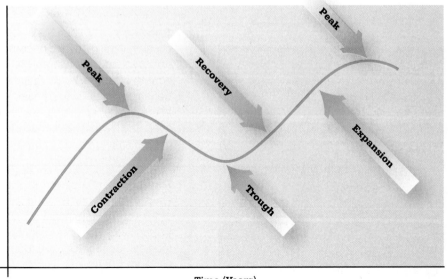

© COMSTOCK IMAGES/JUPITERIMAGES

closely tied to political philosophy. But regardless of politics, most economists agree that lower taxes can boost the economy by leaving more money in people's pockets for them to spend or invest. Most also agree that government spending can boost the economy in the short term by spurring sales of goods and services such as military equipment or advertising, and providing jobs such as mail carrier or national park ranger. Done well, both taxation and spending can offer economic benefits. The tricky part is finding the right balance between the two approaches.

Every year, the government must create a budget, or a financial plan that outlines expected revenue from taxes and fees, and expected spending. If revenue is higher than spending, the government incurs a **budget surplus** (rare in recent years, but usually quite welcome!). If spending is higher than revenue, the government incurs a **budget deficit** and must borrow money to cover the shortfall. The sum of all the money borrowed over the years and not yet repaid is the total **federal debt**. Exhibit 2.5 shows key sources of revenue and key expenses for the federal government in 2005. Note that spending significantly outstrips receipts, creating a 1-year budget deficit of $317.9 billion.[9]

As of August 2008, the total U.S. federal debt stood at more than $9.6 trillion, a staggering $31,600 for every U.S. citizen (see the National Debt Clock at http://brillig .com/debt_clock/ for the latest figures). And the debt has only grown bigger every year since 1957. This matters to each taxpayer because as the government repays the debt—not to mention paying the skyrocketing interest to finance this debt—less and less money will be available for other uses; services may be eliminated (e.g., student loans, veterans' benefits, housing subsidies), or taxes will soar, or perhaps even both.[10]

**fiscal policy**
Government efforts to influence the economy through taxation and spending.

**budget surplus**
Overage that occurs when revenue is higher than expenses over a given period of time.

**budget deficit**
Shortfall that occurs when expenses are higher than revenue over a given period of time.

**federal debt** The sum of all the money that the federal government has borrowed over the years and not yet repaid.

**monetary policy**
Federal Reserve decisions that shape the economy by influencing interest rates and the supply of money.

due largely to infusions of technology that help workers produce more output, more quickly. But keep in mind that that productivity doesn't measure quality. That's why it's so important to examine multiple measures of economic health, rather than relying on simply one or two dimensions.

## LO6 Managing the Economy Through Fiscal and Monetary Policy

While market forces drive performance in a capitalist economy, the national government and the Federal Reserve can help *shape* performance. Effective government policies can strengthen and lengthen economic expansion, and mitigate—or maybe even reverse—economic contraction. The overarching goal is controlled, sustained growth, and both fiscal and monetary policy help achieve this objective.

> 66
> **It's a recession when your neighbor loses his job; it's a depression when you lose your own.**
> —Harry Truman
> 99

### Fiscal Policy

**Fiscal policy** refers to government efforts to influence the economy through taxation and spending decisions that are designed to encourage growth, boost employment, and curb inflation. Clearly, fiscal strategies are

### Monetary Policy

**Monetary policy** refers to actions that shape the economy by influencing interest rates and the supply of money. The Federal Reserve System, better known as the Fed, manages U.S. monetary policy. The Fed is essentially the central bank of the United States. In addition to setting monetary policy, the Fed provides banking

**money supply** The total amount of money within the overall economy.

**M1 money supply** Includes all currency plus checking accounts and traveler's checks.

**M2 money supply** Includes all of M1 money supply plus most savings accounts, money market accounts, and certificates of deposit.

**open market operations** The Federal Reserve function of buying and selling government securities, which include treasury bonds, notes, and bills.

services to member banks and to the federal government.

The Fed is headed by a seven-member Board of Governors. Each member of the Board is appointed by the president to serve a single 14-year term—though a member can also complete an unexpired term and still be appointed to a full term. These terms are staggered, with one expiring every 2 years, so that no single president can appoint all of the members. This structure helps ensure that the Fed can act independently.

In addition to setting monetary policy, the Board of Governors oversees the operation of the 12 Federal Reserve Banks that carry out Fed policies and perform banking services for commercial banks in their districts. Interestingly, the federal government does not own these Federal Reserve Banks. Instead, they're owned by the member commercial banks in their district.

The president appoints one of the seven members of the Board of Governors to serve as its chairman—a position so powerful that many consider him the second most powerful man on earth. For nearly 19 years the chairman was Alan Greenspan. When Greenspan retired in early 2006, President Bush appointed economist Ben Bernanke to take over the role of chairman. Bernanke claims that he will walk in Greenspan's footsteps—tough on inflation—but early indications suggest that he may take a somewhat different approach to guiding the economy. One thing seems sure: unlike Greenspan, Bernanke values clear, direct communication. In contrast, Greenspan once said, "If I seem unduly clear to you, you must have misunderstood what I said."[11]

Regardless of the chairman's communication style, the Fed helps guide the economy by influencing the size of the **money supply**—or the total amount of money within the overall economy. The two most commonly used definitions of the money supply are M1 and M2:

- **M1 money supply** refers to all currency—paper bills and metal coins—plus checking accounts and traveler's checks.

- **M2 money supply** refers to all M1 plus most savings accounts, money market accounts, and certificates of deposit (low risk savings vehicles with a fixed term, typically less than a year).

In practice, the term "money supply" most often refers to M2. Note that credit cards are not part of the money supply, although they do have an unmistakable impact on the flow of money through the economy.

The Fed attempts to reduce the money supply when prices begin to rise. Ideally, if less money is available, interest rates will rise. This will reduce spending, which should bring inflation under control. But when the economy is too sluggish, the Fed typically increases the money supply. If more money is available, interest rates usually drop, encouraging businesses to expand and consumers to spend. Specifically, the Fed uses three key tools that expand and contract the money supply:

- Open market operations.

- Discount rate changes.

- Reserve requirement changes.

**Open Market Operations** This is the Fed's most frequently used tool. **Open market operations** involve buying and selling government securities, which include treasury bonds, notes, and bills. These securities are the IOUs the government issues to finance its deficit spending.

How do open market operations work? When the economy is weak, the Fed *buys* government securities on the open market. When the Fed pays the sellers of these

---

**Exhibit 2.5** Federal Government Revenue and Expenses[12]

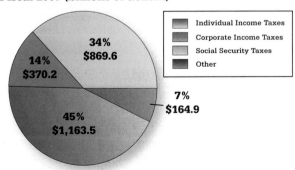

**Federal Government Revenue**
**Fiscal 2007 (billions of dollars)**

- Individual Income Taxes
- Corporate Income Taxes
- Social Security Taxes
- Other

34% $869.6
14% $370.2
45% $1,163.5
7% $164.9

TOTAL=$2,568.2
100%

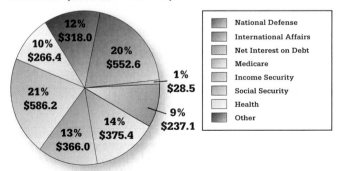

**Federal Government Expenses**
**Fiscal 2007 (billions of dollars)**

- National Defense
- International Affairs
- Net Interest on Debt
- Medicare
- Income Security
- Social Security
- Health
- Other

12% $318.0
10% $266.4
20% $552.6
1% $28.5
21% $586.2
9% $237.1
13% $366.0
14% $375.4

TOTAL=$2,730.2
100%

securities, money previously held by the Fed is put into circulation. This directly stimulates spending. In addition, any of the additional funds supplied by the Fed that are deposited in banks will allow banks to make more loans, making credit more readily available. This encourages even more spending and further stimulates the economy.

When inflation is a concern, the Fed *sells* securities. Buyers of the securities write checks to the Fed to pay for securities they bought, and the Fed withdraws these funds from banks. With fewer funds, banks must cut back on the loans they make, credit becomes tighter, and the money supply shrinks. This reduces spending and cools off the inflationary pressures in the economy.

Open market operations are set by the aptly named Federal Open Market Committee, which consists of the 7 members of the Board of Governors and 5 of the 12 presidents of the Federal Reserve district banks. Each year, the Federal Open Market Committee holds 8 regularly scheduled meetings to make decisions about open market operations, although they do hold additional meetings when the need arises.

**Discount Rate Changes** Just as you can borrow money from your bank, your bank can borrow funds from the Fed. And, just as you must pay interest on your loan, your bank must pay interest on loans from the Fed. The **discount rate** is the interest rate the Fed charges on its loans to commercial banks. When the Fed reduces the discount rate, banks can obtain funds at a lower cost and use these funds to make more loans to their own customers. With the cost of acquiring funds from the Fed lower, interest rates on bank loans also tend to fall. As a result, businesses and individuals are more likely to borrow money and spend it, which stimulates the economy. Clearly, the Fed is most likely to reduce the discount rate during recessions. But in response to inflation—usually a sign of a rapidly expanding economy—the Fed usually increases the discount rate. In response, banks raise the interest rates they charge their customers. Fewer businesses and individuals are willing to take loans, which ultimately slows down the economy and reduces inflation.[13]

**Reserve Requirement Changes** The Fed requires that all of its member banks hold funds, called reserves, equal to a stated percentage of the deposits held by their customers. This percentage is called the **reserve requirement** (or required reserve ratio). The reserve requirement helps protect depositors, who may want to withdraw their money without notice. Currently, the reserve requirement stands at about 10%, depending on the size and type of a bank's deposits. If the Fed increases the reserve requirement, banks must hold more funds, meaning they will have fewer funds available to make loans. This makes credit tighter and causes interest rates to rise. If the Fed decreases the reserve requirement, some of the funds that banks were required to hold become available for loans. This increases the availability of credit and causes interest rates to drop. Since changes in the reserve requirement can have a dramatic impact on both the economy and the financial health of individual banks, the Fed uses this tool quite infrequently.

**Other Fed Functions** In addition to monetary policy, the Fed has several other core functions, including regulating financial institutions, and providing banking services both for the government and for banks. In its role as a regulator, the Fed sets and enforces rules of conduct for banks and oversees mergers and acquisitions to ensure fairness and compliance with government policy. In its role as a banker for banks, the Fed coordinates the check clearing process for checks on behalf of any banks that are willing to pay its fees. And as the government's bank, the Fed maintains the federal government's checking account and keeps the U.S. currency supply in good condition.

**discount rate** The rate of interest that the Federal Reserve charges when it loans funds to banks.

**reserve requirement** A rule set by the Fed, which specifies the minimum amount of reserves (or funds) a bank must hold, expressed as a percentage of the bank's deposits.

**Federal Deposit Insurance Corporation (FDIC)** A federal agency that insures deposits in banks and thrift institutions for up to $100,000 per customer, per bank.

---

## "Looking to Multiply Your Money? Look No Further Than Your Local Bank!"

Everyone knows that banks help people save money, but most people don't realize that banks actually create money. The process is complex, but a simplified example illustrates the point: Say you deposit $5,000 in the bank. How much money do you have? You obviously have $5,000. Now imagine that your neighbor Anne goes to the bank for a loan. In line with Federal Reserve requirements, the bank must hold onto about 10% of its funds, so it loans Anne $4,500. She uses the money to buy a used car from your neighbor Jake, who deposits the $4,500 in the bank. How much money does Jake have? Clearly, he has $4,500. How much money do you have? You still have $5,000. Thanks to the banking system, our "money supply" has increased from $5,000 to $9,500. Multiply this phenomena times millions of banking transactions, and you can see why cold hard cash accounts for only about 11% of the total U.S. money supply.[14]

But what happens if everyone goes to the bank at once to withdraw their money? The banking system would clearly collapse. And in fact, in 1930 and 1931, a run on the banks caused wave after wave of devastating bank failures. Panicked customers lost all their savings, ushering in the worst years of the Great Depression. To restore public confidence in the banking system, Congress established the **Federal Deposit Insurance Corporation (FDIC)** in 1933. The FDIC insures deposits in banks and thrift institutions for up to $100,000 per customer, per bank. Since the FDIC began operations on January 1, 1934, no depositor has lost a single cent of insured funds as a result of a bank failure.[15]

## CHAPTER 3

# The World Marketplace: Business without Borders

## LEARNING OBJECTIVES

After studying this chapter, you will be able to...

**LO1** Discuss business opportunities in the world economy

**LO2** Explain the key reasons for international trade

**LO3** Describe the tools for measuring international trade

**LO4** Analyze strategies for reaching global markets

**LO5** Discuss barriers to international trade and strategies to surmount them

**LO6** Describe the free trade movement and discuss key benefits and criticisms

4ltrpress.cengage.com/busn

A company that keeps its eye on Tom, Dick, and Harry
is going to miss Pierre, Hans, and Yoshio.

–Al Ries, marketing strategist and author

## LO1 An Unprecedented Opportunity...

As access to technology skyrockets and barriers to trade continue to fall, individual economies around the world have become more interdependent than ever before. The result is a tightly woven global economy marked by intense competition and huge, shifting opportunities. The potential for U.S. business is enormous. Even though many domestic markets are saturated, developing countries such as China, India, and Turkey are growing at a torrid rate, and a host of other nations, from Vietnam to Brazil, seem poised on the brink of significant growth spurts.[1]

A quick look at population trends validates the global business opportunity. With about 300 million people, the United States accounts for only 4.6% of the world's total population. More than 6 billion people live beyond our borders, representing more than 95% of potential customers for U.S. firms. But even though the growth rates in many high-population countries are strong, most of these nations remain behind the United States in terms of development and prosperity, posing considerable challenges for foreign firms. (In other words, most of their populations may not have the resources to buy even basic goods and services.) Exhibit 3.1, a comparison of population, growth rate, and per capita income for the world's five largest nations, highlights some of the discrepancies. Note that even though U.S. consumers clearly have money, China and India represent a much bigger opportunity in terms of both sheer size and economic growth.

**Exhibit 3.1** Selected population and GDP figures[2]

| Nation | Population* | Per Capita GDP (U.S Dollars)** | GDP Growth Rate*** |
|---|---|---|---|
| China | 1,330,044,605 | $5,300 | +11.4% |
| India | 1,147,995,898 | $2,700 | +8.5% |
| United States | 303,824,646 | $46,000 | +2.2% |
| Indonesia | 237,512,355 | $3,400 | +6.1% |
| Brazil | 191,908,598 | $9,700 | +4.5% |

*CIA World Factbook, July 2008 Population Estimates, updated April 15, 2008.
**CIA World Factbook, 2007 GDP Estimates, updated April 15, 2008.
***CIA World Factbook, 2007 GDP Growth Estimates, updated April 15, 2008.

The growing number of people with cell phones offers an interesting indicator of economic growth. Not surprisingly, cell phone penetration in India and China is skyrocketing. China currently boasts the world's largest base of cell phone users—about 480 million—and the number is likely to double in the next 5 years. India's current subscriber base is about 250 million; it has grown explosively over the last 5 years, and seems likely to follow suit in the next decade. In the United States, Europe, and Japan, cell phones followed landlines, but large swaths of China and India aren't bothering to build conventional phone service. Rather, they're moving directly to cell phone networks. Padmasree Warrior, Motorola's former chief technology officer, commented that everyone in the developing world "has realized that cellular-telephone service is not a luxury." As economic growth offers more and more people the chance to get connected, better communication will likely feed even more economic growth. The upshot is that millions of people worldwide will have a higher standard of living.[3]

## LO2 Key Reasons for International Trade

Companies engage in global trade for a range of reasons beyond the obvious opportunity to tap into huge and growing new markets. The benefits include better access to factors of production, reduced risk, and an inflow of new ideas.

- *Access to factors of production:* International trade offers a valuable opportunity for individual firms to capitalize on factors of production that simply aren't present in the right amount for the right price in each individual country. India, China, and the Philippines, for example, attract multibillion dollar investments because of their large cohort of technically skilled university graduates who work for about one-fifth the pay of comparable American workers. Russia and the OPEC nations offer a rich supply of oil, and Canada, like other forested nations, boasts an abundant supply of timber. The United States offers plentiful capital, which is less available in other parts of the world. International trade helps even out some of the resource imbalances among nations.

- *Reduced risk:* Global trade reduces dependence on one economy, lowering the economic risk for multinational firms. When the Japanese economy entered a deep, sustained slump in the 1990s, for instance, Sony and Toyota thrived through their focus on other, healthier markets around the world. But a word of caution is key: as national economies con-

## Interesting Choices...

BrandChannel.com, a weekly online branding journal, holds annual Reader's Choice Awards to acknowledge the brands that—for better or worse—have had the most significant impact on people's lives. In the global brands category, the most recent winners were:

1. Google
2. Apple
3. YouTube
4. Wikipedia
5. Starbucks
6. Nokia
7. Skype
8. IKEA
9. Coca-Cola
10. Toyota

The two most notable newcomers to the top ten were YouTube and Wikipedia. Both brands feature user-created content. YouTube, launched in 2005, boasts more than 50 million unique monthly visitors, and was purchased by Google in 2006 for $1.6 billion in stock. Wikipedia, launched in 2001, has become the premier user-developed reference site, with more than 7 million articles in more than 200 languages. Skype, a low cost Internet-based phone service that first hit the top ten in 2005, has doubled its user base, connecting satisfied callers around the globe. And Google, Apple, Starbucks, and Nokia have been top ten stalwarts since BrandChannel launched the survey in 2001.

But a word of caution regarding all of these choices: BrandChannel warns that their reader survey is not scientific... although they do claim that their readers are "above average in intelligence, curiosity, good looks, taste, and charm"![4]

© PHOTODISC/GETTY IMAGES

tinue to integrate, an economic meltdown in one part of the world can have far-reaching impact. For example, after the 9/11 terrorist attacks in the United States, nations around the world experienced economic repercussions along with the United States.

- *Inflow of innovation:* International trade can also offer companies an invaluable source of new ideas. Japan, for instance, is far ahead of the curve regarding cell phone service. Japanese cell phone "extras," including games, ring tones, videos, and stylish new accessories, set the standard for cell service around the world. In Europe, meanwhile, consumers are seeking to bring a top-quality pub experience into their homes with professional quality home beer taps. Companies with a presence in foreign markets experience budding trends like these firsthand, giving them a jump in other markets around the world.[5]

## Competitive Advantage

Beyond individual companies, industries tend to succeed on a worldwide basis in countries that enjoy a competitive advantage. But to understand competitive advantage, you need to first understand how **opportunity cost** relates to international trade. When a country produces more of one good, it must produce less of another good (assuming that resources are finite). The value of the second-best choice—the value of the production that a country gives up in order to produce the first product—represents the opportunity cost of producing the first product.

A country has an **absolute advantage** when it can produce more of a good than other nations, using the same amount of resources. China, for example, has an absolute advantage in terms of clothing production, relative to the United States. But having an absolute advantage isn't always enough. Unless they face major trade barriers, the industries in any country tend to produce products for which they have a **comparative advantage**—meaning that they tend to turn out those goods that have the lowest opportunity cost compared to other countries. The United States, for instance, boasts a comparative advantage versus most countries in movie and television program production, Germany has a comparative advantage in the production of high-performance cars, and South Korea enjoys a comparative advantage in electronics.

But keep in mind that comparative advantage seldom remains static. As technology changes and the workforce evolves (through factors such as education and experience), nations may gain or lose comparative advantage in various industries. China and India, for example, are both seeking to build a comparative advantage versus

> 66
> There's no such thing as a global strategy without China.
> –Bill Roedy, vice chairman, MTV Networks
> 99

other nations in technology production by investing in their infrastructure and their institutions of higher education.

## LO3 Global Trade: Taking Measure

While global trade has grown robustly during the last decade, the World Trade Organization reports that growth began slowing in 2007, due largely to turbulence in the worldwide financial markets. In 2006, world trade growth hit 8.5%, but slid to 5.5% in 2007, and may fall to 4.5% in 2008. The deceleration ties to weakened demand in developed countries—growth in developing countries was nearly three times the rate of developed regions. Measuring the impact of international trade on individual nations requires a clear understanding of balance of trade, balance of payments, and exchange rates.[5a]

### Balance of Trade

The **balance of trade** is a basic measure of the difference between a nation's exports and imports. If the total value of exports is higher than the total value of imports, the country has a **trade surplus**. If the total value of imports is higher than the total value of exports, the country has a **trade deficit**. Balance of trade includes the value of both goods and services, and it incorporates trade with all foreign nations. Although a trade deficit signals the wealth of an economy that can afford to buy huge amounts of foreign products, a large deficit can be destabilizing. It indicates, after all, that as goods and services flow into a nation, money flows out—a challenge with regard to long-term economic health. The United States has had an overall trade deficit since 1976, and as the American appetite for foreign goods has grown, the trade deficit has ballooned.

### Balance of Payments

**Balance of payments** is a measure of the total flow of money into or out of a country. Clearly, the balance of trade plays a central role in determining the balance of payments. But the balance of payments also includes

**opportunity cost** The opportunity of giving up the second-best choice when making a decision.

**absolute advantage** The benefit a country has in a given industry when it can produce more of a product than other nations using the same amount of resources.

**comparative advantage** The benefit a country has in a given industry if it can make products at a lower opportunity cost than other countries.

**balance of trade** A basic measure of the difference in value between a nation's exports and imports, including both goods and services.

**trade surplus** Overage that occurs when the total value of a nation's exports is higher than the total value of its imports.

**trade deficit** Shortfall that occurs when the total value of a nation's imports is higher than the total value of its exports.

**balance of payments** A measure of the total flow of money into or out of a country.

other financial flows such as foreign borrowing and lending, foreign aid payments and receipts, and foreign investments. A **balance of payments surplus** means that more money flows in than out, while a **balance of payments deficit** means that more money flows out than in. Keep in mind that the balance of payments typically corresponds to the balance of trade, since trade is, in general, the largest component.

## Exchange Rates

**Exchange rates** measure the value of one nation's currency relative to the currency of other nations. While the exchange rate does not directly measure global commerce, it certainly has a powerful influence on how global trade impacts individual nations and their trading partners. The exchange rate of a given currency must be expressed in terms of another currency. Here are some examples of how the exchange rate can affect the economy, using the dollar and the euro.

| **Strong Dollar versus Euro: Who Benefits?** (Example: $1.00 = 1.20 euros) | **Weak Dollar versus Euro: Who Benefits?** (Example: $1.00 = .60 euros) |
|---|---|
| *U.S. travelers to Europe:* Their dollars can buy more European goods and services. | *European travelers to the United States:* Their dollars buy more American goods and services. |
| *American firms with European operations:* Operating costs—from buying products to paying workers—are lower. | *European firms with American operations:* Operating costs—from buying products to paying workers—are lower. |
| *European exporters:* Their products are less expensive in the United States, so Europe exports more and we import more. | *American exporters:* Their products are less expensive in Europe, so we export more and Europe imports more. |

## Countertrade

A complete evaluation of global trade must also consider exchanges that don't actually involve money. A surprisingly large chunk of international commerce—as much as 20%—involves the barter of products for products rather than for currency. Companies typically engage in **countertrade** to meet the needs of customers that don't have access to hard currency or credit, usually in developing countries. Individual countertrade agreements range from simple barter to a complex web of exchanges that

end up meeting the needs of multiple parties. Done poorly, countertrading can be a confusing nightmare for everyone involved. But done well, countertrading is a powerful tool for gaining customers and products that would not otherwise be available.[6]

## LO4 Seizing the Opportunity: Strategies for Reaching Global Markets

There is no one right way to seize the opportunity in global markets. In fact, the opportunity may not even make sense for every firm. While international trade can offer new profit streams and lower costs, it also introduces a higher level of risk and complexity to running a business. Being ready to take on the challenge can mean the difference between success and failure.

Firms ready to tap the opportunity have a number of options for how to move forward. One way is to seek foreign suppliers through outsourcing and importing. Another possibility is to seek foreign customers through exporting, licensing, franchising, and direct investment. These market development options fall in a spectrum from low cost–low control to high cost–high control, as shown in exhibit 3.2. In other words, companies that choose to export products to a foreign country spend less to enter that market than companies that choose to build their own factories. But companies that build their own factories have a lot more control than exporters over how their business unfolds. Keep in mind that profit opportunity and risk—which vary along with cost and control—also play a critical role in how firms approach international markets.

Smaller firms tend to begin with exporting, and move along the spectrum as the business develops. But larger firms may jump straight to the strategies that give them more control over their operations. Large firms are also likely to use a number of different approaches in different countries, depending on the goals of the firm and the structure of the foreign market. Regardless of the specific strategy, most large companies—such as General Electric, Nike, and Disney—both outsource with foreign suppliers and sell their products to foreign markets.

© DAVID ROARK/PHOTOSHOT/LANDOV

## Exhibit 3.2 Market Development Options

**LOWER** Risk

Exporting    Licensing    Franchising    Direct Investment

**HIGHER** Risk

**LESS** Control

**MORE** Control

**foreign outsourcing (also contract manufacturing)** Contracting with foreign suppliers to produce products, usually at a fraction of the cost of domestic production.

**importing** Buying products domestically that have been produced or grown in foreign nations.

## Foreign Outsourcing and Importing

**Foreign outsourcing** means contracting with foreign suppliers to produce products, usually at a fraction of the cost of domestic production. Gap, for instance, relies on a network of manufacturers in 50 different countries, mostly in less developed parts of the world, from Asia, to Africa, to Central America. Apple depends on firms in China and Taiwan to produce the iPod. And countless small companies contract with foreign manufacturers as well. The key benefit, of course, is dramatically lower wages, which drive down the cost of production.

But while foreign outsourcing lowers costs, it also involves significant risk. Quality control typically requires very detailed specifications to ensure that a company gets what it actually needs. Another key risk of foreign outsourcing involves social responsibility. A firm that contracts with foreign producers has an obligation to ensure that those factories adhere to ethical standards. Deciding what those standards should be is often quite tricky, given different cultures, expectations, and laws in different countries. And policing the factories on an ongoing basis can be even harder than determining the standards. But companies that don't get it right face the threat of significant consumer backlash in the United States and Europe.

**Importing** means buying products from overseas that have already been produced, rather than contracting with overseas manufacturers to produce special orders. Imported products, of course, don't carry the brand name of the importer, but they also don't carry as much risk. Pier 1 Imports, a large retail chain, has built a powerful brand around the importing concept, creating stores that give the customer the sense of a global shopping trip without the cost or hassle of actually leaving the country.

### The Sleeping Dragon Awakes

With its huge population and its tightly controlled economy, China spent many decades closed off from the rest of the world. But over the last 15 years, the Chinese government has loosened control and actively pursued economic growth. The results have been astounding. Big cities boast space-age skylines, churning factories mark the landscape, and sparkling research centers pursue innovation. In just one generation, per capita income has tripled, pulling 300 million people from poverty with sizzling economic growth of nearly 10% per year. In 2005 revised statistics from the Chinese government indicated that the size of the economy—measured in terms of GDP—is even bigger than anyone thought. The corrected data uncovered about $280 billion in additional value, an amount equivalent to 40% of India's entire economy. Economists believe that in 2005 China's economy will rank fourth largest in the world, trailing only the United States, Japan, and Germany. If growth continues at a similar pace, China will likely surpass the United States by 2035.

Also reflecting China's stunning rise to economic power, its total foreign trade in 2005 surpassed $1.4 trillion. China now ranks third in international commerce, trailing only the United States and Germany. This isn't entirely positive for the rest of the world, since China's trade surplus hit a record $102 billion, thanks in part to China's weak currency. The United States is especially concerned because China accounts for the largest chunk of the alarming U.S. trade deficit—nearly twice the size of second-highest Japan. To slow down their mounting deficits with China, American and European officials have called for China to take active steps to increase the value of its currency. If this happens, one result would be fewer cheap Chinese goods for Western consumers, but another result might be fewer U.S. jobs moving overseas.

Looking ahead, China's sheer size and blistering growth rate will clearly play a pivotal role in shaping—and likely transforming—the world economy of the 21st century. The dragon is awake and roaring.[7]

## Exporting

**Exporting** is the most basic level of international market development. It simply means producing products domestically and selling them abroad. Exporting represents an especially strong opportunity for small and mid-sized companies. Ernest Joshua, for instance, developed a thriving Arkansas-based hair care company that specializes in products for African Americans. Recognizing opportunity abroad, Joshua now exports his products to Africa and the Caribbean.[8]

Even though exporting is relatively basic, it still isn't easy. Exporters must negotiate their way through documentation requirements, shipping standards, content regulations, packaging requirements, and more. Finding the right distributor represents another key challenge. The good news is that the U.S. Commercial Service, a wing of the Department of Commerce, offers companies guidance through the entire export process, providing invaluable advice and connections. The government is clearly quite motivated to provide export assistance, because higher exports can help lower the trade deficit, strengthening the economy by keeping more money in the country.

## Foreign Licensing and Foreign Franchising

Foreign licensing and foreign franchising, the next level of commitment to international markets, are quite similar. **Foreign licensing** involves a domestic firm granting a foreign firm the rights to produce and market its product or to use its trademark/patent rights in a defined geographical area. The company that offers the rights, or the *licensor*, receives a fee from the company that buys the rights, or the *licensee.* This approach allows firms to expand into foreign markets with little or no investment, and it also helps circumvent government restrictions on importing in closed markets. But maintaining control of licensees can be a significant challenge. Licensors also run the risk that unethical licensees may become their competitors, using information that they gained from the licensing agreement. Foreign licensing is especially common in the food and beverage industry. The most high-profile examples include Coke and Pepsi, which grant licenses to foreign bottlers all over the world.

**Foreign franchising** is a specialized type of licensing. A firm that expands through foreign franchising, called a *franchisor*, offers other businesses, or *franchisees,* the right to produce and market its products if the franchisee agrees to specific operating requirements—a complete package of how to do business. Franchisors also often offer their franchisees management guidance, marketing support, and even financing. In return, franchisees pay both a start-up fee and an on-going percentage of sales to the franchisor. A key difference between franchising and licensing is that franchisees take over the identity of the franchisor. A McDonald's franchise in Paris, for instance, is clearly a McDonald's, not, say, a Pierre's Baguette outlet that also carries McDonald's products.

## Foreign Direct Investment

**Direct investment** in foreign production and marketing facilities represents the deepest level of global involvement. The cost is high, but companies with direct investments have more control over how their business operates in a given country. The high dollar commitment also represents significant risk if the business doesn't go well. Most direct investment takes the form of either acquiring foreign firms, or developing new facilities from the ground up. Another increasingly popular approach is strategic alliances or partnerships that allow multiple firms to share risks and resources for mutual benefit.

Foreign acquisitions enable companies to gain a foothold quickly in new markets. In 2005, for instance, eBay purchased Skype Technologies, a Luxembourg-based communications company. The acquisition brought them an instant presence in the Internet telephone business in 225 countries. A number of other global giants, such as Microsoft, General Electric, and Nestle tend to follow a foreign acquisition strategy.[9]

Developing new facilities from scratch—or "offshoring"—is the most costly form of direct investment. It also involves significant risk. But the benefits include complete control over how the facility develops and the potential for high profits, which makes the approach attractive for corporations that can afford it. Intel, for instance, recently announced plans to invest $3.5 billion to build a new plant in Israel to produce specialized computer chips. And foreign car companies, from German Mercedes-Benz, to Korean Hyundai, to Japanese Toyota, have built factories in the southern United States.[10]

**Joint ventures** involve two or more companies joining forces—sharing resources, risks, and profits, but not merging companies—to pursue specific opportunities. A formal, long-term agreement is usually called a

**partnership**, while a less formal, less encompassing agreement is usually called a **strategic alliance**. Joint ventures are a popular, though controversial, means of entering foreign markets. Often a foreign company connects with a local firm to ease its way into the market. In fact, some countries, such as Malaysia, require that foreign investors have local partners. But recent research from Harvard professor Mihir Desai finds that joint ventures between multinational firms and domestic partners can be more costly and less rewarding than they initially appear. He and his team suggest that they only make sense in countries that require local political and cultural knowledge as a core element of doing business.[11]

## LO5 Barriers to International Trade

Every business faces challenges, but international firms face more hurdles than domestic firms. Understanding and surmounting those hurdles is the key to success in global markets. Most barriers to trade fall into the following categories: sociocultural differences, economic differences, and legal/political differences. As you think about these barriers, keep in mind that each country has a different mix of barriers. Often countries with the highest barriers have the least competition, which can be a real opportunity for the first international firms to break through.

### Sociocultural Differences

**Sociocultural differences** include differences among countries in language, attitudes, and values. Some specific and perhaps surprising elements that impact business include nonverbal communication, forms of address, attitudes toward punctuality, religious celebrations and customs, business practices, and expec-

tations regarding meals and gifts. Understanding and responding to sociocultural factors is vital for firms that operate in multiple countries. But since the differences often operate at a subtle level, they can undermine relationships before anyone is aware that it's happening. The best way to jump over sociocultural barriers is to conduct thorough consumer research, cultivate firsthand knowledge, and practice extreme sensitivity. The payoff can be a sharp competitive edge. Hyundai, for instance, enjoys a whopping 17% share of the passenger car market in India. They beat the competition with custom features that reflect Indian culture, such as elevated rooflines to provide more headroom for turban-wearing motorists.[12]

**partnership A** formal, typically long-term agreement between two or more firms to jointly pursue a specific opportunity without actually merging their businesses.

**strategic alliance** An agreement between two or more firms to jointly pursue a specific opportunity without actually merging their businesses. Strategic alliances typically involve less formal, less encompassing agreements than partnerships.

**sociocultural differences** Differences among cultures in language, attitudes, and values.

### Economic Differences

Before entering a foreign market, it's critical to understand and evaluate the local economic conditions. Key factors to consider include population, per capita income, economic growth rate, currency exchange rate, and stage of economic development. But keep in mind that low scores for any of these measures don't necessarily equal a lack of opportunity. In fact, some of today's biggest opportunities are in countries with low per capita income. For example, the Indian division of global giant Unilever gets 50% of its sales from rural India, by selling products to individual consumers in tiny quantities, such as

## Veggie Surprise, Anyone?

Travel around the world and you're likely to find McDonald's—a highly successful international franchise—in virtually every city. But while each restaurant features the Golden Arches, the overall McDonald's experience differs from country to country in response to local culture. Here are a few examples from menus around the world:

- India: Paneer Salsa Wrap (cottage cheese with Mexican-Cajun coating)
- Australia: Bacon and Egg Roll ("rashers of quality bacon and fried egg")
- Hong Kong: Corn Cup (a plastic cup filled with corn off the cob)
- Singapore: Low Fat "Yoghurt" (to "balance out your digestive system")
- Kuwait: Veggie Surprise Burger (no more detailed description...yikes!)
- New Zealand: Hazelnut Mochaccinos (one of several "Winter Delights")
- United Kingdom: Five "Toasted Deli" sandwich options

And the differences don't stop with the menu. In Kuwait, McDonald's promotes free e-greeting cards...and people actually send them! In Malaysia, McDonald's offers free home delivery. And in much of Europe, beer and wine are standard items on the McDonald's menu. While McDonald's faces a number of challenges around the world, they're likely to keep people "lovin' it" for years to come, due to their uncanny ability to adjust to local culture, while maintaining a universal brand.[13]

two-cent sachets of shampoo. And Hewlett Packard has recently joined forces with Unilever to give micro-distributors in rural India the ability to check prices and place orders online from "what are now distinctively offline villages and regions."

Effectively serving less-developed markets requires innovation and efficiency. Emerging consumers often need different product features, and they almost always need lower costs. C.K. Prahalad, an influential business scholar, believes that forward-thinking companies can make a profit in developing countries if they make advanced technology affordable. Many markets are simply so large, that high-volume sales can make up for low-profit margins.

Overall, the profit potential is clear and growing. And as consumers in developing countries continue to gain income, companies that established their brands early will have a critical edge over marketers who enter the market after them.[14]

**Infrastructure** should be another key economic consideration when entering a foreign market. Infrastructure refers to a country's physical facilities that support economic activity. It includes basic systems in each of the following areas:

- Transportation (e.g., roads, airports, railroads, and ports)
- Communication (e.g., TV, radio, Internet, and cell phone coverage)

> Obstacles are those frightful things you see when you take your eyes off your goal.
> –Henry Ford, founder of Ford Motor Company

- Energy (e.g., utilities and power plants)
- Finance (e.g., banking, checking, and credit)

The level of infrastructure can vary dramatically among countries. As of March 31st, 2008, the number for Africa was 51,022,400, a 5.3% penetration rate, compared to a 71% penetration rate in North America. In Vietnam and Thailand, many consumers buy products directly from vendors in small boats, compared to firmly grounded stores in Europe. In China, 4% of merchants can accept electronic payment, compared to 80% in the United States.[15]

## Political and Legal Differences

Political regimes obviously differ around the world, and their policies have a dramatic impact on business. The specific laws and regulations that governments create around business are often less obvious, yet they can still represent a significant barrier to international trade. To compete effectively—and to reduce risk—managers must carefully evaluate these factors, and make plans to respond to them both now and as they change.

**Laws and Regulations** International businesses must comply with international legal standards, the laws of their own countries, and the laws of their host countries. This can be a real challenge, since many developing countries change business regulations with little notice and less publicity. The justice system can pose another key challenge. Companies entering the Russian market are often dismayed by the lack of legal enforcement of ownership rights. And firms in China complain that there is "virtually no court system" to enforce contracts. In the United States, on the other hand, both legislation and the court system actively enforce contracts, reducing risks for both foreign and domestic businesses.[16]

Bribery, the payment of money for favorable treatment, and corruption, the solicitation of money for favorable treatment, are also major issues throughout the world. While bribery and corruption are technically illegal in virtually every major country, they are often accepted as a standard way of doing business. Regardless, U.S. corporations and American citizens are subject to prosecution by U.S. authorities for offering bribes in any nation. See chapter 4 for more details.

**Political Climate** The political climate of any country deeply influences

© ANNIE REYNOLDS/PHOTOLINK/PHOTODISC/GETTY IMAGES

whether that nation is attractive to foreign business. Stability is crucial. A country subject to strife from civil war, riots, or other violence, creates huge additional risk for foreign business. Yet figuring out how to operate in an unstable environment such as Russia, Bolivia, or the Middle East can give early movers a real advantage. Grant Winterton, Coca-Cola's regional manager for Russia, recently commented to *Time* magazine that "the politics do concern us." But having snagged 50% of the $1.9 billion carbonated-soft-drink market, he concludes that "the opportunity far outweighs the risk." Poor enforcement of intellectual property rights across international borders is another tough issue for business. Piracy rates are especially high in Asia and the Middle East, routinely hitting more than 90% for music, movies, and software.[17]

**International Trade Restrictions** National governments also have the power to erect barriers to international business through a variety of international trade restrictions. The arguments for and against trade restrictions—also called **protectionism**—are summarized below. As you read, note that most economists find the reasons to eliminate trade restrictions much more compelling than the reasons to create them.

Just as trade restrictions have a range of motivations, they can take a number of different forms. The most common trade restrictions are tariffs, quotas, voluntary export restraints, and embargos.

- **Tariffs** are taxes levied against imports. Governments tend to use protective tariffs either to shelter fledgling industries that couldn't compete without help, or to shelter industries that are crucial to the domestic economy. In 2002, for instance, the United States imposed tariffs of 8% to 30% on a variety of imported steel products for a period of three years, in order to give some relief to the large, but ailing, U.S. steel industry.

- **Quotas** are limitations on the amount of specific products that may be imported from certain countries during a given time period.

- **Voluntary Export Restraints (VERs)** are limitations on the amount of specific products that one nation will export to another nation. Since importing nations typically compel exporting nations to establish VERs, they aren't as "voluntary" as the name suggests.

- An **embargo** is a total ban on the international trade of a certain item, or a total halt in trade with a particular nation. The intention of most embargoes is to pressure the targeted country to change political policies or to protect national security. The U.S. embargo against trade with Cuba offers a high-profile example.

Embargoes, VERs, and quotas are relatively rare compared to tariffs, and tariffs are falling to new lows. But as tariffs decrease, some nations are seeking to control imports through nontariff barriers such as:

- Requiring red-tape intensive import licenses for certain categories.

- Establishing nonstandard packaging requirements for certain products.

- Offering less-favorable exchange rates to certain importers.

- Establishing standards on how certain products are produced or grown.

- Promoting a "buy national" consumer attitude among local people.

Nontariff barriers tend to be fairly effective because complaints about them can be hard to prove and easy to counter.[18]

## LO6 Free Trade: The Movement Gains Momentum

Perhaps the most dramatic change in the world economy has been the global move toward **free trade**—the unrestricted movement of goods and services across international borders. Even though *complete* free trade is not a reality, the emergence of regional trading blocks, common markets, and international trade agreements has moved the world economy much closer to that goal.

| Reasons to *Create* Trade Restrictions | Reasons to *Eliminate* Trade Restrictions |
|---|---|
| Protect domestic industry (e.g., the U.S. steel industry) | Reduce prices and increase choices for consumers by encouraging competition from around the world |
| Protect domestic jobs in key industries (but perhaps at the cost of domestic jobs in other industries) | Increase domestic jobs in industries with a comparative advantage versus other countries |
| Protect national security interests | Increase jobs—both at home and abroad—from foreign companies |
| Retaliate against countries who have engaged in unfair trade practices | Build exporting opportunities through better relationships with other countries |
| Pressure other countries to change their policies and practices | Use resources more efficiently on a worldwide basis |

**protectionism** National policies designed to restrict international trade, usually with the goal of protecting domestic businesses.

**tariffs** Taxes levied against imports.

**quotas** Limitations on the amount of specific products that may be imported from certain countries during a given time period.

**voluntary export restraints (VERs)** Limitations on the amount of specific products that one nation will export to another nation.

**embargo** A complete ban on international trade of a certain item, or a total halt in trade with a particular nation.

**free trade** The unrestricted movement of goods and services across international borders.

# GATT and the World Trade Organization (WTO)

**GATT**, the General Agreement on Tariffs and Trade, is an international trade accord designed to encourage worldwide trade among its members. Established in 1948 by 23 nations, GATT has undergone a number of revisions. The most significant changes stemmed from the 1986–1994 *Uruguay Round* of negotiations, which took bold steps to slash average tariffs by about 30% and to reduce other trade barriers among the 125 nations that signed.

The Uruguay Round also created the **World Trade Organization (WTO)**, a permanent global institution to promote international trade and to settle international trade disputes. The WTO monitors provisions of the GATT agreements, promotes further reduction of trade barriers, and mediates disputes among members. The decisions of the WTO are binding, which means that all parties involved in disputes must comply to maintain good standing in the organization.

Ministers of the WTO meet every 2 years to address current world trade issues. As the world economy has shifted toward services rather than goods, the emphasis of WTO meetings has followed suit. Controlling rampant piracy of intellectual property is a key concern for developed countries. For less-developed countries, a central issue is U.S. and European agricultural subsidies, which may unfairly distort agricultural prices worldwide.

© RIKO PICTURES/PHOTOGRAPHER'S CHOICE/GETTY IMAGES

In fact, both the broader agenda and the individual decisions of the WTO have become increasingly controversial over the past 10 years. Advocates for less-developed nations are deeply concerned that free trade clears the path for major multinational corporations to push local businesses into economic failure. A local food stand, for instance, probably won't have the resources to compete with a global giant such as McDonald's. If the food stand closes, the community has gained inexpensive hamburgers, but the entrepreneur has lost his livelihood and the community has lost the local flavor that contributes to its unique culture. Other opponents of the WTO worry that the acceleration of global trade encourages developing countries to fight laws that protect the environment and workers' rights, for fear of losing their low-cost advantage on the world market. The concerns have sparked significant protests during the past few meetings of the WTO ministers, and the outcry may well grow louder as developing nations gain economic clout.

## The World Bank

Established in the aftermath of World War II, the **World Bank** is an international cooperative of 185 member countries, working together to reduce poverty in the developing world. The World Bank influences the global economy by providing financial and technical advice to the governments of developing countries for projects in a range of areas including infrastructure, communications, health, and education. The financial assistance usually comes in the form of low interest loans. But to secure a loan, the borrowing nation must often agree to conditions that can involve rather arduous economic reform.

The World Bank sees international trade as a vital tool for decreasing poverty. It actively encourages aid recipients to reduce trade barriers. The World Bank also promotes trade by working with aid recipient governments to strengthen court systems, build financial services, and fight corruption. But over the last decade the World Bank has become controversial as well. Critics suggest that in actual practice, the World Bank—contrary to its mission—undermines local economies by introducing deep-pocketed, global competitors who drive smaller firms out of business. They claim that the ultimate result is a lower standard of living for impoverished citizens. Critics have also accused the World Bank of inadvertently lining the pockets of corrupt officials and their cronies. Other key concerns involve the impact of World Bank projects on the environment and on local working conditions.

## The International Monetary Fund

Like the World Bank, the **International Monetary Fund**, or IMF, is an international organization accountable to the governments of its 185 member nations. The basic mission of the IMF is to promote international economic cooperation and stable growth. Funding comes from the member nations, with the United States contributing more than twice as much as any other country. To achieve these goals, the IMF:

- Supports stable exchange rates.

- Facilitates a smooth system of international payments.

- Encourages member nations to adopt sound economic policies.

- Promotes international trade.

- Lends money to member nations to address economic problems.

Although all of its functions are important, the IMF is best known as a lender of last resort to nations in financial trouble. This policy has come under fire in the past few years. Critics accuse the IMF of encouraging poor countries to borrow more money than they can ever hope to repay, which actually cripples their economies over the long-term, creating even deeper poverty.

The IMF responded to its critics by implementing a historic debt relief program for poor countries at the end of 2005. Under this program, the IMF has extended 100% debt forgiveness to 19 poor countries, erasing about $3.3 billion in debt. The managing director of the IMF pointed out the canceled debt will allow these countries to increase spending in priority areas to reduce poverty and promote growth (although some experts worry that debt cancellation sets a troubling precedent for future lending). The result should have a positive ripple effect on virtually every economy around the world.[19]

© SEBASTIAN D'SOUZA/AFP/GETTY IMAGES

# WITHOUT A MAP... CHARTING AN ETHICAL COURSE

## Farm Support: Fair or Foul?

It's tough farming cotton in Africa. And the United States makes it tougher still by using subsidies to guarantee American farmers a set price for their cotton—currently 72 cents per pound—that is well above the going global rate. With such a rich pledge, American cotton farmers have flooded the world market with so much cotton that the actual price in world markets has plummeted. As a result, farmers in Africa, who produce top-quality cotton for about half the cost of production in the States, sometimes end up getting so little for their crop that they struggle simply to feed their families.

Oxfam, a respected nonprofit organization that promotes fair trade, notes a sad irony: U.S. aid to West African cotton-producing countries is comparable to the export losses that those countries incur from American cotton subsidies. And support for cotton is only a fraction of the $12 billion plus that the United States doles out each year in farm subsidies.

Not surprisingly, developing nations protest that farm subsidies in America and Europe unfairly distort the world agricultural market. And the U.S. has claimed willingness to reduce them, but only in return for greater access to service industries, such as insurance and banking, in developing countries. This solution could improve the health of the agricultural business in countries such as Benin and Mali, but it could also decimate their fledgling service industries.

From a U.S. perspective, the reluctance to eliminate farm subsidies is not surprising. American farmers feel singled out, since European farmers receive over $50 billion in farm subsidies, more than four times the U.S. level. In fact, to highlight the inequity, World Bank chief economist Nicholas Stern estimates that a European cow receives $2.50 a day in government subsidies, while 75% of Africans live on less than $2 a day.

The U.S. cotton industry feels particularly targeted, and has agreed to submit to subsidy cuts only if other sectors get hit as well. But beyond these specific issues lies a broader concern that U.S. farm subsidies help maintain a strong agricultural industry in the United States. A drastic decline in American farming would not be in the best long-term interest of American citizens, and could even represent a threat.

In light of the heated debate, the World Trade Organization has given particular attention to farm subsidies—especially cotton—but negotiations have been painfully slow. As the trade talks drag on, African farmers continue to handpick their cotton, hoping that this year, it will help them earn enough to survive.[20]

© JOHNER/JOHNER IMAGES/GETTY IMAGES

## Trading Blocs and Common Markets

Another major development in the last decade is the emergence of regional **trading blocs**, or groups of countries that have reduced or even eliminated all tariffs, allowing for the free flow of goods among the member nations. A **common market** goes even further than a trading bloc by attempting to harmonize all trading rules. The United States, Mexico, and Canada have formed the largest trading bloc in the world, and the 27 countries of the European Union have formed the largest common market.

NAFTA    The North American Free Trade Agreement, or **NAFTA**, is the treaty that created the free-trading zone among the United States, Mexico, and Canada. The agreement took effect in 1994, gradually eliminating trade barriers and investment restrictions over a 15-year period. Despite dire predictions of American jobs flowing to Mexico, the U.S. economy has grown significantly since the implementation of NAFTA. The Canadian and Mexican economies have thrived as well.

> Over the past 20 years, the absolute number of people living on less than one dollar a day has begun to fall, even as the world's population has grown by more than 1.6 billion people.
>
> —*World Bank FAQs*

But NAFTA critics point out that the U.S. trade deficit with both Mexico and Canada has skyrocketed. While exports to both nations have increased, imports have grown far faster, accounting for nearly 29% of the total U.S. trade deficit, and threatening the long-term health of the American economy. Other criticisms of NAFTA include increased pollution and worker abuse. Companies that move their factories to Mexico to capitalize on lower costs also take advantage of looser environmental and worker protection laws, creating major ethical concerns. But the full impact of NAFTA—for better or for worse—is tough to evaluate, since so many other variables affect all three economies.[21]

European Union    Composed of 27 nations and 493 million people, and boasting a combined GDP of more than $14 trillion, the **European Union (EU)** is the world's largest common market. Exhibit 3.3 shows a map of the 2007 EU countries plus the three countries that have applied to join.[21a]

The overarching goal of the EU is to bolster Europe's trade position and to increase its international political and economic power. To help make this happen, the EU has removed all trade restrictions among member nations and unified internal trade rules, allowing goods and people to move freely among EU countries. The EU has also created standardized policies for import and export between EU countries and the rest of the world, giving the member nations more clout as a bloc than each would have had on its own. Perhaps the EU's most economically significant move was the introduction of a single currency,

## Bono to the Rescue?

Perhaps the best-known champion of debt cancellation for poor countries is U2's Bono. A tireless and stunningly well-informed advocate for global have-nots, Bono has traveled the world, befriending the leaders of the world's richest countries, and badgering and cajoling them to give some relief—lots of relief—to the world's poorest citizens.

In the 1990s, Bono played a key role in persuading President Clinton to write off $6 billion in third world debt to the United States. In 2000 Bono delivered a petition with over 20 million signatures to the United Nations, asking them to cancel third world debt. More recently, he worked backstage to help convince the world's eight strongest economic powers to approve a historic $50 billion aid package for the developing world.

Bono clearly didn't do any of this on his own. But Canadian Prime Minister Paul Martin told *Time* magazine that "it's hard to imagine how much of it would have been done without him." Looking forward, Bono knows that much work has yet to be done to eliminate world poverty. But however long it takes, Bono is sure to leverage his U2 fame and his personal charisma to help make it happen.[22]

BONO    OBASANJO

© AP IMAGES

the euro, in 2002. Of the 15 EU members at the time, 12 adopted the euro (exceptions were the United Kingdom, Sweden, and Denmark). Most economists anticipate that the holdouts plus the 12 newest members of the EU will eventually adopt the euro, creating an even bolder presence on the world market. The EU also impacts the global economy with its leading-edge approach to environmental protection, quality production, and human rights.

**Exhibit 3.3**  European Union 2007

# CHAPTER 4

# Business Ethics and Social Responsibility: Doing Well by Doing Good

## LEARNING OBJECTIVES

After studying this chapter, you will be able to...

**LO1** Define ethics and explain the concept of universal ethical standards

**LO2** Describe business ethics and ethical dilemmas

**LO3** Discuss how ethics relates to both the individual and the organization

**LO4** Define social responsibility and examine the impact on stakeholder groups

**LO5** Explain the role of social responsibility in the global arena

**LO6** Describe how companies evaluate their efforts to be socially responsible

4ltrpress.cengage.com/busn

> In the final analysis, it is your moral compass that counts far more than any bank balance, any resume, and any diploma.
>
> —Elizabeth Dole, U.S. senator

## LO1 Ethics and Social Responsibility: A Close Relationship

Ethics and social responsibility—often discussed in the same breath—are closely related, but they are definitely not the same. Ethics are a set of beliefs about right and wrong, good and bad; business ethics involve the application of these issues in the workplace. Clearly, ethics relate to individuals and their day-to-day decision making. Just as clearly, the decisions of each individual can impact the entire organization.

Social responsibility is the obligation of a business to contribute to society. The most socially responsible firms feature proactive policies that focus on meeting the needs of all of their stakeholders—not just investors but also employees, customers, and the broader community. The stance of a company about social responsibility sets the tone for the organization, and clearly influences the decisions of individual employees.

While this chapter discusses ethics and social responsibility separately, keep in mind that the two areas have a dynamic, interactive relationship that plays a vital role in building both profitable businesses and a vibrant community.

### Defining Ethics: Murkier Than You'd Think...

In the most general sense, **ethics** are a set of beliefs about right and wrong, good and bad. While your individual ethics stem from who you are as a human being, your family, your social group, and your culture also play a significant role in shaping your ethics. And therein lies the challenge: in the United States, people come from such diverse backgrounds that establishing broad agreement on specific ethical standards can be daunting. The global arena only amplifies the challenge.

A given country's legal system provides a solid starting point for examining ethical standards. The function of laws in the United States (and elsewhere) is to establish and enforce ethical norms that apply to everyone within our society. Laws provide basic standards of behavior. But truly ethical behavior goes beyond the basics. In other words, your actions can be completely legal, yet still unethical. But since the legal system is far from perfect, in rare instances your actions can be illegal, yet still ethical. The table on the following page shows some examples of how business conduct can fall within legal and ethical dimensions.

**ethics** A set of beliefs about right and wrong, good and bad.

| | |
|---|---|
| **Legal and Unethical**<br>Promoting R-rated movies to young teens<br>Producing products that you know will break before their time<br>Paying non-living wages to workers in developing countries | **Legal and Ethical**<br>Producing high quality products<br>Rewarding integrity<br>Leading by example<br>Treating employees fairly<br>Contributing to the community<br>Respecting the environment |
| **Illegal and Unethical**<br>Embezzling money<br>Engaging in sexual harassment<br>Practicing collusion with competitors<br>Encouraging fraudulent accounting | **Illegal and Ethical**<br>Providing rock-bottom prices *only* to distributors in underserved areas<br>Collaborating with other medical clinics to guarantee low prices in low-income counties (collusion) |

Clearly, legal and ethical actions should be your goal. Legality should be the floor—not the ceiling—for how to behave in business and elsewhere.

Do all actions have ethical implications? Clearly not. Some decisions fall within the realm of free choice with no direct link to right and wrong, good and bad. Examples might include where you buy your morning coffee, what features your company includes on its new MP3 players, or what new machines your gym decides to purchase.

## Universal Ethical Standards: A Reasonable Goal or Wishful Thinking?

Too many people view ethics as relative. In other words, their ethical standards shift depending on the situation and how it relates to them. Here are a few examples:

- "It's not okay to steal paper clips from the stationery store...*but* it's perfectly fine to "borrow" supplies from the storage closet at work. Why? The company owes me a bigger salary."

- "It's wrong to lie...*but* it's okay to call in sick when I have personal business to take care of. Why? I don't want to burn through my limited vacation days."

- "Everyone should have a level playing field...*but* it's fine to give my brother the first shot at my company's contract. Why? I know he really needs the work."

This kind of two-faced thinking is dangerous because it can help people rationalize bigger and bigger ethical deviations. But the problem can be fixed by identifying **universal ethical standards** that apply to everyone across a broad spectrum of situations. Some people argue that we could never find universal standards for a country as diverse as the United States. But the non-profit, nonpartisan *Character Counts* organization has worked with a diverse group of educators, community leaders, and ethicists to identify six core values, listed at the right, that transcend political, religious, class, and ethnic divisions.

© RYAN MCVAY/DIGITAL VISION/GETTY IMAGES

| | |
|---|---|
| **Trustworthiness** | Be honest.<br>Don't deceive, cheat, or steal.<br>Do what you say you'll do. |
| **Respect** | Treat others how you'd like to be treated.<br>Be considerate.<br>Be tolerant of differences. |
| **Responsibility** | Persevere.<br>Be self-controlled and self-disciplined.<br>Be accountable for your choices. |
| **Fairness** | Provide equal opportunity.<br>Be open-minded.<br>Don't take advantage of others. |
| **Caring** | Be kind.<br>Be compassionate.<br>Express gratitude. |
| **Citizenship** | Contribute to the community.<br>Protect the environment.<br>Cooperate whenever feasible.[1] |

## LO2 Business Ethics: Not an Oxymoron

Quite simply, **business ethics** is the application of right and wrong, good and bad in a business setting. But this isn't as straightforward as it may initially seem. The most challenging business decisions seem to arise when values are in conflict...when whatever you do will have negative consequences, forcing you to choose among bad options. These are true **ethical dilemmas**. (Keep in mind that ethical *dilemmas* differ from ethical *lapses*, which involve clear misconduct.) Here are a couple of hypothetical examples of ethical dilemmas:

- You've just done a great job on a recent project at your company. Your boss has been very vocal about acknowledging your work and the increased revenue that resulted from it. Privately, she said that you clearly earned a bonus of at least 10%, but due to company politics, she was unable to secure the bonus for you. She also implied that if you were to submit inflated expense reports for the next few months, she would look the other way, and you could pocket the extra cash as well-deserved compensation for your contributions.

- One of the engineers on your staff has an excellent job offer from another company and asks your advice on whether or not to accept the position. You need him to complete a project that is crucial to your company (and to your own career). You also have been told—in strictest confidence by senior management—that when this project is complete, the company will lay off all internal engineers. If you advise him to stay, he would lose the opportunity (and end up without a job), but if you advise him to go, you would violate the company's trust (and jeopardize your own career).

## LO3 Ethics: Multiple Touchpoints

Although each person must make his or her own ethical choices, the organization can have a significant influence on the quality of those decisions. The next two sections discuss the impact of both the individual and the organization on ethical decision making, but as you read them, keep in mind that the interaction between the two is dynamic: sometimes it's hard to tell where one stops and the other starts.

### Ethics and the Individual: The Power of One

Ethical choices begin with ethical individuals. Your personal needs, your family, your culture, and your religion all influence your value system. Your personality traits—self-esteem, self-confidence, independence, and sense of humor—play a significant role as well. These factors all come into play as you face ethical dilemmas. The chal-

lenge can be overwhelming, which has led a range of experts to develop frameworks for reaching ethical decisions. While the specifics vary, the key principles of most decision guides are very similar:

- Do you fully understand each dimension of the problem?

- Who would benefit? Who would suffer?

- Are the alternative solutions legal? Are they fair?

- Does your decision make you comfortable at a "gut feel" level?

- Could you defend your decision on the nightly TV news?

- Have you considered and reconsidered your responses to each question?

The approach seems simple, but in practice, it really isn't. Workers—and managers, too—often face enormous pressure to do what's right for the company or right for their career, rather than simply what's right. And keep in mind that it's completely possible for two people to follow the framework and arrive at completely different decisions, each feeling confident that he or she has made the right choice.

**business ethics** The application of right and wrong, good and bad in a business setting.

**ethical dilemma** A decision that involves a conflict of values; every potential course of action has some significant negative consequences.

**The Business Roundtable Association—boasting 10 million skilled workers, and $4 trillion in annual revenue—now stands ready to help when disaster strikes anywhere in the world.**

© JIM BOURG/REUTERS/LANDOV

## Ethics and the Organization: It Takes a Village

**code of ethics** A formal, written document that defines the ethical standards of an organization and gives employees the information they need to make ethical decisions across a range of situations.

Although each person is clearly responsible for his or her own actions, the organization can influence those actions to a startling degree. Not surprisingly, that influence starts at the top, and actions matter far more than words. The president of the Ethics Resource Center states, "CEOs in particular must communicate their personal commitment to high ethical standards and consistently drive the message down to employees through their actions." Any other approach—even just the *appearance* of shaky ethics—can be deeply damaging to a company's ethical climate. Here are a couple of examples from the news:

- **Retirement Perks:** When Jack Welch retired from his post at CEO of General Electric, the Board awarded him a generous financial package, and an eye-popping collection of perks. His perks ranged from use of an $80,000 per month apartment, to food and wine for home entertainment, to corporate jet privileges. These perks did not represent an ethical breach—Welch negotiated them in good faith—but when the list surfaced in the press a year after his retirement, he voluntarily gave up his perks to mitigate a public relations problem that could tarnish his reputation as a tough, ethical, and highly successful CEO.

- **Gross Excess:** In the mid-1990s, Disney CEO Michael Eisner hired his friend Michael Ovitz as Disney's president. Fourteen months later, Disney fired Ovitz for incompetence, and he walked away with a $140 million settlement. Disgruntled stockholders sued the Disney Board for mismanagement, which has led to the release of Ovitz's Disney expense account documents. In 14 months he spent $4.8 million (that's about $80,000 per week!). Specifics included $54,330 for Lakers tickets, a $946 gun for Robert Zemeckis, and $319 for breakfast. Was he stealing? *No.* Was he unethical? You decide.[2]

## Creating and Maintaining an Ethical Organization

Recent research from the Ethics Resource Center (ERC) suggests that organizational culture has more influence than any other variable on the ethical conduct of individual employees. According to the ERC, key elements of a strong culture include displays of ethics-related actions at all levels of an organization and accountability for actions. The impact of these elements can be dramatic. Consider, for example, the following research results:

- Where top management displays certain ethics-related actions, employees are 50 percentage points less likely to observe misconduct.

- Ethics-related actions of coworkers can increase employee willingness to report misconduct, by as much as 10 percentage points.

- When employees perceive that others are held accountable for their actions, their overall satisfaction increases by 32 percentage points.[3]

It takes a lifetime to build a reputation, and only a short time to lose it all.

—Joseph Neubauer, chairman and CEO of Aramark

A strong organizational culture works in tandem with formal ethics programs to create and maintain ethical work environments. A written **code of ethics** is the cornerstone of any formal ethics program. The purpose of a written code is to give employees the information they need to make ethical decisions across a range of situations. Clearly, an ethics code becomes even more important for multinational companies, since it lays out unifying values and priorities for divisions that are rooted in different cultures. But a written code is worthless if it doesn't reflect living principles. An effective code of ethics flows directly from ethical corporate values and leads directly to on-going communication, training, and action.

Specific codes of ethics vary greatly among organizations. Perhaps the best-known code is the Johnson & Johnson Credo, which has guided the company profitably—with a soaring reputation—through a number of crises that would have sunken lesser organizations. One of the striking elements of the Credo is the firm focus on fairness. It carefully refrains from overpromising financial rewards, committing instead to a "fair return" for stockholders.

To bring a code of ethics to life, experts advocate a forceful, integrated approach to ethics that virtually always includes the following steps:

1. Get executive buy-in and commitment to follow-through. Top managers need to communicate—even overcommunicate—about the importance of ethics. But talking only works when it's backed up by action: senior management must give priority to keeping promises and leading by example.

2. Establish expectations for ethical behavior at all levels of the organization from the CEO to the nighttime cleaning crew. Be sure that outside par-

ties such as suppliers, distributors, and customers understand the standards.

3. Integrate ethics into mandatory staff training. From new employee orientation to on-going training, ethics must play a role. Additional, more specialized training helps for employees who face more temptation (e.g., purchasing agents, overseas sales reps).

---

### Ethics at Work: How would you judge the actions of these business leaders?

**Pierre Omidyar**  eBay creator Omidyar has contributed $100 million to the Tufts University Micro Finance Fund.  His goal is to give economic power to poor people around the world through small business loans.  Ultimately, he hopes to create entrepreneurial self-sufficiency as eBay has done for so many avid users.

**Sherron Watkins**  Despite intense pressure and high personal stakes, Watkins, a former vice president of Enron, reported the accounting irregularities that led to the discovery of staggering corporate fraud.

**Dennis Kozlowski**  Kozlowski, former CEO of Tyco, was convicted of looting millions of dollars from company coffers. He spent Tyco dollars on luxuries for his NYC apartment, such as a $6,000 shower curtain, and a $15,000 dog umbrella stand.

**Martha Stewart**  In 2004, Martha Stewart, who is worth over $1 billion, was convicted of obstructing justice and lying to investigators about a suspiciously well-timed stock sale that involved a small profit of $40,000.

**Paul Newman**  In 1982, Newman established Newman's Own food company, producing quality foods and beverages. The company donates 100% of the profits to education and charity, totaling more than $150 million to date.

**Sanjay Kumar**  Appointed CEO of Computer Associates International in 2000, Kumar promised to improve accounting and customer relations. Four years later he resigned in the wake of a federal investigation, and in 2006 he was convicted of massive accounting fraud.

---

4. Ensure that your ethics code is both global and local in scope. Employees in every country should understand both the general principles and the specific applications. Be sure to translate it into as many languages as necessary.

5. Build and maintain a clear, trusted reporting structure for ethical concerns and violations. The structure should allow employees to seek anonymous guidance for ethical concerns and to anonymously report ethics violations.

6. Establish protection for **whistleblowers**, people who report illegal or unethical behavior. Be sure that no retaliation occurs, in compliance with both ethics and the recently passed Sarbanes-Oxley Act (see discussion later in the chapter). Some have even suggested that whistleblowers should receive a portion of the penalties levied against firms that violate the law.

7. Enforce the code of ethics. When people violate ethical norms, companies must respond immediately and—whenever appropriate—publicly to retain employee trust. Without enforcement, the code of ethics becomes meaningless.

## LO4 Defining Social Responsibility: Making the World a Better Place

**Social responsibility** is the obligation of a business to contribute to society. Similar to ethics, the broad definition is clear, but specific implementation can be complex. Obviously, the number one goal of any business is long-term profits; without profits, other contributions are impossible. But once a firm achieves a reasonable return,

---

### Bill Gates: An Ethical Enigma

Bill Gates, founder and head of the Microsoft Corporation, played a pivotal role in building Microsoft into a software powerhouse. In the process, he made some ethically shaky moves that squashed competitors and eliminated options for customers... even to the point of government antitrust action. But this same man became an ethical hero when he and his wife used a chunk of their Microsoft profits to establish the Bill and Melinda Gates Foundation. With an endowment of $37.3 billion (yes billion!), the Gates Foundation has awarded grants totaling more than $16 billion. In terms of both overall size and overall giving, the Gates Foundation is more than twice as large as any other U.S. foundation. So does Bill Gates belong in the Ethics Hall of Shame or the Ethics Hall of Fame? You decide.[3a]

© AP IMAGES

the balancing act begins: how can a company balance the need to contribute against the need to boost profits, especially when the two conflict? The answer depends on the business's values, mission, resources, and management philosophy, which lead in turn to its position on social responsibility. Business approaches fall across the spectrum from no contribution to proactive contributions, as shown in exhibit 4.1.

## The Stakeholder Approach: Responsibility to Whom?

**Stakeholders** are any groups that have a stake—or a personal interest—in the performance and actions of an organization. Different stakeholders have different needs, expectations, and levels of interest. The federal government, for instance, is a key stakeholder in pharmaceutical companies but a very minor stakeholder in local art studios. The community at large is a key stakeholder for a coffee shop chain but a minor stakeholder for a Web design firm. Enlightened organizations identify key stakeholders for their business and consider stakeholder priorities in their decision making. The goal is to balance their needs and priorities as effectively as possible, with an eye toward building their business over the long term. Core stakeholder groups for most businesses are employees, customers, investors, and the broader community.

### Responsibility to Employees: Creating Jobs That Work
Jobs alone aren't enough. The starting point for socially responsible employers is to meet legal standards, and in this case the requirements are significant. Employers must comply with laws that range from equal opportunity, to workplace safety, to minimum wage and overtime requirements, to protection from sexual harass-

ment, to family and medical unpaid leaves. We will discuss these legal requirements (and others) in chapter 16 on Human Resource Management.

But socially responsible employers go far beyond the law. They create a workplace environment that respects the dignity and value of each employee. They ensure that hard work, commitment, and talent pay off. They move beyond minimal safety requirements to establish proactive protections such as ergonomically correct chairs (i.e., chairs that won't hurt your back), and computer screens that reduce eye strain. And the best employers respond to the on-going employee search for a balance between work and the rest of their lives. With an increasing number of workers facing challenges such as raising kids and caring for elderly parents, responsible companies are stepping in with programs such as on-site day care, company-sponsored day camp, and referral services for elder care.

### Responsibility to Customers: Value, Honesty, and Communication
A core responsibility of business is to deliver consumer value by providing quality products at fair prices. Honesty and communication are critical components of this equation. **Consumerism**—a widely

© IMAGE SOURCE BLACK/JUPITERIMAGES

---

**Exhibit 4.1** The Spectrum of Social Responsibility

## LESS
Responsible

**No Contribution**
Some businesses do not recognize an obligation to society and do only what's legally required.

**Responsive Contributions**
Some businesses choose to respond on a case-by-case basis to market requests for contributions.

**Proactive Contributions**
Some businesses choose to integrate social responsibility into their strategic plans, contributing as part of their business goals.

## MORE
Responsible

# Virtual Intruder Alert!

© NICK KOUDIS/PHOTODISC/GETTY IMAGES

As wireless networks become more mainstream, wireless intruders stalk closely behind them. In 2006 there were 242 million wireless subscribers in the United States alone—up from 213 million in 2005. That same year the number of mobile wireless devices with high speed Internet increased more than 600%. Many wireless networks operate in homes, but businesses of every size are going wireless at a rapid pace. Vulnerability to hackers, viruses, and unwanted snooping increases with each new wireless network. Some examples:

• In 2003, two young men hacked a Michigan Lowe's store through the airwaves. From a car in the parking lot, they hooked into the store's wireless network of bar code readers, capturing credit card information as shoppers checked out.

• Demonstrating over-zealous ambition, salespeople have been known to hack into business networks from company lobbies, scanning emails to get the inside scoop on how to tailor their pitches.

• The Wall Street Journal reports that IBM consultants tracked the source of a virus that shut down a company's network to a passing car that connected by accident and transmitted the bug.

How can you protect yourself and your business? The first step is encryption, which means sending your transmissions in code. But remote hacking often starts with face-to-face communication, which can be an easy starting point for intruders. Low-level IT workers and chatty support staff can unwittingly share too much information with potential hackers who don't fit the outdated computer nerd stereotype. And too many forgetful people post their passwords on or near their computers, assuming that no one will notice. (Take a quick stroll through almost any office, and you're likely to spot a number of not-so-cleverly disguised passwords.) Wireless networks often "feel" private, but that deceptive illusion can cost you time and money.[4]

accepted social movement—suggests that consumer rights should be the starting point. In the early 1960s, President Kennedy defined these rights, which most businesses respect in response to both consumer expectations and legal requirements:

• **The Right to Be Safe:** Businesses are legally responsible for injuries and damages caused by their products—even if they have no reason to suspect that their products might cause harm. This makes it easy for consumers to file suits. In some cases, the drive to avert lawsuits has led to absurdities such as the warning on some coffee cups: "Caution! Hot coffee is hot!" (No kidding...)

• **The Right to Be Informed:** The law requires firms in a range of industries—from mutual funds, to groceries, to pharmaceuticals—to provide the public with extensive information. The Food and Drug Administration, for instance, mandates that most grocery foods feature a very specific "Nutrition Facts" label. Beyond legal requirements, many firms use the Web to provide a wealth of extra information about their products. Pizza Hut, for example,

> Nearly 80% of Americans consider corporate citizenship when making investment and purchasing decisions.
>
> —*Community Wealth Ventures/ Cone research*

offers an interactive Nutrition Calculator that works with all of their menu items (and it's fun to use, too).

• **The Right to Choose:** Freedom of choice is a fundamental element of the capitalist U.S. economy. Our economic system works largely because consumers freely choose to purchase the products that best meet their needs. As businesses compete, consumer value increases. Socially responsible firms support consumer choice by following the laws that prevent anticompetitive behavior such as predatory pricing, collusion, and monopolies.

• **The Right to Be Heard:** Socially responsible companies make it easy for consumers to express legitimate complaints. They also develop highly trained customer service people to respond to complaints. In fact, smart businesses view customer complaints as an opportunity to create better products and stronger relationships. Statistics suggest that one in 50 dissatisfied customers takes the time to complain. The other 49 quietly switch brands. By soliciting feedback, you're not only being responsible, but also building your business.[5]

Delivering quality products is another key component of social responsibility to consumers. **Planned obsolescence**—deliberately designing products to fail in order to shorten the time between consumer repurchases—represents a clear violation of social responsibility. In the long term, the market itself weeds out offenders. After all, who would repurchase a product that meets a premature end? But in the short term, planned obsolescence thins consumer wallets and abuses consumer trust.

When businesses do make mistakes, apologizing to consumers doesn't guarantee renewed sales. But a sincere apology can definitely restore a company's reputation, which can ultimately lead to greater profits. Two recent examples make this point clear:

- Basketball Blasphemy? At the end of 2004, Nike ran a TV ad in China that featured NBA star LeBron James fighting and defeating some Kung Fu characters and a pair of dragons. Chinese officials immediately banned the ad, claiming offense to the national dignity of China and citing "strong public indignation." Nike responded with a "deep apology to Chinese consumers" that they released to the general media. In part because of their quick, contrite response, the controversy did nothing to shake Nike's position as the king of cool in China.[6]

- Starbucks Sensitivity: Soon after the 2004 Indian Ocean tsunami, Starbucks sent their customers an e-mail promoting their Sumatran coffee, grown on one of the hardest hit islands in Indonesia. The e-mail addressed their pride in the coffee but didn't even mention the disaster. Less than a week later, Starbucks sent an apology for the appearance of shameless commercialism. They also explained why it happened (the first e-mail had been written months earlier), and detailed their active tsunami relief efforts. As a result, they created a stronger bond between the brand and its customers. John Hennessy of the Retail Wire Website describes it like this: "Even when they trip and fall, Starbucks is able to find a quarter on the sidewalk."[7]

> ❝
> There's no incompatibility between doing the right thing and making money.
> —William Clay Ford, Jr., CEO, Ford Motor Company
> ❞

**Responsibility to Investors: Fair Stewardship and Full Disclosure** The primary responsibility of business to investors is clearly to make money—to create an on-going stream of profits. But companies achieve and maintain long-term earnings in the context of responsibility to *all* stakeholders, which may mean trading short-term profits for long-term success. Responsibility to investors starts by meeting legal requirements, and in the wake of the recent corporate scandals, the bar is higher than ever. The 2002 **Sarbanes-Oxley Act** limits

## Does It Pay to Pay More?

Despite consistently impressive profits, Costco's stock typically performs less well than its rival Wal-Mart. One reason may be that Costco operates on a high wage model, betting that higher pay will mean higher profits. Data compiled by *BusinessWeek* suggests that they're right: Costco pays a lot more than Wal-Mart, but seems to get more from its workers. The statistics:

| | Costco | Wal-Mart's Sam's Club |
|---|---|---|
| Average hourly wage | $15.97 | $11.52 |
| Annual health costs per worker | $5,735 | $3,500 |
| Covered by health plan | 82% | 47% |
| Employee turnover | 6%/yr | 21%/yr |
| Labor and overhead costs | 9.8% of sales | 17% of sales |
| Profits per employee | $13,647 | $11,039 |

Perhaps in time Wall Street will reward Costco as much as Wal-Mart, recognizing that Costco's well compensated employees create more value for their employer.[8]

© AP IMAGES

conflict of interest issues by restricting the consulting services that accounting firms can provide for the companies they audit. Sarbanes-Oxley also requires that financial officers and CEOs personally certify the validity of their financial statements. (See chapter 8 for more detail on the Sarbanes-Oxley Act.)

But beyond legal requirements, companies have a number of additional responsibilities to investors. Spending money wisely would be near the top of the list. For instance, are executive retreats to the South Pacific on the company tab legal? They probably are. Do they represent a responsible use of corporate dollars? Now that seems unlikely. Honesty is another key responsibility that relates directly to financial predictions. No one can anticipate exactly how a company will perform, and an overly optimistic or pessimistic assessment is perfectly legal. But is it socially responsible? It probably isn't, especially if it departs too far from the objective facts—which is, of course, a subjective call.

## Responsibility to the Community: Business and the Greater Good

Beyond increasing everyone's standard of living, businesses can contribute to society in two main ways: philanthropy and responsibility. **Corporate philanthropy** includes all business donations to nonprofit groups, including both money and products. Although tracking the exact amounts can be challenging, the Giving USA Foundation estimates that total corporate donations in 2007 exceeded $12 billion. Corporate philanthropy also includes donations of employee time; in other words, some companies pay their employees to spend time volunteering at nonprofits. Timberland, an outdoor clothing company, is a leader in corporate philanthropy, not only donating goods but also giving employees paid six-month sabbaticals to work for nonprofits.[9]

Some companies contribute to nonprofits through **cause-related marketing**. This involves a partnership between a business and a nonprofit, designed to spike sales for the company and raise money for the nonprofit. Unlike outright gifts, these dollars are not tax deductible for the company, but they can certainly build the company's brands.

**Corporate responsibility** relates closely to philanthropy but focuses on the actions of the business itself rather than donations of money and time. The Home Depot, for instance, employs more Olympic hopefuls than any other U.S. company through its Olympic Job Opportunities Program. The firm offers athletes full-time pay and benefits for a flexible 20-hour workweek to accommodate demanding training and competition schedules. Taking a different approach to corporate responsibility, Cisco Systems has developed relationships with the different branches of the military to help make recruitment and hiring of disabled veterans a standard part of their hiring practices. Both of these policies ultimately benefit society as a whole.

## Responsibility to the Environment

Protecting the environment is perhaps the most crucial element of responsibility to the community. Business is a huge consumer of the world's limited resources, from oil, to timber, to fresh water, to minerals. In some cases, the production process decimates the environment and spews pollution into the air, land, and water, sometimes causing irreversible damage. And the products created by business can cause pollution as well, such as the smog generated by cars, and the sometimes-toxic waste caused by junked electronic parts.

The government sets minimum standards for environmental protection at the federal, state, and local level. But a growing number of companies are going further, developing innovative strategies to build their business while protecting the environment. Many have embraced the idea of **sustainable development**: doing business to meet the needs of this generation without harming the ability of future generations to meet their needs. This means weaving environmentalism throughout the business decision-making process. The results have been impressive across a range of industries. McDonald's, for instance, produces mountains of garbage each year, as do virtually all major fast-food chains. But the Golden Arches stands above the others in their attempts to reduce the problem. An article from the Sustainability Institute reports some encouraging statistics:

**corporate philanthropy** All business donations to nonprofit groups, including money, products, and employee time.

**cause-related marketing** Marketing partnerships between businesses and nonprofit organizations, designed to spike sales for the company and raise money for the nonprofit.

**corporate responsibility** Business contributions to the community through the actions of the business itself rather than donations of money and time.

**sustainable development** Doing business to meet the needs of the current generation, without harming the ability of future generations to meet their needs.

© AP IMAGES

Your purchase of this can will help Campbell make a donation in support of breast cancer awareness. *Together we can make a difference.*

**The Future Forests organization helps companies become "carbon neutral" by planting trees to offset the carbon dioxide they generate and to combat global warming.**

© JOHN FOXX/STOCKBYTE/GETTY IMAGES

**green marketing** Developing and promoting environmentally sound products and practices to gain a competitive edge.

- "The company used to ship orange juice to its restaurants in ready-to-serve containers. Now it ships frozen concentrate, which reduces orange juice packaging by 75% — 4 million pounds less garbage a year."

- "Soft drinks were shipped as syrup in cardboard containers. The local restaurants added the water and the fizz. Now the syrup is delivered by trucks that pump it directly into receiving tanks at the restaurants. No packaging is needed at all. Savings: 68 million pounds of cardboard per year."[10]

Reducing the *amount* of trash is better than recycling, but recycling trash clearly beats dumping it in a landfill. McDonald's participates in this arena as well, through their extensive recycling programs, but more importantly as a big buyer of recycled products.

A growing number of companies use **green marketing** to promote their business. This means marketing environmental products and practices to gain a competitive edge. Patagonia, for example, markets outdoor clothing using 100% organic cotton and natural fibers such as hemp. But green marketing represents a tough challenge: while most people support the idea of green products, the vast majority won't sacrifice price, performance, or convenience to actually buy those products. Sometimes, however, green marketing can be quite consistent with profitability. The Toyota Prius hybrid car provides an interesting example. The Prius costs several thousand dollars more than a standard car, but as gas prices skyrocket, consumers are flooding the dealerships, snapping up Prius hybrids faster than Toyota can ship them.[11]

| Social Responsibility at Work: How would you judge the actions of these firms? | |
|---|---|
| *Ben and Jerry's* <br> Ben and Jerry's operates according to a double bottom line: fair profits and social responsibility. They take their social mission seriously, favoring sustainable farms in their purchasing, minimizing their impact on the environment, and promoting peace and justice. Each year, they donate 7.5% of their pretax profits to charity. | *Enron/Arthur Andersen (now defunct)* <br> Enron, once hailed as a shining example of corporate excellence, collapsed in late 2001 due to massive accounting fraud, which bilked employees and other small investors out of millions of dollars. Arthur Andersen, hired to audit Enron's accountings, participated in the scandal by masking the issues and shredding documents containing potential evidence. |
| *MTV* <br> Tapping the potential of their fans, MTV has drawn millions of young people to the polls through their Choose or Lose campaign during the last four presidential elections. Their tactics include MTV specials, on-air promotion, concert tours, and voter registration drives. Due in large part to their efforts, over 21 million young people voted in the last election, up 42% from 2000. | *WorldCom* <br> A star of the 1990s telecom boom, WorldCom came crashing down at about the same time as Enron. Investors lost $180 billion in WorldCom's collapse, which cost the jobs of about 20,000 workers. Convicted of accounting fraud, Bernie Ebbers, the former CEO of MCI WorldCom, is now in prison and will probably spend the rest of his life there. |
| *Kraft* <br> As obesity among kids spirals out of control, Kraft has taken a brave stand: a pledge to stop advertising unhealthy—yet highly profitable—foods to young children. Kraft also plans to eliminate in-school marketing and drop some unhealthy snacks from school vending machines. As the king of the food business, Kraft has chosen what's right for kids over what's right for its own short-term profits. | *Urban Outfitters* <br> In its ongoing quest for edginess, Urban Outfitters has marketed a number of controversial products. In 2003, for instance, Urban Outfitters introduced "Ghettopoly." Sample card: "You got yo whole neighborhood addicted to crack. Collect $50." They soon pulled the game off the shelves due to complaints from outraged customers and community members. |

# WITHOUT A MAP... CHARTING AN ETHICAL COURSE

## *Choosing between a Loaf of Bread and a Packet of Shampoo*

Three-quarters of the world's population—nearly 4 billion people—earn less than $2.00 per day. But C.K. Prahalad, a well-respected consultant and economist, claims that if the "aspirational poor" had a chance to consume, they could add about $13 trillion in annual sales to the global economy. Unilever, a global marketing company headquartered in Europe, has aggressively pursued this market with consumer products. Their customers might not have electricity, running water, or even enough for dinner, but many of them do have packets of Sunsilk Shampoo and Omo detergent. Electronics companies have experienced marketing success as well. In Dharavi, for instance—one of the largest urban slums in India—more than 85% of households own a television set.

Critics suggest that the corporate push to reach impoverished consumers will enrich multinationals at the expense of their customers, representing exploitation of the world's poorest people. Ashvin Dayal, East Asia director for the antipoverty group Oxfam UK, recently expressed concern to *Time* magazine that corporate marketing might unseat locally produced products or encourage overspending by those who truly can't afford it. Citing heavily marketed candy and soda, he points out that "companies have the power to create needs rather than respond to needs."

But Prahalad counters that many people at the bottom of the economic pyramid accept that some of the basics—running water, for instance—are not likely to ever come their way. Instead, they opt to improve their quality of life through affordable "luxuries" such as single-use sachets of fragrant shampoo. He argues that "It's absolutely possible to do very well while doing good." Furthermore, he suggests that corporate marketing may kick-start the poorest economies, triggering entrepreneurial activity and economic growth. Since globalization shows no signs of slowing, let's hope that he's right.[12]

© AMIT BHARGAVA/BLOOMBERG NEWS/LANDOV

## LO5 Ethics and Social Responsibility in the Global Arena: A House of Mirrors?

Globalization has made ethics and social responsibility even more complicated for workers at every level. Bribery and corruption are among the most challenging issues faced by companies and individuals that are involved in international business. Transparency International, a leading anticorruption organization, publishes a yearly index of "perceived corruption" across 146 countries. No country scores a completely clean 10 out of 10, and the United States scores a troubling 7.2. Not surprisingly, the world's poorest countries fall largely in the bottom half of the index, suggesting rampant corruption is part of their business culture.

Corruption wouldn't be possible if companies didn't offer bribes, so Transparency International also researched the likelihood of firms from industrialized countries to pay bribes abroad. The results indicated that firms from Russia and China are using bribes "on an exceptional and intolerable scale," followed closely by companies from Taiwan and South Korea. U.S. corporations, forbidden to offer bribes since 1977 under the Foreign Corrupt Practices Act, show a disturbing inclination to flout the law. The United States scored a 7.2 out of a possible 10, falling below many Western European countries.[12a]

These statistics raise some thought provoking questions:

- When does a gift become a bribe? The law is unclear, and perceptions differ from country to country.

- How can corporations monitor corruption and enforce corporate policies in their foreign branches?

- What are other ways to gain a competitive edge in countries where bribes are both accepted and expected?

Other challenging issues revolve around business responsibility to workers abroad. At minimum, businesses should pay a living wage for reasonable hours in a safe working environment. But exactly what this means is less clear-cut. Does a living wage mean enough to support an individual or a family? Does "support" mean enough to subsist day to day, or enough to live in modest comfort? Should American businesses mandate no child labor in countries where families depend on their children's wages to survive? Companies must address these questions individually, bringing together their own values with the laws of both the United States and their host countries.

The most socially responsible companies establish codes of conduct for their vendors, setting clear policies for human rights, wages, safety, and environmental impact. In 1991, Levi Strauss became the first global company to establish a comprehensive code of conduct for its contractors. Over the years, creative thinking has helped them maintain their high standards even in the face of cultural clashes. An example from Bangladesh, outlined in the Harvard Business Review, illustrates their preference for win-win solutions. In the early 1990s, Levi Strauss "discovered that two of its suppliers in Bangladesh were employing children under the age of 14 — a practice that violated the company's principles but was tolerated in Bangladesh. Forcing the suppliers to fire the children would not have ensured that the children received an education, and it would have caused serious hardship for the families depending on the children's wages. In a creative arrangement, the suppliers agreed to pay the children's regular wages while they attended school and to offer each child a job at age 14. Levi Strauss, in turn, agreed to pay the children's tuition and provide books and uniforms." This creative solution allowed the suppliers to maintain their valuable contracts from Levi Strauss, while Levi Strauss upheld its values and improved the quality of life for its most vulnerable workers.[13]

Clearly, codes of conduct work best with monitoring, enforcement, and a commitment to finding solutions that work for all parties involved. Gap Inc. offers an encouraging example. In 1996, Gap published a rigorous Code of Vendor Conduct and required compliance from all of their vendors. Their 90 vendor compliance officers strive to visit each of their 3,000 factories at least once a year. They have uncovered a troubling number of violations, proactively pulling contracts from serious violators and rejecting bids from suppliers who don't meet their standards.

Gap and Levi Strauss seem to be doing their part, but the world clearly needs universal standards and universal enforcement to ensure that the benefits of globalization don't come at the expense of the world's most vulnerable people.[14]

© AP IMAGES

## LO6 Monitoring Ethics and Social Responsibility: Who Is Minding the Store?

Actually, many firms are monitoring themselves. The process is called a **social audit**: a systematic evaluation of how well a firm is meeting its ethics and social responsibility objectives. Establishing goals is the starting point for a social audit, but the next step is determining how to measure the achievement of those goals, and measurement can be a bit tricky. *As You Sow,* an organization dedicated to promoting corporate social responsibility, recommends that companies measure their success by evaluating a "double bottom line," one that accounts for traditional financial indicators such as earnings, and one that accounts for social responsibility indicators such as community involvement.

Other groups are watching as well, which helps keep businesses on a positive track. Activist customers, investors, unions, environmentalists, and community groups all play a role. In addition, the threat of government legislation keeps some industries motivated to self-regulate. One example would be the entertainment industry, which uses a self-imposed rating system for both movies and TV, largely to fend off regulation. Many people argue the emergence of salads at fast food restaurants represents an effort to avoid regulation as well.

# More Bang for Your Buck

BUSN has it all, and you can too. Between the text and our online offerings, you have everything you need to successfully pass your course. Make sure you check out all that BUSN has to offer:

- Chapter in Review Cards
- Online Quizzing with Feedback
- Audio Downloads
- Visual Summaries
- Printable and Interactive Flash Cards
- Interactive Games
- Video Downloads
- And More!

Visit **4ltrpress.cengage.com/busn** to find the resources you need today!

## CHAPTER 5

# Business Communication: Creating and Delivering Messages that Matter

## LEARNING OBJECTIVES

After studying this chapter, you will be able to...

**LO1** Explain the importance of excellent business communication

**LO2** Describe the key elements of nonverbal communication

**LO3** Compare, contrast, and choose effective communication channels

**LO4** Choose the right words for effective communication

**LO5** Write more effective business memos, letters, and e-mails

**LO6** Create and deliver successful verbal presentations

4ltrpress.cengage.com/busn

> I know that you believe that you understand what you think I said, but I am not sure you realize that what you heard is not what I meant.
>
> –Unknown

## LO1 Excellent Communication Skills: Your Invisible Advantage

Much of your success in business will depend on your ability to influence the people around you. Can you land the right job? Close the deal that makes the difference? Convince the boss to adopt your idea? Motivate people to buy your products? Excellent communicators are not only influential, but also well liked, efficient, and effective. Great communication skills can dramatically boost your chance for success, while poor communication skills can bury even the most talented people.

So what exactly are "excellent communication skills"? Many students believe that great business communication equates to a knack for speaking or a flair for writing. But if that's where you stop, you're likely to hit a brick wall again and again as you attempt to achieve your goals. Effective **communication** only happens when you transmit meaning—*relevant* meaning—to your audience.

Communication must be dynamic, fluid, and two-way, which includes listening. Seeking and understanding feedback from your audience—and responding appropriately—forms the core of successful business communication. And it isn't as easy as you may think. American novelist Russell Hoban neatly summarized the issue: "When you come right down to it, how many people speak the same language even when they speak the same language?"

### Communication Barriers: "That's Not What I Meant!"

Why is effective communication so challenging? The key issue is **noise**: any interference that causes the message you send to be different from the message your audience understands. Some experts define noise in terms of **communication barriers**, which arise in a number of different forms. As you read the definitions, keep in mind that with a bit of extra effort, most are surmountable, and we'll discuss strategies and tips as we move through the chapter.

- Physical Barriers: These can range from a document that looks like a wall-of-type, to a room that's freezing cold, to chairs in your office that force your visitors to sit at a lower level than you.

- Language Barriers: Clearly, if you don't speak the language you'll have trouble communicating. But even among people who do share the same language, slang, jargon, and regional accents can interfere with meaning.

**communication** The transmission of information between a sender and a recipient.

**noise** Any interference that causes the message you send to be different from the message your audience understands.

**communication barriers** Obstacles to effective communication, typically defined in terms of physical, language, body language, cultural, perceptual, and organizational barriers.

- **Body Language Barriers:** Even if your words are inviting, the wrong body language can alienate and distract your audience so completely that they simply won't absorb the content of your message.

- **Perceptual Barriers:** How your audience perceives you and your agenda can create a significant obstacle to effective communication. If possible, explore their perceptions—both positive and negative—in advance!

- **Organizational Barriers:** Some companies have built-in barriers to effective communication, such as an unspoken rule that the people at the top of the organization don't talk to the people at the bottom. These barriers are important to understand but hard to change.

- **Cultural Barriers:** These can include everything from how you greet colleagues and establish eye contact to how you handle disagreement, eat business meals, and make small talk at meetings. As globalization gains speed, **intercultural communication** will become increasingly pivotal to long-term business success.

Identifying and understanding communication barriers is a vital first step toward dismantling them, in order to communicate more effectively with any audience.

## LO2 Nonverbal Communication: Beyond the Words

Most of us focus on *what* we want to say, but *how* we say it matters even more. In fact, studies cited in the *Wall Street Journal's Career Journal* suggest that during face-to-face communication, only 7% of meaning comes from the verbal content of the message—38% comes from tone of voice and 55% comes from body language such as facial expressions, gestures, and posture.[1]

The goal of **nonverbal communication** should be to reinforce the meaning of your message. Random facial expressions and disconnected body language—arbitrary arm thrusts, for example—are at best distracting, and at worst clownish. But strong, deliberate nonverbal communication can dramatically magnify the impact of your messages. Here are a few examples of how this can work (but keep in mind that these examples do not necessarily translate from culture to culture):

- **Eye Contact:** Within American culture, sustained eye contact (different from a constant cold stare)

indicates integrity, trust, and respectful attention, whether you're communicating with a subordinate, a superior, or a peer.

- **Tone of Voice:** Variation is the key to effectiveness, since paying attention to a monotone takes more concentration than most people are willing to muster. Also, even when you're angry or frustrated, try to keep your voice in a lower pitch to encourage listeners to stay with your message.

- **Facial Expressions:** People vary widely in terms of how much emotion they show on their faces, but virtually everyone communicates, whether or not they know it, through a wide range of expressions that include shy smiles, focused frowns, clenched jaws, squinted eyes, and furrowed brows.

- **Gestures and Posture:** How you handle your body speaks for you. For example, leaning forward can indicate interest, shrugging can suggest a lack of authority, and fidgeting can imply either impatience or nervousness. To increase the power of your message, both your gestures and your posture should be confident, open, and coherent.

As silly as it sounds, one of the easiest, most effective ways to improve your body language is to practice nonverbal communication in front of the mirror. Check out your gestures, notice your facial expressions, and focus on eye contact. If you have the time and ability, it's also helpful (though humbling!) to videotape yourself delivering both a formal and informal message, and ask a trusted friend to dissect the results with you.

> **"** You have two ears and one mouth because you're supposed to listen twice as much as you talk. **"**
> —Old Saying

© KEITH BROFSKY/PHOTODISC/GETTY IMAGES

# TechNotes

## Employment Communication: How Can You Make Your Resume More Tech-Friendly?

Online recruiting may sound a bit scary, but the numbers show that it can work to your advantage. Nearly half of all mid-sized companies and almost all large companies are scanning resumes and using computerized applicant-tracking systems, and the trend is definitely gaining momentum.

You can capitalize on this trend by creating a scannable resume: a version of your traditional resume that a computer will "read" and "file" in a database. Your goal should be to ensure 1) that the computer can easily read every word on your resume, and 2) that your resume uses keywords that recruiters are likely to select in their searches.

### Formatting: Less is more!

Very plain resumes scan much better than fancy ones. Some tips for a scannable format:

- Include only your name on the top line. Your address, email, and phone number should be below your name.

- Use only plain text. Do not include graphics, underlining, bold, or bullet points. Differentiate headings with all caps rather than bold.

- Choose a plain, popular font. Options include Times New Roman, Arial, Helvetica, and Verdana.

- Include plenty of white space. And don't worry about length—multiple pages are fine for a computer!

- Left justify all information on the resume, rather than using indenting, tabs, or columns, which may end up looking like gibberish.

### Keywords: Be specific!

Keywords are specific terms that recruiters are likely to search for when seeking qualified applicants in your field. The ad for your job is the best starting point for finding the right words. Possibilities include job titles, responsibilities, soft skills (e.g., leadership), personality traits (e.g., outgoing), and hard skills (e.g., Linux programming). You don't need to create a separate keywords section—simply make sure that the keywords are integrated into your content.

If you're applying for a job and you're not sure how the employer uses technology, you can either ask or send both versions of your resume, with a note that designates the purpose of each. Bring both copies to your interview, since most human eyes are more comfortable reading a traditional format.[2]

Accurately discerning the body language of others is another powerful business communication tool. But keep in mind that you must evaluate others in the context of common sense. When your boss keeps yawning, she may be bored *or* she may just be tired. When your colleague crosses his arms, he may be indicating defensiveness *or* he might just normally stand that way.

## Active Listening: The Great Divider

How we listen (or don't listen) also sends a high-impact, nonverbal message. In fact, an old Chinese proverb asserts that to listen well is as powerful a means of influence as to talk well. Those who do both are unstoppable.

Strong listening skills—**active listening**—plays an obvious role in business success. The higher you go in an organization, the more you find that people are listening. Hourly employees may spend 30% of their time listening, while managers often spend 60%, and executives might spend 75% or more. Interestingly, top salespeople also tend to spend about 75% percent of their communication time listening.[3]

According to the International Listening Association Web site, *85% of our learning is derived from listening*, yet listeners are distracted, forgetful, and preoccupied 75% of the time. If listening is so crucial, why do most of us have such a hard time engaging completely? One reason may be that people *listen* at about 125 to 250 words per minute, but *think* at about 1,000 to 3,000 words per minute…that's a significant gap. Common ways to fill the void include daydreaming, thinking about the past (e.g., last night), and planning for the future (e.g., later in the day).[4]

When you listen, try to use the extra thinking time to make yourself pay closer attention to the speaker. You'll find that people tend to tell more to those who listen better, so if you polish your listening skills, you're also likely to buff up the quality of what you know and when you know it. The table on the following page highlights some listening do's and don'ts (specific to American culture).[5]

## LO3 Choose the Right Channel: A Rich Array of Options

Figuring out the right way to send a message can be a daunting challenge, especially in light of the growing number of choices. The various options are called **communication channels**. Understanding the impact of each channel will help you make the best decision regarding which to use.

Communication channels differ from one another in terms of how much information—or richness—they

**active listening** Attentive listening that occurs when the listener focuses his or her complete attention on the speaker.

**communication channels** The various ways in which a message can be sent, ranging from one-on-one in-person meetings to Internet message boards.

© RYAN MCVAY/PHOTODISC/GETTY IMAGES

| Listening Do's | Listening Don'ts |
|---|---|
| Use your extra mental capacity to summarize (to yourself!) what the speaker is saying. Ask yourself: Why does this matter? What's the key point? | Don't even glance at your e-mails or text messages. You won't fool anyone with those surreptitious peeks. |
| Take a few notes. It will not only help you concentrate but also communicate to the speaker that his or her thoughts really matter. | Don't begin speaking the moment the person stops talking. Take a brief pause to indicate that you're absorbing the message. |
| Listen with both your ears and your eyes. Notice any inconsistency between the speaker's words and body language. | Don't get overly comfortable. If your body is too relaxed, your mind may wander more easily. |
| Use nonverbal communication—nods, smiles, leaning forward—to indicate interest in the speaker. | Don't pick up your phone—or even look at your phone—when you're listening. And whenever it's practical, set your cell phone to vibrate when others are speaking. |
| Use verbal feedback and questions to indicate understanding and empathy: "So you're saying that...," or "Why do you think that?" | Don't interrupt or finish other people's sentences. There are few better ways to cut off future communication. |

communicate to the recipient. Exhibit 5.1 provides a brief overview of key channels.

What other channels can you identify? Possibilities include intranet postings, WebEx, and text messaging, among others. Where would these additional channels fall on the spectrum? Why?

## Consider the Audience: It's Not about You!

Clearly, the needs and expectations of your audience play a crucial role in your choice of communication channel. Even if the recipient's preferences seem absurd—for example, we probably all know someone who refuses to check e-mail or voice mail—remember that your first priority is to communicate your message. If you send it through a channel that the audience doesn't expect or understand or like, you've crippled your chance for successful communication.

© BIG CHEESE PHOTO/JUPITERIMAGES

Analysis and consideration of your audience should also be a top priority after you choose your channel. Meeting the needs of your audience will give you a crucial edge in developing a message that works.

## LO4 Pick the Right Words: Is That Car Pre-Loved or Just Plain Used?!

Mark Twain once said, "The difference between the right word and almost the right word is the difference between lightning and a lightning bug." Perhaps that's a little extreme, but it may not be too far from the truth. In a business world, where your messages are competing with so many others for the all-too-limited attention of the recipient, the right words can encourage your audience to stay with you long enough to absorb your message.

### Analyze Your Audience

To find the right words, begin with the needs of your audience. Consider:

- **Expectations.** What kind of language do most people use in the organization? Is it formal or informal? Is it direct or roundabout? Should you differ from the norm? Why or why not?

- **Education:** The education level of the audience should drive the level of vocabulary, and the complexity of the message.

- **Profession:** Some professions (e.g., Web site development) are rife with jargon and acronyms. How should this impact your message?

**Exhibit 5.1** Communication Channels

| Communication Channel | Channel Richness | When Should You Use This Channel? |
|---|---|---|
| **Memos/Reports** | Very Low: Your audience won't gain any information from your tone or your body language. | When your content is uncontroversial.<br>When you must reach a number of people with the same message.<br>When you must communicate lengthy or detailed information. |
| **E-Mail** | Very Low: Here, too, your audience learns nothing beyond your words themselves. | When your content is uncontroversial.<br>When you must reach a number of people with the same message. |
| **Instant Message** | Very low: Because so many of us IM with as few words as possible, your audience will only pick up the basics. | When your content is uncontroversial.<br>When you want a quick response regarding relatively simple issues.<br>When you know that your audience won't be annoyed by it. |
| **Voice Mail** | Low: Your audience has the benefit of hearing your tone but not seeing your body language. | When your content is uncontroversial.<br>When you don't need a record of your message (but don't forget that the recipient can easily save or forward your voice mail). |
| **Telephone Conversation** | Moderate: Your audience benefits from hearing your tone and how it changes through the call. | When you have time urgency in terms of either delivering your message or getting a response.<br>When your content is more personal or controversial.<br>When you need or want a spontaneous, dynamic dialogue with the recipient. |
| **Videoconferencing** | High: Especially with state-of-the-art equipment, the channel conveys much of the richness of actually being there. | When you need to reach multiple people with complex or high-priority content.<br>When you need or want a spontaneous, dynamic dialogue with an audience that you cannot reach in person. |
| **In-Person Presentation** | High: Your audience directly experiences every element of your communication, from verbal content, to tone, to body language. | When you need to reach a large audience with an important message.<br>When you need or want to experience the immediate response of your audience. |
| **Face-to-Face Meeting** | Very High: Your audience experiences your full message even more directly. | When your message is personal, emotional, complex, or high priority (but if the recipient might be volatile, you should consider using a less immediate channel).<br>When you need or want instant feedback from your audience. |

NOTE: If you're working in a more global arena, be sure to also consider your audience's comfort level with English.

## Be Concise

Jerry Seinfeld once said, "I will spend an hour editing an eight word sentence into five." While Jerry might be going a bit too far, it pays to be clear and concise in virtually all business communication. But don't be concise at the expense of completeness; include all information that your audience may need (it'll save you time down the road).

## Avoid Slang

Unless you're absolutely certain that your audience will understand and appreciate it, do not use slang in either written or verbal communication. The risk of unintentionally alienating yourself from your audience is simply too high.

## Avoid Bias

Intentionally or unintentionally, words can communicate biases that can interfere with your message, alienate your audience, and call your own character into question. As a result, you will be less effective in achieving the immediate goals of your communication (and possibly any future communication as well). Three kinds of **bias** are common:

Gender Bias Gender bias consists of words that suggest stereotypical attitudes toward a specific gender. Avoiding bias becomes tricky when you simply don't know the gender of your audience, which often happens when you apply for a job in writing. The best solution, of course, is to find out the recipient's name, but if you can't do that, do *not* address your message to "Dear Sir" or "Dear Madam"; rather, use the title of the position (e.g., "Dear Hiring Manager").

Another common dilemma is establishing agreement in your sentences without creating gender bias. Consider the following example:

*The guitarist who loses his instrument must buy a new one.*

Technically, this sentence is correct, but it implies that all guitarists are men. A simple solution would be to convert to plural:

*Guitarists who lose their instruments must buy new ones.*

This approach almost always works to help you sidestep the gender bias issue. In the rare case that it doesn't, you can simply use the "his or her" option.

Age bias Age bias refers to words that suggest stereotypical attitudes toward people of specific ages. In American culture, older people tend to experience negative age bias much more often than younger people. This happens despite specific, federal legislation outlawing employment discrimination against people over 40 years old. The reason may be that American culture associates youth with highly valued qualities such as creativity, speed, independence, and individualism. This bias will become increasingly detrimental as the workforce ages. Here is an example of age bias:

*We need someone young and dynamic in this position!*

You could easily eliminate the negative bias by simply deleting the word "young," or by replacing it with the word "energetic." One clear benefit of eliminating bias in this case would be a broader applicant pool that might include an older person who is more dynamic than any of the younger applicants.

Race, Ethnicity, and Nationality Bias Words can also suggest stereotypical attitudes toward specific races, ethnicities, and nationalities. Leaving aside prejudice—which is clearly wrong—the problems in this area are usually unintentional and stem from unarticulated assumptions about a person's attitudes, opinions, and experiences. Your best plan for avoiding bias would be to forgo any references to race, ethnicity, or nationality unless they are directly relevant and clearly necessary. And of course, never simply assume that a single person embodies the attitudes, opinions, and experiences of a larger group. If you communicate with each person as an individual, you will not only avoid bias, but also develop deeper, more effective channels of communication.

## Use Active Voice Whenever Possible

Active voice facilitates direct, powerful, concise communication. You have used **active voice** when the subject of your sentence *is* doing the action described by the verb. You have used **passive voice** when the subject of your sentence *is not* doing the action described by the verb.

## Language in Flux

As time goes by, language changes to reflect our changing experience. From the serious to the seriously silly, new words and expressions surface continually. For instance, "cyberspace," "wardrobe malfunction," and "soccer moms" entered common language only in the last couple of decades. But familiar words can also be used in new ways. Some clever examples currently circulating on the Internet:

**Abdicate:** to give up all hope of ever having a flat stomach.
**Gargoyle:** olive-flavored mouthwash.
**Balderdash:** a rapidly receding hairline.

Word lovers have also been known to redefine words by playing with the letters to create new meanings. A few witty examples from the Web:

**Sarchasm:** The gulf between the author of sarcastic wit and the person who doesn't get it.
**Dopeler effect:** The tendency of stupid ideas to seem smarter when they come at you rapidly.

© ERIK ISAKSON/RUBBERBALL/JUPITERIMAGES

Here's an example of a sentence that uses active voice:

*Our team made a mistake in the sales forecast.*

Our team, the subject of the sentence, did the action described by the verb (making a mistake). The same sentence in passive voice would read as follows:

*A mistake was made in the sales forecast.*

In this version, the subject of the sentence is the mistake, which clearly did *not* do the action. As you can see from these examples, another benefit of active voice is accountability, which can create deeper trust between you and your audience.

## LO5 Write High-Impact Messages: Breaking through the Clutter

For many businesspeople, checking e-mail—or even regular mail—is like approaching a fire hose for a sip of water. Goal number one is to crank down the pressure to get what you need without being knocked over by all the rest. To attain this goal, many people simply press the delete button.

Your challenge as a writer is to make your message a must-read, and the starting point should be the needs of your audience. Consider how the audience will respond to your message—think about how will they *feel*, not what they will they *do*—and use that information to guide your writing. But keep in mind that it's hard to know for sure how the recipient will respond. For instance, each of the following responses could be reasonable for different people:

| Message | Possible Responses |
|---|---|
| Please note the new computer password procedures. | *Positive:* Great! We've really needed this.<br>*Neutral:* OK, no big deal.<br>*Negative:* Not another change… |
| The company plans to restructure your work team when the project is complete. | *Positive:* I can hardly wait to work with new people!<br>*Neutral:* It's all part of the job...<br>*Negative:* Not another change! |

How do you know how your audience will respond? In most cases you must simply guess based on as much evidence as you can find. The value of making a thoughtful guess is that the chances of achieving your goal will soar if you happen to be correct.

The anticipated audience response should directly affect how you structure your writing.

- If the recipient will feel positive or neutral about your message, the memo or e-mail should begin with your bottom line. What is your request or recommendation or conclusion? Why should the audience care? Once you've clarified those points, follow up with your rationale and explanations (keeping in mind that less is usually more for time-starved businesspeople).

- If the recipient will feel negative about your message, start the memo or e-mail with a couple of lines that present the rationale, before you give the bottom line. Follow up with alternatives if there are any, and be sure to end on a positive note (rather than an apology). This structure is less straightforward, but it's a more effective way to communicate your message.

> " 
> I didn't have time to write a short letter, so I wrote a long one instead.
> –Mark Twain
> "

See exhibit 5.2 for sample e-mails based on different anticipated responses to messages in an Internet game development firm.

### Strike the Right Tone

Good business writing sounds natural—it flows like spoken language, and reads like a conversation on paper. To strike the right tone for any given message, remember that you can choose from a wide variety of conversational styles, from formal to chatty. Imagine yourself speaking to the recipient of your message, and you'll find that the right tone emerges naturally. A few guidelines will also help:

- Use common words in most situations (e.g., *use* versus *utilize*).

- Use active voice (e.g., *We made a mistake* versus *A mistake was made*).

- Use personal pronouns (*I, you*) whenever appropriate.

- Use contractions (*I'll, don't, here's*) as often as you would when speaking.

### Don't Make Grammar Goofs

Grammatical errors will distract your reader from your writing and undermine your credibility. Most businesspeople are aware of the more common grammatical errors, so they tend to jump off the page before the content of the message. But if you're uncertain about a particular point, look at how professionally edited publications handle similar issues. Finally, don't be afraid to do a common-sense check on any grammatical question.

Edward P. Bailey, noted professor and business communication author, points out that many writers make grammar mistakes based on phantom knowledge—"mythical" grammar rules that aren't even in grammar handbooks. His research firmly reassures us that:

**Exhibit 5.2** Sample Emails: Same Message, Different Approach

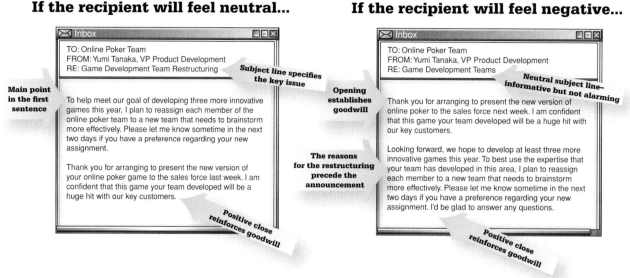

**If the recipient will feel neutral...**

Main point in the first sentence

Subject line specifies the key issue

**Inbox**

TO: Online Poker Team
FROM: Yumi Tanaka, VP Product Development
RE: Game Development Team Restructuring

To help meet our goal of developing three more innovative games this year, I plan to reassign each member of the online poker team to a new team that needs to brainstorm more effectively. Please let me know sometime in the next two days if you have a preference regarding your new assignment.

Thank you for arranging to present the new version of your online poker game to the sales force last week. I am confident that this game your team developed will be a huge hit with our key customers.

Positive close reinforces goodwill

**If the recipient will feel negative...**

Neutral subject line—informative but not alarming

Opening establishes goodwill

**Inbox**

TO: Online Poker Team
FROM: Yumi Tanaka, VP Product Development
RE: Game Development Teams

Thank you for arranging to present the new version of online poker to the sales force next week. I am confident that this game your team developed will be a huge hit with our key customers.

Looking forward, we hope to develop at least three more innovative games this year. To best use the expertise that your team has developed in this area, I plan to reassign each member to a new team that needs to brainstorm more effectively. Please let me know sometime in the next two days if you have a preference regarding your new assignment. I'd be glad to answer any questions.

The reasons for the restructuring precede the announcement

Positive close reinforces goodwill

---

- It is *OK* to end a sentence with a preposition when doing so sounds natural and does not involve excess words (e.g., *Where is this book from?* is much better than *From where is this book?*).

- It is *OK* to begin sentences with "And" or "But" (e.g., *Most teens enjoy videogames with a moderate level of violence. But a small, vocal minority strongly advocates a more clean-cut approach*).

- It is *OK* to split infinitives (e.g., *Try to effectively film the next scene* is a perfectly acceptable sentence, even though "effectively" is inserted between "to" and "film").

Once you accept these principles, your writing not only will sound more natural but also will flow more easily. Winston Churchill, renowned writer and speaker, was on-board with this common-sense approach decades ago, as we can see from his joking comment that poked fun at

tortured writing: "From now on, ending a sentence with a preposition is something up with which I will not put."[6]

## Use Block Paragraphs

There are three elements to block paragraphs: (1) use single spacing, (2) double space between paragraphs, and (3) do not indent the first sentence of your paragraphs. This approach has become standard for business writing over the past decade, as writers have begun to include an increasing number of additional elements such as headings and illustrations. The block paragraphs create a more organized look for your page, guiding the reader's eye through the key elements of your structure.

## Use Headings and Bulleted Lists Wherever Appropriate

Both headings and bulleted lists will guide your reader more easily through your writing. And the easier it is for your reader, the more likely that he or she will absorb your message, which is, of course, your ultimate goal.

- Headings: A heading is not a title; rather, it is a label for one of *several* parts. If you have only one part, skip the heading and use a title or a subject line. Consider using informative headings (e.g., *Recruitment has stalled*, rather than simply *Recruitment*), or question headings (e.g., *Have we met our recruitment goals for this campaign?*). And remember, headings are just as effective for letters and e-mails as they are for memos, and they are perfectly OK in one-page documents.

- Bulleted Lists: Bulleted lists are an invaluable tool that you can use to engage your reader's attention whenever you have more than one of anything in your writing (e.g., next steps, similar sections, questions). By formatting your lists with bullets, you are directing your reader's eye through your writing.

**Always aim to be clear, direct, and concise. Use common words and straightforward sentence construction.**

© LICHTRAUSCH/PREMIUM STOCK/JUPITERIMAGES

## Ten Tips for Excellent E-Mail

1. *Consider both your primary and secondary readers.* In other words, never forget that your reader may forward your e-mail without considering the potential impact on you.

2. *Keep it short!* Many readers won't scroll down past whatever shows on their screen, so be sure to get your bottom line close to the top of your message.

3. *Don't forget to proofread.* This is especially important if you're asking someone to do something for you. And remember that your spell checker won't catch every mistake.

4. *Use standard writing.* Smiley faces, abbreviations, and five exclamation points are all fine if you're e-mailing your buddies, but in more formal messages they can make you look silly (or like you just don't care).

5. *Avoid attachments if possible.* They take time and space to open, and they don't always translate well to cell phones and PDAs. Instead, cut and paste relevant sections of the attachment into your e-mail.

6. *Don't assume privacy.* Think of your e-mails as postcards that anyone (especially system administrators) can read along the way. In that light, try not to use e-mail to communicate negative or critical messages.

7. *Respond promptly to e-mails.* If you don't have time to respond to the e-mail itself, consider sending a message such as "Sorry, but I'm swamped right now—will get back to you early next week."

8. *Assume the best.* Since e-mails are often brief, they can cause unintentional offense. If you receive an off-key message, don't be afraid to inquire: "I'm not sure what you mean…could you please explain?"

9. *Create a compelling subject line.* Make your reader want to open your message. Briefly communicate the topic of your message and why your reader should care.

10. *Think before you write, and think again before you send!* Since it's so easy to send e-mail, too many people send messages in an emotional moment that they later regret. Take time to think and think again.

## LO6 Create and Deliver Successful Verbal Presentations: Hook 'Em and Reel 'Em In!

What do people fear most? The *Book of Lists* asserts that public speaking ranks number one for the majority of people, high above the fear of death at number four. So when people say they would rather die than give a speech, they may really mean it! This section is designed to mitigate any fear you might have about public speaking by giving you guidance on how to create and deliver a high-impact verbal presentation.

As with most communication, the needs of the audience are the best place to begin. How does your audience feel about you and your topic? Are they interested? Hostile? Positive? What were they doing before your presentation? Dragging themselves out of bed after a late night at a sales meeting? Eating lunch? Use this information to guide how you develop your presentation. For instance, an eager, educated audience might not need as much background as a more lethargic, less interested audience.

### Opening

The opening of your presentation gives you a chance to grab the attention of the audience. If your opening hooks them, you've boosted the likelihood that you will hold their attention throughout the presentation. But developing that hook can be a challenge. Following are some suggestions for effective hooks.

- An Interesting or Startling Statistic: In a presentation regarding a risk management program, you could open by sharing that "Your odds of being killed in a plane crash are about 1 in 25 million, while your odds of being killed falling out of bed are about 1 in 2 million. What does this mean for us?"

- Audience Involvement: Pulling the audience into your opening can be very effective. For instance, in a presentation for a clothing company: "Imagine yourself with me at 11 P.M. on a Friday night, standing in line for admission to the hottest club in New York. As we inch forward, we suddenly realize that every other woman in line is wearing…."

- A Compelling Story or Anecdote: This approach works best when it's completely genuine, using specific details that are directly relevant to the audience. For instance, in a presentation about employee benefits, you might want to share the story of a colleague who beat cancer using the company's innovative healthcare program.

- A Relevant Simile or Metaphor: Patricia Fripp, an award-winning keynote speaker, shares a simile that worked well to open a presentation for a colleague: "Being a scientist is like doing a jigsaw puzzle in a snowstorm at night…you don't have all the pieces…and you don't have the picture to work from."

- Engaging Questions: In a presentation about customer service, you could open by asking: "How many of you have spent far too long waiting on hold for customer service that was finally delivered by a surly agent who clearly knew nothing about your question?"

### Body

The most common presentation mistake is to include too many key ideas in the body of your presentation. Audiences simply cannot absorb more than two to four main points, and three are ideal. Specific examples and vivid comparisons will illustrate your points and bring them to life, while trusted sources, specific data, and expert quotations will increase your credibility and persuasiveness. Regardless of the length of your presentation, be sure to use clear transitions as you move from point to point.

Just before launching into the body of your presentation, you should tell the audience your key points, ideally with visual reinforcement. Then as you move to each new point, you can refer to the blueprint that you established upfront. A clear, explicit structure will help the audience track with you as you move through your material.

## Close

Ideally, the close of your presentation will summarize your key points. Then, circle back to your introduction, so that the beginning and the end serve as "book-ends" for the body of your presentation. For instance, if you began by asking questions, end by answering them. If you began with an anecdote, end by referring to the same story. As an alternative (or maybe an addition), consider sharing a quotation or a bit of humor relevant to your content.

Also, keep in mind that you should verbally signal to your audience that you are about to conclude. Once you do so—by saying "in summary," for instance—be sure that you actually do conclude. Nothing alienates an audience more quickly than launching into another point after you've told them you're finished! Your body language will support your conclusion if you turn off your projector, and move toward the audience to answer questions. And even if you aren't so eager to field questions, try to paste a receptive look on your face—it'll increase your credibility and set a positive tone for the Q&A session.

## Questions

At the start of your presentation, decide whether you want to handle questions throughout your talk or save them for the end. Tell your audience your preference upfront; most of the time they will respect it. But if you do receive unwanted questions in the middle of your presentation, don't ignore them.

> ❝ It usually takes me three weeks to prepare an impromptu speech.
> –Mark Twain ❞

Simply remind the questioner that you'll leave plenty of time for questions at the end.

Not surprisingly, the best tip for handling questions is to be prepared. Since it's tough to anticipate questions for your own presentation, you may want to enlist the help of a trusted colleague to brainstorm the possibilities. And don't just come up with the questions—prepare the answers too!

## Visual Aids

Studies suggest that three days after a presentation, people retain 10% of what they heard from an oral presentation, 35% from a visual presentation, and 65% from a combined visual *and* oral presentation. The numbers are compelling: visual aids matter. Depending on your audience, effective, high-impact visual aids could range from props to charts to mounted boards. But in business communication, PowerPoint slides are the most common option. If you use PowerPoint, consider these suggestions:

- Showing Works Better Than Simply Telling: Use pictures and other graphics whenever possible.

- Less Is More: Keep this helpful guideline in mind: no more than seven words per line, no more than seven lines per slide.

- Don't Just Read Your Slides Aloud: Instead, paraphrase, add examples, and offer analysis and interpretation.

- Go Easy on the Special Effects: Too many sounds and too much animation can be painfully distracting.

- Don't Let Your Slides Upstage You: Look at your audience, not at the slides. And dim the screen when you're not specifically using it.[7]

## Handling Nerves

Believe it or not, most experts agree that nervousness can be useful before a presen-

## Death by PowerPoint

While PowerPoint remains the standard in most organizations, a backlash against it has begun to build. Critics point out that its rigid formatting—not to mention its overuse and misuse—stupefies audiences. Taken to an extreme, boring PowerPoint can be dangerous. The Columbia Accident Investigation Board reported that "the endemic use of PowerPoint" at NASA contributed to the space shuttle disaster by taking the place of thorough, meticulous analysis. But even when the stakes are lower than human lives, PowerPoint can be costly. Respected author Dave Paradi conservatively estimates that bad PowerPoint presentations cost companies $252 million a day in wasted time. The lesson for you: If you do use PowerPoint, be sure to use it well.[8]

tation. A little adrenalin can help you perform better, think faster, and focus more completely. But we all know that out-of-control nerves can interfere with effectiveness. Here are some ideas to mitigate speech anxiety:

- Send yourself positive messages; visualize success. Examples: "I will be dynamic and engaging." "They will completely support my new product idea."

- Take ten slow, deep breaths—use the yoga approach of breathing in through your nose and out through your mouth.

- Take a sip of water to loosen your throat muscles and mitigate a shaking voice (water also gives you a way to fill pauses).

- Pick a friendly face or two in the audience, and imagine yourself speaking only to those people (but don't stare at them!).

© NUTS/ICONICA/GETTY IMAGES

### Does Humor Work?

Humor works only if you're really, really sure that it's funny. Even so, double-check that your jokes are appropriate and relevant. You should never, ever laugh at the expense of any member of your audience. Even laughing at yourself is chancy, since you risk diminishing your credibility. (But a joke at your own expense is always effective if you make a mistake; there's no better way to recover the goodwill of your audience.)

- Remind yourself that the audience wants you to succeed. Focus on their needs rather than your own nerves.

### Delivery

Some people are naturals, but for the rest of us, **dynamic delivery** is a learned skill. It begins and ends with preparation, but keep in mind that practice doesn't always make perfect—in fact, practice more often just makes permanent. So be sure that you practice with an eye toward improvement. If possible, you should set up a practice situation that's close to the real thing. If you'll be standing to present, stand while you practice, since standing makes many people feel more vulnerable. Consider practicing in front of a mirror to work on eye contact and gestures. Also, try recording your voice to work on a lively tone. Finally, practice in front of a trusted friend or two who can give you valuable feedback.

### Ten Tips for Dynamic Delivery

1. PRACTICE!
2. Know your material, but never memorize it word for word.
3. Look directly at members of your audience at least 50% of the time.
4. Vary your voice, your facial expressions, and your body language.
5. Use selective notes (but keep them inconspicuous).
6. Stick to your allotted time.
7. Slow down and listen to yourself.
8. Don't apologize (unless you really did something wrong!).
9. Remember to use natural gestures.
10. PRACTICE!

### Handling Hostility

We've all seen hostile questioners who seem determined to undermine presenters. It can be awful to watch, but it's surprisingly easy to handle. Here are a few tips:

- Stay calm and professional. Right or wrong, the hostile questioner has won the day if you get defensive or nervous.
- Don't be afraid to pause before you answer to gather your thoughts and allow the hostility to diffuse (a sip of water can provide good cover for a thought-gathering moment).
- Once you've answered the question, don't reestablish eye contact with the questioner. Doing so would suggest that you are seeking approval for your response, which only invites further hostile follow-up.
- If the questioner insists on follow-up, you may need to agree to disagree. If so, be decisive: "Sounds like we have two different points of view on this complex issue."
- Use body language to reinforce that you are done interacting with the questioner. Take a couple of steps away, and ask another part of the group if they have any questions.

© IMAGE SOURCE BLACK/JUPITERIMAGES

## CHAPTER 6

# Business Formation: Choosing the Form that Fits

## LEARNING OBJECTIVES

After studying this chapter, you will be able to...

**LO1** Discuss the pros and cons of operating a business as a sole proprietorship

**LO2** Describe the basic features of general partnerships, limited partnerships, and limited liability partnerships

**LO3** Explain why corporations have become the dominant form of business ownership

**LO4** Describe how S corporations, statutory closed corporations, and nonprofit corporations differ from general corporations and from each other

**LO5** Explain how a corporation can restructure through mergers and acquisitions

**LO6** Explain why limited liability companies have become increasingly popular

**LO7** Evaluate the advantages and disadvantages of franchising

4ltrpress.cengage.com/busn

A corporation is an artificial being, invisible, intangible, and existing only in the contemplation of the law.
–John Marshall, fourth Chief Justice of the United States

## LO1 Sole Proprietorships: Business at Its Most Basic

One of the most important decisions entrepreneurs must make when they start a new business is the form of ownership they'll use. The form they choose will affect virtually every aspect of establishing and operating the firm. For example, the form of ownership affects the initial cost of setting up the business, the way the profits will be distributed, and the types of taxes (if any) the business must pay. It also affects the degree to which each owner has personal liability for the firm's debts and the sources of funds available to the firm to finance future expansion.

Historically, the vast majority of businesses in the United States have been owned and organized in one of three forms: sole proprietorship, partnership, or corporation. Most companies still operate under one of these arrangements, but toward the end of the twentieth century, some new forms of ownership emerged. In particular, the limited liability company (or LLC) has attracted much attention. This form is so new that the government does not yet provide detailed statistics on it, but given its recent popularity, the "Big 3" forms of business ownership appear on the way to becoming the "Big 4."

Let's begin our discussion with a look at the simplest form of ownership, the **sole proprietorship**. This is a business that is owned, and usually managed, by a single individual. As far as the law is concerned, a sole proprietorship is simply an extension of the owner. Any earnings of the company are treated as income of the owner; likewise, any debts the company incurs are treated as the owner's personal debts.

As you can see from exhibit 6.1 on the following page, the sole proprietorship is by far the most common type of business organization in the United States. In recent years, more than 20 million individuals have reported income from the ownership of a sole proprietorship, and in recent years these businesses have generated well over $1 trillion of revenue and over $248 billion in net income per year. Sole proprietorships are found in almost every sector of the economy, but they're most common in areas such as professional and technical services (such as law firms, architects, management and computer consultants), construction (mostly small specialized contractors), and retail trade (restaurants, book and music stores, hardware and clothing stores).[1]

**sole proprietorship**
**A form of business ownership with a single owner who usually actively manages the company.**

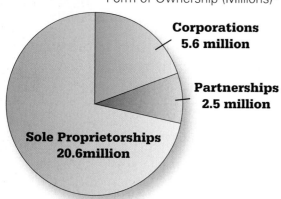

**Exhibit 6.1** Total Number of Businesses by Form of Ownership (Millions)[2]

Corporations 5.6 million

Partnerships 2.5 million

Sole Proprietorships 20.6 million

Even though over 70% of all businesses are organized as sole proprietorships, the size of a typical proprietorship is quite small. According to the U.S. Census Bureau's *Statistical Abstract of the United States: 2007*, more than two-thirds of all sole proprietorships reported revenue of less than $25,000, while far less than 1% reported receipts in excess of $1 million. You can see from exhibit 6.2 that, despite their large numbers, sole proprietorships lag well behind partnerships and corporations in terms of net income (profit).[3]

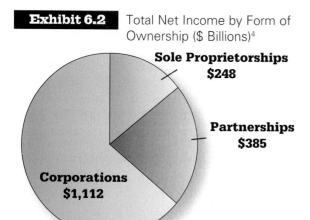

**Exhibit 6.2** Total Net Income by Form of Ownership ($ Billions)[4]

Sole Proprietorships $248

Partnerships $385

Corporations $1,112

These observations raise two questions. First, why are sole proprietorships so popular? Second, why do they usually remain relatively small? A look at the advantages and disadvantages of sole proprietorships can help answer these questions.

## Advantages and Disadvantages of Sole Proprietorships

Sole proprietorships offer some very attractive advantages to people starting a business:

- **Ease of Formation:** Compared to the other forms of ownership we'll discuss, the paperwork and costs involved in forming a sole proprietorship are minimal. No special forms must be filed, and no special fees must be paid.

- **Retention of Control:** As the only owner of a sole proprietorship, you're in control. You have the ability to manage your business the way *you* want.

- **Pride of Ownership:** One of the main reasons many people prefer a sole proprietorship is the feeling of pride and the personal satisfaction they gain from owning and running their own business.

- **Retention of Profits:** If your business is successful *all* the profits go to you—minus your personal taxes, of course.

- **Possible Tax Advantage:** No taxes are levied directly on the earnings of sole proprietorships as a business. Instead, the earnings are taxed only as income of the proprietor. As we'll see when we discuss corporations, this avoids the undesirable possibility of double taxation of earnings.

However, sole proprietorships also have some serious drawbacks:

- **Limited Financial Resources:** Raising money to finance growth can be tough for sole proprietors. Banks and other financial institutions are often reluctant to lend them money, and suppliers may not provide supplies on credit. This leaves sole proprietors dependent on their own wealth plus money that their firms generate.

- **Unlimited Liability:** Because the law views a sole proprietorship as an extension of its owner, the debts of the firm become the personal debts of the owner. If someone sues your business and wins, the court could seize your personal possessions—even those that have nothing to do with your business—and sell them to pay the damages.

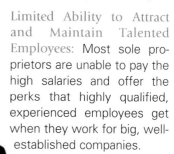

- **Limited Ability to Attract and Maintain Talented Employees:** Most sole proprietors are unable to pay the high salaries and offer the perks that highly qualified, experienced employees get when they work for big, well-established companies.

- **Heavy Workload and Responsibilities:** Being your own boss can be very rewarding, but it can also mean very long hours and a lot of stress. Sole proprietors—as the ultimate authority in their business—often must perform tasks or make decisions in areas where they lack expertise.

© COMSTOCK/JUPITERIMAGES

- **Lack of Permanence:** Because a sole proprietorship is just an extension of the owner, it lacks permanence. If the owner dies, retires, or must withdraw from the business for some other reason, the company legally ceases to exist. Even if the company continues to operate under new ownership, in the eyes of the law it would be a different firm.

## LO2 Partnerships: Two Heads (and Bankrolls) Can Be Better Than One

A **partnership** is a voluntary arrangement under which two or more people act as co-owners of a business for profit. As you can see from exhibit 6.1, partnerships are much less common than sole proprietorships or corporations. Still, about 2.5 million businesses are organized as partnerships in the United States. And partnerships tend to be both larger and more profitable than sole proprietorships. As exhibit 6.2 shows, in recent years partnerships enjoyed substantially higher total net income than sole proprietorships despite the fact that there were over eight times as many sole proprietorships in operation during that period![4a]

Let's look at three types of partnerships, starting with the most basic.

### General Partnerships

In a **general partnership,** all partners have the right to participate in the management of their firm and to share in any profits (or losses) that result from its operations. There is no specific upper limit on the number of partners that can participate in a general partnership, but most partnerships consist of only a few partners—often just two.

General partnerships operate under a voluntary partnership agreement. The partnership agreement usually covers basic issues such as the name of the partnership, the nature of the business, and the term of the agreement. It also spells out the initial financial contributions each partner will make, their specific duties and responsibilities, and how they will share in profits and losses. Finally, it often spells out how the firm will handle disagreements among partners and deal with the death or withdrawal of a partner. A well-written agreement can prevent a lot of misunderstandings, so it's a good idea to seek expert legal assistance when drawing it up.

### Advantages and Disadvantages of General Partnerships

Partnerships offer some key advantages relative to both sole proprietorships and corporations.

- **Ability to Pool Financial Resources:** With more people investing in the company, a partnership is likely to have a stronger financial base than a sole proprietorship.

- **Ability to Share Responsibilities and Capitalize on Complementary Skills:** Partners can share the burden of running the business, which can ease the workload. They can also benefit from complementary skills and interests; the partners can split up the tasks so they use their skills to best advantage.

- **Ease of Formation:** Partnerships are relatively easy to set up. All that's needed is an agreement among two or more people to operate a business as co-owners.

- **Possible Tax Advantages:** Similar to a sole proprietorship, the earnings of a partnership "pass through" the business—untouched by the Internal Revenue Service (IRS)—and are taxed only as the partners' personal income. Again, this avoids the potential for double taxation endemic to corporations.

But general partnerships also have some serious disadvantages. As you read about them, keep in mind that a well-written partnership agreement can mitigate some of the drawbacks.

> ❝ It's very much like a marriage, though I get along better with my wife. ❞
> –Zane Carter, general partner in Carter Cosgrove and Co. on his partnership

**limited partnership**
A partnership that includes at least one general partner and limited partner. Both partners contribute financially and share profits. General partners actively manage the company, accepting unlimited liability for debts while limited partners do not actively manage in exchange for limited liability.

**limited liability**
When owners are not personally liable for claims against their firm. Limited liability owners may lose their investment in the company, but their personal assets are protected.

**limited liability partnership (LLP)**
Form of partnership in which all partners have the right to participate in management and have limited liability for company debts.

- **Unlimited Liability:** All general partners have unlimited liability for the debts and obligations of their business. If the business can't pay its debts, each partner must pay from his or her personal resources. And as a general partner you're not only liable for your own mistakes, but also for the mistakes of your partners. In fact, if you have more personal wealth than the other partners, you could lose more than they do, even if they were at fault!

- **Potential for Disagreements:** If general partners can't agree on how to run the business, the conflict can complicate and delay decision making. Although a well-drafted partnership agreement usually specifies how disputes will be resolved, disagreements among partners can undermine the communication and cooperation needed to manage the business.

- **Difficulty in Withdrawing from a Partnership:** Most partnership agreements specify the terms under which a partner may withdraw. If a withdrawing partner violates those terms, the other partners can sue him or her for breach of contract.

- **Lack of Continuity:** If a current partner leaves the business or a new partner joins, the relationship among the participants will clearly change, potentially ending the partnership. But most agreements allow the partnership to continue under such circumstances, as long as the other partners unanimously agree to the change.

## Limited Partnerships

A **limited partnership** is a business arrangement that includes at least one general partner *and* at least one limited partner. Both types of partners contribute financially to the company and share in its profits. But in other respects they play different roles:

- General partners may contribute money, property and personal services to the partnership. They assume full responsibility for managing the partnership, and they have unlimited personal liability for any of its debts—just like the partners in a general partnership.

- Limited partners may contribute money and property to the company, but *cannot* actively participate in its management. Limited partners have **limited liability**; they are liable for the debts of the firm *only* to the extent of their actual investment. As long as they do not actively participate in management, their personal wealth is not at risk.

## Limited Liability Partnerships

The **limited liability partnership (LLP)** is the newest form of partnership. It is similar to a limited partnership in some ways, but it has the advantage of allowing *all* partners to take an active role in management while also offering *all* partners some form of limited liability. In other words, there's no need to distinguish between limited and general partners in an LLP.

The amount of liability protection offered by LLPs varies among states. In some states, LLPs offer "full shield" protection, meaning that partners have limited liability for all claims against their company except those resulting from *their own* negligence or malpractice. In other states,

### Keeping It in the Family

In recent years, limited partnerships have become increasingly popular in a surprising place: the family. Many families have set up family limited partnerships (sometimes called FLIPs) with the parents as the general partners and the children as the limited partners. Why do this? By using this structure, parents can transfer family assets to their children, thus greatly reducing gift and inheritance taxes. Since the parents are the general partners, they retain control over family assets even though they are now held by the children. Also, because (as limited partners) the children have limited liability, this structure can protect family assets from lawsuits or creditors.

Anyone thinking about setting up a FLIP should seek legal advice; this type of arrangement needs to be carefully structured to avoid problems. The IRS has expressed concern that many people are abusing this type of partnership and has vowed to be diligent in looking for such abuse. Thus, setting up a FLIP is likely to significantly increase your chances of an audit by the IRS![5]

© GEORGE DOYLE/STOCKBYTE /GETTY IMAGES

partners in LLPs have a lesser "partial shield" protection. In these states, each partner has limited liability for the negligence or malpractice of other owners but still has unlimited liability for any other debts. Some states only allow certain types of professional businesses to organize as LLPs. For example, California law allows only accountants, lawyers, and architects to form LLPs.

## LO3 Corporations: An Artificial Reality

A **corporation** is a legal entity created by permission of a state or federal government. (In the United States, most business corporations are created by filing appropriate paperwork with a specific state agency.) Unlike a sole proprietorship or partnership, a corporation is considered to be separate and distinct from its owners. In many ways, it's like an artificial person; it can legally engage in virtually any business activity a natural person can. For example, a corporation can own property, enter into binding contracts, borrow money, and initiate legal actions (such as lawsuits) in its own name.

You can see from exhibit 6.2 that corporations are the dominant form of ownership when it comes to net income. Virtually all of the largest companies in the United States are incorporated. Corporations like Wal-Mart, Exxon, and General Electric have annual sales revenues measured in the hundreds of billions of dollars. But don't assume that all corporations are large. In recent years, about 24% of all corporations have reported total sales revenues of less than $25,000.[6]

There are several types of corporations. The **general corporation** (also called a C corporation) is the most common;

when most people use the term "corporation" without specifying which type, the general corporation is almost certainly what they have in mind. Because it's the most common, we'll devote most of our discussion to the general corporation. However, we'll also describe three other types of corporations: S corporations, statutory close (or closed) corporations, and nonprofit corporations.

### Forming a General Corporation

Forming a corporation is more complex than forming a sole proprietorship or partnership. It requires filing a special form, known in most states as the **articles of incorporation**, with a specific state agency. In addition, incorporators must pay filing fees to the state and must establish **corporate bylaws**—which are the basic rules and procedures governing the way the corporation will operate—and file them with the state as well.

When it comes to the specifics of incorporating, every state has its own forms and requirements. Some states are known for their simple forms, inexpensive fees, low corporate tax rates, and "corporation friendly" laws

**corporation** A form of business ownership in which the business is considered a legal entity that is separate and distinct from its owners.

**general corporation (or C corporation)** The most common type of business corporation, where ownership offers limited liability to all of its owners, also called stockholders.

**articles of incorporation** The document filed with a state government to establish the existence of a new corporation.

**corporate bylaws** The basic rules governing how a corporation is organized and how it conducts its business.

> The limited liability corporation is the greatest single invention of modern times.
> –Nicholas Murray Butler, former president of Columbia University

### All for one...

Does the idea of participating in a business based on ideals such as self-reliance, democracy, and equality appeal to you? If so, you might want to look into becoming a member of a special type of business organization called a cooperative (or co-op). Cooperatives are usually formed as corporations, but they are organized and operated under special bylaws that emphasize open and democratic ownership and control. The goal of co-ops is to provide direct benefits to their member-owners.

You might be surprised by how common co-ops are in the United States. In fact, you might be even more surprised to find out that you already belong to one without knowing it! For example, if you're a member of a credit union, you belong to a co-op. Over 9,300 credit unions operate in the United States, benefiting their 86 million members by paying them higher interest on deposits—and charging them lower interest rates on loans—than most banks and other financial institutions.

But credit unions are only the tip of the co-op iceberg. Cooperatives also play significant roles in such diverse areas of the economy as electric power generation, agriculture, health care, insurance, childcare, legal services, telecommunications, and the Internet. You can find out more about the philosophy behind co-ops and their economic impact on the U.S. economy by visiting the Web sites of the National Cooperative Business Association at http://www.ncba.coop/ and the International Cooperative Alliance at http://www.ica.coop/al-ica/.[7]

and court systems. Not surprisingly, many large companies choose to incorporate in states with such favorable environments—even if they intend to do the majority of their business in other states. Delaware, in particular, has been very successful at attracting corporations. You may not think of Delaware as the home of corporate power, but about half of all publicly traded corporations—and 60% of the firms listed in the Fortune 500—are incorporated in Delaware.[8]

There's one other important complication when doing business as a corporation. When a business that's incorporated in one state does business in other states, it's called a *domestic* corporation in the state where it's incorporated and a *foreign* corporation in the other states. A corporation must register as a foreign corporation and pay a filing fee in *every* state in which it operates other than its state of incorporation.

## Ownership of General Corporations

Ownership of corporations is represented by shares of stock, so owners are called **stockholders** (or shareholders). Common stock represents the basic ownership interest in a corporation, but some firms also issue preferred stock. We'll describe the characteristics of both types of stock and explain how they differ in chapter 10.

Some large, publicly traded corporations issue billions of shares of stock and have hundreds of thousands of stockholders. For example, in 2007 General Electric had 9.98 billion shares of stock outstanding, held by over 607,000 stockholders. But many corporations are owned by a just a handful of stockholders. It's even possible for individuals to incorporate as the sole owner of a corporation. (However, individuals usually incorporate as an S corporation—which we'll describe in the next section—rather than as a general corporation.)[9]

Stockholders don't have to be individuals. For example, organizations such as mutual funds, insurance companies, pension funds, and endowment funds pool money from a large number of individual contributors, and use these funds to buy stocks and other securities. These organizations, called **institutional investors**, own the majority of stock in many large corporations.

## The Role of the Board of Directors

It's not practical for all of the stockholders of a large corporation to actively participate in the management of

The board of directors is responsible for representing the interests of the corporation's stockholders.

their company. Besides, most stockholders don't have the time, management skills, or desire to effectively manage such a complex business enterprise. Thus, in accordance with corporate bylaws, the stockholders elect a **board of directors** and rely on this board to oversee the operation of their company and protect their interests.

The board of directors establishes the corporation's mission and sets its broad objectives but seldom takes an active role in the day-to-day management of the company. Instead, it appoints the chief executive officer (CEO) and other corporate officers, and delegates the responsibility for detailed management of the corporation to them. The board is responsible for monitoring the performance of these corporate officers to ensure that their decisions are consistent with stockholder interests. It also provides advice to these officers on broad policy issues, approves their major proposals, and ensures that the company adheres to major regulatory requirements.

> ❝ Corporation: an ingenious device for obtaining profit without individual responsibility.
>
> –Ambrose Bierce, 19th-century editor and compiler of the *Devil's Dictionary* ❞

## Advantages of General Corporations

There are several reasons why corporations have become the dominant form of business ownership:

- Limited Liability: Because a corporation is legally separate from its owners, stockholders are not personally liable for the debts of their company. If a corporation goes bankrupt, the stockholders might find that their stock is worthless, but their other personal assets are protected.

- Permanence: Unless the articles of incorporation specify a limited duration, corporations can continue operating as long as they remain financially viable and the majority of stockholders want the business to continue. Unlike a sole proprietorship or partnership, a general corporation is unaffected by the death or withdrawal of an owner.

- **Ease of Transfer of Ownership:** It's easy for stockholders of publicly traded general corporations to withdraw from ownership—they simply sell their shares of stock.

- **Ability to Raise Large Amounts of Financial Capital:** Corporations can raise large amounts of financial capital by issuing shares of stock or by selling long-term IOUs called corporate bonds. (We'll discuss how they can do this in chapter 10.) The ability to raise money by issuing these securities gives corporations a major financial advantage over most other forms of ownership.

- **Ability to Make Use of Specialized Management:** Large corporations often find it easier to hire highly qualified professional managers than proprietorships and partnerships. Major corporations can typically offer attractive salaries and benefits, and their permanence and potential for growth offer managers opportunities for career advancement.

## Disadvantages of Corporations

In addition to their significant benefits, corporations also have a number of drawbacks:

- **Expense and Complexity of Formation and Operation:** As we've already seen, establishing a corporation is more complex and expensive than forming sole proprietorships and partnerships. Corporations are also subject to more formal operating requirements. For example, they are required to hold regular board meetings and keep accurate minutes.

- **Double Taxation of Earnings and Additional Taxes:** The IRS considers a general corporation to be a separate legal entity and taxes its earnings accordingly. Then, any dividends (earnings the corporation distributes to stockholders) are taxed *again* as the personal income of the stockholders. In addition to income taxes, states also impose an annual franchise tax on corporations.

- **More Paperwork and More Regulation:** Corporations are more closely regulated than other forms of business. Large, publicly traded corporations are required to send annual statements to all shareholders and to file detailed quarterly and annual reports with the Securities and Exchange Commission (SEC). Anyone can look at the forms filed with the SEC, making it difficult to keep financial information secret from competitors.

- **Possible Conflicts of Interest:** The corporate officers appointed by the board are supposed to further the interests of stockholders. But some top executives pursue policies that further their *own* interests (such as prestige and power, job security, and attractive financial perks) at the expense of the stockholders. The board of directors is *supposed* to look out for the interests of stockholders, but several boards in

# WITHOUT A MAP... CHARTING AN ETHICAL COURSE

### Shareholders Take Aim at Golden Parachutes

A recent study by the Corporate Library, an independent research firm that rates boards of directors of U.S. corporations, suggests that many CEOs receive pay that has little or no relationship to their success at increasing shareholder value. The study found that the CEOs of 12 major U.S. corporations—including Ford Motor Company, Time Warner, Inc., and Home Depot, Inc.—received a total of $1.26 *billion* in pay (over $100 million per CEO) even though their corporations lost $330 billion in shareholder value. Many of these same executives also have clauses in their contracts, called golden handshakes or golden parachutes, which call for millions in severance pay after they quit or are fired. The situation has caused analysts to quip that the goal of granting CEOs "pay for performance" has turned into mere "pay for pulse."

Who's responsible for these lavish payouts? Many critics believe that excessive compensation of CEOs is a sign that the boards have failed in their duty to stockholders to exercise proper control over the senior managers they're supposed to oversee. Stockholders in some corporations have taken matters into their own hands, going to court over the issue. In 2007, a group of Home Depot stockholders sued to prevent former CEO Robert Nardelli from receiving his $210 million severance package. The group said that Nardelli had mismanaged the home-improvement company and that his severance pay amounted to "a final, indefensible step by the board of directors in wrongly overcompensating an unsuccessful CEO." Such actions signal that shareholders may finally be determined to deflate the "golden parachutes" of their executives once and for all.[10]

recent years have been criticized for failure to exercise proper oversight.

## LO4 Other Types of Corporations: Same but Different

Now that we've described general corporations, let's take a quick look at three other types: S corporations, statutory close corporations, and nonprofit corporations.

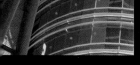

Like general corporations, each is created by filing the appropriate document with a government entity. Also like general corporations, these corporations can enter into contracts, own property, and take legal action in their own names. But in other key respects they are quite different from general corporations—and from each other. Exhibit 6.3 describes the basic features of these corporations.

## LO5 Corporate Restructuring

Large corporations constantly look for ways to grow, operate more efficiently, and achieve competitive advantages. Some corporations work to achieve these goals at least in part through mergers and acquisitions. We'll close our discussion of corporations by taking a quick look at these forms of corporate restructuring.

### Mergers and Acquisitions

In the news and casual conversation, the terms "merger" and "acquisition" are often used interchangeably. However, there's a difference between the two. An **acquisition** occurs when one firm buys another firm. The firm making the purchase is called the *acquiring firm*, and the firm being purchased is called the *target firm*. After the acquisition, the target firm ceases to exist as an independent entity while the purchasing firm continues in operation and its stock is still traded. In a **merger**, instead of one firm buying the other, the two companies agree to a combination of equals, joining together to form a new company out of the two previously independent firms. Exhibit 6.4 describes the three most common types of mergers and acquisitions.[11]

| **Exhibit 6.3** | Characteristics of S, Statutory Close, and Nonprofit Corporations |

| Type | Key Advantages | Limitations |
|---|---|---|
| **S Corporation** | • IRS does not tax earnings of S corporations separately. Earnings pass through the company and are taxed only as income to stockholders, thus avoiding the problem of double taxation associated with C corporations.<br>• Stockholders have limited liability. | • Can have no more than 100 stockholders.<br>• With only a few rare exceptions, each stockholder must be a U.S. citizen or permanent resident of the United States. (No ownership by foreigners or other corporations.) |
| **Statutory Close (or Closed) Corporation** | • Can operate under simpler arrangements than conventional corporations. For example, doesn't have to elect a board of directors or hold an annual stockholders' meeting.<br>• All owners can actively participate in management while still having limited liability. | • Number of stockholders is limited. (The number varies among states but is usually no more than 50.)<br>• Stockholders normally can't sell their shares to the public without first offering the shares to existing owners.<br>• Not all states allow formation of this type of corporation. |
| **Nonprofit (or Not-for-Profit) Corporation** | • Earnings are exempt from federal and state income taxes.<br>• Members and directors have limited liability.<br>• Individuals who contribute money or property to the nonprofit can take a tax deduction, making it easier for these organizations to raise funds from donations. | • Has members (who may pay dues) but cannot have stockholders.<br>• Cannot distribute dividends to members.<br>• Cannot contribute funds to a political campaign.<br>• Must keep accurate records and file paperwork to document tax-exempt status. |

**Exhibit 6.4** Types of Mergers and Acquisitions

| Type of Merger | Definition | Common Objective | Example |
|---|---|---|---|
| **Horizontal merger** | Combination of firms in the same industry | Increase size and market power within industry. Improve efficiency by eliminating duplication of facilities and personnel. | 2006 merger of telecommunications giants SBC and AT&T |
| **Vertical merger** | Combination of firms at different stages in the production of a given good or service, so that the firms have a "buyer-seller" relationship | Provide tighter integration of production and increased control over supply of crucial inputs. | 1996 Merger of Time Warner (a major provider of cable television) with Turner Broadcasting (owner of several cable networks such as CNN and TNT) |
| **Conglomerate merger** | Combination of firms in unrelated industries | Reduce risk by making the firm less vulnerable to adverse conditions in any single market. | GE's move into the entertainment industry by acquiring RCA (to gain control of NBC) in 1986 and Vivendi Universal's movie and television units in 2004 |

**horizontal merger** A combination of two firms that are in the same industry.

**vertical merger** A combination of firms at different stages in the production of a good or service.

**conglomerate merger** A combination of two firms that are in unrelated industries.

**limited liability company (LLC)** Form of business ownership which combines the limited liability of corporations with the tax pass-through of partnerships, eliminating the problem of double taxation.

## LO6 The Limited Liability Company: The New Kid on the Block

Although corporations remain the dominant form of business ownership, the **limited liability company (LLC)**—a relatively new form of ownership—has become a popular alternative. The LLC is a hybrid that is like a corporation in some ways, and like a partnership in others. Because LLCs are neither corporations nor partnerships, their owners are called *members* rather than stockholders or partners.

### Forming and Managing an LLC

In many respects, forming an LLC is similar to forming a corporation. As with corporations, LLCs are created by filing a document (usually called *the articles of organization*) and paying filing fees in the state where the business is organized. Organizers of most LLCs also draft an operating agreement, which is similar to the bylaws established for a corporation. A few states also require LLCs to publish a notice of intent to operate as a limited liability company. Members of LLCs often manage their own company under an arrangement similar to the relationship among general partners in a partnership. However, some LLCs hire professional managers.

### Advantages of LLCs

Why are LLCs becoming so popular? This form of ownership offers significant advantages:

Donald Trump is one of a growing number of business owners who have discovered the many advantages of the LLC form of ownership.

© MARK VON HOLDEN/FILMMAGIC/GETTY IMAGES

**franchising** A contractual relationship in which an established business entity allows others to operate a business using unique resources that it supplies in exchange for monetary payments and other considerations.

**franchisor** The business entity in a franchise relationship that allows others to operate their business using resources it supplies in exchange for money and other considerations.

**franchisee** The party in a franchise relationship that pays for the right to use resources supplied by the franchisor.

**business format franchise** A broad franchise agreement in which the franchisee pays for the right to use the name, trademark, and business and production methods of the franchisor.

- Limited Liability: Similar to a corporation, *all* owners of an LLC have limited liability.

- Tax Pass-Through: LLCs are taxed like a partnership. Members must pay personal income taxes on income they receive from their LLC, but there is no separate tax on the earnings of the company. This eliminates the double taxation of profits that is endemic to general corporations.

- Simplicity in Management and Operation: Unlike corporations, LLCs aren't required to hold regular board meetings. Also, LLCs are subject to less paperwork and fewer reporting requirements than corporations.

- Flexible Ownership: Unlike S corporations, LLCs can have any number of owners. Also unlike S corporations, the owners of LLCs can include foreign investors and other corporations.

## Limitations and Disadvantages of LLCs

Despite their increasing popularity, LLCs have some limitations and drawbacks:

- More Complex to Form than Partnerships: LLCs take more time and effort to form than sole proprietorships and general partnerships.

- Annual Franchise Tax: Like corporations, LLCs typically must pay an annual franchise tax to the state where they're organized.

- Foreign Status in Other States: Also like corporations, LLCs must file as "foreign" companies when they do business in states other than where they were organized. This results in more paperwork and fees.

- Limits on Types of Firms That Can Form LLCs: Some states do not permit certain types of businesses, such as banks, insurance companies, and nonprofit organizations, to operate as LLCs.

- Differences in State Laws: There are significant differences in state laws governing LLCs. In some states, for instance, LLCs must have a limited life, while other states have removed this restriction. States also vary in the way ownership interests in LLCs may be transferred. A move is currently gaining momentum to establish a uniform law for LLCs in all states, but until the majority of states adopt such a

law, operating an LLC in more than one state is likely to remain a complex endeavor.[12]

## LO7 Franchising: Proven Methods for a Price

**Franchising** is an ongoing contractual relationship in which an established firm supplies another business with unique resources in exchange for payment and other considerations. The business that provides the resources is the **franchisor**. Those who acquire the right to use these resources to operate their business are **franchisees**.

Franchising is *not* a form of ownership like the sole proprietorships, partnerships, corporations, and LLCs we've already described. Instead, it's a very popular way to *operate* a business. In 2008 more than 909,000 franchises in the United States contributed almost 21 million jobs and $2.3 trillion dollars in sales to the U.S. economy.[13]

The most common type of franchise arrangement is a **business format franchise**. Under this type of franchise the franchisee uses the franchisor's brand name and trademark and operates the business according to methods and principles provided by the franchisor. You're no doubt very familiar with business format franchises; examples include Subway, 7-Eleven, and Jiffy Lube.

## Franchising in Today's Economy

Franchising is now a well-established method of operating a business—but that doesn't mean it's static. Let's look at some ways the world of franchising is changing.

One of the biggest trends in franchising for the past several years has been an expansion into foreign markets. Franchisors in a variety of industries have found that opportunities for franchise growth are greater in foreign countries because competition is less intense and markets are less saturated than in the United States. At the end of 2007, McDonald's had 10,498 franchise outlets in foreign countries, Subway had 4,659, Jani-King had 1,661, and Curves had 2,474.[14] Of course, operating in foreign countries can pose special challenges. As we explained in Chapter 3, differences in culture, language, laws, demographics, and economic development mean that franchisors, like other types of business owners, must adjust their business methods—and the specific products they offer—to meet the needs of foreign consumers.

Another notable trend has been the growth in the number of women franchisees. Hard data are difficult to find, but the International Franchising Association (IFA) estimates that women now own about 30% of all franchises, and anecdotal evidence suggests that the trend toward more women-owned franchisees is continuing. A number of women, such as JoAnne Shaw (founder of the Coffee Beanery) and Maxine Clark (founder of Build-A-Bear) also have become very successful franchisors. But, despite these highly visible success stories, the number of women franchisors hasn't grown nearly as fast as the number of women-owned franchisees.[15]

Minority participation in franchises, both as franchisees and franchisors, has been relatively low. Although African Americans, Hispanics, Asian Americans, and Native Americans make up about a third of the population, less than 10% of all franchisees are minorities.[16] One of the main reasons for such low minority involvement in franchising is a lack of awareness of franchising opportunities within minority communities. Until recently, most franchisors did a poor job of reaching out to minorities.

In early 2006, the IFA announced an initiative to encourage greater minority involvement in franchising. Called MinorityFran, this program encourages franchisors to actively recruit minority franchisees. The initiative has attracted the cooperation of a variety of organizations interested in promoting minority business ownership, including the National Urban League, the Association of Small Business Development Centers, the U.S. Pan Asian American Chamber of Commerce, and the Minority Business Development Agency. Franchisors participating in the program receive information and training on how to deal with diversity issues. They're also given contact information for community leaders who can help them reach out to various minority communities. As of January 2008, MinorityFran had 247 participating franchisors, including many of the largest franchisors in the United States.[17]

## Advantages of Franchising

The advantages of franchising for the franchisor are fairly obvious. It allows the franchisor to expand the business and bring in additional revenue (in the form of franchising fees and royalties) without investing its own capital. Also, franchisees—business owners who are motivated to earn a profit—may be more willing than salaried managers to do whatever it takes to maximize the success of their outlets.

From the franchisee's perspective, franchising offers several advantages:

- **Less Risk:** Franchises offer access to a proven business system and product. The systems and methods offered by franchisors have an established track record. People who are interested in buying a franchise can do research to see how stores in the franchise have performed and can talk to existing franchisees before investing.

- **Training and Support:** The franchisor normally provides the franchisee with extensive training and support. For example, Subway offers 2 weeks of training at its headquarters and additional training at meetings. It also sends out newsletters, provides Internet support, maintains a toll-free number for phone support, and provides on-site evaluations.[18]

- **Brand Recognition:** Operating a franchise gives the franchisee instant brand name recognition, which can be a big help in attracting customers.

- **Easier Access to Funding:** Bankers and other lenders may be more willing to loan you money if your business is part of an established franchise than a new, unproven business.

### Martha Matilda Harper, First Franchising Superstar

The first true business format franchise was established in 1891 when Martha Matilda Harper began franchising her hair salons, which became known as Harper Method Shops (or just Harper Shops). By the mid 1920s, over 500 Harper Shops were serving customers throughout the United States and Canada, as well as several foreign cities including London and Paris. Many of the era's rich and famous, including Susan B. Anthony, Helen Hayes, and Presidents Woodrow Wilson and Calvin Coolidge, became devoted customers of the franchise.

Harper was a true business innovator. In addition to developing the first business format franchising system, she was among the first employers to offer profit sharing, flexible work schedules, and childcare for the women who worked in her shops. She also invented the reclining shampoo chair that salons still use today. Harper was elected to the National Women's Hall of Fame in 2003 for her entrepreneurial contributions.[19]

**franchise agreement** The contractual arrangement between a franchisor and franchisee that spells out the duties and responsibilities of both parties in detail.

## Disadvantages of Franchising

Franchising also has some drawbacks. From the franchisor's perspective, operating a business with perhaps thousands of semi-independent owner-operators can be complex and challenging. Franchisees are also likely to find some disadvantages:

- **Costs:** Franchisees usually must pay an initial franchise fee and an ongoing royalty, which is usually a percentage of monthly sales, to the franchisor. In addition, the franchisor may assess other fees to support national advertising campaigns or for other purposes. These costs vary considerably, but for high-profile franchises, they can be substantial. For example, in 2008 the initial franchise fee for a McDonald's restaurant was $45,000, and the royalty was 12.5% of sales.[20]

- **Lack of Control:** The **franchise agreement** usually requires the franchisee to follow the franchisor's procedures and methods to the letter. People who want the freedom and flexibility to be their own boss can find these restrictions frustrating.

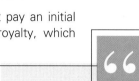

It's not hard to meet expenses. They're everywhere.

–Anonymous franchisee

- **Negative Halo Effect:** The irresponsible or incompetent behavior of a few franchisees can create a negative perception that adversely affects not only the franchise as a whole but also the success of other franchisees.

- **Growth Challenges:** While growth and expansion are possible in franchising (many franchisees own multiple outlets), strings are attached. Franchise agreements usually limit the franchisee's territory and require franchisor approval before expanding into other areas.

- **Restrictions on Sale:** Franchisees are prohibited from selling their franchises to other investors without prior approval from the franchisor.

- **Poor Execution:** Not all franchisors live up to their promises. Sometimes the training and support are of poor quality and sometimes the company does a poor job of screening franchisees, leading to the negative halo effect we mentioned previously.

These considerations suggest that before buying a franchise, potential owners should carefully research the franchise opportunity.

### Some Franchisees Are Quite Happy When They Don't Earn a Profit

While most franchisees are out to make a profit, some nonprofit organizations (including several youth development organizations) have turned to franchising as a new way to raise funds. Everybody seems to win from this arrangement:

- Many customers like doing business with nonprofit franchisees; they get a well-known product while supporting a worthy cause.
- Franchisors view their arrangements with nonprofit franchisees as a good way to meet their social responsibilities and build goodwill within local communities.
- The nonprofits gain access to a business with proven products and methods. This can boost their fundraising efforts at a time when funds from more traditional sources are no longer growing fast enough to keep up with needs. In addition, some nonprofit youth organizations have found that operating a franchise allows them to offer employment opportunities to the teenagers they serve.

Many franchisors now actively seek nonprofit franchisees. Ben & Jerry's has been particularly active in reaching out to nonprofits. It's even established a special program, called PartnerShops, to help nonprofits get started in franchising.[21]

© ANTHONY BLAKE PHOTO LIBRARY/PHOTOLIBRARY

## Entering into a Franchise Agreement

To obtain a franchise, the franchisee must sign a franchise agreement. This agreement is a legally binding contract that specifies the relationship between the franchisor and the franchisee in great detail. There's no standard form for the contract, but it normally covers the following items:

- Terms and Conditions: The franchisee's rights to use the franchisor's trademarks, patents and signage, and any limitations or restrictions on those rights. It also covers how long the agreement will last and under what terms and conditions it can be renewed.

- Fees and Other Payments: The fees the franchisee must pay for the right to use the franchisor's products and methods, and when these payments are due.

- Training and Support: The types of training and support the franchisor will provide to the franchisee.

- Specific Operational Requirements: The methods and standards established by the franchisor that the franchisee is required to follow.

- Conflict Resolution: How the franchisor and franchisee will handle disputes.

- Assigned Territory: The geographic area in which the franchisee will operate and whether the franchisee has exclusive rights in that area.

It's vital that franchisees read through the franchise agreement carefully before signing on the dotted line. In fact, it's a good idea to have a lawyer who is knowledgeable about franchise law review it. You'll have to pay for any legal advice, but entering into a bad franchise agreement can be a lot more expensive (and stressful) than a lawyer's fees.

# Small Business and Entrepreneurship: Economic Rocket Fuel

## CHAPTER 7

## LEARNING OBJECTIVES

After studying this chapter, you will be able to…

**LO1** Explain the key reasons to launch a small business

**LO2** Describe the typical entrepreneurial mindset and characteristics

**LO3** Analyze the opportunities and threats that small businesses face

**LO4** Discuss ways to become a new business owner and tools to facilitate success

**LO5** Discuss funding options for small business

**LO6** Explain the size, scope, and economic contributions of small business

4ltrpress.cengage.com/busn

Business opportunities are like buses. . .
there's always another one coming.
–Richard Branson, founder, Virgin Enterprises

## LO1 Launching a New Venture: What's in It for Me?

The number of new business launches today is increasing faster than ever. Looking forward, the trend should only gain momentum, since research suggests that the majority of American teenagers and young people plan to launch their own enterprise as soon as they can. Make no mistake: starting a new business is tough...very tough. Yet for the right person, the advantages of business ownership far outweigh the risk and hard work. Although people start their own ventures for a variety of reasons, most are seeking some combination of greater financial success, independence, flexibility, and challenge. Others are simply seeking survival.[1]

### Greater Financial Success

Although you can make a pretty good living working for someone else, your chances of getting really rich may be higher if you start your own business. The Forbes annual list of the 400 richest Americans is dominated by **entrepreneurs**, such as Bill Gates and Paul Allen (founders of Microsoft), Phil Knight (founder of Nike), Michael Dell (founder of Dell computer), and Sergey Brin and Larry Page (founders of Google). Well below the top 400, many people feel that their chances of even moderate financial success are higher if they're working for themselves rather than someone else. The opportunity to make more money is a primary motivator for many entrepreneurs, although other factors clearly play a role as well.[2]

### Independence

Being your own boss is a huge benefit of starting your own business. You have to answer to no one other than yourself and any investors that you invite to participate in your business. Bottom line: you are the only one who is ultimately responsible for your success or failure. This setup is especially compelling for people who have trouble being a subordinate because of their personalities (and we probably all know someone who fits that description!). But while independence is nice, it's important to keep in mind that every business depends on meeting the needs of its customers, who can be even more demanding than the toughest boss.

**entrepreneurs** People who risk their time, money, and other resources to start and manage a business.

## Serial Entrepreneur

Wayne Huizenga seems hooked on the challenge and excitement of launching new ventures. Huizenga is the only person in history to found six companies listed on the New York Stock Exchange and three Fortune 500 companies across a range of industries. His successes include Waste Management, Inc. (the global leader in garbage services), AutoNation, and Blockbuster Entertainment.

While you might not see it at first glance, Huizenga seems to follow a consistent model across very different businesses. He focuses on service industries that aren't meeting customer needs and he creates firms that set a new, higher standard of customer service.

An innovative, savvy entrepreneur, Huizenga won the 2005 Ernst & Young World Entrepreneur of the Year award. The judges acknowledged Huizenga not just for his business success, but also for his contributions to humanity. The head of the program commented that Huizenga's "personal qualities, the strength of his family relationships and his business leadership have had far reaching social and economic impact across the globe."[2a]

## Flexibility

The ability to set your own hours and control your own schedule is a hugely appealing benefit for many business owners, especially parents seeking more time with their kids or retirees looking for extra income. Given current technological tools—from e-mail to eBay—it's easy for small business owners to manage their firms on the go or after hours. Of course, there's often a correlation between hours worked and dollars earned (it's rare to work less and earn more). But when more money isn't the primary goal, the need for flexibility can be enough to motivate many entrepreneurs to launch their own enterprise.

## Challenge

Running your own business provides a level of challenge unmatched by many other endeavors. Most business owners—especially new business owners—never find themselves bored! Starting a business also offers endless opportunities for learning that can provide more profound satisfaction for many people than grinding out the hours as an employee.

> 66
> ### Size certainly matters, and not always in a positive way.
> —Michael Powell, founder and owner of Powell Books
> 99

## Survival

Although most entrepreneurs launch their business in response to an opportunity and in hopes of improving their lives, some entrepreneurs launch an enterprise because they believe that starting their own business is their *only* economic option. This segment of "necessity entrepreneurs" includes a range of people from middle-age workers laid off from corporate jobs, to new immigrants with limited English and heavy accents, to those who experience discrimination in the standard workplace. For each of these people, small business ownership can be the right choice in the face of few other alternatives.

## When Less Is Definitely More

Like many other small business owners, Eric Truran, founder of a small New England manufacturing firm and retail store, saw the emergence of the Internet as a huge opportunity. But in Eric's case the Web represented an opportunity to downsize his business and upsize his quality of life. As the Web side of his business began to grow, he closed his retail store to focus strictly on online and telephone sales. While his income dropped by about 50%, his free time more than quadrupled. He went from working 80 to 90 hours a week to working 15 to 20 hours a week. And he uses his free time to pursue other passions, such as playing guitar with his two bands. "My whole business philosophy is, enough is enough," he comments. "Anything more than that, and you just work all the time."[3]

## LO2 The Entrepreneur: A Distinctive Profile

Successful entrepreneurs tend to stand out from the crowd in terms of both their mindset and their personal characteristics. As you read this section, consider whether you fit the entrepreneurial profile.

### The Entrepreneurial Mindset: A Matter of Attitude

Almost every entrepreneur starts as a small businessperson—either launching a firm or buying a firm—but not every small businessperson starts as an entrepreneur. The difference is a matter of attitude. From day one, a true entrepreneur—such as Sam Walton of Wal-Mart, Steve Jobs of Apple, or Jeff Bezos of Amazon—aims to change the world through blockbuster goods or services. That isn't the case for all small business owners; in fact, most people who launch new firms expect to better themselves, but they don't expect huge, transformative growth.

However, classic entrepreneurs who deliver on the promise of their best ideas can dramatically change the economic and social landscape worldwide. Examples of business owners who thought and delivered big include Henry Ford, founder of the Ford Motor Company and originator of assembly line production; Walt Disney, founder of The Walt Disney Company and creator of Mickey Mouse; Bill Gates, founder of Microsoft; Mary Kay Ash, founder of a cosmetics powerhouse; Martha Stewart, lifestyle innovator for the masses; George Lucas, creator of the Star Wars empire; Pierre Omidyar, founder of eBay; and Oprah Winfrey, media mogul.

### Entrepreneurial Characteristics

While experts sometimes disagree about the specific characteristics of successful entrepreneurs, virtually all include vision, self-reliance, energy, confidence, tolerance of uncertainty, and tolerance of failure. (See exhibit 7.1.) Most successful entrepreneurs have all of these qualities and more, but they come in a huge variety of combinations that highlight the complexity of personality: there is no one successful entrepreneurial profile.

**Vision**  Most entrepreneurs are wildly excited about their own new ideas, which many seem to draw from a bottomless well. Entrepreneurs find new solutions to old problems, and they develop brand-new products that we didn't even know we needed until we had them. And entrepreneurs stay excited about their ideas, even when friends and relatives threaten to call the loony bin. For instance, Fred Smith, founder of the FedEx empire, traces the concept for his business to a term paper he wrote at Yale, which supposedly received a C from a skeptical professor. But that didn't stop him from creating a business logistics system that transformed the industry.

**Self-Reliance**  As an entrepreneur, the buck stops with you. New business owners typically need to do everything themselves, from getting permits, to motivating employees, to keeping the books—all in addition to producing the product or service that made them start the business in the first place. Self-reliance seems to come with an **internal locus of control**, or a deep-seated sense that the individual is personally responsible for what happens in his or her life. When things go well, people with an internal locus of control feel that their efforts have been validated, and

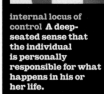

**internal locus of control** A deep-seated sense that the individual is personally responsible for what happens in his or her life.

### The Wild, Wild East!

The sun may be setting on days of opportunity in the west, as the eastern frontier opens for entrepreneurship. Meet Vishal Gondal, 28-year-old founder of Indiagames, one of the leading game development centers in the world. *Rediff India* reports that due to the firm's creative vision and efficient production, Indiagames has bagged exclusive rights to develop games for hot entertainment properties such as *Spiderman* and *Jurassic Park*. The marketing coups will likely continue, judging by the company's close ties to movie studios, handset manufacturers, and major mobile operators. Most of Indiagames' growth to date has come from the European and American markets, with games based on blockbuster films and popular national pastimes such as darts in the United Kingdom and baseball in the United States. But looking to the future, Vishal gazes eastward. As the number of mobile phone users and broadband installations skyrocket in India and China, he plans to ride that wave, boldly declaring, "I think it's now time to forget the West and look east."[4]

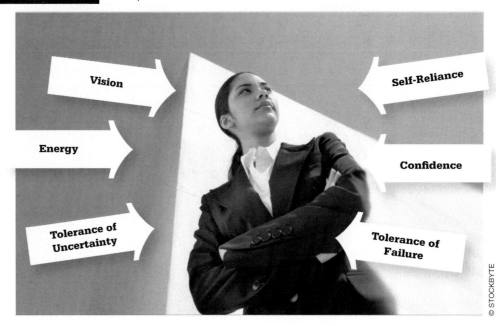

when things go poorly, those same people feel that they need to do better next time. This sense of responsibility encourages positive action. In contrast, people with an **external locus of control** rely less on their own efforts, feeling buffeted by forces such as random luck and the actions of others, which they believe will ultimately control their fate.

**Energy**  Entrepreneurs simply can't succeed without an enormous amount of energy. Six or seven 12-hour workdays are not atypical in the start-up phase of running a business. A recent survey by the Wells Fargo/Gallup Small Business Index recently found that today's small business owner works an average of 52 hours per week, with 57% working at least six days a week, and more than 20% working all seven. But they seem to find it worthwhile: 47% percent of small business owners said that if they won $10 million in the lottery, they would still work in their current job. Only 9% would stop working, and 8% would combine work, volunteering, and other areas of interest.[5]

**Confidence**  Successful entrepreneurs typically have confidence in their own ability to achieve, and their confidence encourages them to act boldly. But too much confidence has a downside. Entrepreneurs must take care not to confuse likelihood with reality. In fact, many could benefit from the old adage to hope for the best and plan for the worst. A recent study for the Small Business Administration Office of Advocacy

confirmed that entrepreneurs are typically overconfident regarding their own abilities. As a result they're willing to plunge into a new business, but they don't always have the skills to succeed.[6]

**Tolerance of Uncertainty**  More often than others, entrepreneurs see the world in shades of gray, rather than simply black and white. They tend to embrace uncertainty in the business environment, turning it to their advantage rather than shying away. Uncertainty also relates to risk, and successful entrepreneurs tend to more willingly accept risk—financial risk, for instance, such as mortgaging their home for the business, and professional risk, such as staking their reputation on the success of an unproven product.

**Tolerance of Failure**  Even when they fail, entrepreneurs seldom label themselves losers. They tend to view failure as a chance to learn, rather than as a sign that they just can't do it (whatever "it" may be for them at any given moment). Interestingly, Isaac Fleischmann, director of the U.S. Patent Office for 36 years, pointed out that "During times of economic decline when unemployment increases, so does the number of patents. Dark days often force us to become more ingenious, to monitor and modify the ways we reached failure and reshape them into a new pattern of success." Failure can actually be an effective springboard for achievement.[7]

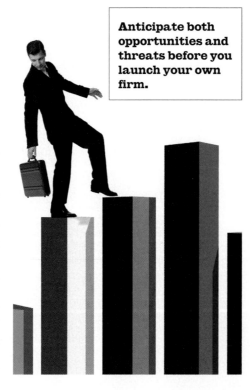

> **Anticipate both opportunities and threats before you launch your own firm.**

## LO3 Opportunities and Threats for Small Business: A Two-Sided Coin

Most small businesses enjoy a number of advantages as they compete for customers. But they also must defuse a range of daunting potential threats in order to succeed long term.

### Small Business Opportunities

Small businesses enjoy a real competitive edge across a range of different areas. Because of their size, many small firms can exploit narrow but profitable market niches, offer personal customer service, and maintain lower overhead costs. And due to advances in technology, small firms can compete more effectively than ever in both global and domestic markets.

**Market Niches** Many small firms are uniquely positioned to exploit small but profitable **market niches**. These sparsely occupied spaces in the market tend to have fewer competitors because they simply aren't big enough—or high enough profile—for large firms. They nonetheless offer more than enough potential for small, specialized companies. For example, Kazoo & Company, a relatively small toy store, competes effectively with Wal-Mart, Target, and Kmart by stocking different—and complementary—products, deliberately zigging when the big players zag.[8]

**Personal Customer Service** With a smaller customer base, small firms can develop much more personal relationships with individual customers. Shel Weinstein, for instance, former owner of a Los Angeles corner pharmacy, knew his customers so well that they would call him at home in the middle of the night for help with medical emergencies. The personal touch can be especially beneficial in some foreign markets, where clients prize the chance to deal directly with top management.

**Lower Overhead Costs** With entrepreneurs wearing so many hats, from CEO to customer service rep, many small firms have lower overhead costs. They can hire fewer managers and fewer specialized employees. Perhaps more importantly, smaller firms—due to a lack of resources—tend to work around costs with tactics such as establishing headquarters in the owner's garage or offering employees flexible schedules instead of costly healthcare benefits.

**Technology** The Internet has played a powerful role in opening new opportunities for small business. Using a wealth of online tools, from eBay to eMachineshop, companies-of-one can create, sell, publish, and even manufacture goods and services more easily than ever before. The Web has also created international opportunities, transforming small businesses into global marketers. The London-based Anything Left-Handed retail store, for instance, evolved into an award-winning global wholesaler of left-handed items within a year of launching its Website. Founder Keith Milsom comments "our Web site has allowed us to communicate with potential customers and market our business worldwide at very little cost, making international development possible."[9]

### Small Business Threats

While small businesses do enjoy some advantages, they also face intimidating obstacles, from a high risk of failure to too much regulation.

> ## Entrepreneurship is the last refuge of the trouble-making individual.
> —Natalie Cifford Barney, author

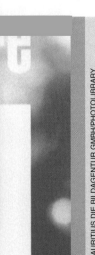

### Failing with Style

A surprising number of 20th century entrepreneurial stars experienced significant failure in their careers, yet bounced back to create wildly successful ventures. Early in his career, for instance, Walt Disney was fired from an ad agency (in hindsight, a rather foolish ad agency), for a "singular lack of drawing ability." Ray Kroc, the man who made McDonald's into a fast food empire, couldn't make a go of real estate, so he sold milkshake machines for much of his life. He was 52 years old, and in failing health, when he discovered the McDonald brothers' hamburger stand and transformed it into a fast food empire. And Steve Jobs, founder of Apple computer, found himself unceremoniously dumped by his board of directors less than ten years after introducing the world's first personal computer. After another decade, he returned in triumph, restoring Apple's polish with blockbuster new products such as the iMac and the iPod. So next time you fail, keep your eyes open for opportunity—your failure may be the first step of the next big thing.[10]

**High risk of failure** Starting a new business involves risk—a lot of risk—but the odds improve significantly if you make it past the 5-year mark. Check out the 10-year survival rate, cited by small business expert Rhonda Abrams in her *USAToday* column. Notice that it declines much more slowly after Year 5:

| Year in Business | Survival Rate | Change vs. Prior Year (percentage points) |
|---|---|---|
| Year 1 | 85% | −15 |
| Year 2 | 70% | −15 |
| Year 3 | 62% | −8 |
| Year 4 | 55% | −7 |
| Year 5 | 50% | −5 |
| Year 6 | 47% | −3 |
| Year 7 | 44% | −3 |
| Year 8 | 41% | −3 |
| Year 9 | 38% | −3 |
| Year 10 | 35% | −3 |

Even though these numbers may look daunting, it's important to remember that owners shut down their businesses for many reasons other than the failure of the firm itself. The possibilities include poor health, divorce, better opportunities elsewhere, and interestingly, an unwillingness to make the enormous time commitment of running a business. Small business expert David Birch jokingly calls this last reason—which is remarkably common—the "I had no idea!" syndrome. It highlights the importance of anticipating what you're in for *before* you open your doors.[11]

**Lack of Knowledge and Experience** People typically launch businesses because they either have expertise in a particular area—like designing Websites or cooking Vietnamese food—or because they have a breakthrough idea—like a new way to develop computer chips or run an airline. But in-depth knowledge in a specific area doesn't necessarily mean expertise in running a business. Successful business owners must know everything from finance to human resources to marketing.

**Too Little Money** The media is filled with stories of business owners who made it on a shoestring, but lack of start-up money is a major issue for most new firms. Ongoing profits don't usually begin for a while, which means that entrepreneurs must plan on some lean months—or even years—as the business develops momentum. That means a real need to manage money wisely and to resist the temptation to invest in fixed assets, such as fancy offices and advanced electronics, before sufficient regular income warrants it. It also requires the nerve to stay the course despite initial losses.[12]

**Bigger Regulatory Burden** Complying with federal regulations can be challenging for any business, but it can be downright overwhelming for small firms. A recent study sponsored by the federal government shows that firms with fewer than 20 employees spend an average of $7,647 per employee abiding by federal regulations, compared with $5,282 spent by firms with more than 500 employees. The overall burden is 45% greater for small business than for their larger business counterparts.[13]

# TechNotes

Running your own business doesn't have to be your only gig. In fact, with digital tools becoming easier to use than ever, millions of Americans have leveraged the Web to create a staggering range of new ventures. These Web-driven entrepreneurs comprise about 25% of all small businesses. Some generate a few extra dollars a week, while others produce a healthy income. But all use the Web to transform people from every background into entrepreneurs.

Many of these ventures couldn't have happened without the Web. Consider, for example, Chris Lindland, founder of Cordaround.com. Chris came up with the concept of corduroy clothing with horizontal rather than vertical stripes. Clothing industry experts scoffed at his idea—they explained that no one would want side-to-side stripes since they would make butts and thighs look wider. But Chris moved forward, launching a funny, irreverent Website that sold 2,000 pairs of horizontal cords in less than a year.

Another oddball example: Pat Misterovich, a stay-at-home dad working from his basement, scored a license from PEZ to make an MP3 player that looks like a PEZ dispenser. His key development goals were 1) Be true to PEZ, and 2) Keep it simple. Hard to imagine that he'll ever get broad distribution, but he does sell his slightly goofy PEZ Pal Boy MP3 players via his Website for $99 a piece—pre-loaded with "all kinds of cool indie music."

While many budding business owners start their own sites, the primary home of small, Web-driven entrepreneurs is eBay. In a recent survey more than 724,000 Americans reported that eBay is their primary or secondary source of income. Beyond these professional eBay sellers, another 1.5 million individuals said they supplement their income to a smaller extent by selling on eBay.

Other highly affordable—yet thoroughly professional—software products make it easy for even neophytes to succeed in areas that range from music production to publishing. Even if your entrepreneurial efforts yield only a fraction of your income, being your own boss for part of the week can be an irresistible lure. And who would say no to a few extra bucks as well?[14]

## Entrepreneurship for Everyone

**Higher Health Insurance Costs**   Administrative costs for small health plans are much higher than for large businesses, making it even tougher for small firms to offer coverage to their employees. Given skyrocketing healthcare costs in general, the best employees are likely to demand a great insurance plan, putting small business at a real disadvantage in terms of building a competitive workforce.[15]

## LO4 Launch Options: Reviewing the Pros and Cons

When you imagine starting a new business, the first thought that comes to mind would probably be the process of developing your own big idea from an abstract concept to a thriving enterprise. But that's not the only option. In fact, it may make more sense to purchase an established business, or even buy a franchise such as a Pizza Hut or Subway restaurant. Each choice, of course, involves pros and cons. The trick is finding the best fit for you: the combination that offers you the least harmful downsides and the most meaningful upsides. Broadly speaking, it's less risky to buy an established business or franchise, but it can be more satisfying to start from scratch. Below is a more detailed overview of the pros and cons.

### Making It Happen: Tools for Business Success

Whatever way you choose to become a small business owner, several strategies can help you succeed over the long term: gain experience in your field, learn from others, educate yourself, access **Small Business Administration (SBA)** resources, and develop a business plan.

*Small Business Administration (SBA) An agency of the federal government designed to maintain and strengthen the nation's economy by aiding, counseling, assisting, and protecting the interests of small businesses.*

**Gain Experience**   Getting roughly three years of experience working for someone else in the field that interests you is a good rule of thumb. That way, you can learn what does and doesn't fly in your industry with relatively low personal risk (and you'd be making any mistakes on someone else's dime). You can also start developing a vibrant, relevant network before you need to ask for favors. But if you stay much longer than three years, you may get too comfortable to take the plunge and launch your own venture.

---

### Starting Your Business from Scratch

| Key Pros | Key Cons |
|---|---|
| It's all *you*: Your concept, your decisions, your structure, and so on. | It's all *you*. That's a lot of pressure. |
| You don't have to deal with the prior owner's bad decisions. | It takes time, money, and sheer sweat equity to build a customer base. |
| | Without a track record, it's harder to get credit from both lenders and suppliers. |
| | From securing permits to hiring employees, the logistics of starting a business can be challenging. |

### Buying an Established Business

| Key Pros | Key Cons |
|---|---|
| The concept, organizational structure, and operating practices are already in place. | Working with someone else's idea can be a lot less fun for some entrepreneurs. |
| Relationships with customers and suppliers and other stakeholders are established. | You may inherit old mistakes that can range from poor employee relations to pending lawsuits. |
| Getting financing and credit is less challenging. | |

### Buying a Franchise

| Key Pros | Key Cons |
|---|---|
| In most cases, you're buying your own piece of a well-known brand and proven way of doing business. | You have less opportunity for creativity since most agreements tie you to franchise requirements. |
| Typically, management expertise and consulting come with the franchise package. | If something goes wrong with the national brand (e.g., *E. coli* at a burger joint), your business will suffer, too. |
| Franchisers occasionally offer not just advice but also the financing that can make the purchase possible. | The initial purchase price can be steep, and that doesn't include the on-going percent-of-sales royalty fee.[16] |
| These advantages add up to a very low 5% first-year failure rate. | |

**Learn from Others** You should actively seek opportunities to learn from people who've succeeded in your field. If you don't know anyone personally, use your network to get introductions. And don't forget industry associations, local events, and other opportunities to build relationships. Also, remember that people who failed in your field may be able to give you valuable insights (why make the same mistakes they did?). As a bonus, they may be more willing to share their ideas and their gaffes if they're no longer struggling to develop a business of their own.

**Educate Yourself** The opportunities for entrepreneurial learning have exploded in the past decade. Many colleges and universities now offer full-blown entrepreneurship programs that help students both develop their plans and secure their initial funding. But education shouldn't stop there. Seek out rel-evant press articles, workshops, Websites, and blogs so that your on-going education will continue to boost your career.

**Access SBA Resources** The SBA offers a number of resources beyond money (which we'll discuss in the next section). The SBA Website, www.sba.gov, provides a wealth of information from industry-specific statistics, to general trends, to updates on small business regulations. The SBA also works hand-in-hand with individual states to fund local **Small Business Development Centers (SBDCs)**. SBDCs provide a range of free services for small businesses from developing your concept, to consulting on your business plan, to helping with your loan applications. And the SBA supports **SCORE**, the *Service Corps for Retired Executives* at www.score.org. They provide free, comprehensive counseling for small businesses from qualified volunteers.

**Develop a Business Plan** Can a business succeed without a plan? Of course. Many do just fine by simply seizing opportunity as it arises and changing direction as needed. Some achieve significant growth without a plan. But a **business plan** does provide an invaluable way to keep you and your team focused on success. And it's absolutely crucial for obtaining outside funding, which is why many entrepreneurs write a business plan after they've used personal funding sources (such as savings, credit cards, and money from family and friends) to get themselves up and running. Even then, the plan may be continually in flux if the industry is rapidly changing.

Writing an effective business plan, which is usually 25 to 50 pages long, takes about six months to write. While the specifics may change by industry, the basic elements of any business plan answer these core questions:

- What service or product does your business provide, and what needs does it fill?
- Who are the potential customers for your product or service, and why will they purchase it from you?
- How will you reach your potential customers?
- Where will you get the financial resources to start your business?
- When can you expect to achieve profitability?[17]

The final document should include all of the following information:

- Executive summary (2 to 3 pages)
- Description of business (include both risks and opportunities)
- Marketing
- Competition (don't underestimate the challenge)
- Operating procedures
- Personnel
- Complete financial data and plan, including sources of start-up money (be realistic!)

**Running a business from your home can offer some valuable advantages, from hanging out with your dog to scoring a home-office tax write-off.**

© ANNIE MARIE MUSSELMAN/STONE/GETTY IMAGES

- Appendix (be sure to include all your research on your industry)[18]

Check out the SBA business-planning site for more information on how to write your own business plan and for samples of actual business plans (www.sba.gov/starting_business/). Other excellent resources (among many) on the Internet include the sample business plan resource center (www.bplans.com/) and the business plan pages of AllBusiness.com (www.allbusiness.com/).

## LO5 Finding the Money: Funding Options for Small Business

For many entrepreneurs, finding the money to fund their business is the top challenge of their start-up year. The vast majority of new firms are funded with the personal resources of their founder. In fact, 94% of companies on the Inc 500 list of fastest growing firms raised start-up funds from personal accounts, family, and friends. Other key funding sources include bank loans, angel investors, and venture capital firms.[19]

### Personal Resources

While the idea of using just your own money to open a business sounds great, the financial requirements of most new firms typically force entrepreneurs to also tap personal resources such as family, friends, and credit cards. If you do borrow from family or friends, virtually every small business expert recommends that you keep the relationship as professional as possible. If the business fails, a professional agreement can preserve personal ties. And if the business succeeds, you'll need top-quality documentation of financing from family and friends to get larger scale backing from outside sources.

Personal credit cards can be an especially handy—though highly risky—financing resource. In fact, a recent survey found that about half of all start-ups are funded with plastic. (It's no wonder, given that those solicitations just keep on coming.) Credit cards do provide fast, flexible money, but watch out—if you don't pay back your card company fast, you'll find yourself socked with financing fees that can take years to pay off.[20]

### Loans

Getting commercial loans for a new venture can be tough. Banks and other lenders are understandably hesitant to fund a business that doesn't have a track record. And when they do, they require a lot of paperwork, and often, a fairly long waiting period. Given these hurdles, only 20% of new business owners launch with commer-

cial loans. And virtually no conventional lending source—private or government—will lend 100% of the start-up dollars for a new business. Most require that the entrepreneur provide a minimum of 25 to 30% of total start-up costs from personal resources.[21]

Another source for loans may be the U.S. Small Business Administration. The SBA doesn't give free money—neither grants nor interest-free loans—but they do partially guarantee loans from local commercial lenders. This reduces risk for the lender, who is, in turn, more likely to lend money to a new business owner. The SBA also has a microloan program that lends small amounts of money—$10,000 on average—to start-up businesses through community nonprofit organizations.[22]

### Angel Investors

**Angel investors** aren't as saintly—or as flighty—as they sound. Angels are wealthy individuals who invest in promising start-up companies for one basic reason: to make money for themselves. According to Jeffrey Sohl, director of the Center for Venture Research, angels look for companies that seem likely to grow at 30 to 40% per year and will then either be bought or go public. He estimates that 10 to 15% of private companies fit that description, but points out that finding those firms isn't easy. It doesn't help, he says, that "80% of entrepreneurs think they're in that 10% to 15%." But the good news for business owners is that angel investors have begun forming investment groups such as the Angel Capital Association, which make them more visible to entrepreneurs. And the percentage of viable proposals that receive funding—an average of $469,000 each—has increased to 18.5% from just 10% in 2003.[23]

### Venture Capital

**Venture capital firms** fund high-potential new companies in exchange for a share of ownership, which can sometimes be as high as 60%. These deals tend to be quite visible, but keep in mind that only about 2% of new businesses receive any venture capital money. And the advice and guidance that comes with the dollars can be quite significant. David Barger, president and chief operating officer of JetBlue Airways, remembers that he and the CEO, David Neeleman, originally planned to call the airline Taxi and to fly bright yellow planes. But an influential venture capitalist changed their minds. He called

> ## Do what you love. This way, whether you make money at it or not, at least you're enjoying yourself.
> –Guy Kawasaki, venture capitalist

them into his office and said, "If you call this airline Taxi, we're not going to invest." The name changed, and the venture capitalist stayed.[24]

## LO6 Small Business and the Economy: An Outsized Impact

The most successful entrepreneurs create goods and services that change the way people live. Many build blockbuster corporations that power the stock market and dominate pop culture through ubiquitous promotion. But small businesses—despite their lower profile—also play a vital role in the U.S. economy. Here are a few statistics from the U.S. Small Business Administration:

- In 2006, 99.9% of the 26,800,000 businesses in the United States had fewer than 500 employees.

- More than three-quarters of those business own-ers—19,500,000 people, totaling more than 6% of the population—ran their businesses without any employees.

- Yet these small businesses generate half of the U.S. gross domestic product.

- Over the last decade, small businesses created 60 to 80% of the net new jobs in the United States.

- In total, small business provides jobs for half of the nation's private workforce.[25]

The statistics, of course, depend on the definition of small business. For research purposes, the SBA defines small business as companies with up to 500 employees, including the self-employed. But the SBA also points out that the meaning of small business differs across industries. To officially count as "small," the number of employees can range from less than 100 to 1,500, and the average revenue can range from $0.75 million to $28.5 million, depending on the type of business. But regardless of the specific definition, the fact is clear: small business is a big player in the U.S. economy.

Beyond the sheer value of the goods and services they generate, small businesses make a powerful contribution to the U.S. economy in terms of creating new jobs, fueling innovation, and vitalizing inner cities.

© AP IMAGES

> Bill Gates, Steve Jobs, and Michael Dell built block-buster firms without a college degree, but 57% of those who start a business in high income countries do have a college degree.
>
> —*Global Entrepreneurship Monitor*

- Creating New Jobs: Small businesses with employees start up at a rate of more than 500,000 per year, generating about 70% of the total new jobs in the economy. Four years after they launch, almost half of those businesses—and many of the jobs they create—remain viable. But while small businesses are quick to add new jobs, they're often the first to contract when times are tough; instability comes with the territory.[26]

- Fueling Innovation: Small businesses develop new innovations at twice the rate of their large business counterparts. Not only that, small patenting firms are more likely to produce "scientifically important" innovations and have produced 13 to 14 times more patents per employee. Small firms tend to be effective innovators for a number of reasons. Perhaps most importantly, their very reason for being often ties to a brand new idea. In the early years, they need innovation in order to simply survive. And they often display a refreshing lack of bureaucracy that allows new thinking to take hold.[27]

- Vitalizing Inner Cities: New research shows that small businesses are the backbone of urban economies, finding opportunity in niches that may not be worthwhile for larger firms. Small business comprises more than 99% of inner city business establishments. In addition to creating new jobs, those small businesses generate 80% of total employment in American inner cities, providing a springboard for economic development.[28]

# Entrepreneurship around the World

Research suggests that entrepreneurship has an economic impact in countries around the world. For the past five years, the Global Entrepreneurship Monitor (GEM) has measured the annual rate of new business start-ups across a range of countries around the globe, adding new nations each year. In 2004 (the most recent year for which data was available), the GEM study included 34 countries. The results demonstrate that entrepreneurship is a global phenomenon: nearly one out of ten adults worldwide start a new business each year. But only about 3% of these ventures are high potential, meaning that they expect fast growth, intend to bring innovations to market, and use state-of-the art technology.

The entrepreneurship rate varies dramatically from country to country, ranging from a high of 40.3% in Peru to a low of 1.5% in Japan.

The differences among countries seem to depend largely on three key factors: What is the national per capita income? What will the entrepreneur need to give up (i.e., the opportunity costs)? How strongly does the national culture and political environment support business start-ups?

Per Capita Income   In low-income countries such as Peru, Uganda, and Ecuador, a high percentage of entrepreneurs start their own businesses because they simply have no other options. This contributes heavily to the startlingly high overall level of entrepreneurship. The rate of such "necessity entrepreneurship" declines in higher income countries such as the United States and Japan, where entrepreneurs are more likely to strike out on their own in response to an opportunity that they spot in the marketplace.

Opportunity Costs   Entrepreneurship rates are significantly lower in countries that provide a high level of employment protection (it's hard to get fired) and strong unemployment insurance (financial support if you do get fired). With these benefits in place, the sense of urgency regarding entrepreneurship tends to fall. The European Union, with a combined entrepreneurship rate of only 5.4%, provides a number of clear examples.

Cultural/Political Environment   Extensive, complex regulations can hinder entrepreneurship by raising daunting barriers. And a lack of cultural support only compounds the problem. These factors certainly contribute to the low entrepreneurship rates in much of the European Union and Japan. Entrepreneurs in more supportive nations such as the United States and New Zealand get a boost from limited regulation and strong governmental support. A thriving "cowboy culture" helps, too—standout individuals who break free of old ways attract attention and admiration in many of the countries with higher entrepreneurship rates.[29]

| Top Ten: Start-up Stars | | Bottom Ten: Start-up Laggards[30] | |
|---|---|---|---|
| **Country** | **Entrepreneurship rate** | **Country** | **Entrepreneurship rate** |
| Peru | 40.3% | 10. Finland | 4.4% |
| Uganda | 31.6% | 9. Hungary | 4.3% |
| Ecuador | 27.2% | 8. Italy | 4.3% |
| Jordan | 18.3% | 7. Portugal | 4.0% |
| New Zealand | 14.7% | 6. Sweden | 3.7% |
| Iceland | 13.6% | 5. Croatia | 3.7% |
| Brazil | 13.5% | 4. Belgium | 3.5% |
| Australia | 13.4% | 3. Hong Kong | 3.0% |
| Argentina | 12.8% | 2. Slovenia | 2.6% |
| United States | 11.3% | 1. Japan | 1.5% |

CHAPTER **8**

# Accounting: Decision Making by the Numbers

## LEARNING OBJECTIVES

After studying this chapter, you will be able to...

**LO1** Define accounting and explain how accounting information is used by a variety of stakeholders

**LO2** Discuss the career opportunities open to accountants

**LO3** Identify the goals of generally accepted accounting principles

**LO4** Describe the key elements of the major financial statements

**LO5** Explain how horizontal, vertical, and ratio analysis can provide insights into financial statements

**LO6** Describe how managerial accounting can help managers with product costing, incremental analysis, and budgeting

118•99
125•99 +
98•97 +
109•99 +
175•99 +
250•99 +
1199•99 +
99•99 +
0•*

4ltrpress.cengage.com/busn

A bank is a place that will only lend you money
if you can prove you don't need it.

–Bob Hope

## LO1 Accounting: Who Needs It?

**Accounting** is a system for recognizing, recording, organizing, summarizing, analyzing, and reporting information about the financial transactions that affect an organization. This system provides its users with relevant, timely information that allows them to make sound economic decisions. In fact, accounting is so important that it's sometimes called the language of business.

Who are the users of this accounting system? It's a long list, since everyone wants to make sound economic decisions. In fact, you're likely to find yourself on that list sometime in the future—that is if you aren't already on it! Key users of accounting information include:

- Managers: Marketing managers, for instance, need information about sales in various regions and for various product lines. Financial managers need up-to-date facts about debt, cash, inventory, and capital.

- Stockholders: As owners of the company, most stockholders have a keen interest in its financial performance, especially as indicated by the firm's financial statements. Has management generated a strong enough return on their investment?

- Employees: Strong financial performance would help employees make their case for nice pay raises and hefty bonuses. But if earnings drop—especially multiple times—many employees might decide to polish their résumés!

- Creditors: Bankers and other lenders want to know that a company has the financial resources needed to pay back what it borrows.

A number of other groups—including the Internal Revenue Service (IRS), the news media, competitors, and suppliers—have a real interest in a firm's accounting information. From your personal perspective, whether you currently are or at some time will be an owner, employee, manager, or creditor of a company, you'll find the ability to understand accounting information to be extremely valuable.

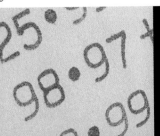

**accounting** A system for recognizing, recording, organizing, analyzing, summarizing, and reporting information about the financial transactions that affect an organization.

## LO2 The Accounting Profession: More Than Just Recording Transactions

Accounting is a popular major among business students. But many students who are just beginning their study of business don't really know much about the profession. What do accountants do, and what kind of education and training do they need to succeed? Let's take a look.[1]

### What Accountants Do

People who have no background in accounting sometimes think it's the same as bookkeeping. But even though the two are related, accounting involves more than bookkeeping. In general, bookkeeping covers the routine procedures involved in recording financial transactions. Accounting goes beyond these functions to organize, analyze, and interpret information and to communicate findings to end users.

Today virtually all firms use computers and specialized accounting software to help perform the routine functions of accounting, such as those normally performed by bookkeepers. In fact, computers have given accountants the ability to store and retrieve vast amounts of data, analyze this data, and create meaningful reports much more quickly than they could with traditional manual systems. But the issues and problems accountants deal with still require a great deal of human insight and expertise. Computers haven't replaced accountants—they've just given them the ability to work more effectively.

Let's look at the duties and responsibilities of several types of accountants.

- Private accountants: Many accountants work within an organization, preparing reports and analyzing financial information specific to that organization. These **private accountants** perform a wide variety of tasks, including the development of budgets, cost and asset management, and the preparation of reports for managers and financial statements for owners and other stakeholders. Most private accountants work within profit-seeking businesses; however, many work for nonprofit organizations, such as charities, private schools, and churches.

- Internal auditors: Internal auditors are private accountants who are responsible for verifying the accuracy of their organization's internal records and the validity of its accounting procedures. They can identify areas where mismanagement, waste, and fraud may exist.

- Public accountants: **Public accountants** provide a broad range of accounting and consulting services to clients on a fee basis. These clients may be individuals, corporations, nonprofit organizations, or government agencies. Typical public accounting services include income tax preparation, external auditing services, and consultation on a variety of accounting issues and problems. Public accountants often help new companies design their accounting systems and procedures and mature companies update and improve their accounting systems.

- Government accountants: As their name implies, government accountants work for a wide variety of government agencies at the local, state, and federal levels. In general, they perform tasks similar to those of public and private accountants. The IRS, the Securities and Exchange Commission, the Federal Bureau of Investigation (FBI), and other government agencies involved in law enforcement and regulation employ *forensic accountants*, who combine knowledge of accounting with investigative skills. Forensic accountants can help detect and investigate white-collar crimes such as tax evasion, embezzlement, money laundering, and securities fraud. They're often called on to serve as expert witnesses in court cases involving these crimes.

### Qualifications for Accounting Positions

Most accounting jobs today require at least a bachelor's degree in accounting plus a solid grasp of spreadsheets

**Computerized systems have reduced the need to enter accounting data manually.**

© STEVE COLE/PHOTODISC/GETTY IMAGES

# TechNotes

## CPA or CSI? A Look at Accounting's Private Eyes

When the National Hockey League had a labor dispute over the compensation of its pro athletes, arbitrators reached an agreement that player salaries would be based on a percentage of team revenues. There was only one problem: NHL teams were at a loss to determine the proportion of box seat revenues earmarked for the hockey league versus other arena entertainment, such as pro basketball or concerts. To solve the mystery, the NHL hired a new breed of financial specialists to analyze the situation and crunch the numbers: forensic accountants.

Businesses, trial lawyers, and government agencies hire these financial sleuths to follow the money trail of potentially explosive cases, from corporate accounting fraud to money laundering to high-stakes divorces. "I liken it to *CSI* or *Law and Order*," says Terry McCarthy, audit partner at Green & Seifter, in Syracuse, NY. "But instead of figuring out the trajectory of a bullet, you're trying to find out how a transaction occurred."

Like the forensic scientists on the television series *CSI*, forensic accountants often have impressive credentials. Many are Certified Public Accountants or Certified Fraud Examiners who also hold additional degrees in fields like law enforcement and criminal justice. They are mystery solvers who must use all of their skills to analyze financial transactions that often are intended to be misleading. "Forensic accountants untangle events and details that are tangled by design," says Barry Mukamal of Rachlin Cohen & Holtz, a forensic accounting practice in Miami.

With billions of dollars being lost to corporate fraud each year and with identity theft on the rise, it's not surprising that forensic accounting is one of the fastest growing occupations in the world of work. *U.S. News & World Report* lists the profession among its "20 Hot Job Tracks," and nearly 40% of the top 100 U.S. accounting firms are beefing up their forensics services. American corporations now spend more than $6 billion a year on forensic accounting, with expenditures growing at a 20% rate annually.

Will the need for this field dry up with increasing government oversight and the emergence of highly skilled numbers narks? According to Andrew Bernstein, a forensics and valuation services director at Miami-based Berkowitz Dick Pollack & Brant, it's not likely. "Fraud is a growth industry," Bernstein remarks. "There's never been a shortage of bad people doing bad things."[2]

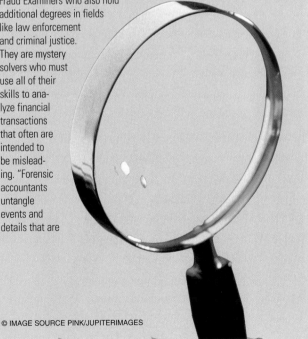

and more specialized accounting software. Many employers in today's job market strongly prefer accountants who have earned a master's in accounting or attained professional certification by becoming a certified public accountant (CPA), certified management accountant (CMA), or certified internal auditor. These professional certifications indicate that an individual has extensive education and experience in the designated field, has passed a rigorous examination, and has satisfied other requirements.

Financial accounting and managerial accounting are the two broad areas in which most accountants employ their skills. We'll spend most of the remainder of this chapter looking at these two fields of accounting.

**financial accounting** The branch of accounting that prepares financial statements for use by owners, creditors, suppliers, and other external stakeholders.

**generally accepted accounting principles (GAAP)** A set of accounting standards that is used in the preparation of financial statements.

**Financial Accounting Standards Board (FASB)** The private self-regulating board that establishes and enforces the generally accepted accounting principles used in the practice of financial accounting.

## LO3 GAAP: Playing by the Rules of Financial Accounting

**Financial accounting** is the branch of accounting that addresses the needs of external stakeholders, including stockholders, creditors, and government regulators. These stakeholders seldom need detailed accounting information about the individual departments or divisions within a company. Instead, they're interested in the financial performance of the firm as a whole. They often want to know how a firm's financial performance has changed over a period of several years or to compare its results to those of other firms in the same industry. The major output of financial accounting is a set of financial statements designed to provide this broad type of information. We'll describe these statements in the next section.

### Role of the Financial Standards Accounting Board

Imagine how confused and frustrated investors, creditors, and regulators would become if every firm could just make up its own financial accounting rules as it went along and change them whenever it wanted! To reduce confusion and provide external stakeholders with consistent and accurate financial statements, the accounting profession has adopted a set of **generally accepted accounting principles (GAAP)** that guide the practice of financial accounting.

Who develops these principles? The ultimate legal authority to do so rests with the Securities and Exchange Commission (or SEC), a government agency that we'll describe in more detail in chapter 10. However, the SEC currently delegates the primary responsibility for this task to a private, self-regulated organization known as the **Financial Accounting Standards Board** (or FASB).

Through GAAP, the FASB aims to ensure that financial statements are:

- Relevant: They must contain information that helps the user understand the firm's financial performance and condition.

- Reliable: They must provide information that is objective, accurate, and verifiable.

- Consistent: They must provide financial statements based on the same core assumptions and procedures over time; if a firm introduces any significant changes in how it prepares its financial statements, GAAP requires it to clearly identify and describe these changes.

- Comparable: They must present accounting statements in a reasonably standardized way, allowing users to track the firm's financial performance over a period of years and compare its results with those for other firms.

The FASB faces a challenging task in setting these principles. Businesses of different sizes and in different industries vary considerably in the ways they operate. Accounting methods that work well for one firm might be less appropriate for another firm. In recognition of this fact, the FASB allows some flexibility in the principles it establishes. In doing so, however, it faces a trade-off: more flexibility means less consistency and comparability.

## Ethics in Accounting

Even well thought-out accounting principles won't result in accurate and reliable information if managers and accountants flaunt them. A series of accounting scandals shocked the American business world during the late 1990s and first few years of the 21st century. Between October of 2001 and July of 2002, several large corporations—Enron, Tyco, Halliburton, WorldCom, and Adelphia to name only a few—were implicated in major scandals. In many cases these firms overstated earnings by billions of dollars or hid billions of dollars in debts. Once their accounting improprieties became known, most of these firms suffered severe financial difficulties. Many went bankrupt, leaving stockholders with worthless stock and employees without jobs or pension plans.[4]

The media rightfully placed much of the blame for these scandals on a small number of senior executives at each company. But these executives couldn't have

> "The upside of the recent scandals is that they have led to widespread public concern about ethical business practices. This heightened level of engagement creates a moment—a unique moment—to make a lasting difference in corporate practice.[3]
> –R. Edward Freeman, academic director of the Business Roundtable for Corporate Ethics

## Closing the Gaps in GAAP?

Some critics believe that the current methods used by the FASB to develop GAAP allow too much input from corporate management and don't pay enough attention to the needs of the stakeholders who use the statements. The results, they claim, are rules that are so flexible that they seriously undermine the FASB's goals of creating consistent and comparable financial statements.

Arthur Levitt, a former chair of the SEC, has been one of the most vocal critics of current practices. He argues that the degree of flexibility that currently exists in GAAP allows managers to manipulate accounting information in ways that make their firm's financial situation look better than it really is. According to Levitt, "What we have seen happening is companies have become more and more creative in terms of the way they present their numbers to the public." Levitt believes this temptation to use creative accounting was a major contributor to the accounting scandals that made headlines in first few years of the 21st century.

In late 2006, the FASB, led by board member Donald M. Young, began looking into ways to change GAAP that will make it more difficult for firms to manipulate results. As you might expect, corporate managers who like the flexibility allowed under current GAAP have tried to block, or at least limit, the reforms. Despite these objections, the FASB seems likely to make some basic changes in GAAP in an effort to move toward greater consistency and comparability. But given the complexity and importance of the rules, any significant reforms are likely to take years to implement.[5]

**In accounting, consistency is better than creativity!**

© AP IMAGES

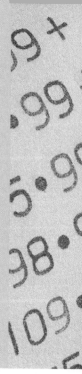

implemented their schemes without the help of accountants. Here's what a *Business Week* article said about the state of the accounting profession at the height of the Enron scandal: "Investor confidence is crucial to the success of our economic system. This confidence is threatened by not only the Enron scandal but by the dramatic decline in accounting standards. People increasingly feel the game is rigged."[6]

These scandals served as a wake-up call, creating awareness within the accounting profession of the need to improve ethical training and standards. In the wake of the scandals, many state accounting boards passed new ethics-related requirements for CPAs. For example, in 2005 the state of Illinois began requiring CPA candidates to pass a separate examination on the rules of professional conduct in addition to the regular CPA exam. Many other states have new rules requiring CPAs to take additional continuing professional education courses in ethics.[7]

## LO4 Financial Statements: the Main Output of Financial Accounting

One of the major responsibilities of financial accounting is the preparation of three basic financial statements: the balance sheet, income statement, and statement of cash flows. Large corporations with publicly traded stock must send an annual report containing these statements to all stockholders. They also must file quarterly and annual reports containing these financial statements with the SEC. Let's take a look at the information each of these statements provides.

### The Balance Sheet: What We Own and How We Got It

The **balance sheet** summarizes a firm's financial position at a specific point in time. It is organized to reflect the most famous equation in all of accounting—so famous that it is usually referred to simply as the **accounting equation**:

Assets =
Liabilities + Owners' Equity

What does each term in the accounting equation mean? And what is the logic of the relationship it represents?

- **Assets** are things of value that the firm owns, such as its cash, inventory of goods available for sale, land, machinery, equipment, and buildings. Accounts receivable, which indicates the amount of money credit customers owe to the firm, is another asset found on many balance sheets.

- **Liabilities** indicate what the firm owes to non-owners—or, put another way, they represent the claims non-owners have against the firm's assets. The amount a firm owes to a bank when it takes out a loan is an example of a liability. Accounts payable—what the firm owes suppliers when it buys supplies on credit—is another example of a liability.

- **Owners' equity** refers to the claims the owners have against their firm's assets. In a corporation, one of the key owners' equity accounts is common stock, which represents the shares of ownership investors have in a business. Retained earnings, which are the earnings that have been reinvested in the company (rather than distributed to owners), are also included in owners' equity.

What's the logic behind the accounting equation? Firms must finance the purchase of their assets, and owners and non-owners are the only two sources of funding. The accounting equation tells us that the value of a firm's assets must equal the amount of financing provided by owners (as measured by owners' equity) plus the amount provided by creditors (as indicated by the firm's liabilities) to purchase those assets.

Because it reflects the logic of the accounting equation, a balance sheet must always "balance." This is true for *all* firms. Whether a company is a huge corporation or a small sole proprietorship, and whether it is highly profitable or suffering huge losses, the dollar value of the assets listed on its balance sheet *must* equal the dollar value of its liabilities and owners' equity.

Exhibit 8.1 on the following page shows the balance sheet for Bigbux, a hypothetical company we'll use in our examples to illustrate the various financial statements. Study each of the key categories included in the balance sheet: *current assets, fixed assets, current liabilities, long-term liabilities,* and *owners' equity.* Note that the balance sheet does indeed balance: total assets equal total liabilities plus owners' equity.

> It sounds extraordinary, but it's a fact that balance sheets can make fascinating reading.
> —Baroness Mary Archer

**Exhibit 8.1:**  The Balance Sheet for Bigbux

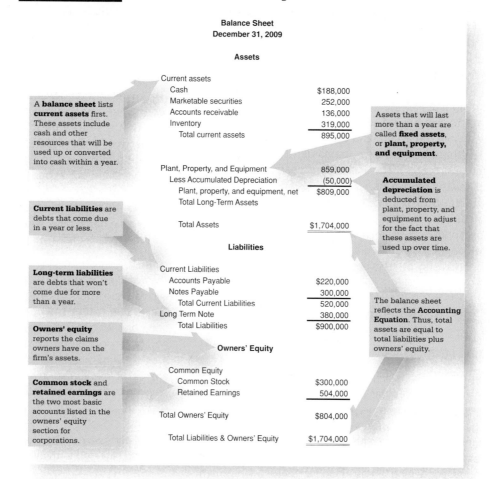

A **balance sheet** lists **current assets** first. These assets include cash and other resources that will be used up or converted into cash within a year.

**Current liabilities** are debts that come due in a year or less.

**Long-term liabilities** are debts that won't come due for more than a year.

**Owners' equity** reports the claims owners have on the firm's assets.

**Common stock** and **retained earnings** are the two most basic accounts listed in the owners' equity section for corporations.

Assets that will last more than a year are called **fixed assets**, or **plant, property, and equipment**.

**Accumulated depreciation** is deducted from plant, property, and equipment to adjust for the fact that these assets are used up over time.

The balance sheet reflects the **Accounting Equation**. Thus, total assets are equal to total liabilities plus owners' equity.

**Balance Sheet**
**December 31, 2009**

**Assets**

Current assets
| | |
|---|---|
| Cash | $188,000 |
| Marketable securities | 252,000 |
| Accounts receivable | 136,000 |
| Inventory | 319,000 |
| Total current assets | 895,000 |

| | |
|---|---|
| Plant, Property, and Equipment | 859,000 |
| Less Accumulated Depreciation | (50,000) |
| Plant, property, and equipment, net | $809,000 |
| Total Long-Term Assets | |
| | |
| Total Assets | $1,704,000 |

**Liabilities**

Current Liabilities
| | |
|---|---|
| Accounts Payable | $220,000 |
| Notes Payable | 300,000 |
| Total Current Liabilities | 520,000 |
| Long Term Note | 380,000 |
| Total Liabilities | $900,000 |

**Owners' Equity**

Common Equity
| | |
|---|---|
| Common Stock | $300,000 |
| Retained Earnings | 504,000 |
| | |
| Total Owners' Equity | $804,000 |
| | |
| Total Liabilities & Owners' Equity | $1,704,000 |

## The Income Statement: How Did We Do?

The **income statement** summarizes a firm's operations over a given period of time in terms of its net income (profit or loss). Just as with the balance sheet, we can use a simple equation to illustrate the logic behind the way the income statement is organized:

Revenue – Expenses = Net Income

In this equation:

- **Revenue** represents the increase in the amount of assets (such as cash and accounts receivable) the firm earns in a given time period as the result of its ongoing operations. A firm normally earns revenue by selling goods or by charging fees for providing services (or both).

- **Expenses** indicate the cash a firm spends or other assets it uses up to carry out the normal business activities necessary to generate its revenue. Many of the expenses on an income statement are referred to as costs.

> Remind people that profit is the difference between revenue and expense. This makes you look smart.
> –Scott Adams, creator of Dilbert

- **Net income** is the profit or loss the firm earns in the time period covered by the income statement. As our equation indicates, it's the difference between the amount of revenue the firm earns and its expenses. If the difference is positive, the firm has earned a profit. If it's negative, the firm has suffered a loss. Net income is often called the "bottom line" of the income statement because it is such an important measure of the firm's operating success.

It's important to realize that the revenue a firm reports on its income statement for a time period is *not* the same thing as the amount of cash it receives in that time period. Accountants use **accrual-basis accounting** when recognizing revenues and expenses. Under the accrual approach, revenues are recorded when they are earned, and payment is reasonably assured. This is not always when cash is actually received. For example, if a firm sells most of its goods on credit, the revenue it earns in a given time period might show up mainly as an increase in accounts receivable rather than as an increase in cash. Also, under the accrual-basis, expenses aren't necessarily recorded when cash is paid. Instead, expenses are matched to the revenue they help generate.

Take a look at exhibit 8.2 to see how an income statement is organized. The most important concepts to understand are *revenue, cost of goods sold, gross profit, operating expenses,* and *net income.*

## Statement of Cash Flows: Show Me the Money

The last major financial statement is the **statement of cash flows**, which shows the cash flowing into and out of the firm from three types of activities: operations, investing, and financing. It also shows the net increase or decrease in cash from all three sources and the total amount of cash on hand at the end of the period.

This statement attracts a lot of attention from external stakeholders. A firm *must* have adequate cash to pay its workers, creditors, suppliers—and an agency called the IRS! It also needs cash to pay dividends to stockholders, take advantage of unexpected investment opportunities, and cope with unexpected problems. If the cash balance falls too low, the firm may find its ability to conduct business severely compromised.

**statement of cash flows** The financial statement that identifies a firm's sources and uses of cash in a given accounting period.

---

| **Exhibit 8.2** | Bigbux's Income Statement |

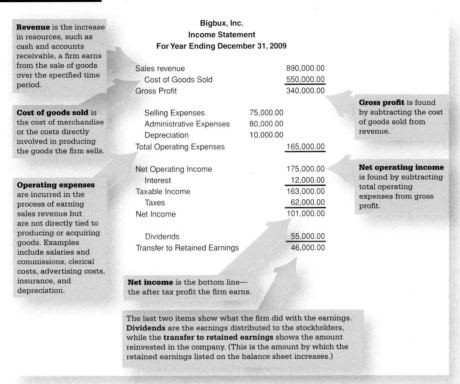

**Revenue** is the increase in resources, such as cash and accounts receivable, a firm earns from the sale of goods over the specified time period.

**Cost of goods sold** is the cost of merchandise or the costs directly involved in producing the goods the firm sells.

**Operating expenses** are incurred in the process of earning sales revenue but are not directly tied to producing or acquiring goods. Examples include salaries and commissions, clerical costs, advertising costs, insurance, and depreciation.

**Gross profit** is found by subtracting the cost of goods sold from revenue.

**Net operating income** is found by subtracting total operating expenses from gross profit.

**Net income** is the bottom line—the after tax profit the firm earns.

The last two items show what the firm did with the earnings. **Dividends** are the earnings distributed to the stockholders, while the **transfer to retained earnings** shows the amount reinvested in the company. (This is the amount by which the retained earnings listed on the balance sheet increases.)

**Bigbux, Inc.**
**Income Statement**
**For Year Ending December 31, 2009**

| | | |
|---|---:|---:|
| Sales revenue | | 890,000.00 |
| Cost of Goods Sold | | 550,000.00 |
| Gross Profit | | 340,000.00 |
| | | |
| Selling Expenses | 75,000.00 | |
| Administrative Expenses | 80,000.00 | |
| Depreciation | 10,000.00 | |
| Total Operating Expenses | | 165,000.00 |
| | | |
| Net Operating Income | | 175,000.00 |
| Interest | | 12,000.00 |
| Taxable Income | | 163,000.00 |
| Taxes | | 62,000.00 |
| Net Income | | 101,000.00 |
| | | |
| Dividends | | 55,000.00 |
| Transfer to Retained Earnings | | 46,000.00 |

---

## Read All About It!

Now that you've learned about financial statements, you might want to use your new knowledge to check out the financial performance of a real company. If the company's stock is publicly traded, finding its financial statements online is usually very easy.

The simplest approach is to start with the company's own Web site. Publicly traded corporations usually have a link to an "Investor Relations" site on their home page that will (after a few mouse clicks) give you access to the company's current annual report containing its most recent financial statements. Another approach is to visit a site that specializes in providing annual reports of publicly traded companies, such as the IRIN Annual Report Resource Center (http://www.irin.com), or AnnualReports.com, (http://www. annualreports.com). These sites give you the ability to access the annual reports of thousands of well-known corporations, offering convenient "one-stop shopping" if you want to search for financial statements of more than one company.

A final resource is the Securities and Exchange Commission's Website. Publicly traded companies are required to file their financial statements in a document called a Form 10-K with the SEC each year. You can view this form online by using the SEC's Edgar database (http://www.sec.gov/edgar.shtml).

Exhibit 8.3 illustrates one common way that a statement of cash flows can be organized. Note that the cash balance at the end of the period matches the amount of cash reported in the current balance sheet (as it always should).

## Other Statements

In addition to the three major statements we've just described, firms usually prepare either a statement of retained earnings or a stockholders' equity statement. Let's take a quick look at each of these statements.

The *statement of retained earnings* is a simple statement that shows how retained earnings have changed from one accounting period to the next. The change in retained earnings is found by subtracting dividends paid to shareholders from net income.

Firms that have more complex changes in the owners' equity section sometimes report these changes in notes to the financial statements in the annual report. But they often disclose these changes by providing a *stockholders' equity statement*. Like the statement of retained earnings, this statement shows how net income and dividends affect retained earnings. But it also shows other changes in stockholders' equity, such as those that arise from the issuance of additional shares of stock.

## LO5 Interpreting Financial Statements: Digging Beneath the Surface

The financial statements we've just described contain a lot of important information. But they don't necessarily tell the whole story. In fact, the numbers they report can be misleading if they aren't put into proper context.

Thus, in addition to looking at the statements, it's also important to check out the independent auditor's report and the notes that accompany these statements. Doing so will give you the background information you need to properly interpret the statements. You can then extend your knowledge by using additional analytical techniques that we'll describe at the end of this section.

## The Independent Auditor's Report: A Necessary Stamp of Approval

Every publicly traded corporation in the United States is required to have a CPA firm (an accounting firm that specializes in providing public accounting services) perform an annual external audit of its financial statements. The results of this audit are presented in an independent auditor's report, which expresses an opinion as to whether

© JOHN KNILL/PHOTODISC/GETTY IMAGES

---

**Exhibit 8.3** The Statement of Cash Flows for Bigbux

**Bigbux Corporation**
**Statement of Cash Flows**
**For Year Ended December 31, 2009**

**Operating cash flows** represent cash generated through the sale of goods and services.

**Investing cash flows** reflect cash flows generated by the purchase or sale of fixed assets, by buying or selling securities issued by other companies, or by making loans or collecting payments on loans.

**Financing cash flows** include any cash received from the firm's sale of its own stocks or bonds and any cash disbursed to repay debt or to pay dividends to stockholders.

| Operating Cash Flow | |
|---|---|
| Net Income | 101,000.00 |
| Non Cash Adjustments | |
|   Depreciation | 10,000.00 |
|   Increase in Accounts Receivable | -5,500.00 |
|   Decrease in Accounts Payable | -2,500.00 |
| Net Cash Provided from Operations | 103,000.00 |
| | |
| **Investing Cash Flow** | |
|   Purchase of Equipment | -45,000.00 |
| Net Cash Used by Investing | -45,000.00 |
| | |
| **Financing Cash Flow** | |
|   Increase in Long Term Loan | 105,000.00 |
|   Payments of Cash Dividends | -55,000.00 |
| Net Cash Provided from Financing | 50,000.00 |
| | |
| Total Cash Flow | 108,000.00 |
| Cash at Beginning of Period | 80,000.00 |
| Cash at End of Period | 188,000.00 |

**Non cash adjustments** to net income are needed because the revenues and expenses used to compute net income under the accrual method don't always represent inflows or outflows of cash.

**Total cash flow** is the sum of the cash flows from operations, investing, and financing activities.

The amount of cash reported at the end of the period should match the amount of cash reported in the current balance sheet.

the information in the firm's financial statements fairly reflects the true financial condition of the firm.

If the audit doesn't find any problems, the report will offer an *unqualified opinion*. If, however, the audit identifies problems with the firm's accounting methods or financial statements, the report may include a *qualified opinion*. Even more serious, if the audit uncovers major and widespread problems, the report may contain an *adverse opinion*. An adverse opinion should set off alarm bells, warning you to view the information in the firm's financial statements with real skepticism.

In order for CPA firms to perform audits with integrity, they must be independent of the firms they audit. During the 1990s, many of the major CPA firms that performed external audits entered into very lucrative consulting contracts with some of the businesses they were audit-ing. It became increasingly difficult for these CPA firms to risk losing these high-paying contracts by raising issues about accounting practices when they audited the books of their clients. In other words, the auditors ceased to be truly independent and objective. The lack of rigorous oversight by external auditors contributed to the accounting scandals we mentioned earlier.

In the aftermath of the scandals, Congress passed the **Sarbanes-Oxley Act of 2002** (commonly referred to as SOX). This law banned business relationships between CPA firms and the companies they audit that might create conflicts of interest. It also established a private sector nonprofit corporation known as the Public Company Accounting Oversight Board (PCAOB). The mission of PCAOB is to "protect the interests of investors and further the public interest in the preparation of informative, fair, and independent audit reports."[8]

**Sarbanes-Oxley Act of 2002 A law passed in the wake of the accounting scandals of the early 21st century that included several provisions designed to improve external auditing procedures and enhance financial reporting for publicly traded firms.**

> I have no use for body guards, but I have very specific use for two highly trained certified public accountants.
>
> –Elvis Presley

## Notes to Financial Statements: Reading the Fine Print

Some types of information can't be adequately conveyed by numbers alone. Annual reports include notes (often *many* pages of notes) to the financial statements that disclose additional information about the firm's operations, accounting practices, and any special circumstances that affected the organization's financial performance. These notes can be *very* revealing. They may provide interesting details about mergers or acquisitions involving the firm.

### Taking a Bite out of Apple's Balance Sheet

Apple Inc.'s 2007 balance sheet reported that its stockholders' equity on September 29, 2007 was \$14.5 billion. But the actual market value of Apple's stock on that date was more than \$133 billion—over nine times the balance sheet figure. What accounts for this huge discrepancy?

Many of Apple's most valuable resources, including the patents it holds on innovative products and the goodwill it's built among its fanatically loyal customers, are "intangible" assets that can't be touched or seen. And most of these assets were created by Apple's own new product design teams, software programmers, and marketers—a fact that creates a big problem for Apple's accountants.

When a company buys an asset from an external seller, the purchase price gives accountants an objective measure of value that they can record on the balance sheet. But when Apple creates intangible assets internally, there is no purchase price for accountants to record. Lacking an objective measure of their value, Apple's accountants (in accordance with today's GAAP) write off the cost of creating these assets as an expense rather than recording their value on the balance sheet.

While Apple's balance sheet ignores the value of internally created intangible assets, investors are keenly aware of how incredibly important they are. These unrecorded intangible assets are the most important reason why the market value of Apple's stock far exceeded the value reported on its balance sheet.[9]

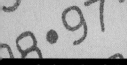

They might also disclose changes in the way it funds the pension plan or health insurance for its employees, or key facts about the status of a lawsuit against the firm. Finally, the notes might disclose changes in accounting methods that could affect the comparability of the current financial statements to those of previous years. Stakeholders who ignore these notes are likely to miss out on important information.

## Beyond the Statements: Horizontal, Vertical, and Ratio Analysis

You can glean a lot of useful information about a firm's financial performance directly from its current financial statements. But you can obtain even greater insights through the application of horizontal analysis, vertical analysis, and ratio analysis.

**Horizontal analysis** compares information in a firm's financial statements over a period of 2 or more years. This type of analysis helps stakeholders identify important changes and trends in key accounts. For example, by looking at balance sheet accounts over a period of years, investors can see whether the firm is using more debt to finance its operations now than in the past, or whether it has increased its investment in plant, property, and equipment. Investors can look at a series of income statements to see how the firm's revenues, expenses, and net income have changed over recent years.

**Vertical analysis** expresses each item on a balance sheet or income statement as a percentage of some key value. For example, vertical analysis normally expresses each individual asset account as a percentage of total assets. Similarly, various costs or expenses on an income statement are expressed as a percentage of total revenue. This makes it easier to see how each item on a financial statement compares, in terms of its relative size, to some key value in the same statement. Vertical analysis also makes it easier to compare the financial statements of companies of different sizes.

**Ratio analysis** provides even more ways to analyze the information reported in financial statements. It compares selected items found in financial statements by computing percentages, rates, or proportions. There are several broad categories of ratios:

- Liquidity ratios measure the ability of firms to pay current liabilities as they come due.

- Asset management ratios provide insights into how effectively firms manage their assets to generate revenue.

- Leverage ratios indicate the extent to which a firm relies on debt financing to finance its operations.

- Profitability ratios provide ways to look at the return a firm earns on its investment relative to its sales, total assets, or stockholders equity.

We'll look at some specific ratios in the next chapter, when we describe how financial managers use ratio analysis to evaluate the performance of their firm.

## LO6 Managerial Accounting: Inside Intelligence

Now that we've looked at financial accounting, let's turn our attention to the other major branch of accounting, **managerial (or management) accounting**. As its name implies, this branch of accounting is designed to meet the needs of a company's managers, though in recent years many firms have empowered other employees and given them access to this information as well. Exhibit 8.4 identifies several ways that managerial accounting differs from financial accounting.

**Exhibit 8.4** Comparison of Financial and Managerial Accounting

| Financial Accounting | Managerial Accounting |
|---|---|
| Is primarily intended to provide information to external stakeholders such as stockholders, creditors, and government regulators | Is primarily intended to provide information to internal stakeholders such as the managers of specific divisions or departments |
| Prepares a standard set of financial statements | Prepares customized reports designed to deal with specific problems or issues |
| Presents financial statements on a predetermined schedule (usually quarterly and annually) | Creates reports upon request by management rather than according to a predetermined schedule |
| Is governed by a set of generally accepted accounting principles | Uses procedures developed internally and is not required to follow GAAP |

Managers throughout an organization rely on information created by managerial accountants to make important decisions. The accuracy and reliability of this information can make a huge difference in the performance of a firm. In fact, many firms view their management accounting systems as a source of competitive advantage and regard the specifics of these systems as highly valuable company secrets.[10]

We'll close this chapter by describing three types of management responsibilities that rely on information provided by managerial accounting: determining product costs, performing incremental analysis, and developing budgets. Keep in mind that this is only a "sampler" of the areas where managerial accounting plays an important role.

## Product Costing

Managers must have an accurate measure of the costs incurred to produce their firm's goods and services. Without good information on costs, managers would be operating in the dark as they try to set prices, determine the most desirable mix of products, and locate areas where efficiency is lagging. While clearly important, the task of assigning meaningful costs to the production of specific products can be surprisingly difficult.

Actually, some costs are easy to assign. The cost of labor and materials used directly in the production of a product are usually easy to identify and measure. These are called *direct labor* and *direct materials costs*. Unfortunately, many other costs a firm incurs aren't tied in such a simple and direct way to the production of a specific product. For example, a firm typically pays property taxes on its factory building and pays premiums on an insurance policy to cover losses due to fire or storm damage. It also incurs general maintenance costs for upkeep of the building. These costs are for the entire production facility and aren't directly tied to the production of any specific product. Such costs are called *overhead costs*.

In the past, managerial accountants often relied on very simple rules to determine how much of the overhead costs to assign to different products. One common approach was to allocate overhead in proportion to the number of direct labor hours involved in the production of each product—products that required the most labor to produce were assigned the most overhead costs. But, while this approach was simple, it often provided misleading information. Many overhead costs aren't related to the amount of direct labor used to produce a product. For example, changes in the amount of labor used to produce a product may have no impact on the cost of an insurance premium or property taxes.

In recent years managerial accountants have developed more sophisticated ways to allocate costs. One promising new approach is called **activity-based costing** (or **ABC**). This approach is more complex and difficult to implement than the direct labor method. However, it's likely to provide more meaningful results because it is based on a systematic examination of what actually *creates* (or drives) overhead costs. It assigns these costs to specific products by linking the production of those products to the specific activities that create the costs.

## Incremental Analysis

**Incremental analysis** evaluates the financial impact of different alternatives in a decision-making situation. Typical examples include analysis of whether a firm should:

- Make parts and components itself, or buy them from suppliers
- Repair its existing equipment or buy new equipment
- Perform warranty repairs itself, or outsource this function to another firm
- Eliminate or sell off an existing product line—or even an entire division or subsidiary

To make the best decision in each of these situations, managers must correctly identify how each alternative would affect the company's revenues and costs. Correctly identifying the impact a decision has on costs and revenues can sometimes lead to surprising results. Let's look at an example to see why.

Suppose an electronics firm produces high definition LCD televisions at a rate of 10,000 per month. It currently makes its own speaker sets for the televisions, and the various types of costs it incurs to produce the speakers are listed in exhibit 8.5. By dividing the total costs by the number of TVs produced per month, we see the average cost of speakers per TV is $26.

**activity-based costing (ABC)** A technique used by managerial accountants to assign product costs based on links between activities that drive costs and the production of specific products.

**incremental analysis** An evaluation and comparison of the financial impact different alternatives would have in a particular decision-making situation.

| Exhibit 8.5 | Costs of Making Television Speakers Per Month |
|---|---|
| Direct labor costs | $120,000 |
| Direct materials costs | 80,000 |
| Manufacturing overhead costs | 60,000 |
| Total costs | 260,000 |
| Costs per unit (at 10,000 units per month) | 26 |

**Consumers also need to analyze all the costs when making an expensive television purchase.**

Now suppose that a supplier offers to sell the firm similar speakers at a cost of $23 per television. An initial comparison might suggest that the firm could lower its costs by buying speakers; after all, $23 is less than $26.

But a more careful look, using incremental analysis, might suggest that this would be a bad move. Why? Incremental analysis would almost certainly find that many of the overhead costs assigned to the production of the speakers are *fixed*, meaning that they're unaffected by how many speakers the company produces. Insurance premiums, property taxes, and depreciation expenses on the production facility are examples. The firm would still incur most of these costs even if it bought the speakers from another firm!

To correctly analyze the impact of buying speakers rather than making them, incremental analysis identifies which costs would actually *change* if the company discontinued its production of the speakers. These are called the *incremental* costs of the decision. The direct labor and materials costs are incremental; if the firm doesn't produce the speakers, it won't incur these costs. But as we've just seen, most of the manufacturing overhead costs aren't incremental.

Let's assume that all of direct material and labor costs but that only 20% of manufacturing overhead costs are incremental. Exhibit 8.6 shows that the decision to

buy speakers would completely eliminate direct labor and direct materials costs, but would reduce overhead costs by only $12,000 (20% of $60,000). The firm will still incur the other $48,000 of overhead costs. When these remaining overhead costs are added to the cost of purchasing the speakers, you can see that the firm's total costs would be higher if it bought the speakers than if it continued to produce them itself.

## Budgeting

Managerial accounting also provides much of the information needed to develop budgets. **Budgeting** is a management tool that explicitly shows how firms will acquire and use the resources needed to achieve its goals over a specific time period. The budgetary process facilitates planning by requiring managers to translate goals into measurable quantities and identify the specific resources needed to achieve these goals. But budgeting offers other advantages as well. If done well, budgeting:

- Requires managers to clearly specify how they intend to achieve the goals they set during the planning process. This should lead to a better allocation of the organization's limited resources.

- Encourages communication and coordination among managers and employees in various departments within the organization. It can give middle and first-line managers and employees an opportunity to provide top managers with important feedback about the needs of their specialized areas.

- Serves as a motivational tool. Good budgets clearly identify goals *and* demonstrate a plan of action for acquiring the resources needed to achieve them. Employees tend to be more highly motivated when they understand the goals their managers expect them to accomplish and when they view these goals as ambitious but achievable.

- Provides an effective way to monitor progress and evaluate performance. Managers can compare actual performance to budgetary figures to determine whether various departments and functional areas are making adequate progress toward achieving their organization's goals. If actual performance falls short of budgetary goals, managers know to look for reasons and take corrective action.

Budgeting actually involves the preparation of several different budget documents. These documents are organized into two broad classes: operating budgets and financial budgets.

**Operating budgets** identify sales and production goals and the various costs the firm will incur in order to meet these goals. The *sales budget* is the first operating budget created during the budgeting process because

| Exhibit 8.6 | Incremental Analysis: Make or Buy Speakers? |
| --- | --- |

| Type of Cost | Make | Buy |
| --- | --- | --- |
| Direct labor costs | $120,000 | $0 |
| Direct materials costs | $80,000 | $0 |
| Incremental manufacturing overhead | $60,000 | $48,000 |
| Cost of purchasing speakers ($23 × 10,000 units) | $0 | $230,000 |
| Total monthly cost | $260,000 | $278,000 |

the production and costs included in the other operating budgets depend on the level of sales. The sales budget indicates the number of units of each product the firm expects to sell, the expected selling price, and the total dollar value of sales. Exhibit 8.7 illustrates a sales budget for Bigbux. Other operating budgets specify the level of production and the direct labor costs, direct materials costs, manufacturing overhead, and other costs and expenses the firm will incur to meet these sales.

**Financial budgets** focus on the firm's financial objectives and identify the resources needed to achieve these goals. The two main financial budget documents are the *cash budget* and the *capital budget*. The cash budget identifies short-term fluctuations in cash inflows and outflows, helping managers identify times when the firm might face cash flow problems—or when it might have extra cash that it could invest. The capital budget

deals with the firm's investments in major fixed assets and long-term projects. We'll describe both of these budgets in chapter 9, where we look at how financial managers use them.

The firm's **master budget** brings together all of the documents in the operating and financial budgets into a unified whole, representing the firm's overall plan of action for a specified time period. In other words, the master budget shows how all of the pieces fit together to form a complete picture.

**financial budgets** The budget documents that identify the cash and other financial resources the firm will acquire and use to finance its operations and make planned investments in fixed assets.

**master budget** A combined statement of an organization's operational and financial budgets that represents the firm's overall plan of action for a specified time period.

| **Exhibit 8.7** | Sales Budget for BIGBUX, INC for the Year Ending December 31, 2009 | | | |
|---|---|---|---|---|
| | **First Quarter** | **Second Quarter** | **Third Quarter** | **Fourth Quarter** |
| Expected Unit Sales | 60,000 | $64,000 | $58,000 | $77,000 |
| Unit Selling Price | $4.00 | $4.00 | $4.00 | $4.00 |
| Projected Sales Revenue | $240,000 | $256,000 | $232,000 | $308,000 |

Developing the sales budget is the first step in the budgeting process, because several other budgets depend on the information it contains.

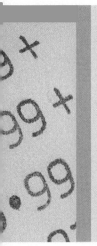

## Budgets Aren't Just for Companies

Achieving your financial goals requires planning and control. Many individuals and households set up a personal budget to gain control of their finances. Working with a budget helps them understand their spending patterns, become more disciplined, and start saving to achieve their long-term goals. If you haven't yet done so, you might find that setting up a personal budget can help you in the same way.

While a personal budget isn't nearly as detailed or complex as a budget for a business, it can be hard for someone new to budgeting to know where to start. One approach is to use commercial software such as Intuit's Quicken or Microsoft's Money. These programs can guide you step-by-step through the creation of a budget. Many Web sites also provide basic budgeting advice and budget templates. While not as comprehensive or sophisticated as the commercial software, many of these budgeting aids can be downloaded at little or no cost.[11]

© COMSTOCK IMAGES/JUPITERIMAGES

# Finance: Acquiring and Using Funds to Maximize Value

## LEARNING OBJECTIVES

After studying this chapter, you will be able to...

**LO1** Explain how maximizing financial value relates to social responsibility

**LO2** Describe how financial managers use key ratios to evaluate their firm

**LO3** Discuss how financial managers use a cash budget

**LO4** Explain the significance of working capital management

**LO5** Explain how financial managers evaluate capital budgeting proposals

**LO6** Identify the key issues involved in determining a firm's capital structure

4ltrpress.cengage.com/busn

The waste of money cures itself, for soon there
is no money to waste.

–M. W. Harrison

## LO1 What Motivates Financial Decisions?

Finance is concerned with answering two basic questions that are crucial to the success of a business organization:

- What types of assets do we need to achieve the goals of our organization?
- How do we get the funds we need to acquire these assets?

In a nutshell, finance is all about finding the best sources and uses of funds for a firm. But what exactly do we mean by the "best" sources and uses? What standards do financial managers rely upon to make financial decisions?

Historically, the goal of financial management has been to find the sources and uses of funds that *maximize the value of the firm to its owners*. This focus may seem to conflict with our discussion of social responsibility in chapter 4. In that chapter we saw that today's business organizations recognize the need to address the needs of all stakeholders, from employees to suppliers, to society as a whole. But many firms recognize that the goal of shareholder wealth maximization *can* be consistent with this broader view of social responsibility—especially if the managers take a long-term perspective. Treating customers, employees, suppliers, creditors, and other stakeholders with fairness and respect can build goodwill. This often results in satisfied customers and higher sales, a more favorable business climate, and more loyal and highly motivated workers, all of which contribute to a more successful and profitable company—and an increase in shareholder value.[1]

Though many financial managers now accept a broader view of social responsibility, finding the right balance among the competing interests of the various groups of stakeholders can be difficult. Different stakeholder groups can have very different goals. When conflicts arise between the long-term interests of owners and those of other stakeholders, even financial managers who support a broad view of social responsibility tend to adopt the position that the interests of owners should come before those of other stakeholders.

In order to make sound financial decisions, managers must perform a number of functions. Specifically, they must:

- Evaluate their firm's recent financial performance
- Plan for the effective use of financial resources
- Manage the firm's working capital
- Evaluate long-run investment opportunities
- Determine the appropriate strategy to meet the firm's long-term financing needs

In the remainder of this chapter we'll take a look at how financial managers perform each of these functions.

## LO2 Evaluating Performance: Where Do We Stand?

Before financial managers can determine the best strategies for their firms, they must identify the existing financial strengths and weaknesses. Ratio analysis, a topic we briefly introduced in Chapter 8, is one of their major tools in this evaluation process. Several key ratios are described in exhibit 9.1. A careful look at this exhibit will help you understand how financial managers compute and use these ratios. Notice that most of the information used to compute these ratios comes from the balance sheet and income statement we described in chapter 8.

There's no single "best" value for a specific ratio. Firms in different industries often face very different market situations, so a ratio value that is acceptable for a firm in one industry may spell big trouble for a firm in another. For example, grocery stores normally have high inventory turnover ratios, meaning goods move through them quickly—a good thing, since few people want to buy bananas, bread, milk, or tomatoes that have been sitting in the store for several months! But it's not unusual for a furniture store to have some expensive and distinctive pieces in stock for months before they are sold. So it's not surprising that the average inventory turnover of food stores is 16.6, while the average for furniture stores is 6.4.[2]

A comparison of a firm's ratios with the average ratios for other firms in the same industry (or with the ratios for a firm recognized as an industry leader) can help determine whether they're in the right ballpark. But even firms in the same industry may face very different circumstances, so ratios of other firms or the industry average should serve only as general guidelines, not as rigid goals. Also, as we showed in chapter 8, generally accepted accounting principles allow firms some flexibility in their accounting methods. Since most of the information used to compute ratios comes from the firm's balance sheet and income statement, two firms with very similar real-world performance might report very different ratios simply because they used different—but equally acceptable—accounting methods to develop their statements.

© RYAN MCVAY/PHOTODISC/GETTY IMAGES

## LO3 Financial Planning: Providing a Road Map for the Future

Financial planning is an important part of the firm's overall planning process. We'll discuss planning in more detail in chapter 15. For now, we'll assume that the overall planning process has established appropriate goals and objectives for the firm. In this context, financial planning must answer the following questions:

- What specific assets must the firm obtain in order to achieve its goals?

- How much additional financing will the firm need to acquire these assets?

- How much financing will the firm be able to generate internally (through additional earnings), and how much must it obtain from external sources?

- When will it need to acquire external financing?

## Avoiding Burn Out!

New firms launch with some cash on hand. But it may take quite a while to generate *more* cash from their operations. At first, firms need to spend money—often, lots and lots of money—to get established. During these crucial first months of heavy spending, smart managers carefully monitor how quickly they're using up their cash.

One way to keep track of cash use is to compute a ratio known as the burn rate. This ratio is found by dividing the decline in the firm's total cash position by the time period over which the decline occurs. The higher the burn rate, the more quickly a firm is using up its cash. An extremely high burn rate indicates that a firm needs to take measures to either conserve its available cash or find ways to generate new cash inflows. Options range from serious cost-cutting measures to selling off assets or seeking funds from new external investors. None of these options are likely to be quick or easy fixes, but they usually beat the alternative of going bankrupt!

The burn rate is not a traditional ratio, but it became popular during the rise and fall of the dot-com boom of the 1990s and early part of the twenty-first century. Investors learned the importance of the ratio as they watched one dot-com company after another "flame out" because (at least in part) they failed to effectively monitor and manage their use of cash.[3]

© COMSTOCK/JUPITERIMAGES

**Exhibit 9.1** Key Financial Ratios

| Ratio | Type | What It Does | How It Is Computed |
|-------|------|--------------|--------------------|
| **Current** | Liquidity: measures ability to pay short-term liabilities as they come due | Compares current assets (which include cash and other assets that are expected to be converted to cash in the next year) to current liabilities (which will require payment of cash in the next year). | $\dfrac{\text{Current Assets}}{\text{Current Liabilities}}$ |
| **Inventory turnover** | Asset management: measures how effectively a firm is using its assets to generate revenue | Compares sales (measured by the cost of the goods sold) to the average size of the firm's inventory. A firm must sell the goods in its inventory to generate revenue. A high inventory ratio usually indicates that a firm is doing a good job of "moving" its goods. But a very high ratio may indicate that the firm is holding too little inventory, which could result in running out of merchandise. | $\dfrac{\text{Cost of Goods Sold}}{\text{Average Inventory}}$ |
| **Debt-to-equity** | Leverage: measures the extent to which a firm relies on debt to meet its financing needs | Compares the total amount of debt financing to the amount of financing provided by ownership. A high ratio indicates that the firm is relying heavily on debt, or is "highly leveraged." | $\dfrac{\text{Total Debt}}{\text{Total Owners' Equity}}$ |
| **Debt-to-assets** | Leverage: measures the extent to which a firm relies on debt to meet its financing needs | Similar to debt-to-equity, but compares debt to assets rather than equity. This is another way of measuring the degree of financial leverage, or debt, the firm is using. | $\dfrac{\text{Total Debt}}{\text{Total Assets}}$ |
| **Return on equity** | Profitability: compares the amount of profit to some measure of resources invested | Indicates the amount of profit earned per dollar invested by the owners of the company. Since common stockholders are the true owners, preferred stockholders' dividends are deducted from net income before computing this ratio. | $\dfrac{\text{Net Income} - \text{Preferred Dividends}}{\text{Average Common Stock Equity}}$ |
| **Return on assets** | Profitability: compares the amount of profit to some measure of resources invested | Indicates the amount of profit earned on each dollar the firm has invested in assets. | $\dfrac{\text{Net Income}}{\text{Average Total Assets}}$ |
| **Earnings per share** | Profitability: compares the amount of profit to some measure of resources invested | Measures the net income per share of common stock outstanding. | $\dfrac{\text{Net Income} - \text{Preferred Dividends}}{\text{Average Number of Common Shares Outstanding}}$ |

**current ratio** A liquidity ratio found by dividing a firm's total current assets by its total current liabilities. The current ratio is one of the most commonly used measures of a firm's ability to pay its short-term obligations as they come due.

**inventory turnover ratio** An asset management ratio that measures the average number of times a firm sells (or "turns over") its inventory in a year.

**debt-to-equity ratio** Measures the extent to which a firm relies on debt financing by dividing total debt by total owners' equity. The higher the value of this ratio, the more the firm is relying on debt.

**debt-to-assets ratio** Measures the extent to which a firm relies on debt financing by dividing total debt by total assets. The closer the ratio is to one, the greater the firm's reliance on debt.

**return on equity** A profitability ratio that is computed by dividing net income by average common stock equity. If the firm issues preferred stock, the dividends paid to preferred stock are subtracted from net income.

**return on assets** A profitability ratio that is found by dividing net income by average total assets.

**earnings per share (EPS)** A profitability ratio that measures how much a firm earns per share of common stock outstanding.

**pro forma statements** Projected financial statements that financial managers use during financial planning.

**cash budget** A detailed projection of cash flows that financial managers use to identify when a firm is likely to experience temporary shortages or surpluses of cash.

**net working capital** The difference between a firm's current assets and its current liabilities.

**cash equivalents** Short-term, very safe, and highly liquid assets that many firms include as part of their cash holdings on their balance sheet.

The planning process involves input from a variety of areas. In addition to seeking input from managers in various functional areas of their business, financial managers usually work closely with the firm's accountants during the planning process.

## Basic Planning Tools: Pro Forma Statements and the Cash Budget

A key element of financial planning is the development of projected financial statements called **pro forma statements.** These statements look much like the financial statements we discussed in chapter 8, but instead of describing the results of a firm's past operations, they present a forecast of what will happen in the future. The two major pro forma statements are the pro forma income statement and the pro forma balance sheet.

- Pro Forma Income Statement: A pro forma income statement forecasts the sales, expenses, and net income for the firm in some future time period.

- Pro Forma Balance Sheet: A pro forma balance sheet projects the types and amounts of assets a firm will need to carry out its future plans and shows the amount that additional financing (liabilities and owners' equity) the firm must obtain to acquire those assets.

The **cash budget** is another important tool of financial planning. Financial managers use cash budgeting to get a better understanding of the *timing* of cash flows within the planning period. Cash budgets normally project cash inflows and outflows for each month—and may look at even shorter time periods, such as weeks or days. This helps financial managers determine when the firm is likely to need additional funds to meet short-term cash shortages, and when surpluses of cash will be available to pay off loans or to invest in other assets.

Even firms with growing sales can experience cash flow problems, especially if many of their customers buy on credit. In order to meet higher sales levels, growing firms must hire more labor and buy more supplies. The firm may have to pay for these additional inputs *before* it receives an inflow of cash from its credit customers, leading to a temporary cash crunch. A cash budget helps financial managers anticipate such cash flow problems so that they can make arrangements to acquire short-term financing.

Exhibit 9.2 illustrates a cash budget for a hypothetical firm called Oze-Moore. Notice that Oze-Moore's sales increase significantly in both March and April, but that most of its customers buy on credit. Most of the cash Oze-Moore receives in March actually is from payments by credit customers for purchases they made in *February*. Because February sales are much lower than sales in March, the cash budget shows that the cash available will fall short of the amount Oze-Moore needs to pay its March bills. In fact, since the cash budget assumes that Oze-Moore wants to maintain at least $10,000 in its cash account at all times, it will have to arrange for a short-term loan of $11,750 to cover the shortfall and maintain its desired cash balance.

A look at the other months in exhibit 9-2 shows that Oze-Moore also will need to arrange additional loans in April. But by May, it will generate a large enough cash surplus to repay the short-term loans it had to obtain in the earlier months. This is valuable information to the firm's financial managers. Knowing in advance that they will need additional funds in March and April gives them time to seek the best sources for the needed funds.

## LO4 Managing Working Capital: Current Events

A firm's **net working capital** is the difference between its current assets and current liabilities. In part, working capital management involves maintaining the appropriate level of current assets such as cash, inventories, and accounts receivable. But another concern is deciding the amount and type of current liabilities needed to finance the firm's activities. Let's look at how a firm manages both current assets and current liabilities.

### Managing Current Assets

Holding current assets involves trade-offs. Either too much or too little can create problems. Effective management of working capital involves making the right investment decisions with respect to the type and amount of each current asset.

Managing Cash   A company must have cash to pay its workers, suppliers, lenders, dividends, and taxes. And firms also want to hold enough cash to meet unexpected contingencies. But cash has one serious shortcoming compared to other assets: it earns little or no return. If a firm holds a lot more cash than is necessary to meet its required payments, stockholders are likely to ask why excess cash isn't being invested in more profitable assets. And if the firm doesn't have any better way to invest the money, the stockholders are likely to ask management why it doesn't use the excess cash to pay them a higher dividend!

In the narrowest sense, a firm's cash refers to its holdings of currency (paper money and coins issued by the government) plus demand deposits (the balance in the company's checking account). However, when firms report their cash holdings on their balance sheet, they take a broader view, including cash equivalents along with their actual cash. **Cash equivalents** are very safe and highly liquid assets that can be converted into cash so easily that firms view them as part of their cash holdings. Commercial paper, U.S. Treasury Bills (T-bills), and

**Exhibit 9.2**   Cash Budget for Oze-Moore

| | February | March | April | May |
|---|---|---|---|---|
| Sales | $75,000 | $95,000 | $110,000 | $90,000 |
| Cash balance at beginning of month | | $10,000 | $10,000 | $10,000 |
| Receipts of Cash | | | | |
| Cash Sales | | $9,500 | $11,000 | $9,000 |
| Collection of accounts receivable | | $67,500 | $85,000 | $99,000 |
| Total Cash Available | | $87,000 | $106,500 | $118,000 |
| Disbursements of cash | | | | |
| Payment of accounts payable | | $57,000 | $60,500 | $49,500 |
| Wages and Salaries | | $23,750 | $27,500 | $22,500 |
| Fixed costs (rent, insurance, etc.) | | $8,000 | $8,000 | $8,000 |
| Purchase of new computers | | | $6,500 | |
| Total cash payments | | $88,750 | $102,500 | $80,000 |
| Excess or deficit of cash for month | | -$1,750 | $4,000 | $38,000 |
| Loans needed to maintain cash balance of $10,000 | | $11,750 | $6,000 | $0 |
| Amount of cash available to repay short-term loans | | $0 | $0 | $28,000 |
| Cash balance at end of month | | $10,000 | $10,000 | $10,250 |
| Cumulative loans | | $11,750 | $17,750 | $0 |

Financial managers want to have at least $10,000 in the cash balance at the beginning of each month.

Oze-Moore's receipts of cash are equal to 10% of this month's sales plus 90% of last month's sales. Total cash available is the sum of cash received plus the balance at the beginning of the month.

While receipts of cash lag behind sales, payments of wages and accounts payable are due in the same month as sales.

Even though Oze-Moore experienced a big increase in sales in March, it suffers a cash shortage because cash payments increased more than cash receipts. Thus, it must borrow $11,750 to make up for the cash shortage.

In May, Oze-Moore has a surplus in cash because it collects payments from April's high level of credit sales. This gives it enough cash to pay off the loans from earlier months.

**commercial paper** Short-term unsecured promissory notes issued by large corporations.

**U.S. Treasury bills (also called T-bills)** Short-term IOUs issued by the U.S. federal government. Treasury bills are marketable and are considered to be very safe securities.

**money market mutual funds** A mutual fund that pools funds from many investors and uses these funds to purchase very safe, highly liquid securities.

money market mutual funds are among the most popular cash equivalents. The advantage of these cash equivalents is that they offer a better financial return (in the form of interest) than currency or demand deposits.

**Commercial paper** consists of short-term unsecured promissory notes (IOUs) issued by major corporations with excellent credit ratings. Even though commercial paper can be issued for up to 270 days, firms usually issue it for much shorter periods—sometimes for as little as two days. Corporations sell commercial paper at a *discount*, meaning that it is initially sold at a lower price than the amount the company will pay the holder when the paper comes due. The difference between the initial price and the price paid to the holder when the paper comes due represents the interest earned on the note.

**T-bills** are short-term IOUs issued by the U.S. government. Most T-bills mature (come due) in 4, 13, or 26 weeks. Like commercial paper, the bills are sold at a discount, and the holder receives the full face value of the bill at maturity. There is a very active market for T-bills, so they are easy to sell for cash on short notice. And, since the U.S. government backs them, they're essentially risk-free, making them very attractive cash equivalents.

**Money market mutual funds** raise funds by selling shares to large numbers of investors. They then pool these funds to purchase a portfolio of short-term, liquid securities. (In fact, many money market mutual funds

## Life in the 21st Century: Faster Ways to Bounce Your Check?

For a law many people have never heard of, the Check Clearing for the 21st Century Act has had a major impact on the cash flows of both businesses and their customers. Until the passage of this law in 2004, banks had to clear checks by shipping the paper checks from the bank where they were deposited to the bank on which the funds were drawn—a slow and cumbersome process. Under Check 21 (as the law is commonly called), banks can process checks electronically.  This means that when you pay a bill by check, the bank can deduct funds from your account and deposit them in the company's account more quickly than in the past.

Recognizing that Check 21 reduces the time needed to process checks, the Fed now requires banks to reduce the holding time before they make funds available to depositors.  This is good news for most companies, since they get their funds faster.  But for those writing the checks, the shorter processing time increases the chances their checks will bounce. The moral of the story: More than ever, these days, you should make sure you have enough money in your account *before* you write the check![4]

© JANIS CHRISTIE/PHOTODISC/GETTY IMAGES

**spontaneous financing** Funds that arise as a natural result of a firm's business operations without the need for special arrangements.

**trade credit** Credit granted by sellers when they provide customers with goods and services for a period of time before requiring payment.

include commercial paper and T-bills within their portfolios.) Money market mutual funds are an affordable way for small investors to get into the market for securities, which would otherwise be beyond their means. This affordability also makes these funds a particularly attractive cash equivalent for smaller firms.

### Managing Accounts Receivable

Accounts receivable represents what credit customers owe the firm. Allowing customers to buy on credit can significantly increase sales. But, as our discussion of the cash budget showed, credit sales can create cash flow problems because they delay the receipt of cash the firm needs to meet its financial obligations. Credit customers who pay late or don't pay at all only exacerbate the problem. Thus, it's important for firms to have a well-thought-out policy that balances the advantages of offering credit with the costs. The key elements of this policy should include:

- **Setting Credit Terms:** For how long should the firm extend credit? What type of cash discount should the firm offer to encourage early payments?

- **Establishing Credit Standards:** How should the firm decide which customers qualify for credit? What type of credit information should it require? How strict should its standards be?

**Accepting debit and credit cards helps retailers speed up their receipt of cash.**

© IMAGE SOURCE PINK/JUPITERIMAGES

- **Deciding on an Appropriate Collection Policy:** How aggressive should the firm be at collecting past-due accounts? At what point does it make sense to take (or at least threaten to take) legal action against late-paying customers, or to turn over the accounts to collection agencies?

In each area, firms face trade-offs. For example, a firm that extends credit for only 30 days will receive its payments faster than a firm that allows customers 60 or 90 days. But setting short credit periods may also result in lost sales, especially if competitors give customers more time to pay. Similarly, setting high credit standards reduces problems with customers who pay late (or not at all). Yet these strict standards may prevent many good customers from getting credit, resulting in lower sales. Finally, an aggressive collection policy may help the firm collect payments that it would otherwise lose. But an aggressive policy might alienate customers who make honest mistakes, causing them to take future business to competitors.

### Managing Inventories

Inventories are the stocks of goods, materials, parts, and work-in-process that firms hold as a part of doing business. Clearly, businesses must hold inventories to operate. For example, merchandising firms, such as clothing stores, hold inventories of finished clothes so that customers can see and try on coats, dresses, and shirts before they buy. A manufacturing firm must hold an inventory of parts and materials to produce its products.

For many firms, the funds tied up in inventories represent a major investment, and the cost of storing and insuring inventory items is a significant expense. Inventory management is an important part of overall working capital management, but it's usually designed and implemented within the broader context of a firm's overall operations management strategy—a concept covered in chapter 18. Thus, we'll discuss strategies to determine the appropriate investment in inventories when we reach that chapter.

### Short-Term Financing

Firms often have several options when it comes to raising short-term financing. Let's look at some of the more important sources.

**Spontaneous Sources of Funds** Certain sources of funding arise naturally, during the normal course of business operations. This type of financing is called **spontaneous financing** because the firm doesn't have to make special arrangements to acquire it. **Trade credit**, which arises when suppliers ship materials, parts, or

> "There's always something to be thankful for. If you can't pay your bills you can be thankful you aren't one of your creditors."
>
> –Anonymous

goods to a firm without requiring payment at the time of delivery, is the major source of spontaneous financing for most firms. In most cases, the terms of trade credit are presented on the invoice for the shipment. For example, an invoice might list the terms as 2/10 net 30. The "net 30" indicates that the supplier allows the buyer 30 days before payment is due. But the "2/10" tells the buyer that the supplier is offering a 2% discount off the invoice price if it pays within 10 days.

At first glance, the 2% discount may not seem like a big deal. But failing to take the discount can be very costly. Consider the terms we mentioned above: 2/10, net 30. If the firm fails to pay within 10 days it loses the discount and must pay the full amount 20 days later. Paying 2% more for the use of funds for only 20 days is equivalent to an annual finance charge of over 37%![5]

Suppliers will grant trade credit only after they've evaluated the creditworthiness of the firm. But once they've granted this credit to a company once, they generally continue offering it as long as the firm satisfies the terms of the credit arrangements. Although firms of all sizes use this

type of financing, trade credit is a particularly important source of financing for small businesses. The Federal Reserve Board's *Survey of Small Business Finances* indicates that about 60% of all small businesses relied on this form of financing—the highest percentage of any source of short-run financial capital.[6]

**Short-Term Bank Loans** Banks are another common source of short-term business financing. Short-term bank loans are usually due in 30 to 90 days, though they can be up to a year in length. When a firm negotiates a loan with a bank, it signs a *promissory note*, which specifies the length of the loan, the rate of interest the firm must pay, and other terms and conditions of the loan. Banks sometimes require firms to pledge collateral, such as inventories or accounts receivable, to back the loan. That way, if the borrower fails to make the required payments, the bank has a claim on specific assets that can be used to pay off the amount due.

Rather than going through the hassle of negotiating a separate loan each time they need more funds, many firms work out arrangements with their bankers to obtain preapproval so that they can draw on funds as needed. One way firms do this is by establishing a **line of credit**. Under this type of arrangement, a bank agrees to provide the firm with funds up to some specified limit, as long as the borrower's credit situation doesn't deteriorate.

A **revolving credit agreement** is another way firms can arrange for bank credit. This is similar to

**Banks are an important source of short-term financing.**

© AP IMAGES

**line of credit** A financial arrangement between a firm and a bank in which the bank preapproves credit up to a specified limit, provided that the firm maintains an acceptable credit rating. The firm can then borrow funds from the bank up to the approved amount without having to negotiate separate loan agreements.

**revolving credit agreement** A guaranteed line of credit in which a bank makes a binding commitment to provide a business with funds up to a specified credit limit at any time during the term of the agreement. In exchange for the bank's commitment, the firm pays a commitment fee.

## Breaking the Rebate Habit

Retailers and manufacturers have long used mail-in rebates to increase their sales. But in recent years rebates have proven less effective, causing companies to change their strategies. What's the reason for the popularity of rebates, and why have many firms made major changes in their rebate policies in the past few years?

From a financial perspective, it's easy to see why mail-in rebates were popular with sellers. Buyers typically pay the full price when they purchase a good offering a rebate, and only get their "cash back" several weeks later. In the meantime the seller has the use of this money, providing big cash flow benefits. In fact, many customers never complete the necessary steps to redeem their rebate, so the firm never has to part with the cash—a result known as "breakage." And some customers who redeem rebates never bother to cash the checks they receive, an outcome known as "slippage."

In the short term, sellers benefit financially when customers don't collect their rebates, since this gives them permanent use of the funds. But high breakage rates ultimately backfire by alienating customers. By early this century many sellers began noticing that frustrated consumers were less responsive to rebates. So merchants adjusted their policies. Some eliminated rebates altogether. Many others—including major retailers such as Staples, OfficeMax, and Best Buy—phased out mail-in rebates, and replaced them with online rebate centers that made the process of redeeming cash-back offers both faster and more convenient.[7]

© PHOTODISC/GETTY IMAGES

**factor** A company that provides short-term financing to firms by purchasing their accounts receivables at a discount.

**capital budgeting** The process a firm uses to evaluate long-term investment proposals.

a line of credit, except that the bank makes a formal, legally binding commitment to provide the agreed-upon funds. A revolving credit agreement is like a *guaranteed* line of credit. In exchange for the binding commitment to provide the funds, the bank requires the borrowing firm to pay a commitment fee based on the *unused* amount of funds. Thus, under the terms of a revolving credit agreement, the firm will pay interest on any funds it borrows, and a commitment fee on any funds it does not borrow. The commitment fee is much lower than the interest on the borrowed funds, but it can amount to a fairly hefty charge if the firm has a large unused balance.

**Factoring**   Firms can also obtain short-term financing by using the services of a factor. A **factor** is a company that buys the accounts receivable of other firms. The factor makes a profit by purchasing the receivables at a discount from the firm and collecting the full amount from the credit customer.

Although firms that use factors don't receive the full amount for their accounts receivables, the use of factors offers some definite advantages. Instead of having to wait for credit customers to pay, the firm gets its money almost immediately. Also, using a factor allows the firm to outsource its collection efforts, so it doesn't have to maintain its own collection department. Factoring now provides more that a trillion dollars in short-term financing to firms—an amount that's more than tripled since the early 1990s.[8]

**Commercial Paper**   We defined commercial paper in our discussion of cash equivalents. Large, well-established corporations often issue commercial paper to meet their short-term financing needs. By far the biggest issuers of commercial paper are financial institutions, but other large corporations also use this form of financing. A key reason commercial paper is popular with large corporations is that the interest rate on this type of financing is usually much lower than the rate charged by commercial banks on short-term loans. The market for commercial paper is huge—in October, 2007 the amount of commercial paper outstanding exceeded $1.9 *trillion*.[9]

Capital budgeting helps managers evaluate the desirability of investments in long run assets.

term financing needs. We'll conclude the chapter with a look at how firms make decisions about investing in fixed assets and how they arrange for long-term financing.

**Capital budgeting** refers to the procedure a firm uses to plan for its investment in assets or projects that it expects will yield benefits for more than a year. The capital budgeting process evaluates proposals such as:

- Replacing existing machinery and equipment with more advanced models
- Buying additional new machinery and equipment to expand production capacity
- Building a new factory, warehouse, or office building
- Introducing an entirely new product line or service into the firm's product mix

> ❝ Sometimes your best investments are the ones you don't make. ❞
> –Donald Trump

A firm that makes a poor capital budgeting choice may need to live with the consequences of its decision for a long time, or to sell expensive assets at a substantial loss. For example, a multibillion-dollar plant Intel builds to fabricate computer chips may be so specialized in its design and layout that firms in other industries couldn't use it without expensive modifications. If Intel found that it really didn't need the extra capacity, it might have a hard time finding a firm interested in buying the plant.

## LO5 Capital Budgeting: In It for the Long Haul

So far we've looked at how a firm manages its current assets and liabilities and how it arranges to meet short-

### Comparing Cash Flows That Occur at Different Times

Financial managers measure the benefits and costs of a long-term investment proposal in terms of the cash flows it will generate. Cash flows are likely to be negative at the start of a project. But a viable project must eventually generate positive cash flows. For example, if a beverage company decides to introduce a new sports drink, it would incur negative cash flows in the first year as it spends money to set up its production facilities, create its distribution system, and begin promotion. Sales are likely to start out slowly but grow over time. If successful, the new drink eventually should result in positive cash flows for many years.

When financial managers compare cash flows that occur at different times, they must take the time value of money into account. The **time value of money** says that a dollar received today is worth *more* than a dollar received in the future because the sooner you receive a sum of money, the sooner you can put that money to work to earn even *more* money.

Let's illustrate the time value of money with a simple example. Suppose your favorite aunt is extremely proud of your decision to enroll in a business course—as well she should be! In fact, she's so pleased that she decides to send you $1,000 to reward your good judgment. Let's also suppose that you decide to invest your aunt's gift in a certificate of deposit (CD) at your local bank that pays 5% interest. (We realize that you have other ways to use the $1,000, but humor us for now.) How much money will you have a year from the day you buy the CD? The answer is $1,050—your original $1,000 *plus* the $50 interest you earned on the CD.

Now let's change our assumptions. Suppose your aunt still gives you $1,000 but doesn't send you the money until next year. Because you receive the money later, you lose the opportunity to earn a year's worth of interest. Receiving your aunt's gift today means that *you're $50 better off next year than you would be if you'd received the $1,000 a year from today.*

Also note that you'd continue earning interest every year your funds remained invested in the CD. In fact, each year your money remains invested at 5%, you earn *more* interest than the year before, because in addition to the interest on the initial $1,000, you'd also earn *interest on the interest from previous years*—a process called **compounding**. For example, in the second year you'd earn interest of $52.50 on your CD (5% of the $1,050 you had at the end of the first year), making your CD worth $1,102.50. And in the third year you'd earn $55.13 of interest (5% of the $1,102.50), raising the value of your CD to $1,157.63. The increases in the amount of interest may seem small in our example, but the longer the money is invested, the greater this compounding effect becomes.

Because of the time value of money, financial managers need a way to take differences in the timing of cash flows into account when they evaluate capital budgeting proposals. The most common way they do this is by converting all cash flows to their present values.

The **present value** of a cash flow received in a future time period is the amount of money which, if invested *today* at a specified rate of interest, would grow to become that future amount of money. For example, if you can earn 5% on your investments, the present value of $1,157.63 received in 3 years is $1,000 because (as we have already shown) if we have $1,000 today and invest it at 5%, then in 3 years the investment will have grown to $1,157.63.

> Time is money.
> –Ben Franklin

**time value of money** The principle that a dollar received today is worth more than a dollar received in the future.

**compounding** Earning interest in the current time period on interest from previous periods.

**present value** The amount of money that, if invested today at a given rate of interest, would grow to become some future amount in a specified number of time periods.

### Creating Interest in Retirement Saving

The time value of money has important implications for how successfully you achieve your long-term financial goals. The sooner you start saving for an important goal like retirement, the longer your money will work for you and the greater the compounding effect will be. The results of compounding can be quite impressive if you allow your money to work over a long time period. For example, suppose you begin saving for retirement at age 25 by putting $2,500 into an individual retirement account (IRA) each year for 40 years and that you can earn 6% interest per year on your savings. If you stick to your plan and retire at age 65, you'd have contributed $100,000 to your retirement fund ($2,500 per year for 40 years). But your fund will be worth about $413,000. The extra $313,000 is due to the compounding effect.

How much difference can a few years make when saving toward a long-term goal? In our example, waiting to start saving until you're 30 will reduce your total retirement savings to about $298,000—a drop of almost $115,000! Notice that waiting 5 years to start saving means you contributed $12,500 less than if you'd begun at age 25 ($2,500 per year for the first 5 years). The rest of the decrease in your retirement savings—over $100,000—comes from the fact that delaying your contributions by 5 years means losing the compounding effect on those early contributions.

**discounting** The process of converting a future cash flow to its present value.

**discount rate** The rate of interest used when computing the present value of some future cash flow. (Note: this term also has another meaning; it refers to the rate of interest the Fed charges when it loans funds to banks.)

**net present value (NPV)** The sum of the present values of expected future cash flows from an investment minus the net cost of that investment. It measures the increase in shareholder value expected to result from an investment.

**capital structure** The mix of equity and debt financing a firm uses to meet its permanent financing needs.

The process of computing the present value of a future cash flow is called **discounting**. It involves dividing the amount of the cash flow by $(1 + r)^N$, where $N$ is the number of time periods in the future that the cash flow will be received and $r$ is the **discount rate**, which is the rate of interest used in the present value computations. (Financial managers typically assume that the discount rate is equal to the firm's cost of obtaining additional financial capital.) Today, financial calculators and spreadsheet software make computing present values easy. All the manager needs to do is enter the amount and timing of the estimated cash flow into the calculator (or spreadsheet) along with the discount rate.

## Using Net Present Value to Evaluate Capital Budgeting Proposals

The most commonly used method to evaluate capital budgeting proposals is to compute their **net present value (NPV)**. The NPV of an investment proposal is found by adding the present values of *all* of its estimated future cash flows and subtracting the initial cost of the investment from the sum. A positive NPV means the present value of the expected cash flows from the project is greater than the cost of the project. In other words, the benefits from the project exceed its cost. Financial managers are likely to approve projects with positive NPVs. A negative NPV means that the present value of the expected future cash flows from the project is less than the cost of the investment. This would indicate that the cost of the project outweighs its benefits. Financial managers would almost certainly reject proposals with negative NPVs. (See exhibit 9.3.)

**Exhibit 9.3** Decision Rule for Capital Budgeting

| Result of NPV Calculation | Decision |
|---|---|
| NPV ≥ 0 | Accept proposal ☑ |
| NPV < 0 | Reject proposal ☒ |

## LO6 Choosing the Sources of Long-term Capital: Loaners vs. Owners

Our last major financial management topic deals with how firms meet their long-term financing needs. Firms use a combination of equity and debt to acquire needed assets and to finance their operations. Owners provide equity financing, while creditors (lenders) provide debt financing. The extent to which a firm relies on various forms of debt and equity to satisfy its financing needs is called that firm's **capital structure**.

To simplify our discussion, we'll focus mainly on the capital structure of corporations, but keep in mind that many of the basic issues and principles apply to any form of ownership. In this chapter, we focus on some of the basic issues that affect a firm's *choice* of debt or equity financing. We'll look at the ways firms actually go about acquiring these funds in chapter 10.

### Sources of Debt Financing

Well-established corporations usually have several options for how to acquire long-term debt financing. These options include:

- Arranging for long-term loans with banks or other financial institutions

- Negotiating private placements, which involve the direct sale of debt to a small number of sophisticated investors

- Issuing notes or bonds in a public offering, which involves selling these securities to the general public in securities markets

When a firm borrows funds, it enters into a contractual agreement with the lenders. This arrangement creates a *legally binding* agreement to repay the money borrowed (called the principal) *plus interest*. In addition, the firm often must pledge collateral, such as real estate, financial securities, or equipment, to back the loan. Should the firm be unable to make the required payments, the lenders can use this collateral to recover what it is owed.

Debt financing offers some advantages. First, the interest payments a firm makes on debt are a tax-deductible expense. So Uncle Sam (in the form of the IRS) subsidizes the interest payments. For example, if the corporation's tax rate is 25%, then each dollar of interest expense reduces the firm's taxes by $.25—meaning the true cost to the firm of each dollar of interest is only $.75.

Another advantage of debt is that it enables the firm to acquire additional funds without requiring the existing owners to contribute more of their own funds. If the firm invests the borrowed funds profitably, the use of debt

© RUSS WILSON/SUPERSTOCK

can substantially improve the return on equity to the shareholders. We'll illustrate this result in our discussion of financial leverage.

An obvious disadvantage of debt is the requirement to make fixed payments. This can create real problems when the firm finds itself in an unexpectedly tight financial situation. Another disadvantage of debt financing is that creditors often impose conditions, called **covenants**, on the borrower. Covenants sometimes place restrictions on the amount of dividends a firm can pay or a limit on the amount of additional debt financing the firm can obtain. They sometimes even limit the level of salaries and bonuses the firm can pay its employees. The purpose of covenants is to protect creditors by preventing the borrower from pursuing policies that might put the lenders' funds at greater risk. Covenants are desirable from the perspective of the lender, but they are a burden to the borrower.

## Sources of Equity Financing

The two primary sources of equity financing are:

- Direct Contributions by Owners: Unincorporated businesses can raise equity capital by having the individual owners directly contribute cash or other resources. Corporations can raise equity capital by issuing new shares of stock and selling them to existing stockholders or to new investors.

- Retained Earnings: **Retained earnings** represent that part of net income (profit) that a firm re-invests in its operations. Retained earnings are classified as equity financing because a firm's profits legally belong to its owners.

Equity financing provides a company with more flexibility and less risk than debt financing. Unlike debt, equity imposes no required payments. A firm can skip dividend payments to stockholders without having to worry that it will be pushed into bankruptcy. And a firm doesn't have to agree to burdensome covenants to acquire equity funds.

On the other hand, equity financing doesn't yield the same tax benefits as debt financing. (You may recall from our discussion of corporations in chapter 6 that dividend payments to stockholders are actually subject to double taxation.) In addition, existing owners may not want a firm to issue additional stock, since doing so might dilute their share of ownership. Finally, a company that relies mainly on equity financing forgoes the opportunity to use financial leverage—the topic of our next section.

**covenants** Conditions lenders place on firms that seek long-term debt financing.

**retained earnings** That part of net income that a firm reinvests.

**financial leverage** The use of debt in a firm's capital structure.

## Financial Leverage: Using Debt to Magnify Gains (And Losses)

**Financial leverage** is the use of debt in a firm's capital structure. A firm that has a lot of debt in its capital structure is said to be *heavily leveraged*. The main advantage of leverage is that it increases the expected return on the stockholders' investment. Its main disadvantage is that it also increases the firm's financial risk.

An example can help us illustrate both the advantages and disadvantages of financial leverage. Exhibit 9.4 shows the revenues, expenses, and earnings two firms would experience under two different levels of sales. We'll call the two firms Eck-Witty Corporation and Oze-Moore International. Let's assume that Eck-Witty and Oze-Moore are *identical* in all respects *except* their capital structure. Thus, any differences in the financial performance of these firms results solely from difference in their use of debt and equity financing. We'll focus on return on equity (ROE) to measure financial performance from the perspective of the firm's stockholders. (Exhibit 9.1 shows how this ratio is computed.)

Note that *both* firms have raised a total of $1.2 million in financing. Eck-Witty uses only common stock and retained earnings in its capital structure. Oze-Moore's capital structure consists of $600,000 in owners' equity and $600,000 in debt. (Eck-Witty uses only equity, and Oze-Moore uses long-term debt, so it "owes more." Granted, the names aren't subtle, but they should help you keep straight which firm uses which type of financing.)

Take a look at exhibit 9.4 and compare the results for the two firms in each scenario. Although the revenue and operating expenses for the firms are identical under both scenarios, Oze-Moore also must pay interest on its debt, which is an additional expense. Eck-Witty has no interest expense, so it has a higher reported taxable income than Oze-Moore under both poor and good market

| **Exhibit 9.4** | Illustration of Financial Leverage |

| Interest Rate: | 10% |
| Tax Rate: | 25% |

**Eck.-Witty** (Capital structure uses only equity)

| Total funds supplied by owners: | $1,200,000 |
| Total debt: | $0 |

| Market Conditions: | Poor | Good |
| --- | --- | --- |
| Sales | $250,000 | $650,000 |
| Operating Expenses | $193,000 | $473,000 |
| Earnings before Interest and Taxes | $57,000 | $177,000 |
| Interest | $0 | $0 |
| Earnings after Interest | $57,000 | $177,000 |
| Taxes | $14,250 | $44,250 |
| Net Profits | $42,750 | $132,750 |
| | | |
| Return on Equity | 3.6% | 11.1% |

**Oze-Moore** (Capital structure contains 50% debt and 50% equity)

| Total funds supplied by owners: | $600,000 |
| Total debt: | $600,000 |

| Market Conditions: | Poor | Good |
| --- | --- | --- |
| Sales | $250,000 | $650,000 |
| Operating Expenses | $193,000 | $473,000 |
| Earnings before Interest and Taxes | $57,000 | $177,000 |
| Interest | $60,000 | $60,000 |
| Earnings after taxes | -$3,000 | $117,000 |
| Taxes | -$750 | $29,250 |
| Net Profits | -$2,250 | $87,750 |
| | | |
| Return on Equity | -0.4% | 14.6% |

conditions. But also keep in mind that the owners of Eck-Witty contributed twice as much of their *own* money as the owners of Oze-Moore.

In the poor sales scenario, Eck-Witty earns a small profit; even though its return on equity (ROE) is low, it is positive. Oze-Moore suffers a loss and has a negative ROE. This illustrates the risk associated with financial leverage. Oze-Moore's $60,000 in required interest payments are a drain on its earnings when sales are low. If it fails to make the interest payments, creditors could force Oze-Moore into bankruptcy.

But look at what happens when sales are good: Oze-Moore's ROE is 14.6%, while Eck-Witty's ROE is only 11.1%. This shows the upside of leverage—it increases the return to owners when sales are strong. This happens because interest payments are fixed; Oze-Moore pays creditors no more in good times than in bad. Once the firm earns enough to cover its fixed interest payments, *all additional earnings* go to the owners. When earnings are strong, this can be a really nice deal for the owners!

# Oops! What were they THINKING?!

## Spider-Man Nets Box-Office Record, Marvel Profits Make Getaway

Moviegoers around the globe got caught in a web of thrills when *Spider-Man 3* opened worldwide to enthusiastic audiences and record profits. The third installment in the Marvel Comics superhero franchise starring Tobey Maguire and Kirsten Dunst earned more than $750 million internationally and snagged a U.S. record $151.1 million on its opening weekend.

Sony Pictures, the film studio behind the *Spider-Man* series, created a pre-release buzz worthy of the insect world. Sony's promotion effort featured crowd-pleasing tie-ins, including a "Which Spidey Suits You?" game at Burger King—a nod to the superhero's red- and black-suit alter egos—and a General Mills partnership that placed movie scenes on packages of Cheerios and Fruit Roll-ups.

Despite the effective marketing push and streams of cash flowing in from all corners of the earth, executives at Marvel Entertainment were noticeably subdued regarding the recent movie success of their superhero. In particular, the company refused to announce its profits from the first two *Spider-Man*

films. Financial analysts reported that the combined total was a mere $62 million—a sign that Sony got the better end of the licensing deal.

Indeed, this result isn't an isolated incident. Marvel characters appear to have special powers for making *other* companies rich. Fox's 2005 movie *The Fantastic Four* grossed hundreds of millions of dollars but delivered only $13 million to Marvel. Likewise the *X-Men* action-film series earned a combined $2 billion, but only $26 million found its way into Marvel's wallet.

Feeling shortchanged by its licensing strategy, Marvel has decided to produce its own films. The first, featuring *Iron Man*, hit the box office in the spring of 2008. Others, featuring Captain America and Nick Fury, will soon follow. The move is a bold attempt to reap the profits generated by Marvel's superheroes, while retaining the merchandising rights. But moviemaking is risky, and Marvel made it riskier when it entered into a $525 million debt financing deal, using the film rights to its superhero characters as collateral. If the gamble works--and the success of *Iron Man's* debut was encouraging--the company's use of financial leverage could provide a truly "marvelous" return on its investment. But if future movies bomb and Marvel can't generate enough cash to pay its debts, financial lenders will own the film rights to Captain America and other Marvel creations.[10]

# Review!

With **BUSN** you have a multitude of study aids at your fingertips. After reading the chapters, check out these ideas for further help:

• **Chapter in Review Cards,** in the back of the book, include all learning objectives, definitions, and visual summaries for each chapter.

• **Online Printable and Interactive Flash Cards** give you additional ways to check your comprehension of key business concepts.

• Other great ways to help you study include **interactive business games, visual summaries, audio downloads, and online tutorial quizzes with feedback.**

You can find more resources at **4ltrpress.cengage.com/busn**.

# 10

# Securities Markets: Trading Financial Resources

## LEARNING OBJECTIVES

After studying this chapter, you will be able to...

**LO1** Describe the three basic types of securities issued by corporations

**LO2** Explain how securities are issued in the primary market and traded on secondary markets

**LO3** Discuss how the government and private organizations regulate securities markets

**LO4** Compare several strategies investors use to invest in securities

**LO5** Explain the investor appeal of mutual funds and exchange traded funds

**LO6** Describe how investors can track the performance of their investments

4ltrpress.cengage.com/busn

If you don't follow the stock market, you
are missing some amazing drama.

–Mark Cuban, owner of the Dallas Mavericks

## LO1 Basic Types of Financial Securities

Securities markets perform a vital function: they transfer funds from investors to firms that need financial resources to achieve their long-term goals. If these markets didn't perform efficiently, firms would find it difficult to obtain the financial resources they need to expand, create jobs, introduce new products, and compete effectively in global markets.

But securities markets don't just benefit the businesses that issue the securities. Investors who buy securities obtain valuable assets that enhance their wealth. You can, and most likely will, become involved in these markets. In fact, doing so is likely to be vital to achieving your financial goals. Making wise investment decisions can help you buy your dream home, put your kids through college, and live comfortably when you retire. A key goal of this chapter is to provide you with basic knowledge about your investment opportunities.

Corporations can raise long-term financial capital through the securities markets in a number of ways. But in this section, we'll focus only on the three key types of securities that firms can issue to meet their financial needs.

### Common Stock

The first type of security we'll examine is **common stock**, which represents the basic form of ownership in a corporation. Exhibit 10.1 is a stock certificate representing ownership in Yahoo! Inc. Owners of common stock have certain key rights.

**Exhibit 10.1**   Common Stock Certificate: A Share of Corporate Ownership

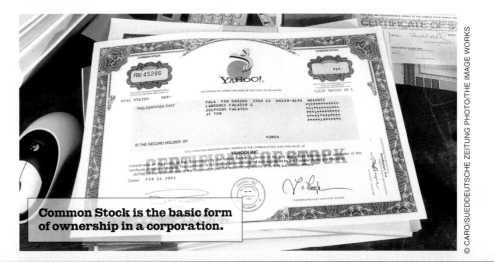

**Common Stock is the basic form of ownership in a corporation.**

**common stock** The basic form of ownership in a corporation.

- Voting Rights: Owners of common stock have the right to vote on important issues in the annual stockholders' meeting. One of the key issues stockholders vote on is the selection of members to the corporation's board of directors. They also may vote on other major issues, such as the approval of a merger with another firm or a change in the corporation's bylaws. Under the most common arrangement, stockholders can cast one vote for each share of stock they own.

- Right to Dividends: Dividends are a distribution of profits to the corporation's owners. Common stockholders have the right to receive a dividend, *if* the board of directors declares one. Of course, if a firm has a bad year, there may not be any profits to distribute. And even if the company is profitable, the board may choose to reinvest the earnings in the company rather than distribute them as dividends. Thus, *there is no guarantee stockholders will receive a dividend.* But many companies have a long history of paying regular dividends. For example, as of mid-2008 Dow Chemical had paid a dividend for 386 consecutive quarters going all the way back to 1912.[1]

- Capital Gains: Stockholders also may receive another type of return on their investment, called a **capital gain**, if the price of the stock rises above the amount they paid for it. Capital gains can create very attractive returns for stockholders. To take an extreme example, someone who bought Google stock in August 2004 would have paid about $100 per share. A little over 2 years later, the investor could have sold each share for well over $400. The potential for capital gains is one of the main reasons for investing in common stock. Of course, stock prices sometimes fall so investors can realize capital losses as well as gains.

- Preemptive Right: If a corporation issues new stock, existing stockholders may have a preemptive right to purchase new shares in proportion to their existing holdings before the stock is offered to the general public. For example, if you own 5% of the existing shares of stock, then the preemptive right gives you the right to purchase 5% of the new shares. This could be important for large stockholders who want to maintain control over a significant share of votes.

- Right to a Residual Claim on Assets: The final stockholder right is a residual claim on assets. If the corporation goes out of business and liquidates its assets, stockholders have a right to share in the proceeds in proportion to their ownership. But note that this is a *residual* claim—it comes *after all other claims* have been satisfied. In other words, the firm must pay any back taxes, legal expenses, wages owed to workers, and debts owed to creditors before the owners get anything. Little or nothing may be left for the owners.

## Preferred Stock

Common stock is the basic form of corporate ownership, but some companies also issue **preferred stock**, so named because—compared to common stock—it offers its holders preferential treatment in two respects:

- Claim on Assets: Holders of preferred stock have a claim on assets that comes before common stockholders if the company goes out of business. This gives preferred stockholders a better chance than common stockholders of recovering their investment if the company goes bankrupt.

- Payment of Dividends: Although a corporation has no legal requirement to pay a dividend to any stockholders, the board of directors normally has a stronger incentive to pay the preferred stock dividend than the common stock dividend. And, unlike the common stock dividend, the preferred stock dividend is a fixed amount.

Most preferred stock includes a *cumulative feature*. This means that when the firm skips a preferred dividend in one quarter, the amount it must pay the next quarter is equal to the dividend for that quarter *plus* the amount of the dividend it skipped in the previous quarter. Any additional skipped dividends continue to accumulate. The firm can't pay *any* dividends to common stockholders until it has paid preferred stockholders *all* of the accumulated dividends it owes them. This provision is one of the reasons the board has a strong incentive to make regular dividend payments to preferred stockholders.

Preferred stock isn't necessarily "preferred" to common stock in all respects. For example, preferred stockholders normally don't have voting rights, so they can't vote on issues that come up during stockholders meetings. And even though preferred stockholders are more likely to receive a dividend, the overall return for common stockholders (including the capital gain) is often higher.

## Bonds

A **bond** is a long-term debt instrument issued by a corporation or governmental entity in exchange for funds. In other words, it's a formal IOU that comes due several years after an organization issues it. The date the bond comes due is called the **maturity date**. Bonds come in many different varieties. We'll only describe the types commonly issued by corporations.

Typically, bonds issued by corporations mature 10 to 30 years after issuance, but bonds with longer maturities are not unusual. The amount the issuer of the bond must pay the bondholder at maturity is known as the principal, and is indicated by the **par value** of the bond. But the par value doesn't necessarily represent what the bondholder would receive for a bond sold to another investor prior to maturity. If the market price of a bond is above its par value, it is said to be selling at a *premium*; if it's below its par value it is selling at a *discount*.

In addition to repaying the principal upon maturity, the issuing firm typically pays interest to bondholders each year until the bond matures. The **coupon rate** expresses this annual interest payment as a percentage of the bond's par value. For example, investors who own a bond with a par value of $1,000 and a coupon rate of 7.5% receive $75 in interest (7.5% of $1,000) each year until the bond reaches maturity—or until they sell their bonds to someone else.

Unlike dividends to stockholders, both the interest on bonds and the repayment of principal are *legally required* payments. Exhibit 10.2 illustrates a bond certificate that shows the maturity date, coupon rate, and principal for a corporate bond. See if you can locate the par value, coupon rate, and maturity date for this bond. Ownership of bonds is now electronically recorded, so bond certificates like this one have become increasingly rare.

Bonds can differ in terms of how firms secure them, how firms retire them, and in certain special features they may possess. Let's look at some common variations.

**Securing bonds**  Many bonds are **secured**, meaning that the issuing firm backs them with a pledge of specific assets such as property or equipment. Should the issuer fail to make the required payments of interest and principal, the bondholders can require it to use these assets to satisfy their claims.

Some bonds, called *debentures,* aren't secured by the pledge of any specific assets. Instead, they are backed only by the earning capacity and general creditworthiness of the issuing firm. Most investors are only willing to buy debentures from businesses with excellent financial reputations—such as General Electric and AT&T. Even so, debentures typically carry a higher coupon rate than similar secured bonds.

## Methods of Retiring Bonds

Corporations that issue bonds usually make specific provisions to ensure an orderly repayment of principal. Firms that fail to do so might find themselves faced with the need to make large repayments at a time when they were strapped for cash. One approach is to offer **serial bonds**, which are issued at the same time but mature in different years. This enables the issuer to spread the repayment over time. Another common method is to establish a **sinking fund**. When a firm uses a sinking fund, it periodically deposits money into a fund that is used to buy back some of the bonds each year. Like a serial bond issue, a sinking fund allows the firm to repay the principal gradually instead of making all of the payments in the same year.

## Special Characteristics of Bonds

Bonds often include special features that can make them more attractive to both the investor and the issuing firm. Let's take a look at two common examples.

**Callable bonds** include a provision that allows the firm to call in (or "redeem") *all* of the bonds at a specified price prior to their maturity date. This allows firms to take advantage of drops in interest rates after they issue their bonds. For example, a firm that issued $100 million in callable bonds that paid 10% interest would have to make $10 million in interest payments each year (10% of $100 million). If interest rates fell to 7%, the firm could issue new bonds at the lower rate and use the proceeds to call in the 10% bonds. This would reduce the firm's annual interest expense from $10 million to $7 million.

Of course, bondholders who own these high interest-earning bonds are likely to be very unhappy when they are called. In order to attract investors, callable bonds typically offer a higher coupon rate than similar bonds that aren't callable.

**Convertible bonds** allow bondholders to exchange their bonds for a

---

**par value (of a bond)** The value of a bond at its maturity; what the firm must pay the bondholder when the bond matures.

**coupon rate** The interest paid on a bond expressed as a percentage of the bond's par value.

**secured bond** A bond backed by the pledge of specific assets.

**serial bonds** A series of bonds issued at the same time but having different maturity dates to spread out the repayment of principal.

**sinking fund** Funds set aside to retire bonds over a period of time. Money deposited into a sinking fund is used to call in bonds or purchase bonds.

**callable bond** A bond that the issuer can redeem at a given price prior to its maturity.

**convertible bond** A bond that gives its holder the right to exchange it for a stated number of shares of common stock in some specified time period.

---

**Exhibit 10.2**  Bond Certificate: A Long Term Corporate IOU

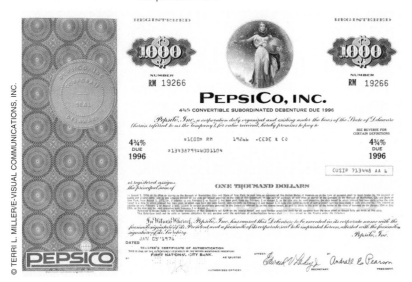

© TERRI L. MILLER/E-VISUAL COMMUNICATIONS, INC.

stated number of shares of the corporation's common stock. The *conversion ratio* states the number of shares of stock exchanged for each convertible bond. For example, if the conversion ratio is 20, then each bond can be exchanged for 20 shares of common stock. Owning a convertible bond allows investors to take advantage of a rise in stock prices, while limiting their risk if stock prices fall. The firm also can benefit from issuing convertible bonds. Since bondholders like the convertible feature, the firm can offer a lower coupon rate on convertible bonds, reducing its interest expense. Also, if the investor exchanges the bonds for stock, the firm no longer has to make interest payments or repay the principal on the bonds.

# LO2 Trading Securities: The Primary and Secondary Markets

The securities markets have two distinct components. The **primary securities market** is where corporations raise additional financial capital by issuing and selling *newly issued* securities. **Secondary securities markets** involve trades of *previously issued* securities. Let's take a look at how each of these markets work.

## The Primary Securities Market

There are two basic methods of issuing securities in the primary market:

- In a **public offering** securities may be sold to anyone in the investing public that is willing (and financially able) to buy them.

- In a **private placement** securities are sold directly to one or more large investors under terms negotiated between the issuing firm and the private investors.

**Public Offerings** Many corporations are initially owned by only a handful of people who don't actively trade the stock to outsiders. But rapidly growing corporations often need to obtain more financial capital than such a small group can provide. Such firms may decide to *go public* by issuing additional stock and offering it to the general pub-

lic. The first time a corporation sells its stock in a public offering, the sale is called an **initial public offering**, or **IPO**. The process typically involves four steps.

- Selecting an Investment Bank: Many firms that go public enlist the help of a financial intermediary known as an **investment bank**. The investment bank assists the firm at every step of the IPO, from the planning and market assessment until the day of the actual offering. Determining how to structure the offer is a key role of the investment bank.

- Preparing the IPO Paperwork: Before going public, a firm must file a registration statement with the Securities and Exchange Commission (SEC)—an agency we will describe later in this chapter. The registration statement provides a detailed description of both the firm and the securities, including the firm's key financial statements plus additional financial information. The investment bank usually helps prepare this long, complex document. The firm later includes much of the information from the registration statement in its *prospectus*, which the firm must give to all investors who are interested in purchasing the securities.

- Arranging for Financing: One of the key responsibilities of the investment bank is to arrange for the actual sale of the securities. The investment bank typically uses either a *best efforts* or a *firm commitment* approach. Under a best efforts agreement, the investment bank provides advice about pricing and marketing and assists in finding potential buyers. But it doesn't guarantee that the firm will sell all of its securities at a high enough price to meet its financial goals. The investment bank earns a commision on all of the shares sold under a best efforts approach. Under a *firm-commitment* arrangement, the investment bank **underwrites** the issue. This means that the investment bank itself purchases *all* of the shares, which guarantees that the firm issuing the stock will receive a known amount of new funds directly from the investment bank. The investment bank makes its profit by reselling the stock to investors at a higher price.

- Carrying Out the Offer: On the day of the actual IPO the investment banker normally takes charge, handling all of the details to ensure that investors receive their securities and copies of the final prospectus, and the firm receives its funding.

**Private Placements** Private placements are usually quicker, simpler, and less expensive than public offerings. In a private placement, the issuing firm negotiates the terms of the offer directly with a small number of investors. An investment banker often helps the firm identify and contact potential investors and assists the firm as it negotiates the terms of the offer.

One reason private placements are simpler and less expensive than public offerings is that privately placed securities are exempt from the requirement to register with the

SEC. The ability to obtain financing without having to prepare complex registration documents can be a real attraction. But a significant drawback is that private placements normally don't raise as much money as public offerings.

Private placements can only be offered to *accredited investors*. These are individuals, businesses, or other organizations that meet specific requirements set by the SEC. The SEC's rationale is that accredited investors are likely to be more knowledgeable than other investors, so they don't need protection provided by the registration process.

## Secondary Securities Markets

The firms issuing the stocks and bonds don't receive any additional funds when their securities are traded in the secondary markets. But secondary markets still matter to the corporations that issue these securities. The price of a firm's stock in the secondary market directly reflects the performance of the management team in building the value of the corporation. And many investors wouldn't have bought newly issued securities on the primary market without the possibility of capital gains in the secondary markets.

Securities exchanges are the biggest secondary market players, but a new arrangement for trading securities, called an **electronic communications network (ECN)**, has recently attracted a lot of attention. Let's take a look at each of these market configurations.

**Securities Exchanges** A securities exchange is an organization that provides a venue for stockbrokers or securities dealers to trade listed stocks and other securities.

Each stock exchange establishes requirements for the stocks it lists. Specific listing requirements vary among the exchanges, but they're typically based on the earnings of the company, the number of shares of stock outstanding, and the number of shareholders. In addition to meeting listing requirements, exchanges also require firms to pay an initial fee at the time its securities are first listed and an annual listing fee to remain listed on the exchange.

The **New York Stock Exchange (NYSE)** and **NASDAQ** are the two largest exchanges in the United States. Most of the nation's largest and best-known corporations, such as Exxon, Wal-Mart, and General Electric, are listed on the NYSE, and many prominent high-tech firms, such as Apple, Google, and Microsoft are listed on the NASDAQ exchange. Both the NYSE and NASDAQ are corporations with publicly traded stock.

NASDAQ and the NYSE have become intense rivals, each claiming to be the biggest and most influential exchange. Exhibit 10.3 on the following page offers some comparisons of their relative size.

Securities exchanges operate around the world. The largest exchange outside the United States is the Tokyo

**Electronic communications network (ECN)** An automated, computerized securities trading system that automatically matches buyers and sellers, executing trades quickly and when markets are closed.

**New York Stock Exchange (NYSE)** The largest securities exchange in the United States. After its 2007 merger with a large European exchange, it is formally known as NYSE Euronext.

**NASDAQ exchange** A major stock exchange that handles trades through a computerized network.

## If It's Tuesday, This Must Be Boston

Several weeks before the IPO actually occurs, representatives of the investment bank accompany corporate officers of the issuing firm on a whirlwind tour of major cities. This tour is called an IPO road show. Its purpose is to create interest in the offering among potential big money investors and to solicit orders for the stock in advance of the actual sale.

For the corporate officers, road shows can be intense, with lots of travel, long hours, and an endless stream of high stakes meetings and presentations. For example, Chris Mottern, the CEO of Peet's Coffee at the time of that company's IPO, made 63 presentations to potential investors in a 3-week period during his company's road show. What was his take on the road show? "The process is really tiring. You want to be on your toes. You want to give a good presentation every time." He found it a tough sell to convince most investors to give his company a serious look. His key challenge is summed up in this directive: "You have twenty minutes. They don't know anything about coffee."

Not only are road shows grueling and expensive, but they also take senior managers away from their company for a number of weeks. Isn't there a better way? WILink, Inc., thinks so. The company has developed a Web site that enables IPO firms to make virtual road show presentations to qualified investors. The Website (http://www.VRoadshow.com) allows investors to participate in conference calls, download podcasts of road show presentations, and sign up for e-mail updates about specific IPO presentations. It is a timely idea for virtually everyone involved.[2]

© RANDALL FUNG/CORBIS

**Exhibit 10.3**  A Comparison of NYSE and NASDAQ[3]

| | NYSE | NASDAQ |
|---|---|---|
| Total number of companies listed (approx.) | 2,800 | 3,200 |
| Total market capitalization of listed firms (end of 2005) | $21.7 trillion | $3.6 trillion |
| Average daily share volume (April, 2007) | 1.91 billion | 2.07 billion |
| Average daily dollar volume (April, 2007) | $78.2 billion | $51.2 billion |

Stock Exchange (TSE). The London Stock Exchange is recognized as the most important exchange in Europe. And the Shanghai Stock Exchange continues to grow rapidly in mainland China. Both the NYSE and NASDAQ have pursued mergers with foreign securities exchanges. In early 2007, the NYSE merged with a large European stock exchange known as Euronext. (After the merger its name was officially changed to NYSE Euronext, but it's still usually just called the NYSE.) NASDAQ attempted to merge with the London Stock Exchange early in 2007; when that deal collapsed, it merged instead with OMX, another European exchange.

The NYSE and NASDAQ have always operated in fundamentally different ways. Until very recently, the vast majority of trades on the NYSE took place at a physical location—a group of trading floors in the heart of New York's financial district—where brokers representing buyers and sellers of listed stocks meet to conduct their business. Each stock listed on the NYSE trades at a particular spot on a floor where a *specialist* for that stock is located. The specialist organizes bidding on the stock, essentially acting as an auctioneer. Because of this arrangement, the traditional method of trading stocks on the NYSE is sometimes called an *auction market*.

The newer NASDAQ exchange has never had a physical trading location. Instead, dealers who participate in NASDAQ are linked by telephone and computer networks. Thus, NASDAQ is often called an *electronic exchange*. It's also sometimes described as a *screen-based exchange* because transactions today are carried out on a computer screen.

**Big Changes at the NYSE**  In 2006 and 2007 the NYSE began implementing a new system for trading securities, known as the **NYSE Hybrid Market**. The Hybrid Market still allows investors to trade securities via the traditional auction market. But it also gives traders the option of using a newer system called NYSE

NASDAQ has no trading floors. All trades on this exchange are carried out through a network of securities dealers linked by phone and computer networks.

© JONATHAN FICKIES/BLOOMBERG NEWS/LANDOV

Direct+. This is a computerized system that automatically matches buyers and sellers, bypassing the brokers and specialists on the floor of the exchange.[4]

From the outset, it was apparent that many investors preferred the speed and convenience of the new Direct+ system to the older auction system. In the first quarter of 2007, 82.1% of all traded shares on the NYSE went through Direct+ while only 17.9% of the shares were traded in the auction market. That's a dramatic change from a year earlier, when the auction market handled trades for about 86% of all shares.[5]

opportunity for growth—and both reacted in much the same way. On April 20, 2005, the NYSE announced plans to buy Archipelago, one of the largest and best-known ECNs. Two days later, NASDAQ announced its intention to buy Instinet, another major ECN. Both exchanges quickly followed through on their plans and have now integrated ECN technology into their operations.

> **over-the-counter market (OTC)** The market in which securities that are not listed on exchanges are traded.

> **Securities Act of 1933** The first major federal law regulating the securities industry.

## LO3 Regulation of Securities Markets: Establishing Confidence in the Market

Securities markets work well only if participants have confidence in the integrity and fairness of the system. To ensure that this confidence is justified, a mix of state, federal, and private efforts regulates the markets. Let's look at some of the major players.

### State Regulations

In the early twentieth century, unscrupulous securities dealers took advantage of the lack of government oversight to sell stocks in highly risky (and sometimes completely fictitious) businesses to naïve customers. The result was financial ruin for many of these investors—and a public outcry calling for government action.

State governments responded to these unethical practices more quickly than the federal government. Kansas passed the first state law dealing with securities fraud in 1911. Over the next few years virtually every state passed similar laws, which soon came to be called *blue sky laws*. Though they varied in the specifics, these laws typically required all securities sold in the state to be registered with a state regulatory agency. They also required all securities dealers and brokerage firms to register with the state and gave investors the right to sue when injured by securities fraud.

### Federal Legislation

The federal government got involved in regulating the securities industry during the depression years, following the great stock market crash that began in October of 1929. The first two federal laws dealing with securities markets were the Securities Act of 1933 and the Securities Exchange Act of 1934. These two laws still provide the foundation for the federal approach to the regulation of securities markets.

A key objective of the **Securities Act of 1933** was to restore public faith and trust in the securities markets that had been battered by the crash in 1929. This act deals mainly with securities issued in the primary market. It prohibits misrepresentation, deceit, or other forms of fraud in the sale of new securities. It also requires firms issuing new stock to file a registration statement with the SEC, as we mentioned in our discussion of initial public offerings.

> Is this type of activity a thing of the past? With the advent of the Hybrid Market, the amount of trading on the floor of the NYSE has fallen dramatically.

© MONIKA GRAFF/UPI/LANDOV

The Over-the-Counter Market  Many corporations don't meet the requirements for listing on an organized exchange; some are too small, and others haven't experienced satisfactory business performance. Other corporations meet requirements to list on the NYSE or NASDAQ but choose not to do so because they don't want to pay the listing fees the exchanges charge. The **over-the-counter market (OTC)** is where the stocks of such companies are traded. OTC stocks are traded through a network of securities dealers much like stocks are traded on the NASDAQ exchange. However, trading of most OTC stocks is much less active than for stocks listed on the major exchanges.

Electronic Communications Networks  Electronic communications networks are a relatively new type of computer-based securities market. ECNs are entirely automated. When an investor places an order for a certain security on an ECN, the system automatically checks to see if there is a matching order to sell. If so, it immediately executes the transaction. This essentially eliminates the need for "middlemen" who operate on the exchanges. The use of ECNs can speed up transactions and lower trading costs.

By early 2005, both the NYSE and NASDAQ saw ECNs as a threat to their market positions *and* as an

The **Securities Exchange Act of 1934** dealt mainly with the regulation of secondary security markets. This law created the **Securities and Exchange Commission** and gave it broad powers to oversee and regulate the securities industry. The law required that all publicly traded firms with at least 500 shareholders and $10 million in assets file quarterly and annual financial reports with the SEC, and that brokers and dealers register with the SEC.

The Securities Exchange Act also gave the SEC the power to prosecute individuals and companies that engaged in fraudulent securities market activities. For example, the SEC has the authority to go after employees or advisors of a company who engage in illegal *insider trading*, which is the practice of using inside information (important information about a company that isn't available to the general investing public) to profit from trading in that company's securities. In a recent case, former Oracle Corporation vice president Christopher Balkenhol paid almost $200,000 to settle charges by the SEC that he used inside information to illegally buy stock in companies Oracle was planning to purchase before the acquisition plans were made public.[6]

### The Role of Self-Regulatory Organizations

Although the SEC retains ultimate regulatory authority over securities markets, it relies on **self-regulatory organizations (SROs)** to oversee the operations of these markets. SROs are non-governmental organizations that develop and enforce the rules governing the behavior of their members. The SEC reviews and approves (or disapproves) any new rules or regulations the SROs propose.

Until recently the National Association of Securities Dealers (NASD) and the NYSE maintained separate SROs. However, in July of 2007, these two SROs merged to form the Financial Industry Regulatory Authority (FINRA). The goal of FINRA was to establish a single authority to regulate all securities dealers and brokers in the United States, thus ensuring more regulatory consistency. The new SRO oversees approximately 5,000 brokerage firms and almost 700,000 brokers and dealers—making it by far the largest non-governmental regulator of U.S. securities markets.[7]

## LO4 Personal Investing

Would investing in stocks, bonds, and other securities make sense for you? If so, how could you get started? What are the potential risks and rewards of various investment strategies? Since this chapter is about securities markets, we'll focus on personal investing in stocks and bonds, but keep in mind that other types of investments could also help you achieve your financial goals.

Investing in securities requires you to think carefully about your specific situation and your personal needs and preferences:

- What are your short-term and long-term goals?
- Given your budget, how much are you able to invest?
- How concerned are you about the tax implications of your investments?
- How much tolerance do you have for risk?

### Symbolic Logic: Do You LUV this HOG's DNA?

Every publicly traded corporation is identified by a unique combination of letters known as its stock symbol. The use of symbols began in the mid-1800s when people began sending information about stock prices via telegraph. The symbols allowed telegraph operators to tap out a few letters rather than having to spell out a company's entire name. Although we no longer rely on the telegraph for stock quotes, the symbols are still used today. For example, symbols are used to quote stock prices on those scrolling tickers at the bottom of many financial news channels on cable TV. And many financial Websites require you to enter a company's symbol in order to get the latest quotes and statistics for its stock.

The combination of letters used in a symbol is usually tied to the company's business, but the connection can be a bit subtle. See if you can identify the well-known corporation that uses each of the symbols listed below. (Answers are given below.)[8]

- GM
- GOOG
- MMM
- BUD
- JAVA
- HOG
- DNA
- LUV

Answers: General Motors, Google, 3M, Anheuser Busch (Budweiser is its best-known brand), Sun Microsystems (JAVA is its best-known programming language), Harley-Davidson (Hog is the nickname for its motorcycles), Genentech (the company specializes in genetic research), Southwest Airlines (its first major hub of operations was Love Field in Dallas, TX.)

© RUBBERBALL/JUPITERIMAGES

The best types of securities for you, and the best investment strategies for you to use, will depend in large part on your answers to questions such as these.

Notice that the last question deals with your attitudes toward risk. Most people are not comfortable with high levels of risk. But no investment strategy completely avoids risk. And in general, the riskier the approach, the greater the *potential* rewards. To achieve your goals, you'll need to find the balance between risk and return that works for you.

Diversification is one common strategy for dealing with risk. This means investing in many different types of securities in many different sectors of the economy. If you put all of your investment dollars into a small number of securities, a setback in one or two could have a devastating financial impact. But if you hold many different securities in different sectors of the economy, then losses on some securities are likely to be offset by gains on others.

### Choosing a Broker

Members of the general public cannot directly trade stocks and other securities on the exchanges we described earlier in the chapter. Thus, most investors enlist the services of a brokerage firm with access to these exchanges. Choosing the right broker is the first step in implementing your investment plans.

A full service broker provides a wide range of services—such as marketing research, investment advice, and tax planning—in addition to carrying out your trades.

Discount brokers provide the basic services needed to buy and sell securities, but offer fewer additional services. As you might expect, discount brokers tend to charge significantly lower commissions than full service brokers. In fact, many discount brokers charge flat fees of only a few dollars per trade for basic transactions.

In recent years, competition among brokerage firms has blurred the distinction between full service and discount brokers. To stop clients from defecting to discount brokers, many full service firms have lowered their commissions. At the same time, many discount brokers have begun offering a broader range of services to attract more clients.

> You've got to go out on a limb sometimes, because that's where the fruit is.
> –Will Rogers

### Buying Securities

Once you've chosen your broker you can place orders to buy or sell securities. To do so, you'd contact your broker and indicate the stock you want to buy and how many shares you want to purchase. You can also specify the type of order you want to place. The most common types of orders are market orders and limit orders:

- **Market orders** instruct the broker to buy or sell a security at the current market price. Placing a market order virtually guarantees that your order will be executed. The downside is that you may end up buying at a higher price than you expected to pay (or selling your stock for less than you expected to receive).

- **Limit orders** place limits on the prices at which orders are executed. A buy limit order tells a broker to buy a stock *only* if its price is at or below a specified value. You'd use this approach if you wanted to make sure you didn't pay more for the stock than you thought it was worth. A sell limit order tells your broker to sell the shares only if the price is at or above a specified value. This prevents your broker from selling your stock at a price you believe is too low.

### Strategies for Investing in Securities

How do you choose specific securities to buy? Should you buy and sell on a regular basis? Or should you hold

© STOCKBYTE/GETTY IMAGES

on to securities and ignore short-term fluctuations? Your answers to these questions will reflect the investing strategy you choose. We'll provide an overview of the more common approaches, but as you'll see, none of these approaches is foolproof—investing in securities will always entail some risk.

## Investing for Income

Some investors focus on buying bonds and preferred stocks in order to generate a steady, predictable flow of income. Recall that bonds pay a stated amount of interest each year and that preferred stock usually pays a fixed dividend on a regular basis. These investors may also buy common stock in large, well-established firms with a reputation for paying regular dividends. This approach is popular with retirees who want to supplement their retirement income. The drawback is that the return on such low-risk securities is relatively low, and their market value seldom increases much over time. Thus, it probably isn't the best strategy for younger investors who are trying to accumulate wealth.

## Market Timing

Investors who rely on market timing use a variety of analytical techniques to try to predict when prices of specific stocks are likely to rise and fall. Market timers try to make quick gains by buying low and selling high over a relatively short time horizon.

The problem with market timing is that so many factors can influence stock prices—some of them random in nature—that it's tough to consistently identify the timing and direction of short-run stock price changes. Market timing also requires investors to make frequent trades. Given the commissions and fees the investor pays on every trade, this approach may do a better job of enriching the broker than enriching the investor!

> Anyone who thinks there is safety in numbers hasn't looked at the stock market pages.
>
> –Irene Peter, American writer

## Value Investing

Investors who favor value investing try to find stocks that are undervalued in the market. They believe other investors will eventually recognize the true value of these stocks. When this happens, the demand for the stocks will increase, and the market value will rise, generating an attractive return. This approach requires a lot of research to identify discrepancies between a company's true (or intrinsic) value and its current market price.

The drawback with value investing is that you are in competition with thousands of other investors trying to do the same thing. Unless you're among the first to discover an undervalued stock, the investors who beat you to it will rush to buy up the stock, increasing demand and driving up the stock's price so that it is no longer undervalued.

## Investing for Growth

Investors who focus on growth look for companies that have the potential to grow much faster than average for a sustained period of time, which they believe will lead to stock price growth. Investors using this strategy often invest in stocks of relatively small new companies with innovative products in a hot sector of the economy.

Investing for growth entails a lot of risk. By their very nature, small new companies don't have an established track record. Rapidly expanding industries also tend to attract a lot of start-up companies, so competition can be intense. It's hard to predict which firms will be winners; even experts often make the wrong choice.

## Do You Really Need a Broker to Buy Securities?

When investors want to purchase more stock, the services of a broker are often the best way—and sometimes the only way—to do so. But that's not always the case. Many corporations offer investors the opportunity to buy stock through a direct stock purchase plan (DSPP). This approach allows you to buy stock from the company without having to place an order with your broker, thus avoiding commissions and fees. It's also nice to know that DSPPs are regulated by the SEC. Not all corporations offer this type of plan, but many well-known companies do.

Many companies also offer dividend reinvestment plans (called DRIPs) that allow current stockholders to automatically reinvest their dividends to purchase additional shares of stock. DRIPs are a convenient way to automatically purchase more stock without having to pay brokerage commissions. But watch out: you'll need to pay taxes on the dividends even though you don't get the cash![9]

**Buying and Holding** If you're a patient person with steady nerves, a buy and hold approach might appeal to you. This strategy involves purchasing a diversified set of securities and holding them for a long period of time. Investors who use the buy and hold approach don't usually worry about detailed analysis of individual stocks. Instead, they invest in a broad range of securities and put their faith in the ability of the *overall market* to continue the long-run upward trend it has exhibited throughout its history. The buy and hold strategy seldom enables someone to "get rich quick," but it does usually result in an attractive financial return over the long haul.

Some people who think they're comfortable with a buy and hold strategy end up getting "happy feet" after a few days of declining stock prices. They panic and sell off their stock—often just days before the market starts to rise again! For the buy and hold strategy to work, you've got to have the mental toughness to ride out short-term downturns in the market.

## LO5 Other Types of Securities-related Investments

So far we've discussed a wide variety of strategies and techniques that involve investing directly in specific securities. But, for reasons we'll describe in this section,

many investors find it more attractive to invest in securities indirectly. Two ways to do this are by investing in mutual funds and exchange traded funds. Let's see why these investment options have become so popular.

**mutual fund** An investment vehicle that pools the contributions of many investors and buys a wide array of stocks or other securities.

### Mutual funds

**Mutual funds** pool money from large numbers of individual investors and invest these funds in a variety of stocks, bonds, government securities, and other assets. Each individual investor then shares in the earnings from these investments in proportion to the amount contributed.

Several features make mutual funds a popular choice for investors:

- **Diversification at Relatively Low Cost:** Since you're pooling your funds with thousands of other investors, investing in mutual funds lets you own a broader portfolio of securities at much lower cost than if you tried to invest as an individual.

- **Professional Management:** Many individual investors don't have the time, inclination, or expertise to make complex investment decisions. Most mutual funds have full-time professional managers to make these decisions.

> ❝ Unless you can watch your stock holding decline by 50% without becoming panic stricken, you should not be in the stock market. ❞
> –Warren Buffet

## Oops! What were they THINKING?!

### How Do You Like Them Apples?

In the first 4 years after the introduction of the iPod, Apple's stock price didn't merely rise: it went to the moon. Shares of the Cupertino, California, company soared an astounding 1,600% between 2003 and 2007, making those who bought Apple stock at the beginning of that period very happy—and some of them extremely wealthy. But lots of people missed the boat, having bailed out on the company during a long period of declining prices at the turn of the century. In early 2003, Apple's stock was selling at a price 80% below its peak of a few years earlier.

Those who sold Apple shares in early 2003 and missed out on the mega-gains may find consolation in knowing that the rapid rise in the company's stock over the next 4 years surprised even Apple insiders. One prominent investor who no doubt regretted his lack of faith in Apple Inc. was the company's CEO himself: Steve Jobs.

A big part of Jobs' compensation between 1999 and 2003 was in the form of stock options to buy 55 million shares of Apple stock at prices ranging from $9.15 to $21.80. But in early 2003, the price of Apple's stock had fallen to about $7.50, making the options appear virtually worthless. (An option to buy a stock at a price that's well above the market price isn't attractive.) So just weeks before Apple's stock began its dramatic turnaround, Jobs negotiated with Apple's board of directors to exchange his options for 10 million actual shares of stock worth about $75 million at the time.

The shares of stock Jobs received as the result of his deal were worth over a billion dollars in mid-2007. Not too bad, right? Well, if Jobs had just held on to the options, they would have been worth well over $5 billion. So, Jobs' deal with Apple's board cost him more than $4 billion. One options analyst called it the worst options trade ever made.

Jobs' misstep illustrates how hard it can be to predict price changes for stocks of specific companies. But the huge gains enjoyed by those who bought Apple's stock in early 2003 also illustrate why so many investors attempt to beat the market despite the odds.[10]

- Variety: There are a wide variety of mutual funds available representing a number of different investment strategies. Whatever your investment philosophy, you can probably find a fund that's a good match.

- Liquidity: It's usually easy to withdraw funds from a mutual fund. In most cases, you can log on to your fund's Website, withdraw a specified amount of your money, and have it deposited directly into your bank account.

Not all mutual funds are truly diversified. Some specialize in a single sector of the economy. When a specific sector performs well, mutual funds that specialize in that sector can yield very attractive returns. But such an approach is risky. Just ask investors who held shares in mutual funds that invested heavily in dot-com firms at the beginning of the twenty-first century. (To say that most of these funds tanked in 2001–2002 is putting it kindly.)

## Exchange traded funds

An **exchange traded fund (ETF)** is a hybrid investment that looks something like a stock and something like a mutual fund. When you buy a share in an ETF, you're buying ownership in a "market basket" of many different stocks, similar to a mutual fund. Just as there are many types of mutual funds, there are many types of ETFs. Most ETFs are based on a highly diversified market basket of stocks, but in recent years more narrowly focused ETFs have appeared on the market.

From an investor's perspective, the major difference between ETFs and mutual funds is that shares of ETFs are sold exactly like securities. Unlike mutual funds, which allow investors to buy and sell only at the end of the day, you can buy and sell ETFs any time of the day. Also unlike most mutual funds, ETFs require no minimum initial investment. However, one drawback of ETFs compared to mutual funds is that you have to pay brokerage commissions every time you buy or sell shares. Thus, while you *could* buy only a few ETF shares at a time, the commissions could take a big bite out of any gains.

In recent years ETFs have become a hot investment option. If you're looking for ways to diversify your investments, you should definitely consider them.

## LO6 Keeping Tabs on the Market

Once you've begun to invest in securities, you'll want to keep track of how your investments are doing. Using the Internet, you can easily access more information than ever before about both general market trends and the performance of specific securities.

### Stock Indices

One of the most common ways to track general market conditions and trends is to follow what's happening to various stock indices. A **stock index** provides a means of tracking the prices of a large group of stocks that are

### How about a Friendly Game of Darts?

That's the challenge the *Wall Street Journal* tossed out to big name stock analysts over a period of several years beginning in the late 1980s. Princeton economist Burton Malkiel inspired this challenge by asserting that "a blindfolded monkey throwing darts at a newspaper's financial pages could select a portfolio that would do just as well as one carefully selected by experts."

Each month the *Journal* gave four well-known stock analysts an opportunity to pick one stock each. In lieu of monkeys, the paper asked four of its own staffers to each throw one dart at a copy of the *Journal's* financial pages to randomly select a stock. The *Journal* then compared the return on each of the stocks over a 6-month period.

So, how did the professional stock pickers do compared to the darts? At first glance, the pros seemed to know what they were doing. One study found that, over a period of 100 challenges, the average return for the pros was 10.9%, while for the darts it was only 4.5%. But more careful analysis suggests that these results may be misleading. One reason the pro picks did well was that the *Wall Street Journal* published the expert picks in one of their popular columns, which artificially increased their demand (and price) over the first few days of the challenge period.

The pros also had another edge; the game computed the return only on the stock's capital gain. It ignored any returns earned from dividends. Since the pros knew this, they didn't waste time picking stocks that paid dividends. But the randomly thrown darts couldn't be so selective. They sometimes landed on stocks that paid nice dividends even though they didn't offer much of a capital gain. If the game had taken returns from dividends into account, the performance of dart-selected stocks would have looked better.

Once these and other factors were taken into account, the average return on the dartboard picks was much closer to the return on the analysts' picks. Of course, we'll never know what would have happened if actual blindfolded monkeys had tossed the darts![11]

related in some way. Let's look at some of the best-known and most widely followed indices.

The **Dow Jones Industrial Average** (often called the DJIA or just the Dow) is the most widely followed stock index. The Dow is based on the adjusted average price of 30 stocks picked by the editors of the *Wall Street Journal*. All of the Dow firms are huge, well-established corporations, such as American Express, General Electric, Coca-Cola, Hewlett-Packard, and Disney.

With 500 stocks instead of just 30, The **Standard and Poor's 500** (S&P 500) is a much broader index than the DJIA. Another difference is that the S&P 500 weights the stock prices to reflect the total market value of each stock (called the stock's market capitalization). Most analysts believe that this approach is a better way to compute an index than to simply take an adjusted average of the prices of each stock as the DJIA does. In fact, like the S&P 500, all other key indices weight the stock prices by market capitalization.

There are many other indices, but we'll mention just two more that focus on the U.S. market. The *NASDAQ Composite Index* includes all the domestic and foreign common stocks traded on the NASDAQ exchange. The *Wilshire 5000* index is sometimes called the total stock market index—and this is only a slight exaggeration. It includes the stocks of almost all large, publicly traded U.S. corporations. In fact, though it's called the Wilshire 5000, it now includes over 6,000 stocks.

Indices are also available for foreign stock markets. The *Nikkei 225* index, which tracks the prices of major stocks on the Tokyo Stock Exchange, is one of the best-known foreign indices. Many investors also follow the *FTSE 100*, which tracks the stocks of 100 of the largest companies listed on the London Stock Exchange.

## Tracking the Performance of Specific Securities

Many newspapers offer daily stock market reports, but you can find more current and detailed informa-tion by visiting one of the many Websites that specialize in financial news. To check out a specific stock you simply type the symbol for that stock into a "Get Quote" box. (Don't worry if you're unsure of the symbol—most sites have a lookup feature that finds the symbol if you type in the company's name.)

Let's see how a popular financial Website, *Yahoo! Finance* (http://finance.yahoo.com/), displays information about a specific stock. (Many other financial Websites provide very similar information.) For our illustration we'll look at the information for the common stock issued by NYSE Euronext, the corporation that owns and operates the NYSE. The symbol for this stock is NYX. Exhibit 10.4 shows the information this Website provided for NYSE Euronext's stock on April 24, 2008.

The Yahoo! Website provides a wealth of up-to-date information about NYSE stock, including its price at the end of the day's trading ($66.82) and the fact that this was a $0.53 increase compared to the previous day's closing price. It also shows the day's volume (the total number of shares traded), the stock's market capitalization, and the annual dividend paid per share. Finally, it reports key ratios such as earnings per share (defined in Chapter 9) and the price-earnings ratio which compares the stock's current price to its most recent earnings. On the right hand side of the screen you can view graphs showing how the price of the stock has changed over various time periods ranging from one day to five years. And on the left side of the display you can click on links to a wide variety of other resources, including a profile of the NYSE, comparisons to its key competitors (e.g., Nasdaq), and documents it must file with the SEC.

Financial Websites also have information about other types of securities such as mutual funds, ETFs, and bonds.

> **Dow Jones Industrial Average** A stock index based on the prices of the stocks of 30 large, well-known corporations.
>
> **Standard & Poor's 500** A stock index based on prices of 500 major U.S. corporations in a variety of industries and market sectors.

---

**Exhibit 10.4**  Stock Quote on Yahoo! Finance[12]

**NYSE EURONEXT** (NYSE: NYX)

After Hours: 67.01 ↑ 0.19 (0.28%) as of 4:50PM ET on 04/24/08

**Charts**
Interactive
Basic Chart
Basic Tech. Analysis

**News & Info**
Headlines
Financial Blogs
Company Events
Message Board

**Company**
Profile
Key Statistics
SEC Filings
Competitors
Industry

| | | | |
|---|---|---|---|
| Last Trade: | **66.82** | Day's Range: | 66.22 - 67.55 |
| Trade Time: | 4:00PM ET | 52wk Range: | 55.12 - 95.25 |
| Change: | ↑ 0.53 (0.80%) | Volume: | 2,429,228 |
| Prev Close: | 66.29 | Avg Vol (3m): | 3,955,120 |
| Open: | 66.22 | Market Cap: | 17.73B |
| Bid: | N/A | P/E (ttm): | 24.73 |
| Ask: | N/A | EPS (ttm): | 2.70 |
| 1y Target Est: | 84.00 | Div & Yield: | 1.20 (1.80%) |

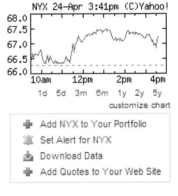

NYX 24-Apr 3:41pm (C)Yahoo!

1d 5d 3m 6m 1y 2y 5y
customize chart

✚ Add NYX to Your Portfolio
🔔 Set Alert for NYX
⬇ Download Data
✚ Add Quotes to Your Web Site

Quotes delayed, except where indicated otherwise. For consolidated real-time quotes (incl. pre/post market data), sign up for a free trial of Real-time Quotes.

## CHAPTER 11

# Marketing: Building Profitable Customer Connections

## LEARNING OBJECTIVES

After studying this chapter, you will be able to...

**LO1** Discuss the objectives, the process, and the scope of marketing

**LO2** Identify the role of the customer in marketing

**LO3** Explain each element of marketing strategy

**LO4** Describe the consumer and business decision-making process

**LO5** Discuss the key elements of marketing research

**LO6** Explain the roles of social responsibility and technology in marketing

4ltrpress.cengage.com/busn

## If opportunity doesn't knock, build a door.
–Milton Berle, actor and comedian

## LO1 Marketing: Getting Value by Giving Value

What comes to mind when you hear the term **marketing**? Most people think of the radio ad they heard this morning, or the billboard they saw while driving to school. But advertising is only a small part of marketing; the whole story is much bigger. The American Marketing Association defines marketing as *an organizational function and a set of processes for creating, communicating, and delivering value to customers and for managing customer relationships in ways that benefit the organization and its stakeholders.*

Let's start at the end of that definition. The key benefit that most businesses seek is long-term profitability. But attaining this benefit is impossible without first delivering value to customers. A successful marketer delivers value by filling customer needs in ways that exceed their expectations. As a result, you get sales today and sales tomorrow and sales the next day, which—across the days and months and years—can translate into long-term profitability. Alice Foote MacDougall, a successful entrepreneur in the 1920s, understood this thinking early on: "In business you get what you want by giving other people what they want." **Utility** is the ability of goods and services to satisfy these wants. And since there is a wide range of wants, products can provide utility in a number of different ways:

- **Form utility** satisfies wants by converting inputs into a finished form. Clearly, the vast majority of products provide some kind of form utility. For example, Jamba Juice pulverizes fruit, juices, and yogurt into yummy smoothies, and McDonald's slices, dices, and sizzles potatoes into french fries.

- **Time utility** satisfies wants by providing goods and services at a convenient time for customers. For example, FedEx delivers some parcels on Sunday, LensCrafters makes eyeglasses within about an hour, 7-Eleven opens early and closes late, and e-commerce, of course, provides the ultimate 24-7 convenience.

- **Place utility** satisfies wants by providing goods and services at a convenient place for customers. For example, ATMs offer banking services in many large supermarkets, Motel 6 lodges tired travelers at the bottom of highway off-ramps, and vending machines

**marketing** An organizational function and a set of processes for creating, communicating, and delivering value to customers and for managing customer relationships in ways that benefit the organization and its stakeholders.

**NOTE:** Visit 4ltrpress.cengage.com/busn to view an alternate page 137 containing the American Marketing Association's new definition of marketing.

**utility** The ability of goods and services to satisfy consumer "wants."

**form utility** The power of a good or a service to satisfy customer "wants" by converting inputs into a finished form.

**time utility** The power of a good or a service to satisfy customer "wants" by providing goods and services at a convenient time for customers.

**place utility** The power of a good or a service to satisfy customer "wants" by providing goods and services at a convenient place for customers.

refuel tired students at virtually every college campus.

- **Ownership utility** satisfies wants by smoothly transferring ownership of goods and services from seller to buyer. Virtually every product provides some degree of ownership utility, but some offer more than others. Apple computer, for example, has created a hassle-free purchase process that customers can follow by phone, by computer, and in-person.

Satisfying customer wants—in a way that exceeds expectations—is a job that never ends. Jay Levinson, a recognized expert at breakthrough marketing, comments, "Marketing is...a process. You improve it, perfect it, change it, even pause it. But you never stop it completely."

## The Scope of Marketing: It's Everywhere!

For many years, businesspeople have actively applied the principles of marketing to goods and services that range from cars, to fast food, to liquor, to computers, to movies. But within the last decade or two, other organizations have successfully adopted marketing strategies and tactics to further their goals.

Nonprofit organizations—in both the private and the public sectors—play a significant role in our economy, employing more people than the federal government and all 50 state governments combined (not to mention an army of volunteers!). These organizations use marketing, sometimes quite assertively, to achieve their objectives. The U.S military's advertising budget, for example, is about $600-$700 million, which ranks on the list of top

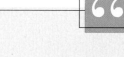

> ## Advertising is the 'wonder' in Wonder Bread.
> –Jef I. Richards, advertising professor and author

U.S. advertisers. Your own college probably markets itself to both prospective students and potential alumni donors. Private sector nonprofit organizations also use marketing strategies for everything from marshaling AYSO soccer coaches for kids, to boosting attendance at the local zoo, to planning cultural events.[1]

Nonprofit organizations play a pivotal role in the expansion of marketing across our economy to include people, places, events, and ideas. But for-profit enterprises have also begun to apply marketing strategies and tactics beyond simply goods and services.

- People Marketing: Sports, politics, and art dominate in this category. Kobe Bryant, for example, could probably use some marketing to rehabilitate his image. Arnold Schwarzenegger marketed himself brilliantly throughout the governor's race in California. And after the 2004 Super Bowl "wardrobe malfunction," effective marketing helped Justin emerge unscathed, while Janet's reputation plummeted. In fact, as you pursue your personal goals—whether you seek a new job or a Friday night date—people marketing principles can help you achieve your objective. Start by figuring out what your "customer" needs, and then ensure that your "product" (you!) delivers above and beyond expectations.

- Place Marketing: This category involves drawing people to a particular place. Cities and states use place marketing to attract businesses. Delaware, for instance, the second smallest state in the union, is home to more than half of the Fortune 500 firms because Delaware deliberately developed a range of advantages for corporations. But more visibly, cities, states, and nations use place marketing to attract tourists. Las Vegas offers an excellent example with its high profile sales pitch: "What happens here, stays here."

## Sin City Goes Back to Its Roots

In 2003 Las Vegas embraced its seedy heritage with the high profile launch of a new positioning: *What Happens Here Stays Here*. With ads splashed across TV and billboards nationwide, the tagline has become a pop culture mainstay. The outsized results have been fitting for a city that celebrates extremes. In 2004, a record 37.4 million visitors passed through Las Vegas, and the number has grown higher each year, even as the economy slowed in 2007. And the visitors have brought open wallets; since 2003, yearly expenditures on shopping, dining, entertainment, lodging, and gambling have increased 35%. With three major new resorts slated to open by 2010, experts expect the growth to continue. So while anything goes in Las Vegas, the money is one thing that definitely stays.[2]

© THINKSTOCK IMAGES/JUPITERIMAGES

The 2008 Beijing Olympics provided a golden opportunity for China to market itself to the world.

© XINHUA/LANDOV

- Event Marketing: This category includes marketing—or sponsoring—athletic, cultural, or charitable events. Partnerships between the public and private sectors are increasingly common. Examples include the Olympics, the Super Bowl, or the MusicForRelief concert to benefit victims of the Indian Ocean tsunami.

- Idea Marketing: A whole range of public and private organizations market ideas that are meant to change how people think or act. Buckle your seatbelt, support our political party, recycle, donate blood, don't pollute, don't smoke; all are examples of popular causes. Often, idea marketing and event marketing are combined, as we see in the annual Avon Walk for Breast

Cancer. The planners actively market the idea of annual mammograms, as they solicit contributions for breast cancer research and participation in the event itself.

## The Evolution of Marketing: From the Product to the Customer

The current approach to marketing evolved through a number of overlapping stages, as you'll see in exhibit 11.1. But as you read about these eras, keep in mind that some businesses have remained lodged—with varying degrees of success—in the thinking of a past era.

Production Era Marketing didn't always begin with the customer. In fact, in the early 1900s, the customer was practically a joke. Henry Ford summed up the prevailing

**Exhibit 11.1**   The Evolution of Marketing

The focus of marketing has evolved over time.

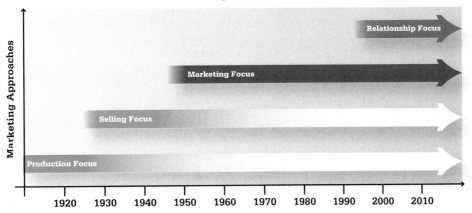

Marketing Approaches

Relationship Focus

Marketing Focus

Selling Focus

Production Focus

1920  1930  1940  1950  1960  1970  1980  1990  2000  2010

While individual firms differ in their approach to marketing, the prevailing view at leading edge firms has changed over time as shown here.

mindset when he reportedly said "You can have your Model T in any color you want as long as it's black." This attitude made sense from a historical perspective, since consumers didn't have the overwhelming number of choices that are currently available; most products were purchased as soon as they were produced and distributed to consumers. In this context, the top business priority was to produce large quantities of goods as efficiently as possible.

**Selling Era** By the 1920s, production capacity had increased dramatically. For the first time, supply in many categories exceeded demand, which caused the emergence of the hard sell. The selling focus gained momentum in the 1930s and 1940s, when the Depression and World War II made consumers even more reluctant to part with their limited money.

**Marketing Era** But the landscape changed dramatically in the 1950s. Many factories that had churned out military supplies converted to consumer production, flooding the market with choices in virtually every product category. An era of relative peace and prosperity emerged, and—as soldiers returned from World War II—marriage and birthrates soared. To compete for the consumer's dollar, marketers attempted to provide goods and services that met customer needs better than anything else on the market. As a result, the marketing concept materialized in the 1950s. The **marketing concept** is a philosophy that makes customer satisfaction—now and in the future— the central focus of the entire organization. Companies that embrace this philosophy strive to delight customers, integrating this goal into all business activities. The marketing concept holds that delivering unmatched value to customers is the only effective way to achieve long-term profitability.

**Relationship Era** The marketing concept has gathered momentum across the economy, leading to the current era, unfolding over the last decade, which zeros-in on long-term customer relationships. Acquiring a new customer can cost five times more than keeping an existing customer. Retaining your current customers—and getting them to spend additional dollars—is clearly cost effective. Moreover, satisfied customers can develop into advocates for your business, becoming powerful generators of positive "word-of-mouth."

# LO2 The Customer: Front and Center

**Customer relationship management (CRM)** is the centerpiece of successful, 21st century marketing. Broadly defined, CRM is the on-going process of acquiring, maintaining, and growing profitable customer relationships by delivering unmatched value. CRM works best when marketers combine marketing communication with one-on-one personalization. Amazon is a champion player at CRM, greeting customers by name, recommending specific products, and providing streamlined checkout. Clearly, information is an integral part of this process—you simply can't do CRM without collecting, managing, and applying the right data at the right time for the right person (and every repeat customer is the "right person"!).

**Limited relationships** Clearly the scope of your relationships will depend not just on the data you gather but also on your industry. Colgate-Palmolive, for example, can't forge a close personal bond with every person who buys a bar of Irish Spring soap. However, they do invite customers to call their toll-free line with questions or comments, and they maintain a vibrant Website with music, an e-newsletter, special offers, and an invitation to contact the company. You can bet that they actively gather data and pursue a connection with customers who do initiate contact.

**Full Partnerships** If you have a high-ticket product and a smaller customer base, you're much more likely to pursue a full partnership with each of your key clients. Colgate-Palmolive, for instance, has dedicated customer service teams working with key accounts such as Wal-Mart and Costco. With a full partnership, the marketer gathers and leverages extensive information about each customer, and often includes the customer in key aspects of the product development process.

## Value

You know you've delivered **value** when your customers believe that your product has a better relationship between the cost and the benefits than any competitor. By this definition low cost does not always mean high value. In fact, a recent survey suggests that loyal customers are often willing to pay *more for* their products rather than switch to lower cost competitors. Apple provides a

© ERICKA MCCONNELL/BOTANICA/JUPITERIMAGES

clear example. We probably all personally know at least a handful of Apple fanatics who gladly pay far more for their Macs (or their PowerBooks or their iPods) than they would pay for a competing product.[3]

*Perceived Value versus Actual Value*   The operative idea here is *perceived*. Simply creating value isn't enough; you also must help customers believe that your product is uniquely qualified to meet their needs. This becomes a particular challenge when you're a new business competing against a market leader with disproportionately strong perceived value.

## Customer Satisfaction

You know you've satisfied your customers when you deliver perceived value above and beyond their expectations. But achieving **customer satisfaction** can be tricky. Less savvy marketers frequently fall into one of two traps:

- The first trap is overpromising. Even if you deliver more value than anyone else, your customers will be disappointed if your product falls short of overly high expectations. The messages that you send regarding your product influence expectations—keep them real!

- The second trap is underpromising. If you don't set expectations high enough, too few customers will be willing to try your product. The result will be a tiny base of highly satisfied customers, which usually isn't enough to sustain a business.

Finding the right balance is tricky, but clearly not impossible. Judging by their high scores on the American Customer Satisfaction Index, the following companies come close to mastering the art of customer satisfaction: eBay, Ford, Apple, Whirlpool, Google, State Farm, and Publix (grocery chain).[4]

## Customer Loyalty

**Customer loyalty** is the payoff from delivering value and generating satisfaction. Loyal customers purchase from you again and again—and they sometimes even pay more for your product. They forgive your mistakes. They provide valuable feedback. They may require less service. They refer their friends (and sometimes even strangers). Moreover, studying your loyal customers can give you a competitive edge for acquiring new ones, since people with a similar profile would likely be a great fit for your products.[5]

## LO3 Marketing Strategy: Where Are You Going And How Will You Get There?

In marketing terms, the question becomes: Who is your target audience and how will you reach them? Many successful firms answer this question by developing a formal **marketing plan**, updated on a yearly basis; other firms handle their planning on a more informal basis. But regardless of the specific approach, the first step in planning your marketing strategy should be to determine where to target your efforts. Who are those people who are most likely to buy your products? The first step is **market segmentation**—dividing your marketing into groups of people, or segments, which are similar to one another and different from everyone else. One or more of these segments will be your target market. Once you've identified your target market, your next step is to determine how you can best use marketing tools to reach them. And finally, you need to anticipate and respond to changes in the external environment. This section will define target market, explain market segmentation, introduce the marketing mix, and review the key factors in the marketing environment. Taken together, these elements will shape an effective marketing strategy, as shown in exhibit 11.2.

**Exhibit 11.2**   Marketing Strategy

The marketer creates the marketing mix but responds to the marketing environment with a single-minded focus on the target market.

**target market** The group of people who are most likely to buy a particular product.

**consumer marketers (also known as business-to-consumer or B2C)** Marketers who direct their efforts toward people who are buying products for personal consumption.

**business marketers (also known as business-to-business or B2B)** Marketers who direct their efforts toward people who are buying products to use either directly or indirectly to produce other products.

**demographic segmentation** Dividing the market into smaller groups based on measurable characteristics about people such as age, income, ethnicity, and gender.

## Target Market

Your **target market** is the group of people who are most likely to buy your product. This is where you should concentrate your marketing efforts. But why not target your efforts toward everyone? After all, even if most middle-aged moms wouldn't buy purple polka-dotted mini skirts, an adventurous few just might do it. Well, you can always hope for the adventurous few, but virtually every business has limited resources, and marketing toward the people who are most likely to buy your flamboyant minis—say, teenage girls—will maximize the impact of each dollar you spend. A well-chosen target market embodies the following characteristics:

- Size: There must be enough people in your target group to support a business.

- Profitability: The people must be willing and able to spend more than the cost of producing and marketing your product.

- Accessibility: Your target must be reachable through channels that your business can afford.

- Limited competition: Look for markets with limited competition; a crowded market is much tougher to crack.

## Consumer Markets versus Business Markets

**Consumer marketers** (B2C) direct their efforts to people who are buying products for personal consumption (e.g., candy bars, shampoo, and clothing), whereas **business marketers** (B2B) direct their efforts to customers who are buying products to use either directly or indirectly to produce other products (e.g., tractors, steel, and cash registers). But keep in mind that the distinction between the market categories is not in the products themselves; rather, it lies in how the buyer will use the product. For instance, shampoo that you buy for yourself is clearly a consumer product, but shampoo that a hair stylist buys for a salon is a business product. Similarly, a computer that you buy for yourself is a consumer product, but a computer that your school buys for the computer lab is a business product. Both B2C and B2B marketers need to choose the best target, but they tend to follow slightly different approaches.

## Consumer Market Segmentation

Choosing the best target market (or markets) for your product begins with dividing your market into segments, or groups of people who have similar characteristics. But people can be similar in a number of different ways, so not surprisingly, marketers have several options for segmenting potential consumers.

Demographic B2C **demographic segmentation** refers to dividing the market based on measurable characteristics about people such as age, income, ethnicity, and gender. Demographics are a vital starting point for most marketers. Mattel, for example, targets kids, while Howard Stern targets young men, and BMW targets the wealthy. Sometimes the demographic make-up of a given market is tough to discern; African American artists, for

### A Marketing Fiesta

You probably already know that in 2001, Latinos surpassed African Americans as the largest minority group in the United States. But you may not know that in key cities and states—especially across the southwest—Hispanics are rapidly becoming the dominant population group. In California, for instance, about one of every two babies born is Hispanic. And this burgeoning market has money. In the past 15 years, U.S. Latino buying power has more than tripled, reaching $686 billion. Experts predict that before the end of the decade, it will grow an additional 45% to $992 billion.

Reaching this market requires an understanding of consumers who have distinctive characteristics well beyond language. Hispanics, for instance, tend to spend more on their children and less on their pets than the general population. They also value different product features. For example, research suggests that nearly two-thirds of Hispanic customers seek highly scented products, compared to about one-third of the general population.

Targeting the surging Latino market may be more efficient than targeting other segments of the population. Latino consumers are much more likely than the overall population to respond to advertising, and to discuss ads with their family and friends. And Spanish-speaking Hispanics are 16% more brand loyal than the general population. Focusing on Latinos can clearly add value. If marketers pay attention, the result could be extra salsa for their bottom lines.[6]

© CREATAS IMAGES/JUPITERIMAGES

instance, create the bulk of rap music, yet Caucasian suburban males form the bulk of the rap music market.

Geographic B2C **geographic segmentation** refers to dividing the market based on where consumers live. This process can incorporate countries, or cities, or population density as key factors. For instance, Toyota Sequoia does not concentrate on European markets, where tiny, winding streets and nonexistent parking are common in many cities. Cosmetic surgeons tend to market their services more heavily in urban rather than rural areas. And finding a great surfboard is easy in California, but more challenging in South Dakota.

Magazine publishers use segmentation to zero in on their specific target audiences.

Psychographic B2C **psychographic segmentation** refers to dividing the market based on consumer attitudes, interests, values, and lifestyles. Porsche, for instance, in preparation for the introduction of the Cayenne, targeted consumers who seek the thrill of driving. A number of companies have found a highly profitable niche providing upscale wilderness experiences for people who seek all the pleasure with none of the pain (you enjoy the great outdoors, while someone else lugs your gear, pours your wine, slices your goat cheese, and inflates your extra-comfy air mattress). And magazine racks are filled with products geared toward psychographic segments, from *People* magazine, to *Sports Illustrated*, to *InfoWorld*, to *Cosmopolitan*. NOTE: Marketers typically use psychographics to complement other segmentation approaches, rather than to provide the core definition.[7]

Behavioral B2C **behavioral segmentation** refers to dividing the market based on how people behave toward various products. This category includes both the benefits that consumers seek from products and how consumers use the product. The Neutrogena Corporation, for example, built a multimillion dollar hair care business by targeting consumers who wanted an occasional break from their favorite shampoo. Countless products such as Miller Lite actively target the low-carbohydrate consumer. But perhaps the most common type of behavioral segmentation is based on usage patterns. Fast food restaurants, for instance, actively target heavy users (who, ironically, tend to be slender): young

men in their 20s and 30s. This group consumes about 17% of their total calories from fast food, compared to 12% for adults in general. Understanding the usage patterns of your customer base gives you the option of either focusing on your core users, or trying to pull light users into your core market.[8]

## Business Market Segmentation

B2B marketers typically follow a similar process in segmenting their markets, but they use slightly different categories:

Geographic B2B geographic segmentation refers to dividing the market based on the concentration of customers. Many industries tend to be highly clustered in certain areas, such as technology in California, and auto suppliers in the "auto corridor" that stretches south from Michigan to Tennessee. Geographic segmentation, of course, is especially common on an international basis where variables such as language, culture, income, and regulatory differences can play a crucial role.

Customer-based B2B customer-based segmentation refers to dividing the market based on the characteristics of customers. This approach includes a range of possibilities. Some B2B marketers segment based on customer size. Others segment based on customer type. Johnson&Johnson, for example, has a group of salespeople dedicated exclusively to retail accounts such as Target and Publix, while other salespeople focus solely on motivating doctors to recommend their products. Other potential B2B markets include institutions—schools and hospitals, for instance, are key segments for Heinz Ketchup—and the government.

Product-use-based B2B product-use-based segmentation refers to dividing the market based on how customers will use the product. Small and mid-sized companies find this strategy especially helpful in narrowing their target markets. Possibilities include the ability to support certain software packages or production systems or the desire to serve certain customer groups such as long-distance truckers or restaurants that deliver food.

## The Marketing Mix

Once you've clearly defined your target market, your next challenge is to develop compelling strategies for product, price, distribution, and promotion. The blending of these elements becomes your **marketing mix**, as shown in exhibit 11.3 on the following page.

**geographic segmentation** Dividing the market into smaller groups based on where consumers live. This process can incorporate countries, or cities, or population density as key factors.

**psychographic segmentation** Dividing the market into smaller groups based on consumer attitudes, interests, values, and lifestyles.

**behavioral segmentation** Dividing the market based on how people behave toward various products. This category includes both the benefits that consumers seek from products and how consumers use the product.

**marketing mix** The blend of marketing strategies for product, price, distribution, and promotion.

Exhibit 11.3 Marketing Mix

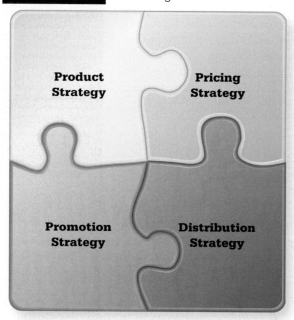

Product Strategy

Pricing Strategy

Promotion Strategy

Distribution Strategy

- **Product Strategy:** Your product involves far more than simply a tangible good or a specific service. Product strategy decisions range from brand name, to product image, to package design, to customer service, to guarantees, to new product development, and more. Designing the best product clearly begins with understanding the needs of your target market.

- **Pricing Strategy:** Pricing is a challenging area of the marketing mix. To deliver customer value, your prices must be fair relative to the benefits of your product. Other factors include competition, regula-

tion, and public opinion. Your product category plays a critical role, as well. A low-cost desk, for instance, might be appealing, but who would want discount-priced knee surgery?

- **Distribution Strategy:** The goal is to deliver your product to the right people, in the right quantities, at the right time, in the right place. The key decisions include shipping, warehousing, and selling outlets (e.g., the Web versus network marketing versus brick-and-mortar stores). The implications of these decisions for product image and customer satisfaction can be significant.

- **Promotion Strategy:** Promotion includes all of the ways that marketers communicate about their products. The list of possibilities is long and growing, especially as the Internet continues to evolve at breakneck speed. Key elements today include advertising, personal selling, sales promotion, public relations, word-of-mouth, and product placement. Successful promotional strategies typically evolve in response to both customer needs and competition. A number of innovative companies are even inviting their customers to participate in creating their advertising through venues such as YouTube. Check out exhibit 11.4 to see how easily you can analyze promotional strategies.

## The Global Marketing Mix

As you decide to enter foreign markets, you'll need to reevaluate your marketing mix for each new country. Should it change? If so, how should it change? Many business goods simply don't require much change in the marketing mix, since their success isn't dependent on culture. Examples include heavy machinery, cement, and farming

Exhibit 11.4 Analyzing Promotional Strategies

Who is the target audience for each of these ads? How does each ad position the product relative to the competition? Which strategy is most effective? Why?

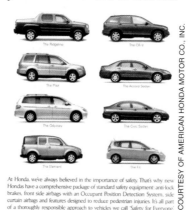

equipment. Consumer products, however, often require completely new marketing mixes to effectively reach their consumers.

Nike's approach to marketing in China offers an interesting example of how one firm managed the complex process of building a successful business in a foreign market. When Nike first entered China in the 1990s, the company seemed to face an insurmountable challenge: Not only did a pair of Nike sneakers cost twice the Chinese average monthly salary, but most Chinese just didn't play sports, according to Terry Rhoads, then director of Nike sports marketing. So he boldly set out to change that. Rhoads created a Nike high school basketball league, which has since spread to 17 cities. To loosen up fans, he blasted canned cheering during games and arranged for national TV coverage of the finals. He leveraged connections with the NBA to bring Michael Jordan for visits.

The gamble quickly paid off, as the Chinese middle class emerged—along with more individualistic values—which are a strong fit with the Nike ethos. By 2001, Nike had dubbed their marketing approach "hip hoop," which they described as an effort to "connect Nike with a creative lifestyle." Sales in 2008 reached an estimated $1 billion, and a recent survey suggests that college students consider Nike the world's coolest brand by more than double the margin of the nearest contender.[9]

## The Marketing Environment

While marketers actively influence the elements of the marketing mix, they must anticipate and respond to the elements of the external environment, which they typically cannot control. **Environmental scanning** is a key tool; the goal is simply to continually collect information from sources that range from informal networks, to industry newsletters, to the general press, to customers, to suppliers, to the competition, among others.

The key elements of the external environment include the following components:

Competitive   The dynamic competitive environment probably affects marketers on a day-to-day basis more than any other element. Understanding the competitive environment often begins with analysis of **market share**, or the percentage of the marketplace that each firm controls. To avoid ambushes—and to uncover new opportunities—you must continually monitor how both dominant and emerging competitors handle each element of their marketing mix. And don't forget indirect competitors, who meet the same consumer needs as you but with a completely different product (e.g., cable TV and Internet games).

Economic   The only certainty in the economic environment is change, but the timing of expansions and contractions is virtually impossible to predict. Your goal as a marketer is to identify and respond to changes as soon as possible, keeping in mind that a sharp eye sees opportunity even in economic downturns. For instance, affordable luxuries and do-it-yourself enterprises can thrive during recessions.

Social/Cultural   The social/cultural element covers a vast array of factors including lifestyle, customs, language, attitudes, interests, and population shifts. Trends can change rapidly, with a dramatic

**environmental scanning** The process of continually collecting information from the external marketing environment.

**market share** The percentage of a market controlled by a given marketer.

### Grassroots Marketing Is a Bunch of Bull...Red Bull!

Creating extraordinary momentum though word-of-mouth, Red Bull single-handedly created the energy drink category, which they continue to dominate on a worldwide basis. Red Bull launched in Europe in 1987 with a novel strategy. They basically gave cases of the product to student advocates and encouraged them to throw parties. This grassroots approach developed credibility for the brand among young consumers who are increasingly cynical about product promotion. And as an added bonus, student advocates helped Red Bull marketers stay closely in touch with their changing market. Before long, Red Bull and vodka were a favorite drink order at European clubs and all-night raves. (To build the buzz, Red Bull marketers sometimes even left empty cans of Red Bull on tables in party hot spots.) After ten years of success in Europe, Red Bull launched in the United States in 1997, where they are now available in all 50 states.

Red Bull continues to leverage word-of-mouth, but the firm also sponsors a number of extreme sports—such as skydiving, mountain biking, and skateboarding—that fit well with their slogan "Red Bull gives you wings." Possibly the most innovative Red Bull event is their annual series of "Flugtags," which encourage competitors to build their own flying machines and fly into a body of water such as the Pacific Ocean in Santa Monica, or the Serpentine in Hyde Park, London. They also sponsor the Red Bull Music Academy, which trains aspiring DJs—an excellent fit with the Red Bull club connection.

Looking ahead, Red Bull's challenge will be to stay connected to the evolving (and fickle) youth culture as the brand becomes increasingly mainstream.[10]

impact on marketing decisions. Anticipating and responding to trends can be especially important in industries such as entertainment, fashion, and technology. Nokia, for instance, lost market share when they failed to respond quickly enough to the shift toward camera phones.

### Technological
Changes in technology can be very visible to consumers (e.g., the introduction of the iPod once MP3 music files emerged on the market). However, technology often impacts marketers in ways that are less directly visible. For example, technology allows for mass customization of Levi's blue jeans at a reasonable price and facilitates just-in-time inventory management for countless companies who see the results in their bottom lines.

### Political/Legal
The political/legal area includes laws, regulations, and political climate. Most U.S. laws and regulations are clear (e.g., dry counties in certain states), but others are complex and evolving (e.g., qualifications for certain tax breaks). Political climate includes changing levels of governmental support for various business categories. Clearly, the political/legal issues affect heavily regulated sectors (e.g., telecommunications and pharmaceuticals) more than others.

### The Global Marketing Environment

As the Internet has grown, the world market has become accessible to virtually every business. This boosts the importance of understanding each element of the marketing environment—competitive, economic, social/cultural, technological, and political/legal—in each of your key markets. Among the biggest global challenges are researching opportunities in other countries, and delivering your product to customers in other countries.

## LO4 Customer Behavior: Decisions, Decisions, Decisions!

If successful marketing begins with the customer, then understanding the customer is critical. Why do people buy one product but not another? How do they use the products they buy? When do they get rid of them? Knowing the answers to these questions will clearly help you better meet customer needs.

### Consumer Behavior

**Consumer behavior** refers specifically to how people act when they are buying products for their own personal consumption. The decisions they make often seem spontaneous (after all, how much thought do you give to buying a pack of gum?), but they often result from a complex set of influences, as shown in exhibit 11.5.

Marketers, of course, add their own influence through the marketing mix. For instance, after smelling pretzels in the mall and tasting pretzel morsels from the sample tray, many of us would at least be tempted to cough up the cash for a hot, buttery pretzel of our own... regardless of any other factors! Similarly, changes in the external environment—for example, a series of hurricanes in Florida—dramatically affect consumer decisions about items such as flashlights, batteries, and plywood.

© RUBBERBALL/JUPITERIMAGES

All these forces shape consumer behavior in each step of the process regarding purchase decisions. Here's how the consumer decision process works:

**Need Recognition**
Your best friend suddenly notices that she is the only person she knows who still wears high-rise blue jeans to class...problem alert!

**Information Search**
Horrified, your friend not only checks out your style, but also notices what the cool girls on campus are wearing. AND she snitches your copy of *Cosmo* to leaf through the ads.

**Evaluation of Alternatives**
Your friend compares the prices and styles of the various brands of blue jeans that she identifies.

**Purchase Decision**
After a number of conversations, your friend finally decides to buy True Religion jeans for $215.

**Postpurchase Behavior**
Three days later, she begins to kick herself for spending so much money on jeans, because she can no longer afford her daily Starbucks habit.

Clearly, marketing can influence the purchase decision every step of the way, from helping consumers identify needs (or problems), to resolving that awful feeling of **cognitive dissonance** (or kicking oneself) after a major purchase. Some marketers attempt to avoid cognitive dissonance altogether by developing specific programs

## Exhibit 11.5 — Elements that Influence the Consumer Decision-Making Process

| Influence | Description |
|---|---|
| Cultural | *Culture:* The values, attitudes, customs shared by members of a society<br>*Subculture:* A smaller division of the broader culture<br>*Social Class:* Societal position driven largely by income and occupation |
| Social | *Family:* A powerful force in consumption choices<br>*Friends:* Another powerful force, especially for high-profile purchases<br>*Reference Groups:* Groups that give consumers a point of comparison |
| Personal | *Demographics:* Measurable characteristics such as age, gender, income<br>*Personality:* The mix of traits that determine who you are |
| Psychological | *Motivation:* Pressing needs that tend to generate action<br>*Attitudes:* Lasting evaluations of (or feelings about) objects or ideas<br>*Perceptions:* How people select, organize, and interpret information<br>*Learning:* Changes in behavior based on experience |

## LO5 Marketing Research: So What Do They REALLY Think?

If marketing begins with the customer, marketing research is the foundation of success. **Marketing research** involves gathering, interpreting, and applying information to uncover opportunities and challenges. The goal, of course, is better marketing decisions: more value for consumers and more profits for businesses that deliver. Companies use marketing research in a number of different areas:

- To identify external opportunities and threats (from competition to social trends).

- To monitor and predict customer behavior.

- To evaluate and improve each area of the marketing mix.

### Types of Data

There are two main categories of marketing research data—**secondary data** and **primary data**—each with its own set of benefits and drawbacks.

| Secondary Data:<br>Existing Data That Marketers Gather or Purchase | Primary Data:<br>New Data That Marketers Compile for the First Time |
|---|---|
| Tends to be lower cost | Tends to be more expensive |
| May not meet your *specific* needs | Customized to meet your needs |
| Frequently outdated | Fresh, new data |
| Available to your competitors | Proprietary—no one else has it |
| *Examples:* U.S. Census, *Wall Street Journal, Time* magazine, your product sales history | Examples: Your own surveys, focus groups, customer comments, mall interviews |

Clearly, it makes sense to gather secondary data before you invest in primary research. Look at your company's internal information. What does previous research say? What does the press say? What can you find on the Web? Once you've looked at the secondary research, you may find that primary research is unnecessary. But if not, your secondary research will guide your primary research and make it more focused and relevant, which ends up saving time and money.

**business buyer behavior** Describes how people act when they are buying products to use either directly or indirectly to produce other products.

**marketing research** The process of gathering, interpreting, and applying information to uncover marketing opportunities and challenges, and to make better marketing decisions.

**secondary data** Existing data that marketers gather or purchase for a research project.

**primary data** New data that marketers compile for a specific research project.

to help customers validate their purchase choices. One example might be postpurchase mailings that highlight the accolades received by an expensive product.

But does every consumer go through every step of the process all the time? That's clearly not the case! People make low involvement decisions (such as buying that pack of gum) according to habit…or even just on a whim. But when the stakes are high—either financially or socially—most people move through the five steps of the classic decision-making process. For example, most of us wouldn't think of buying a car, a computer, or the "right" pair of blue jeans without stepping through the decision-making process.

### Business Buyer Behavior

**Business buyer behavior** refers to how people act when they're buying products to use either directly or indirectly to produce other products (e.g., chemicals, copy paper, computer servers). Business buyers typically have purchasing training and apply rational criteria to their decision-making process. They usually buy according to purchase specifications and objective standards, with a minimum of personal judgment or whim. Often, business buyers are integrating input from a number of internal sources, based on a relatively formal process. And finally, business buyers tend to seek (and often secure) highly customized goods, services, and prices.

## Primary Research Tools

There are two basic categories of primary research: observation and survey.

**Observation Research** **Observation research** happens when the researcher *does not* directly interact with the research subject. The key advantage of watching versus asking is that what people actually *do* often differs from what they *say*—sometimes quite innocently. For instance, if an amusement park employee stands outside an attraction and records which way people turn when they exit, he may be conducting observation research to determine where to place a new lemonade stand. Watching would be better than asking because many people could not honestly say which way they'd likely turn. Examples of observation research include:

- Scanner data from retail sales.
- Traffic counters to determine where to place for billboards.
- Garbage analysis to measure recycling compliance.

Observation research can be both cheap and amazingly effective. A car dealership, for instance, can survey the preset radio stations on every car that comes in for service. That information helps them choose which stations to use for advertising. But the biggest downside of observation research is that it doesn't yield any information on consumer motivation—the reasons behind consumer decisions. The preset radio stations wouldn't matter, for example, if the bulk of drivers listen only to CDs in the car.

**Survey research** happens when the researcher *does* interact with research subjects. The key advantage is that you can secure information about what people are thinking and feeling, beyond what you can observe. For example, a carmaker might observe that the majority of its purchasers are men. They could use this information to tailor their advertising to men, or they could do survey research and possibly learn that even though men do the actual purchasing, women often make the purchase decision...a very different scenario! But the key downside

of survey research is that many people aren't honest or accurate about their experiences, opinions, and motivations, which can make survey research quite misleading. Examples of survey research include:

- Telephone and on-line questionnaires
- Door-to-door interviews.
- Mall-intercept interviews.
    - Focus groups.
        - Mail-in questionnaires.

## An International Perspective

Doing marketing research across multiple countries can be an overwhelming challenge. In parts of Latin America, for instance, many homes don't have telephone connections, so the results from telephone surveys could be very misleading. Door-to-door tends to be a better approach. But in parts of the Middle East, researchers could be arrested for knocking on a stranger's door, especially if they aren't dressed according to local standards. Because of these kinds of issues, many companies hire research firms with a strong local presence (often based in-country) to handle their international marketing research projects.

# LO6 Social Responsibility and Technology: A Major Marketing Shift

Two key factors have had a dramatic impact on marketing in the last couple of decades: A surge in the social responsibility movement and the dramatic emergence of the Internet and digital technology. This section will cover how each factor has influenced marketing.

## Marketing and Society: It's Not Just About You!

Over the past couple of decades the social responsibility movement has accelerated in the United States, demanding that marketers actively contribute to the needs of the broader community. Leading-edge marketers have responded by setting a higher standard in key areas such

© MIKE SEGAL/PHOTOLIBRARY

as environmentalism, abolishment of sweatshops, and involvement in the local community. Starbucks, Nike, and McDonald's, for instance, all publish corporate responsibility reports that evaluate the social impact of how the companies run their businesses, and all highlight their programs on their corporate Websites.

**Green Marketing** Companies employ **green marketing** when they actively promote the ecological benefits of their products. Powered (in part) by rising gas prices, Toyota has been especially successful promoting the green benefits of their Prius. Their strategy highlights fuel economy *and* performance, implying that consumers can "go green" without making any real sacrifices. Environmentally friendly fashion offers another emerging example of green marketing. Over the past few years, a number of designers have rolled out their versions of upscale eco-fashion. In addition to clothing from organic cotton, recent entries include earrings from recycled inner tube cores, bracelets from recycled bike-chain links, and jackets with recycled Coke can sequins. These green marketing items are aimed at a growing number of consumers who make purchase decisions based (at least in part) on their convictions.[11]

> Just over 20% of people say they think most creatively in their cars, while 5% say they think most creatively in the shower, and—surprisingly—only 1% say they think most creatively while listening to music.
>
> —*M.I.T. 2005 Invention Index*

## Technology and Marketing: Power to the People!

The emergence of the digital age has revolutionized every element of marketing. Perhaps the most dramatic change has been a shift in power from producers to customers. The Internet gives customers 24/7 access to information and product choices from all over the world. In response, competition has intensified as marketers strive to meet an increasingly high standard of value.

But technology has also created opportunities for marketers. The Internet has opened the door for **mass customization**: creating products tailored for individual consumers on a mass basis. Using sophisticated data collection and management systems, marketers can now collect detailed information about each customer, which allows them to develop one-on-

**green marketing** The development and promotion of products with ecological benefits.

**mass customization** The creation of products tailored for individual consumers on a mass basis.

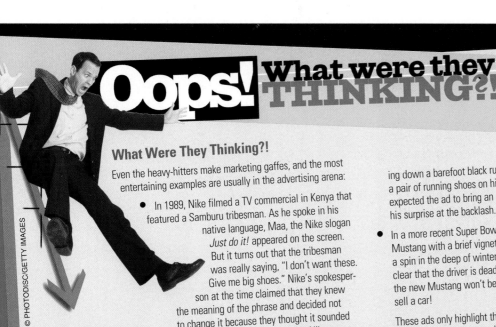

## Oops! What were they THINKING?!

### What Were They Thinking?!

Even the heavy-hitters make marketing gaffes, and the most entertaining examples are usually in the advertising arena:

- In 1989, Nike filmed a TV commercial in Kenya that featured a Samburu tribesman. As he spoke in his native language, Maa, the Nike slogan *Just do it!* appeared on the screen. But it turns out that the tribesman was really saying, "I don't want these. Give me big shoes." Nike's spokesperson at the time claimed that they knew the meaning of the phrase and decided not to change it because they thought it sounded more pleasant than the Maa version of *Just do it!* Apparently Nike never considered that there would be Maa speakers in the United States!

- Ten years later Just for Feet, a rapidly growing footwear chain, made an even bigger blunder. They spent almost $7 million to create, promote, and run an ad during the Super Bowl that showed a group of white men track-

ing down a barefoot black runner, drugging him unconscious, and forcing a pair of running shoes on his feet. Believe it or not, the Just for Feet CEO expected the ad to bring an upsurge of goodwill for the company. Imagine his surprise at the backlash.

- In a more recent Super Bowl ad, Ford introduced their highly hyped new Mustang with a brief vignette that featured a man taking his Mustang for a spin in the deep of winter with the top down. After a moment it becomes clear that the driver is dead…stone cold frozen. The point? To tell us that the new Mustang won't be available until spring. Nothing like a corpse to sell a car!

These ads only highlight the importance of *marketing research.* But sometimes, of course, even research isn't enough to identify marketing issues before they hit. At that point the priority should shift to dealing with the mistake openly, honestly, and quickly, which can help a company win the game, despite the gaffe. Just for the record, Nike and Ford remain corporate giants, while Just for Feet collapsed in bankruptcy and litigation in 2000.[12]

one relationships and to identify high-potential new customers. Through the Web, marketers can tap into (or even create) communities of users that yield valuable information about their goods and services. Technology also helps marketers lower costs, so they can deliver greater value to their customers.

The digital boom has also created an abundance of promotional opportunities as marketers reach out to consumers via new tools such as interactive advertising, virtual reality displays, text-messaging, and video kiosks. We'll discuss these tools in more detail in chapter 14.

## Innovation Unleashed!

In today's hyper-competitive marketplace, businesses must differentiate their products from an astonishing array of alternatives. While life-changing innovation is rare, many successful products simply provide a new twist on an existing product. Examples include Go-Gurt's portable yogurt in a tube, Apple's multi-colored iPod shuffle, and Colgate's pump toothpaste dispenser.

To help you make those kinds of jumps, the game in this box uses Rebus puzzles to stretch your creativity. Rebus puzzles present common words and phrases in novel orientation to each other. The goal is to determine the meaning. The puzzles are below, and the answers are at the bottom of the box.

| ARREST YOU'RE | HISTORY HISTORY HISTORY | Chimadena | RIGHT RIGHT | BAN ANA |
| --- | --- | --- | --- | --- |
| abcdefghjmo pqrstuvwxyz | TimeTime | YYYGuy | MEREPEAT | BPULSEIANSEUSRSE |

Answers: You're under arrest, missing link, history repeats itself, time after time (or double time), made in China, wise guy, equal rights, repeat after me, banana split, mixing business with pleasure

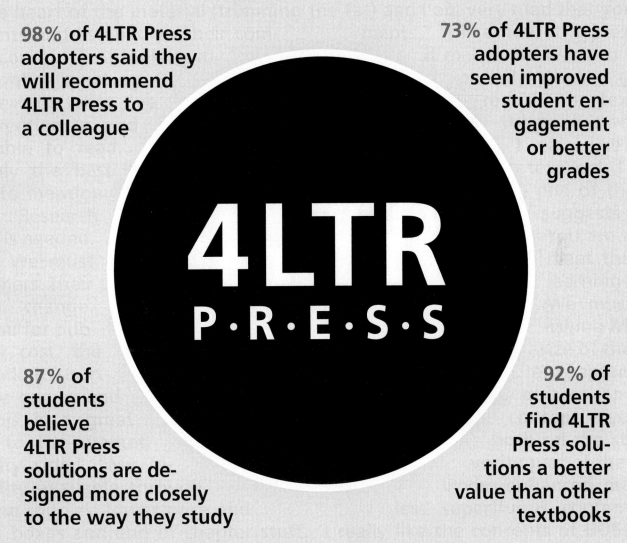
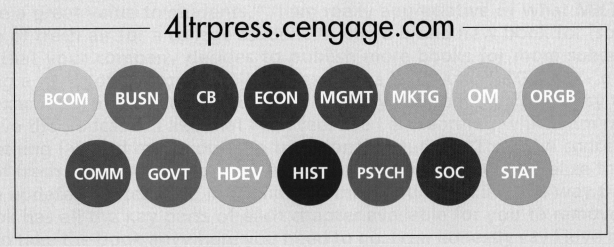

## CHAPTER 12

# Product Strategy: Delivering More Value

## LEARNING OBJECTIVES

After studying this chapter, you will be able to...

**LO1** Explain "product" from a marketing standpoint

**LO2** Identify consumer and business product classifications

**LO3** Describe product differentiation and the key elements of product planning

**LO4** Discuss innovation and the new product development process

**LO5** Describe the product life cycle and its relationship to marketing

# Customers buy for their reasons, not yours.

–Orvel Ray Wilson, consultant

## LO1 Product Definition: It's Probably More Than You Thought

When most people hear the term "product," they immediately think of the material things that we buy and use and consume every day: a can of Coke, a Nokia cell phone, a pair of 7 jeans. But from a marketing standpoint, **product** means much more. A product can be anything that a company offers to satisfy consumer needs and wants; the possibilities include not only physical goods, but also services and ideas. A car wash, laser eye surgery, and a cooking lesson all qualify as products.

When you buy a product, you also "buy" all of the attributes associated with the product. These encompass a broad range of qualities such as the brand name, the image, the packaging, the reputation, and the guarantee. Keep in mind that—from a consumer standpoint—these attributes (or the *lack* of these attributes) are part of their product purchase, even if they don't add to its value. As a marketer, it's worth your while to carefully consider each element of your product to ensure that you're maximizing value without sacrificing profitability. For example, with the introduction of the translucent, multicolored iMac computers in 1998, Apple computer established its reputation for creating value through product design—an attribute that other PC manufacturers completely overlooked as they churned out their inventories of boring, beige boxes. Over the years, Apple has continued to polish its reputation by introducing sleek, elegantly designed products such as their new PowerBooks and their iPod Nanos.

### Services: A Product by Any Other Name...

If a "product" includes anything that satisfies consumer needs, services clearly fit the bill. But services have some obvious differences from tangible goods. You often cannot see, hear, smell, taste, or touch a service, and you can virtually never "own" it. After a haircut, for example, you might possess great looking hair, but you don't own the haircutting experience (at least not literally). Most services embody these qualities:

- Intangibility: As we discussed, you typically cannot see, smell, taste, or touch a service before you buy it. Clearly, this creates a lot of uncertainty. Will the purchase really be worthwhile? Smart marketers mitigate the uncertainty by giving clues that suggest value. For example, the Formosa Café, a funky, old-time Hollywood bar and restaurant, plasters the walls with signed pictures of movie stars, providing "evidence" of its movie biz credentials.

- Inseparability: Try as you might, you simply can't separate the buyer of a service from the person who renders it. Delivery requires interaction between the buyer and the provider, and the customer directly contributes to the quality of the service. Consider a trip to the doctor. If you accurately describe your symptoms, you're likely to get a correct diagnosis. But if you simply say, "I just don't feel *normal*," the outcome will likely be different.

**product** Anything that an organization offers to satisfy consumer needs and wants, including both goods and services.

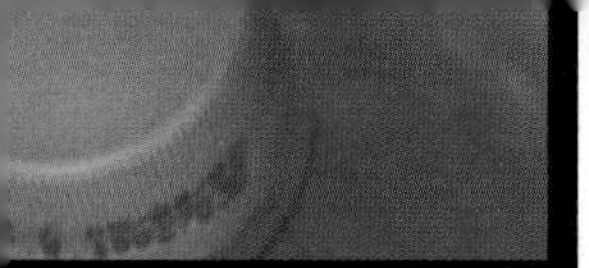

- Variability: This one ties closely to inseparability. A talented masseuse would probably help you relax, whereas a mediocre one might actually create tension. And even the talented masseuse might give better service at the end of the day than at the beginning, or worse service on the day she breaks up with her boyfriend. Variability also applies to the difference among providers. A massage at a top-notch spa, for example, is likely to be better than a massage at your local gym.

- Perishability: Marketers cannot store services for delivery at peak periods. A restaurant, for instance, only has so many seats; they can't (reasonably) tell their 8 P.M. dinner customers to come back the next day at 5 P.M. Similarly, major tourist destinations, such as Las Vegas, can't store an inventory of room service deliveries or performances of Cirque du Soleil. This creates obvious cost issues; is it worthwhile to prepare for a peak crowd but lose money when it's slow? The answer depends on the economics of your business.

## Goods versus Services: A Mixed Bag

Identifying whether a product is a good or a service can pose a considerable challenge, since many products contain elements of both. A meal at your local Italian restaurant, for instance, obviously includes tangible goods: You definitely own that calzone. But someone else took your order, brought it to the table, and (perhaps most importantly) did the dishes! Service was clearly a crucial part of the package.

A goods and services spectrum can provide a valuable tool for analyzing the relationship between the two. (See exhibit 12.1.) At one extreme, **pure goods** don't include any services. Examples include a bottle of shampoo, or a package of pasta. At the other extreme, **pure services** don't include any goods. Examples include financial consulting or math tutoring. Other products—such as a meal at Pizza Hut—fall somewhere between the poles.

## Product Layers: Peeling the Onion

When customers buy products, they actually purchase more than just the good or service itself. They buy a complete product package that includes a core benefit, the actual product, and product augmentations. (See exhibit 12.2.) Understanding these layers is valuable, since the most successful products delight consumers at each one of them.

Core Benefit At the most fundamental level, consumers buy a **core benefit** that satisfies their needs. When you go to a concert, for instance, the core benefit is entertainment. When you buy a motorcycle, the core benefit is transportation. And when you go to the gym, the core benefit is fitness. Most products also provide secondary benefits that help distinguish them from other goods and services that meet the same customer needs. A secondary benefit of a motorcycle, for example, might include the ease of parking.

© PROFIMEDIA INTERNATIONAL S.R.O./ALAMY

---

**Exhibit 12.1** Goods and Services Spectrum

Where on the spectrum would you place each of these products: a rock concert, a hotel, a new car, an alternative clothing boutique, a college class, a coffee shop, a ski resort. Why?

**Pure Goods**
Bottle of Shampoo
Can of Cola

**Pure Service**
Financial Consulting
Math Tutoring

**Exhibit 12.2** The three product layers: Camera Phone

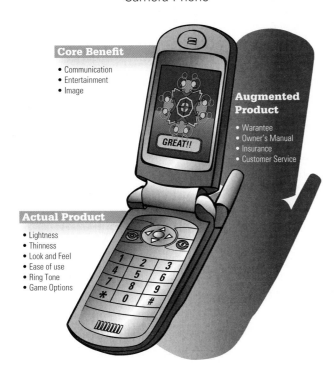

**Core Benefit**
- Communication
- Entertainment
- Image

**Augmented Product**
- Warantee
- Owner's Manual
- Insurance
- Customer Service

GREAT!!

**Actual Product**
- Lightness
- Thinness
- Look and Feel
- Ease of use
- Ring Tone
- Game Options

**Actual Product** This **actual product** layer, of course, is the product itself: the physical good or the delivered service that provides the core benefit. A U2 concert is the actual "service" that provides a live music experience. A Kawasaki Ninja is the actual product that provides a thrilling ride. Sports Club LA is the actual gym that provides fitness. Identifying the actual product is sometimes tough when the product is a service. For example, the core benefit of personal training might be weight loss, but the actual product may be some very fit person haranguing you to do ten more sit-ups. Keep in mind that the actual product includes all of the attributes that make it unique, such as the brand name, the features, and the packaging.

**Augmented Product** Most marketers wrap their actual products in additional goods and services, called the **augmented product**, that sharpen their competitive edge. Augmentations come in a range of different forms, such as warrantees, free service, instruction manuals, installation, and customer help lines. A U2 concert might give fans a chance to win backstage passes. The Kawasaki Ninja usually comes with a 2-year warranty and free dealer prep. And Sports Club LA offers valet parking, overnight laundry service, and delicious smoothies.

In the factory, we make cosmetics; in the store, we sell hope.
–Charles Revson, founder, Revlon Cosmetics

## LO2 Product Classification: It's a Bird, It's a Plane...

Products fall into two broad categories—consumer products and business products—depending on the reason for the purchase. **Consumer products** are purchased for personal use or consumption, while **business products** are purchased to use either directly or indirectly in the production of another product. The bag of chips that you buy to eat, for instance, is a consumer product, while the bag of chips that a Subway owner buys to sell is a business product.

### Consumer Product Categories

Convenience Products **Convenience products** are the inexpensive goods and services that consumers buy frequently with limited consideration and analysis. Distribution tends to be widespread, with promotion by the producers. Examples include staples such as milk and toothpaste, impulse items such as candy bars and magazines, and emergency products such as headache tablets and plumbing services.

Shopping Products **Shopping products** are the more expensive products that consumers buy less frequently. Typically, as consumers shop, they search for the best value and learn more about features and benefits through the shopping process. Distribution is widespread, but more selective than for convenience products. Both producers and retailers tend to promote shopping products. Examples include: computers, appliances, and maid services.

Specialty Products **Specialty products** are those much more expensive products that consumers seldom purchase. Most people perceive specialty products as being so important that they are unwilling to accept substitutes. Because of this, distribution tends to be highly selective (consumers are willing to go far out

**actual product** The physical good or the delivered service that provides the core benefit of any product.

**augmented product** The additional goods and services included with a product to sharpen its competitive edge.

**consumer products** Products purchased for personal use or consumption.

**business products** Products purchased to use either directly or indirectly in the production of other products.

**convenience products** Inexpensive goods and services that consumers buy frequently with limited consideration and analysis.

**shopping products** Moderately expensive products that consumers buy less frequently, after learning about their features and benefits through the shopping process.

**specialty products** Expensive products that consumers seldom purchase. Most people perceive specialty products as so important that they are unwilling to accept substitutes.

of their way for the "right" brand). Both producers and retailers are apt to promote specialty products, but to a highly targeted audience. Some specialty product examples are Lamborghini sports cars, Tiffany jewelry, and Rolex watches.

Unsought Products **Unsought products** are the goods and services that hold little interest (or even negative interest) for consumers. Price and distribution vary wildly, but promotion tends to be aggressive to drum up consumer interest. Home warranties, prepaid legal services, and blood donations are some examples.

## Business Product Categories

Installations **Installations** are large capital purchases designed for a long productive life. The marketing of installations emphasizes personal selling and customization. Examples include industrial robots, new buildings, and railroad cars.

Accessory Equipment **Accessory equipment** includes smaller, movable capital purchases, designed for a shorter productive life than installations. Marketing focuses on personal selling, but includes less customization than installations. Examples include personal computers, copy machines, and furniture.

Maintenance, Repair, and Operating Products The **maintenance, repair, and operating products** category consists of small ticket items that businesses consume on an on-going basis, but don't become part of the final product. Marketing tactics emphasize efficiency. Examples include brooms, nails, pens, and lubricants.

Raw Materials **Raw materials** include the farm and natural products used in producing other products. Marketing emphasizes price and service rather than product differentiation. Examples include milk, cotton, turkeys, oil, and iron.

Component Parts and Processed Materials Finished (or partially finished) products used in producing other products make up this business product category. Marketing emphasizes product quality as well as price and service. Examples include batteries for cars and aluminum ingots for soda cans.

Business Services **Business services** are those services that businesses purchase to facilitate operations. Marketing focuses on quality and relationships; the role of price can vary. Examples include: payroll services, marketing research, and legal services.

## LO3 Product Differentiation and Planning: A Meaningful Difference

While some products have succeeded with little or no forethought, you'll dramatically boost your chance of a hit with careful planning. **Product differentiation** should be a key consideration. Winning products must embody a real or perceived difference versus the glut of goods and services that compete in virtually every corner of the market. As we'll discuss in the next section, areas to consider include product quality, features and benefits, branding, and packaging. But different alone isn't enough; different from *and better than* the competition is the shortest path to success. A quick look at some high-profile product failures illustrates the point.

- Nehru suits: In the 1960s, fashion experts predicted that Nehru suits—with their oddly tailored collars—would be a major hit. Few were disappointed when they died an early death.

- Clear Beer: In the 1990s, several companies introduced clear beers, reflecting an ill-fated obsession with clear products, including shampoo, soap, and the short-lived, clear Crystal Pepsi.

- Funky French Fries: In 2002, Ore-Ida introduced Funky Fries. The flavors included cinnamon-sugar, chocolate, and "radical blue." Not surprisingly, they were off the market in less than a year.

### Product Quality

Product quality relates directly to product value, which comes from understanding your customer. Peter

Drucker, a noted business thinker, writer, and educator, declared:

> Quality in a product or service is not what the supplier puts in. It's what the customer gets out and is willing to pay for. A product is not quality because it is hard to make and costs a lot of money...this is incompetence. Customers pay only for what is of use to them and gives them value. Nothing else constitutes quality.

In other words, a high-quality product does a great job meeting customer needs. Seimans, a huge electronics conglomerate, embodies this thinking in their approach to quality: "Quality is when our customers come back and our products don't."

But the specific definition of quality—and the attributes that indicate quality—change across product categories. Here are a few examples:

| Product Category | Some Quality Indicators |
|---|---|
| Internet search engines | Fast, relevant, far-reaching results |
| Stylish blue jeans | High-profile designer, high price, celebrity customers |
| TV editing equipment | Reliability, flexibility, and customer service |
| Roller coasters | Thrill factor, design, and setting |
| Chain saws | Effectiveness, safety, and reliability |

Regardless of product category, the two key aspects of quality are level and consistency. **Quality level** refers to how well a product performs its core functions. You might think that smart companies deliver the highest possible level of performance, but this is seldom profitable, or even desirable. For instance, only a tiny group of consumers would pay for a jet ski to go 200 mph, when 80 mph offers a comparable thrill (at least for most of us!). The right level of product performance is the level that meets the needs of your consumers, and those needs include price. Decisions about quality level must also consider the competition. The goal is to out-perform the other players in your category, while maintaining profitability.

The second dimension of quality is **product consistency.** How consistently does your product actually deliver the promised level of quality? With a positive relationship between price and performance, consistent delivery can offer a competitive edge at almost any quality level.

> " Quality is remembered long after the price is forgotten.
> –Gucci family slogan "

Toyota offers an excellent example. When most people consider Scion, Toyota, and Lexus—all Toyota-owned brands—quality quickly comes to mind. And all three dominate their markets. But clearly, the quality *level* (and price) is different for each. Scion serves the lower end of the market, Toyota the broad middle, and Lexus the upper crust. In short, Toyota succeeds at delivering product consistency at three markedly different quality levels.

Perhaps the exact opposite of automotive quality was the Yugo, imported from the former Yugoslavia in the mid-1980s. See the *Oops!* box on the next page to learn more.

## Features and Benefits

**Product features** are the characteristics of the product you offer. If a product is well designed, each feature corresponds to a meaningful **customer benefit.** The marketer's challenge is to design a package of features that offer the highest level of value for an acceptable price. And the equation must also account for profitability goals.

One winning formula may be to offer at least some low-cost features that correspond to high-value benefits. Creating an "open kitchen" restaurant, for instance, has limited impact on costs, but gives patrons an exciting, up-close view of the drama and hustle of professional food preparation. The table on the following page lists some other examples of product features and their corresponding customer benefits.

## Product Lines and the Product Mix

Some companies focus all of their efforts on one product, but most offer a number of different products to enhance their revenue and profits. A **product line** is a group of products that are closely related to each other, either in terms of how they work or the customers they serve. Amazon's first product line, for instance, was books. To meet the needs of as many book lovers as possible, Amazon carries well over a million different books in their product line. A **product mix** is the total number of product lines and individual items sold by a single firm. Amazon's product mix includes a wide range of product lines, from books, to electronics, to toys (to name

## Product Features and Customer Benefits

| Product | Product Feature | Customer Benefit |
|---|---|---|
| Subway sandwiches | Lower fat | Looser pants |
| Contact lenses | Different colors | A new-looking you |
| High-definition TV | 46-inch screen | The party's at your house |
| Hybrid car | Lower gas mileage | More cash for other needs |
| Triple latte | Caffeine, caffeine, caffeine | More time to, uh, study |

just a few!). Please see exhibit 12.3 for an illustration of Amazon's product line and product mix.

Decisions regarding how many items to include in each product line and in the overall product mix can have a huge impact on a firm's profits. With too few items in each line, the company may be leaving money on the table. With too many items, the company may be spending unnecessarily to support its weakest links.

One reason that firms add new product lines is to reach completely new customers. Gap, for instance, added Old Navy to reach younger, lower income

> Having a competitive advantage is like having a gun in a knife fight.
> –Anonymous

customers, and Banana Republic to reach older, higher income customers. Each line includes a range of different products designed to meet the needs of their specific customers. But the risk of adding new lines—especially lower priced lines—is **cannibalization**, which happens when a new entry "eats" the sales of an existing line. This is especially dangerous when the new products are lower priced than the current ones. You could see the problem, for instance, if a $20 blue jean purchase from Old Navy replaces a $50 blue jean purchase from Gap; the company has lost more than half its revenue on

# Oops! What were they THINKING?!

### If You Drive a Yugo, Maybe You Will Go and Maybe You Won't Go...

The tiny Yugo hatchback hit the U.S. market with great fanfare in the summer of 1985. Billed as the cheapest new car in the United States, the Yugoslavian import captured the imagination of the consumer market. Eager buyers stormed the dealerships before the first cars were off the boat. The price was an unimaginably low $3,990.

But low price wasn't enough. As buyers began to actually drive their cars, they uncovered flaw after flaw, including major issues such as premature engine failure and poor dealer service. Reviewers described the Yugo as more of a toy than a car. Not surprisingly, sales plummeted, leading to bankruptcy in 1989.

The short life of the Yugo was long enough to establish its place as a cultural icon of cheap. Countless disillusioned owners competed to coin the best description of their Yugo. Sample comments from the CarTalk Website (which featured the Yugo as the worst car of the millennium):

"The Yugo's first stop after the showroom was the service department: `Fill 'er up and replace the engine!'"

"At least it had heated rear windows—so your hands would stay warm while you pushed."

But despite its problems (or perhaps because of them!) the Yugo also spawned a remarkable artistic effort. A professor at the NYC School of Visual Arts challenged his students several years ago to turn discarded Yugos into something useful. The results, displayed for a time in Union Station, included a toaster, a Port-o-Potty, a confessional, a diner, and a submarine.[1]

© PHOTODISC/GETTY IMAGES, © AP IMAGES

**Exhibit 12.3**    Amazon's product line and product mix

"Books" is a key product line for Amazon . . . but "Books" is only one of 40 product lines in the Amazon product mix.

the sale. Like other companies with multiple lines, Gap carefully monitors the cannibalization issue and works to differentiate its lines as fully as possible.

## Branding

At the most basic level, a **brand** is a product's identity that sets it apart from other players in the same category. Typically, brands represent the combination of elements such as product name, symbol, design, reputation, and image. But today's most powerful emerging brands go far beyond the sum of their attributes. They project a compelling group identity that creates brand fanatics: loyal customers who advocate for the brand better than any advertising a marketer could buy. The overall value of a brand to an organization—the extra money that consumers will spend to buy that brand—is called **brand equity**.

Since 2001, *BusinessWeek* and Interbrand, a leading brand consultancy, have teamed up to publish a ranking of the 100 Best Global Brands by dollar value. The top ten brands are listed in the table at the right, but you can find the complete list at *BusinessWeek's* Website (http://bwnt.businessweek.com/interactive_reports/global_brand_2008/?chan=magazine+channel_special+report).

The biggest gainers on the 2008 list were Google (+43%), Apple (+24%), Amazon (+19%), Zara (+15%), and Nintendo (+13%). All five share a common theme with the top ten brands: they create experiences for their customers, rather than simply providing a good or a service. The top decliners, on the other hand—Merrill Lynch (-21%), Gap (-21%), Morgan Stanley (-16%), Citi (-14%), and Ford (-12%)—have struggled to provide value for their customers in a rapidly changing world.[2]

**Brand Name**   A catchy, memorable name is among the most powerful elements of your brand. While the right name will never save a bad business, it can launch a good business to new heights. But finding the right name can be tough. According to the respected Brighter Naming consulting group, the following characteristics can help:

*BusinessWeek/Interbrand Top Ten Global Brands*

| Brand | Country of Ownership |
|---|---|
| Coca-Cola | United States |
| IBM | United States |
| Microsoft | United States |
| GE | United States |
| Nokia | Finland |
| Toyota | Japan |
| Intel | United States |
| McDonald's | United States |
| Disney | United States |
| Google | United States |

1. *Short, sweet, and easy to pronounce and spell:* Examples include Dell, Gap, Nike, Dove, Tide, Kool-Aid.
2. *Unique within the industry:* Think Apple, Monster, Jet Blue, and Victoria's Secret.
3. *Good alliteration, especially for long names:* The words should roll off your tongue. Some examples are Coca-Cola, BlackBerry, and Minute Maid.[3]

Brand names typically fall into four categories, as described in the table on the following page.

Line Extensions versus Brand Extensions As companies grow, marketers look for opportunities to grow their businesses. **Line extensions** are similar products offered under the same brand name. Possibilities include new flavors, sizes, colors, ingredients, and forms. One example is Coca-Cola, which offers versions with lemon, with lime, with vanilla, with caffeine, without caffeine, with sugar, and without sugar. The marketing challenge is to ensure that line extensions steal market share from competitors, rather than from the core brand.

## Brand Name Categories

| Category | Description | Examples |
|---|---|---|
| Location-based | Refers to either the area served or the place of origin | Southwest Airlines, Bank of America, Best Western Hotels |
| Founder's name | Can include first name, last name, or both | McDonald's, Suzy's Sub Sandwiches, Ford, Disney, Hewlett-Packard |
| Descriptive or functional | Describes what the product is or how it works | e-Bay, U.S. News and World Report, Weight Watchers, Krispy Kreme |
| Evocative | Communicates an engaging image that resonates with consumers | Yahoo, Craftsman, Virgin, Intel, Lunchables, Cosmopolitan, Starbucks |

**Brand extensions**, on the other hand, involve launching a product in a new category under an existing brand name. The Bic brand, for instance, is quite elastic, stretching nicely to include diverse products such as pens, glue, cigarette lighters, and disposable razors. The Virgin brand demonstrates similar elasticity, covering 350 companies that range from airlines, to cell phones, to soft drinks, to cars. But the concept of brand extension becomes most clear (and most entertaining) through examining brand extension failures. Examples include Bic perfume, Budweiser Dry, and Harley Davidson Cologne.[4]

Licensing  Some companies opt to license their brands from other businesses. **Licensing** means purchasing—often for a substantial fee—the right to use another company's brand name or symbol. The benefits, of course, are instant name recognition, an established reputation, and a proven track record. On a worldwide basis the best-known licensing arrangements are probably character names, which range from Mickey Mouse to Bart Simpson and appear on everything from cereal, to toys, to underwear. Many movie producers also do high-profile licensing, turning out truckloads of merchandise that features movie properties such as Harry Potter and James Bond.

Another fast-growing area is the licensing of corporate names. Coca-Cola, for instance, claims to have more than 300 licensees who sell over a billion dollars of licensed merchandise each year. The potential benefits for Coca-Cola are clear: more promotion, increased exposure, and enhanced image. But the risk is significant. If licensed products are poor quality or overpriced, the consumer backlash hits the core brand rather than the producer of the licensed product.

## Living, Breathing Brands

Donald Trump has become a brand. Millions of people watch his show "The Apprentice," and millions more probably recognize him and his trademark blond hair. Trump stands for autocratic power and self-indulgent luxury, which translates into a 25% value premium for any property that carries his name. A little ego helps too: Trump had no problem telling BusinessWeek that he is "a bigger brand now than Pepsi Cola or Coca-Cola."

Richard Branson, founder of the Virgin Group, has also become a human brand. He stands for outrageous risk-taking and high-profile fun, reinforced by his flamboyant stunts such as showing up naked to launch his book *Virginity*, or traveling around the world by hot air balloon. Branson, too, sees bottom line benefits. He recently launched a new airline in India and ended up on the front page of every paper. He notes that "the costs of that in advertising terms would have been considerable."

William Arruda, founder of a global branding company, suggests that the key to personal branding success lies in clarity, consistency, and constancy. Human brands are clear about who they are and who they aren't. They are consistent in their message (even Madonna is consistent about always changing). And they are constantly visible to their target markets.[5]

© PUNIT PARANJPE/REUTERS/LANDOV

The Simpsons brand is quirky, provocative, and highly profitable! The Simpsons show has generated about two billion dollars for Fox since its debut in 1990.

© GETTY IMAGES

Cobranding **Cobranding** is when established brands from different companies join forces to market the same product. This cooperative approach has a long history, but is currently enjoying a new popularity. Examples include:

- Dreyer's markets various Girl Scout Cookie flavored ice creams

- Target markets Isaac Mizrahi clothing

- Kmart markets Martha Stewart house wares

Cobranding can offer huge advantages to both partners, by leveraging their strengths to enter new markets and gain more exposure. Through the Target–Mizrahi agreement, for example, Isaac Mizrahi has gained unprecedented exposure to a mass audience (and their shopping dollars), while Target has bolstered its reputation for cheap chic. But cobranding can be risky. If one partner makes a major goof (think Martha Stewart), the fallout can damage the reputation of the other partner as well.

National Brands versus Store Brands **National brands**, also called manufacturers' brands, are brands that the producer owns and markets. Many are well-known and widely available such as Head and Shoulders shampoo, Purina pet food, and Pepsi-Cola. Although most retailers carry lots of national brands, an increasing number have opted to also carry their own versions of

the same products, called **store brands**, or private label. Deep discounters such as Wal-Mart and Costco have had particular success with their private label brands (e.g., Sam's Choice and Kirkland). Private labels play a growing role in grocery stores, as well. In the United States, about one out of five grocery purchases is private label, and in Europe the number reaches about 40%. The growing influence of low-end private label brands increases the pressure on national brands to continually innovate.[6]

At the upper end of the market—especially in the clothing business—key retailers specialize in private brands to create and protect a consistent, upscale image. Examples include Neiman Marcus, Coldwater Creek, and Saks Fifth Avenue. Private label clothing accounts for more than a third of all U.S. apparel sales.[7]

## Packaging

Great packaging does more than just hold the product. It can protect the product, provide information, facilitate storage, suggest product uses, promote the product brand, and attract buyer attention. Great packaging is especially important in the crowded world of grocery stores and mass merchandisers. In the average supermarket, for instance, the typical shopper passes about 300 items per minute and makes more than 60% of purchases on sheer impulse. In this environment, your package must call out to your target customers and differentiate your product from all the others lined up beside it. Yet, in attracting consumer attention, a good package cannot sacrifice the basics such as protecting the product.

Bottom line, great packaging stems from consumer needs, but it usually includes at least a smidge of creative brilliance. Examples include yogurt in a pouch that doesn't need a spoon, soup to-go that can be microwaved in the can, and single-serving baby carrot packets that moms can toss into kids' lunches.

**cobranding** When established brands from different companies join forces to market the same product.

**national brands** Brands that the producer owns and markets.

**store brands** Brands that the retailer both produces and distributes (also called private label brands).

© DANIEL ACKER/BLOOMBERG NEWS/LANDOV

## LO4 New Product Development: Nuts, Bolts, and a Spark of Brilliance

For a business to thrive long term, effective new product development is vital. And the process only works if it happens quickly. As technological advances hit the market at breakneck speed, current products are becoming obsolete faster than ever before. The need for speed compounds as hungry competitors crowd every niche of the market. But the rush is risky, since new product development costs can be in the millions, and the success rate is less than a third. Marketers who succeed in this challenging arena devote painstaking effort to understanding their customers, but they also nurture the creativity they need to generate new ideas. An example of how this can work: The 3M Corporation—makers of Post-It notes and Scotch Tape—introduce about 500 new products per year by pushing their employees to "relentlessly ask 'What if?'" 3M also employs the 15% rule, encouraging workers to spend 15% of their work time (*paid* work time!) on projects of personal interest.[8]

### Types of Innovation

Clearly the first personal computer represented a higher degree of newness than the first personal computer with a color screen. And the computer with a color screen represented a higher degree of newness than the first low-cost knockoff. Levels of innovation fall along a spectrum, as shown in exhibit 12.4.

Discontinuous Innovation **Discontinuous innovations** are brand new ideas that radically change how people live. Examples include the first car, the first plane, the first television, and the first computer. These dramatic innovations require extensive customer learning, which should guide the marketing process.

**Exhibit 12.4** Levels of innovation

Discontinuous Innovation

Dynamically Continuous Innovation

Continuous Innovation

### Free Lunch at Last!

According to the Economist, a growing number of leading-edge companies—from carmaker BMW to game-maker Electronic Arts—have harnessed the creativity of their customers to develop hot new products. Electronic Arts, noticing spontaneous customer innovation, "made a conscious decision to embrace this phenomenon." They began shipping development tools with their games and feeding the new ideas to designers. The result, of course, is better games. General Electric cultivates customer "luminaries" to help develop startling new medical products. And BMW recently invited 15 customers to work with their German engineers in Munich to create in-car technology services. Eric Von Hippel of MIT, author of *Democratizing Innovation*, affirms that user-led innovation has a much higher success rate. And the best part is that most customers are willing to donate their creativity free of charge.[9]

© MARK ELIAS/BLOOMBERG NEWS/LANDOV

**Dynamically Continuous Innovation** **Dynamically continuous innovations** are characterized by marked changes to existing products. Examples include cell phones, MP3 players, and digital cameras. These types of innovations require a moderate level of consumer learning in exchange for significant benefits.

**Continuous Innovation** A slight modification of an existing product is called a **continuous innovation**. Examples include new sizes, flavors, shapes, packaging, and design. The goal of continuous innovation is to distinguish a product from the competition. The goal of a knockoff, on the other hand, is simply to copy a competitor and offer a lower price.

## The New Product Development Process

An efficient, focused development process will boost your chances of new product success. The standard model includes six stages:

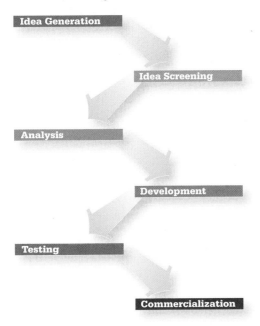

Idea Generation

Idea Screening

Analysis

Development

Testing

Commercialization

Each stage requires management to "green light" ideas before moving forward to ensure that the company doesn't waste resources on marginal concepts.

- **Idea Generation:** Some experts estimate that it takes 50 ideas for each new product that makes it to market, so you should definitely cast a wide net. Ideas can come from almost anywhere, including customer research, customer complaints, salespeople, engineers, suppliers, and competitors.

- **Idea Screening:** The purpose of this stage is to weed out ideas that don't fit with the company's objectives and ideas that would clearly be too expensive to develop. The Walt Disney Company, for instance, would certainly eliminate the idea of a XXX cable channel because it just doesn't fit their mission.

- **Analysis:** The purpose of the analysis stage is to estimate costs and forecast sales for each idea to get a sense of the potential profit and of how the product might fit within the company's resources. Each idea must meet rigorous standards to remain a contender.

- **Development:** The development process leads to detailed descriptions of each concept with specific product features. New product teams sometimes also make prototypes, or samples, that consumers can actually test. The results help fully refine the concept.

- **Testing:** This stage involves the formal process of soliciting feedback from consumers by testing the product concept. Do they like the features? Are the benefits meaningful? What price makes sense? Some companies also test-market their products, or sell them in a limited area to evaluate the consumer response.

**dynamically continuous innovation Existing products with marked changes and significant new product benefits.**

**continuous innovation Existing products with slight modifications.**

## Wacky Labels

As product lawsuits take on a life of their own, manufacturers are responding with warning labels that seem increasingly wacky. To call attention to this trend, a Michigan anti-lawsuit group called M-LAW sponsors the annual Wacky Warning Label Contest. Top finishers over the past few years included the following gems:

- A toilet brush tag that says "Do not use for personal hygiene"
- A small tractor that warns "Danger: Avoid Death"
- A label on a baby-stroller storage pouch that warns "Do not put child in bag"
- A scooter that cautions "This product moves when used"
- A disappearing ink marker which cautions "The Vanishing Fabric Marker should not be used as a writing instrument for signing checks or any legal documents."[10]

© FOODPIX/JUPITERIMAGES

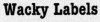

• **Commercialization:** This stage entails introducing the product to the general market. Two key success factors are gaining distribution and launching promotion. But a product that tested well doesn't always mean instant success. The VW Beetle, for example, only sold 330 cars during its first year in the United States, but it later became a hit.

## New Product Adoption and Diffusion

In order to become a commercial success, new products must spread throughout a market after they are introduced. That process is called **diffusion**. But clearly diffusion happens at different speeds, depending on the individual consumer and on the product itself.

**Product Adoption Categories**  Some consumers like to try new things; others seem terrified of change. These attitudes clearly impact the rate at which individual people are willing to adopt (or begin buying and using) new products. The first adopters, about 2.5% of the total, are adventurous risk-takers. The laggards, about 16% of the total, sometimes adopt products so late that earlier adopters have already moved to the next new thing. The rest of the population falls somewhere in between. Keep in mind that individuals tend to adopt different new products at different rates. For instance, we probably all know someone who is an innovator in technology, but a laggard in fashion, or vice-versa.

**Product Diffusion Rates**  Some new products diffuse into the population much more quickly than others. For example, Apple iPods and Segway Human Transporters appeared on the market around the same time, but iPods have become a pop culture icon, while Segways remain on the fringe. What accounts for the difference? Researchers have identified five product characteristics that affect the rate of adoption and diffusion. The more characteristics a product has, the faster it will diffuse into the population.

• **Observability:** How visible is the product to other potential consumers? Some product categories are easier to observe than others. If you adopt a new kind of pillowcase, for example, only your overnight guests are likely to see it. But if you adopt a new kind of car, the whole neighborhood will know, plus anyone else who sees you on the streets and highways.

The Segway Human Transporter hit the market at about the same time as the Apple iPod, but it hasn't been nearly as successful. What characteristics have held up the diffusion process?

© AP IMAGES

> ❝
> **If you're not failing every now and again, it's a sign you're not doing anything very innovative.**
> –Woody Allen, film director
> ❞

• **Trialability:** How easily can potential consumers sample the new product? Trial can be a powerful way to create new consumers, which is why many markets fill their aisles with sample tables during popular shopping hours. Other examples of trial-boosting strategies include test driving cars, sampling music, and testing new fragrances. But creating trial opportunities for some products, such as major appliances, can be almost impossible.

• **Complexity:** Can potential consumers easily understand what your product is and how it works? If your product confuses people—or if they find it hard to explain to others—adoption rates will slow. For example, many people who test-ride Segway Human Transporters love the experience, but they have trouble explaining to others how it works or why it beats other transportation options.

• **Compatibility:** How consistent is your product with the existing way of doing things? MP3 music files, for instance, represented a whole new way of buying music, which continues to pose a barrier for many in the older generation of music lovers. But cordless phones caught on almost instantly, since they were completely consistent with people's prior experiences—only better!

- Relative Advantage: How much better are the benefits of your new product compared to existing products? As gas prices continue to climb, for example, the benefits of a hybrid car take on a much higher value relative to standard cars. As a result, demand skyrockets. But before high gas prices, demand was much lower, since the relative advantage just wasn't as meaningful for most consumers.

## LO5 The Product Life Cycle: Maximizing Results over Time

When marketers introduce a new product, they hope it will last forever, generating sales and profits for years to come. But they also realize that all products go through a **product life cycle**: a pattern of sales and profits that typically changes over time. The life cycle can be dramatically different across individual products and product categories, and predicting the exact shape and length of the lifecycle is virtually impossible. But most product categories do move through the four distinct stages shown in exhibit 12.5 on the following page.

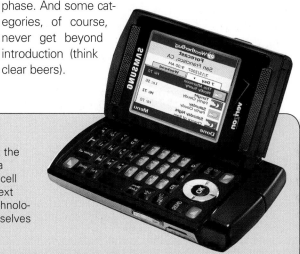

**product life cycle A pattern of sales and profits that typically changes over time.**

- Introduction: This is a time of low sales and nonexistent profits as companies invest in raising awareness about the product and the product category. Some categories, such as the microwave, languish in this phase for years, while other categories, such as computer memory sticks, zoom through this phase. And some categories, of course, never get beyond introduction (think clear beers).

### The Microwave versus the Cell Phone

Many people are surprised to learn that the first microwave oven hit the American consumer market in the mid-1950s. But it didn't become a staple in American homes until the mid-1980s. Compare that to the cell phone, which arrived in 1983 and was virtually everywhere by the next decade. What accounts for the difference? Changes in price and technology clearly played a role, but the characteristics of the products themselves were the defining factors.

| Characteristic | Microwave | Cell Phone |
|---|---|---|
| Observability | To see your microwave, your friends would need to be in your kitchen as you cook…a relatively limited number of people! | It's hard to miss people talking on their cell phones, since the whole point (especially in the early days) was to use them outside the home. |
| Trialability | Marketers took a good 10 years to realize that in-store demos and sampling would encourage consumers to risk the pricey purchase. | Early cell phone adopters were eager to lend others their phones (and those others were constantly asking!). |
| Complexity | Before the tech boom of the 1980s and 1990s, the molecules-and-friction explanation of how microwaves work seemed downright odd to many average consumers. | Cell phones offered such compelling benefits that many just didn't care *how* they worked (only *if* they worked!). |
| Compatibility | Cooking with plastic and paper rather than metal pans and aluminum foil just didn't seem right to many dedicated homemakers. | It did the same thing as a regular phone, but without the tether and with a lot more highly valued convenience. |
| Relative Advantage | When most women were homemakers, the 20-minute dinner held little added appeal. This changed, of course, as women flooded into the workforce in the late 1970s. | In an age where convenience is king, the cell phone offered a priceless advantage that fueled its rapid growth. |

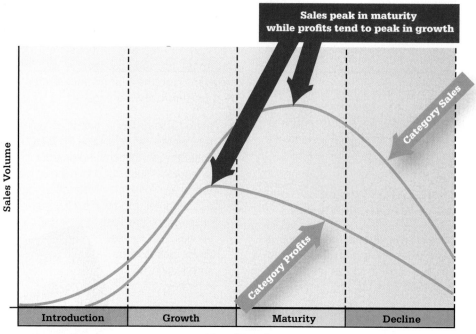

Sales peak in maturity while profits tend to peak in growth

- **Growth:** During the growth period, sales continue to rise, although profits usually peak. Typically, competitors begin to notice emerging categories in the growth phase. They enter the market—often with new variations of existing products—which further fuels the growth. Portable MP3 players, for example, are currently in the growth phase, and a number of competitors are challenging Apple's hold on the market.

- **Maturity:** During maturity, sales usually peak. Profits continue to decline as competition intensifies. Once a market is mature, the only way to gain more users is to steal them from competitors, rather than to bring new users into the category. Weaker players begin to drop out of the category. Gasoline-

powered cars and network TV are in maturity in the United States.

- **Decline:** During this period sales and profits begin to decline, sometimes quite rapidly. The reasons usually relate to either technological change or change in consumer needs. For instance, the introduction of word processing pushed typewriters into decline, and a change in consumer taste and habits pushed hot cereal into decline. Competitors continue to drop out of the category.

Familiarity with the product life cycle helps marketers plan effective strategies for existing products and identify profitable categories for new products. The following table summarizes typical marketing strategies and offers examples for each phase.

| Phase | Examples | Sales/Profits | Key Marketing Strategies |
|---|---|---|---|
| Introduction | Plasma televisions, virtual reality games, fuel cell technology | Low sales, low profits | Build awareness, trial, and distribution |
| Growth | Hybrid cars, video cell phones, Internet gambling | Rapidly increasing sales and profits | Reinforce brand positioning, often through heavy advertising |
| Maturity | Airlines, DVD players, food processors, personal computers, online stock trading | Flat sales and declining profits | Target competitors, while defending franchise with new product features, competitive advertising, promotion, and price cuts |
| Decline | Pagers, videocassettes | Declining sales and profits | Reduce spending and consider terminating the product |

Individual products also have life cycles that usually follow the category growth pattern but sometimes vary dramatically. Clearly, it's in the marketer's best interest to extend the profitable run of an individual brand as long as possible. There are several ways to make this happen: finding new uses for the product, changing the product, and changing the marketing mix. Arm & Hammer baking soda, for example, extended their life cycle by marketing the brand as a refrigerator deodorizer, which completely reversed their decline. And M&Ms created a splash in the market by adding new colors based on customer voting.

# Listen Up!

*BUSN* was designed for students just like you – students who want choices, flexibility, and multiple learning options. *BUSN* delivers concise, focused information in a fresh and contemporary format.

At **4ltrpress.cengage.com/busn**, you'll find electronic resources such as **animated visual summaries** and **audio downloads** for each chapter. These resources will help supplement your understanding of core business concepts in a format that fits your busy lifestyle.

Visit **4ltrpress.cengage.com/busn** to learn more about the multiple *BUSN* resources available to help you succeed!

# Distribution and Pricing: Right Product, Right Person, Right Place, Right Price

## LEARNING OBJECTIVES

After studying this chapter, you will be able to...

**LO1** Define distribution and differentiate between channels of distribution and physical distribution

**LO2** Describe the various types of wholesale distributors

**LO3** Discuss strategies and trends in store and nonstore retailing

**LO4** Explain the key factors in physical distribution

**LO5** Outline core pricing objectives and strategies

**LO6** Discuss pricing in practice, including the role of consumer perceptions

4ltrpress.cengage.com/busn

> Make your product easier to buy than your competition, or you will find customers buying from them, not you.
>
> –Mark Cuban, entrepreneur

Distribution and pricing are not the most glamorous elements of the marketing mix, but managed effectively, they can provide a powerful competitive advantage. While this chapter will cover distribution and pricing strategies separately, keep in mind that the two are linked both with each other, and with the product and promotional strategies of any successful brand.

## LO1 Distribution: Getting Your Product to Your Customer

Next time you go to the grocery store, look around…the average U.S. supermarket carries about 30,000 different products. Is your favorite brand of soda part of the mix? Why? How did it get from the factory to your neighborhood store? Where else could you find that soda? How far would you be willing to go to get it? These are marketing distribution questions that contribute directly to the **distribution strategy**: getting the right product to the right person at the right place, at the right time.

The distribution strategy has two elements: channels of distribution and physical distribution. A **channel of distribution** is the path that a product takes from the producer to the consumer, while **physical distribution** is the actual movement of products along that path. Some producers choose to sell their products directly to their customers through a **direct channel**. No one stands between the producer and the customer. Examples range from Dell computers, to local farmers markets, to factory outlet stores. But most producers use **channel intermediaries** to help their products move more efficiently and effectively from their factories to their consumers. Coppertone, for example, sells sun block to Costco—a channel intermediary—who may in turn sell it to you.

### The Role of Distributors: Adding Value

You might be asking yourself why we need distributors. Wouldn't it be a lot less expensive to buy directly from the producers? The answer, surprisingly, is no. Distributors add value—additional benefits—to products. They charge for adding that value, but typically they charge less than it would cost for consumers or producers to add that value on their own. When distributors add to the cost of a product without providing comparable benefits, the middlemen don't stay in business. Fifteen years ago, for instance, most people bought plane tickets from travel agents. But when the Internet reduced the cost and inconvenience of

**distribution strategy** A plan for delivering the right product to the right person at the right place at the right time.

**channel of distribution** The network of organizations and processes that links producers to consumers.

**physical distribution** The actual, physical movement of products along the distribution pathway.

**direct channel** A distribution process that links the producer and the customer with no intermediaries.

**channel intermediaries** Distribution organizations—informally called middlemen—that facilitate the movement of products from the producer to the consumer.

**utility** The value, or usefulness, that a good or a service offers a customer.

buying tickets directly from airlines, thousands of travel agencies lost their customers.

One core role of distributors is to reduce the number of transactions—and the associated costs—for goods to flow from producers to consumers. As you'll see in exhibit 13.1, even one marketing intermediary in the distribution channel can funnel goods from producers to consumers with far fewer costly transactions.

Distributors add value, or **utility**, in a number of different ways: form, time, place, ownership, information, and service. Sometimes the distributors *deliver* the value (rather than adding it themselves), but often they add new utility that wouldn't otherwise be present. As you read through the various types of utility, keep in mind that they are often interrelated, building on each other to maximize value.

**Form Utility** Form utility provides customer satisfaction by converting inputs into finished products. Clearly, form utility is primarily a part of manufacturing. Kellogg's, for instance, provides form utility by transforming wheat into cereal. But retailers can add form utility as well. Jamba Juice, for example, converts wheat grass into juice and fruit into smoothies.

**Time Utility** Time utility adds value by making products available at a convenient time for consumers. In our 24/7 society, consumers feel entitled to instant gratification, a benefit that distributors can provide more easily than most producers. Consider 1-hour dry cleaning, or even vending machines. These distributors provide options for filling your needs at a time that works for you.

**Place Utility** Place utility satisfies customer needs by providing the right products in the right place. Gas sta-

**Exhibit 13.1** How transactions are reduced through marketing intermediaries

tions and fast food, for instance, often cluster conveniently at the bottom of freeway ramps. ATMs—essentially electronic distributors—are readily available in locations that range from grocery stores to college cafeterias.

**Ownership Utility** Ownership utility adds value by making it easier for customers to actually possess the goods and services that they purchase. Providing credit, cashing checks, and delivering products are all examples of how distributors make it easier for customers to own their products.

**Information Utility** Information utility boosts customer satisfaction by providing helpful information. EB Games, for instance, hires gaming experts to guide their customers to the latest games and systems. Similarly, most skateboard stores hire skater salespeople who gladly help customers find the best board for them.

**Service Utility** Service utility adds value by providing fast, friendly, personalized service. Examples would include placing a special order for that part you need to customize your car, or giving you a makeover in your favorite department store. Distributors who provide service utility typically create a loyal base of customers.

## The Members of the Channel: Retailers versus Wholesalers

Many producers sell their goods through multiple channels of distribution. Some channels have many members, while others have only a few. The main distinction among channel members is whether they are retailers

**Many dry cleaners provide time utility by offering their customers one-hour dry cleaning services.**

© GREGORY JAMES VAN RAALTE/SHUTTERSTOCK

or wholesalers. **Retailers** are the distributors that most of us know and use on a daily basis. They sell products directly to final consumers. Examples include 7-Eleven markets, Starbucks, and Urban Outfitters. **Wholesalers**, on the other hand, buy products from the producer and sell them to businesses (or other nonfinal users such as hospitals, nonprofits, and the government). The businesses that buy from wholesalers can be retailers, other wholesalers, or business users. To complicate this fairly simple concept, some distributors act as both wholesalers and retailers. Sam's Club, for example, sells directly to businesses *and* to consumers.

## LO2 Wholesalers: Sorting out the Options

Some wholesalers are owned by producers and others are owned by retailers, but the vast majority—accounting for about two-thirds of all the wholesale trade—are **independent wholesaling businesses**. These companies represent a number of different producers, distributing their goods to a range of customers. Independent wholesalers fall into two categories: (1) **merchant wholesalers**, who take legal possession, or title, of the goods they distribute, and (2) **agents/brokers**, who don't take title of the goods.

### Merchant Wholesalers

Merchant wholesalers comprise about 80% of all wholesalers. By taking legal title to the goods they distribute, merchant wholesalers reduce the risk for producers that their products might be damaged or stolen…or even that they just won't sell. Taking title also allows merchant wholesalers to develop their own marketing strategies, including price.

- Full-service merchant wholesalers provide a complete array of services to the retailers or business users who typically purchase their goods. This includes warehousing, shipping, promotional assistance, product repairs, and credit.

- Limited service merchant wholesalers provide fewer services to their customers. For example, some might warehouse products, but not deliver them. Others might warehouse and deliver, but not provide credit or marketing assistance. The specific categories of limited service merchant wholesalers include the following:

  - *Drop Shippers:* Drop shippers take legal title of the merchandise, but they never physically process it. They simply organize and facilitate product shipments directly from the producer to

their customers. Drop shippers are common in industries with bulky products, such as coal or timber. Amazon, however, successfully pioneered the use of drop shipping in e-commerce, where it has become a standard shipping method for a number of major Websites.

- *Cash and Carry Wholesalers:* These distributors service customers who are too small to merit in-person sales calls from wholesaler reps. Customers must make the trip to the wholesaler themselves and cart their own products back to their stores. Costco and Staples are both examples.

- *Truck Jobbers:* Typically working with perishable goods such as bread, truck jobbers drive their products to their customers, who are usually smaller grocery stores. Their responsibilities often include checking the stock, suggesting reorder quantities, and removing out-of-date goods.

### Agents and Brokers

Agents and brokers connect buyers and sellers and facilitate transactions in exchange for commissions. But they do *not* take legal ownership of the goods they distribute. Many insurance companies, for instance, distribute via agents, while brokers often handle real estate and seasonal products such as fruits and vegetables.

## LO3 Retailers: The Consumer Connection

Retailers represent the last stop on the distribution path, since they sell goods and services directly to final consumers. Given their tight consumer connection, retailers must keep in especially close touch with rapidly changing consumer needs and wants.

*Smart retailers gain a competitive edge by providing more utility, or added value, than their counterparts. Low prices are only part of the equation. Other elements clearly include customer service,*

**retailers** Distributors that sell products directly to the ultimate users, typically in small quantities that are stored and merchandised on the premises.

**wholesalers** Distributors that buy products from producers and sell them to other businesses or nonfinal users such as hospitals, nonprofits, and the government.

**independent wholesaling businesses** Independent distributors that buy products from a range of different businesses and sell those products to a range of different customers.

**merchant wholesalers** Independent distributors who take legal possession, or title, of the goods they distribute.

**agents/brokers** Independent distributors who do not take title of the goods they distribute (even though they may take physical possession on a temporary basis before).

© AP IMAGES

**multichannel retailing** Providing multiple distribution channels for consumers to buy a product.

product selection, advertising, and location. The look and feel of the retailer—whether online or on-ground—is another critical element.

Retailing falls into two main categories: store and nonstore. But as we discuss each type, keep in mind that the lines between them are not always clear. In fact, **multichannel retailing**—or encouraging consumers to buy through different venues—is an emerging phenomenon. Some marketers have sold their products through multiple channels for many years. For example, on any given day, you could purchase a Coke from a grocery store, a restaurant, or a vending machine. But the emergence of the Internet has provided a host of new opportunities for firms that hadn't previously considered a multichannel approach. An active relationship between on-ground and online outlets has become pivotal for many retailers.

## Store Retailers

While other retail channels are growing, traditional stores remain the 800-pound gorilla of the retail industry, accounting for well over 90% of total retail. Stores range in size from tiny mom-and-pop groceries to multiacre superstores dwarfed only by their parking lots. A sampling of different store types is shown on page 77.

Both retailers and the producers who distribute through them must carefully consider their distribution

> Reed Hastings created Netflix—which revolutionized video distribution—partly out of anger that Blockbuster charged him $40 in late fees on his overdue rental of "Apollo 13."
>
> —*NewsWeek*

strategy. The three key strategic options are intensive, selective, and exclusive.

**Intensive Distribution**   Intensive distribution involves placing your products in as many stores as possible (or placing your stores themselves in as many locations as possible). This strategy makes the most sense for low cost convenience goods that consumers won't travel too far to find. Marketers have chosen this strategy for Starbucks, Charmin, and People magazine, among thousands of other examples.

**Selective Distribution**   Selective distribution means placing your products only with preferred retailers (or establishing your stores only in limited locations). This approach tends to work best for medium and higher priced products or stores that consumers don't expect to find on every street corner. Marketers have chosen this strategy for Nordstrom, Grand Lux Cafe, and most brands of paintball equipment.

**Exclusive Distribution**   Exclusive distribution means establishing only one retail outlet in a given area. Typically that one retailer has exclusive distribution rights, and provides exceptional service and selection. This strategy tends to work for luxury good providers with a customer base that actively seeks their products. Examples include top-end cars such as Bentley, and jewelers such as Tiffany.

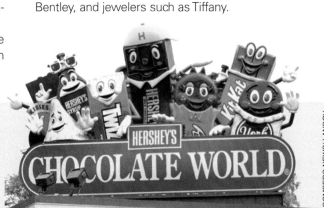

© PAUL CHAPLIN/BLOOMBERG NEWS/ LANDOV

## Shopping or Entertainment?

A growing number of retailers are building a competitive advantage by making the shopping experience just plain fun. Cold Stone Creamery employees, for example, enthusiastically sing for tips in many of their stores. Apple Computer installed whimsical "Genius Bars" in the back of their stores, which a CNET News reporter describes like this:

*This is where perplexed Mac owners can pull up a stool, lean on the bar, and spill their woes to the nodding guru, or "genius." With a smile, the genius—Apple says—will sort through technical problems and find an answer. And for truly baffling troubles, a red "hot line" phone—a concept borrowed from an old Batman episode—connects the genius to presumably higher-level geniuses at Apple's headquarters.*

(The always-busy Genius Bars do make you wonder why a product that bills itself as virtually bug-free requires so much brainpower to fix...)

Many bookstores—both big chains and independent players—have created a distinctive vibe that seems more like a cross between a coffeehouse and a library than a retail establishment (that is, of course, until you get to the cash register!). And in 2005, Hershey's opened Hershey's Chocolate World, which seems more like an interactive theater than a place to buy candy. Dan Papson, Hershey's vice president, says, "This is an entertainment place. We surround you with the sights, smells and magic of our brand."

The healthy growth of "shoppertainment" suggests that the trend is here to stay. The interactivity helps retailers build emotional bonds with their customers. And those bonds keep them coming back...even in the face of higher prices.[1]

## What Do Best Buy, Peet's Coffee and Tea, Lush Cosmetics, and REI Have in Common?

All are masters of multichannel marketing. Best Buy actually asks its on-ground employees to hand out coupons for online-only offers. They motivate the sales associates by giving them credit for online sales. Peet's Coffee and Tea, a small but growing competitor to Starbucks, finds that when their on-ground stores perform well, "Internet, mail order, and grocery businesses go up within a five-mile radius of the outlet." Lush Cosmetics, a growing retail powerhouse, cultivates customers by periodically selling "personal batches" of discontinued items online, making loyal users feel doubly special. Lush also hosts hugely popular online forums, which help them stay ahead of rapidly changing consumer tastes.

The benefits of multichannel marketing have become increasingly clear. A recent study found that "43 percent of multi-channel retailers...credit their offline channels for Internet sales." In other words, the on-ground stores fuel the online sales. And it works the other way, too. REI, a high-end retailer of outdoor adventure gear, finds that customers pick up about 40% of Internet, phone, and catalog sales from their on-ground stores. An REI spokesperson says, "Those customers, on average, spend an additional $90 in the store," which translates into extra profits for REI. Scott Silverman of the Shop.org retailers' network sums up the movement by pointing out, "Multi-channel retailers...that's redundant at this point...isn't it?" Perhaps it's not *yet* redundant, but hordes of retailers have developed a multichannel approach, and they're seeing the results in a healthier bottom line.[2]

© JOE ATLAS/ BRAND X PICTURES/JUPITERIMAGES

## Retail Store Categories

| Store Type | Store Description | Examples |
|---|---|---|
| Category killer | Dominates its category by offering a huge variety of one type of product. | Home Depot, Best Buy, Staples |
| Convenience store | Sells a small range of everyday and impulse products, at easy-to-access locations with long hours and quick checkout. | 7-Eleven, AM/PM markets, and a wide range of local stores |
| Department store | Offers a wide variety of merchandise (e.g., clothes, furniture, cosmetics), plus (usually) a high level of service. | Nordstrom, Neiman Marcus, JC Penney |
| Discount store | Offers a wide array of merchandise at significantly lower prices and with less service than most department stores. | Target, Wal-Mart, Kmart, Mervyn's |
| Outlet store | Producer-owned store sells directly to the public at a huge discount. May include discontinued, flawed, or overrun items. | Nike, Gap, Gucci, Versace, Quicksilver |
| Specialty store | Sells a wide selection of merchandise within a narrow category, such as auto parts. | Barnes & Noble, Victoria's Secret, Hot Topic, AutoZone |
| Supermarket | Offers a wide range of food products, plus limited non-food items (e.g., toilet paper). | Kroger, Safeway, Albertson's, Whole Foods |
| Supercenter | Sells a complete selection of food and general merchandise at a steep discount in a single enormous location. | Wal-Mart Supercenters, Super Target |
| Warehouse club | Sells discounted food and general merchandise in a large warehouse format to club members. | Costco, Sam's Club |

**wheel of retailing A classic distribution theory that suggests that retail firms and retail categories become more upscale as they go through their life cycles.**

The **wheel of retailing** offers another key strategic consideration. The wheel is a classic theory that suggests that retail firms—sometimes even entire retail categories—become more upscale as they go through their life cycles. For instance, it's easiest to enter a business on a shoestring, gaining customers by offering low prices. But eventually businesses trade up their selection, service, and facilities to maintain and build their customer base. Higher prices then follow, creating vulnerability to new, lower priced competitors. And thus the wheel keeps rolling.

Although the wheel of retailing theory does describe many basic retail patterns, it doesn't account for stores that launch at the high end of the market (e.g., Whole Foods) and those that retain their niche as deep discounters (e.g., Big Lots! or McDonald's). But the wheel theory does underscore the core principle that retailers must meet changing consumer needs in a relentlessly competitive environment.

## Nonstore Retailers

While most retail dollars flow through brick-and-mortar stores, a growing number of sales go through other channels, or non-store retailers. The key players represent online retailing, direct response retailing, direct selling, and vending.

**Online retailing** Also known as e-tailing, online retailing grew at the astonishing rate of nearly 25% per year over the past five years. Although the torrid pace began to slow in 2008, experts predict annual growth of more than 10% over the next five years, despite the sluggish economy.[2a]

Online retailers, like their on-ground counterparts, have learned that great customer service can be a powerful differentiator. Simply "getting eyeballs" isn't enough, since less than 5% of the people visiting a Website convert into paying customers. Overstock.com has been a pioneer in online customer service, hiring and training 60 specialists who engage customers in live chats, available 24/7. When a customer has a live chat with one of their specialists, the average purchase doubles in value.[3]

Online retailers have also learned to use technology to create a personal, in-the-moment shopping experience. Nike and Land's End, for instance, encourage customers to custom-create branded merchandise, providing exclusivity at a reasonable price. But perhaps most importantly, technology allows online retailers to reach potential customers—anywhere, anytime—so long as they have a computer and Internet access.

Despite the advantages, online retailers face two major hurdles. The first is that products must be delivered, and even the fastest delivery services typically take at least a couple of days. But the truly daunting hurdle is the lack of security on the Web. As online retailers and software developers create increasingly secure systems, hackers develop more sophisticated tools to crack their new codes.

**Direct Response Retailing** This category includes catalogs, telemarketing, and advertising (such as infomercials) meant to elicit direct consumer sales. While many traditional catalog retailers have also established successful Websites, the catalog side of the business continues to thrive. Victoria's Secret, for instance, sends a mind-boggling 395 million catalogs each year—that's four catalogs for every single American woman between the age of 15 and 64. Telemarketing, both inbound and outbound, also remains a potent distribution channel, despite the popular National Do Not Call list established in 2003.

## A Surprising Reversal: From Online to On-Ground

Although online retail sales have grown at a scorching rate for the past decade, JupiterResearch predicts that the pace will slow over the next few years, leveling out at 10-15% of total retail sales. But even as web retailing loses momentum, online marketing will generate offline sales at a faster rate, influencing 40% of total U.S. retail sales by 2011.

Recognizing the opportunity, a number of cutting-edge cyber retailers have moved to establish their brands on-ground. Threadless, for instance, a quirky online apparel site, opened their first retail store last year. Why? According to their website, they had "a zillion reasons," most of which revolve around building their brand. But cyber-merchants are not opening traditional retail outlets. Instead, a number of them have built a new, more community-based form of brick-and-mortar store. Threadless, for example, teaches design classes, hosts art exhibits, and sponsors events such as in-store stand-up comedy. Looking forward, chances are good that more online retailers will build a compelling offline presence. Lauren Freedman, president of the E-tailing Group consultancy points out that "there's something about showcasing a brand at a good store. When you do it well, you can't match that."[4]

© THREADLESS, A SKINNYCORP LLC COMPANY

A typical Wal-Mart distribution center is more than one million square feet, or the equivalent of 10 Wal-Mart retail stores.

© COMSTOCK/JUPITERIMAGES

**supply chain** All organizations, processes, and activities involved in the flow of goods from their raw materials to the final consumer.

**supply chain management (SCM)** Planning and coordinating the movement of products along the supply chain, from the raw materials to the final consumers.

**logistics** A subset of supply chain management that focuses largely on the tactics involved in moving products along the supply chain.

**Direct Selling** This channel includes all methods of selling directly to customers in their homes or workplaces. Door-to-door sales has enjoyed a resurgence in the wake of the National Do Not Call list, but the real strength of direct selling lies in multilevel marketing or MLM. Multilevel marketing involves hiring independent contractors to sell products to their personal network of friends and colleagues and to recruit new salespeople in return for a percentage of their commissions. Mary Kay Cosmetics and The Pampered Chef have both enjoyed enormous success in this arena, along with pioneering companies such as Tupperware.

**Vending** Until about a decade ago, vending machines in the United States mostly sold soft drinks and snacks. But more recently, the selection has expanded (and the machines have gone more upscale) as marketers recognize the value of providing their products as conveniently as possible to their target consumers. Banana Boat, for example, has placed sunscreen vending units in high traffic spots across sunny southern Florida. But other countries are far ahead of the U.S. in the vending arena. In Japan, for instance, people buy everything from blue jeans to beef from vending machines. As technology continues to roll forward, U.S. consumers are likely to see a growing number of vending machines for products as diverse as fresh cooked french fries, digital cameras, and Starbucks-style coffee.

We own the relationship with the customer and we subcontract to others.
–Kevin Rollins, Dell CEO

## LO4 Physical Distribution: Planes, Trains, and Much, Much More...

Determining the best distribution channels for your product is only the first half of your distribution strategy. The second half is physical distribution strategy: determining *how* your product will flow through the channel from the producer to the consumer.

The **supply chain** for a product includes not only its distribution channels, but also the string of suppliers who deliver products to the producers (see exhibit 13.2). Planning and coordinating the movement of products along the supply chain—from the raw materials to the final consumers—is called **supply chain management** or SCM. **Logistics** is a subset of SCM that focuses more on tactics (the actual movement of products) than on strategy.

At one time, relationships among the members of the supply chain were contentious. But these days, companies that foster collaboration rather than competition have typically experienced more success. Vendor-managed inventory is an emerging strategy—pioneered by Wal-Mart—that allows suppliers to determine buyer needs and automatically ship product. This strategy saves time and money, but also requires an extraordinary level of trust and information sharing among members of the supply chain.

**Exhibit 13.2** Elements of the Supply Chain

The Supply Chain highlights the links among the various organizations in the production and distribution process.

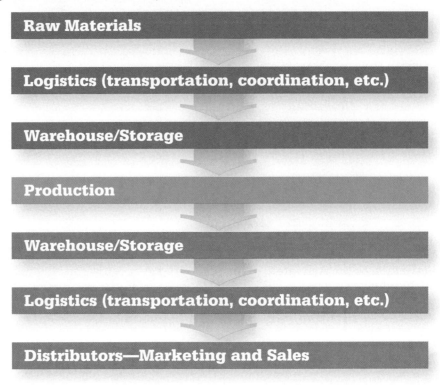

**Raw Materials**

**Logistics (transportation, coordination, etc.)**

**Warehouse/Storage**

**Production**

**Warehouse/Storage**

**Logistics (transportation, coordination, etc.)**

**Distributors—Marketing and Sales**

In our turbo-charged 24/7 society, supply chain management has become increasingly complex. Gap, for instance, contracts with more than 3,000 factories in more than 50 different countries, and distributes their products to about 3,000 stores in five different countries. The coordination requirements are mind-boggling. Key management decisions include the following considerations:

- Warehousing: How many warehouses do we need? Where should we locate our warehouses?

- Materials Handling: How should we move products within our facilities? How can we best balance efficiency with effectiveness?

- Inventory Control: How much inventory should we keep on hand? How should we store and distribute it? What about costs such as taxes and insurance?

- Order Processing: How should we manage incoming and outgoing orders? What would be most efficient for our customers and suppliers?

- Customer Service: How can we serve our customers most effectively? How can we reduce waiting times and facilitate interactions?

- Transportation: How can we move products most efficiently through the supply chain? What are the key tradeoffs?

- Security: How can we keep products safe from vandals, theft, and accidents every step of the way?

And fragile or perishable products, of course, require even more considerations.

## Transportation Decisions

Moving products through the supply chain is so important that it deserves its own section. The various options—trains, planes, and railroads, for instance—are called **modes of transportation**. To make smart decisions, marketers must consider what each mode offers in terms of cost, speed, dependability, flexibility, availability, and frequency of shipments. The right choice, of course, depends on the needs of the business and on the product itself. See the table on the following page for a description of the transportation options.

Depending on factors such as warehousing, docking facilities, and accessibility, some distributors use several different modes of transportation. If you owned a clothing boutique in Las Vegas, for example, chances are that much of your merchandise would travel by boat from China to Long Beach, California, and then by truck from Long Beach to Las Vegas.

## Proactive Supply Chain Management

A growing number of marketers have turned to supply chain management to build a competitive edge through greater efficiency. But given the complexity of the field, many firms choose to outsource this challenge to experts, rather than handling it internally. Companies that specialize in helping other companies manage the supply chain—such as UPS—have done particularly well in today's market.

## LO5 Pricing Objectives and Strategies: A High Stakes Game

Pricing strategy clearly has a significant impact on the success of any organization. Price plays a key role in determining demand for your products, which directly influences a company's profitability. Most people, after all, have a limited amount of money and a practically infinite number of ways they could spend it. Price impacts their spending choices at a more fundamental level than most other variables.

But ironically, price is perhaps the toughest variable for marketers to control. Both legal constraints and marketing intermediaries (distributors) play a role in determining the final price of most products. Marketers must also consider costs, competitors, investors, taxes, and product strategies.

In today's frenetic environment, stable pricing is no longer the norm. Smart marketers continually evaluate and refine their pricing strategies to ensure that they meet their goals. Even the goals themselves may shift in response to the changing market. Common objectives and strategies include building profitability, boosting volume, matching the competition, and creating prestige.

### Building Profitability

Since long-term profitability is a fundamental goal of most businesses, profitability targets are often

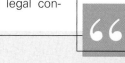

> If automobiles had followed the same development cycle as the computer, a Rolls-Royce would today cost $100, get a million miles per gallon, and explode once a year, killing everyone inside.
>
> —Robert Cringely, technology journalist

the starting point for pricing strategies. Many firms express these goals in terms of either return on investment (ROI) or return on sales (ROS). Keep in mind that profitability is the positive difference between revenue (or total sales) and costs. Firms can boost profits by increasing prices or decreasing costs, since either strategy will lead to a greater spread between the two. Doing both, of course, is tricky, but companies that succeed—such as Toyota—typically dominate their markets.

### Boosting Volume

Companies usually express volume goals in terms of market share—the percent of a market controlled by a company or a product. Amazon.com, for example, launched with volume objectives. Their goal was to capture as many "eyeballs" as possible, in hopes of later achieving profitability through programs that depend on volume, such as advertising on their site. A volume objective usually leads to one of the following strategies:

Penetration pricing **Penetration pricing**, a strategy for pricing new products, aims to capture as much of the market as possible through rock bottom prices. Each individual sale typically yields a tiny profit; the real money comes from the sheer volume of sales. A key benefit of this strategy is that it tends to discourage competitors, who may be scared off by the slim

**penetration pricing** A new product pricing strategy that aims to capture as much of the market as possible through rock bottom prices.

Modes of Transportation

| Mode | Percentage of U.S. Volume* | Cost | Speed | On-time Dependability | Flexibility in Handling | Frequency of Shipments | Availability |
|------|------|------|------|------|------|------|------|
| Rail | 40.2% | Medium | Slow | Medium | Medium | Low | Extensive |
| Truck | 40.0% | High | Fast | High | Medium | High | Most extensive |
| Ship | 9.0% | Lowest | Slowest | Lowest | Highest | Lowest | Limited |
| Plane | 0.2% | Highest | Fastest | Medium | Low | Medium | Medium |
| Pipeline | ** | Low | Slow | Highest | Lowest | Highest | Most limited |

Source: U.S. Department of Transportation, Bureau of Transportation Statistics, *Commodity Flow Survey 2002,* December 2004, www.bts.gov/press_releases/2005/bts003_05/html/bts003_05.html#table_01.
*Amounts shown in share/ton-miles.
**High-quality statistics unavailable for pipeline ton-miles.

margins. But penetration pricing only makes sense in categories that don't have a significant group of consumers who would be willing to pay a premium price (otherwise, the marketer would be leaving money on the table). For obvious reasons, companies that use penetration pricing are usually focused on controlling costs. JetBlue is a key example. Their prices are often unbeatable, but they strictly control costs by using a single kind of jet, optimizing turnaround times at the gate, and using many non-major airports.

### Every-day-low pricing

Also known as sustained discount pricing, **every-day-low-pricing (EDLP)** aims to achieve long-term profitability through volume. Wal-Mart is clearly the king of EDLP with "Always low prices. *Always!*" But Costco uses the same strategy to attract a much more upscale audience. Costco customers boast an average salary of more than $95,000: these people are seeking everyday discounts because they want to, not because they need to. The product mix—eclectic and upscale—reflects the customer base. (Costco sells $600 million of discounted fine wine a year, and 55,000 low-priced rotisserie chickens

a day.) And it works. Costco stock continues to outperform the industry, and earnings show healthy, sustained growth.[5]

### High/Low Pricing

The **high/low pricing** strategy tries to increase traffic in retail stores by special sales on a limited number of products, and higher everyday prices on others. Often used—and overused—in grocery stores, drug stores, and department stores, this strategy can alienate customers who feel cheated when a product they bought for full price goes on sale soon after. High/low pricing can also train consumers to buy only when products are on sale.

### Loss Leader Pricing

Closely related to high/low pricing, **loss leader pricing** means pricing a handful of items—or loss leaders—temporarily below cost to drive traffic. The retailer loses money on the loss leaders, but aims to make up the difference (and then some) on other purchases. To encourage other purchases, retailers typically place loss leaders at the back of the store, forcing customers to navigate past a tempting array of more profitable items. But this strategy can't be used everywhere, since loss leaders are illegal for anti-competitive reasons in a number of states.

### Matching the Competition

The key goal is to set prices based on what everyone else is doing. Usually, the idea is to wipe out price as a point of comparison, forcing customers to choose their product based on other factors. Examples include Coke

## Oops! What were they THINKING?!

© PHOTODISC/GETTY IMAGES

### "Slippery Finger" Pricing Goofs

If a price seems too good to be true, it probably is. But seeking an incredible bargain can still make sense...dollar and cents. Due to "slippery finger" typos, frequent price changes, and programming glitches, online retailers are especially vulnerable to pricing mistakes. Without human cashier confirmation, it's tough to catch the goofs. And to magnify the problem, quick communication on the Web almost ensures a flood of customers placing orders as soon as the wrong price goes live.

A sampling of recent online "deals":

- Free flights from Los Angeles to Fiji
- Round-trip tickets from San Jose, CA to Paris for $27.98
- $1,049 televisions wrongly listed for $99.99 on Amazon
- $588 Hitachi monitors mistakenly marked down to $164
- $379 Axim X3i PDAs wrongly priced at $79 on Dell's site

After the first few high-profile pricing disasters, online retailers have taken steps to protect themselves through specific disclaimers in their terms of use. And the courts have generally ruled that a company need not honor an offer if a reasonable person would recognize that it was a mistake.

But disclaimers and legal protections won't protect a retailer from customers who feel cheated. So companies that post pricing mistakes must choose between losing money by honoring offers or losing customer good will by canceling them...there simply isn't a winning option. But Travelocity—home of those unintended free tickets from Los Angeles to Fuji—has at least found a way to handle snafus with grace. Their Travelocity Guarantee program notes "If, say, we inadvertently advertise a fare that's just 'too good to be true,' like a free trip to Fiji, we'll work with you and our travel partners to make it up to you and find a solution that puts a smile on your face." So...happy shopping![6]

and Pepsi, Honda and Toyota, Delta and United. But sometimes one or two competitors emerge who drive pricing for entire industries. Marlboro, for instance, leads the pack in terms of cigarette pricing, with other brands falling into place behind.

### Creating Prestige

The core goal is to use price to send consumers a message about the high quality and exclusivity of a product... the higher the price the better the product. Of course, this strategy works only if the product actually delivers top quality; otherwise, nobody would buy more than once (and those who do so would clearly spread the word). Rolex watches, Mont Blanc pens, and Bentley cars all use prestige pricing to reinforce their image.

*Skimming Pricing* This new product pricing strategy is a subset of prestige pricing. **Skimming pricing** involves offering new products at a premium price. The idea is to entice price-insensitive consumers—music fanatics, for example—to buy high when a product first enters the market. Once these customers have made their purchases, marketers will often introduce lower-priced versions of the same product to capture the bottom of the market. Apple used this strategy with their iPod, introducing their premium version for a hefty price tag. Once they had secured the big spenders, they introduced the lower priced iPod Minis and Shuffles with a powerful market response. But keep in mind that skimming only works when a product is tough to copy in terms of either design or brand image. Otherwise, the fat margins will attract a host of competitors.

## LO6 Pricing in Practice: A Real World Approach

At this point, you may be wondering about economic theory. How do concepts such as supply and demand

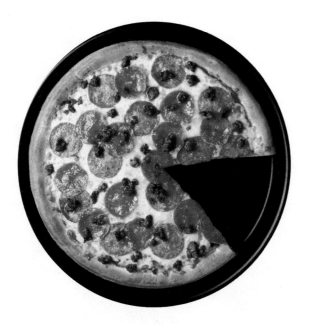

© C SQUARED STUDIOS/PHOTODISC/GETTY IMAGES

and price elasticity impact pricing decisions?

Even though most marketers are familiar with economics, they often don't have the information they need to apply the theories to their specific pricing strategies. Collecting data for supply and demand curves is expensive and time consuming, which may be unrealistic for rapidly changing markets. From a real-world standpoint, most marketers consider market-based factors—especially customer expectations and competitive prices—but they rely on cost-based pricing. The key question is: what price levels will allow me to cover my costs and achieve my objectives?

### Breakeven Analysis

**Breakeven analysis** is a relatively simple process that determines the number of units a firm must sell to cover all costs. Sales above the breakeven point will generate a profit; sales below the breakeven point will lead to a loss. The actual equation looks like this:

$$\text{Breakeven Point (BP)} = \frac{\text{Total fixed costs (FC)}}{\text{Price/Unit (P)} - \text{Variable cost/unit (VC)}}$$

If you were selling pizza, for example, your fixed costs might be $300,000 per year. Fixed costs stay the same regardless of how many pizzas you sell. Specific fixed costs might include the mortgage, equipment payments, advertising, insurance, and taxes. Suppose your variable cost per pizza—the cost of the ingredients and the cost of wages for the baker—were $4.00 per pizza. If your customers would pay $10 per pizza, you could use the breakeven equation to determine how many pizzas you'd need to sell in a year so that your total sales were equal to your total expenses. Remember: a company that is breaking even is not making a profit.

Here's how the breakeven analysis would work for our pizza business:

$$BP = \frac{FC}{P - VC} = \frac{\$300,000}{\$10 - \$4} = \frac{\$300,000}{\$6} = 50,000 \text{ pizzas}$$

Over a one-year horizon, 50,000 pizzas would translate to about 303 pizzas per day. Is that reasonable? Could you do better? If so, fire up those ovens! If not, you have several choices, each with its own set of considerations:

- *Raise Prices:* How much do other pizzas in your neighborhood cost? Are your pizzas better in some way? Would potential customers be willing to pay more?

- *Decrease Variable Costs:* Could you use less expensive ingredients? Is it possible to hire less expensive help? How would these changes impact quality and sales?

- Decrease Fixed Costs: Should you choose a different location? Can you lease cheaper equipment? Would it make sense to advertise less often? How would these changes impact your business?

Clearly, there isn't one best strategy, but a breakeven analysis helps marketers get a sense of where they stand and the hurdles they need to clear before actually introducing a product.

## Fixed Margin Pricing

Many firms determine upfront how much money they need to make for each item they sell. The **profit margin**—which is the gap between the cost and the price on a per product basis—can be expressed as a dollar amount, but more often is expressed as a percent. There are two key ways to determine margins.

- Cost-Based Pricing: The most popular method of establishing a fixed margin starts with determining the actual cost of each product. The process is more complex than it may initially seem, since fixed costs must be allocated on a per product basis and some variable costs fluctuate dramatically on a daily or weekly basis. But once the per product cost is set, the next step is to layer the margin on the cost to determine the price. Costco, for instance, has a strict policy that no branded item can be marked up by more than 14%, and no private-label item by more than 15%. Supermarkets, on the other hand, often mark up merchandise by 25%, and department stores by 50% or more. Margins in other industries can be much thinner.[7]

- Demand-Based Pricing: This approach begins by determining what price consumers would be willing to pay. With that as a starting point, marketers subtract their desired margin, which yields their target costs. This method is more market focused than cost-based pricing, but it's also more risky, since profits depend on achieving those target costs. A number of Japanese companies such as Sony have been very successful with this approach, achieving extraordinarily efficient production.

## Consumer Pricing Perceptions: The Strategic Wild Card

You just don't know if you've found the right price until you figure out how consumers perceive it. And those

perceptions can sometimes defy the straightforward logic of dollars and cents. Two key considerations are price–quality relationships and odd pricing.

The link between price and perceived quality can be powerful. Picture yourself walking into a local sporting goods store, looking for a new snowboard. They have several models of your favorite brand, most priced at around $450. But then you notice another option—same brand, same style—marked down to $79. Would you buy it? If you were like most consumers, you'd probably assume that something was wrong with a board that cheap. Would you be right? It's hard to know. Sometimes the relationship between price and quality is clear and direct, but that is not always the case. Regardless, consumers will use price as an indicator of quality unless they have additional information to guide their decision. Savvy marketers factor this tendency into their pricing strategies.

Marketers also must weigh the pros and cons of **odd pricing**, or ending prices in numbers below even dollars and cents. A home theater speaker package at Target, for instance, costs $99.99. Gasoline, of course, uses odd pricing to 99/100ths of a cent. But wouldn't round numbers be easier? Does that extra penny really make a difference? While the research is inconclusive, many marketers believe that jumping up to the "next" round number sends a message that prices have hit a whole new level. In other words, they believe that the *perceived* gap between $99.99 and $100.00 is much greater than the *actual* gap of one cent. And it certainly makes sense from an intuitive standpoint.

Odd prices have also come to signal a bargain, which is often—but not always—a benefit for the

> There are two kinds of fools in any market. One doesn't charge enough. The other charges too much.
>
> –Russian proverb

© KARL WEATHERLY/PHOTODISC /GETTY IMAGES

## When You Pay MORE to Do It Yourself

Most people assume that the more you do the less you pay. After all, it costs more to hire an accountant than to do your own taxes. It costs more to be served at the luxurious Four Seasons hotel than to pick up your own tray of food at McDonald's. But the relationship between service and cost isn't always as clear-cut as you might think. A master Napa Valley winemaker charges couples $15,000 to spend three days making their own wine at her vineyard. (Assuming 8-hour workdays, that means *you're* paying *her* $625 per hour.) And that's only one example. A high-profile east coast chef charges well over $100 per person for "guests" to cook their own meal before they eat it. The California coast is dotted with summer camps that charge parents upwards of $1,000 a week for their kids to provide hands-on care (e.g., mucking out stalls) for resident animals. For a more down-to-earth example, consider fajitas, a pricey staple for most Mexican restaurants. When you order fajitas, you essentially assemble your own meal, combining goodies from the sizzling tray and the steaming tortilla plate. And you pay *more* for those fajitas than for the tacos and burritos that the restaurant makes for you. Ironically, in our service-based economy, "doing the work" has become so rare, that we're sometimes willing to actually pay for the privilege.[8]

marketer. For instance, a big-screen TV for $999.99 might seem like a great deal, while knee surgery for $4,999.99 sounds kind of scary...you'd probably rather that your doctor charged $5,000. Likewise, a fast food joint might charge $3.99 for their value meal, while fine restaurants almost always end their prices in zeros. Marketers can determine whether odd pricing would work for them by evaluating the strategy in light of the messages it sends to the target market.

## LEARNING OBJECTIVES

After studying this chapter, you will be able to...

**LO1** Explain promotion and analyze the current promotional environment

**LO2** Explain integrated marketing communications

**LO3** Discuss development of the promotional message

**LO4** Discuss the promotional mix and emerging and traditional promotional tools

**LO5** Explain key considerations in choosing an effective promotional mix

4ltrpress.cengage.com/busn

> ## Doing business without advertising is like winking at a girl in the dark. You know what you are doing, but nobody else does.
> –Steuart Henderson Britt, psychologist and marketing expert

## LO1 Promotion: Influencing Consumer Decisions

**Promotion** is the power to influence consumers—to remind them, to inform them, to persuade them. The best promotion goes one step further, building powerful consumer bonds that draw your customers back to your product again and again. But don't forget that great promotion only works with a great product. Bill Bernbach, an ad industry legend, captures this concept by noting that "A great ad campaign will make a bad product fail faster. It will get more people to know it's bad."

Marketers can directly control most promotional tools. From TV advertising to telephone sales, the marketer creates the message and communicates it directly to the target audience. But ironically, marketers *cannot* directly control the most powerful promotional tools: publicity, such as a comment on Oprah, or a review in *Consumer Reports*, and word-of-mouth, such as a recommendation from a close friend or even a casual acquaintance. Marketers can simply influence these areas through creative promotional strategies.

### Promotion in Chaos: Danger or Opportunity?

Not coincidentally, the Chinese symbol for crisis resembles the symbols for danger and opportunity—a perfect description of promotion in today's market. The pace of change is staggering. Technology has empowered consumers to choose how and when they interact with media, and they are grabbing control with dizzying speed. Cable-based video-on-demand continues to soar, and digital movie downloads are poised for explosive growth. In 2007, Internet users spent an average of nearly 33 hours per week surfing the Web, almost twice as much time as watching TV. Meanwhile, more passive forms of entertainment, such as in-theater movies and network television, are slowly losing their audience. And those people who do still watch TV are gleefully changing the schedules and zapping the ads with TiVo or similar devices. As media splinters across an array of entertainment options, usage patterns have changed as well: tech-savvy viewers are more prone to consume media in on-the-fly snacks rather than sit-down meals. Rising consumer power and the breakneck pace of technology have created a growing need—and a stunning opportunity—for marketers to zero in on the right customers, at the right time, with the right message.[1]

**promotion** Marketing communication designed to influence consumer purchase decisions through information, persuasion, and reminders.

**integrated marketing communication** The coordination of marketing messages through every promotional vehicle to communicate a unified impression about a product.

**positioning statement** A brief statement that articulates how the marketer would like the target market to envision a product relative to the competition.

## LO2 Integrated Marketing Communication: Consistency and Focus

How many marketing messages have you gotten in the past 24 hours? Did you flip on the TV or radio? Surf the Web? Notice a billboard? Glance at the logo on a tee shirt or cap? Grab a flyer for a party? Chat with a friend about some product he likes? Marketing exposure quickly snowballs: the typical consumer receives about 3,000 advertising messages each day. Some of those messages are hard to avoid as marketers find new, increasingly creative ways to promote their products to a captive audience. The venues include elevators, taxicabs, golf carts, and other surprising settings.

Given the confounding level of clutter, smart companies use **integrated marketing communication** to coordinate their messages through every promotional vehicle—including their advertising, their Website, their salespeople, and so on—creating a coherent impression in the minds of their customers. Why bother coordinating all of these elements? The answer is clear. Consumers don't think about the specific source of the communication; instead, they combine—or integrate—the messages from *all* the sources to form a unified impression about your product. If the messages are out of sync or confusing, busy consumers won't bother to crack the code. They'll simply move on to the next best option.

Can you really control every message that every consumer sees or hears about your product? It's not likely. But if you accurately identify the key points of contact between your product and your target market, you can focus on those areas with remarkable effectiveness. For instance, the most common points of contact for McDonald's are probably advertising and the in-store experience. From upbeat commercials, to smiling employees, to brightly striped uniforms, they spend millions of dollars to support their core message of fast, tasty food in a clean, friendly environment...heavily concentrated in the areas that are key to their brand.

Other companies are likely to encounter the bulk of their customers through different channels. You'd probably learn about Dell computer, for example, through either their Website or word-of-mouth. Dell has invested heavily in both areas. The company maintains an innovative, user-friendly Website that allows even novice users to create customized systems. And Dell delivers award-winning customer service and technical support, which gets their customers to recommend their products to family and friends.

### Coordinating the Communication

Even after you've identified the key points of contact, coordinating the messages remains a challenge. In many companies completely different teams develop the different promotional areas. Salespeople and brand managers often have separate agendas, even when the same executive manages both departments. And frequently, disconnected outside agencies handle advertising, Web development, and sales promotion programs. Coordinating the messages will only happen with solid teamwork, which must begin at the top of the organization.

Information also plays a crucial role. To coordinate marketing messages, everyone who creates and manages them must have free access to knowledge about the customer, the product, the competition, the market, and the strategy of the organization. Some of this information, such as strategic goals, will come from the top down, but a fair amount, such as information about the customer, should come from the bottom up. Information must also flow laterally, across departments and agencies. The marketing research department, for instance, might have critical information about product performance, which might help the Web management agency create a feature page that might respond to competitive threats identified by the sales force. Smaller companies tend to share information informally, while larger companies often create formal databases that facilitate the information sharing process. But regardless of the mechanism, when all parties have access to the same data, they are much more likely to remain on the same page.

### LO3 A Meaningful Message: Finding the Big Idea

Your promotional message begins with understanding how your product is different from and better than the competition (see chapter 12 for a quick review). But your **positioning statement**—a brief statement that articulates how you want your target market to envision your product relative to the competition—seldom translates directly into the promotional message. Instead it marks the beginning of the creative development process, often spearheaded by ad agency creative professionals. When

it works, the creative development process yields a *big idea*—a meaningful, believable, and distinctive concept that cuts through the clutter. Big ideas are typically based on either a rational or an emotional premise. Here are a few examples:

| Rational: | Science: | Clinique: "Allergy tested. 100% fragrance free." |
|---|---|---|
| | Price: | Wal-Mart: "Always low prices. Always." |
| | Engineering: | BMW: "The ultimate driving machine." |
| Emotional: | Sex: | Carl's Jr.: Paris Hilton. "That's hot." |
| | Security: | Allstate: "You're in good hands." |
| | Humor: | Vonage: "People do stupid things." |

Not surprisingly, funny ads are a consumer favorite, although humor can be risky. For a record 10 years in a row, Budweiser—known for using humor effectively—has nabbed the top spot in *USA Today*'s annual Ad Meter consumer ranking of Super Bowl ads. Their winning ad in 2005 for instance featured a nervous skydiver refusing to jump in pursuit of a six-pack...so the pilot jumped instead. Every year, a wide portfolio of funny ads dominates the top ten.[2]

The best big ideas have entrenched themselves in popular culture, spawning both imitators and parodies. A small sampling includes:

- Nike: "Just do it."
- The Energizer Bunny.
- "Got Milk?"
- Budweiser: "Whasssuuuup?!"
- Motel 6: "We'll leave the light on for you."

Renowned marketing experts Al Ries and Jack Trout offer an interesting perspective on the big idea, narrowing it down to just one word. They claim, "The most powerful concept in marketing is owning a word in the prospect's mind. Not a complicated word. Not an invented one." But it can't be a word that someone else owns; you must drive your stake on unclaimed territory. And it shouldn't be a word like Volkswagen's *fahrvergnugen*, which just isn't worth it. It must be simple and focused. To show how this works, see what word comes to mind when you think of each of the following companies:

- Hershey's
- Nordstrom

Yes. She checks herself out in the mirror.

1 in 5 Americans will develop skin cancer in their lifetime. That's why Jennifer Garner made a promise to herself to examine her skin every month and see her dermatologist for a screening every year.

The Neutrogena Partnership for Skin Health, working with the American Academy of Dermatology (AAD), invites you to join them in their mission to stop skin cancer before it strikes. Empower their cause by wearing broad-spectrum sun protection, covering up and seeking shade between 10:00 am and 4:00 pm. Perform self-examinations regularly and report any changes in existing moles or birthmarks to your doctor. Because with early detection, skin cancer is 99% curable. And that's a statistic we love to share.

**Protect yourself starting today.**
The AAD and the Neutrogena Partnership for Skin Health encourage you to **get a free skin cancer screening** in May, June or July. Find one in your area by visiting aad.org or neutrogenaskinhealth.com. Mark the date of your screening on this slip as a healthy reminder.

**Neutrogena**
PARTNERSHIP FOR SKIN HEALTH

- Domino's Pizza
- Volvo
- Federal Express
- Crest
- Neutrogena

If you're like most other consumers, the words will be chocolate, service, home delivery, safety, overnight, cavities, and healthy. When a company zeros in on the right word, it creates a "hook" for the brand in the consumer's mind, laying the foundation for long-term success.[3]

## An International Perspective

Some big ideas translate well across cultures. The Marlboro Man, for instance, now promotes rugged individualism across the globe. But other big ideas don't travel as smoothly. DeBeers, for example, tried running ads in Japan using their proven strategy in the West: fabulously dressed women smiling and kissing their husbands who have just given them glittering diamonds. The ads failed in Japan because a Japanese woman would be more likely to shed a few tears and feign anger that her husband would spend so much money. The revised DeBeers campaign featured

> " The best way to have a good idea is to have lots of ideas.
> –Linus Pauling, scientist and Nobel Prize winner "

a hard-working man and wife in their tiny apartment. Receiving a diamond, the wife chides her extravagant husband: "Oh, you stupid!" The campaign was a wild success. Johnson & Johnson ran a seemingly innocuous ad in Poland that featured a woman who had just given birth in a hospital. Only later did they realize that Polish women only had babies in the hospital if the woman or her baby was seriously ill. AT&T's "Reach out and touch someone" campaign was a classic in the United States but a dud in Europe where viewers found it overly gushy. Taking a big idea to a foreign market can mean big money and a powerful brand, but careful research should still be your first step.[4]

## LO4 The Promotional Mix: Communicating the BIG IDEA

Once you've nailed your message, you need to communicate the big idea to your target market. The traditional communication tools—or **promotional channels**—include advertising, sales promotion, direct marketing, and personal selling. But more recently, a number of new tools have emerged, ranging from advergaming to Internet minimovies. The combination of communication tools that you choose to promote your product is called your promotional mix. We'll explore each area of the mix, beginning with the newest developments.

### Emerging Promotional Tools: The Leading Edge

In the last decade, the promotional landscape has changed dramatically. Consumer expectations and empowerment have skyrocketed. Consumer tolerance for impersonal

corporate communication has fallen. And digital technology has surged forward at breakneck speed. As a result, new promotional tools have emerged, and previously minor tools have burst into the mainstream.

**Product Placement** **Product placement**—the paid integration of branded products into movies and TV—exploded into big screen prominence in 1982, when Reese's Pieces played a highly visible role in Spielberg's blockbuster *E.T.* Reese's Pieces sales shot up 65% (a major embarrassment for the marketers of M&Ms, who passed on the opportunity). Over the years, product placement in movies has moved rapidly into the limelight. A few notable examples are:

* *Risky Business* (1983): This movie launched Tom Cruise and fueled a run on Ray-Ban sunglasses. The shades got another boost in 1997 with *Men in Black*.

* *You've Got Mail* (1998): AOL scored big in this Tom Hanks–Meg Ryan romance that etched the AOL signature mail call onto the national consciousness.

* James Bond: This longstanding movie icon hawked so many products in recent movies (e.g., Omega watches, Finlandia vodka, and British Airways), that it triggered a backlash from annoyed moviegoers and critics.[5]

Interestingly, product placement sometimes works in reverse. Bubba Gump Shrimp, a fictional brand featured in 1994's *Forrest Gump,* came to life after the movie as an international restaurant chain. Similarly, *Vote for Pedro* shirts from the offbeat hit 2004's *Napoleon Dynamite* became a top seller at T-Shirts.com.

Product placement on TV has catapulted into the mainstream in response to the growing prominence of digital video recorders (DVRs) such as TiVo. By 2009 experts expect that 40% of U.S. households will have DVRs, up from fewer than 10% in 2005. DVRs allow

© IMAGESTATE-PICTOR/JUPITERIMAGES

### Celebrity Pitches and Pitfalls

In celebrity-mad America, even B-listers can be a big idea for their sponsors. Stacie J, for instance, who was fired in the second season of *Apprentice*, hawked Casino Fortune, and boosted clients by 43%. And Zora Andrich, the 2003 winner of *Joe Millionaire*, endorsed NutriSystem weight loss products, and increased sales by 85%. But even B-list celebrities are a gamble because when they make mistakes—or when they don't know your product—it reflects poorly on your brand. Cybill Shepard, former star of the TV series *Moonlighting*, is the queen of the pitching faux pas. As spokesperson for the National Beef Council, she publicly admitted that she doesn't eat red meat. (The beef people replaced her with James Garner, who suffered a heart attack almost immediately.) But perhaps the Beef Council got what they deserved, since Shepard was known to have claimed that she never colored her hair when she was a spokesmodel for L'Oreal hair-coloring products. The bigger the celebrity, the bigger the risk of faux pas or worse: think OJ Simpson and Hertz, or Kobe Bryant and McDonald's. Yet more and more companies are taking the gamble and hitching themselves to a star, in hopes of differentiating themselves in an increasingly crowded consumer market.[6]

**advergaming** A relatively new promotional channel that involves integrating branded products and advertising into interactive games.

Product placement provides Coca-Cola with a starring role in *American Idol.*

consumers not only to watch on their own schedule, but also to zap ads—and 70% of DVR owners take full advantage of that feature. Worried marketers see product placement as chance to "TiVo-proof" their messages by integrating them into the programming. In 2006 they poured $2.4 billion into television product placement, and spending will likely continue to soar.[6a]

Product placement works best for marketers if the product seamlessly integrates into the show as a player rather than simply a prop. Sears has done especially well with *Extreme Makeover*, which features Kenmore appliances and Craftsman tools in starring roles. And it's hard to miss Coke in *American Idol*. The judges are seldom without their Coca-Cola emblazoned cups, and the contestants sit on a Coca-Cola couch in a Coca-Cola room as they wait to hear their fate. The price tag for this exposure—including commercial time and online content—is about $35 million. Media buyers often negotiate product placement deals as part of a package that includes regular ads, which reinforce the product that appeared in the program (unless, of course, the ads are zapped).[7]

Whether in TV or movies, product placement offers marketers huge sales potential in a credible environment. But product placement is risky—if your show is a dud, your placement is worthless. And the cost is high and growing, which only increases the financial risk. The benefits of product placement are tough to measure as well, especially for existing brands. But in the end, the only measure that really counts is consumer acceptance, which may disappear if product placement intrudes too much on the entertainment value of movies and TV.

**Advergaming** Interactive games have exploded into pop culture, with at least one person in 70% of U.S. households playing some kind of videogame. Not surprisingly, marketers have followed closely behind, developing a new promotional channel: **advergaming**. The advergame industry is expected to generate $312.2 million by 2009, up from $83.6 million in 2004.

In 2005, Massive, a start-up New York advertising agency, went live with their new adserving network for digital games. By mid-2006, they were purchased by Microsoft, and by mid-2008 they had signed deals with 40 game developers, including industry giant, Electronic Arts. Best-selling games ship with the Massive technology, which delivers fresh ads as players with an Internet connection move through the games. Massive's advertising clients include industry giants such as Coca-Cola, Paramount Pictures, and Dell.

Massive research shows that advergaming works for marketers. Gamers exposed to embedded ads show a 64% increase in brand familiarity, a 37% increase in brand rating, and a 41% increase in purchase consideration. But Massive isn't the only game in town. In early 2007, Google purchased AdScape, a nimble video game advertising company, and independent agency Double Fusion also provides fierce competition. Given the effectiveness of advergaming and the explosive growth, gamers may soon see a cyber world filled with as much promotion as the real world.[8]

**Minimovies** Branded minimovies—complete with engaging storylines and A-list talent—are creating a new cachet for a number of top brands. BMW pioneered the concept with its trailblazing online film series *The Hire*. The series included eight minimovies by edgy directors such as Ang Lee and Guy Ritchie, released sequentially on the BMW Website. The positive publicity was so powerful that BMW opted to turn the story's shadowy Driver character into a branded entertainment comic book series. Here is a sampling of other recent high-profile minimovies:

- **Chanel No. 5:** Dressed to the nines, Nicole Kidman stars as a movie star fleeing the paparazzi in this 2-minute Web film.

- **Amazon:** Just in time for Christmas, Amazon released a series of online shorts featuring top talent such as Minnie Driver using goods sold on the site.

- **Volkswagen Jetta:** This engaging 6-minute film, distributed to consumers via DVD, features Kevin Connolly and Joe Pantoliano (from *The Matrix*).[9]

Buzz Marketing   A recent study defined "buzz" as the transfer of information from someone who is in the know to someone who isn't. Buzz is essentially word-of-mouth, which now influences two-thirds of all consumer product purchases. And it makes sense. In a world that's increasingly complex, people turn to people they know and trust to help sort the garbage from the good stuff. Other popular terms for **buzz marketing** are guerrilla marketing and viral marketing.

Not surprisingly, marketers have actively pursued buzz for their brands, especially with the rising cost and diminishing effectiveness of more traditional media channels. Innovative buzz campaigns are typically custom-designed to meet their objectives, and they often cost significantly less than more traditional approaches. Here are some notable examples:

- The Subservient Chicken: In line with their "Have it your way" slogan, Burger King launched the Subservient Chicken Website to introduce their new TenderCrisp Chicken sandwich. The site shows an actor in a chicken suit who invites the viewer to "Get chicken the way you want it. Type in your command here." With a few obvious exceptions, the chicken will do just about anything you ask, from laying an egg to throwing pillows. After the link was seeded in some popular chat rooms, it exploded across the Web. The site has garnered more than 14 million unique visitors, becoming a pop culture favorite. And even though Burger King hasn't released specific sales results, they do report "significantly increased" chicken sandwich sales.[10]

- The Drugs I Need: In an unexpectedly funny musical online cartoon, Consumers Union parodies prescription drug marketing by poking fun at the inflated promises and scary list of side effects included in drug advertising. The lyrics for the soundtrack, sung by the Austin Lounge Lizards, include:

  *It's a life enhancing miracle, but there are some things you should know: It may cause agitation, palpitations, excessive salivation, constipation, male lactation, rust-colored urination, hallucinations, bad vibrations, mild electric shock sensations.*

  The goal of the cartoon was to encourage consumers to take action against drug marketing. The site makes it easy, with a direct link to send letters to Congress about drug safety. Less than a month after its launch, visitors had played the song more than 250,000 times.[11]

- Tremor: Proctor & Gamble, known for their traditional marketing, has now mobilized buzz marketing on an unprecedented scale. Its Tremor marketing group, launched in 2001, has recruited 280,000 kids, ages 13 to 19, to talk up products to their peers. Tremor looks for teens with "a wide social circle and a gift of gab." And these teens talk for free…or if not for free, for the chance to influence companies and get the early, inside scoop on new products. In addition to P&G brands, Tremorites have worked on heavy-hitters such as Sony Electronics, DreamWorks SKG, and Coca-Cola. While Tremor's revenues are relatively small at $12 million, P&G is convinced that they're on to something big: P&G's global marketing officer recently announced "The mass marketing model is dead. This is the future." The Dairy Foods Association is a true believer. One of their members introduced a new chocolate malt milk in Phoenix and Tucson with the same marketing mix and the same spending level. One exception: they used Tremor teens in Phoenix. After six months, sales in Phoenix were 18% higher than Tucson. That kind of success tells its own story.[12]

## Second Place: A Winning Strategy?

Unseating the top player in a crowded category can be an overwhelming challenge. But the number two slot holds powerful potential for building a brand. The trick is to embrace second place. Avis Rent-A-Car pioneered this strategy in 1963. For years they lost money competing with the number one rent-a-car agency, Hertz. Then, they decided to simply own their position in the market, changing their message to "Avis is number two in rent-a-cars. So why go with us? We try harder." The *We Try Harder* campaign turned around the business and was hailed by *Advertising Age* as one of the 100 greatest advertising mottos of the 20th century. Neutrogena took a similar approach to a different category: shampoo. Knowing that women are notoriously fickle shampoo users, they established themselves in the 1980s by promoting their brand as a second choice shampoo. They built a multi-million dollar business by essentially telling their prospects, "When your favorite shampoo stops working, try using Neutrogena. When you return to your favorite, you'll find it works better." The number one position is nice, but smart promotion can build the number two spot into a profitable branding winner.[13]

**Sponsorships** **Sponsorships** certainly aren't new, but they are among the fastest growing categories of promotional spending, increasing nearly 400% since 1990. The reasons are clear. Sponsorships provide a deep association between a marketer and a partner (usually a cultural or sporting event). Even though sponsors can't usually provide more than simply their logo or slogan, consumers tend to view them in a positive light, since they are clearly connected to events that matter to the target audience. The best sponsorship investments, of course, occur when the target audience for the marketer completely overlaps the target audience for the event.

The high level of integration between the sponsors and events provides valuable media coverage, justifying the hefty price—often in the neighborhood of $50 million per year. NASCAR, for instance, has attracted a host of Fortune 500 corporate sponsors, including McDonald's, Visa, America Online, Anheuser-Busch, and Dupont. NASCAR's appeal lies both in its committed fans, and in the five billion dollars of television exposure for its sponsors.[14]

## Traditional Promotional Tools: A Marketing Mainstay

Although new tools are gaining prominence, traditional promotional tools—advertising, sales promotion, public relations, and personal selling—remain powerful. In fact, many marketers use the new tools in conjunction with the traditional to create a balanced, far-reaching promotional mix.

**Advertising** The formal definition of **advertising** is paid, nonpersonal communication, designed to influence a target audience with regard to a product, service, organization, or idea. Most major brands use advertising not only to drive sales, but also to build their reputation, especially with a broad target market. Television (network broadcasts and cable combined) remains the number one advertising media, with direct mail and newspapers following close behind. As mass media prices increase and audiences fragment, fringe media is roaring toward the mainstream. But measurement is tough, since alternative media tactics are buried in other categories, including magazines, outdoor, and Internet. The overall media spending patterns for 2006 are shown in the table below.

Overall ad spending is on the rise. Note the strong growth in Internet advertising. This category, as tracked by *Advertising Age*, does **not** include paid search advertising, such as you see on Google. Industry expert *eMarketer* anticipates that search advertising will hit $10 billion by 2009, representing extraordinary growth.[14a]

Each type of media offers advantages and drawbacks, as summarized in the table on the next page. Your goal as a marketer should be to determine which media options reach your target market efficiently and effectively, within the limits of your budget.

**Sales Promotion** **Sales promotion** stimulates immediate sales activity through specific short-term programs aimed at either consumers or distributors. Traditionally, sales promotion has been subordinate to other promotional tools, but spending has accelerated in the past decade. Sales promotion falls into two categories: consumer and trade.

**Consumer promotion** is designed to generate immediate sales. Consumer promotion tools

**sponsorship** A deep association between a marketer and a partner (usually a cultural or sporting event), which involves promotion of the sponsor in exchange for either payment or the provision of goods.

**advertising** Paid, nonpersonal communication, designed to influence a target audience with regard to a product, service, organization, or idea.

**sales promotion** Marketing activities designed to stimulate immediate sales activity through specific short-term programs aimed at either consumers or distributors.

**consumer promotion** Marketing activities designed to generate immediate consumer sales, using tools such as premiums, promotional products, samples, coupons, rebates, and displays.

© DONALD MIRALLE/GETTY IMAGES

| Measured Media* | 2006 Spending (millions) | Percentage Change vs. 2005 |
|---|---|---|
| Broadcast TV | $25,900 | +3.4% |
| Cable TV | $16,700 | +3.4% |
| Spot TV | $18,500 | +11.1% |
| Syndicated TV | $4,200 | +.3% |
| Newspapers | $29,800 | −2.2% |
| Radio | $11,100 | +.3% |
| Magazines | $29,800 | +3.8% |
| Outdoor | $3,800 | +8.6% |
| Internet | $9,800 | +17.3% |
| TOTAL | $149,600 | +3.8%[15] |

*Includes media monitored by national reporting services

Major Media Categories

| Major Media | Advantages | Disadvantages |
|---|---|---|
| Broadcast TV | **Mass audience:** Season finales for top-rated shows garnered more than 30 million viewers in 2005.<br>**High impact:** TV lends itself to vivid, complex messages that use sight, sound, and motion. | **Disappearing viewers:** In 2005, top-rated shows drew about 30 million viewers, compared to the 1983 record of 105 million (the finale of *M*A*S*H*).<br>**Jaded viewers:** Consumers who aren't zapping ads with TiVo are prone to simply tuning them out.<br>**High cost:** A 30-second ad during Super Bowl 2005 cost a record $2.4 million, and a typical prime time ad cost around $400,000. |
| Cable TV | **Targeted programming:** Cable helps advertisers target highly specialized markets (Zhong Tian Channel, anyone?)<br>**Efficient:** The cost per contact is relatively low, especially for local buys.<br>**High impact:** Cable offers the same sight, sound, and motion benefits as broadcast. | **DVRs:** As with broadcast TV, many viewers simply aren't watching ads.<br>**Uneven quality:** Many cable ads are worse than mediocre, providing a seedy setting for quality products. |
| Newspapers | **Localized:** Advertisers can tailor their messages to meet local needs.<br>**Flexible:** Turnaround time for placing and pulling ads is very short.<br>**Consumer acceptance:** Readers expect and even seek newspaper ads. | **Short life span:** Readers quickly discard their papers.<br>**Clutter:** It takes 2 or 3 hours to read the average metro paper from cover to cover. Almost no one does it.<br>**Quality:** Even top-notch color newsprint leaves a lot to be desired. |
| Direct mail | **Highly targeted:** Direct mail can reach very specific markets.<br>**International opportunity:** Less jaded foreign customers respond well to direct mail.<br>**E-mail option:** Opt-in e-mail can lower direct mail costs. | **Wastes resources:** Direct mail uses a staggering amount of paper. And most recipients don't even read it before they toss it.<br>**High cost:** Cost per contact can be high, although advertisers can limit the size of the campaign.<br>**Spam:** Unsolicited e-mail ads have undermined consumer tolerance for all e-mail ads. |
| Radio | **Highly targeted:** In L.A., for example, the dial ranges from Vietnamese talk radio, to urban dance music, each station with dramatically different listeners.<br>**Low cost:** Advertisers can control the cost by limiting the size of the buy.<br>**Very flexible:** Changing the message is quick and easy. | **Low impact:** Radio relies only on listening.<br>**Jaded listeners:** Many of us flip stations when the ads begin. |
| Magazines | **Highly targeted:** From *Cosmo* to *Computerworld*, magazines reach very specialized markets.<br>**Quality:** Glossy print sends a high-quality message.<br>**Long life:** Magazines tend to stick around homes and offices. | **High cost:** A full-page, four-color ad in *People* can cost more than $200,000.<br>**Inflexible:** Advertisers must submit artwork months before publication. |
| Outdoor | **High visibility:** Billboards and building sides are hard to miss.<br>**Repeat exposure:** Popular locations garner daily viewers.<br>**Breakthrough ideas:** Innovative approaches include cars and busses "wrapped" in ads, video billboards, and blimps. | **Simplistic messages:** More than an image and a few words will get lost.<br>**Visual pollution:** Many consumers object to outdoor ads.<br>**Limited targeted:** It's hard to ensure that the right people see your ad. |
| Internet | **24/7 global coverage:** Offers a remarkable level of exposure.<br>**Highly targeted:** Search engines are especially strong at delivering the right ad to the right person at the right time.<br>**Interactive:** Internet ads can empower consumers. | **Intrusive:** The annoyance factor from tough-to-close pop-ups alienates consumers, infuriating many.<br>**Limited readership:** Web surfers simply ignore the vast majority of ads. |

include premiums, promotional products, samples, coupons, rebates, and displays.

- **Premiums** are items that consumers receive free of charge—or for a lower than normal cost—in return for making a purchase. Upscale cosmetics companies use the gift-with-purchase approach on a regular basis. And fast food companies use premiums pretty much every time the major studios release a family movie. Successful premiums create a sense of urgency—"Buy me now!"—while building the value of the brand.

- **Promotional products** are also essentially gifts to consumers of merchandise that advertises a brand name. Nightclub promoters, for instance, often distribute free tee shirts plastered with their slogan. Or pizza delivery places give away refrigerator magnets with their logo and phone number. Promotional products work best when the merchandise relates to the brand, and it's so useful or fun that consumers will opt to keep it around.

- **Samples** reduce the risk of purchasing something new by allowing consumers to try a product before committing their cash. L'Oreal, for instance, distributed thousands of samples of the Garnier Fructis shampoo when they introduced the brand in Europe. Sampling also drives immediate purchases. At one time or another, most of us have probably bought food we didn't need after tasting a delicious morsel in the supermarket aisle. Costco and Trader Joe's do especially well with this angle on sampling.

- **Coupons** offer immediate price reductions to consumers. Instant coupons require even less effort, since they are attached to the package right there in the store. The goal is to entice consumers to try new products. But the downside is huge. Marketers who depend on coupons encourage consumers to focus on price rather than value, which makes it harder to differentiate brands and build loyalty. In categories with frequent coupons (such as soap and cereal), too many consumers wait for the coupon in order to buy. They end up getting great deals, but marketers pay the price in reduced profits.

- **Rebates**, common in the car industry and the electronics business, entice consumers with cash back offers. This is a powerful tactic for higher priced items, since rebates offer an appealing purchase motivator. And rebates provide an incentive for marketers as well: breakage. Most people who buy a product because of the rebate don't actually follow through and do the paperwork to get the money (some estimates suggest that breakage rates are as high as 90 to 95%). This means that marketers can offer hefty discounts without actually coughing up the cash, so it isn't surprising that rebates are a popular promotional tool!

## TechNotes

### If you're not blogging, you're slogging...

For those of you not yet in the know, blogs are Web logs, or personal online journals on every topic imaginable.

Blog search engine Technorati estimates that there are more than 100 million blogs on the Web, and thousands of new ones pop up each day. This booming phenomenon impacts companies across the globe. If the postings are in any way juicy, other bloggers link up, creating an instant surge of networked information. The good news: great ideas spread every bit as quickly as scandal, creating a huge opportunity for savvy firms. How can you use blogs to build your business? Five tips:

1. Surf through the blogosphere every day. Know what your customers are saying about you. Keep tabs on your competition. Harvest new ideas. Seek the support of bloggers who matter in your industry.

2. Consider launching a company blog. Be sure your postings are fair—especially when you respond to criticism—and let your readers post comments,

too. For a great example, check out GM's Fast Lane blog at http://fastlane.gmblogs.com/.

3. Consider advertising on blogs. Since the audience is fragmented, the opportunities are limited (at least for now), but highly focused.

4. Consider using the blogosphere to generate word-of-mouth. But be very, very careful. The backlash can be brutal if bloggers perceive that you're pushing your products on the sly. Being aboveboard—but not crass—simply works better.

5. Draw up commonsense blogging guidelines for your employees...make sure that they're not dishing inside info about your company or trashing your reputation online.

Whether or not you choose to participate, the blogosphere will continue to influence marketers in every industry, from car parts to online poker. Join the conversation![16]

© TATIANA POPOVA/SHUTTERSTOCK

**trade promotion** Marketing activities designed to stimulate wholesalers and retailers to push specific products more aggressively over the short term.

**public relations (PR)** The ongoing effort to create positive relationships with all of a firm's different "publics," including customers, employees, suppliers, the community, the general public, and the government.

**publicity** Unpaid stories in the media that influence perceptions about a company or its products.

- Displays generate purchases in-store. Most experts agree that consumers make about 70% of their purchase decisions as they shop, which means that displays can play a crucial role in sales success. Marketers of consumer products often give prefabricated display materials to grocery stores and mass merchandisers to encourage promotion.

**Trade Promotion** is designed to stimulate wholesalers and retailers to push specific products more aggressively. Special deals and allowances are the most common form of trade promotion, especially for consumer products. The idea is that if you give your distributors a temporary price cut, they will pass the savings on to consumers via a short-term "special."

Trade shows are another popular form of trade promotion. Usually organized by industry trade associations, trade shows give exhibitors a chance to display and promote their products to their distributors. They typically attract hundreds of exhibitors and thousands of attendees. Trade shows are especially common in rapidly changing industries such as toys and consumer electronics. Every year, for instance, the Consumer Electronics Association hosts "The world's largest annual trade show for consumer electronics!" in Las Vegas, and the American Toy Association hosts the American International Toy Fair in New York.

Other forms of trade promotion include contests, sweepstakes, and special events for distributors. A soda company, for instance, might sponsor a contest to see which grocery store can build the most creative summer display for their soda brands. Or a cable TV programmer might take a group of system managers to Key West to "learn more about their programming" (really an excuse for a great party that makes the system managers more open to the programmer's pitch).

**Public Relations** In the broadest sense, **public relations** (or PR) involves the ongoing effort to create positive relationships with all of a firm's different "publics," including customers, employees, suppliers, the community, the general public, and the government. But in a more focused sense, PR aims to generate positive **publicity**, or unpaid stories in the media that create a favorable impression about a company or its products. The endgame, of course, is to boost demand.

For the most part, the media covers companies or products that they perceive as newsworthy. To get coverage, smart firms continually scan their own companies for potential news—a hot product, for example, or a major corporate achievement—and present that news to the media. But finding news on a regular basis can be tough. To fill the gaps, innovative PR people sometimes simply create "news." PR guru Bill Stoller offers some interesting ideas for how to invent stories that will grab media attention:

- Launch a Hall of Fame: Induct some luminaries from your industry, create a simple Website, and send your press release to the media. Repeat each year, building your reputation along the way.

- Make a List: The best, the worst, the top 10, the bottom 10...the media loves lists, and the possible topics are endless! Just make sure that your list is relevant to your business.

### A Mini Campaign with Maximum Punch

When BMW introduced the Mini in the United States in 2002, their promotional budget was about 10% of a typical BMW budget—not nearly enough to fund a TV campaign. Instead, the Mini team relied on quirky print and outdoor ads and irreverent stunts, all with the same playful core message: Let's Motor! The Mini "sat" in the stands at Major League football games. It cruised around major cities perched atop SUVs. It swerved through day-glo orange staples in *Rolling Stone* magazine. And it appeared in a six-page *Playboy* "centerfold," complete with the little car's likes and dislikes. Offbeat billboards celebrated high performance in small packages, reminding consumers that "Napoleon was only 5'2" and "Bruce Lee. Only 135 pounds." And a 40-page booklet, inserted into a number of U.S. magazines spread "rumors" about giant robots made of Mini parts roaming the streets in Oxford, England (the home of the Mini factory). Adding even more punch, the Mini played a featured role in the popular 2003 crime movie, *The Italian Job*. The innovative, low-budget campaign yielded blockbuster results. In the first two years, brand awareness in the United States shot up from 2% to 60%. Total Mini sales have exceeded initial expectations by more than 50%. And the new Mini convertible has garnered impressive results. All in all, the Mini team has used integrated marketing communication to lay solid groundwork for a mighty brand.[17]

- Create a Petition: The Web makes this tactic easy. Harness a growing trend or identify a need in your industry, and launch your petition. The more signatures you get, the better your chances for publicity.[18]

The biggest advantage of publicity is that it is usually credible. Think about it: Are you more likely to buy a product featured on the news or a product featured in a 30-second ad? Are you more likely to read a book reviewed by the *New York Times* or featured on a billboard? Publicity is credible because most people believe that information presented by the media is based on legitimate opinions and facts rather than on the drive to make money. And it also helps that publicity is close to free (excluding any fees for a PR firm).

But publicity has a major downside: the marketer has no control over how the media presents the company or its products. For example, in an effort to protect customers from a growing tide of solicitors in front of its stores, Target banned Salvation Army bell ringers in front of all its stores in 2004. The press cried foul, focusing not on the service to consumers, but rather on the disrespect to a venerable charity. Target's archrival Wal-Mart, spotting an opportunity for themselves at Target's expense, announced that they would match customer donations to the Salvation Army at all of their locations.

> In B2B sales, only 14% of buyers consider the lowest price to be the primary reason for making a purchase.
>
> —The Marketing Edge

### Personal Selling

**Personal selling**—the world's oldest form of promotion—is person-to-person presentation of products to potential buyers. But successful selling typically begins long before the actual presentation and ends long afterwards. In today's competitive environment, selling means building relationships on a long-term basis.

Creating and maintaining a quality sales force is expensive. Experts estimate that each business-to-business sales call costs nearly $400. So why are more than 10% of Americans employed in sales? Because nothing works better than personal selling for high-ticket items, complex products, and high-volume customers. In some companies, the sales team works directly with customers; in other firms, the sales force works with distributors who buy large volumes of products for resale.

Salespeople fall along a spectrum that ranges from order takers who simply process sales to order seekers who use creative selling to persuade customers. Most department stores, for instance, hire order takers who stand behind the counter and ring up sales. But Nordstrom hires creative order seekers who actively garner sales by offering extra services such as tasteful accessory recommendations for a clothing shopper.

A separate category of salespeople focuses on **missionary selling**, which means promoting goodwill for a company by providing information and assistance to customers. The pharmaceutical industry, for instance, hires a small army of missionary salespeople who call on doctors to explain and promote their products, even though the actual sales move through pharmacies.

**personal selling** The person-to-person presentation of products to potential buyers.

**missionary selling** Promoting goodwill for a company by providing information and assistance to customers.

### The Public Relations Hall of Fame

Following his own advice, Bill Stoller created a PR Hall of Fame on his Publicity Insider Website. Here are some highlights:

- National Discount Brokers (NDB), a buttoned-up Wall Street firm with a mallard logo, added a quacking duck as option 7 on its automated phone tree. The publicity was overwhelming. NDB estimated that the exposure was the equivalent of 100 television commercials, yielding a 75% increase in new customers.
- When the Mir Space Station crash landed in 2001, Taco Bell set up a 40 foot by 40 foot target—emblazoned with the company's logo and the words "Free Taco Here!"—10 miles off the coast of Australia. They promised free tacos to every American if the debris hit their mark. The result was millions of dollars of free media coverage (but not a single free taco!).
- P.T. Barnum was the PR master of the 1800s. In addition to creating inventive PR stunts, Barnum pioneered advance PR. He sent teams to each town ahead of his show, planted stories in the local press, and provided behind-the-scenes previews of the show for local journalists (he would have been completely at home in Hollywood today!)[19]

© GETTY IMAGES

**consultative selling**
A sales approach that uses active listening to offer practical solutions to customer problems.

**team selling** A sales approach that includes a group of specialists from key functional areas of a company, such as engineering, finance, customer service, and others.

The sales process typically follows six key stages. But as we explore each one, keep in mind that well before the process begins, effective salespeople seek a complete understanding of their products, their industry, and their competition. A high level of knowledge permeates the entire selling process.

1. Prospect and Qualify: Prospecting means identifying potential customers. Qualifying means choosing those who are most likely to buy your product. Choosing the right prospects makes salespeople more efficient, since it helps them focus their limited time in areas that will yield results. Companies find prospects in a number of different ways, from trade shows, to direct mail, to cold calling. In a retail environment, everyone who walks in the door is a prospect, so salespeople either ask questions or look for visual cues to qualify customers.

2. Prepare: Before making a sales call, research is critical, especially in a business-to-business environment. What are your prospect's wants and needs? What are his or her current product lines? Who are the key competitors? What are the biggest internal and external challenges? How much time is your prospect willing to give you? The answers to these questions will help you customize your presentation for maximum effectiveness.

3. Present: You've probably heard that you don't get a second chance to make a good first impression, and that's especially true in sales. With so many options and so little time, buyers often look for reasons to eliminate choices; a weak first impression provides an easy reason to eliminate you. Your presentation itself should match the features of your product to

the benefits that your customer seeks (a chance to use all that preparation). Testimonials, letters of praise from satisfied current customers, can push forward the sale by reducing risk for your prospect. And in many categories, a demonstration can be the clincher. For some products, a demonstration is a no-brainer—test-driving cars, for example. But in other categories, technology can help demonstrate products that are too big to move.

4. Handle Objections: The key to success here is to view objections as opportunities rather than criticism. Objections give you a chance to learn more about the needs of your prospects and to elaborate on the benefits of your product. You should definitely anticipate as many objections as possible and prepare responses. One response may be connecting prospects with others in your company who can better handle their concerns. This approach offers the additional benefit of deepening ties between your prospect and your company.

5. Close Sale: Closing the sale—or asking the prospect to buy—is at the heart of the selling process. The close should flow naturally from the prior steps, but often it doesn't—sealing the deal can be surprisingly tough. One approach may be a trial close: "Would you like the 15-inch screen or the 17-inch screen?" If your prospect is still reluctant to buy, you may want to offer another alternative, or a special financial incentive. Even if the prospect doesn't actually make the purchase, remember that he or she may be willing in the future, so keep the door open.

6. Follow-up: The sales process doesn't end when the customer pays. The quality of service and support play a crucial role in future sales from the same customer, and getting those sales is much easier than finding brand new prospects. Great relationships with current customers also lead to testimonials and referrals that build momentum for long-term sales success.

Two personal selling trends are gathering momentum in a number of organizations: consultative selling and team selling. **Consultative selling** involves shifting the focus from the products to the customers. On a day-to-day basis, the practice involves a deep understanding of customer needs. Through lots and lots of active listening, consultative salespeople offer practical solutions to customer problems—solutions that use their products. While consultative selling generates powerful customer loyalty, it involves a significant—and expensive—time investment from the sales force.

**Team selling** tends to be especially effective for large, complex accounts. The approach includes a group of specialists from key functional areas of the company— not just sales, but also engineering, finance, customer service, and others. The goal is to uncover opportunities and respond to needs that would be beyond the capacity of a single salesperson. In these situations, a key part of

**Best Buy's switch to non-commissioned salespeople revolutionized the consumer electronics business by eliminating the impression of bias.**

© BILL GREENBLATT/UPI/LANDOV

the salesperson's role is to connect and coordinate the right network of contacts.

## LO5 Choosing the Right Promotional Mix: Not Just a Science

There are no failsafe rules for choosing the right combination of promotional tools. The mix varies dramatically among various industries, but also within specific industry segments. The best approach may simply be to consider the following questions in developing the mix that works best for your products.

- **Product Characteristics:** How can you best communicate the features of your product? Is it simple or complex? Is it high priced or inexpensive? A specialized, high priced item, for example, might require an investment in personal selling, whereas a simple, low-cost product might lend itself to TV or billboard advertising.

- **Product Life Cycle:** Where does your product stand in its lifecycle? Are you developing awareness? Are you generating desire? What about driving purchases? And building loyalty? The answers will clearly impact your promotional focus. For instance, if you're developing awareness, you might focus more on advertising, but if you're aiming to drive immediate sales, you'll probably emphasize sales promotion.

- **Target Audience:** How big is your target audience? Where do they live and work? A small target audience—especially if it's geographically dispersed—would lend itself to personal selling or direct mail. A sizable target audience might suggest advertising as an effective way to reach large numbers. Audience expectations should also play a role in your promotional mix decisions.

- **Push versus Pull:** Does your industry emphasize push or pull strategies? A **push strategy** involves motivating distributors to "push" your product to the final consumers, usually through heavy trade promotion and personal selling. A **pull strategy** involves creating demand from your final consumers so that they "pull" your products through the distribution channels. Many successful brands use a combination of push and pull strategies to achieve their goals. P&G, for example, recently launched a consumer marketing campaign for Crest toothpaste featuring an "Irresistibility IQ" quiz for clubgoers, but they also promote heavily to dentists, hoping that those dentists will recommend Crest to their patients.

- **Competitive Environment:** How are your key competitors handling their promotional strategies? Would it make more sense for you to follow their lead or to forge your own promotional path? If all your competitors offer coupons, for instance, your customers may expect you to offer them as well. Or if the environment is cluttered, you might want to focus on emerging promotional approaches such as advergaming.

- **Budget:** What are your promotional goals? How much money will it take to achieve them? (Answering this question is tough, but it's clearly important.) How much are your competitors spending in each area of the mix? And how much money do you have for promotion? Even though available budget shouldn't drive the promotional mix, it plays a crucial role, especially for smaller businesses.

**push strategy** A marketing approach that involves motivating distributors to heavily promote—or "push"—a product to the final consumers, usually through heavy trade promotion and personal selling.

**pull strategy** A marketing approach that involves creating demand from the ultimate consumers so that they "pull" your products through the distribution channels by actively seeking them.

I know half the money I spend on advertising is wasted, but I can never find out which half.

–John Wanamaker, department store magnate

CHAPTER **15**

# Management
## Motivation and Leadership: Bringing Business to Life

## LEARNING OBJECTIVES

After studying this chapter, you will be able to…

**LO1** Discuss the role of management and its importance to organizational success

**LO2** Explain key theories and current practices of motivation

**LO3** Outline the categories of business planning and explain strategic planning

**LO4** Discuss the organizing function of management

**LO5** Explain the role of managerial leadership and the key leadership styles

**LO6** Describe the management control process

4ltrpress.cengage.com/busn

A typical day at the office for me begins by asking:
What is impossible that I'm going to do today?
—Daniel Lamarre, president and COO, Cirque du Soleil

## LO1 Bringing Resources to Life

To grow and thrive every business needs resources—money, technology, materials—and an economic system that helps enterprise flourish. But those resources, or factors of production, are nothing without management to bring them to life. Managers provide vision and direction for their organizations, they decide how to use resources to achieve goals, and they inspire others—both inside and outside their companies—to follow their lead. While you probably know a number of managers on a personal basis, a more formal definition may help you understand their role: **Management** Achieving the goals of an organization through planning, organizing, leading, and controlling organizational resources including people, money, and time.

In simple terms, **planning** means figuring out where to go and how to get there. **Organizing** means determining a structure for both individual jobs and the overall organization. **Leading** means directing and motivating people to achieve organizational goals. And **controlling** means checking performance and making adjustments as needed. In today's chaotic, hyper-competitive business environment, managers face daunting challenges. But for the right people, management positions can provide an exhilarating—though sometimes exhausting—career.

As the business pace accelerates and the environment continues to morph, the role of management has radically transformed. The successful manager has changed from boss to coach, from disciplinarian to motivator, from dictator to team builder. But the bottom line goal has remained the same: to create value for the organization.

### Management Hierarchy: Levels of Responsibility

Most medium and large companies have three basic levels of management: top management, middle management, and first line (or supervisory) management. The levels typically fall into a pyramid of sorts, with a small number of top managers and a larger number of supervisory managers. Responsibilities shift as managers move up the hierarchy, and the skills that they use must shift accordingly. Here are the three key levels.

**management** Achieving the goals of an organization through planning, organizing, leading, and controlling organizational resources including people, money, and time.

**planning** Determining organizational goals and action plans for how to achieve those goals.

**organizing** Determining a structure for both individual jobs and the overall organization.

**leading** Directing and motivating people to achieve organizational goals.

**controlling** Checking performance and making adjustments as needed.

**top management** Managers who set the overall direction of the firm, articulating a vision, establishing priorities, and allocating time, money, and other resources.

**middle management** Managers who supervise lower-level managers and report to higher-level managers.

**first line management** Managers who directly supervise nonmanagement employees.

**technical skills** Expertise in a specific functional area or department.

**human skills** The ability to work effectively with and through other people in a range of different relationships.

**conceptual skills** The ability to grasp a big picture view of the overall organization, the relationship between its various parts, and its fit in the broader competitive environment.

- **Top management** are the people who set the overall direction of the firm. They must articulate a vision, establish priorities, and allocate time, money, and other resources. Typical titles include chief executive officer (CEO), president, and vice president.

- **Middle management** are the people who manage the managers. While they must communicate up and down the pyramid, their primary contribution often involves coordinating teams and special projects with their peers from other departments. Typical titles include director, division head, and branch manager.

- **First line management** are the people who manage the people who do the work. They must train, motivate, and evaluate nonmanagement employees, so they are heavily involved in day-to-day production issues. Typical titles include supervisor, foreman, and section leader.

## Management Skills: Having What It Takes to Get the Job Done

Given the turbulence of today's business world, managers must draw on a staggering range of skills to do their jobs efficiently and effectively. Most of these abilities cluster into three broad categories: technical skills, human skills, and conceptual skills.

- Technical Skills: **Technical skills** refer to expertise in a specific functional area or department. Keep in mind that technical skills don't necessarily relate to technology. People can have technical skills—or specific expertise—in virtually any field, from sales, to copy writing, to accounting, to airplane repair, to computer programming.

- Human Skills: **Human skills** refer to the ability to work with and through other people in a range of different relationships. Human skills include communication, leadership, coaching, empathy, and team building. A manager with strong human skills can typically mobilize support for initiatives and find win-win solutions for conflicts.

- Conceptual Skills: **Conceptual skills** refer to the ability to grasp a big picture view of the overall organization and the relationship between its various parts. Conceptual skills also help managers understand how their company fits into the broader competitive environment. Managers with strong conceptual skills typically excel at strategic planning.

All three categories of skill are essential for management success. But their importance varies according to the level of the manager. Front line managers must have a high degree of technical skills, which help them hire, train, and evaluate employees; avoid mistakes; and ensure high-quality production. Middle-level managers need an especially high level of human skills. They typically act as the bridge between departments, coordinating people and projects that some-

© AP IMAGES

### Avoiding the Dilbert Syndrome

You may be asking yourself why senior managers need *any* technical skills. After all, the people at the top get the people further down to do the day-to-day work for them. And even if senior managers wanted to, they couldn't possibly have technical skills in more than a handful of key fields...after all, even the most senior manager must rise from some area of specialty. But technical skills still do matter at the top—especially when they fit with the core business. Bill Gates, for instance, no longer does much computer programming himself, yet Microsoft still benefits from his programming expertise. As Chairman of Microsoft, his technical background helps him speedily recognize new opportunities, and evaluate and prioritize Microsoft products. And as importantly, his history as a programming star builds the respect of the cubicle dwellers who are essential to the success of the business.

A manager without technical skills risks becoming the "pointy-haired boss," or PHB, that celebrated cartoonist Scott Adams mocks in his comic strip *Dilbert*. According to the *Dilbert* website, the top priorities of the PHB are "the bottom line and looking good in front of his subordinates and superiors (not necessarily in that order)...the Boss is technologically challenged but he stays current on all the latest business trends, even though he rarely understands them." Not the right role model for a successful senior manager.[1]

times have mismatched priorities. Top-level managers must demonstrate excellent conceptual skills in order to formulate a vision, interpret marketplace trends and plan for the future. To move up in an organization, managers must constantly learn and grow, nurturing skills that reflect their new tasks.

Across all three skill sets, critical thinking and decision-making abilities have become increasingly important. Critical thinking helps managers find value in even an overload of information, while decision-making skills help them respond wisely and rapidly, with an unwavering focus on customer satisfaction.

## LO2 Motivation: Lighting the Fire

Standout managers motivate others to reach for their best selves—to accomplish more than they ever thought possible. Motivated workers tend to feel great about their jobs, and workers who feel great tend to produce more. But the thinking about *how* to motivate workers has changed dramatically over time. In the early 1900s, key management thinkers focused on efficiency and productivity, dictating precisely how workers should do each element of their jobs. But more recent research suggested that people's thoughts and feelings play a vital role in motivation, which led to a range of new theories.

## Theories of Motivation

**Maslow's Hierarchy of Needs Theory** Noted psychologist Abraham Maslow theorized that people are only motivated to satisfy unmet needs. He proposed a hierarchy of human needs—from basic to abstract—suggesting that as each need is met, people become motivated to meet the next highest need in the pyramid. Maslow's five specific needs are shown in the following table. While he didn't develop his theory based on the workplace, Maslow's ideas can illuminate the needs behind motivation at work. The table on the following page explains each need and gives examples of how employers can meet that need.

**Maslow's hierarchy of needs theory** Motivation theory that suggests human needs fall in a hierarchy and that as each need is met, people become motivated to meet the next highest need in the pyramid.

> " If everybody just loves you, you're probably not doing a very good job. "
> —Marin Alsop, renowned symphony conductor

# Oops! What were they THINKING?!

© PHOTODISC/GETTY IMAGES

## Bad Decisions, Big Impacts

Every day, managers around the globe make high stakes decisions, from expanding overseas, to introducing new products, to closing factories. The great decisions have become the stuff of legends, shaping the business world as we know it today. Bad choices also abound, though we tend to hear a lot less about them. Consider these five business decisions that made history for their silliness:

- Faced with the opportunity to buy rights to the telephone in 1876, Western Union, the telegraph behemoth, rejected the newfangled device: "This 'telephone' has too many shortcomings to be seriously considered as a means of communication. The device is inherently of no value to us."

- In 1899 two young attorneys approached Asa Chandler—owner of the briskly selling new fountain drink, Coca-Cola—with an innovative proposal to bottle the beverage. Chandler sold them exclusive rights to bottle Coke across most of the United States for the grand sum of $1. Oops.

- Reviewing technology at the dawn of the television age, the *New York Times*—a bellwether for key trends in business and otherwise—decided that TV just wasn't happening: "The problem with television is that people must keep their eyes glued to a screen; the average American family hasn't time for it." Imagine their surprise a few short years later...

- Gordon Moor of Intel sheepishly admits to a major gaffe: "In the mid-1970's, someone came to me with an idea for what was basically the PC. I personally didn't see anything useful in it, so we never gave it another thought."

- A true believer in the new media future, Jerry Levin, CEO of Time Warner, struck a deal in 2000 to merge with AOL. As soon as he signed the papers, the Internet bubble burst and AOL stock plummeted. Disgruntled Time Warner stockholders have seen the value of their shares decrease by more than 50%.

With the help of hindsight, momentous decisions may seem almost inevitable. But these bloopers clearly show that in the fog of the moment, the right choice can be anything but clear.[2]

**Maslow's Hierarchy of Needs Relates to the Workplace**

| Maslow's Need | Description | Workplace examples |
|---|---|---|
| Physiological | Need for basic survival—food, water, clothing, and shelter | A job with enough pay to buy the basics |
| Safety | Need to feel secure—free of harm and free of fear | Safety equipment, healthcare plans, retirement plans, job security |
| Social (Belonging) | Need to feel connected to others—accepted by family and friends | Teamwork, positive corporate culture, company lunchroom |
| Esteem | Need for self-respect and respect from others—recognition and status | Acknowledgement, promotions, perks |
| Self-Actualization | Need for fulfillment, the need to realize one's fullest potential | Challenging, creative jobs, work that ties to a greater good |

**Theory X and Theory Y** Motivation theory that suggests that management attitudes toward workers fall into two opposing categories based on management assumptions about worker capabilities and values.

**job enrichment** The creation of jobs with more meaningful content, under the assumption that challenging, creative work will motivate employees.

From a workplace perspective, the idea that people are only motivated by unmet needs clearly holds true for the first two levels of the hierarchy. Finding a job that pays the bills, for instance, is the primary motivator for most people who don't have any job at all. People who have a job, but no healthcare, would find health insurance much more motivating than, say, a company picnic geared toward meeting social needs.

But once physiological and safety needs are met, the other needs are motivating to different degrees in different people. An employee with strong social connections outside work, for instance, might be more motivated by a promotion that meets esteem needs than by a company outing that meets social needs. A number of firms actually use self-actualization needs as a starting point for motivating employees, by creating a mission statement that communicates the importance of the work. Google, for instance, inspires employees through its lofty purpose: to organize the world's information and make it universally accessible and useful.

**Theory X and Theory Y** Psychologist Douglas McGregor, one of Maslow's students, studied workplace motivation from a different angle. He proposed that management attitudes toward workers would directly impact worker motivation. His research suggested that management attitudes fall into two opposing categories, which he called **Theory X and Theory Y**.

McGregor proposed that managers should employ Theory Y assumptions in order to capitalize on the imagination and intelligence of every worker. In American business today, some organizations use a Theory X approach, but a growing number have begun to at least experiment with Theory Y, tapping into a rich pool of employee input.

**Job Enrichment** A number of researchers have focused on creating jobs with more meaningful content, under the assumption that challenging, creative work will motivate employees to give their best effort. **Job enrichment** typically includes the following factors:

1. **Skill Variety:** Workers can use a range of different skills.

2. **Task Identity:** Workers do complete tasks with clear beginnings and endings.

3. **Task Significance:** Workers understand the impact of the task on others.

4. **Autonomy:** Workers have freedom and authority regarding their jobs.

| Theory X Assumptions about Workers | Theory Y Assumptions about Workers |
|---|---|
| • Workers dislike work and will do everything they can to avoid it. | • Work is as natural as play or rest—workers do not inherently dislike it. |
| • Fear is motivating—coercion and threats are vital to get people to work toward company goals. | • Different rewards can be motivating—people can exercise self-direction and self-control to meet company goals. |
| • People prefer to be directed, avoiding responsibility and seeking security. | • People can accept and even seek responsibility. |
| | • The capacity for imagination, creativity, and ingenuity is widely distributed in the population. |
| | • The intellectual capacity of the average workers is underutilized in the workplace. |

**Richard Branson, founder of the Virgin Group, believes that people flourish with praise and shrivel under criticism.**

to performance, and performance will lead to a meaningful reward.

Effort ➠ Performance ➠ Reward

The theory suggests that if any link in the chain is broken, the employee will not be motivated.

Retailer Hot Topic has done a great job implementing every step of the equation, especially the link between effort and performance. A Hot Topic employee describes the connection, saying, "I've worked for HT for 5 years and the best thing I've learned is that if you work hard enough and dedicate enough of yourself to something, you can achieve your goals!" IBM, on the other hand, has recently strengthened the link in their company between performance and rewards. Bonuses now count for up to 30% of annual salary, in an effort to ensure that IBM richly rewards their highest producers.[4]

**Equity Theory** Pioneered by J. Stacy Adams, **equity theory** proposes that perceptions of fairness directly impact worker motivation. The key idea is that people won't be motivated if they believe that the relationship between what they contribute and what they earn is different from the relationship between what others contribute and what others earn. For example, if you work 10-hour days, and earn less than the guy in the next cube who works 7-hour days, you'd probably think it was pretty unfair. To restore a sense of balance, you might:

- Demand a raise
- Start working 7-hour days
- Convince yourself that the other guy is about to be fired
- Look for another job

The response to perceived inequity almost always involves trying to change the system, changing your own work habits, distorting your perceptions, or leaving the company.

But keep in mind that equity theory is based on perceptions, which are not always on the mark. People are all too prone to overestimate their own contributions, which throws perceived equity out of balance. The best way to combat equity issues is through clear, open communication from management.[5]

**expectancy theory** Motivation theory that deals with the relationship among individual effort, individual performance, and individual reward.

**equity theory** Motivation theory that proposes perceptions of fairness directly impact worker motivation.

5. **Feedback:** Workers receive clear, frequent information about their performance.

Richard Branson, maverick founder of the Virgin Group, relies on job enrichment—especially autonomy and feedback—to keep people motivated at his 350-company empire (which includes a startling range of firms, such as Virgin Atlantic Airlines, Virgin Music, Virgin mobile phones, and Virgin Galactic space travel). Branson gives his managers a stake in their companies and then tells them "to run it as if it's their own." He says, "I intervene as little as possible. Give them that, and they will give everything back." Due in large part to Branson's motivational approach, the Virgin workforce is fully engaged with the company, contributing to its remarkable long-term success.[3]

> " Leadership is the art of getting someone else to do something you want done because he wants to do it.
> —Dwight D. Eisenhower "

**Expectancy Theory** Usually attributed to researcher Victor Vroom, **expectancy theory** deals with the relationship among individual effort, individual performance, and individual reward. The key concept is that a worker will be motivated if he or she believes that effort will lead

**Motivation Today**

Companies today use a range of approaches to motivation, although several key themes have emerged. Most firms no longer seek to make their employees happy;

instead, they want their workers to be productive and engaged. Yet for employees, work is about more than just productivity. University of Michigan business school professor David Ulrich points out that even in today's hyper-competitive environment, "people still want to find meaning in their work and in the institutions that employ them."[6]

A growing emphasis on corporate culture has captured the best of both worlds for companies that do it right. A distinctive, positive culture tends to create productive employees who are deeply attached to their work and their companies. Biotechnology firm Genentech, for instance, *Fortune* magazine's best company to work for in 2006, aims "to make drugs that really matter," actively shunning a profit-driven approach to science. The corporate culture features Friday-night keggers, tee shirts to celebrate each company milestone, and a strong collaborative spirit.

In fact, a look at *Fortune*'s entire list of "100 Best Companies to Work For" uncovers a number of unique, motivating corporate culture elements. First Horizon National bank, headquartered in Memphis, has a "first-power" culture that puts bank employees ahead of both customers and shareholders. American Express encourages employees who work 12 to 24 months in one position to apply to rotate to a different job—or even a different nation—which keeps workers fresh and excited about the company. And any worker at the Four Seasons can stay free at any of their hotels, anywhere in the world, along with immediate family.[7]

Finally, a growing number of businesses have expanded their range of employee incentives beyond just cash. While money certainly matters, *Fortune* magazine

© PNC/BRAND X PICTURES/JUPITERIMAGES

points out that "telling employees they're doing a great job costs nothing but counts big." Employee training is a noncash motivational tactic gaining momentum across the economy in response to the growing array of complex skills needed by the workforce. The emphasis on training and education is especially motivating given that more and more employees identify themselves based on their field of expertise rather than their organization.[8]

## LO3 Planning: Figuring Out Where to Go and How to Get There

The planning function—figuring out where to go and how to get there—is the core of effective management. A recent survey in the *Wall Street Journal* found that 80% of executives identify planning as their most valuable management tool. But even though planning is critical, it's also highly risky in light of cutthroat competition, rapid change, and economic uncertainty. The best plans keep the organization on track, without sacrificing flexibility and responsiveness; they incorporate ways to respond to change both inside and outside the organization.[9]

Although all managers engage in planning, the scope of the process changes according to the manager's position as shown in the table below. Top-level managers focus on **strategic planning**. They establish a vision for the company, define long-term objectives and priorities, determine broad action steps, and allocate resources. Middle managers focus on **tactical planning**, or applying the strategic plan to their specific areas of responsibility. And first line managers focus on **operational planning**, or applying the tactical plans to daily, weekly, and monthly operations. Successful firms often encourage a flow of feedback up and down the organization to ensure that all key plans are sound and that all key players "buy in." Some typical planning decisions and timeframes are in the table below.

| Type of Planning | Management Level | Scope of Planning | Examples of Planning Questions and Concerns |
|---|---|---|---|
| Strategic Planning | Senior management | Typically 5-year timeframe | Should we acquire a new company? Should we begin manufacturing in China? Should we take our company public? |
| Tactical Planning | Middle management | Typically 1-year timeframe | Should we invest in new production equipment? Should we spend more time servicing each customer? Should we spend fewer ad dollars on TV and more on the Web? |
| Operational Planning | First line management | Daily, weekly, and monthly timeframe | How should we schedule employees this week? When should we schedule delivery for each batch of product? How should customer service people answer the phones? |

A fourth category of planning has gained new prominence in the last decade: **contingency planning**, or planning for unexpected events. Senior management usually spearheads contingency planning, but with input from the other levels of management. Contingency plans consider what might go wrong—both inside the business and with the outside environment—and develop responses. Potential issues include:

- How should we respond if our competitors start a price war?

- What should we do if the government regulates our industry?

- How can we restart our business if a natural disaster destroys our plant?

- How will we evacuate employees if terrorists strike our headquarters?

Clearly, anticipating every potential problem is impossible (and impractical!). Instead, effective contingency plans tend to focus only on the issues that are most probable, most potentially harmful, or both (see exhibit 15.1 on the following page). For example, a Southern California amusement park might concentrate their contingency plans on earthquake response, while a national airline might focus their plans on responding to a pilots' strike.

contingency planning Planning for unexpected events, usually involving a range of scenarios and assumptions that differ from the assumptions behind the core plans.

## Strategic Planning: Setting the Agenda

Strategic planning is the most fundamental part of the planning process, since all other plans—and most major management decisions—stem from the strategic plan. The strategic planning process typically includes these steps:

1. Define the mission of the organization.

2. Evaluate the organization's competitive position.

3. Set goals for the organization.

4. Create strategies for competitive differentiation.

5. Implement strategies.

6. Evaluate results and incorporate lessons learned.

## Attitude and Expectations

Generation Y—which includes the 29 million kids born between 1978 and 1998—is changing the face of the workforce. These self-confident, outspoken young people have posed a new set of challenges for managers across the economy. A quick profile of Generation Y—also known as millennials and echo-boomers—highlights their key characteristics. As you read, keep in mind that no general overview can clearly describe each member of Generation Y. Yet chances are strong that you recognize at least parts of yourself in this profile. Companies that understand you and your peers—and figure out how to harness your talents—will find themselves with a sharp competitive edge in the years to come.

© IMAGE SOURCE BLACK/JUPITERIMAGES

- *Goal Driven:* Gen Yers expect to perform for their rewards. But they tend to find smaller, short-term goals much more motivating than long-term goals. The reason: a week in their fast-paced world is more like a year was for their parents.
- *NOW Focused:* Gen Yers often look for instant gratification. They typically expect to make an impact in their companies right away, and they aren't willing to "pay dues" or "suck up" to people they don't respect in order to make it happen.
- *Change Oriented:* Gen Yers actively embrace change and excitement. Many anticipate—even hope—to change jobs frequently. They don't share the expectation of long term employment that disillusioned so many of their parents.
- *Tech Savvy:* Gen Yers are masters of the Internet and the iPod. They often expect top technology in the workplace, and they use virtually all of it (often at the same time!) to boost their performance.
- *Diverse:* Gen Y is among the most diverse demographic groups—one in three is a minority—and most don't believe that their ethnicity defines their character. Many were born in other countries and speak multiple languages fluently.
- *Idealistic:* Gen Yers grew up in a scary world, marked by violence in their own backyards. Yet they remain convinced that they can make a positive difference, seeking solutions through a refreshing commitment to volunteerism.
- *Fulfillment Focused:* Gen Yers tend to deeply value their families and their personal lives. They fully expect to achieve their lofty career goals without sacrificing time for themselves and the people they care about.[10]

**Exhibit 15.1** Contingency planning paradigm

Businesses tend to focus their contingency plans on issues that are most probable *and* most potentially harmful.

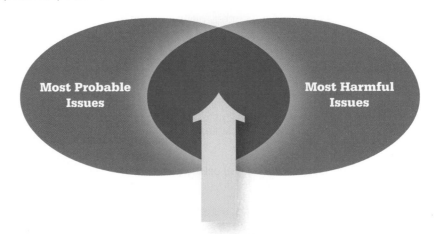

**Most Probable Issues**

**Most Harmful Issues**

**Focus Area for Contingency Plans**

**Defining Your Mission** The mission of an organization articulates its essential reason for being. The **mission** defines the organization's purpose, values, and core goals, providing the framework for all other plans. Most large companies present their mission as a simple, vivid, compelling statement, that everyone involved with the company—from the janitor to the CEO, from customers to investors—can easily understand. Mission statements tend to vary in their length, their language, and even their names, but they share a common goal: to provide a clear, long-term focus for the organization.

Examples of Mission Statements

| | |
|---|---|
| **House of Blues** | To create a profitable, principled, global entertainment company<br>To celebrate the diversity and brotherhood of world culture<br>To promote racial and spiritual harmony through love, peace, truth, righteousness, and non-violence |
| **State Farm Insurance** | State Farm's mission is to help people manage the risks of everyday life, recover from the unexpected, and realize their dreams. |
| **Google** | Google's mission is to organize the world's information and make it universally accessible and useful. |

**Evaluating Your Competitive Position** Strategy means nothing in a vacuum—every firm must plan in the context of the marketplace. Many companies use a **SWOT analysis** to evaluate where they stand relative to the competition. SWOT stands for strengths, weakness, opportunities, and threats. Strengths and weaknesses are internal to the organization, and they include factors that would either build up or drag down the firm's

performance. Opportunities and threats are external, and they include factors that would affect the company's performance, but are typically out of the company's control. The following table offers some examples.

| **Potential internal strengths:**<br>• Premium brand name<br>• Proven management team<br>• Lower costs/higher margins | **Potential external opportunities:**<br>• Higher consumer demand<br>• Complacent competitors<br>• Growth in foreign markets |
|---|---|
| **Potential internal weaknesses:**<br>• Low employee satisfaction<br>• Inadequate financial resources<br>• Poor location | **Potential external threats:**<br>• A powerful new competitor<br>• A deep recession<br>• New government regulations |

Initial information about internal strengths and weaknesses usually comes from careful analysis of internal reports on topics such as budget and profitability. But to better understand strengths and weaknesses, executives should actively seek firsthand information—on a personal basis—from key people throughout the company, from front line workers to the board of directors.

Gathering information about external opportunities and threats can be more complex, since these areas include both current and potential issues (which can be tough to predict). Information about external factors can come from many different sources, including the news, government reports, customers, and competitors.

**Setting Your Goals** **Strategic goals** represent concrete benchmarks that managers can use to measure performance in each key area of the organization. They must fit the firm's mission and tie directly to its competitive position. The most effective goals are:

1. **Specific and Measurable:** Whenever possible, managers should define goals in clear numerical terms that everyone understands.

2. **Tied to a Timeframe:** To create meaning and urgency, goals should be linked to a specific deadline.

3. **Realistic but Challenging:** Goals that make people stretch can motivate exceptional performance.

The following table offers examples of how weak goals can transform into powerful goals.

| Goal Setting "Don't" | Goal Setting "Do" |
| --- | --- |
| Improve customer satisfaction. | Increase average customer satisfaction ratings to 4.5 by the end of the fiscal year. |
| Reduce employee turnover. | Retain 90% of new employees for two or more years. |
| Increase market share. | Become the #1 or #2 brand in each market where we compete by the end of 2010. |

**Creating Your Strategies** **Strategies** are action plans that help the organization achieve its goals by forging the best fit between the firm and the environment. The underlying aim, of course, is to create a significant advantage versus the competition. Sources of competitive advantage vary, ranging from better product quality, to better technology, to more motivated employees. The most successful companies build their advantage across several fronts. Southwest Airlines, for example, has a more motivated workforce and a lower cost structure. Nordstrom has better customer service and higher product quality. And Toyota has better product quality and lower costs.

The specifics of strategy differ by industry and by company, but all strategies represent a roadmap. The SWOT analysis determines the starting point, and the objectives signify the immediate destination. Since speed matters, you must begin mapping the next leg of the journey even before you arrive. For added complexity, you never know—given the turbulent environment—when you might hit roadblocks. This means that strategies must be dynamic and flexible. Top managers have responded to this challenge by encouraging front line managers to participate in the process more than ever before.

**Implementing Your Strategies** Implementation should happen largely through tactical planning. Middle managers in each key area of the company must develop plans to carry out core strategies in their area. If the strategic plan, for example, calls for more new products, marketing would need to generate ideas, finance would need to find funding, and sales would need to prepare key accounts. And all of these steps would require tactical planning.

**Evaluating Your Results and Incorporating Lessons Learned** Evaluation of results should be a continual process, handled by managers at every level as part of their controlling function, covered further in this chapter. But for evaluation to be meaningful, the lessons learned must be analyzed objectively and factored back into the next planning cycle.

# LO4 Organizing: Fitting Together the Puzzle Pieces

The organizing function of management means creating a logical structure for people, their jobs, and their patterns of interaction. And clearly, the pieces can fit together in a number of different ways. In choosing the right structure for a specific company, management typically considers many factors, including the goals and strategies of the firm, its products, its use of technology, its size, and the structure of its competitors. Given the potential for rapid change in each of these factors, smart companies

## Creative "Mosh Pits"

Innovation alone is no longer enough for companies to thrive long term. The breakthroughs must happen faster to keep pace with consumers and competitors. The need for speed has led major firms from Mattel to Boeing to rethink how they organize the innovation process, shattering traditional barriers and churning out successful innovations at a record pace.

Not long ago, companies would handle innovation sequentially, with ideas moving slowly from engineers, to production, to marketing, to sales. The new approach brings together experts from each area in open, high-energy innovation labs, which often feature amenities such as foosball tables, and eliminate private offices. The result: a constant open flow of communication. People from every function brainstorm opportunities and problems, often finding solutions within hours rather than months. Some innovation labs are permanent facilities, while others function as temporary retreats. But all share a common goal of changing the organization to jump-start innovation and fuel the momentum.[11]

© C SQUARED STUDIOS/PHOTODISC/GETTY IMAGES

continually reexamine their structure and make changes whenever necessary. Microsoft, for instance, restructures its organization every couple of years as new challenges emerge.

To be effective, reorganizations—and their purpose—must be clear to employees throughout the company. In order to help employees understand how they and their jobs fit within the broader organization, most firms issue an **organization chart**, or a visual representation of the company's formal structure, as shown in exhibit 15.2.

Looking at the company represented by exhibit 15.2, you would probably assume that the vice president of production has more power than a regular employee in the marketing department. And in terms of formal power, you'd be absolutely right. But if the marketing employee baby-sits on the weekend for the president's granddaughter, the balance of power may actually be a bit different than it seems. Make no mistake: the formal structure matters. But knowing how power flows on an informal basis could dramatically impact your effectiveness as well, by helping you target your ideas to the right managers and marshal the support of the most influential employees.

## Key Organizing Considerations

In developing the organizational structure, management must make decisions about the degree of centralization, the span of management control, and the type of departmentalization that makes the most sense at any given time.

## Centralization

The **degree of centralization** relates directly to the source of power and control. In centralized companies, a small number of people at the top of the organization have the power to make decisions. This approach is simple and efficient, and the result tends to be a strong corporate image and a uniform customer approach across the front lines. But the downside is that centralized companies typically respond more slowly to customer needs and have lower employee morale. The trade-off may be worthwhile in steady, stable markets, but those are rare.

Faced with today's turbulent environment, most firms are moving toward greater decentralization, pushing power to the lower levels of the organization. Employees with the power to make decisions can respond to customer needs more quickly and effectively. They can also capitalize on opportunities that would likely vaporize in the time it would take to get permission to act. But for decentralization to work, every employee must fully understand the firm's mission, goals, and strategy; otherwise, the company could develop a fragmented image, which would undermine its strength long term. Also, active communication across departments is essential so that all employees can benefit from innovations in other parts of the organization.

## Span of Control

The **span of control**, or span of management, refers to the number of people that a manager supervises. There is no ideal number for every manager. The "right" span of control varies based on the abilities of both the manager and the subordinates, the nature of the work being done, the location of the employees, and the need for planning and coordination. Across industries the general trend has moved toward wider spans of control as a growing number of companies have pruned layers of middle management to the bare minimum.

## Departmentalization

**Departmentalization** means breaking workers into logical groups. A number of different options make sense, depending on the organization.

**Exhibit 15.2** Sample organization chart

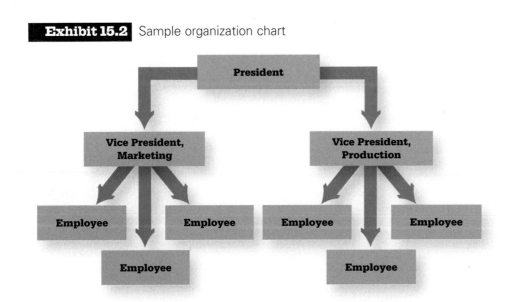

- **Functional:** Dividing employees into groups based on area of expertise, such as marketing, finance, and engineering, tends to be efficient and easy to coordinate. For those reasons it works especially well for small to medium firms.

- **Product:** Dividing employees into groups based on the products that a company offers helps workers develop expertise about products that often results in especially strong customer relations.

- **Customer:** Dividing employees into groups based on the customers that a company serves helps companies focus on the needs of specific customer groups. Many companies have separate departments for meeting the needs of business and consumer users. This approach is related to product departmentalization.

- **Geographical:** Dividing employees into groups based on where customers are located can help different departments better serve specific regions within one country. Similarly, many international firms create a separate department for each different country they serve.

- **Process:** Dividing into groups based on what type of work employees do is common in manufacturing, where management may divide departments by processes such as cutting, dying, and sewing.

As companies get larger, they usually adopt several different types of departmentalization at different levels of the organization. This approach, shown in exhibit 15.3 on the following page, is called hybrid departmentalization.

## Organization Models

Company structures tend to follow one of three different patterns: line organizations, line-and-staff organizations,

***Fast Company* compares business strategy to chess: "Think fast. Think under pressure. Think several moves ahead."**

and matrix organizations. But these organizational models are not mutually exclusive. In fact, many management teams build their structure using elements of each model at different levels of the organization.

**Line Organizations** A **line organization** typically has a clear, simple chain of command from top to bottom. Each person is directly accountable to the person immediately above, which means quick decision making and no fuzziness about who is responsible for what. The downside is a lack of specialists to provide advice or support for line managers. This approach tends to work well for small businesses, but for medium and large companies the result can be inflexibility, too much paperwork, and even incompetence since experts aren't available to give their input into key decisions.

**Line-and-Staff Organizations** A **line-and-staff organization** incorporates the benefits of a line organization without all the drawbacks. **Line managers** supervise the functions that contribute directly to profitability: production and marketing. **Staff managers**, on the other hand, supervise the functions that provide advice and assistance to the line departments. Examples include legal, accounting, and human resources. In a line-and-staff organization, the line managers form the primary chain of authority in the company. Staff departments work alongside line departments, but there is no direct reporting relationship (except at the top of the company). Since staff people don't report to line people, their authority comes from their know-how. This approach, which overlays fast decision making with additional expertise, tends to work well for medium and large companies. But in some firms, the staff departments gain so much power that they become dictatorial, imposing unreasonable limitations on the rest of the company.

**Matrix Organizations** **Matrix organizations** build on the line-and-staff approach by adding a lot more flexibility. A matrix structure brings together specialists from different areas of the company to work on individual projects on a temporary basis. A new product development team, for instance, might include representatives from sales, engineering, finance, purchasing, and advertising. For the course of the project, each specialist reports to the project manager *and* to the head of his or her own department (e.g., the vice president of marketing). The

**line organizations** Organizations with a clear, simple chain of command from top to bottom.

**line-and-staff organizations** Organizations with line managers forming the primary chain of authority in the company, and staff departments working alongside line departments.

**line managers** Managers who supervise the functions that contribute directly to profitability: production and marketing.

**staff managers** Managers who supervise the functions that provide advice and assistance to the line departments.

**matrix organizations** Organizations with a flexible structure that brings together specialists from different areas of the company to work on individual projects on a temporary basis.

**Exhibit 15.3** An example of hybrid departmentalization

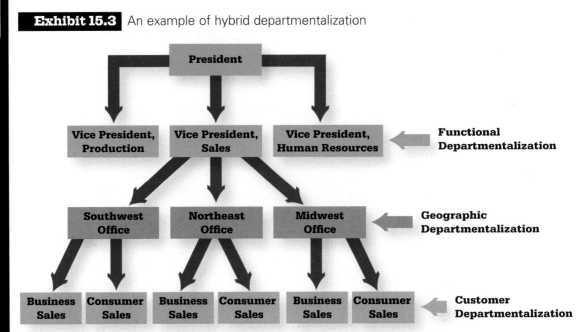

President

Vice President, Production — Vice President, Sales — Vice President, Human Resources ← **Functional Departmentalization**

Southwest Office — Northeast Office — Midwest Office ← **Geographic Departmentalization**

Business Sales — Consumer Sales — Business Sales — Consumer Sales — Business Sales — Consumer Sales ← **Customer Departmentalization**

**autocratic leaders** Leaders who hoard decision-making power for themselves and typically issue orders without consulting their followers.

**democratic leaders** Leaders who share power with their followers. While they still make final decisions, they typically solicit and incorporate input from their followers.

**free-reign leaders** Leaders who set objectives for their followers but give them freedom to choose how they accomplish those goals.

matrix approach has been particularly popular in the high tech and aerospace industries.

The matrix structure offers several key advantages. It encourages teamwork and communication across the organization. It offers flexibility in deploying key people. It lends itself to innovative solutions. And not surprisingly—when managed well—the matrix structure creates a higher level of motivation and satisfaction for employees. But these advantages have a clear flip side. The need for constant communication can bog down a company in too many meetings. The steady state of flux can be overwhelming for both managers and employees. And having two bosses can cause conflict and stress for everyone.[12]

# LO5 Leadership: Directing and Inspiring

While most people easily recognize a great leader, defining the qualities of leaders can be more complex, since successful leaders have a staggering range of personalities, characteristics, and backgrounds. Most researchers agree that true leaders are trustworthy, visionary, and inspiring. After all, we don't follow people who don't know where they're going, and we definitely don't follow people we don't trust. Other key leadership traits include empathy, courage, creativity, intelligence, and fairness.

## Leadership Style

How a leader uses power defines his or her leadership style. While the range of specific styles is huge, most seem to cluster into three broad categories: autocratic, democratic, and free-reign. The categories fall along a continuum of power, with the manager at one end and the employees at the other, as shown in exhibit 15.4.

**Autocratic leaders** hoard decision-making power for themselves, and they typically issue orders without consulting their followers. **Democratic leaders** share power with their followers. Even though they still make final decisions, they typically solicit and incorporate input from their followers. **Free-reign leaders** set objectives for their followers but give them freedom to choose how they accomplish those goals.

Interestingly, the most effective leaders don't use just one approach. They tend to shift their leadership style, depending on the followers and the situation. When a quick decision is paramount, autocratic leadership may make the most sense. An army officer, for example, probably shouldn't take a vote on whether to storm a hill in the middle of a firefight. But when creativity is the top priority—during new product brainstorming, for instance—free-reign management would probably work best. Likewise, a brand-new worker might benefit from autocratic (but friendly) management, while a tal-

**Exhibit 15.4** The continuum of leadership and power

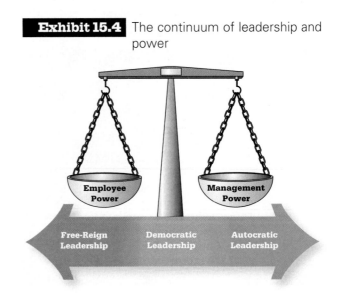

Employee Power — Management Power

Free-Reign Leadership — Democratic Leadership — Autocratic Leadership

ented, experienced employee would probably work best under free-reign leadership.

Another vital consideration is the customer. When the customer seeks consistency in the delivery of the product—in fast food, for instance—the autocratic leadership style may be appropriate. But when the customer needs flexibility and problem-solving assistance—a consulting client, for example—the free-reign leadership style may be most effective. The democratic leadership style typically provides customers with a balance of consistency and flexibility, which works across a wide range of industries.

> Management is doing things right; leadership is doing the right things.
> –Peter Drucker, management researcher, writer, and speaker

## LO6 Controlling: Making Sure It All Works

Controlling may be the least glamorous of the management functions, but don't be fooled: it's critically important. Controlling means monitoring performance of the firm—or individuals within the firm—and making improvements when necessary. As the environment changes, plans change. And as plans change, the control process must change as well, to ensure that the company achieves its goals. The control process includes three key steps:

1. Establish clear performance standards.

2. Measure actual performance against standards.

3. Take corrective action if necessary.

Establishing clear standards—or performance goals—begins with planning. At every level of planning, objectives should emerge that are consistent with the company's mission and strategic plan. The objectives must be (1) specific and measurable, (2) realistic but challenging, and (3) tied to a timeframe. Individual managers may need to break these goals into smaller parts for specific employees, but the subgoals should retain the same three qualities as the original objective.

Measuring performance against standards should happen well before the end of the timeframe attached to the goal. A strong information tracking system is probably management's best tool in this phase of the control process.

If the company or individual is not on track to meet the goals, management's first response should be communication. Employees with full information are far more likely to improve their performance than employees who never learn that they're falling behind. But sometimes workers need more than information—they may need additional resources or coaching in order to meet their goals. If they still don't succeed, perhaps the goals themselves need reexamination as part of a dynamic planning process. Given the expense in both human and financial terms, disciplining employees for poor performance should only come after exploring the reasons for not meeting goals and making changes if necessary.

### Power Play

Leadership traits and practices go hand-and-hand with power and influence. Power in business—the ability to push forward ideas, generate change, and influence others—can come from a number of sources:

- **Position:** The power of position gives a leader formal authority to either reward or punish employees with tools such as pay and job schedules. The chief financial officer, for example, has position power over the accountants.
- **Expertise:** The power of expertise comes from a person's abilities and experience. The best computer programmer, for instance, tends to have power in technology-dependent organizations.
- **Personality:** The power of personality comes from a person's character. Some people—often those with great communication skills and well-developed empathy—influence others simply through who they are.

While any one of these types of power could be effective alone, leaders have the best chance of success if they cultivate all three sources.

When you build your own base of power, don't forget that powerful leaders are seldom bullies. Research suggests that the nice guys do get ahead: A recent study showed that companies with farsighted, tolerant, humane, and practical CEOs yielded a 758% return over the course of a decade, versus a 128% return for the S&P 500.[13]

## CHAPTER 16

# Human Resource Management: Building a Top-Quality Workforce

## LEARNING OBJECTIVES

After studying this chapter, you will be able to...

**LO1** Explain the importance of human resources to business success

**LO2** Discuss key human resource issues in today's economy

**LO3** Outline challenges and opportunities that the human resources function faces

**LO4** Discuss human resource planning and core human resources responsibilities

**LO5** Explain the key federal legislation that impacts human resources

4ltrpress.cengage.com/busn

> If you hire good people, give them good jobs, and pay them good wages, something good is going to happen.
>
> –Jim Sinegal, founder of Costco

### LO1 Human Resource Management: Bringing Business to Life

As competition accelerates across the globe, leading firms in every business category have recognized that a quality workforce can vault them over the competition. Southwest Airlines was early to recognize the untapped potential of their people. Executive Chairman Herb Kelleher declared, "We value our employees first. They're the most important, and if you treat them right, then they treat the customers right, and if you treat the customers right, then they keep coming back and shareholders are happy." His attitude has more than paid off. Southwest Airlines has posted profits for 35 consecutive years, flying high even as other airlines have spiraled into decline.

Companies that get the most from their people typically consider their human resources an investment—often their biggest investment. They view the core goal of **human resource (HR) management** in a similar light: to nurture their human investment so that it yields the highest possible return. HR can achieve that goal by recruiting world-class talent, promoting career development, and boosting organizational effectiveness. But clearly this can only happen in partnership with key managers throughout the company, especially senior executives. (In smaller companies, of course, the owners usually do HR management in addition to their other responsibilities.)

### LO2 Human Resource Management Challenges: Major Hurdles

Building a top-quality workforce can be tougher than it may initially seem. Human resource managers—and their counterparts throughout the company—face huge challenges. The best strategies still aren't clear, but forward-thinking firms tend to experiment with new approaches.

**human resource management** The management function focused on maximizing the effectiveness of the workforce by recruiting world-class talent, promoting career development, and determining workforce strategies to boost organizational effectiveness.

## Older Workers

As the oversized baby boom generation begins turning 60, their employers—which include virtually every major American company—face a potential crisis: the loss of key talent and experience through massive retirements. Enlightened companies have responded with programs to retain their best employees through flexible schedules, training opportunities, and creative pay schedules. But the Society for Human Resource Management reports that 65% of their members surveyed don't do anything specific to retain older workers. By the time they get on board it may be too late to hang on to their competitive edge.[1]

## Younger Workers

As twentysomethings enter the workforce, they often bring optimism, open minds, technological know-how, a team orientation, and a multicultural perspective. But a number of them also bring an unprecedented sense of entitlement. This can translate into startlingly high expectations for their pay, their responsibilities, and their job flexibility, but little willingness to "pay dues." Many have no expectation that their employers will be loyal to them, and they don't feel that they owe their companies strong loyalty. Managing this group can sometimes be a challenge, but companies that do it well stand to deliver results for years to come.[2]

## Women Workers

Over the last few decades, women have made enormous strides in terms of workplace equality. But several large-scale studies confirm that women continue to face daunting discrimination in terms of both pay and promotions. While unfair treatment has been an issue for many years, recent legal changes have made it easier for women to sue, costing companies millions of dollars in the last decade alone. And the flood of lawsuits shows no signs of slowing. Many women have responded to the unfriendly business environment by leaving the workforce to raise children, start their own companies, or pursue other interests. As a result, we are experiencing a harmful, on-going brain drain.[3]

When people have come to me and said, 'I want to work with people,' I say, 'Good, go be a social worker.' HR isn't about being a do-gooder.
–Arnold Kanarick, HR executive

## Need for Flexibility

Across all ages and both genders, workers are actively pursuing more flexibility and work-life balance in their jobs. But from a management standpoint, this can be tough, since the job still needs to get done. Providing flexibility can also mean coping with hidden—or even not so hidden—biases against it. In spite of this issue, insightful HR managers try hard to offer enough flexibility to keep their best workers without jeopardizing their company's business goals.[4]

## Wage Gap

Comparing CEO pay to worker pay demonstrates a startling wage gap, bigger in the U.S. than in any other developed country. In 2006, the average CEO earned 364 times the average worker (up from 107 in 1990). Most observers don't object to the pay gap when top CEO pay ties to top performance. But when the link is missing, the gap can demoralize workers, infuriate stockholders, and may even undermine corporate performance. It clearly represents a strategic challenge for HR management.[5]

## Outsourcing

As high-tech, high-end jobs follow low-tech, low-end jobs out of the country—or even just to local contractors—human resources find themselves in turmoil. What kind of training makes sense in this still-unfolding economy? How can companies boost the morale of the employees who are left behind? Does less job security translate to less worker loyalty? How can human resources continue to add value as the ground shifts beneath them?[6]

## Lawsuits

The United States has become a wildly litigious society, with employees, customers, and shareholders levying lawsuit after lawsuit against firms of all sizes. Even though many of the lawsuits are legitimate—some profoundly important—a good number are just plain silly. But even if a lawsuit is frivolous, even if it's thrown out of court, it can still cost a company millions of dollars. Even more importantly, a frivolous lawsuit can cost a business its reputation. Avoiding employee lawsuits by knowing the law and encouraging legal practices is a growing human resources challenge.

## LO3 Human Resources Managers: Corporate Black Sheep?

### The Problem

The human resource management *function* is clearly critical, but human resources *departments*—and the people who work in them—face major challenges. Leading edge firms expect every department to offer "big picture," strategic contributions that boost company value. But a recent report in *Fast Company* suggests that most HR professionals lack sufficient strategic skills. Among other data, the report quotes a respected executive at a top U.S. company: "Business acumen is the single biggest factor that HR professionals in the U.S. lack today."

But even highly qualified, strategically focused HR managers face daunting perception problems. A management professor at a leading school comments that "The best and the brightest just don't go into HR." Once in the workforce, many employees see the human resources department as irrelevant…or even worse, as the enemy. And interestingly, human resources professionals seem to think more highly of themselves than others think of them. A recent survey asked various parties to rate the strategic value of HR within a company on a scale of 1 to 10. Human resources executives gave themselves a close 9, while senior management gave them a 7, and finance executives gave them a 6.

### The Solution

To gain respect from both senior management and their peers, human resources executives must earn a seat at the table. The first step is to know the company. What are the strategic goals? Who is the core customer? Who is the competition? Respected HR departments typically figure out ways to quantify their impact on the company in dollars and cents. They determine how to raise the value of the firm's human capital, which in turn increases the value of the firm itself. Effective HR people also remain open to exceptions even as they enforce broad company policies.

But clearly, these solutions will only work if senior management recognizes the potential value of effective human resource management. One simple test of senior management commitment is the reporting relationship. If the HR department reports to the CFO, it may be on the fast track to outsourcing. But if the HR department reports to the CEO, the strategic possibilities are unlimited.

## LO4 Human Resource Planning: Drawing the Map

Great human resource management begins with great planning: Where should you go? And how should you get there? Your objectives, of course, should flow from the company's master plan, and your strategies must reflect company priorities.

One of the first steps in the HR planning process should be to figure out where the company stands in terms of human resources. What skills does the workforce already have? What skills do they need? A company-wide **job analysis** often goes hand-in-hand with evaluating the current workforce. Job analysis examines what exactly needs to be done in each position to maximize the effectiveness of the organization—independent of who might be holding each job at any specific time. Smaller companies often handle job analysis on an informal basis but larger companies typically specify a formal **job description** and **job specifications** (or specs). A

### Success Stories!

HR mavericks across a range of industries have demonstrated that human resources can indeed make a strategic difference. Libby Sartain, the "Chief People Yahoo" at Yahoo!, has built a world-class human resources team, transforming the HR function into a corporate profitability driver. Her recommendations for HR professionals include:

- Cultivate powerful relationships.
- Release your company from the tyranny of too many policies.
- Brand and sell your department and its value to the organization.

Betty Lou Smith, VP of corporate HR at Hunter Douglas, created a mentoring program that reduced the employee turnover rate from 70 to 16%. She says, "HR has to step up and assume responsibility, not wait for management to knock on our door."

J. Steele Alphin, global personnel executive at Bank of America, assembled a top-level HR team of executives who then move into other business functions such as real estate and acquisitions. He positions HR as a branding function: "Every year we hire about 40,000 people externally…. That's a branding opportunity. If you interview people, even if you do not hire them, the experience should be such that they would want to bank with us." Clearly—when done right—the human resource management function creates a powerful and measurable competitive advantage.[7]

© AP IMAGES

**internal recruitment** The process of seeking employees who are currently within the firm to fill open positions.

**external recruitment** The process of seeking new employees from outside the firm.

job description defines the jobholder's *responsibilities*, and job specs define the *qualifications* for doing the job. Consider your professor's position. The job description might include the number of classes to be taught as well as other required campus activities. The job specs might include the type of education and teaching experience required. Thus, the job description might look something like this:

| Job Description | Job Specifications |
|---|---|
| Teach 5 business classes each semester either face-to-face or online | A master's degree in business from an accredited graduate school |
| Consult with students for 5 hours each week on an individual basis | A minimum of 3 years business teaching experience |
| Participate actively in college governance | Excellent interpersonal and communication skills |

The next step is to forecast future human resource requirements. The forecasting function requires a deep understanding of the company goals and strategies. HR managers must also assess the future supply of workers. Assessing supply can be a real challenge, since the size and quality of the workforce shifts continually. But key considerations should include retirement rates, graduation rates in relevant fields, and the pros and cons of the international labor market.

A complete HR plan—which falls under the company's strategic planning umbrella—must cover each core area of human resource management (see exhibit 16.1):

- Recruitment
- Selection
- Training
- Evaluation
- Compensation
- Benefits
- Separation

## Recruitment: Finding the Right People

Finding people to hire is easy, but finding *qualified* employees can be tough. The U.S. Census Bureau points out that a college degree typically doubles earning power, and the U.S. Bureau of Labor Statistics attests that the fastest growing fields in the next decade will require college graduates. But only 28% of adults over the age of 25 have a college degree. And as hordes of highly trained, college-educated baby boomers hit retirement, HR recruiters will face a real

hiring crunch. Even in the face of a shortage, recruiters also must find new employees who fit with the company culture in terms of both personality and style.[8]

New employees come from two basic sources: internal and external. **Internal recruitment** involves transferring or promoting employees from other positions within the company. This approach offers several advantages:

- Boosts employee morale by reinforcing the value of experience within the firm.
- Reduces risk for the firm since current employees have a proven track record.
- Lowers costs of both recruitment and training.

But companies often find that they don't have the right person within their organization. The firm may be too small, or perhaps no one has the right set of skills to fill the immediate needs. Or maybe the firm needs the fresh thinking and energy that can only come from outside. When this is the case, companies turn to external recruitment.

**External recruitment**, or looking for employees outside the firm, usually means tapping into a range of different resources. The possibilities include employment Websites, newspaper ads, trade associations, college and university employment centers, and employment agencies. But the most promising source of new hires may be referrals from current employees. A growing number of

**Exhibit 16.1** Human resource management

In 2005, job seekers posted 16.4 million new resumes on the Monster Board, averaging 40,000 new resumes *every day!*

organizations offer their current employees a cash bonus— typically $1,000 to $2,000—for each person they refer to the company who makes it past a probationary period. As an added benefit, employees who come through referrals have an excellent chance at success, since the person who recommended them has a stake in their progress. Employee referral programs also represent a real bargain for employers, compared to the average cost per new hire of more than $7,000. Not surprisingly, a higher level of employee referrals correlates to a higher level of shareholder returns, although lack of diversity may become a long-term problem with relying on employee referrals.[9]

## Selection: Making the Right Choice

Once you have a pool of qualified candidates, your next step is to choose the best person for the job. This, too, is easier said than done, yet making the *right* selection is crucial. The costs of a bad hire—both the direct costs such as placing ads and the intangibles such as lost productivity and morale—can drain company resources. A typical selection process includes accepting applications, interviewing, testing, checking references and background, and making the job offer. Keep in mind, though, that small businesses often follow a more streamlined process.

Applications Many companies use written applications simply as an initial screening mechanism. Questions about education and experience will determine whether a candidate gets any further consideration. In other words, the application is primarily a tool to reject unqualified candidates, rather than to actually choose qualified candidates.

Interviews Virtually every company uses interviews as a central part of the selection process. In larger companies, the HR department does initial interviews and then sends qualified candidates to the hiring manager for the actual selection. The hiring manager usually recruits co-workers to participate in the process.

Although employers frequently give interviews heavy weight in hiring decisions, interviews often say surprisingly little about whether a candidate will perform on the job. Too many managers use the interview as a get-to-know-you session, rather than focusing on the needs of the position. To help ensure that interviews better predict performance, experts recommend a **structured interview** process: developing a list of questions beforehand and asking the same questions to each candidate. The most effective questions are typically behavioral: they ask the candidate to describe a situation that he or she faced at a previous job—or a hypothetical situation at the new job—and to explain the resolution. Interviewers should gear the specific questions toward behaviors and experiences that are key for the new position. Consider the following examples of how this could work:

- Describe a time when you had to think "outside the box" to find a solution to a pressing problem.

- If you realized that a co-worker was cheating on his expense report, how would you handle the situation?

- What would you do if your boss asked you to complete a key project within an unreasonable timeframe?

Cultural differences also impact interview performance. As the U.S. labor pool becomes more diverse, even domestic companies must be aware of cultural differences. And it isn't simply a matter of legality or ethics. Firms that hire the best people regardless of cultural background will gain a critical edge in our increasingly competitive world.

**Testing** Either before or after the interview process (and sometimes at both points), a growing number of companies have instituted employment testing of various sorts. The main categories include skills testing, personality testing, drug testing, and physical exams. Skills testing and personality testing carry a fair amount of legal risk, since these tests must measure skills and aptitudes that relate directly to the job itself. Virtually 100% of Fortune 500 companies do pre-employment drug testing, as do most other companies. Physical exams are also standard but are highly regulated by state and federal law to ensure that firms don't use them just to screen out certain individuals.

**References and Background Checks** Even if you feel absolutely *certain* that a candidate is right for the job, don't skip the reference check before you make an offer. Outplacement firm Challenger, Gray & Christmas estimates that 10 to 30% of job applicants either shade the truth or out-and-out lie on their resumes. Although it may be tough to verify contributions and accomplishments at former jobs, it's pretty easy to uncover lies about education, job titles, and compensation. And it's quite worthwhile, given that the costs of bringing an unethical employee on-board can be staggering. Furthermore, if you happen to hire a truly dangerous employee, you can open the door to negligent hiring lawsuits for not taking "reasonable care." But surprisingly—despite the high risk—only about 15% of candidates are thoroughly vetted by the companies that consider them.[10]

> " In order to grow, you have to be trained or you'll be trapped in the present.
> —John Bachmann, managing partner of Edward Jones "

**Job Offers** After a company finds the right person, the next hurdle is designing the right job offer and getting your candidate to accept it. To hook an especially hot contender, you may need to get creative. A phone call from top management, the royal treatment, and special perks go a long way, but most superb candidates also want to know in very specific terms how their contributions would impact the business. And no matter how excited you are about your candi-

---

# Oops! What were they THINKING?!

© PHOTODISC/GETTY IMAGES

## Interview Gaffes: The Top Ten Things NOT to Do

As you get ready to interview for your dream job, you'll almost certainly find yourself awash in a torrent of advice from family and friends, and slog through a flood of tips on the Web and elsewhere. Don't be late, don't be early… Don't ask too many questions, don't ask too few… Don't look too casual, don't look too stuffy…. And whatever you do, never let anyone see that you're nervous! But however you actually feel—and whatever you actually say—take heart from knowing that you probably won't top these "real-life" interview blunders:

1. Question: "What five or six adjectives best describe you?"
   Answer: "Really, really, really, really, really cool!"

2. Question: "Were you late because you got lost?"
   Answer: "No. It was such a nice day that I didn't mind driving slowly."

3. Question: "Why should I hire you?"
   Answer: "Because they say you should always hire people better than yourself."

4. Question: "What do you find interesting about this job?"
   Answer: "The money. I don't really care what your company does."

5. Question: "Is it important to you to get benefits right away?"
   Answer: "I don't believe in healthcare. If I broke my leg, I'd just live with it."

6. Question: "What is your greatest strength?"
   Answer: "I'm a quick learner if I'm in the mood to pay attention."

7. Question: "What can you tell me about your creative ability?"
   Answer: "My answers to most of your questions are pretty good indicators."

8. Question: "Would you be willing to take a drug test?"
   Answer: "Sure. What kind of drugs do I get to test?"

9. Question: "What would your boss say about you?"
   Answer: "That I'm insubordinate."

10. Question: "How would you define a 'problem person'?"
    Answer: "Anyone who disagrees with me."[11]

date, be certain to establish a **probationary period** upfront. This means a specific timeframe (typically 3 to 6 months) during which a new hire can prove his or her worth on the job. If everything works out, the employee will move from conditional to permanent status; if not, the company can fire the employee fairly easily.

**Contingent Workers**   Companies that experience a fluctuating need for workers sometimes opt to hire **contingent workers**—or employees who don't expect regular, full-time jobs—rather than permanent, full-time workers. Specifically, contingent employees include temporary full-time workers, independent contractors, on-call workers, and temporary agency or contract agency workers. As a group, these contingent workers comprise a little over 4% of total U.S. employment.

Employers appreciate contingent workers because they offer flexibility, which can lead to much lower costs. But the hidden downside can be workers who are less committed and less experienced. Too much reliance on contingent workers could unwittingly sabotage company productivity and the customer experience.

## Training and Development: Honing the Competitive Edge

For successful companies in virtually every field, training and development has become an on-going process rather than a one-time activity. As the pace of change accelerates, training and development must also gather speed for companies and individuals to maintain their competitive edge. Experts offer five key reasons that relate directly to a healthy bottom line:

1. Increased innovation in strategies and products.

2. Increased ability to adopt new technologies.

3. Increased efficiency and productivity.

4. Increased employee motivation and lower employee turnover.

5. Decreased liability (e.g., sexual harassment lawsuits).

Training programs take a number of different forms, from orientation to skills training, to management development, depending on the specific employee and the needs of the organization.

**Orientation**   Once you hire new employees, **orientation** should be the first step in the training and development process. Effective orientation programs typically focus on introducing employees to the company culture (but without sacrificing need-to-know administrative information). Research consistently shows that strong orientation programs significantly reduce employee turnover, which lowers costs.[12]

The Boeing aerospace company has mastered the art of employee orientation. Boeing Military Aircraft and Missile Systems recently revamped their orientation process to include mentoring, meetings with senior executives, and an after-work social program. A highlight of the orientation—meant to crystallize the "wow" factor of working at Boeing—is the chance to take the controls of an F/A-18 fighter plane flight simulator. Management rightfully sees the program as a chance to develop "future leaders…the ones who will make sure that Boeing continues to be a great place to work."[13]

**On-the-Job Training**   **On-the-job training** is popular because it's very low cost: employees simply begin their jobs—sometimes under the guidance of more experienced employees—and learn as they go. For simple jobs this can make sense, but simple jobs are disappearing from the U.S. market due to the combined impact of off-shoring and technology. On-the-job training can also compromise the customer experience. Have you ever waited for much too long in a short line at the grocery store because the clerk couldn't figure out how to use the

**probationary period** A specific timeframe (typically 3 to 6 months) during which a new hire can prove his or her worth on the job before the hire becomes permanent.

**contingent workers** Employees who do not expect regular, full-time jobs, including temporary full-time workers, independent contractors, and temporary agency or contract agency workers.

**orientation** The first step in the training and development process, designed to introduce employees to the company culture, and provide key administrative information.

**on-the-job training** A training approach that requires employees to simply begin their jobs—sometimes guided by more experienced employees—and to learn as they go.

## Pulling Skeletons out of the Closet

With criminal convictions for CEOs splashed across the headlines, companies are spending a lot more time and money on background checks for key executives. According to *Forbes*, top investigative firms find that 10 to 20% of their executive searches expose issues that range from fake degrees to criminal filings. Peter Turecek, a managing partner of a business intelligence and investigations practice, comments, "We came across…an executive at an acquisition target company who turned out to have been a bagman in a murder. We also discovered a CFO that stole his neighbor's sod because he couldn't wait to finish his lawn. What's he doing if he can't meet his quarterly numbers?" That's a scary thought…[14]

© STOCKBYTE/GETTY IMAGES

**apprenticeships** Structured training programs that mandate that each beginner serve as an assistant to a fully trained worker before gaining full credentials to work in the field.

**management development** Programs to help current and potential executives develop the skills they need to move into leadership positions.

**performance appraisal** A formal feedback process that requires managers to give their subordinates feedback on a one-to-one basis, typically by comparing actual results to expected results.

Though nearly always rewarding, some apprenticeships are clearly more stressful than others!

© AP IMAGES

cash register? Multiplied across hundreds of customers, this kind of experience undermines the value of a company's brand.

Formal apprenticeship programs tend to be a more effective way of handling on-the-job training. **Apprenticeship** programs mandate that each beginner serve as an assistant to a fully trained worker for a specified period of time before gaining full credentials to work in the field. In the United States, apprenticeships are fairly common in trades such as plumbing and bricklaying. But in Europe, apprenticeships are much more common across a wide range of professions, from bankers to opticians.

Off–the-Job Training   Classroom training happens away from the job setting, but typically during work hours. Employers use classroom training—either on- or off-site—to teach a wide variety of topics from new computer programming languages, to negotiation skills, to stress management, and more. Going one step further than classroom training, some employers train workers off-site on "real" equipment (e.g., robots) similar to what they would actually use on the job. This approach is called vestibule training. Police academies, for instance, often use vestibule training for firearms. Job simulation goes even further than vestibule training, by attempting to duplicate the *exact* conditions that the trainee will face on the job. This approach makes sense for complex, high-risk positions such as astronaut or airline pilot.

Computer-Based Training   Computer-based training—mostly delivered via the Web—now plays a crucial role in off-the-job training. Broadband technology has turbocharged audio and visual capabilities, which support

engaging and interactive online training programs. Online training also standardizes the presentation of the material, since it doesn't depend on the quality of the individual instructor. And the Web helps employers train employees wherever they may be in the world, at their own pace and convenience. But there is a key drawback: it takes a lot of discipline to complete an online program, and some people simply learn better through direct human interaction.

Management Development   As the bulk of top-level U.S. executives move toward retirement, developing new leaders has become a priority in many organizations. **Management development** programs help current and potential executives develop the skills they need to move into leadership positions. These programs typically cover specific issues that face the business, but also less tangible—yet equally important—topics, such as communication, planning, business-analysis, change-management, coaching, and teambuilding skills.

## Evaluation: Assessing Employee Performance

Straightforward, frequent feedback is a powerful tool to improve employee performance. The best managers provide informal feedback on a constant basis so that employees always know where they stand. But most companies also require that managers give formal feedback through periodic **performance appraisals**, usually every 6 months or once a year. Typically, managers conduct the appraisals by sitting down with each employee on a one-to-one basis, and comparing actual results to expected results. The performance appraisal impacts decisions regarding compensation, promotions, training, transfers, and terminations.

The HR role in performance appraisals begins with the strategic process of creating evaluation tools that tie directly into the company's big picture objectives. Then, on a day-to-day basis, HR coordinates the actual appraisal process, which typically involves volumes of paperwork. HR must also ensure that managers are trained in how to provide relevant, honest, objective feedback, and that workers at every level know how to respond if they believe their appraisal is not fair.

Both giving and receiving evaluations tend to be awkward for everyone involved, and unfortunately, uncomfortable people tend to make mistakes. As you read the following list, you'll probably find that you've been at the receiving end of at least a couple of the most common appraisal goofs.

1. **Gotcha!** Too many managers use the performance appraisal as a chance to catch employees doing something wrong, rather than doing something right.

2. **The Once-a-Year Wonder.** Many companies mandate annual reviews, but some managers use that as an excuse to only give feedback once a year.

3. **Straight from the Gut.** Although "gut feel" can have real value, it's no substitute for honest, relevant documentation of both expectations and accomplishments.

4. **What Have You Done for Me Lately?** Many managers give far too much weight to recent accomplishments, discounting the early part of the review period.

5. **The "Me Filter."** While appraisals are a bit subjective by their very nature, some managers filter every comment through their personal biases. Here are some examples:

- **Positive Leniency:** "I'm a nice guy so I give everyone great scores."
- **Negative Leniency:** "I have high expectations so I give everyone low scores."
- **Halo Effect:** "I like this employee so I'll give her top scores across the board."

For a performance appraisal to be effective, the manager must focus on fairness, relevance, objectivity, and balance. Equally important, the manager should give feedback on a continual basis to eliminate surprises and maximize performance.

## Compensation: Show Me the Money

The term **compensation** covers both pay and benefits, but when most people think about compensation, they think about cash. Yet your paycheck is only part of the picture. Many companies also offer noncash benefits such as healthcare, which can be worth up to 30% of each employee's pay. Researching, designing, and managing effective compensation systems are core HR functions.

**compensation** The combination of pay and benefits that employees receive in exchange for their work.

© BRIAN HAGIWARA/BRAND X PICTURES/JUPITERIMAGES

## Getting out of the Doghouse

Moving far beyond the standard perks, a number of companies offer unique benefits that create a fun, vibrant corporate culture. A sampling:

- Google encourages its employees to bring their dogs to work—one of many creative perks that range from free gourmet meals to an on-site massage therapist.
- Oklahoma's Chesapeake Energy Corp offers workers scuba diving certification classes in its on-site Olympic-size pool.
- Discover Financial Services has a 1.2 million-square-foot work campus with outside basketball and volleyball courts and a 1.6-mile running trail.
- Camden Property Trust gives employees a 20% discount on rent when they live in one of its upscale apartment communities.
- New Belgium Brewing in Colorado gives each employee a case of beer a week, and after five years, takes workers to Belgium to sample the firm's inspirational brews.
- Outdoor outfitter Patagonia in California will "under certain circumstances," pay bail for workers jailed for civil disobedience related to environmental activism.
- Colorado's Chipotle Mexican Grill pays each pet-owning employee up to $30 per month toward veterinary insurance.
- Gould Evans architectural firm provides "spent tents": comfy rest areas with sleeping bags, pillows, and alarm clocks for workers who need a quick snooze.

Nothing can replace a great healthcare and a strong retirement program, but a nice nap and a quick doggie kiss can certainly make work more fun![5]

© BANANASTOCK/JUPITERIMAGES

**wages** The pay that employees receive in exchange for the number of hours or days that they work.

**salaries** The pay that employees receive over a fixed period, most often weekly or monthly. Most professional, administrative, and managerial jobs pay salaries.

**benefits** Noncash compensation, including programs such as health insurance, vacation, and childcare.

From a company perspective, compensation—both cash and non-cash—represents a big chunk of product costs, especially in labor-intensive businesses such as banks, restaurants, and airlines. Although many firms opt to cut labor costs as far as possible, others boost compensation above the norm to find and keep the best workers. For example, Costco pays its average worker nearly 40% more than Wal-Mart, and covers almost twice as many workers with health insurance. The extra compensation seems to pay off, since Costco's profits per employee are $13,647, versus $11,039 at Wal-Mart. In fact, research suggests that companies that offer higher than average compensation generally outperform their competitors in terms of total return to shareholders—both stock price and dividend payouts.[16]

Regarding specific individuals and positions, companies typically base compensation on a balance of the following factors:

- **Competition:** How much do competing firms offer for similar positions?

- **Contribution:** How much does a specific person contribute to the bottom line?

- **Ability to Pay:** How much can the company afford?

- **Cost of Living:** What would be reasonable in light of the broader local economy?

- **Legislation:** What does the government mandate?

The most common compensation systems in the United States are wages and salaries. **Wages** refer to pay in exchange for the number of hours or days that an employee works. Variations can be huge, starting at the federal minimum wage of $5.85 per hour (as of mid-2007) and ranging up to more than $50 per hour. Jobs that require less education—such as flipping burgers—typically pay hourly wages. Federal law requires companies to pay wage earners overtime, 50% more than their standard wage, for every hour worked over 40 hours per week.

**Salaries** on the other hand, cover a fixed period, most often weekly or monthly. Most professional, administrative, and managerial jobs pay salaries. While salaries are usually higher than wages, salaried workers do not qualify for overtime, which means that sometimes a low-level manager's overall pay may be less than the pay of wage-based employees who work for that manager.

**Pay for Performance** In addition to wages and salaries, many organizations link some amount of worker pay directly to performance. The idea, of course, is to motivate employees to excel. The following table lists some common approaches.

| Variable Pay System | Description |
| --- | --- |
| Commission | Commission involves payment as a percentage of sales. Usually, larger commissions go with smaller base pay. |
| Bonuses | Bonuses are lump sum payments, typically to reward strong performance from individual employees. |
| Profit sharing | Profit sharing plans reward employees with a share of company profits above and beyond predetermined goals. |
| Stock options | Stock options are the right to buy shares of company stock at some future date for the price of the shares on the day that the company awarded the options. |
| Pay for knowledge | This approach involves awarding bonuses and pay increases in exchange for increases in knowledge such as earning an MBA. |

As you look over the various variable pay options, which would you find most motivating? Why? What type of business might use each form of variable pay? Why?

> ❝
> Money is better than poverty, if only for financial reasons.
> —Woody Allen, filmmaker
> ❞

## Benefits: From Birthday Cakes to Death Benefits

While **benefits** represent a significant chunk of change for employers, many employees take them for granted. But keep in mind that employers don't *need* to give you sick days, vacations, or overtime pay for working on Christmas. In fact, a number of budget-minded employers stick to the legally mandated basics: Social Security and Medicare contributions, payments to state unemployment and workers' compensation programs, and job protection per the Federal Family and Medical Leave Act. However, socially responsible employers—and companies who seek a competitive advantage through a top-notch workforce—tend to offer far more. Optional benefits usually include some or all of the following:

- Paid vacation days and holidays
- Paid sick days
- Health insurance
- Retirement programs
- Product discounts

A smaller number of companies also offer less traditional benefits such as discounted childcare facilities, elder care assistance, fitness programs, tuition reimbursement, and paid time off for volunteering.

In the past decade, a growing number of companies have begun to offer **cafeteria-style benefits**. This approach involves giving their employees a set dollar amount per person that they must spend on company benefits. The key to these plans is choice, which allows employees to tailor their benefits to their individual needs.

Over the past couple of decades, employees across the U.S. economy have demanded more flexibility from their employers, and companies have responded. According to the U.S. Bureau of Labor Statistics, only 15% of full-time U.S. workers had flexible work schedules in 1991, but by 2004 the number had almost doubled to nearly 28%. Flexible scheduling options include flextime, telecommuting, and job sharing plans.[17]

Flextime  A **flextime** plan gives workers some degree of freedom in terms of when they start and finish their workday, as long as they complete the required number of hours. Typically, companies with flextime scheduling oblige their employees to start work between mandated hours in the morning—say, anytime between 7 A.M. and 10 A.M.—to take lunch between certain hours in the middle of the day, and to complete work at the end of 8 hours. This approach ensures that everyone is present during core hours for communication and coordination, but provides choice outside those parameters. Flextime tends to increase employee

morale and retention. But it makes less sense in jobs that entail extensive teamwork and customer interaction. It also requires careful management to avoid abuse.

The **compressed workweek**, another version of flextime scheduling, allows employees to work a full-time number of hours in less than the standard workweek. The most popular option is to work four 10-hour days rather than five 8-hour days. Major companies such as Intel have developed successful compressed workweek programs at a number of their facilities.

Telecommuting  Working remotely—most often from home—is a growing phenomenon on a global basis. Booming technological advances allow employees to "commute" to the office via phone lines, FAX machines, and broadband networks. In 2006 roughly 20% of the U.S. workforce engaged in some level of **telecommuting**, according to a report by World at Work based on data collected by The Dieringer Research Group. The bottom line benefits for companies that embrace the approach can be significant. AT&T, for example, encourag-

## Sugar and Spice and Everything Nice...but Only If You Ask

Surprisingly, the pay gap between men and women remains quite wide. Women working full-time earn just $0.755 per hour for every dollar a man earns. Even correcting for factors such as time off to have kids, women consistently earn less than men as they progress through their careers. Here are some examples:

- *Psychologists:* Women earn 83 cents to the male dollar.
- *College Professors:* Women earn 75 cents to the male dollar.
- *Lawyers and Judges:* Women earn 69 cents to the male dollar.
- *Secretaries:* Women earn 84 cents to the male dollar.
- *Retail Managers:* Women earn 70 cents to the male dollar.

The reasons for the pay gap include stereotypes and assumptions, exclusion from male networks, and possibly less interest in the whole idea of competition. But the most significant reason seems to be that women are far less willing to negotiate their salaries. A recent Carnegie Mellon study reported that male graduate students were eight times more likely than women to negotiate a starting salary, leading to beginning pay that was on average 7.4% more than their female classmates. Making up that difference over time can be tough. Lesson learned: if you ask for what you want you might not get it, but if you don't ask, you *definitely* won't get it.[18]

© GEORGE DOYLE/STOCKBYTE/GETTY IMAGES

es much of its workforce to telecommute, which has led to operational savings of $180 million per year through increased productivity and lower real-estate costs.[19]

While telecommuting sounds great at first glance, it offers benefits and drawbacks for organizations and employees alike, as you'll see in the table below.

Job Sharing   Job sharing allows two or more employees to share a single full-time job. Typically job share participants split salary equally, but they often need to allocate full benefits to just one of the partners. On a nationwide basis, about 17% of employers (e.g., American Express and Quaker Oats) offer job-sharing programs and reap the benefits such as higher morale and better retention.[20]

## Separation: Breaking Up Is Hard to Do

Employees leave jobs for a number of different reasons. Experiencing success, they may be promoted or lured to another firm. Experiencing failure, they may be fired. Or in response to changing business needs, their employer might transfer them or lay them off. And of course, employees also leave jobs for completely personal reasons such as family needs, retirement, or a change in career aspirations.

When companies terminate employees, they must proceed very carefully to avoid wrongful termination lawsuits. The best protection is honesty and documentation. Employers should always document sound business reasons for termination and share those reasons with the employee.

But employees can still lose their jobs for reasons that have little to do with their individual performance. Over the last 5 years, employers eliminated more than 10 million positions through mass layoffs. Reasons include economic slumps, global competition, and the efficiencies of outsourcing. As companies have become leaner, the remaining workers have experienced enormous stress. Managers can mitigate the trauma most effectively by showing empathy and concern for employees who remain, and by treating the laid-off employees with visible compassion.[21]

## LO5 Legal Issues: HR and the Long Arm of the Law

Even when the company is right—even when the company *wins*—employment lawsuits can cost millions of dollars and deeply damage the reputation of your organization, as we briefly discussed earlier in this chapter. To avoid employment lawsuits, most firms rely on HR to digest the complex, evolving web of employment legislation and court decisions, and to ensure that management understands the key issues.

The bottom line goal of most employment legislation is to protect employees from unfair treatment by employers. Some would argue that the legislation goes so far that it hinders the ability of companies to grow. But regardless of your personal perspective, the obligation of an ethical employer is to understand and abide by the law as it stands…even if you're working within the system to change it.

An Analysis of Telecommuting

|  | Benefits | Drawbacks |
|---|---|---|
| **Organization** | • Lower costs for office space, equipment, and upkeep<br>• Higher employee productivity due to better morale, fewer sick days, and more focused performance<br>• Access to a broader talent pool (not everyone needs to be local) | • Greater challenges maintaining a cohesive company culture<br>• Greater challenges fostering teamwork<br>• Greater challenges monitoring and managing far-flung employees |
| **Employee** | • Much more flexibility<br>• Zero commute time (less gas money)<br>• Better work-family balance<br>• Every day is casual Friday (or even pajama day!)<br>• Fewer office politics and other distractions | • Less fast-track career potential<br>• Less influence within the organization<br>• Weaker connection to the company culture<br>• Isolation from the social structure at work[22] |

The most influential piece of employment law may be the **Civil Rights Act of 1964. Title VII** of this act—which only applies to employers with 15 or more workers—outlaws discrimination in hiring, firing, compensation, apprenticeships, training, terms, conditions, or privileges of employment based on race, color, religion, sex, or national origin. Over time, Congress has supplemented Title VII with legislation that prohibits discrimination based on pregnancy, age (40+), and disability.

Title VII also created the **Equal Employment Opportunity Commission (EEOC)** to enforce its provisions. And in 1972, Congress beefed up the EEOC with additional powers to regulate and to enforce its mandates, making the EEOC a powerful force in the human resources realm.

Here are some additional key pieces of employment legislation:

- Fair Labor Standards Act of 1938: Established a minimum wage and overtime pay for employees working more than 40 hours a week.

- Equal Pay Act of 1963: Mandated that men and women doing equal jobs must receive equal pay.

- Occupational Safety and Health Act of 1970: Required safety equipment for employees and established maximum exposure limits for hazardous substances.

- Immigration Reform and Control Act of 1986: Required employers to verify employment eligibility for all new hires.

- Americans with Disabilities Act of 1990: Prohibited discrimination in hiring, promotion, and compensation against people with disabilities and required employers to make "reasonable" accommodations for them.

- Family and Medical Leave Act of 1996: Required firms with 50 or more employees to provide up to 12 weeks of job-secure, unpaid leave upon the birth or adoption of a child or the serious illness of a spouse, child, or parent.

Human resource managers are responsible for not only knowing this legislation in detail, but also for ensuring that management throughout their firm implements the legislation effectively, wherever it's applicable.

## Affirmative Action: The Active Pursuit of Equal Opportunity

The term affirmative action refers to policies meant to increase employment and educational opportunities for minority groups—especially groups defined by race, ethnicity, or gender. Emerging during the American civil rights movement in the 1960s, affirmative action seeks to make up for the systematic discrimination of the past, by creating more opportunities in the present.

Over the past couple of decades, affirmative action has become increasingly controversial. Opponents have raised concerns that giving preferential treatment to some groups amounts to "reverse discrimination" against groups who do not get the same benefits. They claim that affirmative action violates the principle that all individuals are equal under the law. But supporters counter that everyone who benefits from affirmative action must—by law—have relevant and valid qualifications. They argue that proactive measures are the only workable way to right past wrongs, and to ensure truly equal opportunity.

Recent Supreme Court decisions have supported affirmative action, pointing out that government has a "compelling interest" in assuring racial diversity. But the Supreme Court has rejected "mechanistic" affirmative action programs that amount to quota systems based on race, ethnicity, or gender.

The long-term fate of affirmative action remains unclear, but achieving the underlying goal—a diverse workplace with equal opportunity for all—stands to benefit both business and society as a whole.[22]

## Sexual Harassment: Eliminating Hostility

Sexual harassment—which violates Title VII of the Civil Rights Act of 1964—involves discrimination against a person based on his or her gender. According to the EEOC, sexual harassment can range from requests for sexual favors to the presence of a hostile work environment. The EEOC also points out that a sexual harasser may be either a woman or a man, and the harasser doesn't need to be the victim's supervisor. The victim could be anyone affected—either directly or indirectly—by the offensive conduct. And clearly, to qualify as sexual harassment, the conduct must be unwelcome. The total number of sexual harassment charges filed with the EEOC in the last decade dropped 21% from 1997 to 2007, but the number of charges filed by men rose from 11.6% to 16.0%.

Not just the perpetrator is liable for sexual harassment; employers may share accountability if they did not take "reasonable care" to prevent and correct sexually harassing behavior, or if they did not provide a workable system for employee complaints. Simply adopting a written policy against sexual harassment is not enough. Taking "reasonable care" also means taking proactive steps—such as comprehensive training—to ensure that everyone in the organization understands 1) that the firm does not tolerate sexual harassment, 2) that the firm has a system in place for complaints and will not tolerate retaliation against those who complain.[23]

## CHAPTER 17

# Managing Information and Technology: Finding New Ways to Learn and Link

## LEARNING OBJECTIVES

After studying this chapter, you will be able to...

**LO1** Explain the basic elements of computer technology—including hardware, software, and networks—and analyze key trends in each area

**LO2** Describe how data becomes information and how decision support systems can provide high-quality information that helps managers make better decisions

**LO3** Discuss the role of information technology in e-commerce

**LO4** Describe the problems posed by the rapid changes in Internet-based technologies, and explain ways to deal with these problems

**LO5** Discuss the business opportunities created by new technologies

4ltrpress.cengage.com/busn

> Any sufficiently advanced technology
> is indistinguishable from magic.
>
> –Arthur C. Clarke, science fiction author

## LO1 Information Technology: Explosive Change

Over the past few decades, computer and communications hardware and software have changed dramatically. The capabilities of hardware have increased by orders of magnitude. In 1956, for example, you would have needed fifty 24-inch disks—costing tens of thousands of dollars—to store five megabytes of data. Today, you can buy a flash memory device the size of your finger that stores several gigabytes of data—hundreds of times more data than that whole 1956 disk farm—for considerably less than $100. A basic calculator—or even your cell phone—has more processing power than early megacomputers that took up a whole room and weighed several tons. Software has taken advantage of these dramatic improvements in hardware to become more versatile and powerful, and much easier to use. Despite these huge changes, the most basic vocabulary of computing has remained essentially the same: hardware, software, networks, data, and information.

### Hardware and Software

**Hardware** refers to the physical components used to collect, store, organize, and process data and to distribute information. This hardware includes the various components of a computer system, as well as communications and network equipment. Examples include central processing units, hard drives, keyboards, modems, smartphones, and printers.

**Software** refers to computer programs that provide instructions to a computer so that it can perform a desired task. There are two broad categories of software: system software and application software.

**System Software** **System software** performs the critical functions necessary to operate the computer at the most basic level. The fundamental form of system software is the *operating system*, which controls the overall operation of the computer. It implements vital tasks such as managing the file system, reading programs and data into main

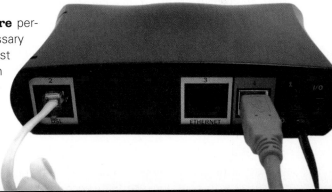

**hardware** The physical tools and equipment used to collect, store, organize, and process data and to distribute information.

**software** Programs that provide instructions to a computer so that it can perform a desired task.

**system software** Software that performs the critical functions necessary to operate the computer at the most basic level. The two basic types of system software are the operating system and utility programs.

memory, and allocating system memory among various tasks to avoid conflicts. Operating system software also provides the interface that enables users to interact with the computer.

*Utility programs*, another type of system software, supplement operating system software in ways that increase the security or abilities of the computer system. High-profile examples include firewalls, antivirus software, spam blockers, and antispyware programs. Over the years operating systems have incorporated basic versions of many of these utility programs.

### Applications Software

**Applications software** is the software that helps users perform a desired task. The two broad types of application software are horizontal market software and vertical market software.

- Horizontal market software applies broadly across many markets or industries. You're probably already familiar with several types of horizontal market software, including word processors, spreadsheets, and personal information managers. Other examples include accounting, inventory management, payroll, and human resource management software.

- Vertical market software consists of specialized applications that are used in a particular industry. For instance, there are certain types of software designed specifically to meet the needs of the construction industry, other applications designed for retail trade, and yet others used only by the finance industry. Doctors, lawyers, and accountants also have unique needs and use highly specialized applications.

### Networks

Today, most firms (and many households) use networks to enable users to communicate with each other and share both files and hardware resources. A network links computer resources using either a wired or wireless connection. As we'll show later in the chapter, firms sometimes allow customers or suppliers partial access to their private networks to strengthen their relationships with these important stakeholders.

**The Internet and the World Wide Web** The development and growth of the Internet is one of the great networking stories of the last two decades. The Internet is essentially the world's largest computer network. It's

actually a network of networks, consisting of hundreds of thousands of smaller networks, operating under a common set of rules so that they can communicate with each other.

You probably experience the Internet through the World Wide Web. In fact, many people think that the Internet and the Web are the same thing, but they aren't. The Internet supports the Web and provides access to it, but it also includes many sites that aren't on the Web. Still, the Web is big enough in its own right; it consists of billions of documents written and linked together using Hypertext Markup Language (HTML).

The increased availability of broadband Internet connections has fueled the popularity of the Web in the United States and other developed countries. Broadband connections allow users to quickly load pages with graphic or audio content and to download huge files such as music, games, and movies. A survey by the Pew Internet and American Life Project in early 2007 found that almost half of all U.S. households had a broadband connection, and experts expect that number only to grow.[1]

**Intranets and Extranets** Many organizations have set up **intranets**. An intranet is a network that has the same look and feel as the Internet and uses the same browser software to locate and display documents. But the network is confined to sites on internal Web servers and is only available to the firm's employees. When properly implemented, intranets are an effective way to distribute information, forms, and applications to employees.

Firms sometimes also create **extranets** by opening up their intranets to give limited access to certain groups of stakeholders, such as key customers and suppliers. Extranets help firms provide extra services and information to their stakeholders. For example, the firm might allow customers to check on the status of their order, or suppliers to check on the state of the firm's inventory to plan shipments of parts and materials.

## LO2 Information Technology and Decision Making: A Crucial Aid

One of the vital functions of information technology—at least in relationship to business—is to transform data into useful information for decision makers. In order to make decisions, managers must have information about the current state of their business, their competitive environment, and the trends and market conditions that offer new opportunities. Where does this information come from? How can it be made more useful? How can managers process the information to make better decisions?

### Data and Information

Let's start by distinguishing between data and information. **Data** are the facts and figures a firm collects. Data in their raw form have limited usefulness because they lack the context needed to give them meaning. Data become **information** when they are processed, orga-

---

**intranet** A network that has the look and feel of the Internet and is navigated using a Web browser but that is confined to documents located on a single company's servers and is only available to the firm's employees.

**extranet** An intranet that allows limited access to a selected group of stakeholders, such as suppliers or customers.

**data** Raw, unprocessed facts and figures.

**information** Data that have been processed in a way that make them meaningful to their user.

nized, and presented in a way that makes them useful to a decision maker.

Data come from many different sources. Internally, every department of an organization generates facts and figures that the firm must store and track. To store all of these data, businesses maintain **databases**, which are files of related data organized according to a logical system and stored on hard drives or some other computer-accessible storage media. Most firms have many different databases, each maintained by a different department or functional area to meet its specific needs. For example, the human resources department might have a database of employee pay rates, and the marketing department may have another database of customer history.

Once all these data are stored, the firm must convert them into information. One common method is to *query* a database. A query is a request for the database management software to search for data that matches criteria that the user specifies. Suppose, for instance, that a marketing manager plans to introduce a product upgrade. She can enter a query that asks for the e-mail addresses of all customers who have purchased the product in the past year. She can use this information to send a targeted e-mail blast, promoting the upgrade to the customers who are most likely to buy it.

Decision makers can also obtain information from a variety of outside sources. Most major industries are served by a variety of publications and websites that provide information about trends, new technologies, and news (and rumors) about what the movers and shakers in the industry are doing. Twenty years ago, decision makers got this information primarily by subscribing to hard copies of magazines and newspapers. Today, several **push technologies** automatically deliver information quickly and conveniently to the user's computer desktop. Given

today's competitive environment, the speed with which managers obtain good quality information can be a crucial competitive advantage.

### Characteristics of Good Information

We've seen that businesses have many sources of information. But not all information is of good quality. High-quality information is:

- **Accurate:** It should be free of errors and omissions.
- **Relevant:** It should focus on issues that are important to making a decision.
- **Timely:** It should be available in time to make a difference.
- **Understandable:** It must help the user grasp its meaning.
- **Secure:** Confidential information must be secure from hackers and competitors.

### Dealing with Information Overload

"Too much of a good thing" can definitely be the case with information. In fact, if you're like most people, you may often find yourself with *information overload*, or so much information that you feel overwhelmed. One study, conducted by University of London psychiatrist Glenn Wilson, suggested that when workers were constantly bombarded with new information, their ability to complete tasks was disrupted. In fact, he found information overload could actually temporarily reduce the worker's IQ by up to ten points![2]

Consider these suggestions to help you avoid information overload:

- Rather than constantly interrupting work to check e-mail, read RSS (Rich Site Summary) feeds, and surf the Web, try to set aside a few specific times each day to absorb information.
- Prioritize: think carefully about what is really important, and avoid the temptation to get distracted by irrelevant (though often interesting) topics.
- Set up folders to store content in an organized way so that if you find information that you think is relevant, you can easily find it later.
- Resist the urge to subscribe to information sources just because they are available—they won't help you if you never have time to read them.

> Technology is so much fun but we can drown in our technology. The fog of information can drive out knowledge.
>
> –Daniel Boorstin, historian and former Librarian of Congress

database A file consisting of related data organized according to a logical system and stored on a hard drive or some other computer-accessible media.

push technologies Computer applications that allow information to be delivered via the Internet directly to a user's computer desktop.

© STEVE COLE/RISER/GETTY IMAGES

**Managers and employees can sometimes become swamped by information overload.**

A company's information technology (IT) department frequently works closely with managers throughout the organization to support decision making. In fact, many companies develop **decision support systems (DSS)** that give managers access to large amounts of data and the processing power to convert the data into high quality information.

Over the past two decades, a new class of decision support system has evolved to take advantage of the dramatic increase in data storage and processing capabilities. Called **business intelligence systems**, these systems help businesses discover subtle and complex relationships hidden in their data.

One of the most common approaches to implementing a business intelligence system is to create a data warehouse and use data mining to discover unknown relationships. A **data warehouse** is a very large, organization-wide database that provides a centralized location for storing data from both the organization's own databases and external sources. **Data mining** uses powerful statistical and mathematical techniques to analyze the vast amounts of data in a data warehouse to identify useful information that had been hidden. In recent years, data mining has had considerable success in areas as diverse as fraud and crime detection, quality control, and scientific research.[3]

## Expert Systems

In general, managers who use decision support systems already know quite a bit about the problem and how they want to solve it. They just need access to the right data and a system to "crunch the numbers" in a way that provides relevant, accurate, and timely information to help them make their decisions. But what happens when the problem is beyond the expertise of the manager? One way to deal with this problem is to set up an **expert system (ES)** to actually solve problems for the manager.

To develop expert systems, programmers ask experts in the relevant area to explain how they solve problems. They then devise a program to mimic the expert's approach, incorporating various rules or guidelines that the human expert uses. The finished program will ask a user a series of questions, basing each question on the response to the previous question. The program continues to ask questions until it has enough information to reach a decision and make a recommendation.

Expert systems routinely solve problems in areas as diverse as medical diagnoses, fraud detection, and consumer credit evaluation. The troubleshooting systems many companies have on the customer support pages of their Websites are another type of expert system. If your product doesn't work, the troubleshooter will ask a series of questions designed to diagnose the problem and suggest solutions. Based on your responses to each question, the system selects the next question as it starts narrowing down the possible reasons for the problem until it identifies the cause and offers a solution. Often you can solve your problem without waiting on hold to talk to a human expert over the phone.[4]

Despite impressive results in many fields, expert systems have their limitations. Programming all of the decision rules into the system can be time consuming, complicated, and expensive. In fact, it's sometimes impossible because the experts themselves can't clearly explain how they make their decisions—they just "know" the answer based on their years of experience. If the experts can't clearly explain how they reach their conclusions, then programmers can't include the appropriate decision rules in the system. Finally, an expert system has little flexibility and no commonsense. It probably won't be able to find a solution to a problem that's even a little different from the specific type of problem it was programmed to solve.[5]

## LO3 Information Technology and the World of e-Commerce

Over the past 20 years, advances in information technology have had a dramatic and widespread effect on how companies conduct their business. But in this chapter, we'll just concentrate on one key area: the growth and development of e-commerce.

**E-commerce** refers to using the Internet to facilitate the exchange of goods and services. You're probably most familiar with **business-to-consumer (B2C) e-commerce**. You participate in this form of e-commerce when you purchase some songs from iTunes, use Travelocity or Expedia to make travel arrangements, or buy stocks through an online broker such as Charles Schwab. However,

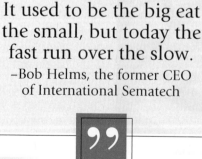

It used to be the big eat the small, but today the fast run over the slow.
—Bob Helms, the former CEO of International Sematech

**business-to-business (B2B) e-commerce**, which consists of markets where businesses sell supplies, components, machinery, equipment, or services to other businesses, actually accounts for a *much* larger volume of business.

While both B2C and B2B involve exchanging goods over the Internet, they differ in some important ways, as shown in exhibit 17.1. Given these structural differences, it isn't surprising that the two markets operate so differently.

## Using Information Technology in the B2C Market

Firms in the B2C market use information technology in a variety of ways. In this section, we'll see how firms use technology in general, and the Internet in particular, to attract new customers, manage customer relationships, and handle customer payments.

**Advertising on the Internet**  Since successful B2C companies typically sell to a large target market, advertising and product promotion are important. The Internet has provided a new advertising medium. Though total Internet advertising is still small by the standards of television and print media, it's growing rapidly. According to PricewaterhouseCoopers, in 2002 total spending on Internet advertising was $6.0 billion for the entire year. In 2007, Internet advertising was $10 billion *in the first 6 months*. The most popular form of Internet advertising, accounting for about 40% of all Internet advertising expenditures, consists of ads placed on pages containing search engine results. Google, in particular, has been very successful with Adwords, a program that targets advertising messages according to key search words and phrases.[6]

Firms in B2C markets also use opt-in e-mail as an advertising medium. Opt-in e-mails are messages that the receiver has explicitly chosen to receive. Customers often opt-in when they register their products online and click to indicate that they would like to receive product information from the company. Since the customer has agreed to receive the message, opt-in e-mails tend to reach interested consumers. And, because e-mail requires no envelopes, paper, or postage, it's much less expensive than direct mail.

**Viral Marketing**  The Internet has also proven to be an effective medium for **viral marketing**, which attempts to get customers to communicate a firm's message to friends, family, and colleagues. Despite its name, legitimate viral marketing doesn't use computer viruses. Effective viral marketing campaigns can generate a substantial increase in consumer awareness of a product.

**business-to-business (B2B) e-commerce** E-commerce in markets where businesses buy from and sell to other businesses.

**viral marketing** An Internet marketing strategy that tries to involve customers and others not employed by the seller in activities that help promote the product.

---

| **Exhibit 17.1** | Key Differences Between B2C and B2B E-Commerce[7] |

| | B2C | B2B |
|---|---|---|
| Type of customers | Individual final consumers | Other businesses |
| Number of customers in target market | Very large | Often limited to a few major business customers |
| Size of typical individual transaction | Relatively small (usually a few dollars to a few hundred dollars) | Potentially very large (often several thousand dollars, sometimes several million dollars) |
| Customer behavior | May do some research, but many purchases may be based on impulse. | Usually does careful research and compares multiple vendors. May take bids. |
| Complexity of negotiations | Purchase typically involves little or no negotiation. Customer usually buys a standard product and pays the listed price. | Often involves extensive negotiation over specifications, delivery, installation, support, and other issues. |
| Nature of relationship with customers | Firm wants to develop customer loyalty and repeat business but seldom develops a close working relationship with individual customers. | Buyers and sellers often eventually develop close and long-lasting relationships that allow them to coordinate their activities. |

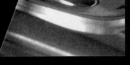

**customer relationship management (CRM)** The strategy of building relationships with customers by learning more about them and using this knowledge to provide products and services that match their preferences.

**cybermediary** An Internet-based firm that specializes in the secure electronic transfer of funds.

**electronic bill presentment and payment** A method of bill payment that makes it easy for the customer to make a payment, often by simply clicking on a payment option contained in an e-mail.

As a strategy, viral marketing isn't unique to the Internet; buzz marketing, which we discussed in chapter 14, represents a similar approach. But the Internet has made it possible to implement such strategies in clever ways and reach large numbers of people very quickly.

## Customer Relationship Management

The idea behind **customer relationship management (CRM)** is to attract customers and build loyalty by making it easy and enjoyable to do business with the company, providing high-quality service and support, and offering products and services that precisely match each consumer's preferences. The growth of the Internet has been a major boost to CRM. It enables firms to provide a level of service and convenience that would have been impossible only a few years ago. Customers can shop at the firm's site from home, 24-7. They also can access customer support at any time of day—perhaps to use expert systems to troubleshoot a problem, or to place an order for a replacement part, or to check the status of an order.

Doing business over the Internet allows firms to track all of the links (including purchases) that a customer clicks on while visiting the company's Website. Many sites today use this information to offer suggestions to customers. For example, Audible.com, a site that sells audio books that can be downloaded over the Internet and played on MP3 players, tracks and analyzes customer purchases to find patterns and determine preferences. Using this business intelligence, it recommends books the next time the customer visits.[8]

**Handling Payments Electronically** B2C e-commerce normally requires customers to pay at the time the purchase is made. Clearly, the use of cash and paper checks isn't practical. In the United States, most payments in the B2C market are made by credit cards. To ensure that such transactions are secure, most sites transmit payment information using a *secure socket layer (SSL)* protocol. You can tell if a site on which you're doing business is using SSL in two fairly subtle ways. First, the URL will begin with https:// instead of simply http://. (Note the "s" after http in the address.) Also, a small closed lock icon will appear near the bottom of your web browser (the exact location depends on the specific browser you are using). 🔒

Another common approach to sending electronic payments is to use a **cybermediary**—an Internet-based company that specializes in the secure electronic transfer of funds. By far the best-known cybermediary is PayPal. According to figures on its Website, more than 100 million subscribers now have PayPal accounts.[9]

A final way of making electronic payments is **electronic bill presentment and payment.** This is a relatively new method in which bills are sent to customers via e-mail. The bill includes a simple mechanism (such as clicking on a button) that allows the

> ## What new technology does is create new opportunities to do a job that customers want done.
> –Tim O'Reilly, founder and CEO of O'Reilly Media

## Viral Marketing: To B2B or Not To B2B

B2B marketing has a reputation for relying on traditional methods. So people tend to be surprised when they learn that many B2B marketers have developed edgy and creative viral marketing tactics. As with B2C viral marketing, the goal is to generate buzz and get outsiders to help spread the message.

The first really successful viral campaign in the B2B market was developed by Internet marketing company e-tractions in 2000. The firm wanted to attract new corporate clients, and hit upon the idea of developing an Internet game called Whack a Flack. The game—designed to appeal to journalists and public relations specialists—became so popular that several leading newspapers wrote about the phenomenon. More importantly, a game-related survey helped the company generate over 1,500 sales leads.

In terms of the sheer numbers of campaigns, B2C viral marketing still holds a sizable edge over B2B efforts. But the best B2B campaigns now are now widely recognized for their creativity and impact. For example, B2B campaigns by NetQoS and Exeros were both listed in Marketing Sherpa's Top Ten Viral Efforts list for 2007.[10]

customer to make a payment once the amount of the bill has been verified. Many banks now offer this service, as do services such as Checkfree and Quicken.

## Using Information Technology in the B2B Market

Businesses that participate in B2B e-commerce typically don't surf multiple sites on the Web to find customers or suppliers. Instead, many participate in **e-marketplaces**, which are specialized Internet sites where many buyers and sellers in a specific B2B market can exchange information and buy and sell goods and services.

E-marketplaces provide a number of advantages to their participants:

- Compared to older methods, they reduce time, effort, and cost of doing business for both buyers and sellers.

- Because they are Internet based, they don't require expensive dedicated connections between firms, so even smaller firms can afford to participate.

- They enable sellers and buyers to contact and negotiate with a large number of market participants on the other side of the market.

- They often provide additional services—beyond simple trade—that allow firms to exchange information and collaborate.

Once buyers and sellers have reached agreement in an e-marketplace, they may eventually develop a long-term working relationship that requires close coordination and collaboration. This is where the extranets mentioned earlier become important. Extranets allow suppliers to keep tabs on shipments and inventory levels so that they can time their deliveries to precisely meet the needs of their customers.

## LO4 Challenges and Concerns Arising from New Technologies

So far we've concentrated on the benefits of advances in information technology—and it's clear that these benefits are enormous. But rapid technological advances also pose challenges and create opportunities for abuse. These problems affect businesses, their customers, and their employees, as well as the general public. In this section, we'll look at annoyances, security concerns, and legal and ethical issues.

## Cookies, Adware, Spyware, and Viruses

As you almost certainly know, the Internet—for all its advantages—creates the possibility that unwanted files and programs may land on your computer. In many cases, this happens without your knowledge, much less your permission. Some of these files and programs are relatively benign (even useful), but others can create major problems.

**Cookies** are small text files that are placed on your computer when you visit Websites. They help the Website identify you when you visit again and track your behavior while on the site. Unlike adware, spyware, and viruses, *cookies contain no programming code;* they're simply text files. Modern Web browsers allow users to easily delete cookies or even to refuse to accept them. But doing so may reduce the functionality of some Websites. For example, many Web B2C sites rely on cookies to keep track of items in your shopping cart and make purchases without filling in all of the order information every time you visit. Amazon's popular One-Click shopping option wouldn't work without cookies.

If you download and install free software on the Internet, you're probably familiar with adware—whether you want to be or not. **Adware** is software that's installed on your computer to show you advertisements. When you download and install freeware, you agree to terms in the end user licensing agreement. A provision is usually buried somewhere in the agreement allowing the supplier of the freeware to install the adware along with the program you actually want.

Adware can slow down your computer and your Internet connection as it diverts memory, processing power, and bandwidth to retrieve and display ads. The pop-up ads may cover part of the Website you want to view until you close it. And because some adware is poorly programmed, it can lead to system instability and crashes.

**e-marketplace** A specialized Internet site where buyers and sellers engaged in business-to-business e-commerce can communicate and conduct business.

**cookies** Small text files that are placed on a user's computer by a Website, usually to allow the Website to identify the user.

**adware** A software program that is placed on a computer for the purpose of generating advertisements; frequently included with free programs downloaded from Internet sites.

**spyware** Software that is installed on a computer without the user's knowledge or permission for the purpose of tracking the user's behavior.

**virus** Computer software that can be spread from one computer to another without the knowledge or permission of the computer users.

**spam** Unsolicited e-mail advertisements usually sent to very large numbers of recipients, many of whom may have no interest in the message.

**phishing** A scam in which official-looking e-mails are sent to individuals in an attempt to get them to divulge private information such as passwords, user names, and account numbers.

**Spyware** is software that installs itself on your computer without permission and then tracks your computer behavior in some way. It might track which Internet sites you visit to learn more about your interests and habits in order to send you targeted ads. Or, more alarmingly, it might log every keystroke (thus capturing passwords, account numbers, and user names to accounts as you enter them), allowing someone to steal your identity. Some spyware even goes beyond passive watching and takes control of your computer, perhaps sending you to Websites you didn't want to visit.[11]

**Viruses** are small programs that install themselves on computers without the users' knowledge or permission and spread from one computer to another—sometimes very rapidly. (This ability to spread automatically to other computers is the key difference between virus software and adware or spyware.) Some viruses are little more than pranks, but others can cause great harm. They can erase or modify data on your hard drive, prevent your computer from booting up, or find and send personal information you've stored on your computer to people who want to use it for identity theft. Viruses are often hidden in e-mails, instant messages, or files downloaded from the Internet.

How can you protect yourself from adware, spyware, and viruses? Take these commonsense steps:

- Perform regular backups. This can come in handy should a virus tamper with (or erase) the data on your hard drive. Store the backed up data in a separate place.

- Install high-quality antivirus and antispyware software and keep them updated.

- Update your operating system regularly so that any security holes it contains are patched as soon as possible.

- Don't open e-mail messages or attachments if you don't know and trust the sender.

- Read the licensing agreement of any programs you install. These agreements will often divulge if adware or spyware will be installed with your free program.

## Spam and Phishing

**Spam** refers to unsolicited commercial e-mails, usually sent to huge numbers of people with little regard to whether they would have any interest in the product. It's hard to get exact measures of the amount of spam that is sent each year, but experts agree that it now comprises the vast majority of all e-mail in the United States. It clogs e-mail inboxes and makes it tough for people to find legitimate messages among all the junk. Spam filters exist that help detect and eliminate spam, but spammers are very good at eventually finding ways to fool these filters.[12]

The U.S. Congress enacted the Controlling the Assault of Non-Solicited Pornography and Marketing Act (usually called the CAN-SPAM Act) in 2003. This act requires senders of unsolicited commercial e-mail to label their messages as ads and to tell the recipient how to decline further messages. It also prohibits the use of false or deceptive subject lines. But the rapid increase in the amount of spam in recent years suggests this law hasn't been an effective deterrent.

**Phishing** is another common use of spam. Phishers send e-mail messages that appear to come from a legitimate business, such as a bank or retailer. The e-mail attempts to get recipients to disclose personal information, such as their social security or credit card numbers, by claiming that there is a problem with their account. The messages appear authentic; in addition to official sounding language, they include official-looking graphics, such as corporate logos. The e-mail also usually provides a link to a Website where the recipient is supposed to log in and enter the desired information. When the victims of the scam click on this link, they go to a Website that can look amazingly like

## Sickening Developments for Cell Phones?

Computers aren't the only devices plagued by security and privacy problems. When unwary cell phone users download games or ringtones or use Bluetooth to link to other devices their phones can become infected with viruses capable of deleting stored information or sending unintended text messages. Another annoying problem is spam text messages. In early 2008 experts predicted that U.S. cell phone users would receive at least 1.5 billion spam messages over the next year. And, unlike e-mail spam, many cell phone users end up paying extra for these unwanted messages.[13]

**How can you avoid getting hooked by phishing scams?**

© BOB ELSDALE/STONE/GETTY IMAGES

the site for the real company—but it's not. It's a clever spoof of the site where the phishers collect personal information and use it to steal identities.

Current versions of major Web browsers include filters to block phishing scams, but phishers (like spammers in general) are very clever at finding ways to get around filters so you need to take extra precautions. In addition to using a browser with an antiphishing filter, remember that reputable businesses almost never ask you for private information via e-mail. Also, never click on a link in an e-mail message to go to a Website where you have financial accounts.

## Hackers

**Hackers** are skilled computer users who use their expertise to gain unauthorized access to other people's computers. Not all hackers intend to do harm, but some—called black hat hackers, or crackers—definitely have malicious intent. They may attempt to break into a computer system to steal identities or to disrupt a business. *Cyberterrorists* are hackers motivated by political or ideological beliefs who try to cause harm to those who don't share their beliefs. Some experts predict that cyberterrorists may attempt to launch attacks on key industries (such as energy, finance, or transportation) that could cripple a nation's economy.[14]

Protecting against hackers requires individuals and businesses to be security conscious. Some of the precautions used against hackers, such as making frequent backups, are similar to those used to protect against viruses. Another key to protecting against hackers is to make sure that all data transmitted over a network is encrypted, or sent in code. Security experts also suggest that organizations restrict access to computer resources by requiring users to have *strong passwords*, and change them on a regular basis. According to Microsoft, a strong password:

- Is relatively long (at least seven characters)

- Consists of a mix of lower- and uppercase letters, numbers, and special characters (such as #, @, &, ~)

- Doesn't include the user's real name, user name, or a common word

- Differs significantly from other passwords

But strong passwords not only make it difficult for hackers to gain unauthorized access to a system, they also pose a challenge to legitimate users—it's tough to remember long random strings of letters, numbers, and characters. One security expert found that many people have such a hard time keeping up with their passwords that they simply write them down and hide them under their mouse pads—hardly a secure location![15]

Given these problems with passwords, many firms are now relying on *biometrics*—the use of personal characteristics to uniquely identify an individual to determine whether they should have access to computer resources. The most common current example of biometrics is the use of fingerprint readers, but other approaches, such as iris or retina scans may become more common in the future.

**Firewalls** are another important tool against hackers and other security threats. A firewall uses hardware or software (or sometimes both) to create a barrier that prevents unwanted messages or instructions from entering a computer system. As threats from spyware, hackers, and other sources have developed, the use of firewalls has become commonplace.

## Ethical and Legal Issues

Information technology raises a number of legal and ethical challenges, such as the need to deal with privacy issues and to protect intellectual property rights. These issues are controversial and don't have simple solutions.

**Personal Privacy** We've already mentioned that firms now have the ability to track customer behavior in ways that were never before possible. So far, we've discussed the advantages to the firm and customer by emphasizing that such knowledge often allows firms to offer better, more personalized service. But all of this extra information comes at the expense of your privacy. Does the fact that firms know so much about your preferences and behavior make you a bit nervous?

Does it also bother you that your e-mail messages lack confidentiality? When you send an e-mail, it's likely to be stored on at least four computers: your personal computer, the server of your e-mail provider, the server of your recipient's provider, and your recipient's own computer. If you send the e-mail from your company's system, it's also likely to be stored when the company backs up its information. If you thought that deleting an e-mail message from your own computer erased it permanently and completely, you need to think again.

Legal opinions about e-mail are still evolving. A ruling by a U.S. federal appeals court in 2007 found that the Fourth Amendment protects e-mails from unreasonable

**hacker** A skilled computer user who uses his or her expertise to gain access to the computer (or computer system) of others, sometimes with malicious intent.

**firewall** Software, hardware, or both designed to prevent unwanted access to a computer or computer system.

**intellectual property** Property that is the result of creative or intellectual effort, such as books, musical works, inventions, and computer software.

search and seizure by the government. But federal law enforcement agencies have indicated they plan to appeal the ruling, claiming that such protection makes it more difficult to monitor e-mails by terrorists and criminals. This issue promises to remain controversial.[16]

The list of other ways you can lose your privacy is long and getting longer. For example, your employer can probably track everything you do on your office computer. Unfortunately, there's no simple way to solve privacy concerns. Privacy is an elusive concept, and there is no strong consensus about how much privacy is enough.

**Protecting Intellectual Property Rights Intellectual property** refers to products that result from creative and intellectual efforts. There are many types of intellectual property, but we'll focus on forms of intellectual property that are protected by copyright law, such as books, musical works, computer programs, and movies. Copyright law gives the creators of this property the exclusive right to produce, record, perform, and sell their work for a specified time period.

The rationale for copyright protection is that creators of intellectual property will receive little or no compensation for their efforts if their work can be copied, distributed, and used by others without permission and without payment. Without the chance to get paid for their work, many talented people might decide it's not worth the effort to create anything new.

The rise and fall of Napster in the early 2000s highlighted both how easy it was for literally millions of

**The music we listen to is the intellectual property of its creators.**

© AP IMAGES

people to use the Internet to share musical works without permission and how aggressively the music industry would try to prevent such practices. The subsequent development of other music file sharing networks and the lawsuits the music industry has filed against individual file swappers in recent years suggests that the struggle between those on opposite sides of this issue is far from over.[17]

Unauthorized music sharing isn't the only form of piracy. The Business Software Alliance estimates that 35% of all software installed on personal computers in 2006 was illegally obtained, resulting in the loss of over $40 billion in revenue to software companies. Many software publishers, including Microsoft, have become very aggressive at prosecuting firms and individuals engaged

# Oops! What were they THINKING?!

## The Perks and Pitfalls of E-mail

For more than a decade, the Internet has enabled computer users to connect to others anywhere around the globe. Though tools such as instant messaging and video conferencing have gained wide-spread usage over the past few years, e-mail continues to be the Internet's "killer app." The speed and convenience with which people send e-mail messages is unlike anything businesses have ever experienced with traditional forms of written communication. Moreover, electronic messages provide a written record that is digitally stored and easily retrieved using a simple search.

Yet for all its strengths, e-mail presents many challenges in the workplace. In a survey conducted by the International Association of Business Communicators, a full 85% of respondents said that e-mail is having a negative impact on work productivity. Forty percent of those surveyed said they spend 2 hours each workday responding to e-mail. BlackBerry users who accessed e-mail while away from the office faced even greater difficulties getting away from their inboxes.

The potential for lower productivity is enough to worry e-mail and BlackBerry users alike, but other common pitfalls are equally troubling. One in three companies claim to have terminated employees for violating corporate e-mail policies—a powerful reminder that bosses are monitoring workers' inboxes. In some cases, e-mail misuse occurs at the top of the organization— during 2006, nearly 400 employees of Radio Shack opened their inboxes and found the following message: "The workforce reduction notification is currently in progress. Unfortunately your position is one that has been eliminated."

Like all business applications, e-mail is merely a tool. And, as with other tools, the benefit e-mail offers depends largely on the good sense and skillful handling of the user.[18]

© PHOTODISC/GETTY IMAGES

in software piracy. Exhibit 17.2 includes some tips that can help you identify unauthorized software. But many software pirates have become quite good at making their wares look authentic, so identifying pirated software isn't always as easy as the tips in this table suggest.[19]

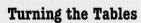

**Exhibit 17.2**  Someone's Trying to Sell You Pirated Software If:[20]

It is sold in a clear CD-ROM jewel case with no accompanying documentation or certificate of authenticity.

The software is labeled OEM (meaning original equipment manufacturer).

The documentation accompanying the software appears to be photocopied.

Labels on the CD-ROMs or DVDs are handwritten or the packaging is of poor quality.

Multiple software programs from different publishers are included on the same CD-ROM(s).

Video game and motion picture producers also face significant problems with piracy. Nintendo estimated that it lost almost $1 billion in revenues in 2007 due to the sale of pirated versions of games for its DS and Wii game systems. In late 2007 a raid on a factory in Hong Kong seized 10,000 machines used to illegally copy the company's games.[21]

Given how lucrative piracy can be, it's unlikely that this problem will go away anytime soon. You can expect the companies hurt by these practices to continue aggressively prosecuting pirates and to work on new technologies that make pirating digital media more difficult.

## LO5 New Developments—What's around the Corner?

The information technologies we've described in this chapter have already revolutionized many aspects of business. But more change is on the way. There are some amazing technologies on the horizon that will open up a host of new opportunities (and possibly some new threats, if the wrong people get their hands on them!). We'll focus on three major areas just to give you a taste of what's likely to be on the horizon:

- Radio frequency identification
- Holographic storage
- Next generation Internet technologies

Each of these technologies has the potential to revolutionize business.

### Radio Frequency Identification

**Radio frequency identification (RFID)** is a technology that stores information on a microchip and transmits it to a reader when it's within range—which is usually limited to a few feet. While the chip can store and send all sorts of information, in most cases its main purpose is to transmit a serial number that *uniquely* identifies a person, product, or device. These microchips can be embedded in most types of tangible products. In many cases, they don't even need their own power supply—they're powered by the energy in the radio signal sent by the reader.

How might RFID technology work in the future? One of its biggest uses will be for supply chain management,

**radio frequency identification (RFID)** Use of microchips to transmit information about a device, product, or person to an RFID reader.

## Turning the Tables

High school and college students often get caught up in intellectual property disputes. In most cases, they are the ones accused of violating the property rights of creators of music, movies, software, or video games by downloading pirated copies of these works. But recently the shoe has been on the other foot—many students claim that *their* intellectual property rights have been violated. According to these students the culprit is a plagiarism detection service called Turnitin offered by a company called iParadigms.

Schools that use iParadigm's Turnitin service routinely provide the company with copies of student papers—even those that contain no plagiarism. The service uses these papers to help detect future plagiarism. Students at some schools have objected to this practice, arguing that iParadigm was making money by using their intellectual property without permission. A group of students at a Virginia high school launched a lawsuit against the company in 2007 claiming copyright infringement. But the courts ultimately sided with iParadigm, ruling that the use of student papers was permissible under fair use provisions of copyright law.[22]

© RAY OOMS/MASTERFILE

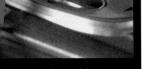

**holographic storage** A relatively new technology that stores data in three dimensions rather than two, thus greatly expanding storage capacity.

**Internet2** A new Internet utilizing technologies that give it a speed and capacity far exceeding the current Internet.

an application we'll discuss in chapter 18. But RFID technology is also likely to directly affect the way you shop. Within a few years, shopping carts at many stores will probably have a video display equipped with an RFID reader. As you put each item in your cart, the display will communicate with the RFID chip on the product and display the price of the item. It will also keep a running total of the cost of all the items in your cart. When you're finished shopping, you'll walk past a reader where the total amount will automatically be charged to a debit or credit card in your wallet or purse that has its own RFID chip, allowing you to bypass the checkout lane.

## New Hardware Technologies

Hard drives and other forms of conventional data storage technology have improved tremendously in recent years, but most experts predict that it is nearing the limits of its ability. The most promising new storage technique appears to be **holographic storage**.

In today's storage technologies, everything is stored on the *surface* of a magnetic or optical disk. This limits the storage capacity to two dimensions. Holographic storage uses three dimensions, giving it a much greater capacity. Even early versions of holographic storage can hold the equivalent of more than 60 DVDs worth of data on a single disk the size of a DVD; in the near future the capacity should reach 1.6 terabytes, equivalent to about 340 DVDs. Holographic storage also allows faster read and write times than conventional optical storage such as CDs and DVDs, and appears to be very security friendly.[23]

The best way to predict the future is to invent it.
–Alan Kay, computer scientist

Early uses of holographic storage are likely to be for data backup and archiving. For example, Turner Entertainment plans to store all of its movies and other digital video footage on holographic media. Turner has over 200,000 movies and thousands of other programs and commercials. As holographic storage develops and prices drop, consumer products are likely to use it extensively. Imagine being able to store *all* your movies, music, and pictures on a single portable disk that could play on portable players.

## Internet2

Even today's broadband connections are too slow and inefficient for many advanced business and scientific applications. Such applications often require high-definition video and audio files to be shared among multiple sites at the same time. Beginning in 1996, several leading universities, corporations, and other organizations formed a coalition to create a new generation of Internet technology, which they dubbed **Internet2**. Internet2 is up and running, but access is limited to dues-paying members.[24]

Internet2 isn't just a faster way to surf the Web or send e-mail. In fact, these routine uses of the current Internet aren't even allowed on it. Instead, it focuses on ways to use high-speed connectivity to improve education, research, and collaboration. Businesses with facilities around the world see the Internet2 as a way to bring together their researchers, scientists and engineers at various locations in a way that allows real-time collaboration on complex and important topics. It also allows corporations to collaborate with other companies, universities, and organizations located thousands of miles apart.[25]

### We Bet This Use of RFIDs Will Surprise You!

Some casinos already use RFID technology in their chips. This enables them to spot counterfeit chips, catch bettors who try to sneak additional chips into their pile after cards are dealt, and even track the gambling behavior of patrons to see which games they prefer and how often they win and lose at each game. The casinos can use this betting information to identify their most valuable customers (the ones who have a habit of making large bets and losing) and offer them rewards (such as free meals or hotel rooms) to keep them coming back.[26]

© IMAGE SOURCE

# Speak Up!

BUSN was built on a simple principle: to create a new teaching and learning solution that reflects the way today's faculty teach and the way you learn.

Through conversations, focus groups, surveys, and interviews, we collected data that created the current version of BUSN you are using today.

But it doesn't stop there – in order to make an even better learning experience, we'd like you to **SPEAK UP** and tell us how BUSN worked for you. What did you like about it? What would you change? Are there additional ideas you have that would help us build a better product for next semester's introduction to business students?

At **4ltrpress.cengage.com/busn** you'll find all of the resources you need to succeed in your introduction to business classroom – **visual summaries, audio downloads, printable and interactive flash cards,** and more!

*Speak Up!* Go to **4ltrpress.cengage.com/busn/survey**.

## CHAPTER 18

# Operations Management: Putting It All Together

## LEARNING OBJECTIVES

After studying this chapter, you will be able to...

**LO1** Discuss the role of operations management in business

**LO2** Describe the key responsibilities of operations managers

**LO3** Explain how technology has influenced operations management

**LO4** Discuss the coordination and integration of operations systems

**LO5** Explain the role of quality in operations management

**LO6** Explain the movement toward lean production

4ltrpress.cengage.com/busn

> # Success is simple. Do what's right, the right way, at the right time.
>
> –Arnold H. Glasgow, American psychologist

## LO1 Operations Management: It Isn't Glamorous, But It Definitely Matters...

**Operations management** is concerned with all of the activities involved in creating goods and services and distributing them to customers. It doesn't have a glamorous reputation, but it's still extremely important. When operations managers do their job well, a firm uses the most effective and efficient methods to produce the right goods and services in the right quantities—and to distribute them to the right customers at the right time. Obviously, the decisions of operations managers can have a major impact on the firm's revenues and its costs, and thus on its overall profitability.

Over the past few decades, operations management has seen dramatic changes. Emerging technology and global competition have fueled a range of new strategies. But before examining them in detail, let's look at some operations management basics.

### Goods vs. Services

In chapter 12, we briefly discussed the differences between goods and services from a marketing perspective. Exhibit 18.1 revisits some of these differences, but from an operations perspective. As we move through the chapter, we'll see that the differences between goods and services directly affect many operations management decisions.

**Exhibit 18.1** Differences between Goods and Services

| Goods | Services |
| --- | --- |
| Are tangible: they have a physical form and can be seen, touched, handled, etc. | Are intangible: they can be "experienced," but they don't have a physical form. |
| Can be stored in an inventory. | Must be consumed *when* they are produced. |
| Can be shipped. | Must be consumed *where* they are provided. |
| Are produced independently of the consumer. | Often require the customer to be actively involved in their production. |
| Can have at least *some* aspects of their quality determined objectively by measuring defects or deviations from desired values. | Intangible nature means quality is based mainly on customer perceptions. |

**operations management** **The activities involved in creating goods and services and distributing them to customers.**

The differences between goods and services are not always as clear-cut as exhibit 18.1 suggests. As we pointed out in chapter 12, many products are a mix of both goods *and* services. You might think of General Motors as a classic example of a firm that produces tangible goods. But when you buy a GM car, you're also buying several services that go with it, including a 100,000 mile warranty, free roadside assistance for 5 years, and a free year of the OnStar wireless service that can (among other things) track your car if it is stolen and dispatch that free roadside assistance if your car breaks down.

## Effectiveness vs. Efficiency

You may be surprised to learn that efficiency and effectiveness are two different concepts. In operations management, **efficiency** refers to completing a task or producing a product at the *lowest cost*. **Effectiveness** means completing tasks and producing products that *create the greatest value*. Both efficiency and effectiveness are important, but being effective is more crucial to a firm's success. A firm can produce *any* good efficiently by ensuring that it produces it at the lowest cost. But if no one wants to buy that good, it just won't matter.

The relationship between efficiency and effectiveness is subtle and complex. In the short run, improving effectiveness is likely to increase costs, which would seem to reduce efficiency. But over the long haul, efficiency and effectiveness may go hand in hand; creating value can sometimes actually reduce costs. We'll show an important example of this when we discuss the role of quality in operations management later in this chapter.

## LO2 What Do Operations Managers Do?

Operations management is a broad field. This section will focus on only some of the issues that managers typically

encounter, but it should still give you a sense of how important operations managers are to the success of their organizations.

## Facility Location

For some types of facilities, the location decision is a no-brainer. A coal mine, for instance, must be located where there's coal. But for many other types of facilities, the decision is more complex, requiring numerous considerations. Exhibit 18.2 identifies several key factors operations managers look at when they decide where to locate a facility.

The importance of each factor in exhibit 18.2 varies depending on the specific type of industry. Because of their need for direct interaction with customers, many service firms place primary interest on locating close to their markets. But manufacturing firms may be more concerned about the availability of land or the cost of labor.

Locating Overseas Low-wage labor is one of the reasons firms look at overseas sites for manufacturing and other facilities, but it's certainly not the only reason. Land and other resources may also be much less expensive in developing nations than in the United States. And as we pointed out in chapter 3, many foreign markets are growing much more rapidly than the relatively mature U.S. market.

But operations managers must balance the advantages of locating in foreign countries against possible drawbacks. Locating production facilities in foreign countries may require a firm to deal with unfamiliar laws, languages, and customs. Social unrest and unstable governments beset some developing nations. The infrastructure may be in poor shape, and utilities may be unreliable.

It's also important to realize that the low *wages* in some foreign nations may not always translate into low costs of production. Workers in some developing

There is nothing so useless as doing efficiently that which should not be done at all.
–Peter F. Drucker

### "Mmmmmm...Efficient?!"

A recent television ad campaign by Steak n Shake, a restaurant chain with outlets mainly in the Midwest and South, shows that the firm clearly understands the distinction between efficiency and effectiveness. One of its ads shows two different ways to make a milkshake. The fast food way involves pulling a lever to dispense pre-mixed "milkshake" directly from a machine into a paper cup. The Steak n Shake way involves hand dipping premium ice cream into a large glass, pouring fresh milk, adding a thick, rich looking chocolate syrup, mixing the ingredients, then topping it all off with whipped cream and a cherry. A Steak n Shake waitress in the commercial says, "We admit their way is more efficient." Then she holds a rich looking Steak n Shake milkshake squarely in front of the camera, and continues, "But when is the last time you sipped a milkshake and said, 'Mmmmm, that tastes...efficient'?"[1]

## Exhibit 18.2 — Factors That Affect Location Decisions

| General Location Factors | Examples of Specific Considerations |
| --- | --- |
| Adequacy of utilities | Is the supply of electricity reliable? Is clean water available? |
| Land | Is adequate land available for a facility? How much does the land cost? |
| Labor market conditions | Are workers with the right skills available? How expensive is labor? |
| Transportation factors | Is the location near customers and suppliers? Is appropriate transportation nearby? |
| Quality of life factors | What is the climate like? Are adequate health care facilities available? |
| Legal and political environment | Does the local government support new businesses? What are the local taxes, fees, and regulations? |

nations have less education, less experience, and poorer health than American workers. For these reasons, they may be much less productive than American workers. If foreign workers earn two-thirds less than American workers but only produce a fourth as much output per hour, then their low wage isn't really a bargain. That's particularly true if the market for the goods is in the United States. The costs of shipping goods from foreign markets back to the United States can sometimes more than offset the advantages of low-cost labor.

## Process Selection and Facility Layout

A **process** is a set of activities or steps that combine inputs (e.g., labor, machinery, and equipment) to create a good or service. Well-designed processes enable a firm to produce high-quality products effectively and efficiently, giving it a competitive advantage. Poorly designed processes can result in production delays, problems with quality, high costs, and other problems. Many factors influence the type of process that works best, but two key considerations are the volume of production and the degree of standardization of the product.

Firms use **flow shop processes** when products are relatively standardized and produced in large volumes—a process sometimes called *mass production*. These processes use specialized machinery and equipment to produce a large quantity of a specific good very efficiently. An **assembly line** is the best-known type of flow shop process. On an assembly line, the product being produced moves from one station to another in a fixed sequence, with the machinery and workers at each station performing specialized tasks.

Flow shop processes aren't suited for the production of goods that require customization or that are produced individually or in small batches. Firms producing goods or services with these characteristics often use **job shop processes**. A job shop uses general-purpose equipment, sacrificing the efficiency of specialization for a greater degree of flexibility. Also, job shops don't require production to occur in a specific sequence of steps. Instead, the sequence of steps can be altered so that the shop can produce a variety of different goods without expensive retooling. Because they use general-purpose tools and perform a wider variety of tasks, workers in job shops must be more versatile than workers in flow shops.

**process** A set of activities or steps that combine inputs in order to create a desired output.

**flow shop process** A production process that uses specialized machinery and equipment to produce a large quantity of a specific good very efficiently.

**assembly line** A production process in which the product moves from one station to another in a fixed sequence, with the machinery and workers at each station performing specialized tasks.

**job shop process** A production process designed to produce goods or services in relatively small batches using general-purpose machinery and equipment.

## A Strain on India, Inc.?

India's remarkable economic growth of the 1990s was nearly derailed at the turn of the new century because of serious problems with infrastructure—especially power, transportation, and water. In 2003, large firms in India reported an average of 17 power outages a month—a situation so bad that 61% of these firms chose to invest in their own private power generators. Some of the fastest growing regions also suffered from severely overcrowded roads and railways and had to ration water supplies. Over the past few years, India's government has begun to invest more heavily in infrastructure, so these problems are likely to improve. But it'll be a while before India's infrastructure is up to the standards of most Western nations.[2]

© AP IMAGES

**inventory** Stocks of finished items, work-in-process, parts, materials, or other resources held by an organization.

Some services use job shop processes. The chef and other kitchen personnel in upscale restaurants are highly trained, and usually prepare meals to the specifications of individual customers—do you want your steak rare, medium or well done? What type of dressing do you want on your salad? Similarly, auto mechanics must be able to perform a variety of repairs that use general-purpose tools and require different steps to complete.

Although we won't describe them in depth, let's briefly mention two other types of processes. Companies tend to use a *continuous flow process* when production is even more standardized than a flow shop process and the rate of production is very high; in fact, the good essentially flows continuously through the process. (Oil and sugar refineries are well-known examples.) At the other extreme, a *project* involves the coordination of many complex activities to produce a large-scale good or service. A project is usually expensive and is produced in very low volumes; it often involves producing a one-of-a-kind product. The rebuilding of the levees around New Orleans is an example of a project that produces a good. The creation of a Broadway play is an example of a project for a service.

*Special Characteristics of Service Processes* Because services can't be shipped or stored, they often require

Services such as medical care often require customers to interact directly with the service provider.

© LARRY WILLIAMS/BLEND IMAGES/JUPITERIMAGES

the customer to directly interact with the provider at the time the service is created. The inclusion of the customer in the process means that the creators of most services have less control over how the process is carried out, how long it takes to complete, and whether the result is satisfactory. For instance, the accuracy of a doctor's diagnosis often depends on how honestly and completely the patient answers the doctor's questions. And the amount of time the doctor spends with each patient will depend on the nature and severity of the illness.

## Inventory Control: Don't Just Sit There

**Inventories** are stocks of items or resources held by an organization. Manufacturing firms usually hold inventories of raw materials, components and parts, work-in-process, and finished goods. Retail firms are unlikely to hold work-in-process or raw materials, but they usually do hold large inventories of finished goods and basic supplies that their business needs. Since services are consumed at the time they are created, service firms usually don't have inventories of work-in-process or finished goods. But they may hold inventories of supplies needed to perform the services. Restaurants, for example, hold inventories of breads, meats, vegetables, fruit, seasonings, and other items.

Deciding how much inventory to hold can be a real challenge for operations managers. Here are some of the reasons for holding large inventories:

- To Smooth Out Production Schedules: A candy maker might produce more candy than it needs in August and September and hold the excess in inventory. That way it can meet the surge in demand in the weeks before Halloween without investing in more production capacity.

- To Meet Unexpected Increases in Demand: Firms may lose sales to competitors if they run out of stock. They might hold additional inventory to meet unexpected increases in demand.

- To Reduce Costs Associated with Switching Processes: Rather than incurring frequent set up costs to produce items in small batches, firms may produce more than they need right now, holding the rest in inventory for future periods.

- To Compensate for Forecast Errors: Many firms base production schedules on sales forecasts. But sales forecasts aren't perfectly accurate. Any unsold goods will end up in inventory, at least for the short term.

But holding large inventories involves costs as well as benefits:

- Items in inventory don't generate revenue until they're sold, so holding large inventories can tie up funds that could be better used elsewhere within the organization.

- Large inventories require the firm to rent, buy, or build more storage space—which can also mean extra costs for heating, cooling, taxes, insurance, and so on.

- Holding large inventories exposes the firm to the risk of losses due to spoilage, depreciation, and obsolescence.

Operations managers determine the optimal amount of inventory by comparing the costs and benefits associated with different levels of inventory. In our discussion of lean manufacturing, we'll see that a recent trend has been toward finding ways to reduce inventory levels at every stage of the supply chain.

## Project Scheduling

Projects, such as the construction of a new office building or filming a movie, are usually complex, important, and expensive. It's vital to plan and monitor them carefully to avoid major delays or cost overruns.

Gantt charts and Critical Path Method (CPM) networks are two key tools that operations managers rely on to keep tabs on projects. A simple example can illustrate how both tools are used. We'll assume that the administration of a college wants to build a new sports arena and must complete several activities before it can hire a contractor and begin construction. Exhibit 18.3 lists the specific activities involved in the college's project.

Notice that exhibit 18.3 identifies **immediate predecessors** for all of the activities except A. Immediate predecessors are activities that must be completed before other activities can begin. For example, the

administration believes that it must survey users of the arena to determine their needs and location preferences *before* they develop a preliminary design or select a site. Thus the survey of needs is an immediate predecessor for both the selection of the site and preliminary design.

### Using a Gantt Chart to Get the Big Picture
Exhibit 18.4 on the following page illustrates a Gantt chart for this project. The **Gantt chart** lists all of the activities down its left margin, and shows the elapsed time since the project began across the bottom of the chart. A bar is drawn for each activity, showing when it is expected to start and end. Notice that activities can't start until their immediate predecessors have been completed.

Once a project has begun, the bars for the activities on a Gantt chart can be filled in to indicate progress. In our example, the solid orange bars represent activities that are completed, the solid gray bars represent activities that haven't yet begun, and the bars that are part orange and part gray indicate activities that are currently under way. The chart shows us that as of week 22 the college is about a week behind schedule in finalizing its design since the orange part of the bar for this activity only extends to week 21. We can also see that the college is two weeks ahead of schedule in arranging final financing.

### Using the Critical Path Method to Focus Efforts
Now look at exhibit 18.5 on the following page, which is a **Critical Path Method** diagram for the arena project. One benefit of a CPM network is that it clearly shows how all of the activities are related to each other. The direction of the arrows shows the immediate predecessors for each activity. For example, notice that arrows go from activities F *and* G to activity H. This indicates that *both* F (selection of the architect) and G (establishing the budget) must be completed before activity H (obtaining final financing) can begin. But also notice that no arrow links activities H and I. This shows that these are independent activities, so the college could arrange financing and finalize the design for the arena at the same time.

We can use exhibit 18.5 to illustrate some basic concepts used in CPM analysis. A *path* is a sequence of connected activities that *must be completed in the order specified by the arrows* for the overall project to be completed. You can trace several paths in our example by following a series of arrows from start to finish. For example, one path is A → B → E → G → I → J and another path is A → C → D → E → G → H → J.

**Exhibit 18.3** Activities Involved in College Arena Project

| Activity | Immediate Predecessor(s) | Time (Weeks) |
|---|---|---|
| A. Survey of needs | None | 2 |
| B. Determine site for arena | A | 5 |
| C. Preliminary design developed | A | 5 |
| D. Obtain major donation for funding | C | 6 |
| E. Obtain board approval | B,D | 4 |
| F. Select architect | E | 3 |
| G. Establish budget | E | 2 |
| H. Obtain remaining financing | F,G | 10 |
| I. Finalize design | G | 6 |
| J. Hire contractor | H,I | 2 |

All paths in a project are important, but some need more attention than others. The **critical path** consists of the sequence of activities that takes the longest to complete. *A delay in any activity on a critical path is likely to delay the completion of the entire project.* Thus operations managers watch activities on the critical path very carefully and take actions to help ensure that they remain on schedule. We've shown the critical path for the arena project (A → C → D → E → F → H → J) with red arrows on our diagram.

Activities that aren't on the critical path can be delayed without causing a delay in the overall completion of the project—as long as the delay isn't too great. In CPM terminology, these activities have *slack*. When operations managers see delays in critical path activities, they sometimes divert manpower and other resources from activities with slack to activities on the critical path.

## LO3 The Technology of Operations

Now let's take a close look at how technology has revolutionized operations management. Some of the new technologies involve automated machinery and equipment. Others are advances in software and information technology. But the biggest recent changes have involved efforts to link the new machinery to the new software.

---

**Exhibit 18.4**    A Gantt Chart for the College Arena Project

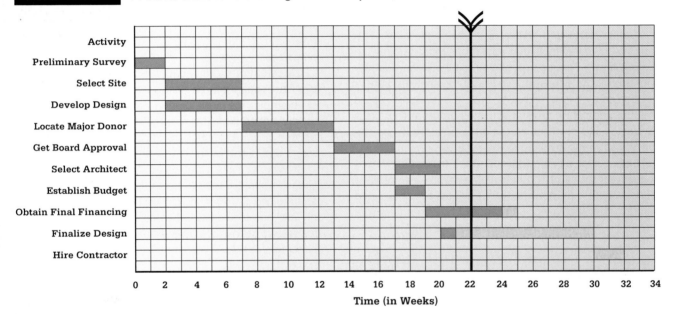

---

**Exhibit 18.5**    CPM Chart for the College Arena Project

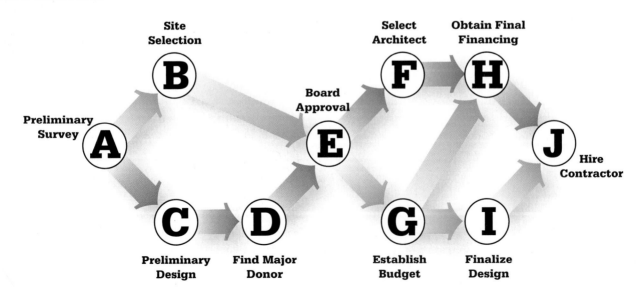

## Automation: Let the Machines Do It

For the past half century, one of the biggest trends in operations management has been increased **automation** of many processes. Automation means replacing human operation and control of machinery and equipment with some form of programmed control. Over the years, the use of automated systems has become increasingly common, and increasingly sophisticated.

Automation began in the early 1950s with primitive programmed machines. But in recent decades, **robots** have taken automation to a whole new level. Robots are reprogrammable machines that can manipulate materials, tools, parts, and specialized devices in order to perform a variety of tasks. Some robots have special equipment that allows them to sense their surroundings by "seeing," "hearing," or "feeling." Many robots are mobile and can even be guided over rugged terrain.

Firms have found that robots offer many advantages:

- They often perform jobs that most human workers find tedious, dirty, dangerous, or physically demanding.

- They don't get tired, so they can work very long hours while maintaining a consistently high level of performance.

- They are flexible; unlike old dogs, robots *can* be taught new tricks because they are reprogrammable.

Robots perform a variety of tasks. Common uses include welding, painting, and assembling, but other uses range from packaging frozen pizza to disposing of hazardous wastes or searching for and defusing bombs.

### Software Technologies

Several types of software have become common in operations management:

- **Computer-aided design (CAD)** software provides powerful drawing and drafting tools that enable users to create and edit blueprints and design drawings quickly and easily. Current CAD programs allow users to create three-dimensional drawings.

- **Computer-aided engineering (CAE)** software enables users to test, analyze, and optimize their designs. CAE software can help engineers find and correct design flaws *before* production.

- **Computer-aided manufacturing (CAM)** software takes the electronic design for a product and creates the programmed instructions that robots must follow to produce that product as efficiently as possible.

Today, computer-aided design and computer-aided manufacturing software are often combined into a single system, called **CAD/CAM**. This enables CAD designs to flow directly to CAM programs, which then send instructions directly to the automated equipment on the factory floor to guide the production process.

When a CAD/CAM software system is integrated with robots and other high-tech equipment, the result is **computer-integrated manufacturing (CIM)** in which the whole design and production process is highly automated. The speed of computers and the integration of all these functions make it possible to switch from the design and production of one good to another quickly and efficiently. CIM is a key element of the *mass customization* strategy we mentioned in chapter 11 because it enables the firm to produce custom-designed products for individual consumers quickly and at costs almost as low as those associated with mass production techniques.

## LO4 Integrated Operating Systems: Coordinating Efforts

The computer-integrated manufacturing we just discussed is one example of another important trend in operations management: the integration of formerly independent functions into highly coordinated systems. Two other major examples of this trend are supply chain management and enterprise resource planning (ERP).

### How Operations Managers View Supply Chains

Although we briefly discussed supply chain management in chapter 13, we'll look at it now in more detail from an operations manager's perspective. From this standpoint, it's important to realize that supply chains involve not only the flow of materials and physical goods through all the organizations involved in production and distribution but also the corresponding flows of *services*, *financial resources*, and *information*.

Supply chains can be very complex, involving many firms, located in many countries, performing a wide range of production and distribution functions. Coordinating all of the flows among these organizations can be a real challenge. But some of the technologies we mentioned in chapter 17 promise to help. For instance, e-marketplaces have proven effective at bringing together firms at different stages of a supply chain, enabling them to negotiate, communicate, and collaborate.

**automation** Replacing human operation and control of machinery and equipment with some form of programmed control.

**robot** A reprogrammable machine that is capable of manipulating materials, tools, parts, and specialized devices in order to perform a variety of tasks.

**computer-aided design (CAD)** Drawing and drafting software that enables users to create and edit blueprints and design drawings quickly and easily.

**computer-aided engineering (CAE)** Software that enables users to test, analyze, and optimize their designs.

**computer-aided manufacturing (CAM)** Software that takes the electronic design for a product and creates the programmed instructions that robots must follow to produce that product as efficiently as possible.

**CAD/CAM** Computer-aided design/ computer-aided manufacturing; a combination of software that can be used to design output and send instructions to automated equipment to perform the steps needed to produce this output.

**computer-integrated manufacturing (CIM)** A combination of CAD/CAM software with flexible manufacturing systems to automate almost all steps involved in designing, testing, and producing a product.

RFID chips, another technology we introduced in chapter 17, also promise to improve the efficiency of many aspects of supply chain management. RFID chips are already helping many organizations track the movement of parts, materials, and finished goods through a supply chain with great accuracy. And when this technology becomes more common it will make taking inventory a snap; using RFID, inventory procedures that used to take days will be accomplished in hours (or perhaps even minutes). Wal-Mart, Target, and other major retailers view RFID technology as so important that they now are requiring all of their major suppliers to include RFID chips with their shipments.[3]

Different types of products call for different approaches to the supply chain. Dell Computer became famous for its innovative supply chain strategy that eliminated most intermediaries by taking orders directly from customers over the Internet, manufacturing computers to order, and shipping directly to the customer. Would that same strategy work for Kellogg's? Can you imagine the giant cereal maker selling cornflakes online to individual buyers? The shipping costs for single boxes of cereal would be higher than price of the cereal itself! Consumers find it cheaper and more convenient to buy their cereal at a grocery store.

One of the most important issues operations managers must consider when looking at how to improve supply chains is the trade-off between vertical integration and outsourcing. **Vertical integration** occurs when a firm attempts to gain more control over its supply chain by either performing the activities itself or acquiring the organizations that do. **Outsourcing** is essentially the opposite of vertical integration; it involves arranging for other organizations in the supply chain to perform functions that were previously performed internally.

In recent years, the trend has been to rely more on outsourcing and less on vertical integration. Outsourcing allows a firm to shed functions it doesn't perform well in order to focus on its areas of strength. It also frees people and money that had been tied up in the outsourced activities, allowing these resources to be employed in more profitable ways.

But heavy reliance on outside organizations can complicate supply chains and create coordination problems. It can also expose the firm to certain types of risks, especially when outsourcing involves firms located in foreign countries. When a firm outsources important functions, it may have

These amazingly small **RFID** chips can store and transmit a **38** digit number that uniquely identifies a product.

© ALBERT LOZANO/SHUTTERSTOCK

## Doc Robot Is in the House

Robots are revolutionizing the practice of medicine. Doctors at many hospitals now use a robot developed by InTouch Health to check on their patients at times when they're unable to get to the hospital. The robot uses video cameras and a wireless Internet hookup to send information back to the doctor. The "head" of the robot is a video screen that allows the patient to see the physician, who can talk to the patient through the Internet hookup. Children, in particular, seem comfortable with this arrangement. When the robot rolls into the pediatric wing of one hospital decked out in a stethoscope and superhero cape the typical response is a roomful of giggles.

Almost 900 hospitals now use a medical robot developed by Intuitive Systems to perform complex surgeries, including heart bypasses. Doctors use a console with a 3-D monitor to control the robot's movements. The robot can perform the surgeries with smaller incisions and steadier "hands" than unaided human surgeons. A study by the University of Maryland found that the use of robots in heart bypass surgery resulted in shorter recovery times, fewer complications, and a better chance that the bypassed blood vessels would remain open.[4]

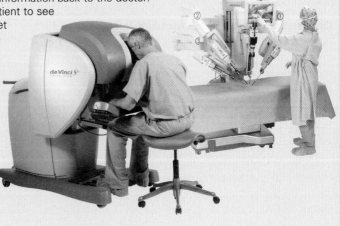

© 2008 INTUITIVE SURGICAL, INC.

to entrust others in its supply chain with confidential information and intellectual property such as copyrighted material or patented products. These strategic assets have less legal protection in some countries than in the United States, so providing access to foreign firms may increase the risk that the firm's intellectual property will be pirated or counterfeited. This issue has been of greatest concern when firms have outsourced some of their supply chain functions to organizations in China.[5]

Some labor leaders and politicians claim that outsourcing to foreign producers results in widespread job losses for American workers. But many economists and business leaders point out that outsourcing ultimately may create more jobs than it eliminates. Their argument is based on the idea that outsourcing increases the efficiency of the supply chain, enabling firms to become more competitive and generate more growth. This growth then creates more jobs within the company than were lost by the outsourcing. While this argument is logical, it's been a tough sell to the American workforce. One problem is that the workers who lose jobs to outsourcing may not have the skills to qualify for the new jobs that are created by the growth.[6]

> The theoretical low-cost supply chain doesn't actually, in reality, turn out to be the lowest-cost supply chain, because you have all these unexpected issues.
>
> –Beth Enslow, Senior Vice President of The Aberdeen Group

## Enterprise Resource Planning: Creating One Big System

**Enterprise resource planning** represents an even higher degree of operations integration than supply chain management. The goal of ERP is to integrate the information flows of *all* aspects of a business's operations—accounting, finance, sales and marketing, production, and human resources. In fact, the newest versions of ERP even include supply chain management as part of their system.

When one department enters data into the ERP system, it becomes immediately available to other departments, eliminating the need for each group to enter the data separately. In addition, the common information system makes it easier for departments throughout the enterprise to communicate and coordinate their activities. Once their ERP systems are fully in place, firms can see dramatic improvements in performance. But for many companies, the problem has been to get their systems up and running.

ERP systems can be very difficult and expensive to implement. Though it's now using ERP successfully,

**enterprise resource planning (ERP)** Software-based approach to integrate an organization's systems in order to improve communication and coordination among all departments and operating units.

---

# Oops! What were they THINKING?!

© PHOTODISC/GETTY IMAGES

### Supply Chain 101: Are You In or Out?

During the 1990s and 2000s, one American firm after another moved manufacturing and technical support jobs to foreign shores. But lately some of these firms have begun to have second thoughts. While it's far too soon to say the offshoring trend has been reversed, some U.S. firms are now finding that there's no place like home.

Consider the case of Hot Kiss, provider of trendy women's clothing to leading U.S. retailers. Until recently it imported the vast majority of its fashions from China. Now it makes 60% of its garments in the U.S.—doubling its domestic production in just a few years. Hot Kiss CEO Moshe Tsabag believes that U.S. apparel manufacturing is on the way back, noting that "Three years ago we were losing jobs in the industry. Now I think we're going through a revival."

Several computer and communications companies are also rethinking their decade-long trend of sending call center jobs overseas. Over the past few years several leading firms, including AT&T, Dell, and Apple, have either brought call center jobs back to the U.S. or cancelled previously announced plans to open call centers overseas.

What explains these reversals? In the case of the fashion industry, the driving force was the desire to reduce the time it takes to get goods to market. Switching from China to the U.S. allowed fashion suppliers to cut delivery times from 120 days to 45 days—a critical competitive advantage in an industry where trends change quickly. For call centers, many customers complained that the accents of the foreign support personnel were difficult to understand. In addition, years of double-digit wage inflation in the high tech sectors of both India and China, coupled with a weaker dollar, have eroded much of the labor savings that attracted many firms to offshore their operations in the first place.[7]

Hershey's initial attempts to build a sophisticated ERP system ended in a near disaster. Because of glitches and delays in its new ERP system, Hershey's found itself with serious supply chain problems that left it unable to ship over $100 million of its candy in September and October of 1999—at the height of the Halloween selling season.[8]

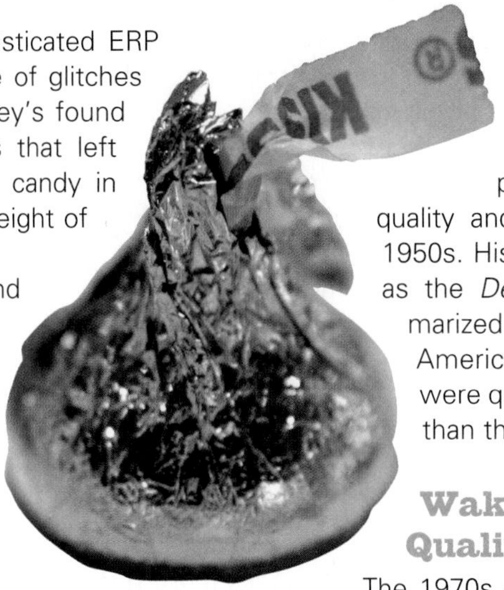

Several factors contribute to the cost and challenge of implementing ERP systems:

- The scope and complexity of the software makes it expensive even without modifications. But most firms want to customize the software to meet their specific needs, adding to the complexity, cost, and timeframe.

- All the data from the old system must be transferred to the new system. Given that the data from different departments is often stored in different formats, this can be a time-consuming task.

- ERP software requires employees throughout the organization to learn new ways of entering and accessing data. Productivity often falls until workers learn how to use the new system.[9]

Despite these problems, most firms that adopt ERP systems ultimately come to view them in a positive light. In a recent survey of over 600 chief financial officers and other top managers, three-fourths of the respondents rated their implementations of an ERP system as a success.[10]

## LO5 Focus on Quality

Almost everyone agrees that quality is important. But the concept of quality is tough to define—even expert opinions differ. For our purposes, we'll adopt the view that quality is defined in terms of how well a good or service satisfies customer preferences.

Why is quality so important? Improvements in quality are a key to achieving competitive advantage because they enable a firm to improve both its effectiveness *and* its efficiency. The fact that high quality improves effectiveness (creates value) probably doesn't surprise you—consumers tend to place a high value on quality. But you might be surprised to learn that improved quality also can lower costs. After all, it's expensive to train workers in quality improvement, to install better equipment, set higher standards, and to implement more rigorous procedures.

But poor quality also comes with costs. When a firm detects defective products, it must scrap, rework, or repair them—all costly options. And the costs can be even higher when a firm *doesn't* catch defects before shipping products to consumers. These costs include handling customer complaints, warranty repair work, loss of goodwill, and the possibility of bad publicity or lawsuits. In the long run, firms often find that improving quality reduces these costs by more than enough to make up for their investment.

These ideas aren't especially new. W. Edwards Deming, viewed by many as the father of the quality movement, first proposed the relationship between quality and business success in the early 1950s. His ideas, which came to be known as the *Deming Chain Reaction*, are summarized in exhibit 18.6. Unfortunately for American firms, Japanese companies were quicker to heed Deming's message than the Americans were.

### Waking Up to the Need for Quality

The 1970s and early 1980s were a wake-up call for many American companies. During this period, Japanese firms in several key industries, including automobiles, electronics, and heavy machinery, rapidly gained global market share at the expense of American firms that had once faced little competition. One of the major reasons for the success of Japanese firms was that the quality of their goods was clearly superior. This was a remarkable turnaround because in the decades immediately after World War II Japanese goods had a reputation for being downright shoddy.

How did the Japanese quality revolution occur? During the 1950s, many Japanese firms listened to quality experts such as W. Edwards Deming. They took the message to heart and began treating quality improve-

**Exhibit 18.6** The Deming Chain Reaction: Improved Quality Helps the Business's Bottom Line

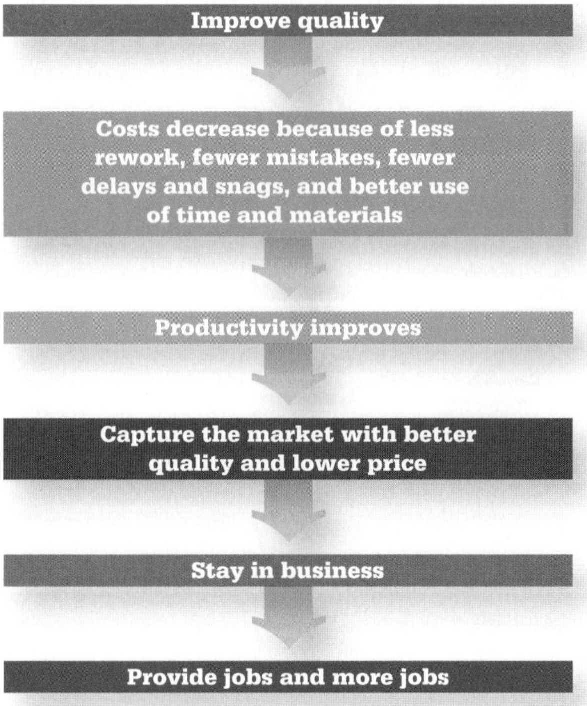

Improve quality

↓

Costs decrease because of less rework, fewer mistakes, fewer delays and snags, and better use of time and materials

↓

Productivity improves

↓

Capture the market with better quality and lower price

↓

Stay in business

↓

Provide jobs and more jobs

ment as a *continuous* process—and as a goal that concerned *every* employee. It took a while, but the quality of Japanese goods slowly and steadily improved. By the early 1970s, when most American firms still treated quality as something to check only at the end of the production process, many Japanese firms had achieved quality levels that exceeded those of companies in most other countries by a wide margin.

## How American Firms Responded to the Quality Challenge

When key American firms realized how far they trailed the Japanese in quality, they made a real effort to change their ways. Like the Japanese a few decades earlier, American business leaders adopted a broader view of quality than they had previously held.

Total Quality Management The first result of this newfound emphasis on quality was the development of an approach called **total quality management**, better known as TQM. There are several variations, but all of them share the following characteristics:

- Customer Focus: TQM recognizes that quality should be defined by the preferences and perceptions of customers.

- Emphasis on Building Quality throughout the Organization: TQM views quality as the concern of every department and every employee.

- Empowerment of Employees: Most TQM programs give teams of workers the responsibility and authority to make and implement decisions to improve quality.

- Focus on Prevention Rather Than Correction: TQM pursues a strategy of preventing mistakes that create defects.

- Long-Run Commitment to Continuous Improvement: TQM requires firms to adopt a focus on making improvements in quality a way of life.

In many cases, American firms using TQM attempt to reduce defects by using **poka-yokes**—the Japanese term for "mistake proofing." Poka-yokes are simple procedures built into the production process that either prevent workers from making mistakes or quickly catch and correct mistakes if they do occur. A simple example of a poka-yoke would be providing assembly workers with "kits" that contain exactly enough parts to complete one unit of work at a time. If the worker completes an assembly and sees a part left over, it's clear that a mistake has been made, and he or she can correct it on the spot.[11]

The Move to Six Sigma During the 1990s, another approach to total quality, known as **Six Sigma**, became increasingly popular. Six Sigma includes some of the same elements as TQM, such as an organization-wide focus on quality, emphasis on finding and eliminating causes of errors or defects (prevention rather than correction), and a long-term focus on continuous quality improvement. Also like TQM, it relies on teams of workers to carry out specific projects to improve quality. At any given time, a firm may have several Six Sigma projects under way, and the goal of each is to achieve the Six Sigma level of quality.

**total quality management (TQM)** An approach to quality improvement that calls for everyone within an organization to take responsibility for improving quality and emphasizes the need for a long-term commitment to continuous improvement.

**poka-yokes** Simple methods incorporated into a production process designed to eliminate or greatly reduce errors.

**Six Sigma** An approach to quality improvement characterized by very ambitious quality goals, extensive training of employees, and a long-term commitment to working on quality-related issues.

## Six Sigma Belts Quality Concerns

Six Sigma quality programs rely on sophisticated techniques that require highly trained and experienced leadership. Much like karate, Six Sigma identifies the proficiency of its practitioners with belt colors:

- **Yellow Belts** have some basic training in six sigma concepts, but are not proficient enough to take responsibility for a project.
- **Green Belts** have a higher level of training than yellow belts, and work on six sigma projects as part of their regular jobs. But they haven't acquired the depth of training needed to become Black Belts.
- **Black Belts** have a high enough level of training and experience to take charge of a Six Sigma team working on a specific project. They work full time on Six Sigma projects.
- **Master Black Belts** have achieved the highest level of expertise in the statistical methods, quality improvement strategies, leadership, and other techniques needed to carry out Six Sigma projects. They are the teachers and mentors of black belts. Master Black Belts can achieve an almost superstar status within their organizations.[12]

© J & L IMAGES/PHOTODISC/GETTY IMAGES

But Six Sigma differs from TQM in other respects. Unlike TQM, it has a single unifying measure: to reduce defects of any operation or process to a level of no more than 3.4 per million opportunities. Attaining this level of quality represents a rigorous and challenging goal. Six Sigma also differs from TQM in its reliance on extensive (and expensive) employee training and reliance on expert guidance. The techniques used in the Six Sigma approach are quite advanced and their application requires a high level of expertise.

## Quality Standards and Quality Initiatives

Another way firms try to implement quality improvement is to launch programs designed to achieve certification or recognition from outside authorities. Two common approaches are to participate in the Baldrige National Quality Program and to seek certification under the International Organization for Standardization's ISO 9000 standards.

### The Baldrige National Quality Program

Congress passed the Malcolm Baldrige National Quality Improvement Act of 1987 in an effort to encourage American firms to become more competitive in the global economy by vigorously pursuing improvements in quality and productivity. Winners of the Baldrige Award must demonstrate excellence in seven criteria: leadership; strategic planning; customer and market focus; measurement, analysis, and knowledge management; human resource focus; process management; and business results.

Firms that participate in the **Baldrige National Quality Program** receive benefits even if they don't win the award. Every participating firm receives at least 300 hours of evaluation and review from highly qualified business and quality experts. At the end of the process, they receive a detailed report identifying areas of strength and areas where improvement is needed. Considering the normal fees high-powered consulting firms charge for similar reports, the information and advice a firm gets for the fee charged to participate in the Baldrige program (which ranges from $1,000 to $6,000 depending on the type of organization) is a tremendous bargain![13]

> You seldom improve quality by cutting costs, but you can often cut costs by improving quality.
> –Karl Albrecht, author and futurist

### ISO 9000 Certification

Founded in 1947, ISO is a network of national standards institutes in over 150 nations that work together to develop international standards for a wide array of industries. ISO standards ensure that goods produced in one country will meet the requirements of buyers in another country. This benefits consumers by giving them the ability to buy from foreign sellers with confidence, giving them a wider array of choices. It also benefits sellers by allowing them to compete more successfully in global markets.

Most of the standards established by the ISO are industry-specific. But in 1987 the ISO developed generic standards for quality management systems that could be applied to virtually any company in any industry in any country. Firms that satisfy these broad standards receive **ISO 9000** certification. Similar to many other quality initiatives, ISO 9000 standards define quality in terms of the ability to satisfy customer preferences and require the firm to implement procedures for continuous quality improvement. Since 1987, the ISO 9000 standards have been updated and modified several times. The latest version is called ISO 9000:2005.

In the late 1990s the International Organization for Standardization published another set of standards called ISO 14000. This newer set of standards focuses on environmental management. The goal is to ensure that qualifying firms minimize harm to the natural environment and achieve continuous improvement in environmental practices.

**Many leading companies now make quality the responsibility of every employee in every department.**

© COURTESY OF STONER, INC. AND NIST

# LO6 Lean Production: Cutting Waste to Improve Performance

**Lean production** refers to a set of strategies and practices to eliminate waste, which is defined as any function or activity that uses resources but doesn't create value. Eliminating waste can lead to dramatic improvements in efficiency. For example, Sanford, the maker of PaperMate pens and Sharpie markers and highlighters, used lean thinking to dramatically cut its packaging costs. Before adopting lean thinking, Sanford developed different blister packs for every single product, resulting in literally hundreds of different packages. After applying lean thinking the company was able to cut the number of package configurations down to 15, reducing setup time for packaging by 50%, cutting tooling costs by up to 80%, and reducing warehousing costs by up to 25%.[14]

## Identifying Sources of Waste: Value Stream Mapping

Lean production begins by looking at all aspects of an organization's operations from the time parts and raw materials first arrive until the production process is completed. The purpose of this process is to find and eliminate sources of waste. Value stream mapping is one of lean production's most important tools in this effort. A **value stream map** is a diagram that provides a detailed picture of the flows of all parts, materials, and information through an entire production process. A value stream map also identifies the amount of labor and other resources used to carry out each activity and indicates activity cycle time (the length of time needed to complete one full cycle of an activity).

Once the firm has identified areas of waste and developed solutions, operations managers draw a future state value map that incorporates the proposed changes. This allows them to visualize the new flow of activities, check for inconsistencies, and communicate their strategy to others in the organization.

## Reducing Investment in Inventory: Just-in-Time to the Rescue

One of the hallmarks of lean systems is a tight control on inventories. In part, this reflects recognition of the inventory holding costs that we discussed earlier. But the lean approach also offers another reason for minimizing inventories. Large inventories serve as a buffer that enables the firm to continue operations when problems arise due to poor quality, faulty equipment, or unreliable suppliers. In the lean view, it's more efficient in the long run to improve quality, keep equipment in good working order, and develop reliable supply relationships than to continue compensating for these problems by holding large inventories.

Lean manufacturing avoids overproduction and holding large inventories of finished goods by using **just-in-time (JIT) production** methods. The JIT approach produces only enough goods to satisfy current demand. This approach is called a *pull system* because actual orders "pull" the goods through the production process. The workers at the end of the production process produce just enough of the final product to satisfy actual orders and use just enough parts and materials from preceding stages of production to satisfy their needs. Workers at each earlier stage are expected to produce just enough output at their workstations to replace the amount used by the processes further along the process—and in so doing they withdraw just the needed amount of parts and other supplies from even earlier processes.

JIT techniques obviously result in very small inventories of finished goods and work-in-process. But lean firms also hold only small inventories of materials and parts, counting on suppliers to provide them with these items as they need them to meet current demand. In a lean system, all organizations in the supply chain must meet the needs of their customers for current production. Thus, only minimum inventories are held at each stage.

## Lean Thinking in the Service Sector

Employing lean principles in the service sector can be quite a challenge because customers often participate in providing the service. This means a service firm usually has less control over how processes are conducted. But many service firms have benefited from creatively applying lean techniques. Southwest Airlines is well known for its efforts to reduce waste. It uses only one type of aircraft (the Boeing 737) to standardize maintenance and minimize training costs. It also has an extremely simple ticketing system (no assigned seating) and, when possible, flies into smaller or older airports where there is less congestion. This means less time (and less fuel) are spent circling airports waiting to land or sitting on runways waiting to take off. Despite a no-frills approach, Southwest almost always ranks near the top of the list in terms of airline customer satisfaction.[15]

**lean production** An approach to production that emphasizes the elimination of waste in all aspects of production processes.

**value stream mapping** A tool used in lean production to show the flows of materials and information from the beginning to the end of a production process; used to identify where waste occurs within a production system.

**just-in-time (JIT) production** A production system that emphasizes the production of goods to meet actual current demand, thus minimizing the need to hold inventories of finished goods and work-in-process at each stage of the supply chain.

© C SQUARED STUDIOS/PHOTODISC/GETTY IMAGES

# Endnotes

## Chapter 1

1. Entrepreneurship alive and well in the U.S., *Business Wire*, April 21, 2005, http://galenet.galegroup.com/servlet/BCRC?vrsn=149&locID=tlearn_trl&srchtp=glb&c=4&ste=25&tab=2&tbst=tsAS&mst=start+their+own+business+&docNum=A131787386&bConts=0; Small business resources for faculty, students, and researchers, SBA Office of Advocacy, http://www.sba.gov/advo/stats/arsbfaq.pdf, accessed September 16, 2005.

2. The 400 Richest Americans ed. by Matthew Miller, *Forbes* Website, September 20, 2007, http://www.forbes.com/lists/2007/54/richlist07_The-400-Richest-Americans_Rank.html, accessed August 16, 2008.

3. Nonprofits start making painful cuts by Sue Kirchhoff, *USA Today* Website September 16, 2003, http://www.usatoday.com/money/economy/2003-09-16-nonprofits2_x.htm; Area nonprofits play large economic role by Jacqueline Salmon, February 23, 2005, *Washington Post* Website, http://www.washingtonpost.com/wp-dyn/articles/A45611-2005Feb22.html; Nonprofits job engine transforms PA economy by Bob Fernandez and Patricia Horn, August 28, 2005, *Philadelphia Inquirer* Website, http://www.philly.com/mld/inquirer/news/local/12493895.htm; Nonprofit Sector Fast Facts, National Council of Nonprofit Associations Website, http://www.ncna.org/index.cfm?fuseaction=Page.viewPage&pageId=734, accessed August 16, 2008; Occupational Employment Statistics, U.S. Department of Labor Bureau of Labor Statistics Website, http://www.bls.gov/oes/home.htm#overview, accessed August 16, 2008.

4. Inflatable Dartboard, Innovation Gone Wrong Website, posted June 13, 2008, http://innovationgonewrong.wordpress.com/2008/06/13/i-couldnt-believe-itinflatable-dart-board/, accessed October 23, 2008; Kamov Ka-50, Wikipedia Website, posting modified October 14, 2008, http://en.wikipedia.org/wiki/Kamov_Ka-50, accessed October 23, 2008; Security Briefcase, Safe Case Corporation Website, http://www.safecasecorp.com/secucase.html, accessed October 23, 2008.

5. Kraft Foods Website, http://kraft.com/responsibility/cc_grants2005.aspx, accessed September 20, 2005; Polo Ralph Lauren Website, http://about.polo.com/philanthropy/star_banner.asp, accessed September 20, 2005; *Los Angeles Times* Website, http://www.latimes.com/extras/readingby9/who.html, accessed September 20, 2005.

6. GNI Per Capita, World Bank Data, http://www.worldbank.org/data/databytopic/GNIPC.pdf, accessed September 24, 2005; CIA World Factbook China, updated August 30, http://www.cia.gov/cia/publications/factbook/geos/ch.html; CIA World Factbook Russia, updated August 30, 2005, http://www.cia.gov/cia/publications/factbook/geos/rs.html.

7. Concluding statement of the IMF mission, May 25, 2005, International Monetary Fund Website, http://www.imf.org/external/np/ms/2005/052505a.htm; Our hidden savings by Michael Mandel, January 17, 2005, *BusinessWeek* Website, http://www.businessweek.com/magazine/content/05_03/b3916043_mz011.htm; The zero savings problem by Chris Isadore, August 3, 2005, http://money.cnn.com/2005/08/02/news/economy/savings/; Were the good old days that good? by Louis Uchitelle, July 3, 2005, *NYT* Website, http://select.nytimes.com/gst/abstract.html?res=FB0C16F939550C708CDDAE0894DD404482); CEO : worker pay shoots up to 431 : 1, United for a Fair Economy Website, http://www.faireconomy.org/press/2005/EE2005_pr.html; Personal savings rate, Bureau of Economic Analysis, December 21, 2006, http://www.bea.gov/briefrm/saving.htm; The Bear Trap by Justin Fox, *NewsWeek*, March 31, 2008, pages 32–35; Why Americans Are Going Broke by Jennifer Barrett, *NewsWeek* Web Exclusive, February 1, 2008.

8. American Customer Satisfaction Index, ASCI Scores, http://www.theacsi.org/first_quarter.htm, accessed September 26, 2005.

9. Coping with the competition by Jack Trout, September 26, 2005, Forbes.com Entrepreneurs Newsletter, http://www.forbes.com/2005/09/23/marketing-advertising-business-cx_jt_0926trout.html?partner=smallbusiness_newsletter.

10. Best Global Brands by David Kiley, *BusinessWeek* Website, August 6, 2007, http://www.businessweek.com/magazine/content/07_32/b4045401.htm, accessed October 8, 2008.

11. Get creative! by Bruce Nussbaum, August 1, 2005, *BusinessWeek* Website, http://www.businessweek.com/magazine/content/05_31/b3945401.htm.

12. Why Webvan drove off a cliff by Joanna Glasner, Wired News, July 10, 2001, http://www.wired.com/news/business/0,1367,45098,00.html.

13. Honey, I shrunk the iPod. A lot by Steven Levy, *NewsWeek*, September 19, 2005; Behind Apple's strategy: be second to market by John Boddie, Harvard Business School Working Knowledge, August 29, 2005, http://hbswk.hbs.edu/item.jhtml?id=4970&t=technology.

14. Giving employees what they want: the returns are huge, Knowledge@Wharton, Human Resources, May 4, 2005, http://knowledge.wharton.upenn.edu/article/1188.cfm.

15. Star search by Nanette Burns, *BusinessWeek* online, October 10, 2005, http://www.businessweek.com/magazine/content/05_41/b3954001.htm?campaign_id=nws_insdr_sep30&link_position=link1.

16. E-Commerce growth, Strategic E-Commerce Solutions Website, http://www.sescommerce.com/pages/main_page.asp?nID=46, accessed October 2, 2005; What impact will e-commerce have on the U.S. economy? by Jonathan Willis, Federal Reserve Bank Economic Review, 2nd Quarter 2004, http://www.kc.frb.org/publicat/econrev/Pdf/2q04will.pdf; Quarterly Retail E-Commerce Sales: 4th Quarter 2007, U.S. Census Bureau Website, February 15, 2008, http://www.census.gov/mrts/www/data/pdf/07Q4.pdf, accessed August 16, 2008.

17. Annual estimates of the population, July 1, 2004, U.S. Census Website, http://www.census.gov/popest/ states/asrh/tables/SC-EST2004-04.xls; The face of our population, October 13, 2004, U.S. Census Website, http://factfinder.census.gov/jsp/saff/SAFFInfo.jsp? _pageId=tp9_race_ethnicity.

18. Texas moves closer to "majority-minority" status, U.S. Census Press Release, September 30, 2004, http://www.census.gov/Press-Release/www/releases/ archives/population/002897.html; Annual estimates of the population, July 1, 2004, U.S. Census Website, http://www.census.gov/popest/states/asrh/tables/ SC-EST2004-04.xls; The face of our population, October 13, 2004, U.S. Census Website, http:// factfinder.census.gov/jsp/saff/SAFFInfo.jsp? _pageId=tp9_race_ethnicity.

19. Translating Hispanic marketing into shareholder value, Hispanic PR Wire/Business Wire, December 4, 2006, http://www.hispanicprwire.com/print .php?l=in&id=7660.

20. Diversity awareness, Hershey Foods Corporation Website, https://www.hersheysjobs.com/Career/ ControlPanel.aspx?ModuleCategoryID=1999999, accessed October 4, 2005.

21. Attitudes of young people toward diversity, CIRCLE fact sheet, February 2005, http://www.civicyouth.org/ PopUps/FactSheets/Attitudes%202.25.pdf.

22. The U.S. population is growing older, October 12, 2004, U.S. Census Website, http://factfinder.census .gov/jsp/saff/SAFFInfo.jsp?_pageId=tp2_aging; China faces up to aging population, January 7, 2005, Xinhua News Agency, http://www.china.org.cn/english/2005/ Jan/117070.htm; The coming demographic: how aging populations will reduce global savings, January 2005, McKinsey Global Institute Website, http://www .mckinsey.com/mgi/publications/demographics/ index.asp.

23. Editors name the greatest inventions of all time, Encyclopedia Britannica News Release, January 30, 2003, http://corporate.britannica.com/press/ releases/invention.html, accessed August 16, 2008; Encyclopedia Britannica's Great Inventions, October 11, 2005, http://corporate.britannica.com/press/ inventions.html, accessed August 16, 2008.

24. Pending job flexibility act received mixed reviews by Sue Shellenbarger, WSJ Career Journal, http://www .careerjournal.com/columnists/workfamily/ 20010426-workfamily.html, accessed October 4, 2005; Bad attitudes in the workplace by Les Christie, September 6, 2005, CNNMoney, http:// money.cnn.com/2005/08/24/pf/workplace_ morale/?section=money_pf; Inspiring worker loyalty one tough job by John Ellis, July 1, 2005, East Bay Business Times Website, http://www.bizjournals.com/ eastbay/stories/2005/07/04/focus1.html.

25. When good will is also good business by Katie Hafner and Claudia Deutsch, New York Times, September 14, 2005, http://www.nytimes.com/2005/09/14/ business/14give.html?ex=1128657600&en=b2f4f8a7c b6c3b24&ei=5070&th=&emc=th&pagewanted=print.

26. Generation C, Trendwatching Website, http://www .trendwatching.com/trends/GENERATION_C.htm, accessed October 5, 2005; The Podfather: part one by Laura Locke, Inside Business, Time, October 2005.

27. Just how cheap is Chinese labor by Peter Coy, December 2, 2004, BusinessWeek Website, http://

www.businessweek.com/bwdaily/dnflash/dec2004/ nf2004122_6762_db039.htm.

28. Asian tsunami devastates Sri Lankan fishing industry by Jason Beaubien, NPR Morning Edition, January 10, 2005, http://www.npr.org/templates/story/story .php?storyId=4276161; Phuket tourism industry crippled by mass cancellations by Sally Pook, Cyber Diver News Network, January 8, 2005, http://www .cdnn.info/news/travel/t050111.html; Homeland security scuffle by Veronique de Rugy, October 15, 2004, National Review Website, http://www .nationalreview.com/comment/rugy200410150840 .asp; Bush brushes aside rebuilding cost concerns, September 19, 2005, Reuters News Service, MSNBC Website, http://www.msnbc.msn.com/id/9374106/.

29. Pomp and circumspect by Daniel Pink, June 4, 2005, New York Times Website, http://select.nytimes.com/ gst/abstract.html?res=F60C1FFD3F5C0C778CDDAF08 94DD404482.

Pg. 13 Fact Box: The Rise of a Fierce Yet Agile Superpower by Fareed Zakaria, NewsWeek, January 7, 2008, page 38.

## Chapter 2

1. Tollbooths on the Internet Highway, Editorial, New York Times Website, February 20, 2006, http://select .nytimes.com/gst/abstract.html?res=F30F16FD3A5A0C 738EDDAB0894DE404482, accessed October 8, 2008; Net Neutrality by Adam Thierer, Cato Institute Policy Analysis, January 12, 2004, http://www.cato.org/pubs/ pas/pa507.pdf, accessed August 16, 2008; Network Neutrality Now by Jeff Chester and Gary Larson, In These Times Website, July 6, 2005, http://www .inthesetimes.com/site/main/article/2203/, accessed August 16, 2008.

2. We woz wrong, The Economist, December 16, 1999, http://investor.google.com/fin_data.html; Google Investor Relations, Financial Data, Income Statement, http://investor.google.com/fin_data.html, accessed March 19, 2006; The Year's ten worst predictions, BusinessWeek Online, December 13, 2005, http:// images.businessweek.com/ss/05/12/worst_predictions/ index_01.htm; World Crude Oil Prices, U.S. Department of Energy, http://tonto.eia.doe.gov/dnav/ pet/pet_pri_wco_k_w.htm, accessed August 16, 2008.

3. Happy cows can get happier by Dennis Pollock, The Fresno Bee, April 12, 2005, http://www .realcaliforniacheese.com/allAboutCheese/happynews _assets/FresnoBee_041205.pdf; California cheese wizards unveil new ad campaign by PSBJ Staff, Puget Sound Business Journal, March 21, 2003, http://www .bizjournals.com/seattle/stories/2003/03/24/tidbits. html; California Sets New Cheese Record in 2007, TransWorld News Website, http://transworldnews .com/NewsStory.aspx?id=35653&cat=1, accessed August 16, 2008.

4. Changes ahead for a theater near you by David Leonhardt, New York Times, February 15, 2006, http:// select.nytimes.com/gst/abstract.html?res=FA0C1EFF 385A0C768DDDAB0894DE404482; Movie Tuesdays, Cool News, Reveries Magazine, 2/15/06, http://www .reveries.com/?p=344.

5. Federal Government, excluding Postal Services, U.S. Department of Labor Bureau of Labor Statistics Website, March 12, 2008, http://stats.bls.gov/oco/ cg/cgs041.htm, accessed August 16, 2008; Postal Service Workers, U.S. Department of Labor Bureau of

Labor Statistics Website, December 18, 2007, http://stats.bls.gov/oco/ocos141.htm, accessed August 16, 2008; Job Opportunities in the Armed Forces, U.S. Department of Labor Bureau of Labor Statistics Website, December 18, 2007, http://stats.bls.gov/oco/ocos249.htm, accessed August 16, 2008.

6. Russia's flat tax miracle by Daniel J. Mitchell, PhD, The Heritage Foundation, March 24, 2003, http://www.heritage.org/Press/Commentary/ed032403.cfm; Russians do taxes right by Deroy Murdock, National Review Online, March 1, 2002, http://www.nationalreview.com/murdock/murdock030102.shtml; Russia: income taxes and tax laws, July 2005, Worldwide-Tax Website, http://www.worldwide-tax.com/russia/russia_tax.asp; History of the U.S. tax system, U.S. Treasury Website, http://www.ustreas.gov/education/fact-sheets/taxes/ustax.html, accessed March 9, 2006.

6a. Rank Order Estimates: 2007 GDP Estimates, CIA—The World Factbook Website, updated April 15, 2008, https://www.cia.gov/library/publications/the-world-factbook/geos/us.html, accessed May 27, 2008.

7. Labor Force Statistics from the Current Population Survey: Unemployment Rate Table, U.S. Department of Labor Bureau of Labor Statistics Website, http://data.bls.gov/PDQ/servlet/SurveyOutputServlet?request_action=wh&graph_name=LN_cpsbref3, accessed August 16, 2008.

8. Economists call it recession, CNN/Money Website, November 26, 2001, http://money.cnn.com/2001/11/26/economy/recession/.

9. Table B-80—Federal receipts and outlays by major category, and surplus or deficit, fiscal years 1940–2007, Economic Report of the President, February 2006, page 377, http://www.gpoaccess.gov/eop/2006/2006_erp.pdf.

10. Historical Debt Outstanding—Annual, TreasuryDirect Website, http://www.treasurydirect.gov/govt/reports/pd/histdebt/histdebt.htm, accessed May 27, 2008.

11. Five ways the new Fed chairman will be different by Daniel Kadlec, Time Magazine, November 7, 2005, http://www.time.com/time/archive/preview/0,10987,1124334,00.html.

12. Table B-80 Federal receipts and outlays, by major category, and surplus or deficit, fiscal years 1940–2009, Economic Report of the President, February 2008, page 321, http://www.gpoaccess.gov/eop/2008/2008_erp.pdf, accessed August 16, 2008.

13. Historical changes of the target federal funds and discount rates, Federal Reserve Bank of New York Website, http://www.ny.frb.org/markets/statistics/dlyrates/fedrate.html, accessed January 26, 2007.

14. Money stock measures, Federal Reserve Statistical Release, February 8, 2007, http://www.federalreserve.gov/releases/h6/current/.

15. Money stock measures, Federal Reserve Statistical Release, February 8, 2007, http://www.federalreserve.gov/releases/h6/current/.

## Chapter 3

1. United States pleased with Vietnam's efforts to join WTO, U.S International Information Programs, January 18, 2006, http://usinfo.state.gov/eap/Archive/2006/Jan/18-424539.html; Brazil in the midst of sustained economic growth by Eric Green, U.S International Information Programs, March 4, 2005, http://usinfo.state.gov/wh/Archive/2005/Mar/04-311354.html.

2. Rank Order Estimates, CIA—The World Factbook Website: https://www.cia.gov/library/publications/the-world-factbook/rankorder/2119rank.html, accessed August 16, 2008, https://www.cia.gov/library/publications/the-world-factbook/rankorder/2004rank.html, accessed August 16, 2008, https://www.cia.gov/library/publications/the-world-factbook/rankorder/2003rank.html, accessed August 16, 2008.

3. The spark plug by Jyoti Thottam, Inside Business, *Time*, December 2005, pages A22–A29; A new world economy by Pete Engardio, *BusinessWeek* Online, August 22, 2005, http://www.businessweek.com/magazine/content/05_34/b3948401.htm; Cell phone penetration ratio hits 35.3%, *China Daily* Website, May 29, 2007, http://www.chinadaily.com.cn/bizchina/2007-05/29/content_883201.htm, accessed August 16, 2008; Indian cell population: 246 million and counting by Om Malik, GigaOm Website, March 19, 2008, http://gigaom.com/2008/03/19/indian-cell-population-246-million-and-counting, accessed August 16, 2008.

4. Similar Search Results: Google Wins by Anthony Zumpano, BrandChannel.com, January 29, 2007, http://www.brandchannel.com/start1.asp?fa_id=352, accessed August 16, 2008; Readers Pick Apple in 2004 by Robin Rusch, BrandChannel.com, January 31, 2005, http://www.brandchannel.com/start1.asp?fa_id=248, accessed August 16, 2008.

5. Insperiences, Trendwatching newsletter, http://www.trendwatching.com/trends/INSPERIENCE.htm, accessed January 12, 2006.

5a. Developing, Transition Economies Cushion Trade Slowdown, World Trade 2007, Prospects for 2008, World Trade Organization Press Release, April 17, 2008, http://www.wto.org/english/news_e/pres08_e/pr520_e.htm, accessed August 16, 2008.

6. Countertrade—an innovative approach to marketing by Dan West, Chairman American Countertrade Association, BarterNews issue #36, 1996, http://barternews.com/approach_marketing.htm; Global Offset and Countertrade Association Website, http://www.globaloffset.org/index.htm, accessed January 27, 2006.

7. That blur? It's China, moving up in the pack by David Barboza and Daniel Altman, *New York Times*, December 21, 2005, http://select.nytimes.com/gst/abstract.html?res=F50B1EFC3F540C728EDDAB0994DD404482; While U.S. exports to China rise, imports from China rise faster by Bruce Odessey, U.S. International Information Programs, March 17, 2005, http://usinfo.state.gov/eap/Archive/2005/Mar/03-517799.html; A new world economy by Pete Engardio, *BusinessWeek* Online, August 22, 2005, http://www.businessweek.com/magazine/content/05_34/b3948401.htm; Trade surplus tripled in '05, China says by David Barboza, *New York Times*, January 12, 2006, http://select.nytimes.com/gst/abstract.html?res=F30C13F63D5B0C718DDDA80894DE404482.

8. Thinking outside the border by Curtis, Minority Business Entrepreneur, September/October 2005, http://www.export.gov/comm_svc/pdf/MBE_article.pdf.

9. eBay to acquire Skype, Press Release, September 12, 2005, Skype Website, http://www.skype.com/company/news/2005/skype_ebay.html.

10. High tech industry in Israel goes from bust to boom by Greg Myre, New York Times, December 26, 2005, http://select.nytimes.com/gst/abstract.html?res=FA0F12FF39540C758EDDAB0994DD404482.

11. Rethink the value of joint ventures by Cynthia Churchwell, Harvard Business School Working Knowledge, May 10, 2004, http://hbswk.hbs.edu/item.jhtml?id=4113&t=globalization.

12. Hyundai grows up by Michael Schuman, Time Global Business, July 2005, http://www.time.com/time/globalbusiness/article/0,9171,1074141,00.html; At 5 feet 10 inches, I was too tall for Tokyo by Cathie Gandel, My Turn, *NewsWeek*, December 12, 2005.

13. McDonald's country/market sites, http://www.mcdonalds.com./countries.html, accessed January 26, 2006.

14. Selling to rural India, Springwise Newsletter, June 2003, http://www.springwise.com/newbusinessideas/2003/06/shakti.html; Red herring: selling to the poor, April 11, 2004, The Next Practice Website, http://www.thenextpractice.com/news/red_herring_selling_to_the_poor.php; Are you ready for globalisation 2.0 by Tim Weber, January 28, 2005, BBC News Website, http://news.bbc.co.uk/1/hi/business/4214687.stm.

15. Internet Usage Statistics for the Americas, Internet World Stats, March 31, 2008, http://www.internetworldstats.com/stats2.htm, accessed August 16, 2008; Internet Usage Statistics for Africa, Internet World Stats, March 31, 2008, http://www.internetworldstats.com/stats1.htm, accessed August 16, 2008; Internet usage statistics, the Big Picture, Internet World Stats, December 31, 2005, http://www.internetworldstats.com/stats.htm; Red herring: selling to the poor, The Next Practice Website, April 11, 2004, http://www.thenextpractice.com/news/red_herring_selling_to_the_poor.php.

16. Tricks of the trade by Barney Gimbel, *NewsWeek*, June 28, 2004; Case studies, Genesis Technology Group, July 1, 2005, http://www.genesis-technology.net/case_studies.asp; A new frontier, by Peter Gumbel, Global Business, Time, July 2005.

17. Microsoft's cultural revolution by Sarah Schafer, *NewsWeek Enterprise*, June 28, 2004; It's all free! by Lev Grossman, Time magazine, May 5, 2003, http://www.time.com/time/archive/preview/0,10987,1004761,00.html; A new frontier by Peter Gumbel, Time Global Business, July 2005, pages A15–A16.

18. USTR releases 2002 inventory of trade barriers, Press Release, April 2, 2002, http://www.useu.be/Categories/Trade/Apr0202USTRReportForeignTradeBarriers.html; U.S. targets non-tariff barriers to global trade, News Release, April 3, 2002, http://www.usconsulate.org.hk/pas/pr/2002/040301.htm.

19. IMF to extend 100 percent debt relief for 19 countries under the multilateral debt relief initiative, IMF Press Release, December 21, 2005, http://www.imf.org/external/np/sec/pr/2005/pr05286.htm.

20. The farm fight by Simon Robinson, Global Business, *Time*, December 2005, pages A13–A16; The WTO cotton case and U.S. domestic policy by Darren Hudson, C. Parr Rosson III, John Robinson, and Jaime Malaga, Choices magazine, 2nd Quarter, 2005, http://www.choicesmagazine.org/2005-2/wto/2005-2-10.htm; "Cotton four" preparing new proposal on domestic support, WTO 2006 News Item, January 31, 2006, http://www.wto.org/english/news_e/news06_e/cotton_31jan06_e.htm.

21. U.S. Total Trade Balance in Goods and Services (Exhibit 1) Seasonally Adjusted: January 1994 to March 2008, U.S. Census Website, accessed June 3, 2008; Trade with NAFTA with Mexico (Consump): 2007, U.S. Census Website, accessed June 3, 2008; Trade with NAFTA with Canada (Consump): 2007, U.S. Census Website, accessed June 3, 2008.

21a. Rank Order Estimates, CIA—The World Factbook Website, https://www.cia.gov/library/publications/the-world-factbook/rankorder/2119rank.html, accessed August 16, 2008, https://www.cia.gov/library/publications/the-world-factbook/geos/ee.html#Econ, accessed August 16, 2008.

22. The constant charmer by Josh Tyrangiel, Time magazine, December 19, 2005, http://www.time.com/time/magazine/printout/0,8816,1142270,00.html; Bono campaigns at debt relief summit, February 3, 2002, BBC News Website, http://news.bbc.co.uk/1/hi/entertainment/1799103.stm.

Pg. 40 Fact Box: About the World Bank, FAQs, World Bank Website, http://web.worldbank.org/WBSITE/EXTERNAL/EXTSITETOOLS/0,,contentMDK:20147466~menuPK:344189~pagePK:98400~piPK:98424~theSitePK:95474,00.html#14, accessed August 16, 2008.

## Chapter 4

1. http://www.charactercounts.org/defsix.htm.

2. Why We'll Miss the Disney Trial by Barney Gimbel, Fortune, December 27, 2004, retrieved from CNNMoney Website, http://money.cnn.com/magazines/fortune/fortune_archive/2004/12/27/8217949/index.htm; Disney's Basket Cases by Peter Bart, Variety, March 7, 2004, http://www.variety.com/article/VR1117901299.html?categoryid=1&cs=1.

3. National Business Ethics Survey: How Employees View Ethics in Their Organizations, 1994–2005, Ethics Resource Center, October 12, 2005, http://www.ethics.org/research/2005-press-release.asp.

3a. Bill & Melinda Gates Foundation, Fact Sheet, http://www.gatesfoundation.com/MediaCenter/FactSheet, accessed August 25, 2008; Foundation Growth and Giving Estimates, 2008 edition, Foundation Center Website, http://foundationcenter.org/gainknowledge/research/pdf/fgge08.pdf, accessed August 25, 2008.

4. Remarks of FCC Chairman Kevin J. Martin, CTIA Wireless 2008, April 1, 2008, http://www.fcc.gov/Daily_Releases/Daily_Business/2008/db0401/DOC-281259A1.pdf, accessed August 25, 2008; Wireless mischief, *Wall Street Journal*, December 7, 2004; Wireless hacking bust in Michigan by Kevin Poulsen, November 12, 2003, Security Focus Website, http://www.securityfocus.com/news/7438, accessed August 25, 2008; Wireless hacking techniques book (excerpt) by Dr. Cyrus Peikari and Seth Fogie, May 17, 2004, *ComputerWorld* Website, http://www.computerworld.com/mobiletopics/mobile/story/0,10801,91313,00.html, accessed August 25, 2008.

5. Complaining Customers Are Good for Business by Bob Leduc, Virtual Marketing Newsletter, May 11, 2004, http://www.marketingsource.com/newsletter/05-11-2004.html.

6. Nike Apologises to China for Ad, December 9, 2004, BBC News World edition Website, http://news.bbc.co.uk/2/hi/asia-pacific/4083265.stm; Nike Apologises

for Footwear Ad in China, December 9, 2004, China Daily Website, http://www.chinadaily.com.cn/english/doc/2004-12/09/content_398845.htm.

7. Loyalty Means Saying You're Sorry by John Hennessy, January 11, 2005, RetailWire Website, http://www.retailwire.com/Print/PrintDocument.cfm?DOC_ID=10370.

8. The Costco Way; Higher Wages Mean Higher Profits. But Try Telling Wall Street, by Stanley Holmes and Wendy Zelner, BusinessWeek, April 12, 2004.

9. Robust Economy = Robust Giving by Jane Lampman, The Christian Science Monitor, June 20, 2006 edition, CSM Website, http://www.csmonitor.com/2006/0620/p25s01-lign.html; The Giving USA Foundation releases its 2006 statistics, Benevon Website, http://sforce.benevon.com/images/GivingUSA2007.htm, accessed August 25, 2008.

10. Bad and Good Environmental Marks for McDonald's by Donalla Meadows, Sustainability Institute Website, http://www.sustainer.org/dhm_archive/search.php?display_article=vn304mcdonaldsed, accessed May 15, 2005.

11. Marketing, Business and Sustainable Development Website, http://www.bsdglobal.com/markets/green_marketing.asp, accessed May 15, 2005.

12. Selling to the Poor by Kay Johnson, Time Bonus Section, May 2005; The Payoff for Investing in Poor Countries by C.K. Prahalad and Allen Hammond, Harvard Business School Working Knowledge Website, http://hbswk.hbs.edu/item.jhtml?id=3180&t=nonprofit&noseek=one.

12a. Corruption Perceptions Index 2007, Transparency International Website, http://www.transparency.org/policy_research/surveys_indices/cpi/2007, accessed August 25, 2008; Bribe Payers Index 2006, Transparency International Website, http://www.transparency.org/policy_research/surveys_indices/bpi/bpi_2006, accessed August 25, 2008.

13. Values in Tension: Ethics Away from Home by Thomas Donaldson, Harvard Business Review, September/October 1996.

14. Gap, Inc. Social Reporting Award, December 20, 2004, Business Ethics Website, http://www.business-ethics.com/annual.htm#Gap%20Inc.

Pg. 49 Fact Box: Community Wealth Ventures Website, Corporations page, http://www.communitywealth.org/corporations.htm, accessed September 5, 2008.

## Chapter 5

1. Body Language Tactics That Sway Interviewers by Eugene Raudsepp, Wall Street Journal CareerJournal, December 5, 2002, http://www.careerjournal.com/jobhunting/interviewing/20021205-raudsepp.html.

2. Electronic Resumes by Pat Criscito, Career Know How Website, http://www.careerknowhow.com/resumes/elecres.htm, accessed October 23, 2008; Scannable Resume Fundamentals: How to Write Text Resumes by Randall S. Hansen, Ph.D., Quintessential Careers Website, http://www.quintcareers.com/scannable_resumes.html, accessed October 23, 2008; How to Make a Resume by Laura Schneider, About.com Website, http://jobsearchtech.about.com/od/gettingthejob/a/HowToMakeResume.htm, accessed October 23, 2008.

3. The Listener Wins by Michael Purdy, Monster contributing writer, Monster.com, http://

featuredreports.monster.com/listen/overview/, accessed August 22, 2006; The Human Side of Business by Stephen D. Boyd, Agency Sales Magazine, February 2004, page 35, accessed via Infotrac College Edition.

4. We Learn More by Listening Than Talking by Harvey Mackay, The Daily Herald, January 16, 2005, page E6[SB14], http://old.heraldextra.com/modules.php?op=modload&name=News&file=article&sid=45313; Listening Factoids, International Listening Association, http://www.listen.org/pages/factoids.html, accessed August 22, 2006.

5. The Human Side of Business by Stephen D. Boyd, Agency Sales Magazine, February 2004, page 35, accessed via Infotrac College Edition; Learn to Listen: Closing the Mouth and Opening the Ears Facilitates Effective Communication by Marjorie Brody, Incentive, May 2004, page 57, accessed via Business and Company Resource Center.

6. Edward P. Bailey, Writing and Speaking at Work, (Prentice Hall, 2005), pages 82–89.

7. Presenting Effective Presentations with Visual Aids, U.S. Department of Labor, Occupational Safety and Health Administration, http://www.osha.gov/doc/outreachtraining/htmlfiles/traintec.html, accessed August 22, 2006.

8. PowerPoint: Killer Ap? By Ruth Marcus, August 30, 2005, Washington Post Website, http://www.washingtonpost.com/wp-dyn/content/article/2005/08/29/AR2005082901444.html; PowerPoint is Evil by Edward Tufte, Wired Website, September 2003, http://www.wired.com/wired/archive/11.09/ppt2.html; Tips for PowerPoint—Please Spare Us by Jared Sandberg, Career Journal Website, November 15, 2006, http://www.careerjournal.com/columnists/cubicleculture/20061115-cubicle.html.

## Chapter 6

1. Sole Proprietorship Returns by Kevin Pierce, Statistics of Income Bulletin, Summer 2005, Table 1, page 19; http://www.irs.gov/pub/irs-soi/03solp.pdf; Statistical Abstract of the United States: 2008, U.S. Census Bureau Website, http://www.census.gov/compendia/statab/tables/08s0721.pdf, accessed August 25, 2008.

2. Statistical Abstract of the United States: 2008, Table 721, U.S. Census Bureau Website, http://www.census.gov/compendia/statab/tables/08s0721.pdf, accessed August 25, 2008.

3. Statistical Abstract of the United States: 2008, U.S. Census Bureau Website, http://www.census.gov/compendia/statab/tables/08s0722.pdf, accessed August 25, 2008.

4. Statistical Abstract of the United States: 2008, Table 721, U.S. Census Bureau Website, http://www.census.gov/compendia/statab/tables/08s0721.pdf, accessed August 25, 2008.

4a. Statistical Abstract of the United States: 2008, Table 722, U.S. Census Bureau Website, http://www.census.gov/compendia/statab/tables/08s0722.pdf, accessed August 25, 2008.

5. Is a Family Limited Partnership the Right Estate Tool for You, Baby Boomer News Website, http://www.babyboomers.com/news/1008f.htm; Protect Your Assets with a Family Partnership by Jeff Schnepper, MSN Money Central Website, http://articles.moneycentral.msn.com/Taxes/TaxShelters/ProtectYourFamilyWithPartnership.aspx.

6. *Statistical Abstract of the United States: 2008*, Table 722, U.S, Census Bureau Website, http://www.census.gov/compendia/statab/tables/08s0722.pdf, accessed August 25, 2008.

7. Cooperative Businesses In the United States…A 2005 Snapshot, National Cooperative Month Planning Committee Website, http://www.uwcc.wisc.edu/info/stats/uscoopbus05.pdf, accessed August 25, 2008; About Cooperatives: Legal Considerations When Forming a Cooperative, National Cooperative Business Association Website, http://www.ncba.coop/abcoop_ab_legal.cfm, accessed August 25, 2008; What is a Co-operative?, International Co-operative Alliance Website, http://www.ica.coop/coop/index.htm, accessed August 25, 2008.

8. Delaware Secretary of State Website, http://www.state.de.us/corp/.

9. GE's form 10-K for 2007, Yahoo! Finance Website, http://yahoo.brand.edgar-online.com/displayfilinginfo.aspx?FilingID=5743489-72609-77865&type=sect&dcn=0000040545-08-000011, accessed April 11, 2008, and http://yahoo.brand.edgar-online.com/displayfilinginfo.aspx?FilingID=5743489-292838-297335&type=sect&dcn=0000040545-08-000011, accessed August 25, 2008.

10. Board of Hard Knocks; Activist Shareholders, Tougher Rules, and Anger over CEO Pay Have Put Directors on the Hot Seat by Nanette Byrnes and Jane Sasseen, *BusinessWeek,* January 22, 2007, page 37; Final Score: CEOs Up $1.26 Billion, Shareholders Down $330 Billion; The Corporate Library's Latest Study—'Pay for Failure II: The Compensation Committees Responsible'—Highlights Twelve of the Largest Companies in the U.S. That Combined High Levels of CEO Compensation and Poor Performance Over the Past Five Years," Internet Wire, May 7, 2007; Home Depot Shareholders Sue to Stop $210 Million Severance Package for Nardelli, *Bloomberg News*, January 11, 2007, http://www.iht.com/articles/2007/01/11/business/depot.php, accessed May 21, 2007.

11. Mergers and Acquisitions: Definition, Investopedia Website, http://www.investopedia.com/university/mergers/mergers1.asp.

12. Types of Businesses—Legal Structures, https://www.wellsfargo.com/biz/education/new_biz/legal_structures; Limited Liability Company 101 by Darrell Zahorsky, About.com Website, http://sbinformation.about.com/cs/ownership1/a/LLC.htm.

13. Economic Impact of Franchised Businesses—Total Contributions to the U.S. Economy, Building Opportunity Website, http://www.buildingopportunity.com/download/National%20Views.pdf, accessed August 25, 2008.

14. Individual franchisors pages, Entrepreneur.com Website, http://entrepreneur.com/franchises/mcdonalds/282570-0.html, http://entrepreneur.com/franchises/subway/282839-0.html, http://entrepreneur.com/franchises/janiking/282472-0.html, http://entrepreneur.com/franchises/curves/282265-0.html, accessed August 25, 2008.

15. Franchising Attracts More Women, Minorities by Julie Bennett, Startup Journal, http://www.startupjournal.com/columnists/franchiseinsight/20030409-bennett.html; Win with Franchising by Rebecca Gardyn, http://www.womensfranchises.com/PR_wmm.cfm (originally in www.WorkingMother.com); Female Franchisors Few and Far Between by Julie M. Young, August, 19,

2002, e-magnify.com Website: http://www.e-magnify.com/resources_viewarticle.asp?ID=423.

16. Boosting Diversity in Franchising by Joan Szabo, December 5, 2006, Franchise Update Website, http://www.franchise-update.com/articles/188/.

17. MinorityFran Participants as of January 2008, IFA Website link to spreadsheet, http://www.franchise.org/uploadedFiles/Franchise_Industry/Resources/Education_Foundation/MinorityFranCompanies_web_03_18_08.xls, accessed August 25, 2008.

18. Subway, Entrepreneur.com Website, http://www.entrepreneur.com/franchises/subway/282839-2.html.

19. Women of the Hall: Martha Matilda Harper, National Women's Hall of Fame Website, http://www.greatwomen.org/women.php?action=viewone&id=203; Martha Matilda Harper, National Women's History Museum Education Resources Website, http://www.nwhm.org/Education/biography_mmharper.html.

20. Entrepreneur.com Website, http://entrepreneur.com/franchises/mcdonalds/282570-1.html, accessed August 25, 2008.

21. Ben & Jerry's Website, http://www.benjerry.com/scoop_shops/partnershops/; Nonprofit Owned Franchises: A Strategic Business Approach, prepared by Community Wealth Ventures and IFA Educational Foundation, March 2004, http://www.franchise.org/uploadedFiles/Files/nonprofit_owned.pdf; Franchise Chains: Nonprofits Team Up by Laura Sydell, Morning Edition, javascript:launchPlayer('1644017', '1', '05-Feb-2004', '&topicName=Business&subtopicName=Business&prgCode=ME&hubId=-1&thingId=1644016', 'RM,WM');February 5, 2004, http://www.npr.org/templates/story/story.php?storyId=1644016.

## Chapter 7

1. Small Business Drives the U.S. Economy, SBA Office of Advocacy NewsRelease, August 4, 2005, http://www.sba.gov/advo/press/05-37.html; 2005 Interprise Poll on Teens and Entrepreneurship, JA Worldwide, September 13, 2005, http://www.ja.org/files/polls/entrepreneurship_2005.pdf; Is Entrepreneurship for You? U.S. Small Business Administration, http://www.sba.gov/starting_business/startup/areyouready.html, accessed December 15, 2005.

2. The 400 Richest Americans edited by Matthew Miller and Peter Newcomb, September 22, 2005, Forbes Website, http://www.forbes.com/400richest/.

2a. Wayne Huizenga biography, About.com Website, http://entrepreneurs.about.com/od/famousentrepreneurs/p/waynehuizenga.htm, accessed August 29, 2008; American dream comes true as Wayne Huizenga wins Ernst & Young World Entrepreneur of the Year, Ernst & Young Website, May 28, 2005, http://www.ey.com/global/content.nsf/International/World_Entrepreneur_Of_The_Year_Awards_2005_-_Winner_of_WEOY_2005, accessed August 29, 2008.

3. He Figured That Business Is So Good, Who Needs a Store? by Katie Zezima, November 16, 2005, New York Times Website, http://select.nytimes.com/gst/abstract.html?res=F00F16F83B5A0C758DDDA80994DD404482.

4. Meet Vishal Gondal, India's King of Gaming by Manu A B, September 20, 2005, Rediff Website, http://inhome.rediff.com/money/2005/sep/20inter.htm.

5. More than Half of Small Business Owners Work At Least Six-Day Weeks, Still Find Time for Personal Life, Wells Fargo News Release, August 9, 2005, https://www.wellsfargo.com/press/20050809_GallupPersonalLife.

6. Entrepreneurial Risk and Market Entry by Brian Wu and Anne Marie Knott, SBA Office of Advocacy, January 2005, http://www.sba.gov/advo/research/wkpbw249.pdf.

7. Failure: Use It as a Springboard to Success, U.S. SBA Online Library, no attribution, http://www.sba.gov/library/successXIII/19-Failure-Use-it.doc, accessed December 28, 2005.

8. Amplestuff Website, http://www.amplestuff.com/; Kazoo v. Wal-Mart, Reveries Magazine, November 29, 2005, http://www.reveries.com/?p=232.

9. E-Commerce Award—June 2002, Anything Left-Handed Website, http://www.anythingleft-handed.co.uk/pressreleases.html.

10. Failure: Use It as a Springboard to Success, U.S. SBA Online Library, no attribution, http://www.sba.gov/library/successXIII/19-Failure-Use-it.doc, accessed December 28, 2005.

11. Focus on Success, Not Failure by Rhonda Abrams, May 7, 2004, USA Today Website money section, http://www.usatoday.com/money/smallbusiness/columnist/abrams/2004-05-06-success_x.htm.

12. Is Entrepreneurship for You? U.S. Small Business Administration, http://www.sba.gov/starting_business/startup/areyouready.html, accessed December 15, 2005.

13. Small Business Hit Hard by Federal Regulatory Compliance Burden, NewsRelease, September 19, 2005, U.S. SBA Office of Advocacy, http://www.sba.gov/advo/press/05-43.html.

14. Minipreneurs, Trendwatching.com Website, http://www.trendwatching.com/trends/MINIPRENEURS.htm, accessed August 29, 2008; New Study Reveals 724,000 Americans Rely on eBay Sales for Income, eBay Press Release, July 21, 2005, http://investor.ebay.com/ReleaseDetail.cfm?ReleaseID=170073&Fyear, accessed August 29, 2008; Nice (horizontal) pants! by Christopher Null, Business 2.0 on CNNMoney.com Website, December 1, 2005, http://money.cnn.com/magazines/business2/business2_archive/2005/12/01/8364593/index.htm, accessed August 29, 2008; PEZ MP3 Website, http://www.pezmp3.com/, accessed August 29, 2008.

15. Entrepreneurship in the 21st Century, Conference Proceedings, March 26, 2004, SBA Office of Advocacy and the Kauffman Foundation, http://www.sba.gov/advo/stats/proceedings_a.pdf.

16. Five Reasons Why Franchises Flop by Steve Strauss, February 28, 2005, USA Today Money Website, http://www.usatoday.com/money/smallbusiness/columnist/strauss/2005-02-28-franchise_x.htm.

17. Business Plan Basics, U.S. SBA, http://www.sba.gov/starting_business/planning/basic.html, accessed December 28, 2005.

18. Business Plan Basics, U.S. SBA, http://www.sba.gov/starting_business/planning/basic.html, accessed December 28, 2005.

19. What Makes Them Tick by Keith McFarland, Inc 500, 2005, Inc Website, http://www.inc.com/resources/inc500/2005/articles/20051001/tick.html.

20. Charging Ahead by Bobbie Gossage, January 2004, Inc. Magazine, http://www.inc.com/magazine/20040101/gettingstarted.html.

21. Start-up Info, Delaware Small Business Development Center, http://www.delawaresbdc.org/startup_info.html, accessed December 16, 2005.

22. SBA Loans for Your Startup by Asheesh Advani, August 1, 2005, Entrepreneur Website, http://www.entrepreneur.com/article/0,4621,322752,00.html.

23. Angels with Angles by Jim Melloan, July 2005, Inc. Magazine Website, http://www.inc.com/magazine/20050701/angels-index.html.

24. The Steady, Strategic Assent of JetBlue Airways, Strategic Management Knowledge at Wharton, December 14, 2005–January 10, 2006, http://knowledge.wharton.upenn.edu/article/1342.cfm; Charging Ahead by Bobbie Gossage, January 2004, Inc. Magazine, http://www.inc.com/magazine/20040101/gettingstarted.html.

25. The SMALL BUSINESS ECONOMY, For Data Year 2006, A Report to the President December 2007, SBA Office of Advocacy, http://www.sba.gov/advo/research/sb_econ2007.pdf, accessed August 29, 2008; SBA Office of Advocacy Frequently Asked Questions, http://www.sba.gov/advo/stats/sbfaq.pdf, accessed August 29, 2008.

26. Top Ten Reasons to Love Small Business, NewsRelease, February 13, 2004, U.S. SBA Office of Advocacy, http://www.sba.gov/advo/press/04-06.html.

27. Entrepreneurship in the 21st Century, Conference Proceedings, March 26, 2004, SBA Office of Advocacy and the Kauffman Foundation, http://www.sba.gov/advo/stats/proceedings_a.pdf; "Green" Ice Cream Helps Celebrate Earth Day, NewsRelease, April 20, 2005, U.S. SBA Office of Advocacy, http://www.sba.gov/advo/press/05-19.html.

28. Small Business Drives Inner City Growth and Jobs, NewsRelease, October 11, 2005, U.S. SBA Office of Advocacy, http://www.sba.gov/advo/press/05-32.html.

29. Global Entrepreneurship Monitor, 2004 Executive Report by Zoltan J. Acs, Pia Arenius, Michael Hay, and Maria Minniti, Babson College and London School of Economics, May 27, 2005, http://www.gemconsortium.org/download/1134024938062/GEM_2004_Exec_Report.pdf.

30. Global Entrepreneurship Monitor, 2004 Executive Report by Zoltan J. Acs, Pia Arenius, Michael Hay, and Maria Minniti, Babson College and London School of Economics, May 27, 2005, http://www.gemconsortium.org/download/1134024938062/GEM_2004_Exec_Report.pdf.

Pg. 92 Fact Box: Global Entrepreneurship Monitor, 2004 Executive Report, http://www.gemconsortium.org/download/1133331987906/GEM_2004_Exec_Report.pdf, published May 27, 2005, accessed August 29, 2008.

## Chapter 8

1. Source for material in this section is based on U.S. Bureau of Labor Statistics, *Occupational Outlook Handbook*: 2006-2007[SB32]. The Website for the accounting information in this handbook is http://www.bls.gov/oco/ocos001.htm.

2. Forensic Teams Dig into Legal Disputes for Clients; Multidisciplinary Investigations Are Now a $6 Billion

Business by Stan Luxenberg, *Crain's New York Business,* September 25, 2006; Forensic Accounting: Exponential Growth: The Work Varies Widely, the Credentials to Practice Are Sophisticated, Unique Marketing Is Needed, but the Engagements Are Very Lucrative by Jeff Stimpson, The Practical Accountant, February 2007; CFE: Certified Fraud Examiner? Forensic Accounting Is Catching On by Peter Vogt," MSN Encarta, August 2006, http://www.investigation.com/articles/library/2006articles/articles6.htm, accessed May 17, 2007.

3. Business Roundtable Institute for Corporate Ethics, Institute Media Releases, http://www.darden.edu/corporate-ethics/Enron_media_roundup_freeman.htm.

4. Scandal Sheet, CBS Marketwatch Website, http://www.marketwatch.com/news/features/scandal_sheet.asp; Corporate Scandal Sheet, Citizen Works Website[SB36], http://www.citizenworks.org/enron/corp-scandal.php; The Corporate Scandal Sheet by Penelope Patsuris, Forbes, August 26, 2002, http://www.forbes.com/2002/07/25/accountingtracker.html.

5. Generally Improvable Accounting Principles, *BusinessWeek,* November 20, 2006, http://www.businessweek .com/magazine/content/06_47/b4010075.htm; Arthur Levitt, interviewed by Hedrick Smith, Frontline, PBS, March 12, 2002, http://www.pbs.org/wgbh/pages/frontline/shows/regulation/interviews/levitt.html.

6. Can You Trust Anybody Anymore? *BusinessWeek* Online, January 28, 2002, http://www.businessweek.com/magazine/content/02_04/b3767701.htm.

7. Illinois Board of Examiners Required Exam on Rules of Professional Conduct, http://www.illinois-cpa-exam.com/files/ethics.pdf ; Ethics: A Crucial Test for New CPAs by Jacqueline A. Burke and Jill D'Aquila, The CPA Journal, January 2004, http://www.nysscpa.org/cpajournal/2004/104/text/p58.htm.

8. Mission statement on PCAOB Website, http://www.pcaobus.org/index.aspx.

9. When Balance Sheets Collide with the New Economy by Denise Caruso, *The New York Times,* Section 3, page 4, September 9, 2007; Albrecht, Stice, Stice and Swain, *Accounting Concepts and Applications,* 9th ed. (Cengage Learning), page 482; The Hidden Value of Intangibles by Ben McClure, Investopedia Website, http://www.investopedia.com/articles/03/010603 .asp, accessed August 29, 2008. The market value of Apple stock was computed by the author using information for the number of shares of common stock outstanding reported on Apple's form 10-K in the SEC's Edgar Database, and historical prices for Apple stock accessed on Yahoo! Finance.

10. Albrecht, Stice, Stice, and Swain, *Accounting Concepts and Applications,* 9th ed. (Cengage Learning), page 758.

11. Put Savings (and Yourself) First with a Budget, Yahoo! Finance Website, http://finance.yahoo.com/how-to-guide/banking-budgeting/12832 ; 12 Money-Management Tips for College Students by Lucy Lazarony, Bankrate.com, http://www.bankrate.com/brm/news/sav/20000814b.asp.

## Chapter 9

1. See, for example, Moyer, McGuigan, and Rao, *Fundamentals of Contemporary Financial Management,* 2nd ed. (South-Western, Cengage Learning), page 3; Brigham and Houston, Fundamentals of Financial Management, 11th ed., page 2.

2. Inventory Turnover Ratios & Days Sales in Ending Inventories: U.S. National Averages, Bizstats.com Website, http://www.bizstats.com/inventory.htm; Financial ratios for specific industries: Food and beverage stores, Bizstats.com Website, http://www.bizstats.com/reports/corp.asp?industry=Food+and+beverage+stores&profType=ratios&var=&coding=44.5.115; Financial ratios for specific industries: Furniture and home furnishings, Bizstats.com Website, http://www.bizstats.com/reports/corp.asp?industry=Furniture+and+home+furnishings+stores&profType=ratios&var=&coding=44.2, accessed August 29, 2008.

3. Don't Get Burned by the Burn Rate by Ben McClure, Investopedia, February 25, 2004, http://www.investopedia.com/articles/fundamental/04/022504.asp; How Long Can I Keep Going? by F. John Reh, About.Com:Management, http://management.about.com/cs/money/a/CanKeepGoing.htm.

4. Check Clearing for the 21st Century Act FAQs, Federal Reserve Board of Governors Website, http://www.federalreserve.gov/paymentsystems/truncation/faqs2.htm#ques1, accessed August 29, 2008; Consumer Alerts—Check Clearing for the 21st Century (Check 21 Act), Federal Deposit Insurance Corporation Website, http://www.fdic.gov/consumers/consumer/alerts/check21.html, accessed August 29, 2008; Questions and Answers About the Check Clearing for the 21st Century Act, "Check 21," ConsumersUnion.org Website, http://www.consumersunion.org/finance/ckclear1002.htm, accessed August 29, 2008.

5. The approximate cost of not taking the discount on credit can be computed using the following formula:

$$\text{Cost of not taking discount} = \frac{\% \text{ discount}}{(100 - \% \text{ discount})} \times \frac{365}{(\text{Credit\_Period} - \text{Discount\_Period})}$$

where % discount is the discount the buyer receives for paying on or before the last day the discount is available, the Credit_Period is the number of days before payment of full invoice amount is due.

6. Financial Services Used by Small Businesses: Evidence from the 2003 Survey of Small Business Finances by Traci Mack and John D. Wolken, *Federal Reserve Bulletin,* October 2006, page A181.

7. The Great Rebate Runaround by Brian Grow, *BusinessWeek* Website, November 23, 2005, http://www.businessweek.com/bwdaily/dnflash/nov2005/nf20051123_4158_db016.htm, accessed August 29, 2008; SmartMoney: Goodbye, Mail-In Rebates by Aleksandra Todorova, *Wall Street Journal*: Sunday Edition [New York, N.Y.], page A.3, August 27, 2006; Rebates on the Way to Expiring by Damon Darlin, *New York Times* Website, November 11, 2006, http://people.ischool.berkeley.edu/~hal/Courses/StratTech07/Lectures/Pricing/Articles/rebates-expiring.html, accessed August 29, 2008.

8. Taking the Fear Out of Factoring by Martin Mayer, Inc.com Website, http://www.inc.com/magazine/20031201/factoring.html.

9. Commercial Paper Outstanding, Federal Reserve Bulletin, February 2008, http://www.federalreserve.gov/pubs/supplement/2008/02/table1_32.htm, accessed August 29, 2008.

10. Calling All Superheroes: The Spider-Man Movies Have Made a Mint—But Not for Spidey's Publisher by Devin

Leonard, Fortune, May 23, 2007, http://money.cnn .com/magazines/fortune; Sony lets retail promos fly for Spider-Man sequel: push relies on retail exclusives and Burger King promo by Todd Wasserman, *Brandweek*, April 16, 2007, page 8(1); "Spider-Man 3" on Track to Beat Predecessors by Dean Goodman, Reuters, May 2, 2007, http://www.reuters.com; Form 10-K, http:// yahoo.brand.edgar-online.com/fetchFilingFrameset .aspx?dcn=0001116679-07-000580&Type=HTML.

## Chapter 10

1. Dow Website News Center Website, http://news .dow.com/dow_news/corporate/2008/20080214a.htm, accessed April 21, 2008.

2. Emily Barker, "Making the Most of an IPO Road Show," Inc., May, 2002. Copyright 2002 by Mansueto Ventures LLC. Reproduced with permission of Mansueto Ventures LLC in the format Textbook via Copyright Clearance Center; and Investor Calendar, http://www.vcall.com/VR/ipocalendar.asp.

3. http://www.nysedata.com/nysedata/asp/factbook/ viewer_edition.asp?mode=table&key=3009&category= 5, http://ir.NASDAQ.com/faq.cfm; NYSE 2005 Year End Review, http://www.nyse.com/press/1135252289621. html, NYSEData.com; Factbook, http://www .nysedata .com/nysedata/asp/factbook/viewer_edition .asp?mode=table&key=3000&category=3; http://www .NASDAQtrader.com/dynamic/dailyfiles/daily2007.csv.

4. Hybrid Market Advances at NYSE, October 2006, NYSE Euronext Website, http://www.nyse.com/about/ publication/1159265937111.html.

5. How Much Volume Is Hybrid? by Ray Pellecchia, Hybrid Talk, May 7, 2007, blog on NYSE Website http://exchanges.nyse.com/archives/2007/05/ how_much.php; Bear Stearns to Take Write-Off on Specialist Unit by and Yalman Onaran, Bloomberg .com, May 14, 2007, http://www.bloomberg.com/apps/ news?pid=20601087&sid=aXo3iKbjzt8A&refer=home.

6. Former Oracle VP Settles Stock Trading Charge, by Ben Ames, PC World Website, May 15, 2007, http:// www.pcworld.com/article/id,131811-c,companynews/ article.html, accessed August 29, 2008.

7. About the Financial Industry Regulatory Authority, FINRA Website, http://www.finra.org/AboutFINRA/ index.htm, accessed August 29, 2008.

8. What Is a Stock Symbol and How Do I Find the Symbol for a Company?, BusinessKnowledgeSource .com Website, http://businessknowledgesource .com/investing/what_is_a_stock_symbol_and_how_ do_i_find_the_symbol_for_a_company_021903.html, accessed August 29, 2008; Stock Symbol Identifiers, StockMaven.com Website, http://www.stockmaven .com/symbols.htm, accessed August 29, 2008; Stock Tickers and Ticker Symbols, Money-zine.com Website, http://www.money-zine.com/Investing/Stocks/Stock- Tickers-and-Ticker-Symbols/, accessed August 29, 2008.

9. Moyer, McGuigan and Kretlow, *Contemporary Financial Management,* 10th ed. (South-Western, Cengage Learning), page 534; also http://www. investopedia.com/terms/d/directstockpurchaseplan. asp and http://beginnersinvest .about.com/cs/brokers1/ a/042501a.htm.

10. Options Trade Cost Steve Jobs $4 Billion by Brett Arends, The Street.com, June 13, 2007, http:// www.thestreet.com; How Steve Jobs Lost Over $4 billion, SeekingAlpha.com, May 27, 2007, http:// ce.seekingalpha.com/article/36615.

11. The Performance of Stocks: Professional Versus Dartboard Picks by Youguo Liang, Sanjay Ramchander and Jandhyala Sharma, *Journal of Financial and Strategic Decisions* Website, Volume 8, Number 1, Spring 1995, pages 55-63, http://www.studyfinance .com/jfsd/pdffiles/v8n1/liang.pdf; Investor Home Website, http://www.investorhome.com/darts.htm.

12. Stock quote, Yahoo! Finance Website, http://finance .yahoo.com/q?s=NYX, accessed April 24, 2008.

## Chapter 11

1. Boone Ch 1, High School Recruiting, Online NewsHour, December 13, 2004, http://www.pbs. org/newshour/bb/military/july-dec04/recruit_12-13. html; Northern California Teens Scrutinize Billion Dollar Military Recruitment Campaign Aimed at Youth, ACLU of Northern California Press Release, August 6, 2007, http://www.aclunc.org/news/press_releases/ northern_california_teens_scrutinize_billion_dollar_ military_recruitment_campaign_aimed_at_youth.shtml, accessed August 29, 2008.

2. The Pied Piper of Las Vegas Seems to Have Perfect Pitch by John Broder, *New York Times*, June 4, 2004; Las Vegas Cashes in by Abram Sauer, BrandChannel Website, July 10, 2006, http://www.brandchannel .com/features_profile.asp?pr_id=292, accessed August 29, 2008; Las Vegas Looks Ahead As Growth Boom Hits a Bump by Talea Miller, NewsHour.com Website, November 9, 2007, http://www.pbs.org/newshour/ vote2008/july-dec07/vegas_development_11-09.html, accessed August 29, 2008; Stats & Facts: Year-end Summaries 2003-2007, Las Vegas Convention and Visitors Authority Website, http://www.lvcva.com/ press/statistics-facts/index.jsp?whichDept=stats, accessed August 29, 2008.

3. Who Do You Love by Paul R. La Monica, September 20, 2004, CNNMoney.com, http://money.cnn .com/2004/09/20/technology/loyalty/.

4. The American Customer Satisfaction Index, http:// www.theacsi.org/overview.htm; Q4 2005, http://www .theacsi.org/fourth_quarter.htm#auc; Q1 2006, http:// www.theacsi.org/first_quarter.htm#air; Q2 2006, http:// www.theacsi.org/second_quarter.htm#nin.

5. Eight Reasons to Keep Your Customers Loyal by Rama Ramaswami, January 12, 2005, http:// opsandfulfillment.com/advisor/Brandi-custloyal/.

6. Abstract of La Nueva California, by David Hayes-Bautista, 2004 Regents of the University of California, http://www.ucpress.edu/books/pages/10120/10120. intro.html; Diapers for Fatima by Sean Gregory, *Time Inside Business,* February 2005.

7. Great View, Less Sweat by Brad Tuttle, *NewsWeek*, June 28, 2004; Porsche Steers Marketing Message to Thrill of Driving in Prep for SUV by Aaron Baar, *Brandweek*, September 16, 2002.

8. Fast-Food Lovers, Unite by Jennifer Ordonez, *NewsWeek*, May 24, 2004; Scientific Update by Reed Mangels, The Vegetarian Journal, http://www.vrg .org/journal/vj2003issue1/vj2003issue1scientific.htm, accessed March 2, 2005.

9. How Nike Figured Out China by Matthew Forney, Bonus Section, *Time,* November 2004; Nike Sales Reach 1 Billion in China, Thomson Reuters Website, March 19, 2008, http://www.reuters.com/article/

companyNews/idUSN1944277620080319, accessed August 29, 2008.

10. A look at a key feature of Red Bull's business, Biz/Ed (no author), http://www.bized.ac.uk/compfact/redbull/redbull7.htm; Raging Bull by Libby Estell, *Incentive,* January 2002; SHOWCASE; Red Bull Flugtag by Mike Fletcher, *Marketing Event,* September 29, 2003; Red Bull North America: The Company That Gave the US Energy Drink Market Wings by Heather Todd, *Beverage World,* May 15, 2003; It's a (Red) Bull Market After All by Anni Layne Rodgers, 2001, http://pf.fastcompany.com/articale/2001/10/redbull.html, accessed March 5, 2005.

11. Green and Still Chic by Sarah Childress and Ginanne Brownell, *NewsWeek,* March 14, 2005; Eco-Friendly/Environmentally-Friendly Fashion, Natural Healthcare Canada, http://naturalhealthcare.ca/fashion.phtml, accessed March 14, 2005.

12. If the Shoe Fits. . . Snopes Website, http://www.snopes.com/business/hidden/nike.asp, accessed March 14, 2005; The Ad from Hell by Ruth Shalit, May 28, 1999, Salon Website, http://www.salon.com/media/col/shal/1999/05/28/kenya/; Super Bowl Special by Seth Stevenson, February 7, 2005, Slate Website, http://slate.msn.com/id/2113214/.

Pg. 149 Fact Box: Lemulson-M.I.T. 2005 Invention Index, http://web.mit.edu/invent/n-pressreleases/n-press-05index.html, accessed August 29, 2008.

## Chapter 12

1. The Years 1980, Histmobile Website, http://www.histomobile.com/histomob/internet/87/histo02.htm, accessed April 16, 2005; Yugo Redux by Doug Donovan, April 23, 2002, Forbes Website, http://www.forbes.com/2002/04/23/0423yugo.html; Worst Cars of the Millennium, CarTalk Website, http://www.cartalk.com/content/features/Worst-Cars/results5.html; First Chinese Cars to Hit US Shores by Bill Vlasic, The Detroit News Website, January 2, 2005, http://www.detnews.com/2005/autosinsider/0501/02/A01-47455.htm; Yugo Art photos from http://magliery.com/Graphics/YugoArt/diner.jpg.

2. Best Global Brands 2008, Interactive Table, *BusinessWeek* Website, September 18, 2008, http://bwnt.businessweek.com/interactive_reports/global_brand_2008/?chan=magazine+channel_special+report, accessed September 24, 2008.

3. Characteristics of a Great Name, The Brand Name Awards by Brighter Naming, http://www.brandnameawards.com/top10factors.html, accessed April 10, 2005.

4. Brand Extensions: Marketing in Inner Space by Adam Bass, Brand Channel Website, http://www.brandchannel.com/papers_review.asp?sp_id=296 accessed March 25, 2007; Brand Extensions We Could Do Without by Reena Jana, August 7, 2006, BusinessWeek Website, http://www.businessweek.com/magazine/content/06_32/b3996420.htm.

5. The Importance of Being Richard Branson: Leadership and Change, Wharton Website, January 12, 2005, http://knowledge.wharton.upenn.edu/index.cjm?fa=printArticle&ID=1109, accessed August 29, 2008; Trump: Bigger Than Coke or Pepsi? Interview by Diane Brady, *BusinessWeek* Website, December 14, 2004, http://www.businessweek.com/bwdaily/dnflash/dec2004/nf20041214_9031_db049.htm, accessed August 29, 2008; The three "c's" of personal branding by Richard Arruda, BrandChannel Website, http://www.brandchannel.com/papers_review.asp?sp_id=318, accessed August 29, 2008.

6. Private Label Brands Captivate Europe's Consumers by Maria Nemeth-Ek, October 14, 2004, USDA Website, http://www.fas.usda.gov/info/agexporter/2000/Jan/private.html; Private label groceries, American Public Radio Website: Marketplace, October 12, 2007, http://marketplace.publicradio.org/display/web/2007/10/12/private_label_groceries/, accessed August 29, 2008.

7. Brand Management and Brand Extension, Deloitte Website, July 29, 2004, http://www.deloitte.com/dtt/article/0,2297,sid%253D2240%2526cid%253D55447,00.html.

8. 3M: Commitment to Sustainability, GreenBiz Leaders Website, 1999.

9. The rise of the Creative Consumer, Economist Website, March 10, 2005, http://www.economist.com/business/displayStory.cfm?story_id=3749354.

10. Toilet Brush Wins Wacky Bowl, CNN Money Website, January 6, 2005, http://money.cnn.com/2005/01/06/news/funny/warning_labels/; Wacky Warning Labels, M-LAW Website, http://www.mlaw.org/wwl/index.html, accessed August 29, 2008.

## Chapter 13

1. Moseying up to Apple's Genius Bar by Joe Wilcox, May 16, 2001, CNET News Website, http://news.com.com/2100-1040-257742.html?legacy=cnet; Gift Retailing in the 21st Century by Erica Kirkland, July/August 2004, Retail News, TrendWatching Website, http://www.trendwatching.com/press/trendarticles/RetailNews_summer2004.html; Borders Group Website, http://www.bordersgroupinc.com/about/index.html; Cold Stone Creamery, the Scoop by Alycia del Mesa, June 21, 2004, BrandChannel Website, http://www.brandchannel.com/features_profile.asp?pr_id=185; Hershey Finds Experiential Retailing Oh, So Sweet by Chris Jones, June 12, 2005, Chicago Tribune Website, http://www.chicagotribune.com/travel/chi-0506120436jun12,1,4383703.story.

2. Starbucks & Peetniks, Reveries Magazine, Cool News of the Day, June 6, 2005, http://www.reveries.com/cool_news/2005/june/jun_6a.html; Reverse Commerce, Reveries Magazine, Cools News of the Day, June 22, 2005, http://www.reveries.com/cool_news/2005/june/jun_22b.html; Lush Cosmetic, Reveries Magazine, Cool News of the Day, July 6, 2005, http://www.reveries.com/cool_news/2005/july/jul_6a.html.

2a. Online Sales to Climb Despite Struggling Economy, Forrester Research, Inc. Press Release, April 8, 2008, http://www.forrester.com/ER/Press/Release/0,1769,1205,00.html, accessed September 4, 2008; Offline Sales Influenced by Online Research to Hit $1 Trillion, eBusiness News Website, April 15, 2008, http://www.ebusinessnews.info/?action=read&article=320, accessed September 4, 2008.

3. E-Tailing: It's All about Service by Sarah Lacy, July 6, 2005, *BusinessWeek* Website, http://www.businessweek.com/technology/content/jul2005/tc2005076_1187.htm.

4. E-tailers expand beyond cyberspace, open storefronts by Sandra Jones, Chicago Tribune Website, April 30, 2007, http://www.trendwatching.com/about/inmedia/articles/online_oxygen/internet_merchants_decide_to_g.html, accessed September 4, 2008; Offline Sales Influenced By Online Research To Hit $1 Trillion,

eBusiness News Website, April 15, 2008, http://www.ebusinessnews.info/?action=read&article=320, accessed September 4, 2008; Threadless Website, http://www.threadless.com/, accessed September 4, 2008.

5. Shop the Vote by Daniel Gross, August 10, 2004, Slate Website, http://slate.msn.com/id/2104988/; The Only Company Wal-Mart Fears by John Helyar, Fortune Website, http://www.fortune.com/fortune/investing/articles/0,15114,538834,00.html, accessed July 19, 2005.

6. Fare errors on the Web: Savvy fliers run with 'em by Laura Bly, *USA Today* Website, May 6, 2005, http://www.usatoday.com/travel/flights/2005-05-05-fare-mistakes_x.htm, accessed September 4, 2008; Dell Axim mis-pricing sparks customer furore by Matt Loney, ZD Net UK Website, November 26, 2003, http://news.zdnet.co.uk/internet/ecommerce/0,39020372,39118131,00.htm, accessed September 4, 2008; Oops! The legal consequences of and solutions to online pricing errors by Benjamin Groebner, *Shidler Journal for Law, Commerce and Technology* Website, May 26, 2004, http://www.lctjournal.washington.edu/Vol1/a002groebner.htm, accessed September 4, 2008.

7. How Costco Became the Anti-Wal-Mart by Steven Greenhouse, July 17, 2005, New York Times Website, http://www.nytimes.com/2005/07/17/business/yourmoney/17costco.html?adxnnl=1&pagewanted=1&adxnnlx=1122004143-8Vfn2DFl1MJfernM1navLA; Consequences of the Internet for Investors by Whitney Tilson, June 5, 2000, Motley Fool Website, http://www.fool.com/boringport/2000/boringport000605.htm.

8. A Wine of Your Own by Sandy Edry, *NewsWeek,* June 27, 2005.

Pg. 172 Fact Box: Rewinding a video giant by Daniel McGinn, *NewsWeek*, June 27, 2005.

## Chapter 14

1. With Popcorn, DVDs, and TiVo, Moviegoers Are Staying Home by Laura Holson, New York Times, May 27, 2005; How Kids Set the (Ring) Tone by Jyoti Thottam, Time, April 4, 2005; New Ways to Drive Home the Message by Brad Stone, *NewsWeek*, May 30, 2005; U.S. Consumer Online Behavior Survey Results 2007—Part One: Wireline Usage, International Data Corporation Website, February 19, 2008, http://www.idc.com/getdoc.jsp?containerId=prUS21096308, accessed September 4, 2008; Studios Are Trying to Stop DVDs From Fading to Black by Brooks Barnes and Matt Richtel, *New York Times* Website, February 25, 2008, http://www.nytimes.com/2008/02/25/business/media/25dvd.html, accessed September 4, 2008; Claritas Convergence Audit Finds That Video-On-Demand Is Increasingly in Demand, Claritas Website, November 22, 2006, http://www.claritas.com/claritas/Default.jsp?ci=5&si=1&pn=convergence-audit-vod, accessed September 4, 2008.

2. Budweiser's dog and pony show takes top Ad Meter spot by Bruce Horovitz, *USA Today* Website, February 6, 2008, http://www.usatoday.com/money/advertising/admeter/2008admeter.htm, accessed September 4, 2008.

3. The 22 Immutable Laws of Marketing by Al Ries and Jack Trout, HarperBusiness 1993, pages 26–33.

4. Professor Paul Herbig, Tristate University, International Marketing Lecture Series, Session 6, International Advertising, http://www.tristate.edu/faculty/herbig/pahimadvstg.htm, accessed June 1, 2005; Taking Global Brands to Japan by Karl Moore and Mark Smith, The Conference Board Website, http://www.conference-board.org/worldwide/worldwide_article.cfm?id=243&pg=1, accessed June 1, 2005.

5. Brandchannel's 2004 Product Placement Awards by Abram Sauer, February 21, 2005, http://www.brandchannel.com/start1.asp?fa_id=251; A Product Placement Hall of Fame by Dale Buss, BusinessWeek Online, June 22, 1998, http://www.businessweek.com/1998/25/b3583062.htm.

6. The Celebrity Pitch by Darren Dahl, Inc. Magazine, April 2005; The Only Good Celebrity Is a Dead Celebrity by Joe Mullich, Business First, January 9, 1998, http://www.bizjournals.com/louisville/stories/1998/01/12/smallb5.html?page=1.

6a. PQ Media Market Analysis Finds Global Product Placement Spending Grew 37% in 2006; Forecast to Grow 30% in 2007, Driven by Relaxed European Rules, Emerging Asian Markets; Double-Digit Growth in U.S. Decelerates, PQ Media Website, March 14, 2007, http://www.pqmedia.com/about-press-20070314-gppf.html, accessed September 4, 2008.

7. TVs New Brand of Stars by Johnnie L. Roberts, *NewsWeek*, November 22, 2004; Prime-time Peddling by Daren Fonda, *Time*, May 30, 2005; New Ways to Drive Home the Message by Brad Stone, *NewsWeek*, May 30, 2005; American Idol Offers Hefty Price Tag to Sponsors by Apryl Duncan, About.com Website, January 16, 2008, http://advertising.about.com/b/2008/01/16/american-idol-offers-hefty-price-tag-to-sponsors.htm, accessed September 4, 2008.

8. Microsoft Completes Deal to Buy Ad Firm by Dina Bass and Jonathan Thaw, *Washington Post* Website, May 5, 2006, http://www.washingtonpost.com/wp-dyn/content/article/2006/05/04/AR2006050402001.html, accessed September 4, 2008; Massive Summary Research—Significant Findings, Massive Website, http://www.massiveincorporated.com/casestudiesa.html, accessed September 4, 2008; Massive Client List, Massive Website, http://www.massiveincorporated.com/clients.html, accessed September 4, 2008; Microsoft, EA sign sports game ad deal by Scott Hillis, Thomson Reuters Website, July 25, 2007, http://www.reuters.com/article/ousiv/idUSN2421994920070725, accessed September 4, 2008; Google to Buy Adscape by Nick Gonzalez, TechCrunch Website, February 16, 2007, http://www.techcrunch.com/2007/02/16/google-to-buy-adscape-for-23-million/, accessed September 4, 2008.

9. A Plot Twist in the World of Advertising by Elaine Dutka, *Los Angeles Times,* March 22, 2005; Sales by Cinema by Elizabeth Sampson, *Time*, November 22, 2004; BMW Morphs Online Film Concept into Comic Books by Jean Halliday, AdAge.com, http://adage.com/news.cms?newsId=44744.

10. Dissecting "Subservient Chicken" by Mae Anderson, March 7, 2005, AdWeek Website, http://www.adweek.com/aw/national/article_display.jsp?vnu_content_id=1000828049.

11. Special Report: Microsites Maximizing Online Participation by Craig Causer, April 1, 2005, The Non Profit Times Website, http://www.nptimes.com/Apr05/sr1.html; Catching the Online Cartoon Virus by Nat Ives, *New York Times,* March 14, 2005.

12. Kid Nabbing by Melanie Wells, February 2, 2004, Forbes Website, http://www.forbes.com/free_forbes/2004/0202/084.html.

13. The 22 Immutable Laws of Marketing by Al Ries and Jack Trout, HarperBusiness, 1993; Quotable Facts, Avis Website, http://www.avis.com/AvisWeb/JSP/US/en/aboutavis/corp_info/quotable_facts.jsp, accessed September 4, 2008; Neutrogena Hair Care, Neutrogena Website, http://www.neutrogena.com/ProductsDetails_16.asp, accessed September 4, 2008.

14. As Cingular Ads Parody, Not All Sponsorships Fit the Brand-Building Bill by Brent Pickett, MarketingProfs Website, http://www.marketingprofs.com/print.asp?source=%2Ftutorials%2Fprophet4%2Easp, accessed June 6, 2005; NASCAR Sponsors: Drive-by Marketing by Chris Jones, March 7, 2004, Las Vegas Review-Journal Website, http://www.reviewjournal.com/lvrj_home/2004/Mar-07-Sun-2004/business/23380897.html.

14a. Paid Search Ad Spend Will Hit $10 Billion by 2000, eMarketer Website, March 7, 2006, http://www.emarketer.com/Article.aspx?id=1003861, accessed September 4, 2008.

15. Total U.S. Advertising Spending by Medium, *Advertising Age* Website, June 21, 2007, http://adage.com/datacenter/article?article_id=118652, accessed September 4, 2008.

16. Blogs will change your business by Stephen Baker and Heather Green, *BusinessWeek* Website, May 2, 2005, http://www.businessweek.com/magazine/content/05_18/b3931001_mz001.htm, accessed September 4, 2008; Technofile: Blogging for business by Anne Stuart, Inc. Website, July 2003, http://www.inc.com/articles/2003/07/bblogs.html, accessed September 4, 2008; Blogging for milk by Rob Walker, Slate Website, April 14, 2003, http://slate.msn.com/id/2081419/, accessed September 4, 2008; Welcome to Technorati, Technorati Website, http://technorati.com/about, accessed September 4, 2008.

17. Small Mini Marketing Campaign Packs a Punch by John McCormick, October 4, 2004, Autos Insider, Detroit News Website, http://www.detnews.com/2004/insiders/0410/31/insiders-292427.htm; MINI USA Launch Exceeds Expectations, May 7, 2003, The Online BMW Forum, http://www.bmwboard.com/news/view.asp?linkid=351; BMW's Mini Just Keeps Getting Mightier by Gail Edmondson, April 5, 2004, BusinessWeek Online, http://www.businessweek.com/magazine/content/04_14/b3877075_mz054.htm.

18. Publicity from Thin Air (Don't Just Wait for News to Happen) by Bill Stoller, Article Point Website, http://www.articlepoint.com/articles/public-relations/publicity-from-thin-air.php, accessed June 15, 2005.

19. The Public Relations Hall of Fame, Publicity Insider Website, http://www.publicityinsider.com/HallOfFame.asp#5, accessed June 15, 2005.

Pg. **193 Fact Box:** Selling Facts You Should Know, The Marketing Edge Website, http://www.marketingedge.biz/stran_selling_facts.html, accessed September 4, 2008.

## Chapter 15

1. Can a Manager Be a Techie and Survive? by C.J. Kelly, ComputerWorld Website, November 20, 2006, http://www.computerworld.com/action/article.do?command=viewArticleBasic&articleId=272778&intsrc=hm_ts_head, accessed October 23, 2008; Gates/Ballmer Succession Watch by Joe Wilcox, Microsoft Watch Blog, June 23, 2008, http://www.microsoft-watch.com/content/corporate/gates_ballmer_succession_watch.html, accessed October 23, 2008.

2. Decisions, Decisions by Stuart Crainer, Entrepreneur, November 1999, http://www.findarticles.com/p/articles/mi_m0DTI/is_11_27/ai_57475879#continue; 20 That Made History by Jerry Useem, Kate Bonamici, Nelson D. Schwartz, Cait Murphy, Brent Schlender, Corey Hajim, Ellen Florian Kratz, Stephanie N. Mehta, and Barney Gimbel, *Fortune,* June 27, 2005, page 58. http://galenet.galegroup.com/servlet/BCRC?vrsn=149&locID=tlearn_trl&srchtp=art&c=8&ste=21&tab=2&tbst=tsAS&atp=KT&docNum=A133228996&art=20+that+made+history&bConts=0).

3. The Importance of Being Richard Branson, Leadership and Change, Knowledge@Wharton, January 12, 2005, http://knowledge.wharton.upenn.edu/article/1109.cfm.

4. Featured Employee Rap Sheet, Hot Topic Website, http://www.hottopic.com/community/rapsheets/emp_jodi.asp?LS=0&, accessed April 11, 2006; A New Game at the Office: Many Young Workers Accept Fewer Guarantees by Steve Lohr, New York Times, December 5, 2005, http://select.nytimes.com/gst/abstract.html?res=F00F12FE38550C768CDDAB0994DD404482.

5. Motivate Your Staff by Larry Page, How to Succeed in 2005, Business 2.0 magazine, December 1, 2004, http://money.cnn.com/magazines/business2/business2_archive/2004/12/01/8192529/index.htm.

6. A New Game at the Office: Many Young Workers Accept Fewer Guarantees by Steve Lohr, *New York Times,* December 5, 2005, http://select.nytimes.com/gst/abstract.html?res=F00F12FE38550C768CDDAB0994DD404482.

7. The 100 Best Companies to Work, *Fortune,* January 23, 2006, pages 79–86, 89–108.

8. The 100 Best Companies to Work For 2006, Fortune magazine, January 23, 2006, p. 71-74; Why the Economy is a Lot Stronger Than You Think by Michael Mandel, BusinessWeek Online, February 13, 2006, http://www.businessweek.com/magazine/content/06_07/b3971001.htm.

9. Don't Get Hammered by Management Fads by Darrell Rigby, *Wall Street Journal,* May 21, 2001.

10. Managing Generation Y—Part 1, Book Excerpt by Bruce Tulgan and Carolyn A. Martin, *BusinessWeek* Online, September 28, 2001, http://www.businessweek.com/smallbiz/content/sep2001/sb20010928_113.htm; Managing Generation Y—Part 2, Book Excerpt by Bruce Tulgan and Carolyn A. Martin, *BusinessWeek* Online, October 4, 2001, http://www.businessweek.com/smallbiz/content/oct2001/sb2001105_229.htm; Generation Y: They've Arrived at Work with a New Attitude by Stephanie Armour, USA TODAY, November 6, 2005, http://www.usatoday.com/money/workplace/2005-11-06-gen-y_x.htm.

11. "Mosh pits" of creativity by Joseph Weber, *BusinessWeek* Website, November 7, 2005, http://www.businessweek.com/magazine/content/05_45/b3958078.htm, accessed September 4, 2008.

12. Cross Functional Structures: A Review and Integration of Matrix Organization and Project Management by R. Ford and A. Randolph, *Journal of Management,* June 1992, http://www.findarticles.com/p/articles/mi_m4256/is_n2_v18/ai_12720959/pg_3.

13. The CEO's new clothes by Yukio Shimizu, Fast Company Website, September 2005, http://www

.fastcompany.com/magazine/98/open_essay.html, accessed September 4, 2008.

## Chapter 16

1. Old. Smart. Productive by Peter Coy, June 27, 2005, *BusinessWeek* Website, http://www.businessweek.com/magazine/content/05_26/b3939001_mz001.htm.

2. Facing Young Workers' High Job Expectations from Associated Press, *Los Angeles Times,* June 27, 2005.

3. How Corporate America Is Betraying Women by Betsy Morris, *Fortune,* January 10, 2005.

4. Pending Job Flexibility Act Received Mixed Reviews by Sue Shellenbarger, WSJ Career Journal, http://www.careerjournal.com/columnists/workfamily/20010426-workfamily.html, accessed August 9, 2005.

5. CEO Pay Charts 1990-2005, United for a Fair Economy Website, http://www.faireconomy.org/news/ceo_pay_charts, accessed September 11, 2008; CEO pay "business as usual" by Gary Strauss and Barbara Hansen, *USA Today* Website, March 30, 2005, http://www.usatoday.com/money/companies/management/2005-03-30-ceo-pay-2004-cover_x.htm, accessed September 11, 2008; Executive Excess 2007, United for a Fair Economy Website, August 29, 2007, http://faireconomy.org/files/pdf/ExecutiveExcess2007.pdf, accessed September 11, 2008.

6. Get Creative! by Bruce Nussbaum, August 1, 2005, *BusinessWeek* Website, http://www.businessweek.com/magazine/content/05_31/b3945401.htm.

7. Why We Hate HR by Keith Hammonds, Fast Company, August 2005, http://pf.fastcompany.com/magazine/97/open_hr.html; HR from the Heart Book Review, SHRM Store Website, http://shrmstore.shrm.org/shrm/product.asp?dept_id=23&pf_id=48.15046, accessed September 5, 2005; Is Your HR Department Friend or Foe? Depends Who's Asking the Question, Human Resources Knowledge@Wharton, August 10, 2005, http://knowledge.wharton.upenn.edu/article/1253.cfm.

8. College Degree Nearly Doubles Annual Earnings, Census Bureau reports, Census Bureau press release, March 28, 2005, http://www.census.gov/Press-Release/www/releases/archives/education/004214.html; College at Work: Outlook and Earnings for College Graduates, 2000–2010 by Arlene Dohm and Ian Wyatt, *Occupational Quarterly Outlook,* Fall 2002, http://www.bls.gov/opub/ooq/2002/fall/art01.pdf.

9. Human Capital Benchmarking Study, Society for Human Resource Management, http://www.shrm.org/research/benchmarks/, accessed August 13, 2005; Study: Moderation in Hiring Practices Boosts Business Performance by Todd Raphael, *Workforce Management*, August 19, 2005, http://www.workforce.com/section/00/article/24/14/03.html.

10. Top Five Resume Lies by Jeanne Sahadi, December 9, 2004, CNN Money Website, http://money.cnn.com/2004/11/22/pf/resume_lies/.

11. The Questions: How Not to Answer, compiled by Barry Shamis of Selecting Winners, Inc., FacilitatorGuy Resume Resource Center, http://resume.bgolden.com/res/interview-bloopers.php, accessed September 1, 2005; Interview Bloopers: What Not to Do! by Maureen Bauer, Channel 3000 Website, http://html.channel3000.com/sh/employment/stories/employment—20001002-144946.html, accessed September 1, 2005; More Interview Bloopers, by Maureen Bauer, Channel 3000 Website, http://html.channel3000.com/sh/employment/stories/employment—20001002-152818.html.

12. Orientation: Not Just a Once-over-Lightly Anymore by Matt DeLuca HRO Today, April/May 2005, http://www.hrotoday.com/Magazine.asp?artID=928.

13. Show and Tell—Disney Institute's Four-Day Seminar on HR Management by Leon Rubis, *HR magazine,* April 1998; New Employee Experience Aims for Excitement Beyond the First Day by Daryl Stephenson, Boeing Frontiers Online, May 2002, http://www.boeing.com/news/frontiers/archive/2002/may/i_mams.html.

14. Investigating the Executives by Penelope Patsuris, April 21, 2005, Forbes Website, http://www.forbes.com/smallbusiness/2005/04/21/cx_pp_0421ceosearch.html.

15. Extreme Extras by David Jacobson, *MONEY Magazine* Website, April 12, 2006, http://money.cnn.com/2006/04/07/pf/bestjobs_moneymag_perks/index.htm, accessed September 11, 2008; Unusual Perks by Anne Fisher, *Fortune* Website, January 22, 2008, http://money.cnn.com/galleries/2008/fortune/0801/gallery.BestCo_unusual_perks.fortune/, accessed September 11, 2008.

16. Labor-Intensive by Sean McFadden, Boston Business Journal, November 19, 2004, http://www.bizjournals.com/boston/stories/2004/11/22/smallb1.html; The Costco Way; Higher Wages Mean Higher Profits. But Try Telling Wall Street by Stanley Holmes and Wendy Zelner, *BusinessWeek,* April 12, 2004; Study: Moderation in Hiring Practices Boosts Business Performance by Todd Raphael, *Workforce Management,* August 19, 2005, http://www.workforce.com/section/00/article/24/14/03.html.

17. Workers on Flexible and Shift Schedules in May 2004, Bureau of Labor Statistics, July 1, 2005, http://www.bls.gov/news.release/flex.nr0.htm; Incidence of Flexible Work Schedules Increases, Bureau of Labor Statistics Monthly Labor Review, September 30, 1999, http://www.bls.gov/opub/ted/1999/Sept/wk5/art04.htm.

18. How Corporate America Is Betraying Women by Betsy Morris, *Fortune,* January 10, 2005, pages 65–70; What Women Want by John Tierney, *New York Times,* May 24, 2005, http://www.nytimes.com/2005/05/24/opinion/24tierney.html?ex=1125115200&en=470a6bcb3a66f0b2&ei=5070&n=Top%2fOpinion%2fEditorials%20and%20Op%2dEd%2fOp%2dEd%2fColumnists%2fJohn%20Tierney&oref=login.

19. Telework Trending Upward, Survey Says, World at Word Press Release, February 8, 2007, http://www.workingfromanywhere.org/, accessed March 07, 2007; Work at Home Grows in Past Year by 7.5% in U.S.; Use of Broadband for Work at Home Grows by 84%, ITAC Press Release, September 2, 2004, http://www.telecommute.org/news/pr090204.htm; Remote Working Increasing across Enterprises, According to Global Survey of Senior Executives, AT&T news release, December 1, 2004, http://www.att.com/news/2004/12/01-1.

20. Moms Go to the Office to Reduce Stress, At Work Harvard, September 21, 2004, http://atwork.harvard.edu/awards/WM-PR-092104.shtml; Can Executives Share a Job? by Cynthia Cunningham and Shelley

S. Murray, May 30, 2005, Harvard Business School Working Knowledge, http://hbsworkingknowledge.hbs.edu/item.jhtml?id=4824&t=career_effectiveness.

21. Archived News Releases for Mass Layoffs (monthly), U.S. Department of Labor, Bureau of Labor Statistics, http://www.bls.gov/schedule/archives/mmls_nr.htm#2005; Managing Morale after Downsizing by Janet Harrell, Monster Website, http://hr.monster.com/articles/manage%5Fmorale/, accessed August 30, 2005.

22. Flexible Hours and Telecommuting—Not the Ticket to the Top of Corporate America, Five Questions for Susan DePhillips, Workforce Management, September 2005, http://www.workforce.com/section/02/article/24/14/66.html.

23. Affirmative Action by Paul Finkelman, Ph.D., Microsoft® Encarta® 2007 © 1997-2007 Microsoft Corporation, http://encarta.msn.com/encyclopedia_761580666/affirmative_action.html, accessed September 11, 2008; Affirmative Action Under Attack by Dan Froomkin, *Washington Post* Website, October 1998, http://www.washingtonpost.com/wp-srv/politics/special/affirm/affirm.htm#how, accessed September 11, 2008; The Origins of Affirmative Action by Marquita Sykes, National Organization for Women Website, August 1995, http://www.now.org/nnt/08-95/affirmhs.html, accessed September 11, 2008.

24. Sexual Harassment Statistics, EEOC Website, updated February 26, 2008, http://www.eeoc.gov/stats/harass.html, accessed September 11, 2008; Sexual Harassment EEOC Website, updated March 4, 2008, http://www.eeoc.gov/types/sexual_harassment.html, accessed September 11, 2008.

## Chapter 17

1. Home Broadband Adoption by John Horrigan and Aaron Smith, The Pew Internet and American Life Project, June 2007, http://www.pewinternet.org/pdfs/PIP_Broadband%202007.pdf; Half of All U.S. Households Will Have Broadband This Year by Nate Anderson, http://arstechnica.com/news.ars/post/20070219-8874.html.

2. E-mail Addles the Mind by Benjamin Pimentel, May 4, 2005, SFGate.com, http://sfgate.com/cgi-bin/article.cgi?file=/c/a/2005/05/04/BUGOSCJGA41.DTL&type=printable; The Modern Brain, Besieged by Robert MacMillan, April 25, 2005, washingtonpost.com, http://www.washingtonpost.com/wp-dyn/content/article/2005/04/25/AR2005042500342_pf.html.

3. Data Mining Ready for a Comeback by Curt Monash, ComputerWorld, September 11, 2006, http://www.computerworld.com/action/article.do?command=viewArticleBasic&articleId=112733&pageNumber=2.

4. Effy Oz, *Management Information Systems*, 5th ed. (Course Technology, Cengage Learning, 2006), pages 332–338; Expert Systems," AlanTuring.Net, http://www.cs.usfca.edu/www.AlanTuring.net/turing_archive/pages/Reference%20Articles/what_is_AI/What%20is%20AI07.html.

5. David M. Kroenke, *Experiencing MIS* (Pearson Prentice Hall, 2008), pages 340–341; What Are Expert Systems? http://library.thinkquest.org/11534/expert.htm.

6. *IAB Internet Advertising Revenue Report*, pages 6–8, PricewaterhouseCoopers Website, September 2006, http://www.iab.net/resources/adrevenue/pdf/

IAB_PwC%202006Q2.pdf, accessed September 11, 2008; Internet Advertising Revenues Again Reach New Highs, Estimated to Pass $21 Billion in 2007 and Hit Nearly $6 Billion in Q4 2007, Internet Advertising Bureau Website, February 25, 2008, http://www.iab.net/about_the_iab/recent_press_releases/press_release_archive/press_release/195115, accessed September 11, 2008; IAB Internet Advertising Revenue Report, PricewaterhouseCoopers Website, http://www.pwc.com/extweb/pwcpublications.nsf/docid/0D548FE1F2EC5446852573FC0060CA34/$FILE/IAB_PwC2007Q2.pdf, accessed September 11, 2008.

7. B2B, B2C Comparison, http://www.generixsol.com/comparison.php; How B2B Differs from B2C, IBM iSeries Information Center, http://publib.boulder.ibm.com/iseries/v5r2/ic2924/index.htm?info/rzalg/b2bdifferb2c.htm; Marketing for B2B vs. B2C—Similar but Different by Debra Murphy, Vista Consulting, http://www.vista-consulting.com/marketing-articles/b2b-b2c-marketing.htm.

8. Viral Marketing by Steve Jurvetson and Tim Draper, http://www.dfj.com/cgi-bin/artman/publish/steve_tim_may97.shtml; Are You Using the Dynamic Power of Viral Marketing? by Tim Lloyd, Businessknowhow.com, http://www.businessknowhow.com/marketing/viralmark.htm.

9. Audible Privacy Statement, December 19, 2005, http://www.audible.com/adbl/store/privacy.jsp?BV_SessionID=@@@@1643509719.1185370133@@@@&BV_EngineID=cccgaddligimhgdcefecekjdffidfgf.0&Type=policy.

10. MarketingSherpa's Viral Marketing Hall of Fame 2007: Top 10 Efforts & Results Data to Inspire You, Marketingsherpa Website, April 25, 2007, http://www.marketingsherpa.com/article.html?ident=29947, accessed September 11, 2008; Is "Flack Whacking" Good Public Relations? by Seth Schiesel, *New York Times* Website, October 2, 2000, http://query.nytimes.com/gst/fullpage.html?res=9F00E7D6153DF931A35753C1A9669C8B63&partner=rssnyt&emc=rss, accessed September 11, 2008; 3 Examples of Awesome B2B Marketing Viral Videos, Hubspot Website, http://blog.hubspot.com/blog/tabid/6307/bid/2192/3-Examples-of-Awesome-B2B-Marketing-Viral-Videos.aspx, accessed September 11, 2008.

11. PayPal home page, https://www.paypal.com/.

12. Spammers Target Email Newsletters by David Utter, January 19, 2007, WebProWorld Security Forum, http://www.securitypronews.com/insiderreports/insider/spn-49-20070119SpammersTargetEmailNewsletters.html; Spammers Turn to Images to Fool Filters by Anick Jesdanun, USA Today, June 28, 2006, http://www.usatoday.com/tech/news/computersecurity/wormsviruses/2006-06-28-spam-images_x.htm.

13. Advertising Sent to Cell Phones Opens New Front in War on Spam by Kim Hart, Washingtonpost.com Website, March 10, 2008, http://www.washingtonpost.com/wp-dyn/content/article/2008/03/09/AR2008030902213.html, accessed September 11, 2008; Gone Smishing: Cell Phone Spam, p2pnet Website, April 25, 2008, http://www.p2pnet.net/story/15230, accessed September 11, 2008; The Ten Biggest Security Threats You Don't Know About by Andrew Brandt, *PC World* Website, June 22, 2006, http://www.pcworld.com/article/id,126083-page,8/article.html, accessed September 11, 2008; Cell Phone Virus Threats: Why They Shouldn't Be Dismissed by Christopher Brandt, Microsoft Small Business Center

Website, http://www.microsoft.com/smallbusiness/resources/technology/security/cell-phone-virus-threats-why-they-shouldnt-be-dismissed.aspx#Cellphonevirusthreatswhytheyshouldntbedismissed, accessed September 11, 2008.

14. The Different Shades of Hackers, WindowSecurity.com, http://www.windowsecurity.com/articles/Different-Shades-Hackers.html; Preparing for Cyberterrorists, Christian Science Monitor, February 3, 2004, http://www.csmonitor.com/2004/0203/p08s01-comv.html; Cyberterrorism: How Real Is the Threat? by Gabriel Weimann, The United States Institute of Peace, December 2004, http://www.usip.org/pubs/specialreports/sr119.html; White Hat, Gray Hat, Black Hat by Michael Arnone, October 3, 2005, FCW.com, http://www.fcw.com/article90994-10-03-05-Print.

15. http://www.microsoft.com/resources/documentation/windows/xp/all/proddocs/en-us/windows_password_tips.mspx?mfr=true; http://www.smat.us/sanity/pwdilemma.html#anchor12895273; http://msdn2.microsoft.com/en-us/library/bb416446.aspx.

16. E-mail Privacy Gets a Win in Court by Reynolds Holding, June 21, 2007, Time Magazine Website, http://www.time.com/time/nation/article/0,8599,1636024,00.html; Federal Court: Stored E-Mails Are Protected by Martin Kaste, June 19, 2007, NPR.org, http://www.npr.org/templates/story/story.php?storyId=11181164.

17. Anti-Napster Ruling Draws Mixed Reaction by Sam Costello, PCWorld.com. http://www.pcworld.com/article/id,41327-page,1/article.html; 23 New Schools to Receive Latest Round of RIAA Pre-Lawsuit Letters, RIAA Pressroom, July 18, 2007, http://www.riaa.com/newsitem.php?news_year_filter=&resultpage=&id=780E8751-0E03-4258-D651-F991B66E1708.

18. E-mail Abuse: An Overwhelming Inbox Can Get in Way of Work by Christina Salerno, Modesto Bee, December 5, 2006; RadioShack Lays Off Employees Via E-mail, USAToday, August 30, 2006, http://www.usatoday.com/tech/news/2006-08-30-radioshack-email-layoffs_x.htm; Employees get canned for e-mailing by Maria Gavrilovic, CNNMoney.com, June 7, 2006, http://money.cnn.com/2006/06/05/news/companies/email_firings/index.htm?cnn=yes.

19. Fourth Annual Piracy Study, Business Software Alliance, http://w3.bsa.org/globalstudy//; Microsoft Ramps Up Anti-Piracy Efforts by Erika Morphy, July 18, 2006, Technewsworld.com, http://www.technewsworld.com/story/51864.html.

20. Software & Information Industry Association Anti-Piracy Division, http://www.siia.net/piracy/pubs/AvoidInfringingSoftware.pdf.

21. Nintendo Wants Action on Piracy by Emma Boyes, GameSpot Website, February 15, 2008, http://www.gamespot.com/news/6186098.html, accessed September 11, 2008; Nintendo Raid Hong Kong Pirates by Anthony Dickens, Nintendo Life Website, October 24, 2007, http://www.nintendolife.com/articles/2007/10/24/nintendo_raid_hong_kong_pirates, accessed September 11, 2008.

22. High School Students Take on Turnitin, The Wired Campus, Chronicle of Higher Education Website, March 30, 2007, http://chronicle.com/wiredcampus/index.php?id=1968; Plagiarism Screener Gets Passing Grade in Copyright Lawsuit by John Timmer, Ars Technica Website, March 26, 2008, http://arstechnica.com/news.ars/post/20080326-plagiarism-screener-gets-passing-grade-in-copyright-lawsuit.html; iParadigm Wins Turnitin Lawsuit by Jonathan Bailey, Plagiarism Today Website, March 25, 2008, http://www.plagiarismtoday.com/2008/03/25/iparadigms-wins-turnitin-lawsuit/, accessed September 11, 2008.

23. Turner Entertainment Turns to Holographic Storage by Lucas Merian, ComputerWorld, November 17, 2005, http://www.computerworld.com/hardwaretopics/storage/story/0,10801,106288,00.html; A Tiger's Speed, an Elephant's Memory: Holographic Storage Ready for Market by Benjamin Alfonsi, October 2005, IEEE Distributed Systems Online, http://csdl2.computer.org/comp/mags/ds/2005/10/ox004.pdf.

24. Internet2 Membership Fees and Network Participation Fees, http://www.internet2.edu/membership/dues.html; About Internet2, http://www.internet2.edu/about/.

25. Next-Generation Cyberspace by Samuel Greengard, Edtech Magazine, March–April 2007, http://www.edtechmag.com/higher/march-april-2007/tech-trends.html.

26. Vegas Casino Bets on RFID by Alorie Gilbert, February 9, 2005, CNet.com, http://news.com.com/Vegas+casino+bets+on+RFID+-+page+2/2100-7355_3-5568288-2.html?tag=st.num; Casino Chips to Carry RFID Tags by Jeff Hecht, January 2004, Newscientist.com, http://www.newscientist.com/article.ns?id=dn4542.

## Chapter 18

1. The Secret's Out: Steak 'n Shake TV Ads Rock to a Different Tune by Gregg Cebrzynski, Nation's Restaurant News, May 12, 2003, page 16; the ad itself is available at the Young and Laramore Website, http://www.youngandlaramore.com/snstv/videos/shakes_Hi-wmv.html.

2. Will Infrastructure Be a Problem by Adil S. Zainulbhai, rediff.com Website, http://www.rediff.com/money/2006/jan/05adil6.htm; India Battles Infrastructure Woes by Satinder Bindra, CNN.com Website.

3. The Strategic Implications of Wal-Mart's RFID Mandate by David H. Williams, Directions Magazine Website, http://www.directionsmag.com/article.php?article_id=629&trv=1; Target Issues RFID Mandate by Carol Silwa, Computerworld, March 1, 2004, page 7.

4. Robot Reinvents Bypass Surgery by Steve Sternberg, USA Today Website, April 29, 2008, http://www.usatoday.com/news/health/2008-04-29-robot-surgery_N.htm, accessed September 11, 2008; Meet Mr. Rounder by Arlene Weintraub, BusinessWeek Website, March 25, 2005, http://www.businessweek.com/magazine/content/05_13/b3926011_mz001.htm, accessed September 11, 2008; Report: For Heart Surgery Robot Beats Doctor by Sharon Gaudin, Computer World Website, April 28, 2008, http://www.computerworld.com/action/article.do?command=viewArticleBasic&taxonomyName=development&articleId=9081302&taxonomyId=11&intsrc=kc_top, accessed September 11, 2008; Dr. Robot. Paging Dr. Robot by Anna Marie Kukek, Daily Herald Website, April 10, 2008, http://www.dailyherald.com/story/?id=169962, accessed September 11, 2008.

5. Outsourcing: Ripoff Nation, BW Smallbiz Front Line, Winter 2006, BusinessWeek Website, http://www.businessweek.com/magazine/content/06

_52/b4015435.htm?chan=rss_topStories_ssi_5; Outsourcing in China: Five Basic Rules for Reducing Risk by Steve Dickinson, ezinearticles.com Website, http://ezinearticles.com/?Outsourcing-in-China: -Five-Basics-for-Reducing-Risk&id=17214.

6. Top Economists Square Off in Debate Over Outsourcing, CareerJournal.com Website, http://www.careerjournal.com/hrcenter/articles/20040520-aeppel.html; Outsourcing Creates Jobs, Study Says, March 30, 2004, CNNMoney.com Website, http://money.cnn.com/2004/03/30/news/economy/outsourcing/.

7. Is Made in the USA Back in Vogue? by Parija Bhatnagar, CNNMoney.com Website, March 1, 2006, http://money.cnn.com/2006/02/28/news/economy/retail_localsourcing/index.htm, accessed September 11, 2008; AT&T decides to bring broadband call center back onshore by Eric Bangeman, Ars Technica Website, September 25, 2006, http://arstechnica.com/news.ars/post/20060925-7826.html, accessed September 11, 2008; Onshoring: Bucking the Trend by Keven Meyer, Evolving Excellence Website, March 4, 2008, http://www.evolvingexcellence.com/blog/2008/03/onshoring-bucki.html, accessed September 11, 2008.

8. Blaming ERP by Andrew Osterwald, CFO, January 2000, page 89; Supply Chain: Hershey's Bittersweet Lesson by Christopher Koch, CIO Magazine, November 15, 2002, http://www.cio.com/article/31518/Supply_Chain_Hershey_s_Bittersweet_Lesson.

9. Cost of ERP—What Does ERP Really Cost? Systopia Website, http://www.sysoptima.com/erp/cost_of_erp.php; Causes of ERP Failures, BusinessKnowledgeSource.com Website, http://businessknowledgesource.com/technology/causes_of_erp_failures_006086.html.

10. Financial Executive Survey: Most Businesses Lack IT Plan, CSC.com Website, http://www.csc.com/features/2005/62.shtml.

11. Poka Yoke Mistake Proofing by Kerri Simon, iSixSigma Website, http://www.isixsigma.com/library/content/c020128a.asp; Make No Mistake by Mark Hendricks, *Entrepreneur Magazine*, October 1996, http://www.entrepreneur.com/magazine/entrepreneur/1996/october/13430.html , accessed July 30, 2007.

12. Six Sigma Training by Charles Waxer, iSixSigma Website, http://www.isixsigma.com/library/content/c010225a.asp, accessed September 11, 2008; What is Six Sigma?, GE Website, http://www.ge.com/sixsigma/SixSigma.pdf, accessed September 11, 2008; Six Sigma Black Belt Certification, ASQ Website, http://www.asq.org/certification/index.html, accessed September 11, 2008.

13. Why Apply? Baldrige National Quality Program Website, http://www.quality.nist.gov/Why_Apply.htm; Answers to Frequently Asked Questions for the Baldrige National Quality Program: 2007, National Institute of Standards and Technology, http://www.quality.nist.gov/Ambassador/Word_Files/2007_FAQs.doc.

14. Sanford "Pens" an Improved Blister-Pack Tale by Lauren R. Hartman, Packaging Digest, January 2007, page 43.

15. David A Collier and James R. Evans, *Operations Management*, 2nd ed. (Mason, OH: South-Western, Cengage Learning, 2007), pages 751–753.

# Subject Index

Entries in boldface are key terms.

**absolute advantage,** 31
**accessory equipment,** 156
**accounting,** 94–107
  defined, 95
  financial statements in, 99–104
  generally accepted accounting
    principles (GAAP) and, 97–99
  managerial, 104–107
  professions in, 96–97
**accounting equation,** 99
accounts receivable, 114
**accrual-basis accounting,** 100–101
**acquisitions,** 76
**active listening,** 59
**active voice,** 60–61
**activity-based costing (ABC),** 105
**actual product,** 155
**advergaming,** 187
**advertising,** 187, 189
**adware,** 231
affirmative action, 223
African Americans
  demographics of, 10
  marketing to, 142
**agents,** 171
aging population, 11–12
Americans with Disabilities Act of
  1990, 223
**angel investors,** 91
annual reports, finding, 101
antitrust laws, 19
**applications software,** 226
**apprenticeship,** 218
**articles of incorporation,** 73
**articles of organization,** 77
Asians, demographics of, 10
**assembly lines,** 241
asset management ratios, 104, 111
**assets,** 99–103
auction markets, 128
audience. *see also* target markets
  business communication and,
    60–63
  target audience and marketing
    promotion, 195
audit reports, 102–103
**augmented product,** 155
**autocratic leaders,** 208
auto industry, 34, 37
**automation,** 245

**balance of payments,** 31–32
**balance of payments deficit,** 32
**balance of payments surplus,** 32

**balance of trade,** 31
**balance sheets,** 99–103
**Baldrige National Quality
  Program,** 250
**behavioral segmentation,** 143
**benefits,** 220–221
**bias,** 60
"big ideas," in marketing promotion,
  184–186
bleeding edge, 9
blogging, 191
blue sky laws, 129
**board of directors,** 74
body, of presentations, 65–66
**bonds,** 124–126
**brand equity,** 159
**brand extensions,** 160
**brands,** 8, 30, 159, 188
breakage rates, 115
**breakeven analysis,** 179
**brokers,** 131, 171
**budget deficit,** 25
**budgeting,** 106–107
**budget surplus,** 25
bulleted lists, 64–65
burn rate, 110
**business,** defined, 3
**business buyer behavior,** 147
business communication, 56–67
  audience and, 60–63
  communication channels for,
    59–60, 61
  communication skills for, 57–58
  effectiveness of, 63–64
  e-mail for, 61, 62, 64, 65, 229, 234
  hostility in, 67
  listening dos and don'ts, 60
  nonverbal communication and,
    58–59
  PowerPoint presentations for, 66
  verbal presentations for, 65–67
**business cycle,** 23–24
**business environment,** 7–13
**business ethics,** 45
**business format franchises,** 78–81
business formation, 68–81
  corporate restructuring and, 76–77
  corporations, 70, 73–75
  ethics and, 75
  franchises, 78–81
  limited liability companies (LLC),
    77–78
  limited partnerships, 72
  nonprofit corporations, 5, 75–76

  partnerships, 70, 71–73
  S corporations, 75–76
  sole proprietorships, 69–71
  statutory close corporations,
    75–76
**business intelligence systems,** 228
**business marketers (B2B),** 142, 230
**business plans,** 90–91
**business products,** 155
**business services,** 156
**business technology,** 9
**business-to-business (B2B)
  e-commerce,** 229–231
**business-to-consumer (B2C)
  e-commerce,** 228–231
**buzz marketing,** 188

**CAD/CAM,** 245
**cafeteria-style benefits,** 221
**callable bonds,** 125
**cannibalization,** 158
capital, as factor of production, 6
**capital budgeting,** 116
**capital gains,** 124
**capitalism,** 16–20
**capital structure,** 118
cash and carry wholesalers, 171
**cash budgets,** 112
cash burn rate, 110
**cash equivalents,** 112–113
casinos, 236
**cause-related marketing,** 51
C corporations, 73
cell phones
  penetration ratios, 30
  product strategy and, 165
  viruses on, 232
CEOs (chief executive officers)
  boards of directors and, 74, 75
  ethics and, 46
  executive searches for, 217
  wage gap and, 212
certified internal auditors (CMA), 97
Certified Public Accountants (CPA), 97
change, 2–13
  business environment and, 7–13
  evolution of business and, 4–5
  factors of production and, 5–7
  pace of business and, 3–4
  personal financial success and, 13
**channel intermediaries,** 169, 170
**channel of distribution,** 169
check clearing time, 113
China, 13, 30, 33

business ethics and, 50, 53
marketing and, 145
offshoring to, 247
**Civil Rights Act of 1964 (Title VII),** 223
Clayton Antitrust Act of 1914, 19
closing, of presentations, 66
**cobranding,** 161
**code of ethics,** 46
code of conduct, 54
**cognitive dissonance,** 146–147
collection policy, 114, 115
**commercial paper,** 113, 116
**common markets,** 40
**common stocks,** 123–124
**communication,** 57, 184. *see also* business communication
**communication barriers,** 57–58
**communication channels,** 59–60, 61
**communism,** 21–22
*Communist Manifesto* (Marx), 22
**comparative advantage,** 31
**compensation,** 219–221
competition
 competitive environment, 8–9
 degrees of, in economics, 18–19
**compounding,** 117
**compressed workweek,** 221
**computer-aided design (CAD),** 245
**computer-aided engineering (CAE),** 245
**computer-aided manufacturing (CAM),** 245
**computer-integrated manufacturing (CIM),** 245
**conceptual skills,** 198
conglomerate mergers, 77
**consultative selling,** 194
**consumer behavior,** 146, 180–181
**consumerism,** 48–49
**consumer price index (CPI),** 24
**consumer products,** 155
**consumer promotion,** 189–192
content, 12
**contingency planning,** 203, 204
**contingent workers,** 217
**continuous innovation,** 163
**contraction,** 23
**controlling,** management and, 197, 209
**convenience products,** 155
conversion ratio, 126
**convertible bonds,** 125–126
**cookies,** 231
cooperatives, 73
**core benefit,** 154, 155
**corporate bylaws,** 73
**corporate philanthropy,** 51
**corporate responsibility,** 51
**corporations,** 70, 73–75
corruption, 7
**countertrade,** 32

**coupon rate,** 125
coupons, 191
**covenants,** 119
creativity, 5, 8, 11, 205
credit. *see* finance
creditors, 95. *see also* finance
criminal background checks, 217
**Critical Path Methods (CPM),** 243, 244
**critical paths,** 244
culture
 communication and, 58
 corporate, 219
 franchising and, 78–79
 small business and, 93
cumulative features, of stocks, 124
**current ratio,** 111
**customer benefits,** 157
**customer loyalty,** 141
**customer marketers (B2C),** 142
**customer relationship management (CRM),** 140–141, 230
**customer satisfaction,** 141
**cybermediary,** 230
cyberterrorists, 233

**data,** 226–228
**databases,** 227
**data mining,** 228
**data warehouse,** 228
debt, 118–119
**debt-to-assets ratio,** 111
**debt-to-equity ratio,** 111
decision making. *see* consumer behavior
**decision support systems (DSS),** 228
**deflation,** 24
**degree of centralization,** 206
delivery, in business communication, 67
**demand,** 20–21
**demand curve,** 20–21
Deming, W. Edwards, 248–249
Deming Chain Reaction, 248
**democratic leaders,** 208
**demographics,** 10
**demographic segmentation,** 142–143
**departmentalization,** 206–207, 208
**depression,** 23
**diffusion,** 164
**direct channels,** 169
**direct investment,** 34
direct stock purchase plans (DSPP), 132
direct response retailing, 174
**discontinuous innovations,** 162
**discounting,** 118
**discount rate,** 27, 118
**disinflation,** 24
displays, 192

distribution and pricing, 168–181
 distribution, defined, 169
 distributors' role in, 169–170
 elements of supply chain, 176
 modes of transportation and, 177
 online pricing mistakes, 178
 physical distribution and, 175–177
 pricing in practice, 179–181
 pricing objectives and strategies, 177–179
 retailers, retail store categories, 173
 retailers and, 171–175
 retailers *vs.* wholesalers in, 170–171
 service and cost, 181
 wholesalers and, 171
**distribution strategy,** 144, 169
**distributors.** *see also* distribution and pricing
 role of, 169–170
 wholesalers *vs.,* 170–171
diversity, 10–12
dividends, 124
dollar, 32
"double bottom line," 54
**Dow Jones Industrial Average,** 135
drop shippers, 171
**dynamically continuous innovations,** 163
**dynamic delivery,** 67

**earnings per share ratio,** 111
**e-commerce,** 8, 10, 228–231
**economics,** 14–27
 business environment and, 7
 capitalism and, 16–20
 defined, 15
 evaluating performance in, 22–25
 FDIC and, 27
 forecasting, 17
 importance of, 15–16
 managing, through fiscal and monetary policy, 25–27
 marketing and, 19
 mixed, 22
 planned, 20–22
 small business and, 92
 transformational trends in, 16
**economic systems,** 16
**economy,** 15. *see also* economics
**effectiveness,** 240
**efficiency,** 240
**electronic bill presentment and payment,** 230
**electronic communications networks (ECN),** 127, 129
e-mail, 61, 62, 64, 65
 opt-in, 229
 pros and cons of, 234
**e-marketplaces,** 231
**embargoes,** 37
employees
 accounting and, 95

competitive environment and, 9
e-mail usage on the job, 234
employment level and economics, 23
ethics toward, 48
online recruiting of, 59
salaries of, 7
in small businesses, 92
technological environment and, 10–12
workforce competition and, 9
**enterprise resource planning (ERP),** 245, 247–248
**entrepreneurs.** *see also* small businesses
defined, 3–4, 83
entrepreneurship as factor of production, 6
Entrepreneurship Era, 4
globalization and, 93
profile of, 85–86
serial, 84
Web-driven, 88
**environmental scanning,** 143
**Equal Employment Opportunity Commission (EEOC),** 223
Equal Pay Act of 1963, 223
**equilibrium price,** 20–21
**equity theory,** 201
**ethical dilemmas,** 45
**ethics,** 12, 42–54
accounting and, 99–100
business environment and, 7
business ethics, defined, 45
business formation and, 75
defined, 43
globalization and, 39, 53, 54
impact of, 45–47
information technology and, 233–234
monitoring, 54
social responsibility and, 43–44, 47–54
Ethics Resource Center (ERC), 46
ethnicity, 10–11, 62
euro, 32
**European Union (EU),** 40–41
**everyday-low-pricing (EDLP),** 178
**exchange rates,** 32, 38–39
**exchange traded funds (ETF),** 134
exclusive distribution, 172
**expansion,** 23–24
**expectancy theory,** 201
**expenses,** 100
**expert system (ES),** 228
**exporting,** 32, 34–37
**external locus of control,** 86
**external recruitment,** 214–215
**extranets,** 226
eye contact, 58

facial expression, 58
**factors,** 116
**factors of production**

defined, 5–7
globalization and, 30–31
Fair Labor Standards Act of 1938, 223
Family and Medical Leave Act of 1996, 223
family limited partnerships (FLIPs), 72
farm subsidies, 39
**federal debt,** 25
**Federal Deposit Insurance Corporation (FDIC),** 27
Federal Reserve System (Fed), 25–27, 115
finance, 108–120
capital budgeting, 116–118
credit unions, 73
evaluating performance and, 110
financial decision making and, 109
financial planning and, 110–112
financial ratios, 111
long-term capital, 118–120
working capital, 112–116
**Financial Accounting Standards Board (FASB),** 97–99
**financial budgets,** 107
Financial Industry Regulatory Authority (FINRA), 130
**financial leverage,** 119
**firewalls,** 233
firm-commitment arrangements, 126
**first line management,** 198
**fiscal policy,** 25
**flextime,** 221
**flow shop processes,** 241
**foreign franchising,** 34
**foreign licensing,** 34
**foreign outsourcing,** 33
forensic accountants, 96
**form utility,** 137, 170
**franchise agreement,** 80
**franchisees,** 78–81
**franchising,** 34, 78–81
**franchisors,** 78–81
**free-reign leaders,** 208
**free trade,** 11, 37–41
*FTSE 100,* 135
full-service merchant wholesalers, 171
fundamental rights, of capitalism, 17–18

gaming, marketing through, 187, 230
**Gantt charts,** 243, 244
**GATT (General Agreement on Tariffs and Trade),** 38
gender bias, 62
**General Agreement on Tariffs and Trade (GATT),** 11
**general corporations,** 73
**generally accepted accounting principles (GAAP),** 97–99
**general partnerships,** 71–72
Generation C, 12
Generation Y, 203
**geographic segmentation,** 143

gestures, 58
globalization, 28–41. *see also* business formation; *individual names of countries*
business ethics and, 54 (*see also* ethics)
as business opportunity, 29–30, 32–35
entrepreneurship and, 6–7, 93
free trade and, 37–41
global environment and, 12–13
international trade, reasons for, 30–31
international trade barriers and, 35–37
marketing and, 148
marketing promotion and, 185–186
measuring global trade, 31–32
operations management and, 240
population and, 29–30
socialism and, 21
global marketing mix, 144–145
"golden parachutes," 75
goods, operations management and, 239
government accountants, 96
grammar, 63–64
grassroots marketing, 145
**green marketing,** 52, 149
**gross domestic product (GDP),** 22–23, 30
growth investing, 132

**hackers,** 233
headings, in written communication, 64–65
Hierarchy of Needs (Maslow), 199–200
Hispanics, demographics of, 10
**holographic storage,** 236
**horizontal analysis,** 104
horizontal market software, 226
horizontal mergers, 77
hostility, in business communication, 67
**human resource (HR) management,** 210–223
affirmative action, 223
challenges of, 211–213
corporate culture and, 219
defined, 211
human resources as factor of production, 6
legal issues, 212, 222–223
online recruiting, 59
planning, 213–222
**human skills,** 198
humor, in public speaking, 67
**hyperinflation,** 24

**immediate predecessors,** 243
Immigration Reform and Control Act of 1986, 223

**importing,** 33–37
income investing, 132
**income statements,** 100–101
**incremental analysis,** 105–106
**independent wholesaling
businesses,** 171
India, 13, 30, 85, 241, 247
individuals, ethics and, 45
Industrial Revolution, 4
**inflation,** 24
**information,** 226–228
information technology, 224–236. see
also technology
challenges of, 231–235
for decision making, 226–228
e-commerce and, 228–231
hardware and software changes
in, 225–226
new developments in, 235–236
information utility, 170
**infrastructure,** 36
**initial public offerings (IPO),** 126
innovation, 5, 11, 150, 162–165, 205
**installations,** 156
instant messages (IM), 61
**institutional investors,** 74
intangible assets, 103
**integrated marketing
communication,** 184
**intellectual property,** 234
intensive distribution, 172
**intercultural communication,** 58
internal auditors, 96
**internal locus of control,** 85
**internal recruitment,** 214
international business. see
globalization
**International Monetary Fund (IMF),**
38–41
Internet. see also technology
marketing on, 189, 229, 230
blogging, 191
e-mail pros and cons, 234
Internet2, 236
network neutrality, 16
online recruiting, 59
small businesses and, 87
stock tracking on, 135
wireless network security, 49
World Wide Web, 9–10
**Internet2,** 236
interviews, human resources and,
215–216
**intranets,** 226
inventions, 11
**inventories,** 242
**inventory turnover ratio,** 111
investing. see securities markets
**ISO 9000,** 250

Japan, 31, 93, 248–249
**job analysis,** 213
**job description,** 213–214

**job enrichment,** 200
**job shop processes,** 241
**job specifications,** 213–214
**joint ventures,** 34–35
**just-in-time (JIT) production,** 251

labels, 163
language, for business
communication, 60–63
Latinos, marketing to, 142
**leading,** 197, 208–209
leading edge, 9
**lean production,** 251
legal issues. see also business
formation
accounting and, 96, 97–99
antitrust laws, 19
globalization and, 36–37
human resources and, 212,
222–223
information technology and,
233–234
limited liability corporations (LLC)
and, 78
marketing and, 146
regulation of securities, 129–130
leverage ratios, 104, 111
**liabilities,** 99–102
liability protection. see business
formation
**licensing,** 34, 160
**limited liability,** 72
**limited liability companies (LLC),**
77–78
**limited liability partnerships
(LLP),** 72–73
**limited partnerships,** 72
limited service merchant wholesalers,
171
**limit orders,** 131
**line-and-staff organization,** 207
**line extensions,** 159
**line managers,** 207
**line of credit,** 115
**line organization,** 207
liquidity ratios, 104, 111
listening
active, 59
dos and don'ts, 60
loans, 91
**logistics,** 175
London Stock Exchange, 128, 135
**loss,** 3
**loss leader pricing,** 178

**macroeconomics,** 15
**maintenance, repair, and operating
products,** 156
**management,** 196–208
contingency planning and,
203, 204
controlling and, 197, 209
defined, 197

hierarchy of, 197–198
human resources and, 212–213
leadership and, 197, 208–209
Maslow's Hierarchy of Needs and,
199–200
motivation and, 199–202
organizing and, 197, 205–208
planning and, 197, 202–205
skills of, 198–199
Theory X and Theory Y, 200
**management development,** 218
**managerial (or management)
accounting,** 95, 104–107
manufacturers brands, 161
**marketing,** 136–150
blogging, 191
California Milk Board "happy cow"
campaign, 19
customer behavior and, 146–147
customer relationship
management (CRM) and,
140–141
defined, 137–138
evolution of, 139–140
marketing research, 147–148
marketing strategy, 141–146
scope of, 138–139
social responsibility and, 148–150
viral, 229, 230
**marketing concept,** 140
Marketing Era, 5
**marketing mix,** 143–144
**marketing plans,** 141
marketing promotion, 182–195
celebrities for, 186
integrated marketing
communication, 184
media categories for, 189–190
positioning statements for,
184–186
promotion, defined, 183
promotional mix and, 186–195
**marketing research,** 147, 149
**market niches,** 87
**market orders,** 131
**market segmentation,** 141
**market share,** 145
market timing, 132
Marx, Karl, 22
Maslow, Abraham, 199–200
**mass customization,** 149–150, 245
**master budgets,** 107
**matrix organizations,** 207–208
**maturity date,** 124
media, marketing promotion and,
189–190
memos, 61
**merchant wholesalers,** 171
**mergers,** 76, 77
messages, high-impact, 63–64
**microeconomics,** 15–16
microwave ovens, product strategy
and, 165

middle management, 198
mission, 204
missionary selling, 193
mixed economies, 22
M1 money supply, 26
M2 money supply, 26
modes of transportation, 176–177
monetary policy, 25–26
money market mutual funds, 113–114
money supply, 26
monopolistic competition, 18
monopoly, 19
motivation, management and, 199–202
movie industry, piracy and, 235
multichannel retailing, 172
mutual funds, 133

NAFTA (North American Free Trade Agreement), 40
NASDAQ, 127–129
  NASDAQ Composite Index, 135
  NYSE and, 128
National Association of Securities Dealers (NASD), 130
national brands, 161
National Debt Clock, 25
National Discount Brokers (NDB), 193
nationality, bias and, 62
national savings rate, 7
natural disasters, 13
natural monopoly, 19
natural resources, as factor of production, 5–6
"necessity entrepreneurs," 84
nervousness, during presentations, 66–67
net income, 100
net present value (NPV), 118
net working capital, 112
New York Stock Exchange (NYSE), 127–129, 130
  NYSE Hybrid Market, 128
  NYSE vs., 128
  NYX symbol of, 135
  Nikkei 225 stock index, 135
noise, 57
nonprofits, 5, 75–76
nonverbal communication, 58–59
North American Free Trade Agreement (NAFTA), 13
notes (financial statements), 103–104
not-for-profit organizations, marketing and, 138
NYSE Hybrid Market, 128

observation research, 148
Occupational Safety and Health Act of 1970, 223
odd pricing, 180
"offshoring," 34, 247
oligopoly, 19

on-the-job training, 217
opening, for presentations, 65
open market operations, 26–27
operating budgets, 106–107
operational planning, 202
operations management, 238–251
  defined, 239
  globalization and, 241
  goods and services, 239
  importance of, 239–240
  inventory control and, 242–243
  lean production and, 251
  location decisions and, 240–241
  process selection and, 241–242
  project scheduling and, 243–244
  quality and, 248–250
  technology of, 245–248
opportunity cost, 31
opt-in e-mail, 229
organization chart, 206
organizing, management and, 197, 205–208
orientation, 217
outsourcing, 246
over-the-counter market (OTC), 129
owners' equity, 99
ownership. see business formation
ownership utility, 137–138, 170

packaging, 161
paragraphs, construction of, 64
partnerships, 35, 70, 71–73
par value, 125
passive voice, 60–61
patents, 86
penetration pricing, 177
per capita income, 93
performance appraisals, 218–219
personal branding, 160
personal finance. see also finance
  budgeting for, 107
  success and, 13
personal selling, 193
Peru, 93
phishing, 232
physical distribution, 169
piracy, 235
place utility, 137–138, 170
plagiarism, 235
planned obsolescence, 50
planning, financial, 110–112
planning, management and, 197, 202–205
poka-yokes, 249
political issues
  globalization and, 36–37
  marketing and, 146
population
  of China, 33
  global, 29–30 (see also globalization)
  U.S., 10–11

positioning statements, 184–186
posture, 58
power, leadership and, 208, 209
PowerPoint, 66
preemptive rights, 124
preferred stocks, 124
premiums, 191
present value, 117
pricing. see distribution and pricing
primary data, 147
primary security market, 126–129
principal, 118, 124–125
privacy, information technology and, 233–234
private accountants, 96
private placements, 126–127
private placement securities, 126
privatization, 22
probationary period, 217
processes, 241
producer price index (PPI), 24
product consistency, 157
product costing, 105
product differentiation, 156–161
product features, 157
Production Era, 4–5
productivity, 24–25
product life cycle, 165–167
product lines, 157
product mix, 157–158
product placement, 186
products, 153
product strategy, 152–167
  goods and services spectrum, 154
  new product development, 162–165
  product classification, 155–156
  product definition, 153–155
  product differentiation, 156–161
  product life cycle, 165–167
profit, 3
profitability ratios, 104, 111
profit margin, 180
profit motive, 49
pro forma statements, 112
project scheduling, 243–244
promissory notes, 115
promotion, 183. see also marketing promotion
promotional channels, 186
promotional products, 191
promotion strategy, 144. see also marketing
protectionism, 37
psychographic segmentation, 143
public accountants, 96
Public Company Accounting Oversight Board (PCAOB), 103
publicity, 192–193
public offerings, 126
public relations (PR), 192, 193
public speaking, 66–67. see also business communication

pull strategy, 194, 251
pure competition, 18
pure goods, 154
pure services, 154
push strategy, 194
push technologies, 227

quality level, 157
quality of life, 4
quotas, 37

race, bias and, 62
radio frequency identification
    (RFID), 235, 246
ratio analysis, 104
raw materials, 156
rebates, 115, 191
recession, 7, 23
recovery, 23
recruitment, human resources and,
    214–215
Relationship Era, 5
reserve requirement, 27
resources
    allocation of, 16
    as factor of production, 5
resumes, online, 59
retailers, 171–175
    defined, 171
    nonstore retailers, 174
    online pricing mistakes, 178
    retail store categories, 173
    wholesalers vs., 170–171
retained earnings, 119
retirement
    for CEOs, 46
    rates, 11–12
    saving for, 117
return on assets ratio, 111
return on equity ratio, 111
revenue, 100–101
revolving credit agreement,
    115–116
rights to residual claims on
    assets, 124
robots, 245, 246

salaries, 84, 220
sales promotion, 189
samples, 191
Sarbanes-Oxley Act, 47, 50–51, 102
secondary data, 147
secondary security markets,
    126–129
secured, 125
secure socket layer (SSL)
    protocol, 230
Securities Act of 1933, 129
Securities and Exchange
    Commission (SEC),
    97–98, 130
Securities Exchange Act of 1934,
    129, 130

securities markets, 122–135
    analysis of, 134
    basic types of securities, 123–126
    bond stock certificate
        example, 125
    common stock certificate
        example, 123
    exchange traded funds (ETF), 134
    mutual funds and, 133–134
    NYSE vs. NASDAQ, 128
    personal investing and, 130–133
    price-earnings ratio, 135
    primary and secondary markets,
        126–129
    regulation of, 129–130
    stock quote example, 135
    stock symbols, 130, 135
    tracking, 134–135
selective distribution, 172
self-regulatory organizations
    (SROs), 130–131
serial bonds, 125
services, 153–154
    operations management and, 239
    pure, 154
service utility, 170
sexual harassment, 223
Shanghai Stock Exchange, 128
Sherman Antitrust Act of 1890, 19
shopping products, 155
short-term financing, 114–115
sinking funds, 125
Six Sigma, 249–250
skimming pricing, 179
slang, 61–62
slippage rates, 115
Small Business Administration
    (SBA), 89, 92
Small Business Development
    Centers (SBDCs), 90
small businesses, 82–93
    economy and, 92–93
    entrepreneur profile and, 85–86
    funding for, 91–92
    launching of, 83–84, 89–91
    opportunities of and threats to,
        87–89
social audit, 54
social environment, 10
socialism, 21
social responsibility, 47–48. see
    also ethics
    globalization and, 53
    marketing and, 148–150
    monitoring, 54
    spectrum of, 48, 52
    stakeholder approach and, 48–53
sociocultural differences, 35
software, 225–226, 235
sole proprietorships, 69–71
South Korea, 53
spam, 232
span of control, 206

specialty products, 155–156
speed-to-market, 9
sponsorships, 189
spontaneous financing, 114–115
spyware, 232
staff managers, 207
stakeholders, 48
Standard and Poorís 500 (S&P
    500), 135
standard of living, 4
statement of cash flows, 101
statement of retained earnings,
    102
stockholders, 74, 95, 102
stock indexes, 134–135
store brands, 161
store retailers, 172
strategic alliances, 35
strategic goals, 204–205
strategic planning, 202
strategies, 205
structured interviews, 215–216
supply, 20
supply chain, 175, 176
supply chain management (SCM),
    175, 245
supply curve, 20
survey research, 148
sustainable development, 51
SWOT (strengths, weaknesses,
    opportunities, threats)
    analysis, 204, 205
system software, 225–226

tactical planning, 202
Taiwan, 53
target markets, 141, 142
tariffs, 37
taxes. see business formation
T-bills, 113
team selling, 194
technical skills, 198
technology. see also information
    technology; Internet
    computer-based training, 218
    human resources and, 212
    marketing and, 146
    promotion and, 183
    technological environment, 9–10
telecommuting, 221, 222
telemarketing, 174
telephone use, 61
termination, of employees, 222
terrorism, 13
Theory X/Theory Y, 200
time utility, 137, 170
time value of money, 117
Title VII (Civil Rights Act of 1964),
    223
Tokyo Stock Exchange, 127–128, 135
tone of voice, 58, 63
top management, 198
total quality management (TQM),
    249–250

trade credit, 114–115
trade deficit, 31
trade promotion, 192
trade surplus, 31
trading blocs, 40
truck jobbers, 171

underwriting, 126
unemployment rate, 23
universal ethical standards, 44
unsought products, 156
U.S. Food and Drug Administration, 49
utility, 137–138

value, 3, 8, 141–142
value investing, 132

value stream maps, 251
vending, 175
venture capital firms, 91–92
vertical analysis, 104
vertical integration, 246
vertical market software, 226
vertical mergers, 77
videoconferencing, 61
viral marketing, 229, 230
viruses, 232
visual aids, 66
voice mail, 61
Voluntary Export Restraints, 37

wages, 220
wealth, 4
wheel of retailing, 174
whistleblowers, 47

wholesalers
    defined, 171
    types of, 171
Wilshire 5000, 135
women
    economics and, 17
    as franchisees, 79
    pay gap between sexes, 221
    in workplace, 212
word choice, 60–63
World Bank, 38–41
world economy. see globalization
World Trade Organization (WTO), 11, 38–41, 39
World Wide Web, 9–10. see also Internet
written communication, for business, 63–64

# BUSN
What if...?

# What happened?

**"A billion here and a billion there, and pretty soon you're talking real money."**
*–U.S. Senator Everett Dirksen*

In September 2008 the U.S. economy plunged into the worst fiscal crisis since the Great Depression. Huge, venerable financial institutions faced collapse, spurring unprecedented bailouts by the Federal Reserve. On September 29, October 9, and October 15, the stock market plummeted—each day, the Dow Jones Industrial average dropped about 7%, posting three of its all-time largest losses. Economic turmoil in the United States spread quickly around the world, causing sequential economic shocks from Europe to Far East Asia.

# How did this happen?

**"If it sounds too good to be true, it probably is."**
*–old adage*

Through the last half of the 1990s, America enjoyed a period of unprecedented growth and prosperity. Unemployment was low, productivity was high, inflation was low, and the real standard of living for the average American rose significantly. The American GDP, a key measure of economic performance, increased $2,382 billion, growing from $7,325 billion to $9,708 billion, a jump of nearly 33% in just five years. But the scene changed for the worse when the dot com bubble burst in 2000, followed by the 9/11 terrorist attacks in 2001. As the stock market dropped and unemployment rose, economic experts feared that the country was hovering on the brink of a full-blown recession.

In an effort to avert recession by increasing the money supply and encouraging investment, the Federal Reserve decreased interest rates from 6.5% in mid-2000 to 1.25% by the end of 2002. As a result, the economy was awash with money, but opportunities to invest yielded paltry returns. This is when *subprime mortgage loans* came into play. Most experts define subprime mortgages as loans to borrowers with low credit scores, high debt-to-income ratios, or other signs of a reduced ability to repay the money they borrow.

These subprime mortgage loans were attractive to borrowers and lenders alike. Hundreds of thousands of people could afford homes for the first time ever. Banks were all too willing to give them mortgage loans, sometimes with little or no documentation (such as proof of income), and sometimes with little or no money down. As demand skyrocketed, home prices continued to rise year after year. Borrowers took on adjustable rate loans assuming that when their loans adjusted up—usually sharply up—they could simply refinance their now more valuable homes for a new low starter rate, and maybe even pull out some equity to buy expensive new toys.

Subprime loans were attractive to lenders because they provided a higher return than many other investments, and—given the growth in housing prices—they seemed relatively low risk. Banks and investment houses invented a range of stunningly complex financial instruments to slice up and resell the mortgages as specialized securities. Hedge funds swapped the new securities, falsely confident that they were virtually risk-free. With a lack of regulation—or any sort of government oversight—financial institutions did not maintain reserves in case those mortgage-backed funds lost value.

And they did indeed lose value. In 2006 housing prices peaked and in the months that followed, prices began falling precipitously. Increasing numbers of subprime borrowers found themselves "upside down"—and once they owed their lenders more than the value of their homes, they were unable to refinance to lower their payments. Foreclosure rates climbed at an increasing pace. RealtyTrac, a

## Federal Funds Rate

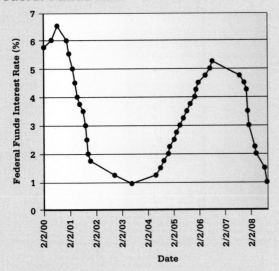

Source: Based on data from Historical Changes of the Target Federal Funds and Discount Rates, 1971 to present, Federal Reserve Bank of New York Website, http://www.newyorkfed.org/markets/statistics/dlyrates/fedrate.html, accessed November 6, 2008.

## Home Price Index (Base Period: January 2000)

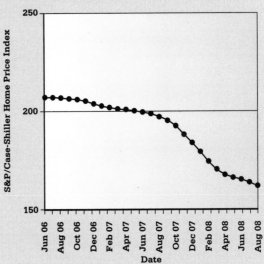

Source: Based on data from S&P/Case-Shiller Home Price Indices, August 2008 data, Standard & Poor's Website, http://www2.standardandpoors.com/portal/site/sp/en/us/page.topic/indices_csmahp/0,0,0,0,0,0,0,0,0,1,1,0,0,0,0,0.html, accessed November 6, 2008.

Visit **4ltrpress.cengage.com/busn** for additional study tools!

leading online marketplace for foreclosure properties, reported that foreclosure rates through August 2008 were 50% higher than the same period in 2007, and they anticipate that rates will continue to climb throughout 2008 and beyond.

As mortgage values dropped, financial institutions began to feel the pressure—especially firms such as Bear Stearns that specialized in trading mortgage backed securities, and firms such as Washington Mutual that focused on selling subprime mortgages. When financial institutions actually began to face collapse, a wave of fear washed over the entire banking industry. Banks became unwilling to lend money to each other or to clients, which meant that funds were not available for businesses to finance either day-to-day operations or longer term growth. Company after company—from General Motors to Yahoo!, American Express, and countless other small employers—began to announce layoffs. The October 2008 unemployment rate hit 6.5%, a 14-year high, and the GDP for the third quarter of 2008 dropped by 0.3%, with greater losses expected in the months to come. Experts anticipate that the negative impact will continue to ripple throughout the economy, despite a $700 billion federal government bailout package.

## Unemployment Rate

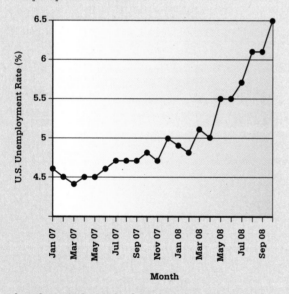

Source: Based on data from Labor Force Statistics from the Current Population Survey, Bureau of Labor Statistics Website, http://data.bls.gov/PDQ/servlet/SurveyOutputServlet?data_tool=latest_numbers&series_id=LNS14000000, accessed November 6, 2008.

## What have we learned?

**"We are all faced with a series of great opportunities brilliantly disguised as impossible situations."**
*–Charles R. Swindoll*

The key drivers of the 2008 credit crisis suggest the need for some fundamental changes by all sectors of our nation's economy—changes that can lay the foundation for long-term prosperity. In particular, we've learned that we need:

- **Greater Federal Fiscal Responsibility:** Deficit spending can be a powerful, positive force during wars and economic crises. But the federal debt now exceeds $10 trillion. Reduced deficit spending could help free up financial capital for the private sector, decrease American dependence on foreign nations, and lessen the burden on future generations.

- **More Conservative Money Supply Management:** The Federal Reserve must have the flexibility to increase the money supply and cut interest rates when the economy faces a severe downturn. But long-term reliance on cheap money can encourage risky speculation that leaves the economy vulnerable to financial crises.

- **Wise Regulation of Financial Markets:** From credit cards to financial markets, deregulation has been disastrous. A new, more effective regulatory approach would allow the economy to thrive long-term without reckless risk-taking.

- **More Emphasis on Personal Responsibility:** Over the last two decades many American families incurred a mountain of debt, and were unprepared for financial setbacks. The recent crisis may spur households to re-set their priorities and emphasize savings rather than consumption.

- **Investment in the Future:** Targeted government spending could help upgrade our nation's crumbling infrastructure, educate our labor force, clean up and preserve our environment, and develop renewable energy sources. Focusing on these priorities would lay solid groundwork for a more competitive national economy.

Despite recent turmoil, the American economy has historically proven to be flexible and resilient; phenomenal opportunities may arise from even the most adverse economic climate, giving us all reason for measured optimism.

## Sources

*Subprime Collapse to Global Financial Meltdown: Timeline* by Chris Dolmetsch, *Bloomberg* Website, October 13, 2008, http://www.bloomberg.com/apps/news?pid=20601208&sid=aleqkSjAAw10, accessed November 6, 2008.

*There Is a Silver Lining* by Fareed Zakaria, *Newsweek* Website, October 20, 2008, http://www.newsweek.com/id/163449/output/print, accessed November 6, 2008.

*GDP Declines 0.3 Percent in Third Quarter,* "Advance" Estimate of GDP, Bureau of Economic Analysis Website, October 30, 2008, http://www.bea.gov/newsreleases/national/gdp/gdphighlights.pdf, accessed November 6, 2008.

*Credit Crisis—The Essentials, The New York Times* Website, http://topics.nytimes.com/top/reference/timestopics/subjects/c/credit_crisis/index.html, accessed November 6, 2008.

*Table 10.1—Gross Domestic Product and Deflators Used in the Historical Tables: 1940-2009,* White House Office of Management and Budget Website, http://www.whitehouse.gov/omb/budget/fy2005/hist.html, accessed November 6, 2008.

*What Is Subprime Lending?* Monetary Trends, Federal Reserve Bank of St. Louis Website, June 2007, http://research.stlouisfed.org/publications/mt/20070601/cover.pdf, accessed November 6, 2008.

*Subprime woes could spill over into other sectors* by John Waggoner, *USAToday* Website, March 15, 2007, http://www.usatoday.com/money/perfi/columnist/waggon/2007-03-15-subprime-woes_N.htm, accessed November 6, 2007.

*RealtyTrac's James J. Saccacio to Discuss Foreclosure Crisis Fallout at AFSA State Government Affairs Forum* by RealtyTrac staff, RealtyTrac Website, October 1, 2008, http://www.realtytrac.com/ContentManagement/pressrelease.aspx?ChannelID=9&ItemID=5284&accnt=64847, accessed November 6, 2008.

*Greatest DJIA % Losses of All Time,* Md Leasing Corp. Website, October 28, 2008, http://www.mdleasing.com/djia-losses.htm, accessed November 6, 2008.

## LO1

**profit**
The money that a business earns in sales (or revenue), minus expenses, such as the cost of goods, and the cost of salaries. Revenue – Expenses = Profit (or Loss)

**loss**
When a business incurs expenses that are greater than revenue.

**entrepreneurs**
People who risk their time, money, and other resources to start and manage businesses.

**standard of living**
The quality and quantity of goods and services available to a population.

**quality of life**
The overall sense of well being experienced by either an individual or a group.

© AP IMAGES

## LO3

**nonprofits**
Business-*like* establishments that employ people and produce goods and services with the fundamental goal of contributing to the community rather than generating financial gain.

## LO4

**factors of production**
Four fundamental elements—natural resources, capital, human resources, and entrepreneurship—that businesses need to achieve their objectives. Some combination of these factors is crucial for an economic system to create wealth.

### LO1 Define business and discuss the role of business in the economy.

A **business** is any activity that provides goods and services in an effort to earn a profit. *Profit* is the money that a business earns in sales, minus expenses such as the cost of goods, and the cost of salaries. Profit potential provides a powerful incentive for people to start their own businesses, or to become *entrepreneurs*. Successful businesses create wealth, which increases the standard of living for virtually all members of a society.

### LO2 Explain the evolution of modern business.

Business historians typically divide the history of American business into five distinct eras, which overlap during the periods of transition.

- *Industrial Revolution:* From the mid-1700s to the mid-1800s, technology fueled a period of rapid industrialization. Factories sprang up in cities, leading to mass production and specialization of labor.
- *Entrepreneurship Era:* During the second half of the 1800s, large-scale entrepreneurs emerged, building business empires that created enormous wealth, but often at the expense of workers and consumers.
- *Production Era:* In the early 1900s, major businesses focused on further refining the production process, creating huge efficiencies. The assembly line, introduced in 1913, boosted productivity and lowered costs.
- *Marketing Era:* After WWII, consumers began to gain power. As goods and services flooded the market, the marketing concept emerged: a consumer-first orientation as a guide to business decision-making.
- *Relationship Era:* With the technology boom in the 1990s, businesses have begun to look beyond the immediate transaction, aiming to build a competitive edge through long-term customer relationships.

### LO3 Discuss the role of nonprofit organizations in the economy.

Nonprofit organizations often work hand-in-hand with business to improve the quality of life in our society. Nonprofits are business-like establishments that contribute to economic stability and growth. Similar to businesses, nonprofits generate revenue and incur expenses. Their goal is to use any revenue above and beyond expenses to advance the goals of the organization, rather than to make money for its owners. Some nonprofits—such as museums, schools, and theaters—can act as economic magnets for communities, attracting additional investment.

### The Relationship Between Nonprofits and Businesses

**Advance Goals of Organization**

**Generate Revenue Incur Expenses Provide Employment**

**Create Profit for Owners**

**business environment**
The setting in which business operates. The five key components are economic environment, competitive environment, technological environment, social environment, and global environment.

**value**
The relationship between the price of a good or a service and the benefits that it offers its customers.

**speed-to-market**
The rate at which a new product moves from conception to commercialization.

**business technology**
Any tools—especially computers, telecommunications, and other digital products—that businesses can use to become more efficient and effective.

**World Wide Web**
The service that allows computer users to easily access and share information on the Internet in the form of text, graphics, video, and animation.

**e-commerce**
Business transactions conducted online, typically via the Internet.

**demographics**
The measurable characteristics of a population. Demographic factors include population size and density, and specific traits such as age, gender, and race.

**free trade**
An international economic and political movement designed to help goods and services flow more freely across international boundaries.

**General Agreement on Tariffs and Trade (GATT)**
An international trade agreement that has taken bold steps to lower tariffs and promote free trade worldwide.

## L04 Outline the core factors of production and how they impact the economy.

The four factors of production are the fundamental resources that both businesses and nonprofits use to achieve their objectives.

- *Natural resources:* All inputs that offer value in their natural state, such as land, fresh water, wind, and mineral deposits. The value of natural resources tends to rise with high demand, low supply, or both.
- *Capital:* The manmade resources that an organization needs to produce goods or services. The elements of capital include machines, tools, buildings, and technology.
- *Human resources:* The physical, intellectual, and creative contributions of everyone who works within an economy. Education and motivation have become increasingly important as technology replaces manual labor jobs.
- *Entrepreneurship:* Entrepreneurs take the risk of launching and operating their own businesses. Entrepreneurial enterprises can create a tidal wave of opportunity by harnessing the other factors of production.

## L05 Describe today's business environment and discuss each key dimension.

Accelerating change marks every dimension of today's business environment.

- *Economic environment:* The U.S. economy is a global powerhouse, largely because the government actively supports free enterprise and fair competition.
- *Competitive environment:* As global competition intensifies, leading-edge companies have focused on long-term customer satisfaction as never before.
- *Technological environment:* The recent technology boom has transformed business, establishing new industries and burying others.
- *Social environment:* The U.S. population continues to diversify. Consumers are gaining power, and society has higher standards for business behavior.
- *Global environment:* The U.S. economy works within the context of the global environment. A key factor is rapid economic growth in China and India.

### The Business Environment

## L06 Explain how current business trends might impact your career choices.

With automation picking up speed, many traditional career choices have become dead ends. But some things—including empathy, creativity, change management, and great communication—can't be digitized. Having these skills can provide you with personal and financial opportunity.

## LO1

**economy**
A financial and social system of how resources flow through society, from production, to distribution, to consumption.

**economics**
The study of the choices that people, companies, and governments make in allocating society's resources.

**macroeconomics**
The study of a country's overall economic issues, such as the employment rate, the gross domestic product, and taxation policies.

**microeconomics**
The study of smaller economic units such as individual consumers, families, and individual businesses.

**economic system**
A structure for allocating limited resources.

## LO2

**capitalism**
An economic system—also known as the private enterprise or free market system—based on private ownership, economic freedom, and fair competition.

**pure competition**
A market structure with many competitors selling virtually identical products. Barriers to entry are quite low.

**monopolistic competition**
A market structure with many competitors selling differentiated products. Barriers to entry are low.

**oligopoly**
A market structure with only a handful of competitors selling products that are either similar or different. Barriers to entry are typically high.

**monopoly**
A market structure with one producer completely dominating the industry, leaving no room for any significant competitors. Barriers to entry tend to be virtually insurmountable.

**natural monopoly**
A market structure with one company as the supplier of a product because the nature of that product makes a single supplier more efficient than multiple, competing ones. Most natural monopolies are government sanctioned and regulated.

**supply**
The quantity of products that producers are willing to offer for sale at different market prices.

**supply curve**
The graphed relationship between price and quantity from a supplier standpoint.

**demand**
The quantity of products that consumers are willing to buy at different market prices.

**demand curve**
The graphed relationship between price and quantity from a customer demand standpoint.

### LO1 Define economics and discuss the impact of economics on business

Economics—the study of how people, companies, and governments allocate resources—offers vital insights regarding the forces that impact every business on a daily basis. Understanding economics helps businesspeople make better decisions, which can lead to greater profitability both short-term and long-term. Macroeconomics is the study of broad economic trends. Microeconomics focuses on the choices made by smaller economic units such as individual consumers, families, and businesses.

### LO2 Explain and evaluate the free market system and supply and demand

Capitalism, also known as the free market system, is based on private ownership, economic freedom, and fair competition. In a capitalist economy, individuals, businesses, or nonprofit organizations privately own the vast majority of enterprises. As businesses compete against each other, quality goes up, prices remain reasonable, and choices abound, raising the overall standard of living.

The interplay between the forces of supply and demand determines the selection of products and prices available in a free market economy. Supply refers to the quantity of products that producers are willing to offer for sale at different market prices at a specific time. Demand refers to the quantity of products that consumers are willing to buy at different market prices at a specific time. According to economic theory, markets will naturally move toward the point at which supply and demand are equal: the equilibrium point.

**Equilibrium**

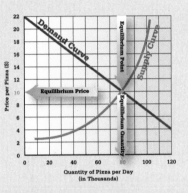

### LO3 Explain and evaluate planned market systems

In planned economies, the government—rather than individual choice—plays a pivotal role in controlling the economy. The two main types of planned economies are socialism and communism. While planned economies aim to create more equity among their citizens, they tend to be more prone to corruption and less effective at generating wealth than market-based economies.

### LO4 Describe the trend toward mixed market systems

Most of today's nations have mixed economies, falling somewhere along a spectrum that ranges from pure planned at one extreme to pure market at the other. Over the past 30 years, most major economies around the world have moved toward the market end of the spectrum.

**equilibrium price**
The price associated with the point at which the quantity demanded of a product equals the quantity supplied.

## LO3

**socialism**
An economic system based on the principle that the government should own and operate key enterprises that directly affect public welfare.

**communism**
An economic and political system that calls for public ownership of virtually all enterprises, under the direction of a strong central government.

## LO4

**mixed economies**
Economies that embody elements of both planned and market-based economic systems.

**privatization**
The process of converting government-owned businesses to private ownership.

## LO5

**gross domestic product (GDP)**
The total value of all final goods and services produced within a nation's physical boundaries over a given period of time.

**unemployment rate**
The percentage of people in the labor force over age 16 who do not have jobs and are actively seeking employment.

**business cycle**
The periodic contraction and expansion that occurs over time in virtually every economy.

**contraction**
A period of economic downturn, marked by rising unemployment and falling business production.

**recession**
An economic downturn marked by a decrease in the GDP for two consecutive quarters.

**depression**
An especially deep and long-lasting recession.

**recovery**
A period of rising economic growth and employment, following a contraction.

**expansion**
A period of robust economic growth and high employment.

**inflation**
A period of rising average prices across the economy.

**hyperinflation**
An average monthly inflation rate of more than 50%.

**disinflation**
A period of slowing average price increases across the economy.

**deflation**
A period of falling average prices across the economy.

**consumer price index (CPI)**
A measure of inflation that evaluates the change in the weighted-average price of goods and services that the average consumer buys each month.

**producer price index (PPI)**
A measure of inflation that evaluates the change over time in the weighted-average wholesale prices.

**productivity**
The basic relationship between the production of goods and services (output) and the resources needed to produce them (input), calculated via the following equation: output/input = productivity.

## LO6

**fiscal policy**
Government efforts to influence the economy through taxation and spending.

**budget surplus**
Overage that occurs when revenue is higher than expenses over a given period of time.

**budget deficit**
Shortfall that occurs when expenses are higher than revenue over a given period of time.

## LO5 Discuss key terms and tools to evaluate economic performance

Since economic systems are so complex, no one measure captures all the dimensions of economic performance. But each measure yields insight on overall economic health.

- *Gross Domestic Product (GDP):* The total value of all goods and services produced within a nation's physical boundaries over a given period of time.
- *Unemployment Rate:* The percentage of the labor force who don't have jobs and are actively seeking employment.
- *Business Cycle:* The periodic expansion and contraction that occur over time in virtually every economy.
- *Inflation Rate:* The rate at which prices are rising across the economy. The government tracks the consumer price index and the producer price index.
- *Productivity:* The relationship between the goods and services that an economy produces and the inputs needed to produce them.

### Business Cycle

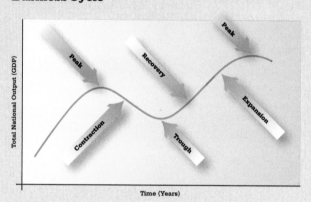

## LO6 Analyze the impact of fiscal and monetary policy on the economy

Fiscal policy and monetary policy refer to efforts to shape the health of the economy. Fiscal policy involves government taxation and spending decisions designed to encourage growth and boost employment. Monetary policy refers to decisions by the Federal Reserve that influence the size of the money supply and the level of interest rates. Effective fiscal and monetary policies can play a powerful role in sustaining economic expansions and mitigating economic contractions.

**federal debt**
The sum of all the money that the federal government has borrowed over the years and not yet repaid.

**monetary policy**
Federal Reserve decisions that shape the economy by influencing interest rates and the supply of money.

**money supply**
The total amount of money within the overall economy.

**M1 money supply**
Includes currency plus checking accounts and travelers checks.

**M2 money supply**
Includes all of M1 money supply plus most savings accounts, money market accounts, and certificates of deposit.

**open market operations**
The Federal Reserve function of buying and selling government securities, which include treasury bonds, notes, and bills.

**discount rate**
The rate of interest that the Federal Reserve charges when it loans funds to banks.

**reserve requirement**
A rule set by the Fed, which specifies the minimum amount of reserves (or funds) a bank must hold, expressed as a percentage of the bank's deposits.

Visit **4ltrpress.cengage.com/busn**
for additional study tools!

## LO2

**opportunity cost**
The cost of giving up the second-best choice when making a decision.

**absolute advantage**
The benefit a country has in a given industry when it can produce more of a product than other nations using the same amount of resources.

**comparative advantage**
The benefit a country has in a given industry if it can make products at a lower opportunity cost than other countries.

## LO3

**balance of trade**
A basic measure of the difference in value between a nation's exports and imports, including both goods and services.

**trade surplus**
Overage that occurs when the total value of a nation's exports is higher than the total value of its imports.

**trade deficit**
Shortfall that occurs when the total value of a nation's imports is higher than the total value of its exports.

**balance of payments**
A measure of the total flow of money into or out of a country.

**balance of payments surplus**
Overage that occurs when more money flows into a nation than out of that nation.

**balance of payments deficit**
Shortfall that occurs when more money flows out of a nation than into that nation.

**exchange rates**
A measurement of the value of one nation's currency relative to the currency of other nations.

**countertrade**
International trade that involves the barter of products for products rather than for currency.

## LO4

**foreign outsourcing (also contract manufacturing)**
Contracting with foreign suppliers to produce products, usually at a fraction of the cost of domestic production.

**importing**
Buying products domestically that have been produced or grown in foreign nations.

**exporting**
Selling products in foreign nations that have been produced or grown domestically.

**foreign licensing**
Authority granted by a domestic firm to a foreign firm for the rights to produce and market its product or to use its trademark/patent rights in a defined geographical area.

**foreign franchising**
A specialized type of foreign licensing in which a firm expands by offering businesses in other countries the right to produce and market its products according to specific operating requirements.

### LO1 Discuss business opportunities in the world economy

Advancing technology and falling trade barriers have created unprecedented international business opportunities. The most populous developing countries, such as China, India, and Turkey, offer the most potential due to both their size and their high economic growth rates.

### LO2 Explain the key reasons for international trade

The benefits of international trade for individual firms include access to factors of production, reduced risk, and an inflow of new ideas from foreign markets. Overall industries tend to succeed on a global basis in countries that enjoy either an absolute or a comparative competitive advantage.

### LO3 Describe the tools for measuring international trade

Measuring the impact of international trade on individual nations requires a clear understanding of balance of trade, balance of payments, and exchange rates.

- *Balance of Trade:* A basic measure of the difference between a nation's exports and imports.
- *Balance of Payments:* A measure of the total flow of money into or out of a country, including the balance of trade, plus other financial flows such as foreign loans, foreign aid, and foreign investments.
- *Exchange Rates:* A measure of the value of one nation's currency relative to the currency of other nations. The exchange rate has a powerful influence on how global trade impacts both individual nations and their trading partners.

### LO4 Analyze strategies for reaching global markets

Firms can enter global markets by developing foreign suppliers, foreign customers, or both. Two strategies for acquiring foreign suppliers are outsourcing and importing. Key strategies for developing foreign markets include exporting, licensing, franchising, and direct investment. Exporting is relatively low cost and low risk, but it offers little control over how the business unfolds. Direct investment, at the other end of the spectrum, tends to be high cost and high risk, but it offers more control and higher potential profits.

**Market Development Options**

LOWER Risk — HIGHER Risk

Exporting  Licensing  Franchising  Direct Investment

LESS Control — MORE Control

### LO5 Discuss barriers to international trade and strategies to surmount them

Most barriers to trade fall into the following categories: sociocultural differences, economic differences, and legal/political differences. Each country has a different mix of barriers. Often countries with the highest barriers have the least competition, which can be a real opportunity for the first international firms to break through. The best way to surmount trade barriers is to cultivate a deep understanding of a country before beginning business. And since conditions change rapidly in many nations, learning and responding is a continual process.

**direct investment (or foreign direct investment)**
When firms either acquire foreign firms or develop new facilities from the ground up in foreign countries.

**joint ventures**
When two or more companies join forces—sharing resources, risks, and profits, but not actually merging companies—to pursue specific opportunities.

**partnership**
A formal, typically long-term agreement between two or more firms to jointly pursue a specific opportunity without actually merging their businesses.

**strategic alliance**
An agreement between two or more firms to jointly pursue a specific opportunity without actually merging their businesses. Strategic alliances typically involve less formal, less encompassing agreements than partnerships.

## LO5

**sociocultural differences**
Differences among cultures in language, attitudes, and values.

**infrastructure**
A country's physical facilities that support economic activity.

**protectionism**
National policies designed to restrict international trade, usually with the goal of protecting domestic businesses.

**tariffs**
Taxes levied against imports.

**quotas**
Limitations on the amount of specific products that may be imported from certain countries during a given time period.

**voluntary export restraints (VERs)**
Limitations on the amount of specific products that one nation will export to another nation.

**embargo**
A complete ban on international trade of a certain item, or a total halt in trade with a particular nation.

## LO6

**free trade**
The unrestricted movement of goods and services across international borders.

**GATT**
General Agreement on Tariffs and Trade. An international trade treaty designed to encourage worldwide trade among its members.

**World Trade Organization (WTO)**
A permanent global institution to promote international trade and to settle international trade disputes.

**World Bank**
An international cooperative of 184 member countries, working together to reduce poverty in the developing world.

## LO6 Describe the free trade movement and discuss key benefits and criticisms

Over the past two decades, the emergence of regional trading blocks, common markets, and international trade agreements has moved the world economy much closer to complete free trade. Key players include:
- *GATT and the WTO*
- *The World Bank*
- *The International Monetary Fund (IMF)*
- *The North American Free Trade Agreement (NAFTA)*
- *The European Union (EU)*

The free trade movement has raised the global standard of living, lowered prices, and expanded choices for millions of people, but critics are troubled by the growing economic gap between the haves and the have-nots, worker abuse, large-scale pollution, and cultural homogenization.

### European Union 2007

**International Monetary Fund (IMF)**
An international organization of 184 member nations that promotes international economic cooperation and stable growth.

**trading bloc**
Group of countries that has reduced or even eliminated tariffs, allowing for the free flow of goods among the member nations.

**common market**
Group of countries that has eliminated tariffs and harmonized trading rules to facilitate the free flow of goods among the member nations.

**NAFTA**
North American Free Trade Agreement. The treaty among the United States, Mexico, and Canada that eliminated trade barriers and investment restrictions over a 15-year period starting in 1994.

**European Union (EU)**
The world's largest common market, composed of 27 European nations.

## LO1

**ethics**
A set of beliefs about right and wrong, good and bad.

**universal ethical standards**
Ethical norms that apply to all people across a broad spectrum of situations.

## LO2

**business ethics**
The application of right and wrong, good and bad in a business setting.

**ethical dilemma**
A decision that involves a conflict of values; every potential course of action has some significant negative consequences.

## LO3

**code of ethics**
A formal, written document that defines the ethical standards of an organization and gives employees the information they need to make ethical decisions across a range of situations.

**whistleblowers**
Employees who report their employer's illegal or unethical behavior to either the authorities or the media.

### LO1 Define ethics and explain the concept of universal ethical standards

Ethics is a set of beliefs about right and wrong, good and bad. Who you are as a human being, your family, and your culture all play a role in shaping your ethical standards. The laws of each country usually set minimum ethical standards, but truly ethical standards typically reach beyond minimum legal requirements. Despite some significant cultural and legal differences, people around the globe tend to agree on core values, which can serve as a starting point for universal ethical standards across a wide range of situations: trustworthiness, respect, responsibility, fairness, caring, and citizenship.

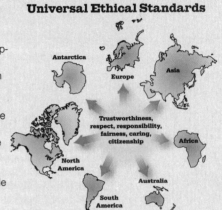

**Universal Ethical Standards**

### LO2 Describe business ethics and ethical dilemmas

Business ethics is the application of right and wrong, good and bad in a business setting. Ethical dilemmas arise when you face business decisions that throw your values into conflict. These are decisions that force you to choose among less than ideal options because whatever choice you make will have some significant negative consequences.

**Ethical Dilemma**

### LO3 Discuss how ethics relates to both the individual and the organization

Ethical choices begin with ethical individuals. To help people make good choices, experts have developed frameworks for reaching ethical decisions. While the specifics vary, the core principles of most decision guides are similar:

- Do you fully understand the problem and how various solutions would affect each party?
- Are the alternatives legal and fair?
- Could you defend your choice to the general public?
- Could you defend it to people who matter to you?

While each person is responsible for his or her own actions, the organization can also have a dramatic influence on the conduct of individual employees. An ethical culture—which includes ethical leadership from top executives, and accountability at every level of the organization—has an outsized impact on individual conduct. But formal ethics programs also play a crucial role. A written code of ethics—a document that lays out the values and priorities of the organization—is the cornerstone of a formal ethics program. Other key elements include ethics training and a clear enforcement policy for ethical violations.

## LO4

**social responsibility**
The obligation of a business to contribute to society.

**stakeholders**
Any groups that have a stake—or a personal interest—in the performance and actions of an organization.

**consumerism**
A social movement that focuses on four key consumer rights: (1) the right to be safe, (2) the right to be informed, (3) the right to choose, and (4) the right to be heard.

**planned obsolescence**
The strategy of deliberately designing products to fail in order to shorten the time between purchases.

**Sarbanes-Oxley Act**
Federal legislation passed in 2002 that sets higher ethical standards for public corporations and accounting firms.

**corporate philanthropy**
All business donations to nonprofit groups, including money, products, and employee time.

**cause-related marketing**
Marketing partnerships between businesses and nonprofit organizations, designed to spike sales for the company and raise money for the nonprofit.

**corporate responsibility**
Business contributions to the community through the actions of the business itself rather than donations of money and time.

**sustainable development**
Doing business to meet the needs of the current generation, without harming the ability of future generations to meet their needs.

**green marketing**
Developing and promoting environmentally sound products and practices to gain a competitive edge.

## LO6

**social audit**
A systematic evaluation of how well a firm is meeting its ethics and social responsibility goals.

## LO4 Define social responsibility and examine the impact on stakeholder groups

Social responsibility is the obligation of a business to contribute to society. Enlightened companies carefully consider the priorities of all stakeholders—groups who have an interest in their actions and performance—as they make key decisions. Core stakeholder groups for most businesses are listed below, along with key obligations.

- *Employees:* Treat employees with dignity, respect, and fairness. Ensure that hard work and talent pay-off. Help workers balance emerging work-life priorities.
- *Customers:* Provide quality products at a fair price. Ensure that customers are safe and informed. Support consumer choice and consumer dialogue.
- *Investors:* Create an on-going stream of profits. Manage investor dollars according to the highest legal and ethical standards. Support full disclosure.
- *Community:* Support non-profit groups that improve the community and fit with your company. Minimize the environmental impact of your business.

### The Spectrum of Social Responsibility

**LESS** Responsible — **No Contribution** — Some businesses do not recognize an obligation to society and do only what's legally required. — **Responsive Contributions** — Some businesses choose to respond on a case-by-case basis to market requests for contributions. — **Proactive Contributions** — Some businesses choose to integrate social responsibility into their strategic plans, contributing as part of their business goals. — **MORE** Responsible

## LO5 Explain the role of social responsibility in the global arena

Social responsibility becomes more complex in the global arena due largely to differences in the legal and cultural environments. Bribery and corruption are key issues, along with concern for human rights and environmental standards.

### Social Responsibility Issues in the Global Arena

Cultural Differences • Bribery • Legal Differences • Corruption • Environmental Standards • Human Rights

## LO6 Describe how companies evaluate their efforts to be socially responsible

Many companies—even some entire industries—monitor themselves. The process typically involves establishing objectives for ethics and social responsibility and then measuring achievement of those objectives on a systematic, periodic basis. Other groups play watchdog roles as well. Key players include activist customers, investors, unions, environmentalists, and community groups.

**WATCHDOG GROUPS**
- Activist Customers
- Investors
- Unions
- Environmentalists
- Community Groups

## LO1

**communication**
The transmission of information between a sender and a recipient.

**noise**
Any interference that causes the message you send to be different from the message your audience understands.

**communication barriers**
Obstacles to effective communication, typically defined in terms of physical barriers, language barriers, body language barriers, cultural barriers, perceptual barriers, and organizational barriers.

**intercultural communication**
Communication among people with differing cultural backgrounds.

## LO2

**nonverbal communication**
Communication that does not use words. Common forms of nonverbal communication include gestures, posture, facial expressions, tone of voice, and eye contact.

**active listening**
Attentive listening that occurs when the listener focuses his or her complete attention on the speaker.

## LO3

**communication channels**
The various ways in which a message can be sent, ranging from one-on-one in-person meetings to Internet message boards.

### LO1 Explain the importance of excellent business communication

Effective communication happens when you transmit *relevant meaning* from the sender to the receiver. Skillful communicators save time and money, and develop deeper, more trusting relationships with their colleagues. Anything that interferes with the correct transmission of your message is a barrier to communication. Barriers can be physical, verbal, non-verbal, cultural, perceptual, or organizational. To communicate effectively, you should be able to identify and surmount any barriers that stand between you and your audience. The result? Greater long-term success in every aspect of business.

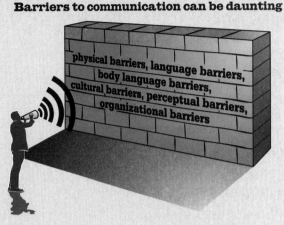

**Barriers to communication can be daunting**

physical barriers, language barriers, body language barriers, cultural barriers, perceptual barriers, organizational barriers

### LO2 Describe the key elements of nonverbal communication

The key elements of non-verbal communication include eye contact, tone-of-voice, facial expressions, gestures, and posture. Studies suggest that on average only 7% of meaning during face-to-face communication comes from the verbal content of the message, which magnifies the importance of every element of non-verbal communication. Active listening also plays an influential role. The starting point is empathy: a genuine attempt to understand and appreciate the speaker. You should signal your focus to the speaker through verbal cues such as "I understand your point," and non-verbal cues such as nods, eye contact, and leaning forward. The result will be better relationships, and better information for you.

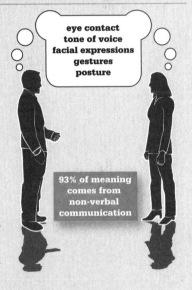

eye contact
tone of voice
facial expressions
gestures
posture

93% of meaning comes from non-verbal communication

### LO3 Compare, contrast, and choose effective communication channels

Communication channels differ significantly in terms of richness: the amount of information that they offer the audience. The spectrum ranges from written communication at the low end to face-to-face meetings at the high end. The best choice depends on your objective, your message, and your audience. To ensure that your communication achieves your goals, always consider the needs and expectations of your audience. If you tailor each message with the audience in mind, you'll give yourself a competitive edge in terms of the time, attention, and response of your audience.

**Communication Channels Have Different Levels of Richness**

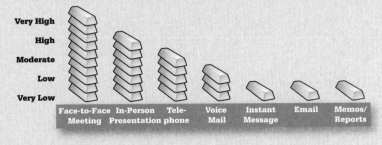

Very High / High / Moderate / Low / Very Low

Face-to-Face Meeting | In-Person Presentation | Telephone | Voice Mail | Instant Message | Email | Memos/Reports

## LO4

**bias**
A preconception about members of a particular group. Common forms of bias include gender bias, age bias, and race, ethnicity, or nationality bias.

**active voice**
Sentence construction in which the subject performs the action expressed by the verb (e.g., *My sister wrote the paper*). Active voice works better for most business communication.

**passive voice**
Sentence construction in which the subject does not do the action expressed by the verb; rather the subject is acted upon (e.g., *The paper was written by my sister*). Passive voice tends to be less effective for business communication.

**Always aim to be clear, direct, and concise. Use common words and straightforward sentence construction.**

## LO6

**dynamic delivery**
Vibrant, compelling presentation delivery style that grabs and holds the attention of the audience.

## LO4 Choose the right words for effective communication

The right words can make the difference between a message your audience absorbs, and a message your audience ignores. Keep these considerations in mind: analyze your audience, be concise, avoid slang, avoid bias, and use active voice.

## LO5 Write more effective business memos, letters, and e-mails

Here, too, you should begin with the needs of your audience; their anticipated response should drive the structure of your writing. Determine the "bottom line" of your communication, and be sure to deliver it upfront. Your message itself should have a natural tone, completely free of grammatical errors.

### Sample Emails: Same Message, Different Approach

**If the recipient will feel positive or neutral about your message...**

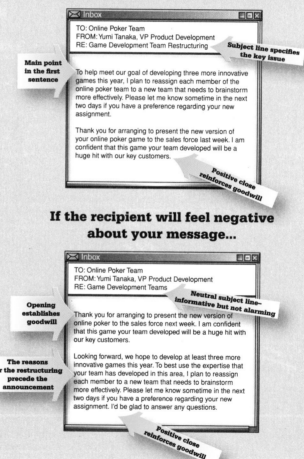

## LO6 Create and deliver successful verbal presentations

A great presentation begins with a hook that draws in your audience and engages their attention. The body of the presentation typically focuses on three key points, supported by credible information and persuasive arguments. The close summarizes the key points, and often refers back to the opening hook. Dynamic delivery is simply a matter of practice, with a focus on knowing your material.

Visit **4ltrpress.cengage.com/busn**
for additional study tools!

## LO1

**sole proprietorship**
A form of business ownership with a single owner who usually actively manages the company.

## LO2

**partnership**
A voluntary agreement under which two or more people act as co-owners of a business for profit.

**general partnership**
A partnership in which all partners can take an active role in managing the business and have unlimited liability for any claims against the firm.

**limited partnership**
A partnership that includes at least one general partner and limited partner. Both partners contribute financially and share profits. General partners actively manage the company, accepting unlimited liability for debts while limited partners do not actively manage in exchange for limited liability.

**limited liability**
When owners are not personally liable for claims against their firm. Limited liability owners may lose their investment in the company, but their personal assets are protected.

**limited liability partnership (LLP)**
Form of partnership in which all partners have the right to participate in management and have limited liability for company debts.

## LO3

**corporation**
A form of business ownership in which the business is considered a legal entity that is separate and distinct from its owners.

**general corporation (or C corporation)**
The most common type of business corporation, where ownership offers limited liability to all of its owners, also called stockholders.

**articles of incorporation**
The document filed with a state government to establish the existence of a new corporation.

**corporate bylaws**
The basic rules governing how a corporation is organized and how it conducts its business.

**stockholder**
An owner of a corporation.

**institutional investor**
An organization that pools contributions from investors, clients, or depositors and uses these funds to buy stocks and other securities.

**board of directors**
The individuals who are elected by stockholders of a corporation to represent their interests.

## LO4

**S corporation**
A form of corporation that avoids double taxation by having its income taxed as if it were a partnership.

### LO1 Discuss the pros and cons of operating a business as a sole proprietorship

A sole proprietorship is the simplest and least expensive form of ownership to establish. It offers the owner the flexibility of running the business without having to seek the approval of other owners, and all of the profits go to the single owner. But a sole proprietor has unlimited liability for the debts of the business. The sole owner often must work long hours and assume heavy responsibilities. Also sole proprietorships normally have limited ability to raise funds for expansion.

### LO2 Describe the basic features of general partnerships, limited partnerships, and limited liability partnerships

In a general partnership, each partner takes an active role in management and shares in the profits and each partner has unlimited liability for the firm's debts. A limited partnership has at least one general partner, who participates actively in managing the company and assumes unlimited liability, and at least one limited partner who gives up the right to participate in management in exchange for limited liability. The limited liability partnership (LLP) is a relatively new form of partnership that allows all partners to participate in management while retaining some degree of limited liability.

### LO3 Explain why corporations have become the dominant form of business ownership

A corporation is a legal entity created by permission of a state or federal government. Corporations are considered legally separate and distinct from their owners, who are called stockholders. The general corporation is the dominant type of corporation. This form of ownership offers limited liability to all owners (called stockholders). Corporations have the ability to raise financial capital through issuing shares of stocks and bonds, giving them an advantage when it comes to financing growth. Another advantage is that corporations have unlimited life.

### LO4 Describe how S corporations, statutory closed corporations, and nonprofit corporations differ from general corporations and from each other

Unlike a conventional corporation, an S corporation avoids the problem of double taxation. However, there are several restrictions on the ownership of S corporations. Statutory close (or closed) corporations are corporations held by a small number of stockholders that can operate less formally than a C corporation. Unlike a C corporation, a nonprofit (or not-for-profit) corporation can't have stockholders and can't pay dividends. Also unlike a C corporation, its earnings are exempt from state and federal income taxes.

### LO5 Explain how corporations can restructure using mergers and acquisitions

An acquisition occurs when one corporation buys controlling interest in another firm. The firm being acquired ceases to exist as an independent entity, while the acquiring firm continues to operate. A merger occurs when two formerly independent firms agree to combine and form a new business entity. A horizontal merger (or acquisition) is a merger between firms in the same industry. A vertical merger is between firms that are at different stages in the production process for a good or service. A conglomerate merger is between firms that are in unrelated industries.

### LO6 Explain why limited liability companies have become increasingly popular

Limited liability companies (LLCs) are attractive because they give owners limited liability while avoiding the problem of double taxation endemic to C corporations. They are similar to S corporations, but have fewer ownership restrictions. LLCs also are subject to fewer regulations and have less strict management requirements than C corporations.

**statutory close (or closed) corporation**
A corporation with a limited number of owners that files special articles of incorporation allowing it to operate under simpler, less formal rules than a general corporation.

**nonprofit corporation**
A corporation that does not seek to earn a profit and differs in several fundamental respects from general corporations.

## LO5

**acquisition**
A corporate restructuring in which one firm buys another. After the acquisition, the target firm (the one being purchased) ceases to exist as an independent entity, while the acquiring firm continues to operate.

**merger**
A corporate restructuring that occurs when two formerly independent business entities combine to form a new organization.

**horizontal merger**
A combination of two firms that are in the same industry.

**vertical merger**
A combination of firms at different stages in the production of a good or service.

**conglomerate merger**
A combination of two firms that are in unrelated industries.

## LO6

**limited liability company (LLC)**
Form of business ownership which combines the limited liability of corporations with the tax pass-through of partnerships, eliminating the problem of double taxation.

## LO7

**franchising**
A contractual relationship in which an established business entity allows others to operate a business using unique resources that it supplies in exchange for monetary payments and other considerations.

**franchisor**
The business entity in a franchise relationship that allows others to operate their business using resources it supplies in exchange for money and other considerations.

**franchisee**
The party in a franchise relationship that pays for the right to use resources supplied by the franchisor.

**business format franchise**
A broad franchise agreement in which the franchisee pays for the right to use the name, trademark, and business and production methods of the franchisor.

**franchise agreement**
The contractual arrangement between a franchisor and franchisee that spells out the duties and responsibilities of both parties in detail.

## Summary of Characteristics of 4 Major Forms of Business Ownership

| Form of Business | Number of Owners | Participation in Management | Owners' Liability | Tax Implications | State Filing Requirements |
|---|---|---|---|---|---|
| Sole proprietorship | 1 | Proprietor typically manages the company. | Unlimited | Taxed only as income to the owner. | No special filing required with state. |
| General Partnership | 2 or more (no limit on maximum) | All general partners have the right to participate in management. | Unlimited | Taxed only as income to the owners. | No special filing required with state. |
| General (or C) Corporation | No limit on number of stockholders | Most stockholders do not take an active role in management. Stockholders elect Board of Directors, which sets policy and appoints and oversees corporate officers who actively manage the corporation. | Limited | Earnings subject to double taxation: all earnings are taxed as income to corporation. Any dividends are also taxed as income to stockholders. | Must file articles of incorporation (or similar document) with state and pay filing fee. |
| Limited Liability Company (LLC) | No limit | May be member-managed, or may be manager-managed, similar to a corporation. | Limited | Taxed only as income to owners. | Must file articles of organization with state and pay filing fee. |

## LO7 Evaluate the advantages and disadvantages of franchising

Franchising is an ongoing contractual relationship in which an established firm (the franchisor) allows another business (the franchisee) to use its unique resources in exchange for payments and other considerations. The franchisor gains revenue without the need to invest its own money. Franchisees gain the right to use a well-known brand name and proven business methods and receive training and support from franchisors. On the downside, franchisors often find that dealing with a large number of franchisees can be complex and challenging. Also, if a few franchisees behave irresponsibly, their actions can have a negative impact on the entire organization. For franchisees, the main drawbacks are the fees they must pay to the franchisor and the loss of control over management of their business.

# CHAPTER IN REVIEW

## Small Business and Entrepreneurship

**7**

## LO1

**entrepreneurs**
People who risk their time, money, and other resources to start and manage a business.

## LO2

**internal locus of control**
A deep-seated sense that the individual is personally responsible for what happens in his or her life.

**external locus of control**
A deep-seated sense that forces other than the individual are responsible for what happens in his or her life.

## LO3

**market niche**
Small segment of a market with fewer competitors than the market as a whole. Market niches tend to be quite attractive to small firms.

### LO1 Explain the key reasons to launch a small business

Launching a business is tough, but the advantages of business ownership can far outweigh the risk and hard work. Most people who take the plunge are seeking some combination of greater financial success, independence, flexibility, and challenge. But some are seeking survival, and simply have no other options.

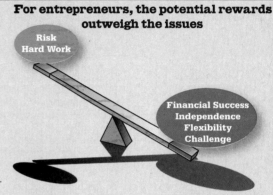

**For entrepreneurs, the potential rewards outweigh the issues**

Risk Hard Work

Financial Success Independence Flexibility Challenge

### LO2 Describe the typical entrepreneurial mindset and characteristics

Not all small business owners are entrepreneurs. The difference is attitude: from day one, true entrepreneurs aim to dominate their industry. The entrepreneurial personality typically includes some combination of the following characteristics: vision, self-reliance, energy, confidence, tolerance of uncertainty, and tolerance of failure. While these qualities are very helpful, they aren't essential: it's clearly possible to succeed with a number of different personality types.

**Entrepreneurial Characteristics**

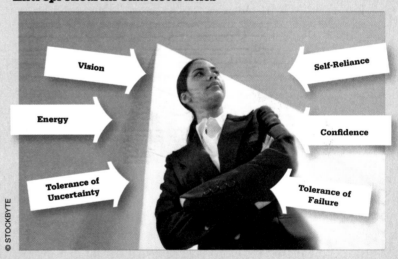

Vision
Self-Reliance
Energy
Confidence
Tolerance of Uncertainty
Tolerance of Failure

© STOCKBYTE

### LO3 Analyze the opportunities and threats that small businesses face

Small businesses enjoy some key advantages, but also face daunting obstacles as they fight for a foothold in the turbulent marketplace.

**Opportunities:**
- *Market Niches:* Many small firms are uniquely positioned to exploit small but profitable market niches.
- *Personal Customer Service:* With a smaller customer base, small firms can develop much more personal relationships with individual customers.
- *Lower Overhead Costs:* Many small firms can hold down overhead costs by hiring fewer managers and fewer specialized employees.
- *Technology:* The Web has played a powerful role in opening new opportunities for small business in both local and global markets.

**Threats:**
- *High risk of failure:* Starting a new business involves a lot of risk, but the odds improve significantly after the five-year mark.

## New Business Survival Rates

- *Lack of knowledge and experience:* Entrepreneurs often have expertise in a particular area, but lack the background to run a successful business.
- *Too little money:* Lack of start-up money is a major issue for

| Year in Business | Survival Rate | Change vs. Prior Year (percentage points) |
|---|---|---|
| Year 1 | 85% | –15 |
| Year 2 | 70% | –15 |
| Year 3 | 62% | –8 |
| Year 4 | 55% | –7 |
| Year 5 | 50% | –5 |
| Year 6 | 47% | –3 |
| Year 7 | 44% | –3 |
| Year 8 | 41% | –3 |
| Year 9 | 38% | –3 |
| Year 10 | 35% | –3 |

most new firms, since ongoing profits don't usually begin for months or even years.
- *Bigger regulatory burden:* Small firms spend 45% more per employee than big firms, simply complying with federal regulations.
- *Higher health insurance costs:* Small-scale health plans are much more expensive, making it harder to offer employees competitive coverage.

## LO4

**Small Business Administration (SBA)**
An agency of the federal government designed to maintain and strengthen the nation's economy by aiding, counseling, assisting and protecting the interests of small businesses.

**Small Business Development Centers (SBDCs)**
Local offices—affiliated with the Small Business Administration—that provide comprehensive management assistance to current and prospective small business owners.

**SCORE (The Service Corps for Retired Executives)**
An organization—affiliated with the Small Business Administration—that provides free, comprehensive business counseling for small business owners from qualified volunteers.

**business plan**
A formal document that describes a business concept, outlines core business objectives, and details strategies and timelines for achieving those objectives.

## LO5

**angel investors**
Individuals who invest in start-up companies with high growth potential in exchange for a share of ownership.

**venture capital firms**
Companies that invest in start-up businesses with high growth potential in exchange for a share of ownership.

## LO4 Discuss ways to become a new business owner and tools to facilitate success

Starting a business from scratch comes to mind first for most people. But buying an established business, or even a franchise, can be excellent choices as well. Each choice involves a range of pros and cons, but broadly speaking, it's less risky to buy an established business or franchise, but more satisfying (at least for some people) to start a new venture from scratch. Whichever path you choose—whether you're an ambitious entrepreneur or simply a small business owner—several strategies can help you succeed over the long term: gain experience in your field, learn from others, educate yourself, access SBA resources, and develop a business plan.

### BUSINESS LAUNCH OPTIONS
- **Starting from scratch**
- **Buying an established business**
- **Buying a franchise**

### STRATEGIES FOR SUCCESS:
- **Gain experience**
- **Learn from others**
- **Educate yourself**
- **Access SBA resources**
- **Develop a plan**

## LO5 Discuss funding options for small business

For many entrepreneurs, finding the money to fund their business is the top challenge of their start-up year. The vast majority of new firms are funded by the personal resources of the founder, including personal accounts (e.g., credit cards), family, and friends. Other key funding sources include bank loans, angel investors, and venture capital firms.

## LO6 Explain the size, scope, and economic contributions of small business

Small businesses play a vital role in the American economy, generating more than half of the U.S. gross domestic product and accounting for 60 to 80% of all new jobs over the past decade. In addition to fueling employment growth, small businesses contribute innovations to the economy at more than twice the rate of their big business counterparts. They also form the backbone of many inner city economies, finding opportunities—and offering products and services—in places where most large firms opt not to operate. Across the globe, nearly one out of ten adults worldwide start a new business each year. But the entrepreneurship rate varies dramatically from country to country, ranging from a high of 40.3% in Peru to a low of 1.5% in Japan.

## LO1

**accounting**
A system for recognizing, recording, organizing, analyzing, summarizing, and reporting information about the financial transactions that affect an organization.

## LO2

**private accountants**
Accountants who work within a business organization, preparing reports and analyzing financial information for the company that employs them.

**public accountants**
Accountants who provide accounting services for clients on a fee basis.

## LO3

**financial accounting**
The branch of accounting that prepares financial statements for use by owners, creditors, suppliers, and other external stakeholders.

**generally accepted accounting principles (GAAP)**
A set of accounting standards that are used in the preparation of financial statements.

**Financial Accounting Standards Board (FASB)**
The private board that establishes the generally accepted accounting principles used in the practice of financial accounting.

## LO4

**balance sheet**
A financial statement that reports the financial position of a firm at a particular point in time by identifying and reporting the value of the firm's assets, liabilities, and owners' equity.

**accounting equation**
Assets = Liabilities + Owners' Equity. This states that the value of a firm's assets is equal to the financing provided by creditors and owners for the purchase of those assets.

**assets**
Resources owned by a firm.

**liabilities**
Claims that outsiders have against a firm's assets.

**owners' equity**
The claims a firm's owners have against their company's assets.

**income statement**
The financial statement that reports the revenues, expenses, and net income that resulted from a firm's operations over an accounting period.

**revenues**
Increases in a firm's assets that result from the sale of goods, provision of services, or other activities intended to earn income.

**expenses**
Resources that are used up as the result of business operations.

**net income**
The difference between the revenue a firm earns and the expenses it incurs in a given time period.

### LO1 Define accounting and explain how accounting information is used by a variety of stakeholders

Accounting is a system for recognizing, recording, organizing, analyzing, summarizing, and reporting information about the financial transactions that affect an organization. This information is used by virtually all of the firm's stakeholders. For example, marketing managers want to know about sales figures for various products and regions. Owners want to know whether their firm made a profit or loss. Creditors want to make sure that the firm has the capacity to repay any loans they make. Employees want to know whether their company is performing well enough to provide job security and a good pay raise. Finally, the IRS wants to know the amount of taxable income the firm earns during each period.

### LO2 Discuss the career opportunities open to accountants

Private accountants work within an organization, analyzing financial information and preparing reports and statements for that organization. Public accountants provide a broad range of accounting and consulting services to clients on a fee basis. They may help clients set up accounting systems or assist in tax preparation. Government accountants work for a wide variety of government agencies at the local, state, and federal levels. In general, they perform tasks similar to those of public and private accountants.

### LO3 Identify the goals of generally accepted accounting principles

Generally accepted accounting principles are rules that govern the practice of financial accounting. The goal of these rules is to ensure that the information generated by financial accounting is relevant, reliable, consistent, and comparable.

### LO4 Describe the key elements of the major financial statements

The major financial statements are the balance sheet, income statement, and statement of cash flows. The balance sheet shows the firm's financial position at a specific point in time by reporting the value of its assets, liabilities, and owners' equity. The income statement shows the net income (profit or loss) the firm earns over a stated period of time by deducting costs and expenses from revenues. The statement of cash flows shows

#### Financial Accounting Statements

| Financial Statement | Purpose | Key Components | Basic Relationship |
|---|---|---|---|
| Balance Sheet | Shows the value of a firm's assets at a particular point in time, and identifies the claims owners and outsiders have against those assets. | • **Assets:** things of value owned by the firm.<br>• **Liabilities:** claims outsiders have against the firm's assets.<br>• **Owners' Equity:** claims the owners of a firm have against its assets. | Assets = Liabilities + Owners' Equity |
| Income Statement | Reports the profit or loss earned by the firm over a given time period. | • **Revenues:** increases in cash and other assets that the firm earns from its operations.<br>• **Expenses:** the cash and other resources used up to generate revenue.<br>• **Net Income:** the profit or loss earned by a firm in a given time period. | Revenues – Expenses = Net Income |
| Statement of Cash Flows | Shows how and why the amount of cash held by the firm changed over a given period of time. | Inflows and outflows of cash due to:<br>• **Operations:** the cash flows that arise from producing and selling goods and services.<br>• **Investments:** the cash flows resulting from buying and selling fixed assets, and from buying and selling financial securities of other companies.<br>• **Financing:** cash a firm receives from selling its own securities and cash the firm disburses to pay dividends and interest. | Net change in cash = Total inflow of cash – total outflow of cash. |

**accrual-basis accounting**
The method of accounting that recognizes revenue when it is earned and matches expenses to the revenues they helped produce.

**statement of cash flows**
The financial statement that identifies a firm's sources and uses of cash in a given accounting period.

## LO5

**Sarbanes-Oxley Act of 2002**
A law that includes several provisions designed to improve external auditing procedures and improve financial reporting for publicly traded firms.

**horizontal analysis**
Analysis of financial statements that compares account values reported on these statements over a period of years to identify changes and trends.

**vertical analysis**
Analysis of information in financial statements that involves expressing various accounts as a percentage of some base amount.

**ratio analysis**
A technique for analyzing information in financial statements that involves expressing account values as ratios of other account values.

## LO6

**managerial (or management) accounting**
The branch of accounting that provides reports and analysis to managers to help them make informed business decisions.

**activity-based costing (ABC)**
A technique used by managerial accountants to assign product costs based on links between activities that drive costs and the production of specific products.

**incremental analysis**
An evaluation and comparison of the financial impact different alternatives would have in a particular decision-making situation.

**budgeting**
A management tool that explicitly shows how firms will acquire and use the resources needed to achieve its goals over a specific time period.

**operating budgets**
The budget documents that communicate an organization's sales and production goals and the resources needed to achieve these goals.

**financial budgets**
The budget documents that identify the cash and other financial resources the firm will acquire and use to finance its operations and make planned investments in fixed assets.

**master budget**
A combined statement of an organization's operational and financial budgets that represents the firm's overall plan of action for a specified time period.

the inflows and outflows of cash that result from a firm's operations, its financing activities and its investing activities in a given time period. This statement also shows the net change in the amount of cash the firm has over that time period.

## LO5 Explain how horizontal, vertical, and ratio analysis can provide insights into financial statements

Horizontal analysis compares information in a firm's financial statements over a period of two or more years to identify changes and trends in key accounts. Vertical analysis expresses each item on a balance sheet or income statement as a percentage of some key value to see how each item compares, in terms of its relative size, to other items in the same section. Ratio analysis uses information from financial statements to compute percentages or proportions that provide insights into the firm's financial condition and performance, such as its ability to pay debts coming due, how effectively it manages its assets, the extent to which it relies on debt in its overall financial structure, and its overall profitability.

## LO6 Describe how managerial accounting can help managers with product costing, incremental analysis, and budgeting

Managers must have an accurate measure of the costs incurred to produce their firm's goods and services in order to set prices and evaluate efficiency [exhibit 8.4]. In recent years, managerial accountants have begun using a technique called activity-based costing to help assign costs more accurately. Incremental analysis helps managers evaluate and compare the impact different alternatives have on costs and revenues in a decision-making situation [exhibits 8.5 and 8.6]. A budget facilitates planning by translating goals into measurable quantities and requiring managers to identify the specific resources needed to achieve them.

## Comparison of Financial and Managerial Accounting

| Financial Accounting | Managerial Accounting |
|---|---|
| Is primarily intended to provide information to external stakeholders such as stockholders, creditors, and government regulators | Is primarily intended to provide information to internal stakeholders such as the managers of specific divisions or departments |
| Prepares a standard set of financial statements | Prepares customized reports designed to deal with specific problems or issues |
| Presents financial statements on a predetermined schedule (usually quarterly and annually) | Creates reports upon request by management rather than according to a predetermined schedule |
| Is governed by a set of generally accepted accounting principles | Uses procedures developed internally and is not required to follow GAAP |

## LO2

**current ratio**
A liquidity ratio found by dividing a firm's total current assets by its total current liabilities. The current ratio is one of the most commonly used measures of a firm's ability to pay its short-term obligations as they come due.

**inventory turnover ratio**
An asset management ratio that measures the average number of times a firm sells (or "turns over") its inventory in a year.

**debt-to-equity ratio**
Measures the extent to which a firm relies on debt financing by dividing total debt by total owners' equity. The higher the value of this ratio, the more the firm is relying on debt.

**debt-to-assets ratio**
Measures the extent to which a firm relies on debt financing by dividing total debt by total assets. The closer the ratio is to one, the greater the firm's reliance on debt.

**return on equity**
A profitability ratio that is computed by dividing net income by average common stock equity. If the firm issues preferred stock, the dividends paid to preferred stock are subtracted from net income.

**return on assets**
A profitability ratio that is found by dividing net income by average total assets.

**earnings per share (EPS)**
A profitability ratio that measures how much a firm earns per share of common stock outstanding.

## LO3

**pro forma statements**
Projected financial statements that financial managers use during financial planning.

**cash budget**
A detailed projection of cash flows that financial managers use to identify when a firm is likely to experience temporary shortages or surpluses of cash.

## LO4

**net working capital**
The difference between a firm's current assets and its current liabilities.

**cash equivalents**
Short-term, very safe, and highly liquid assets that many firms include as part of their cash holdings on their balance sheet.

**commercial paper**
Short-term unsecured promissory notes issued by large corporations.

**U.S. Treasury bills (also called T-bills)**
Short-term IOUs issued by the U.S. federal government. Treasury bills are marketable and are considered to be very safe securities.

**money market mutual funds**
A mutual fund that pools funds from many investors and uses these funds to purchase very safe, highly liquid securities.

### LO1 Explain how maximizing financial value relates to social responsibility

Meeting social responsibilities can be good for shareholder value. When a company treats it workers, suppliers, and customers with honesty, fairness, and respect, it builds goodwill. This can translate to lower turnover and higher motivation among workers, more customer loyalty, and other advantages that lead to a more valuable company.

### LO2 Describe how financial managers use key ratios to evaluate their firm.

Financial managers look at four basic types of ratios. Liquidity ratios, such as the current ratio, provide insights into whether the firm will have enough cash to pay its short-term liabilities as they come due. Asset management ratios, such as inventory turnover, tell financial managers how effectively a firm is using various assets to generate revenues for their firm. Leverage ratios measure how heavily the firm relies on debt in its capital structure. Finally, profitability ratios, such as return on assets and return on equity, measure the firm's overall success at using resources to create a profit for its owners.

### LO3 Discuss how financial managers use cash budgets

Financial managers use the cash budget to get a better understanding of the *timing* of cash flows within the year. They project cash inflows and outflows on a monthly basis, helping financial managers determine when the firm is likely to need additional funds to meet short-term cash shortages, and when surpluses of cash will be available to pay off loans or to invest in other assets.

#### Major Financial Planning Tools

| Tool | Purpose |
|------|---------|
| Pro Forma Income Statement | Forecasts the sales, expenses and revenue for a firm in some future time period. |
| Pro Forma Balance Sheet | Projects the types and amounts of assets a firm will need in order to carry out its plans, and shows the amount of additional financing the firm will need to acquire these assets. |
| Cash Budget | Projects the timing and amount of cash flows so that management can determine when it will need to arrange for external financing, and when it will have extra cash to pay off loans or invest in other assets. |

### LO4 Explain the significance of working capital management

Net working capital refers to the difference between a firm's current assets and its current liabilities. Current assets include cash and other assets expected to be converted into cash in the next year. Current liabilities represent debts that will come due in the next year such as accounts, taxes, and notes payable. These debts represent an important source of short-term financing to the firm, but they also represent obligations that must be repaid in the near future.

### LO5 Explain how financial managers evaluate capital budgeting proposals

Capital budgeting is the process by which financial managers evaluate major long-term investment proposals. Because these projects generate cash flows for several years, a proper evaluation must take the time value of money into account. This is done by computing the present values of all cash flows. The most common way to decide whether to accept a proposal is to calculate its net present value (NPV), which is the sum of the

**spontaneous financing**
Funds that arise as a natural result of a firm's business operations without the need for special arrangements.

**trade credit**
Credit granted by sellers when they provide customers with goods and services for a period of time before requiring payment.

**line of credit**
A financial arrangement between a firm and a bank in which the bank preapproves credit up to a specified limit, provided that the firm maintains an acceptable credit rating. The firm can then borrow funds from the bank up to the approved amount without having to negotiate separate loan agreements.

**revolving credit agreement**
A guaranteed line of credit in which a bank makes a binding commitment to provide a business with funds up to a specified credit limit at any time during the term of the agreement. In exchange for the bank's commitment, the firm pays a commitment fee.

**factor**
A company that provides short-term financing to firms by purchasing their accounts receivables at a discount.

## LO5

**capital budgeting**
The process a firm uses to evaluate long-term investment proposals.

**time value of money**
The principle that a dollar received today is worth more than a dollar received in the future.

**present value**
The amount of money that, if invested today at a given rate of interest, would grow to become some future amount in a specified number of time periods.

**discounting**
The process of converting a future cash flow to its present value.

**discount rate**
The rate of interest used when computing the present value of some future cash flow. (Note: this term also has another meaning; it refers to the rate of interest the Fed charges when it loans funds to banks.)

**net present value (NPV)**
The sum of the present values of all relevant cash flows an investment is expected to generate, including the initial cost of the investment (which is negative). The NPV measures the increase in shareholder value expected to result from an investment.

## LO6

**capital structure**
The mix of equity and debt financing a firm uses to meet its permanent financing needs.

**covenants**
Conditions lenders place on firms that seek long-term debt financing.

**retained earnings**
That part of net income that a firm reinvests.

**financial leverage**
The use of debt in a firm's capital structure.

present values of all the estimated future cash flows minus the initial cost of the investment. If the NPV of a project is positive, it will increase the value of the firm. If the NPV is negative, it will decrease the value of the firm.

| Decision Rule for Capital Budgeting | |
|---|---|
| NPV: the sum of the present values of all relevant cash flows resulting from a proposal including the initial cost. | |
| Result of NPV Calculation | Decision |
| NPV ≥ 0 | Accept proposal ☑ |
| NPV < 0 | Reject proposal ☒ |

## LO6 Identify the key issues involved in determining a firm's capital structure

A firm's capital structure refers to the extent to which a firm relies on various forms of debt and equity to satisfy its permanent financing needs. Debt financing offers tax advantages because interest payments on debt are tax deductible. It also offers the opportunity to use leverage to increase the return to owners during good times. However, debt is risky. The required interest payments can be a real burden during times when cash is tight. Also, lenders often require firms to agree to covenants that can restrict the flexibility of management. Equity financing is contributed by ownership. It offers more flexibility and is less risky than debt financing. However, existing owners might not want to dilute their share of ownership by selling additional stock. In addition, use of equity financing means that the firm is forgoing the opportunity to use financial leverage to increase the return to owners.

### Impact of Capital Structure

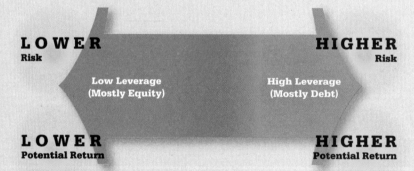

**LOWER**
Risk

**Low Leverage (Mostly Equity)**

**HIGHER**
Risk

**High Leverage (Mostly Debt)**

**LOWER**
Potential Return

**HIGHER**
Potential Return

## LO1

**common stock**
The basic form of ownership in a corporation.

**capital gain**
The return on an asset that results when its market price rises above the price the investor paid for it.

**preferred stock**
A type of stock that gives its holder preference over common stockholders in terms of dividends and claims on assets.

**bond**
A long-term debt instrument issued by a corporation or government entity.

**maturity date**
The date when a bond will come due.

**par value (of a bond)**
The value of a bond at its maturity; what the firm must pay the bondholder when the bond matures.

**coupon rate**
The interest paid on a bond expressed as a percentage of the bond's par value.

**secured bond**
A bond backed by the pledge of specific assets.

**serial bonds**
A series of bonds issued at the same time but having different maturity dates to spread out the repayment of principal.

**sinking fund**
Funds set aside to retire bonds over a period of time. Money deposited into a sinking fund is used to call in bonds or purchase bonds.

**callable bond**
A bond that the issuer can redeem at a given price prior to its maturity.

**convertible bond**
A bond that gives its holder the right to exchange it for a stated number of shares of common stock in some specified time period.

## LO2

**primary securities market**
The market where newly issued securities are traded. The primary market is where the firms that issue securities raise additional financial capital.

**secondary securities market**
The market where previously issued securities are traded.

**public offering**
A primary market issue in which new securities are offered to any investors who are willing and able to purchase them.

**private placement**
A primary market issue that is negotiated between the issuing corporation and a small group of accredited investors.

**initial public offering (IPO)**
The first time a company issues stock that may be bought by the general public.

**investment bank**
A financial intermediary that specializes in helping firms raise financial capital in primary markets.

### LO1 Describe the three basic types of securities issued by corporations

The three basic types of securities are common stock, preferred stock, and bonds. Common stock represents the basic ownership in a corporation. Owners of common stock usually have voting rights and the right to receive a dividend if the corporation's board declares one. Some corporations also issue preferred stock. Owners of preferred stock are more likely to receive a dividend than common stockholders. They also have a preferred claim on assets over common stockholders should the company go bankrupt. However, they normally do not have voting rights. Bonds are long-term IOUs issued by corporations or government entities. Stockholders are considered owners of a corporation, and bondholders are considered creditors. Firms must pay interest on the bonds they issue and must pay the principal to the bondholder when the bond matures.

#### Characteristics of Corporate Securities

| Security | Type | Basic Return | Claim on Assets If Firm Is Liquidated | Voting Rights |
|---|---|---|---|---|
| Common Stock | Equity (ownership) | Dividend (distribution of profits), but only if declared by Board of Directors. | Residual claim (after claims of preferred stockholders and bondholders are satisfied). | Yes |
| Preferred Stock | Equity (ownership) | Dividend—not guaranteed, but with preference in payment over common dividend. | Claim on assets before common stockholders but after bondholders. | No |
| Corporate Bond | Debt (long-term IOU) | Interest: legally required payment expressed as a percentage of the bond's par value. | Claim on assets must be satisfied before common or preferred stockholders. Claim is sometimes secured by pledge of specific assets. | No |

### LO2 Explain how securities are issued in the primary market and traded on secondary markets

The primary market is where corporations obtain financial capital by selling newly issued securities. There are two different ways securities can be sold in primary markets. In public offerings, the securities are sold to the general public. In private placements, the securities are sold to a select group of accredited investors. Most firms hire a financial intermediary known as an investment bank to help them sell securities in the primary market. Secondary markets are where previously issued securities are traded. The corporations that issue stocks and bonds do not receive any funds from sales on the secondary market. The two major types of secondary markets are securities exchanges and the over-the-counter market. Exchanges only list stocks of corporations that satisfy their listing requirements and pay listing fees. The stocks of corporations not listed on an exchange are sold on the over-the-counter market through a network of securities dealers. See chart on the following page.

### LO3 Discuss how the government and private organizations regulate securities markets

The securities industry is subject to both state and federal laws. States typically have laws requiring all securities sold within their borders to be registered with a state authority. They also require securities dealers and brokers to register. The two key federal laws governing securities markets are the Securities Act of 1933 and the Securities

Visit **4ltrpress.cengage.com/busn**
for additional study tools!

**underwriting**
An arrangement under which an investment banker agrees to purchase all shares of a public offering at an agreed upon price. The investment banker will then sell the securities to other investors at a higher price.

**electronic communications network (ECN)**
An automated, computerized securities trading system that automatically matches buyers and sellers, executing trades quickly and when markets are closed.

**New York Stock Exchange (NYSE)**
The largest securities exchange in the United States. After its 2007 merger with a large European exchange, it is formally known as NYSE Euronext.

**NASDAQ exchange**
A major stock exchange that handles trades through a computerized network.

**NYSE Hybrid Market**
A new trading system established by the NYSE Group, Inc., in 2006 that allows investors to execute trades through the traditional floor trading (the auction market) or through a newer automated trading system.

**over-the-counter market (OTC)**
The market in which securities that are not listed on exchanges are traded.

## LO3

**Securities Act of 1933**
The first major federal law regulating the securities industry.

**Securities Exchange Act of 1934**
A federal law dealing with securities regulation that established the Securities and Exchange Commission to oversee the securities industry.

**Security and Exchange Commission**
The federal agency with primary responsibility for regulating the securities industry.

**Self-regulatory organizations**
Nongovernmental organizations operating in the securities industry that develop rules and standards governing the behavior of their members.

## LO4

**market order**
An order telling a broker to buy or sell a specific security at the best available price.

**limit order**
An order to a broker to buy a specific stock only if its price is below a certain level, or to sell a specific stock only if its price is above a certain level.

## LO5

**mutual fund**
An investment vehicle that pools the contributions of many investors and buys a wide array of stocks or other securities.

**exchange traded fund (ETF)**
Certificates traded on securities markets that represent the legal right of ownership over part of a basket of individual stock certificates or other securities.

### Characteristics of Primary and Secondary Security Markets

| Type of Market | What is traded? | Who receives the funds? | How are securities traded? |
|---|---|---|---|
| Primary | Newly issued stocks and bonds | The firm issuing the securities. | • Public offering: securities of issuing firm sold to public investors.<br>• Private placement: sale of securities negotiated between issuing firm and one or more accredited investors. |
| Secondary | Previously issued stocks and bonds | The investor who sells the stocks or bonds. | • Securities of most large, well-known corporations are traded on organized exchanges such as the NYSE or NASDAQ.<br>• Securities for smaller corporations are usually traded in the over the counter (OTC) market. |

Exchange Act of 1934. The Securities Act of 1933 requires firms selling securities to the general public in the primary market to file a registration statement and prospectus. The Securities Exchange Act of 1934 established the Securities and Exchange Commission (SEC) and gave it primary responsibility for regulating securities markets. The SEC delegates much of its regulatory authority to private organizations known as self-regulatory organizations (SROs).

## LO4 Compare several strategies investors use to invest in securities

Income investors choose securities such as bonds and preferred stocks that tend to generate relatively steady and predictable flows of income. Market timers try to time their purchases of specific stocks to buy low and sell high on a short-term basis. Value investors try to find undervalued stocks. Growth investors often look for stocks in small companies with innovative products and the potential for exceptional growth. Finally, investors using a buy and hold approach invest in a broad portfolio of securities with the intention of holding them for a long period of time.

## LO5 Explain the investor appeal of mutual funds and exchange traded funds

Though they are actually created through very different processes, mutual funds and exchange traded funds (ETFs) share some similar benefits from an investor's perspective. Both allow individual investors to invest in a wide "market basket of securities" at a relatively low cost. Investors who buy shares of index mutual funds or index ETFs can achieve the risk-reducing benefits of diversification without having to buy a large number of stocks in separate companies. And both mutual funds and ETFs are highly liquid, meaning they can be easily converted into cash. One difference between ETFs and mutual funds is that ETFs trade just like stocks. You can buy and sell them at any time, with no minimum investment required—but you pay a commission to your broker every time you do.

## LO6 Describe how investors can track the performance of their investments

Investors can find information about actively traded stocks in the financial sections of most major city newspapers. However, many Websites now provide more in-depth information about actively traded securities than newspapers can provide. Many of these Websites allow investors to see current information about price and volume (as well as a host of other statistics and facts) by simply typing in the stock's symbol in a search box.

### LO6

**stock index**
A statistic that tracks how the prices of a specific set of stocks have changed.

**Dow Jones Industrial Average**
A stock index based on the prices of the stocks of 30 large, well-known corporations.

**Standard & Poor's 500**
A stock index based on prices of 500 major U.S. corporations in a variety of industries and market sectors.

Visit **4ltrpress.cengage.com/busn** for additional study tools!

## LO1

**marketing**
An organizational function and a set of processes for creating, communicating, and delivering value to customers and for managing customer relationships in ways that benefit the organization and its stakeholders.

**utility**
The ability of goods and services to satisfy consumer "wants."

**form utility**
The power of a good or a service to satisfy customer "wants" by converting inputs into a finished form.

**time utility**
The power of a good or a service to satisfy customer "wants" by providing goods and services at a convenient time for customers.

**place utility**
The power of a good or a service to satisfy customer "wants" by providing goods and services at a convenient place for customers.

**ownership utility**
The power of a good or a service to satisfy customer "wants" by smoothly transferring ownership of goods and services from buyer to seller.

**marketing concept**
A business philosophy that makes customer satisfaction—now and in the future—the central focus of the entire organization.

## LO2

**customer relationship management (CRM)**
The on-going process of acquiring, maintaining, and growing profitable customer relationships by delivering unmatched value.

**value**
A customer perception that a product has a better relationship than its competitors between the cost and the benefits.

**customer satisfaction**
When customers perceive that a good or service delivers value above and beyond their expectations.

**customer loyalty**
When customers buy a product from the same supplier again and again—sometimes paying even more for it than they would for a competitive product.

## LO3

**marketing plan**
A formal document that defines marketing objectives and the specific strategies for achieving those objectives.

**market segmentation**
Dividing potential customers into groups of similar people, or segments.

**target market**
The group of people who are most likely to buy a particular product.

**consumer marketers (also known as business-to-consumer or B2C)** Marketers who direct their efforts toward people who are buying products for personal consumption.

### LO1 Discuss the objectives, the process, and the scope of marketing

Marketing means delivering value to your customers with the goal of satisfying their needs and achieving long-term profitability for your organization. Goods and services meet customer needs by providing "utility" (or satisfaction) on an on-going basis. Marketing has moved well beyond the scope of traditional goods and services, to include people, places, events, and ideas. Much non-traditional marketing involves both public and private not-for-profit organizations, which measure their success in non-monetary terms. Over the last century, marketing has evolved through a number of phases. The marketing era gave birth to the marketing concept, which is still in force today: a philosophy that customer satisfaction—now and in the future—should be the central focus of the entire organization.

### The Evolution of Marketing

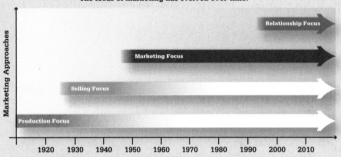

The focus of marketing has evolved over time.

Relationship Focus

Marketing Focus

Selling Focus

Production Focus

Marketing Approaches

1920  1930  1940  1950  1960  1970  1980  1990  2000  2010

While individual firms differ in their approach to marketing, the prevailing view at leading edge firms has changed over time as shown here.

### LO2 Identify the role of the customer in marketing

Successful marketers always place the customer front and center, with a focus on customer relationship management: acquiring, maintaining, and growing profitable customer relationships by consistently delivering unmatched value. Effective data management and one-on-one personalization are key customer relationship tools.

### LO3 Explain each element of marketing strategy

Marketing strategy essentially involves determining who your *target audience* is and how you will reach them. Choosing the right target begins with *market segmentation:* dividing your market into segments or groups of people with similar characteristics. Then, you need to determine the best *marketing mix*—the most effective combination of product, pricing, distribution, and promotion strategies to reach your target market. Finally, you must continually monitor each element of the *marketing environment* to ensure that you respond quickly and effectively to change.

### Consumer Decision Making Process

Competitive

Social/Cultural

Product Strategy

Pricing Strategy

Economic

**TARGET MARKET**

Distribution Strategy

Technological

Political/Legal

**business marketers (also known as business-to-business or B2B)** Marketers who direct their efforts toward people who are buying products to use either directly or indirectly to produce other products.

**demographic segmentation** Dividing the market into smaller groups based on measurable characteristics about people such as age, ethnicity, and gender.

**geographic segmentation** Dividing the market into smaller groups based on where consumers live.

**psychographic segmentation** Dividing the market into smaller groups based on consumer attitudes, interests, values, and lifestyles.

**behavioral segmentation** Dividing the market based on how people behave toward various products, including both the benefits that consumers seek from products and how consumers use the product.

**marketing mix** The blend of marketing strategies for product, price, distribution, and promotion.

**environmental scanning** The process of continually collecting information from the external marketing environment.

**market share** The percentage of a market controlled by a given marketer.

## LO4

**consumer behavior** Description of how people act when they are buying, using, and discarding goods and services for their own personal consumption. Consumer behavior also explores the reasons behind people's actions.

**cognitive dissonance** Consumer discomfort with a purchase decision, typically for a higher priced item.

**business buyer behavior** Describes how people act when they are buying products to use either directly or indirectly to produce other products.

## LO5

**marketing research** The process of gathering, interpreting, and applying information to uncover marketing opportunities and challenges, and to make better marketing decisions.

**observation research** Marketing research that *does not* require the researcher to interact with the research subject.

**survey research** Marketing research that requires the researcher to interact with the research subject.

**primary data** New data that marketers compile for a specific research project.

**secondary data** Existing data that marketers gather or purchase for a research project.

## LO4 Describe the consumer and business decision-making process

Understanding how customers make decisions will help you meet their needs. When people buy for their own personal consumption, a number of forces influence them, including cultural, social, personal, and psychological factors. For high-risk decisions, they generally follow a decision process, but for low-risk decisions, they often just follow rules of thumb. When people buy for business, they typically are more methodical, driven by product specifications.

### Elements that Influence the Consumer Decision-Making Process

| Influence | Description |
|---|---|
| Cultural | *Culture:* The values, attitudes, customs shared by members of a society<br>*Subculture:* A smaller division of the broader culture<br>*Social Class:* Societal position driven largely by income and occupation |
| Social | *Family:* A powerful force in consumption choices<br>*Friends:* Another powerful force, especially for high-profile purchases<br>*Reference Groups:* Groups that give consumers a point of comparison |
| Personal | *Demographics:* Measurable characteristics such as age, gender, income<br>*Personality:* The mix of traits that determine who you are |
| Psychological | *Motivation:* Pressing needs that tend to generate action<br>*Attitudes:* Lasting evaluations of (or feelings about) objects or ideas<br>*Perceptions:* How people select, organize, and interpret information<br>*Learning:* Changes in behavior based on experience |

## LO5 Discuss the key elements of marketing research

Marketing research involves gathering, interpreting, and applying information to uncover opportunities and challenges. Primary and secondary data offer complementary strengths and weaknesses. Observation research tools involve gathering data without interacting with the research subjects, while survey tools involve asking research subjects direct questions.

| **Secondary Data:**<br>Existing Data That Marketers Gather or Purchase | **Primary Data:**<br>New Data That Marketers Compile for the First Time |
|---|---|
| Tends to be lower cost | Tends to be more expensive |
| May not meet your *specific* needs | Customized to meet your needs |
| Frequently outdated | Fresh, new data |
| Available to your competitors | Proprietary—no one else has it |
| *Examples:* U.S. Census, *Wall Street Journal*, *Time* magazine, your product sales history | Examples: Your own surveys, focus groups, customer comments, mall interviews |

## LO6 Explain the roles of social responsibility and technology in marketing

The surging social responsibility movement and dramatic advances in technology have had a significant influence on marketing. In addition to seeking long-term profitability, socially responsible marketers actively contribute to meeting the needs of the broader community. Key areas of concern include fair labor practices (especially in foreign markets), environmentalism, and involvement in local communities. The digital boom of the past decade has revolutionized marketing, shifting the balance of power from producers to consumers. The Internet has also created marketing opportunities, helping businesses realize new efficiencies, facilitating more customized service, and generating new promotional opportunities.

## LO6

**green marketing** The development and promotion of products with ecological benefits.

**mass customization** The creation of products tailored for individual consumers on a mass basis.

Visit **4ltrpress.cengage.com/busn** for additional study tools!

## LO1

**product**
Anything that an organization offers to satisfy consumer needs and wants, including both goods and services.

**pure goods**
Products that do not include any services.

**pure services**
Products that do not include any goods.

**core benefit**
The basic benefit component of any product that consumers buy to satisfy their needs.

**actual product**
The physical good or the delivered service that provides the core benefit of any product.

**augmented product**
The additional goods and services included with a product to sharpen its competitive edge.

## LO2

**consumer products**
Products purchased for personal use or consumption.

**business products**
Products purchased to use either directly or indirectly in the production of other products.

**convenience products**
Inexpensive goods and services that consumers buy frequently with limited consideration and analysis.

**shopping products**
Moderately expensive products that consumers buy less frequently, after learning about their features and benefits through the shopping process.

**specialty products**
Expensive products that consumers seldom purchase. Most people perceive specialty products as so important that they are unwilling to accept substitutes.

**unsought products**
Goods and services that hold little interest for consumers.

**installations**
Large capital purchases designed for a long productive life.

**accessory equipment**
Smaller, movable capital purchases, designed for a shorter productive life than installations.

**maintenance, repair, and operating products (MROs)**
Small ticket items that businesses consume on an on-going basis, but don't incorporate into the final product.

**raw materials**
Farm and natural products used in producing other products.

**component parts and processed materials**
Finished (or partially finished) products used in producing other products.

**business services**
Services that businesses purchase to facilitate operations.

### LO1 Explain "product" from a marketing standpoint

A product can be anything that a company offers to satisfy to consumer needs and wants; the possibilities not only include physical goods, but also services and ideas. A product also includes all the attributes that consumers associate with it, such as name, image, service, packaging, and guarantees. Goods and services fall along a spectrum from pure goods, such as ketchup and pencils, to pure services, such as a doctor's exam. Most products fall somewhere between the two ends, incorporating elements of both goods and services. Products typically encompass three layers. The innermost layer is the core benefit—the basic need that the product satisfies. The next layer is the actual physical good or delivered service. And the outermost layer is the augmented product, which includes additional goods and services included with the actual product.

**Goods and services spectrum**

### The three product layers: Camera Phone

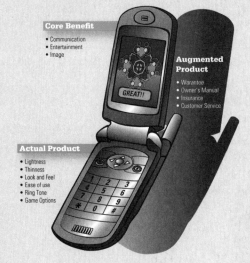

**Core Benefit**
- Communication
- Entertainment
- Image

**Augmented Product**
- Warantee
- Owner's Manual
- Insurance
- Customer Service

**Actual Product**
- Lightness
- Thinness
- Look and Feel
- Ease of use
- Ring Tone
- Game Options

**Pure Goods** — Bottle of Shampoo / Can of Cola · Financial Consulting / Math Tutoring — **Pure Service**

### LO2 Identify consumer and business product classifications

The key difference between the two categories is buyer motivation. Customers buy consumer products for personal consumption, and business products to contribute to the production of other products. Consumer product classifications are convenience products, shopping products, specialty products, and unsought products. Business product classifications are installations; accessory equipment; maintenance, repair, and operating products; raw materials; component parts and processed materials; and business services.

**Consumer Product Summary**

| Type | convenience | shopping | specialty |
|------|-------------|----------|-----------|
| **Price** | low | moderate | high |
| **Availability** | widespread | limited | very limited |
| **Purchase Frequency** | often | moderate | seldom |
| **Examples** | candy bars, plumbing service | computers, cleaning service | sports car, cosmetic surgery |

## LO3

**product differentiation**
The attributes that make a good or service different from or better than other products that compete to meet the same or similar customer needs.

**quality level**
How well a product performs its core functions.

**product consistency**
How reliably a product delivers its promised level of quality.

**product features**
The specific characteristics of a product.

**customer benefit**
The advantage that a customer gains from specific product features.

**product line**
A group of products that are closely related to each other, either in terms of how they work, or the customers they serve.

**product mix**
The total number of product lines and individual items sold by a single firm.

**cannibalization**
When a producer offers a new product that takes sales away from its existing products.

**brand**
A product's identity—including product name, symbol, design, reputation, and image—that sets it apart from other players in the same category.

**brand equity**
The overall value of a brand to an organization.

**line extensions**
Similar products offered under the same brand name.

**brand extension**
A new product, in a new category, introduced under an existing brand name.

**licensing**
Purchasing the right to use another company's brand name or symbol.

**cobranding**
When established brands from different companies join forces to market the same product.

**national brands**
Brands that the producer owns and markets.

**store brands**
Brands that the retailer both produces and distributes (also called private label brands).

## LO4

**discontinuous innovation**
Brand-new products that radically change how people live.

**dynamically continuous innovation**
Existing products with marked changes and significant new product benefits.

**continuous innovation**
Existing products with slight modifications.

**diffusion**
The spread of new products throughout a market after they are introduced.

## LO5

**product life cycle**
A pattern of sales and profits that typically changes over time.

---

### LO3 Describe product differentiation and the key elements of product planning

Product differentiation means making your product different from—and better than—the competition. Product planning offers the opportunity to achieve differentiation through elements such as better quality, better features and benefits, and a stronger brand. These elements are the foundation of an effective product strategy.

### Differing Quality Indicators

| Product Category | Some Quality Indicators |
| --- | --- |
| Internet search engines | Fast, relevant, far-reaching results |
| Stylish blue jeans | High-profile designer, high price, celebrity customers |
| TV editing equipment | Reliability, flexibility, and customer service |

### LO4 Discuss innovation and the new product development process

Innovation can range from small modifications of existing products to brand new products that change how people live. Either way, for a business to thrive long-term, effective new product development is vital. The new product development process is meant to streamline product development. The six steps include idea generation, idea screening, analysis, development, testing, and commercialization. For a new product to succeed, a significant chunk of its target market must adopt it.

### LO5 Describe the product life cycle and its relationship to marketing

During the *introduction* phase, a product first hits the market. Marketing generates awareness and trial. During the *growth* phase, sales rise rapidly and profits usually peak. Competitors enter the category. Marketing focuses on gaining new customers. During the *maturity* phase, sales usually peak, while profits fall. Competition intensifies as growth stops. Marketing aims to capture customers from competitors. During the *decline* phase, sales and profits drop. Marketers consider discontinuing products.

### Levels of innovation

### Product life cycle for a typical product category

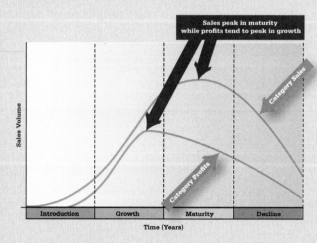

Sales peak in maturity while profits tend to peak in growth

Sales Volume

Category Sales

Category Profits

Introduction | Growth | Maturity | Decline

Time (Years)

## LO1

**distribution strategy**
A plan for delivering the right product to the right person at the right place at the right time.

**channel of distribution**
The network of organizations and processes that links producers to consumers.

**physical distribution**
The actual, physical movement of products along the distribution pathway.

**direct channel**
A distribution process that links the producer and the customer with no intermediaries.

**channel intermediaries**
Distribution organizations—informally called middlemen—that facilitate the movement of products from the producer to the consumer.

**utility**
The value, or usefulness, that a good or a service offers a customer.

**retailers**
Distributors that sell products directly to the ultimate users, typically in small quantities that are stored and merchandised on the premises.

**wholesalers**
Distributors that buy products from producers and sell them to other businesses or nonfinal users such as hospitals, nonprofits, and the government.

## LO2

**independent wholesaling businesses**
Independent distributors that buy products from a range of different businesses and sell those products to a range of different customers.

**merchant wholesalers**
Independent distributors who take legal possession, or title, of the goods they distribute.

**agents/brokers**
Independent distributors who do not take title of the goods they distribute (even though they may take physical possession on a temporary basis).

## LO3

**multichannel retailing**
Providing multiple distribution channels for consumers to buy a product.

**wheel of retailing**
A classic distribution theory that suggests that retail firms and retail categories become more upscale as they go through their life cycles.

### LO1 Define distribution and differentiate between channels of distribution and physical distribution

Distribution is the element of the marketing mix that involves getting the right product to the right customers in the right place at the right time. A channel of distribution is the path that a product takes from the producer to the consumer, while physical distribution is the actual movement of products along that path. Distributors add value by reducing the number of transactions—and the associated costs—required for goods to flow from producers to consumers. Distributors can also add a range of different utilities:

**How transactions are reduced through marketing intermediaries**

- *Form Utility:* Provides customer satisfaction by converting inputs into finished products.
- *Time Utility:* Adds value by making products available at a convenient time for consumers.
- *Place Utility:* Satisfies customer needs by providing the right products in the right place.
- *Ownership Utility:* Adds value by making it easier for customers to actually possess the goods and services that they purchase.
- *Information Utility:* Boosts customer satisfaction by providing helpful information.
- *Service Utility:* Adds value by providing fast, friendly, personalized service.

### LO2 Describe the various types of wholesale distributors

Wholesalers buy products from the producer and sell them to other businesses and organizations. The two key categories of wholesalers are:
- *Merchant wholesalers* who take legal title to the goods they distribute. Full-service merchant wholesalers provide a wide array of services, whereas limited-service merchant wholesalers offer more focused services.
- *Agents and brokers* who connect buyers and sellers in exchange for commissions, but without taking legal ownership of the goods they distribute.

### LO3 Discuss strategies and trends in store and nonstore retailing

Retailers are the final stop before the consumer on the distribution path. The two main retail categories are store and non-store, but the line between the two has blurred as more and more retailers are pursuing a multi-channel approach with online and off-line outlets supporting each other. Key non-store retail approaches include online retailing, direct response retailing, direct selling, and vending. As competition intensifies, a growing segment of retailers (both store and non-store) have distinguished themselves by offering their customers an entertainment-like experience.

**Retailers Add Value for Consumers**

*Product Selection*
*Look and Feel*
*Customer Service*
*Location*
*Promotion*
*Pricing*
*TARGET MARKET*

**RETAILING**

Store          Nonstore

## LO4

**supply chain**
All organizations, processes, and activities involved in the flow of goods from their raw materials to the final consumer.

**supply chain management (SCM)**
Planning and coordinating the movement of products along the supply chain, from the raw materials to the final consumers.

**logistics**
A subset of supply chain management that focuses largely on the tactics involved in moving products along the supply chain.

**modes of transportation**
The various transportation options—such as planes, trains, and railroads—for moving products through the supply chain.

## LO5

**penetration pricing**
A new product pricing strategy that aims to capture as much of the market as possible through rock bottom prices.

**every-day-low pricing (EDLP)**
Long-term discount pricing, designed to achieve profitability through high sales volume.

**high/low pricing**
A pricing strategy designed to drive traffic to retail stores by special sales on a limited number of products, and higher everyday prices on others.

**loss leader pricing**
Closely related to high/low pricing, loss leader pricing means pricing a handful of items—or loss leaders—temporarily below cost to drive traffic.

**skimming pricing**
A new product pricing strategy that aims to maximize profitability by offering new products at a premium price.

## LO6

**breakeven analysis**
The process of determining the number of units a firm must sell to cover all costs.

**profit margin**
The gap between the cost and the price of an item on a per product basis.

**odd pricing**
The practice of ending prices in numbers below even dollars and cents in order to create a perception of greater value.

## LO4 Explain the key factors in physical distribution

As marketers manage the movement of products through the supply chain, they must make decisions regarding each of the following factors:

- *Warehousing:* How many warehouses do we need? Where should we should we locate our warehouses?
- *Materials handling:* How should we move products within our facilities? How can we best balance efficiency with effectiveness?
- *Inventory control:* How much inventory should we keep on hand? How should we store and distribute it? What about taxes and insurance?
- *Order processing:* How should we manage incoming and outgoing orders? What would be most efficient for our customers and suppliers?
- *Customer service:* How can we serve our customers most effectively? How can we reduce waiting times and facilitate interactions?
- *Transportation:* How can we move products most efficiently through the supply chain? What are the key tradeoffs?

Key considerations in each area include efficiency and effectiveness.

### Elements of the Supply Chain

Raw Materials

↓

Logistics (transportation, coordination, etc.)

↓

Warehouse/Storage

↓

Production

↓

Warehouse/Storage

↓

Logistics (transportation, coordination, etc.)

↓

Distributors–Marketing and Sales

## LO5 Outline core pricing objectives and strategies

Many marketers continually evaluate and refine their pricing strategies to ensure that they meet their goals. Even the goals themselves may shift in response to the changing market. Key objectives and strategies include:

- Building profitability
- Driving volume
- Meeting the competition
- Creating prestige

### Pricing Considerations

## LO6 Discuss pricing in practice including the role of consumer perceptions

While most marketers are familiar with economics, they often don't have the information they need to apply the theories to their specific pricing strategies. Because of those limitations, most companies *consider* market-based factors—especially customer expectations and competitive prices—but they rely on cost-based pricing: what should we charge to cover our costs and make a profit? Common approaches include breakeven analysis and fixed margin pricing. Many marketers also account for consumer perceptions, especially the link between price and perceived quality, and odd pricing. If no other information is available, consumers will often assume that higher priced products are higher quality. Odd pricing means ending prices in dollars and cents rather than round numbers (e.g. $999.99 versus $1,000) in order to create a perception of greater value.

$$\text{Breakeven Point} = \frac{\text{Total Fixed Costs}}{\text{Price/Unit} - \text{Variable Cost/Unit}}$$

"It's a deal!"  "It's higher quality!"

$29.⁹⁹  $30.⁰⁰

## LO1

**promotion**
Marketing communication designed to influence consumer purchase decisions through information, persuasion, and reminders.

## LO2

**integrated marketing communication**
The coordination of marketing messages through every promotional vehicle to communicate a unified impression about a product.

## LO3

**positioning statement**
A brief statement that articulates how the marketer would like the target market to envision a product relative to the competition.

## LO4

**promotional channels**
Specific marketing communication vehicles, including traditional tools, such as advertising, sales promotion, direct marketing, and personal selling, and newer tools such as product placement, advergaming, and Internet minimovies.

**product placement**
The paid integration of branded products into movies, television, and other media.

**advergaming**
A relatively new promotional channel that involves integrating branded products and advertising into interactive games.

**buzz marketing**
The active stimulation of word-of-mouth via unconventional, and often relatively low-cost tactics. Other terms for buzz marketing are guerrilla marketing and viral marketing.

**sponsorship**
A deep association between a marketer and a partner (usually a cultural or sporting event), which involves promotion of the sponsor in exchange for either payment or the provision of goods.

**advertising**
Paid, nonpersonal communication, designed to influence a target audience with regard to a product, service, organization, or idea.

**sales promotion**
Marketing activities designed to stimulate immediate sales activity through specific short-term programs aimed at either consumers or distributors.

**consumer promotion**
Marketing activities designed to generate immediate consumer sales, using tools such as premiums, promotional products, samples, coupons, rebates, and displays.

**trade promotion**
Marketing activities designed to stimulate wholesalers and retailers to push specific products more aggressively over the short term.

### LO1 Explain promotion and analyze the current promotional environment

Promotion is marketing communication that influences consumers by informing, persuading, and reminding them about products. The most effective promotion builds strong relationships between customers and companies, drawing customers back to the company again and again. The current promotional environment is changing at breakneck speed. Thanks to technology, consumers have more control over how, when, and even if they receive promotional messages. Media has splintered across an array of entertainment options, and consumer viewing patterns have changed. As a result marketers are seeking increasingly creative means to reach their target customers. Their goal is to zero in—ever more precisely—on the right customers, at the right time, with the right message.

### LO2 Explain integrated marketing communications

The goal of integrated marketing communications (IMC) is to ensure that consumers receive a unified, focused message regardless of the message source. To make this happen, marketers must break through a confounding level of clutter, coordinating their messages through various promotional vehicles. (If messages are out-of-sync, busy consumers won't bother to sort through them.) Since it can be tough to control *every* message the consumer gets about a product, smart marketers identify the key points of contact between them and their target market, and focus on those areas. Coordinating those key points of contact requires that everyone who manages the marketing messages must have information about the customer, the product, the competition, the market, and the strategy of the organization. And clearly, solid teamwork—beginning at the top of the organization—is crucial. The result of effective IMC is a relevant, coherent image in the minds of target customers.

**Integrated Marketing Communications**

### LO3 Discuss development of the promotional message

The promotional message should be a big idea—a meaningful, believable, and distinctive concept that cuts through the clutter. Finding the big idea begins with the positioning statement—a brief statement that articulates how you want your target market to envision your product relative to the competition. A creative development team—often spearheaded by advertising agency professionals—uses the positioning statement as a springboard for finding a big idea. The ideas themselves are typically based on either a rational or an emotional premise, with humor as a recurrent favorite.

**BIG IDEA:**
- **Meaningful**
- **Believable**
- **Distinctive**

### LO4 Discuss the promotional mix and emerging and traditional promotional tools

The promotional mix is the combination of promotional tools that a marketer chooses to best communicate the big idea to the target audience. In today's rapidly changing promotional environment, new promotional tools have emerged and secondary promotional tools have burst into the mainstream. Examples:

- Product placement: Paid integration of branded products into movies and TV
- Advergaming: Advertising and branded products embedded into interactive games

**public relations (PR)**
The ongoing effort to create positive relationships with all of a firm's different "publics," including customers, employees, suppliers, the community, the general public, and the government.

**publicity**
Unpaid stories in the media that influence perceptions about a company or its products.

**personal selling**
The person-to-person presentation of products to potential buyers.

**missionary selling**
Promoting goodwill for a company by providing information and assistance to customers.

**consultative selling**
A sales approach that uses active listening to offer practical solutions to customer problems.

**team selling**
A sales approach that includes a group of specialists from key functional areas of a company, such as engineering, finance, customer service, and others.

## LO5

**push strategy**
A marketing approach that involves motivating distributors to heavily promote—or "push"—a product to the final consumers, usually through heavy trade promotion and personal selling.

**pull strategy**
A marketing approach that involves creating demand from the ultimate consumers so that they "pull" your products through the distribution channels by actively seeking them.

- Mini-movies: Short digital movies that with storylines that revolve around brands
- Buzz marketing: Stimulation of word-of-mouth through unconventional tactics
- Sponsorships: Growing at lightening speed, sponsorships connect brands to events

Yet traditional promotional tools retain enormous clout in terms of both spending and impact on the market. Advertising—designed to influence a target market with regard to a product, service, organization, or idea—has split among a growing array of media options. Sales promotion, designed to stimulate immediate sales, represents a quickly growing area, visible to consumers through premiums, promotional products, samples, coupons, and store displays. Public relations, designed to generate positive, unpaid media stories about a company or its products, also aims to boost brand awareness and credibility. Personal selling, designed to close sales and build relationships, continues to play a dominant role in the promotional mix. Across all of these broad promotional tools, specific approaches continually change to meet new market needs.

### LO5 Explain key considerations in choosing an effective promotional mix

Selecting the right mix of promotional tools poses an ongoing challenge for many marketers. Key considerations include the following:

- Product characteristics: How can you best communicate your product features?
- Product lifecycle: Where does your product stand in its lifecycle?
- Target audience: How big is it? Where do they live? What do they expect?
- Push versus pull: Does your industry emphasize push or pull strategies?
- Competitive environment: How does your strategy relate to competitive strategies?
- Budget: How much money will it take to achieve your goals?

**Emerging Marketing Tools Expand Promotional Reach**

**Media dollars are flooding to cable TV and Internet**

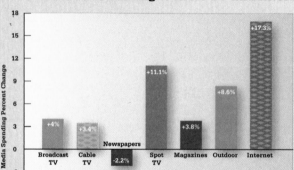

**Buzz marketing travels along social networks**

**Promotional Mix Considerations**

- Product Characteristics
- Product Lifecycle
- Target Audience
- Push vs. Pull Strategy
- Competitive Environment
- Budget

Visit **4ltrpress.cengage.com/busn**
for additional study tools!

## LO1

**management**
Achieving the goals of an organization through planning, organizing, leading, and controlling organizational resources including people, money, and time.

**planning**
Determining organizational goals and action plans for how to achieve those goals.

**organizing**
Determining a structure for both individual jobs and the overall organization.

**leading**
Directing and motivating people to achieve organizational goals.

**controlling**
Checking performance and making adjustments as needed.

**top management**
Managers who set the overall direction of the firm, articulating a vision, establishing priorities, and allocating time, money, and other resources.

**middle management**
Managers who supervise lower-level managers and report to higher-level managers.

**first line management**
Managers who directly supervise nonmanagement employees.

**technical skills**
Expertise in a specific functional area or department.

**human skills**
The ability to work effectively with and through other people in a range of different relationships.

**conceptual skills**
The ability to grasp a big picture view of the overall organization, the relationship between its various parts, and its fit in the broader competitive environment.

## LO2

**Maslow's hierarchy of needs theory**
Motivation theory that suggests human needs fall in a hierarchy, and that as each need is met, people become motivated to meet the next highest need in the pyramid.

**Theory X and Theory Y**
Motivation theory that suggests that management attitudes toward workers fall into two opposing categories based on management assumptions about worker capabilities and values.

**job enrichment**
The creation of jobs with more meaningful content, under the assumption that challenging, creative work will motivate employees.

**expectancy theory**
Motivation theory that deals with the relationship among individual effort, individual performance, and individual reward.

**equity theory**
Motivation theory that proposes perceptions of fairness directly impact worker motivation.

### LO1 Discuss the role of management and its importance to organizational success

The formal definition of management is to achieve the goals of an organization through planning, organizing, leading, and controlling organizational resources. Managers provide vision for their company and inspire others to follow their lead. Most medium and large companies have three basic management levels: top management, middle management, and first line (or supervisory)

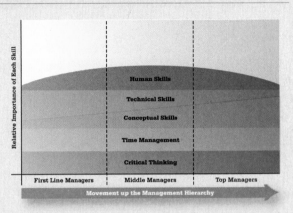

management. Managers must draw on a wide range of skills, but most of their abilities cluster into three key categories: technical skills, human skills, and conceptual skills. All three skill sets are essential for management success, but in different proportions at each managerial level.

### LO2 Explain key theories and current practices of motivation

Research suggests that people's thoughts and feelings play a vital role in motivation. Key theories that incorporate this perspective include Maslow's hierarchy of needs, Theory X and Theory Y, job enrichment, expectancy theory, and equity theory. In today's business environment, leading-edge firms nourish distinctive, positive cultures that tend to create productive employees who are deeply attached to both their work and their companies. Many also focus on training and education, which are especially motivating for the growing cadre of employees who identify themselves based on their field of expertise rather than their organization.

#### Maslow's Hierarchy of Needs

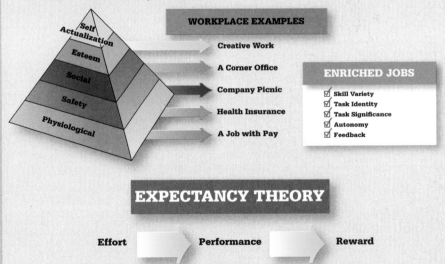

### LO3 Outline the categories of business planning and explain strategic planning

The four main categories of business planning are strategic planning, tactical planning, operational planning, and contingency planning. Strategic planning, handled by top managers, sets the broad direction of the organization, typically over a 5-year horizon.

## LO3

**strategic planning**
High-level, long-term planning that establishes a vision for the company, defines long-term objectives and priorities, determines broad action steps, and allocates resources.

**tactical planning**
More specific, shorter term planning that applies strategic plans to specific functional areas.

**operational planning**
Very specific, short term planning that applies tactical plans to daily, weekly, and monthly operations.

**contingency planning**
Planning for unexpected events, usually involving a range of scenarios and assumptions that differ from the assumptions behind the core plans.

**mission**
The definition of an organization's purpose, values, and core goals, which provides the framework for all other plans.

**SWOT analysis**
A strategic planning tool that helps management evaluate an organization in terms of internal strengths and weakness, and external opportunities and threats.

**strategic goals**
Concrete benchmarks that managers can use to measure performance in each key area of the organization.

**strategies**
Action plans that help the organization achieve its goals by forging the best fit between the firm and the environment.

## LO4

**organization chart**
A visual representation of the company's formal structure.

**degree of centralization**
The extent to which decision-making power is held by a small number of people at the top of the organization.

**span of control**
Span of management; refers to the number of people that a manager supervises.

**departmentalization**
The division of workers into logical groups.

**line organizations**
Organizations with a clear, simple chain of command from top to bottom.

**line-and-staff organizations**
Organizations with line managers forming the primary chain of authority in the company, and staff departments working alongside line departments.

**line managers**
Managers who supervise the functions that contribute directly to profitability: production and marketing.

**staff managers**
Managers who supervise the functions that provide advice and assistance to the line departments.

Strategic planning guides the entire planning process, since all other plans—and most major management decisions—stem from the strategic plan. Given fierce competition and often-unpredictable change, most large firms revise their strategic plans on a yearly basis.

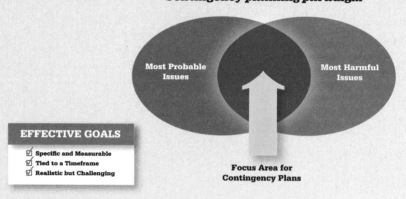

**Contingency planning paradigm**

Most Probable Issues

Most Harmful Issues

Focus Area for Contingency Plans

**EFFECTIVE GOALS**
- ☑ Specific and Measurable
- ☑ Tied to a Timeframe
- ☑ Realistic but Challenging

### LO4 Discuss the organizing function of management

The organizing function of management means creating a logical structure for people, their jobs, and their patterns of interaction. In choosing the right structure for a specific company, management must consider many different factors, including the goals and strategies of the firm, its products, and its size. Management must also make decisions about the degree of centralization, the span of management control, and the type of departmentalization. Company structures tend to follow one of three different patterns: line organizations, line-and-staff organizations, and matrix organizations.

### LO5 Explain the role of managerial leadership and the key leadership styles

Effective business leaders motivate others to achieve the goals of their organization. Most experts agree that true leaders are trustworthy, visionary, and inspiring. Other key leadership traits include empathy, courage, creativity, intelligence, fairness, and energy. While leaders have a range of different styles, three main approaches include autocratic, democratic, and free-reign. The best leaders tend to use all three approaches, shifting style in response to the needs of the followers and the situation.

### LO6 Describe the management control process

Controlling means monitoring performance of the firm—or individuals within the firm—and making improvements when necessary. As the environment changes, plans change. And as plans change, the control process must change to ensure that the company achieves its goals. The control process has three main steps:
1. Establish clear performance standards.
2. Measure actual performance against standards.
3. Take corrective action if necessary.

**matrix organizations**
Organizations with a flexible structure that brings together specialists from different areas of the company to work on individual projects on a temporary basis.

## LO5

**autocratic leaders**
Leaders who hoard decision-making power for themselves and typically issue orders without consulting their followers.

**democratic leaders**
Leaders who share power with their followers. While

they still make final decisions, they typically solicit and incorporate input from their followers.

**free-reign leaders**
Leaders who set objectives for their followers but give them freedom to choose how they accomplish those goals.

Visit **4ltrpress.cengage.com/busn**
for additional study tools!

## LO1

**human resource management**
The management function focused on maximizing the effectiveness of the workforce by recruiting world-class talent, promoting career development, and determining workforce strategies to boost organizational effectiveness.

## LO4

**job analysis**
The examination of specific tasks that are assigned to each position, independent of who might be holding the job at any specific time.

**job description**
An explanation of the responsibilities for a specific position.

**job specifications**
The specific qualifications necessary to hold a particular position.

**internal recruitment**
The process of seeking employees who are currently within the firm to fill open positions.

**external recruitment**
The process of seeking new employees from outside the firm.

**structured interviews**
An interviewing approach that involves developing a list of questions beforehand and asking the same questions in the same order to each candidate.

**probationary period**
A specific timeframe (typically 3 to 6 months) during which a new hire can prove his or her worth on the job before the hire becomes permanent.

**contingent workers**
Employees who do not expect regular, full-time jobs, including temporary full-time workers, independent contractors, and temporary agency or contract agency workers.

**orientation**
The first step in the training and development process, designed to introduce employees to the company culture, and provide key administrative information.

**on-the-job training**
A training approach that requires employees to simply begin their jobs—sometimes guided by more experienced employees—and to learn as they go.

**apprenticeships**
Structured training programs that mandate that each beginner serve as an assistant to a fully trained worker before gaining full credentials to work in the field.

**management development**
Programs to help current and potential executives develop the skills they need to move into leadership positions.

**performance appraisal**
A formal feedback process that requires managers to give their subordinates feedback on a one-to-one basis, typically by comparing actual results to expected results.

### LO1 Explain the importance of human resources to business success

A world-class workforce can lead straight to world-class performance. Human resource managers can directly contribute to that goal by recruiting top talent, promoting career development, and boosting organizational effectiveness. Yet human resource departments typically face numerous challenges in making this happen.

### LO2 Discuss key human resource issues in today's economy

As the economy and society continue to change rapidly, a number of issues have emerged that directly affect human resources. Older workers have begun to retire, while younger workers often bring an unprecedented sense of entitlement. Many women are leaving traditional jobs. Workers are actively seeking more flexibility and a better work-life balance. The growing wage gap between senior managers and the average employee has created tension for a number of stakeholders. Outsourcing remains challenging. And the number of costly employee lawsuits has skyrocketed in the last couple of decades.

### LO3 Outline challenges and opportunities that the human resources function faces

While HR workers tend to have strong people skills, many lack the business acumen to contribute directly to broad company objectives, and other departments often view HR as either irrelevant or adversarial. HR can respond to these issues by demonstrating that they understand the strategic goals of the company, the core customers, and the competition. The best HR departments use this knowledge to raise the value of the firm's human capital, which in turn increases the value of the firm itself.

### LO4 Discuss human resource planning and core human resources responsibilities

Human resource planning objectives must flow from the company's master plan, and the HR strategies must reflect company priorities. The first step should be to determine where the firm currently stands in terms of human resources, and to forecast future needs. Other key areas of focus follow:

- *Recruitment:* The key to recruitment is finding *qualified* candidates who fit well with the organization. The right people can come from either internal or external labor pools.

- *Selection:* Choosing the right person from a pool of candidates typically involves applications, interviews, tests, references. The terms of the job offer itself play a role as well.

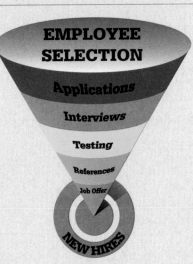

**compensation**
The combination of pay and benefits that employees receive in exchange for their work.

**wages**
The pay that employees receive in exchange for the number of hours or days that they work.

**salaries**
The pay that employees receive over a fixed period, most often weekly or monthly. Most professional, administrative, and managerial jobs pay salaries.

**benefits**
Noncash compensation, including programs such as health insurance, vacation, and childcare.

**cafeteria-style benefits**
An approach to employee benefits that gives all employees a set dollar amount that they must spend on company benefits. Employees can choose to allocate their spending however they wish within broad limitations.

**flextime**
A scheduling option that allows workers to choose when they start and finish their workdays, as long as they complete the required number of hours.

**compressed workweek**
A version of flextime scheduling that allows employees to work a full-time number of hours in less than the standard workweek.

**telecommuting**
Working remotely—most often from home—and connecting to the office via phone lines, fax machines, and broadband networks.

## LO5

**Civil Rights Act of 1964**
Federal legislation that prohibits discrimination in hiring, firing, compensation, apprenticeships, training, terms, conditions, or privileges of employment based on race, color, religion, sex, or national origin.

**Title VII**
A portion of the Civil Rights Act of 1964 that prohibits discrimination in hiring, firing, compensation, apprenticeships, training, terms, conditions, or privileges of employment based on race, color, religion, sex, or national origin for employers with 15 or more workers.

**Equal Employment Opportunity Commission (EEOC)**
A federal agency designed to regulate and to enforce the provisions of Title VII.

- *Training:* The training process begins with orientation, but should continue throughout each employee's tenure. Options include on-the-job training, off-the-job training, and management development.
- *Evaluation:* Performance feedback should happen constantly. But most firms also use formal, periodic performance appraisals to make decisions about compensation, promotions, training, transfers, and terminations.
- *Compensation:* Compensation includes both pay and benefits. Interestingly, companies that offer higher compensation generally outperform their competitors in terms of total return to shareholders.
- *Separation:* Employees leave their jobs for both positive and negative reasons. When the separation is not voluntary—e.g., layoffs or termination—fairness and documentation are critical.

**EMPLOYEE EVALUATION**

Employee     Manager
Feedback should be continual

### Considerations for Compensation

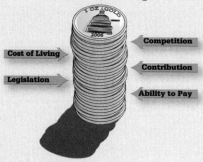

Cost of Living

Legislation

Competition

Contribution

Ability to Pay

### Variable Pay System
- Commission
- Bonuses
- Profit sharing
- Stock options
- Pay for knowledge

**FLEXIBLE SCHEDULING**

- Flextime
- Telecommuting
- Job Sharing

---

## LO5 Explain the key Federal legislation that impacts human resources

Perhaps the most influential piece of employment legislation is the Civil Rights Act of 1964. Title VII of this act prohibits discrimination in hiring, firing, compensation, apprenticeships, training, terms, conditions, or privileges of employment based on race, color, religion, sex, or national origin. Additional legislation prohibits discrimination based on pregnancy, age, and disability. The Equal Employment Opportunity Commission (EEOC) enforces the provisions of Title VII.

## LO1

**hardware**
The physical tools and equipment used to collect, store, organize and process data and to distribute information.

**software**
Programs that provide instructions to a computer so that it can perform a desired task.

**system software**
Software that performs the critical functions necessary to operate the computer at the most basic level.

**applications software**
Software that helps a user perform a desired task.

**intranet**
A network that has the look and feel of the Internet and is navigated using a Web browser but that is confined to documents located on a single company's servers.

**extranet**
An intranet that allows limited access to a selected group of stakeholders, such as suppliers or customers.

## LO2

**data**
Raw, unprocessed facts and figures.

**information**
Data that have been processed in a way that make them meaningful to their user.

**database**
A file consisting of related data organized according to a logical system and stored on a hard drive or some other computer-accessible media.

**push technologies**
Computer applications that allow information to be delivered via the Internet directly to a user's computer desktop.

**decision support system**
A system that gives managers access to large amounts of data and the processing power to convert these data into high-quality information, thus improving the decision-making process.

**business intelligence system**
A sophisticated form of decision support system that usually takes advantage of data mining techniques to help decision makers discover information that was previously hidden.

**data warehouse**
A large, organization-wide database that stores data in a centralized location.

**data mining**
The use of sophisticated statistical and mathematical techniques to analyze data and discover hidden patterns and relationships among data, thus creating valuable information.

**expert system (ES)**
A system that guides decision makers so that they can make good decisions in an area where they lack expertise.

---

**LO1 Explain the basic elements of computer technology—including hardware, software, and networks—and analyze key trends in each area.**

Hardware is the physical equipment used to collect, store, organize, and process data and to distribute information. Examples include hard drives, keyboards, and printers. Software consists of computer programs that provide instructions to a computer. System software performs the critical functions necessary to operate the computer at the most basic level. Applications software helps users perform a desired task. Both hardware and software have become much more powerful, easier to use, and less expensive over the last several decades. Most firms (and many households) now use networks to enable users to communicate with each other and share both files and hardware resources. The Internet is a vast network of computer networks. The part of the Internet used most by the general public is the World Wide Web, which consists of billions of documents written and linked together using Hypertext Markup Language (HTML). In recent years the availability of broadband connections to the Web has made it possible to share large video and audio files. Many organizations have developed intranets that have the same look and feel as the Internet but are limited to servers within an organization. Extranets are intranets which provide limited access to specific stakeholders, such as customers or suppliers.

**LO2 Describe how data becomes information and how decision support systems can provide high-quality information that helps managers make better decisions.**

Data refers to the facts and figures a firm collects. Data become information when they are processed, organized, and presented in a way that is meaningful to a decision maker. Many companies develop decision support systems (DSS) that give managers access to large amounts of data and the processing power to convert the data into high-quality information. Business intelligence systems are the newest version of DSS. These systems usually take advantage of data mining techniques to discover information that was previously buried in masses of data. Firms sometimes develop expert systems to actually solve problems that are beyond the expertise of the decision maker. To develop expert systems, programmers ask experts in the relevant area to explain how they solve problems; then the programmers devise a program to mimic the expert's approach.

| High Quality Information Is: | |
|---|---|
| 1. Accurate | Free from errors and omissions. |
| 2. Relevant | Deals with issues that are important to the decision maker. |
| 3. Timely | Available in time to make a difference to the decision maker. |
| 4. Understandable | Presented in a way that allows decision makers to grasp its meaning and significance. |
| 5. Secure | Stored and presented in a way that makes it difficult for hackers and competitors to obtain it. |

**LO3 Discuss the role of information technology in e-commerce.**

Information technology, and especially the Internet, has revolutionized the way firms interact with their customers in both the business-to-consumer (B2C) and business-to-business (B2B) markets. However, B2C and B2B have very different characteristics, so the way firms use information technology in these two types of markets tends to be quite different. In the B2C market, the Internet has enabled firms to reach broader markets, advertise in new ways, and take customer relationship marketing to a new level. In the B2B market, e-marketplaces enable firms to negotiate with suppliers or customers more effectively and share information that leads to better coordination and collaboration.

---

Visit **4ltrpress.cengage.com/busn** for additional study tools!

## LO3

**e-commerce**
The marketing, buying, selling, and servicing of products over a network (usually the Internet).

**business-to-consumer (B2C) e-commerce**
E-commerce in which businesses and final consumers interact.

**business-to-business (B2B) e-commerce**
E-commerce in markets where businesses buy from and sell to other businesses.

**viral marketing**
An Internet marketing strategy that tries to involve customers and others not employed by the seller in activities that help promote the product.

**customer relationship management (CRM)**
The strategy of building relationships with customers by learning more about them and using this knowledge to provide products and services that match their preferences.

**cybermediary**
An Internet-based firm that specializes in the secure electronic transfer of funds.

**electronic bill presentment and payment**
A method of bill payment that makes it easy for the customer to make a payment, often by simply clicking on a payment option contained in an e-mail.

**e-marketplace**
A specialized Internet site where buyers and sellers engaged in business-to-business e-commerce can communicate and conduct business.

## LO4

**cookies**
Small text files that are placed on a user's computer by a Website, usually to allow the Website to identify the user.

**adware**
A software program that is placed on a computer for the purpose of generating advertisements; frequently included with free programs downloaded from Internet sites.

**spyware**
Software that is installed on a computer without the user's knowledge or permission for the purpose of tracking the user's behavior.

**virus**
Computer software that can be spread from one computer to another without the knowledge or permission of the computer users.

**spam**
Unsolicited e-mail advertisements usually sent to very large numbers of recipients, many of whom may have no interest in the message.

**phishing**
A scam in which official-looking e-mails are sent to individuals in an attempt to get them to divulge private information such as passwords, user names, and account numbers.

## LO4 Describe the problems posed by the rapid changes in Internet-based technologies, and explain ways to deal with these problems.

The rapid development of Internet-based technologies has created enormous business opportunities, but it has also created several challenges and raised several controversial issues. The Internet has made it easier for spyware and viruses to land on your computer, undermining the security and stability of your system and perhaps stealing your personal information. Regular backups of hard drives, the use of updated antivirus and antispyware software, and frequent updating of the computer's operating system can reduce (but not eliminate) these threats. Spam consists of unsolicited commercial e-mails, usually sent to huge numbers of people with little regard for whether they have any interest in the message. Spam filters are available, but spammers are good at finding ways to fool the filters. Phishing is the sending of official-looking (but fake) e-mails to people to get them to divulge private information. It's important to be suspicious of requests to divulge private information via e-mail—they are very likely to be part of a phishing scam. One of the most controversial impacts of information technology has been on the loss in personal privacy. For example, e-mail messages are usually stored on many computers, making it easy for people to locate and view messages that their senders believed were private communications. A final issue involves intellectual property. The Internet makes it possible to share videos, music, and computer programs with huge numbers of people. This has led to a surge in the illegal sharing of copyrighted material. Owners of copyrighted materials have tried to develop methods to make illegal file sharing more difficult. They've also become very aggressive at prosecuting those involved in piracy.

## LO5 Discuss the business opportunities created by new technologies.

Radio frequency identification (RFID) is a technology that stores information on a microchip and transmits it to a reader when it's within range. In most cases, its main purpose is to transmit a serial number that *uniquely* identifies a person, product, or device. The widespread use of RFID will help firms track shipments and manage inventory and will reduce waiting time for customers. Holographic storage promises to greatly improve storage capacity while reducing the time it takes to access the data; it will also improve data security. Finally, Internet2 is a new version of Internet technology which offers much greater bandwidth. It is limited to institutions that participate in a consortium and is used to allow participants to share huge amounts of data and collaborate quickly and efficiently over great distances.

**hacker**
A skilled computer user who uses his or her expertise to gain access to the computer (or computer system) of others, sometimes with malicious intent.

**firewall**
Software, hardware, or both designed to prevent unwanted access to a computer or computer system.

**intellectual property**
Property that is the result of creative or intellectual effort, such as books, musical works, inventions, and computer software.

### LO5

**radio frequency identification (RFID)**
Use of microchips to transmit information about a device, product, or person to an RFID reader.

**holographic storage**
A technology that stores data in three dimensions rather than two, thus greatly expanding storage capacity.

**Internet2**
A new Internet that utilizes technologies that give it a speed and capacity far exceeding the current internet.

## LO1

**operations management**
The activities involved in creating goods and services and distributing them to customers.

**efficiency**
Producing output or achieving a goal at the lowest cost.

**effectiveness**
Using resources to create the greatest value.

## LO2

**process**
A set of activities or steps that combine inputs in order to create a desired output.

**flow shop process**
A production process that uses specialized machinery and equipment to produce a large quantity of a specific good very efficiently.

**assembly line**
A production process in which the product moves from one station to another in a fixed sequence, with the machinery and workers at each station performing specialized tasks.

**job shop process**
A production process designed to produce goods or services in relatively small batches using general-purpose machinery and equipment.

**inventory**
Stocks of finished items, work-in-process, parts, materials, or other resources held by an organization.

**immediate predecessors**
Activities in a project that must be completed before some other specified activity can begin.

**Gantt chart**
A chart that can be used to track the progress of activities involved in completing a project.

**critical path method (CPM)**
A project management tool that illustrates the relationships among all the activities involved in completing a project in a network and enables managers to identify the activities most likely to create delays in the completion of the overall project.

**critical path**
The sequence of activities in a project that is expected to take the longest to complete.

## LO3

**automation**
Replacing human operation and control of machinery and equipment with some form of programmed control.

**robot**
A reprogrammable machine that is capable of manipulating materials, tools, parts, and specialized devices in order to perform a variety of tasks.

**computer-aided design (CAD)**
Drawing and drafting software that enables users to create and edit blueprints and design drawings quickly and easily.

### LO1 Discuss the role of operations management in business

Operations management oversees all of the activities involved in creating the right goods and services in the right quantities and distributing them to the right customers. The decisions of operations management can have a major impact on both the revenue and costs a firm incurs, and therefore on the firm's financial success.

### Differences between Goods and Services

| Goods | Services |
|---|---|
| Are tangible: they have a physical form and can be seen, touched, handled, etc. | Are intangible: they can be "experienced," but they don't have a physical form. |
| Can be stored in an inventory. | Must be consumed *when* they are produced. |
| Can be shipped. | Must be consumed *where* they are provided. |
| Are produced independently of the consumer. | Often require the customer to be actively involved in their production. |
| Can have at least *some* aspects of their quality determined objectively by measuring defects or deviations from desired values. | Intangible nature means quality is based mainly on customer perceptions. |

### LO2 Describe the key responsibilities of operations managers

Operations management is a very broad field. Operations managers perform a wide variety of tasks including (but not limited to) the selection of the appropriate production process and the design of the facility layout to ensure efficient flows of materials and parts, and work-in-process during the production process, the selection of locations for facilities, controlling inventory, and the monitoring and scheduling of complex projects using tools such as Gantt charts and CPM networks.

### LO3 Explain how technology has influenced operations management

Rapid changes in both machinery and equipment and in software and information technologies have revolutionized operations management. The biggest change in machinery and equipment has been the increasing use of automation, which means replacing human operation and control of machinery and equipment with programmed control. Robots, which are reprogrammable machines that can manipulate materials, tools, parts, and specialized devices in order to perform a variety of tasks, are a key example of automation. The development of software applications to allow computer-aided design (CAD), computer-aided engineering (CAE), and computer-aided manufacturing (CAM) have given firms the flexibility to design, test, and produce goods more quickly and efficiently than ever before. When these powerful software applications are integrated with robots and other automated equipment, the result is called computer integrated manufacturing. This tight integration allows firms to produce customized goods quickly and at low cost, a process called mass customization.

### LO4 Discuss the coordination and integration of operations systems

Two key examples of integrated operations systems are supply chain management systems and enterprise resource planning (ERP). Supply chains involve the flow of materials, goods, services, financial resources, and information among all of the organizations involved in production and distribution of a good or service. From an operations management perspective, one of the most important elements of supply chain management is

**computer-aided engineering (CAE)**
Software that enables users to test, analyze, and optimize their designs.

**computer-aided manufacturing (CAM)**
Software that takes the electronic design for a product and creates the programmed instructions that robots must follow to produce that product as efficiently as possible.

**CAD/CAM**
Computer-aided design/computer-aided manufacturing; a combination of software that can be used to design output and send instructions to automated equipment to perform the steps needed to produce this output.

**computer-integrated manufacturing (CIM)**
A combination of CAD/CAM software with flexible manufacturing systems to automate almost all steps involved in designing, testing, and producing a product.

## LO4

**vertical integration**
The performance of functions in a supply chain internally rather than having them performed by other organizations.

**outsourcing**
Arranging for other organizations to perform supply chain functions that were previously performed internally.

**enterprise resource planning (ERP)**
Software-based approach to integrate an organization's systems in order to improve communication and coordination among all departments and operating units.

## LO5

**total quality management (TQM)**
An approach to quality improvement that calls for everyone within an organization to take responsibility for improving quality and emphasizes the need for a long-term commitment to continuous improvement.

**poka-yokes**
Simple methods incorporated into a production process designed to eliminate or greatly reduce errors.

**Six Sigma**
An approach to quality improvement characterized by very ambitious quality goals, extensive training of employees, and a long-term commitment to working on quality-related issues.

## LO6

**Baldrige National Quality Program**
A national program established by the U.S. Congress in 1987 to encourage American firms to focus on quality improvement.

**ISO 9000**
A set of generic standards for quality management systems established by the International Organization for Standardization.

**lean production**
An approach to production that emphasizes the elimination of waste in all aspects of production processes.

determining which functions to perform internally and which functions to outsource. The goal of enterprise resource planning is to integrate the information flows from *all* aspects of a business's operations—accounting, finance, sales and marketing, production, and human resources. Such systems greatly reduce the duplication of data entry and make it easier for the various departments and divisions to communicate and coordinate their actions. But ERP systems can be challenging and expensive to implement.

### LO5 Explain the role of quality in operations management

Quality can be defined in many ways, but operations managers usually define it in terms of how well a good or service satisfies customer preferences. Improvements in quality are a key to competitive advantage because they enable a firm to improve both its effectiveness *and* its efficiency. Better quality improves effectiveness because high quality creates value to the customer. It improves efficiency because good quality tends, in the long run, to be less expensive than poor quality. In recent years U.S. firms have adopted programs such as total quality management (TQM) and Six Sigma to improve quality. Another approach firms have taken to improve efficiency has been to launch programs designed to achieve certification or recognition from outside authorities. Two common approaches are to participate in the Baldrige National Quality Program and to seek certification under the International Organization for Standardization's ISO 9000 standards.

**The Deming Chain Reaction**

Improve quality

Costs decrease because of less rework, fewer mistakes, fewer delays and snags, and better use of time and materials

Productivity improves

Capture the market with better quality and lower price

Stay in business

Provide jobs and more jobs

### LO6 Explain the movement toward lean production

Lean production refers to a set of strategies and practices to eliminate waste and thus make organizations more efficient, responsive, and flexible. Operations managers who implement lean production often use value stream mapping to identify waste, which refers to activities or functions that use resources but don't create value. They then work to find ways to redesign processes to reduce or eliminate the waste. Inventory control is one of the key areas where waste often occurs. Many lean firms have adopted just-in-time production methods to minimize the amount of parts, work-in-process, and finished products they hold in inventory.

**value stream mapping**
A tool used in lean production to show the flows of materials and information from the beginning to the end of a production process; used to identify

where waste occurs within a production system.

**just-in-time (JIT) production**
A production system that emphasizes the production of goods to meet actual

current demand, thus minimizing the need to hold inventories of finished goods and work-in-process at each stage of the supply chain.